Statutes, Decrees, and Regulations of the University of Oxford 2000

This book is no longer republished annually, but as occasion requires.

[*Important Note*. Substantial changes in the governance structures of the University have been introduced with effect from 1 October 2000. A number of consequential changes in legislation, for example references to the General Board (which no longer exists), have still to be made. In the meantime Council has delegated the relevant functions and powers to the appropriate body under the provisions of Tit. IV, Sect. I, cll. 3 and 4.]

OXFORD UNIVERSITY PRESS

OXFORD
UNIVERSITY PRESS
Great Clarendon Street, Oxford OX2 6DP

Oxford University Press is a department of the University of Oxford.
It furthers the University's objective of excellence in research, scholarship,
and education by publishing worldwide in

Oxford New York

Athens Auckland Bangkok Bogotá Buenos Aires Calcutta
Cape Town Chennai Dar es Salaam Delhi Florence Hong Kong Istanbul
Karachi Kuala Lumpur Madrid Melbourne Mexico City Mumbai
Nairobi Paris São Paulo Shanghai Singapore Taipei Tokyo Toronto Warsaw

with associated companies in Berlin Ibadan

Oxford is a registered trade mark of Oxford University Press
in the UK and in certain other countries

ISBN 0 19 951860 2

Printed in Great Britain by
J. W. Arrowsmith Ltd., Bristol

CONTENTS

INTRODUCTION

STATUTES

DECREES AND REGULATIONS

INTRODUCTION

Extracts from the Universities of Oxford and Cambridge Act, 1923

5. The powers of the Commissioners shall continue in force until the end of the year nineteen hundred and twenty-five and no longer.

Provided that His Majesty in Council may, on the application of the Commissioners, continue their powers for such further period as His Majesty may think fit, but not beyond the end of the year nineteen hundred and twenty-seven.

6. (1) Subject to the provisions of this Act, the Commissioners shall, from and after the first day of January, nineteen hundred and twenty-five, make statutes and regulations for the University, its colleges and halls, and any emoluments, endowments, trusts, foundations, gifts, offices, or institutions in or connected with the University in general accordance with the recommendations contained in the Report of the Royal Commission, but with such modifications (not being modifications directly dealing with the curriculum or course of study in the University) as may, after the consideration of any representations made to them, appear to them expedient.

(2) In making any statutes or regulations under this Act, the Commissioners shall have regard to the need of facilitating the admission of poorer students to the Universities and colleges.

7. (1) After the cesser of the powers of the Commissioners, a statute affecting the University made by the Commissioners or by any other authority, not being a statute made for a college, shall be subject to alteration from time to time by statute made by the University under this Act, but, if and in so far as any such statute (not being a statute prescribing the scale or basis of assessment of the contributions to be made by the colleges to University purposes) affects a college, it shall not be subject to alteration except with the consent of the college.

(2) After the cesser of the powers of the Commissioners, a statute for a college made by the Commissioners, and any statute, ordinance or regulation made by or in relation to a college under any authority other than that of this Act, shall be subject to alteration from time to time by statute made by the college under this Act and passed at a general meeting of the governing body of the college specially summoned for the purpose by the votes of not less than two-thirds of the number of persons present and voting:

Provided that—

(*a*) notice of any proposed statute for a college shall be given to the University before the statute is submitted to His Majesty in Council; and

(*b*) a statute made for a college which affects the University shall not be altered except with the consent of the University.

(3) The provisions contained in this Act (including the provisions of the Schedule to this Act other than the section numbered thirty-five therein) with

respect to the making of statutes by the Commissioners and to the proceedings to be taken after the making thereof in connection with statutes made by the Commissioners, and to the effect thereof after approval, shall, with the necessary substitutions, apply to the making of statutes by the University or by a college and to the proceedings to be taken in connection with statutes made by the University or a college, and to the effect of such statutes.

8. (1) No statute shall be made under any of the provisions of this Act for altering a trust, except with the consent of the trustees or governing body of the trust, unless sixty years have elapsed since the date on which the instrument creating the trust came into operation, but nothing in this subsection shall prevent the making of a statute increasing the endowment of any emolument or otherwise improving the position of the holder thereof.

(2) In the making of any statute, whether by the Commissioners or by the University, prescribing or altering the scale or basis of assessment of contributions to be made by the colleges to University purposes, regard shall be had in the first place to the needs of the several colleges in themselves for educational and other collegiate purposes.

9. The exemption from the obligation to obtain a licence in mortmain which is given by section sixty of the Universities of Oxford and Cambridge Act, 1877, in respect of certain purchases of land by the University or a college shall extend, and be deemed always to have extended, to all assurances of land to the University or a college.

10. The provisions of the Universities of Oxford and Cambridge Act, 1877, shall, as set out with modifications in the Schedule to this Act, apply to the Commissioners appointed under this Act and to their procedure, powers and duties and to any statutes made by them as if they were re-enacted with the said modifications in this Act.

11. (1) It shall be lawful for the University to make a scheme for establishing a superannuation fund for the benefit of persons in the employment of the University not being members of its administrative or teaching staff, and for a college to adopt in relation to persons in the employment of the college, not being members of its administrative or teaching staff, any scheme so made.

(2) The provisions of this Act relating to the making of statutes, ordinances and regulations by the University or a college shall not apply to any statutes, ordinances or regulations made for the purposes of this section.

(3) Nothing in this section shall be taken to be in derogation of or to affect the duties of the Commissioners or the powers of the University or a college under the foregoing provisions of this Act.

12. This Act may be cited as the Universities of Oxford and Cambridge Act, 1923.

SCHEDULE

PROVISIONS OF THE UNIVERSITIES OF OXFORD AND CAMBRIDGE ACT, 1877, APPLIED FOR PURPOSES OF THIS ACT[1]

2. In this Act—

'The University' means the University of Oxford and the University of Cambridge respectively, or one of them separately (as the case may require):

'The Senate' means the Senate of the University of Cambridge:

'College' means a College in the University, and includes the Cathedral or House of Christ Church in Oxford:

'Hall' means St. Edmund Hall, in the University of Oxford:

'The Governing Body' of a College means, as regards the Colleges in the University of Oxford, except Christ Church, the head and all actual fellows of the College, being graduates, and as regards Christ Church, means the dean, canons, and students:

'The Governing Body' of a College means, as regards the Colleges in the University of Cambridge, except Downing College, the head and all actual fellows of the College, bye-fellows excepted, being graduates, and as regards Downing College, the head, professors, and all actual fellows thereof, bye-fellows excepted, being graduates:

'Emolument' includes—

(1) A headship, professorship, lecturership, readership, prælectorship, fellowship, bye-fellowship, tutorship, studentship, scholarship, exhibition, demyship, postmastership, taberdarship, Bible clerkship, servitorship, sizarship, sub-sizarship, or other place in the University or a College or the Hall, having attached thereto an income payable out of the revenues of the University or of a College or the Hall, or being a place to be held and enjoyed by a head or other member of a College or the Hall as such, or having attached thereto an income to be so held and enjoyed, arising wholly or in part from an endowment, benefaction, or trust; and

(2) The income aforesaid, and all benefits and advantages of every nature and kind belonging to the place, and any endowment belonging to, or held by, or for the benefit of, or enjoyed by, a head or other member of a College or the Hall as such, and any fund, endowment, or property held by or on behalf of the University or a College or the Hall, for the purpose of advancing, rewarding, or otherwise providing for any member of the University or College or Hall, or of purchasing any advowson, benefice, or property to be held for the like purpose, or to be in any manner applied for the promotion of any such member; and

(3) As regards the University of Oxford a bursary appropriated to any College in Scotland:

'School' means a school or other place of education beyond the precincts of the University, and includes a College in Scotland:

'Advowson' includes right of patronage, exclusive or alternate.

6. If any person nominated a Commissioner by this Act dies, resigns, or becomes incapable of acting as a Commissioner, it shall be lawful for His Majesty to appoint a person to fill his place, and so from time to time as regards every person appointed under this section:

[1] As amended by the Keble College Oxford Act 1988 and the Selwyn College Cambridge Act 1988.

Provided that the name of every person so appointed shall be laid before the Houses of Parliament within ten days after the appointment, if Parliament is then sitting, or if not, then ten days after the next meeting of Parliament.

8. The Commissioner first named in this Act, as regards each of the two bodies of Commissioners, shall be the Chairman of the respective body of Commissioners; and in case of his ceasing from any cause to be a Commissioner, or of his absence from any meeting, the Commissioners present at each meeting shall choose a chairman.

The powers of the Commissioners may be exercised at a meeting at which three or more Commissioners are present.

In case of an equality of votes on a question at a meeting, the chairman of the meeting shall have a second or casting vote in respect of that question.

9. The Commissioners shall have a common seal, which shall be judicially noticed.

10. Any act of the Commissioners shall not be invalid by reason only of any vacancy in their body, but if at any time, and as long as, the number of persons acting as Commissioners is less than four, the Commissioners shall discontinue the exercise of their powers.

11. Until the end of the year one thousand nine hundred and twenty-four, the University and the Governing Body of a College shall have the like powers in all respects of making statutes for the University or the College respectively, and of making statutes for altering or repealing statutes made by them, as are, from and after the end of that year, conferred on the Commissioners by this Act, but every statute so made shall, before the end of that year, be laid before the Commissioners, and the same, if approved before or after the end of that year by the Commissioners by writing under their seal, but not otherwise, shall, as regards the force and operation of the statute, and as regards proceedings prescribed by this Act to be taken respecting a statute made by the Commissioners after (but not before) the statute is made, be deemed to be a statute made by the Commissioners.

If within one month after a statute so made by a College is laid before the Commissioners, a member of the Governing Body of the College makes a representation in writing to the Commissioners respecting the statute, the Commissioners, before approving of the statute, shall take the representation into consideration.

In considering a statute so made by a College, the Commissioners shall have regard to the interests of the University and the Colleges therein as a whole.

14. The Commissioners, in exercising their power to make a statute, shall have regard to the main design of the founder of any institution or emolument which will be affected by the statute, except where that design has ceased to be observed before the passing of this Act, or where the trusts, conditions, or directions affecting the institution or emolument have been altered in substance by or under any other Act.

15. The Commissioners, in making a statute, shall have regard to the interests of education, religion, learning and research, and in the case of a statute which affects a College or the Hall shall have regard, in the first instance, to the maintenance of the College or Hall for those purposes.

20. Nothing in or done under this Act shall prevent the Commissioners from making in any statute made by them for a College such provisions as they think expedient for the voluntary continuance of any voluntary payment that has been used to be made out of the revenues of the College in connection with the College estates or property.

30. A statute made by the Commissioners may, if the Commissioners think fit, be in part a statute for the University, and in part a statute for a College or the Hall.

The Commissioners shall in each statute made by them declare whether the same is a statute, wholly or in any and what part, for the University or for a College or the Hall therein named; and the declaration in that behalf of the Commissioners shall be conclusive, to all intents.

If any statute is in part a statute for a College or the Hall, it shall, for the purposes of the provisions of this Act relative to the representation of Colleges and the Hall, and of the other provisions of this Act regulating proceedings on the statute, be proceeded on as a statute for the College or Hall.

31. Where the Commissioners contemplate making a statute for the University or a statute for a College or the Hall containing a provision for any purpose relative to the University, or a statute otherwise affecting the interests of the University, they shall, one month at least (exclusive of any University vacation) before adopting any final resolution in that behalf, communicate the proposed statute in the University of Oxford to the Hebdomadal Council, and to the Head and to the Visitor of the College affected thereby, or to the Principal of the Hall, and in the University of Cambridge to the Council of the Senate and to the Governing Body of the College affected thereby.

The Commissioners shall take into consideration any representation made to them by the Council, College, Visitor, Principal, or Governing Body respecting the proposed statute.

Within seven days after receipt of such communication by the Council, the Vice-Chancellor of the University shall give public notice thereof in the University.

32. Where the Commissioners contemplate making a statute for a College or the Hall, they shall, one month at least (exclusive of any University vacation) before adopting any final resolution in that behalf, communicate the proposed statute to the Vice-Chancellor of the University and to the Head, and in the University of Oxford the Visitor of the College, and to the Principal of the Hall.

Within seven days after receipt of such communication the Vice-Chancellor shall give public notice thereof in the University.

33. The Commissioners may, if they think fit, by writing under the seal, from time to time authorize and direct the University or any College or the Hall to suspend the election or appointment to, or limit the tenure of, any emolument therein mentioned for a time therein mentioned within the continuance of the powers of the Commissioners as then ascertained; and the election or appointment thereto or tenure thereof shall be suspended or limited accordingly.

34. Any statute made by the Commissioners shall operate without prejudice to any interest possessed by any person by virtue of his having, before the statute comes into operation, become a member of a College or the Hall, or been elected or appointed to a University or College emolument, or acquired a vested right to be elected or appointed thereto.

35. The Commissioners, in the exercise of their authority, may take evidence, and for that purpose may require from any officer of the University or of a College or the Hall the production of any documents or accounts relating to the University or to the College or Hall (as the case may be), and any information relating to the revenues, statutes, usages, or practice thereof, and generally may send for persons, papers, and records.

36. Eight weeks at least (exclusive of any University vacation) before the Commissioners, in the first instance, enter on the consideration of a statute to be made by the Commissioners for a College or the Hall, they shall, by writing under their seal, give notice to the Governing Body of the College, and in the University of Oxford to the Visitor of the College, and in the case of the Hall to the Principal thereof, of their intention to do so.

The Governing Body of the College, at any time after receipt of the notice, may, at an ordinary general meeting, or at a general meeting specially summoned for this purpose, elect three persons to be Commissioners to represent the College in relation to the making by the Commissioners of statutes for the College.

But, in the case of a College, any actual member of the foundation whereof is nominated a Commissioner in this Act, no more than two persons shall be so elected, while that member is a Commissioner.

If during the continuance of the powers of the Commissioners a vacancy happens by death, resignation, or otherwise, among the persons so elected, the same may be filled up by a like election; and so from time to time.

Each person entitled to vote at an election shall have one vote for every place to be then filled by election, and may give his votes to one or more of the candidates for election, as he thinks fit.

The persons elected to represent a College, and the Principal of the Hall, shall be, to all intents, Commissioners in relation to the making by the Commissioners of statutes for the College or Hall, before and after the making thereof, but not further or otherwise, save that they shall not be counted as Commissioners for the purposes of the provisions of this Act requiring four Commissioners to be acting and three to be present at a meeting.

37. Where the Commissioners propose at any meeting, not being an adjourned meeting, to make a statute for a College or the Hall, they shall give to the Governing Body of the College or to the Principal of the Hall, by writing under the seal of the Commissioners, or under the hand of their secretary, fourteen days' notice of the meeting.

38. Any act of the Commissioners shall not be invalid by reason only of any failure to elect any person to be a Commissioner to represent a College, or the failure of any person elected to represent a College, or of the Principal of the Hall, to attend a meeting of the Commissioners.

45. The Commissioners, within one month after making a statute, shall cause it to be submitted to His Majesty in Council, and notice of it having been so submitted shall be published in the *London Gazette* (in this Act referred to as the gazetting of a statute).

The subsequent proceedings under this Act respecting the statute shall not be affected by the cesser of the powers of the Commissioners.

46. At any time within eight weeks (exclusive of any University vacation) after the gazetting of a statute, the University or the Governing Body of a College, or the trustees, governors, or patron of a University or College emolument, or the Principal of the Hall, or the Governing Body of a school, or any other person or body, in case the University, College, emolument, Hall, school, person, or body, is directly affected by the Statute, may petition His Majesty in Council for disallowance of the statute, or of any part thereof.

47. It shall be lawful for His Majesty in Council to refer any statute petitioned against under this Act to the Universities Committee.[1]

The petitioners shall be entitled to be heard by themselves or counsel in support of their petition.

It shall be lawful for His Majesty in Council to make from time to time, rules of procedure and practice for regulating proceedings on such petitions.

[1] The Universities Committee was set up by the Act of 1877 and consists of the President of the Privy Council, the Archbishop of Canterbury, the Lord Chancellor of Great Britain, the Chancellors of the Universities of Oxford and Cambridge (if members of the Privy Council), and such other member or two members of the Privy Council as Her Majesty from time to time thinks fit to appoint in that behalf, that other member, or one at least of those two other members, being a member of the Judicial Committee of the Privy Council.

The costs of all parties of and incident to such proceedings shall be in the discretion of the Universities Committee; and the orders of the Committee respecting costs shall be enforceable as if they were orders of a Division of the High Court of Justice.

48. If the Universities Committee report their opinion that a statute referred to them, or any part thereof, ought to be disallowed, it shall be lawful for His Majesty in Council to disallow the statute or that part, and thereupon the statute or that part shall be of no effect.

If, during the continuance of the powers of the Commissioners, the Universities Committee report their opinion that a statute referred to them ought to be remitted to the Commissioners with a declaration, it shall be lawful for His Majesty in Council to remit the same accordingly; and the Commissioners shall reconsider the statute, with the declaration, and the statute, if and as modified by the Commissioners, shall be proceeded on as an original statute is proceeded on, and so from time to time.

49. If a statute is not referred to the Universities Committee, then, within one month after the expiration of the time for petitioning against it, the statute shall be laid before both Houses of Parliament, if Parliament is then sitting, and if not, then within fourteen days after the next meeting of Parliament.

If a statute is referred to the Universities Committee, and the Committee do not report that the same ought to be wholly disallowed or to be remitted to the Commissioners, then, as soon as conveniently may be after the report of the Universities Committee thereon, the statute, or such part thereof as is not disallowed by Order in Council, shall be laid before both Houses of Parliament.

50. If neither House of Parliament, within four weeks (exclusive of any period of prorogation) after a statute or part of a statute is laid before it, presents an address praying His Majesty to withhold his consent thereto, it shall be lawful for His Majesty in Council by Order to approve the same.

51. Every statute or part of a statute made by the Commissioners, and approved by Order in Council, shall be binding on the University and on every College and on the Hall, and shall be effectual notwithstanding any instrument of foundation or any Act of Parliament, Order in Council, decree, order, statute, or other instrument, or thing constituting wholly or in part an instrument of foundation, or confirming or varying a foundation, or endowment, or otherwise regulating the University or a College or the Hall.

52. If after the cesser of the powers of the Commissioners any doubt arises with respect to the true meaning of any statute made by the Commissioners for the University of Cambridge, the Council of the Senate may apply to the Chancellor of the University for the time being, and he may declare in writing the meaning of the statute on the matter submitted to him, and his declaration shall be registered by the Registrary of the University, and the meaning of the statute as therein declared shall be deemed to be the true meaning thereof.

56. Every statute, ordinance, and regulation made as follows, namely:

(1) Every statute, ordinance, and regulation made by or in relation to the University or a College under any former Act before the passing of this Act, and required by any former Act to be submitted to His Majesty in Council, but not so submitted before the passing of this Act; and

(2) Every statute, ordinance, and regulation made by or in relation to the University or a College under any former Act after the passing of this Act, and before the cesser of the powers of the Commissioners, and required by any former Act to be submitted to His Majesty in Council; and

(3) Every statute, ordinance, and regulation made by or in relation to a College under any former Act or any ordinance since the first day of January, one thousand nine hundred and twenty-three, and before the passing of this Act,

shall, in lieu of being submitted to His Majesty in Council under and according to any former Act or any ordinance, and whether or not a submission to His Majesty in Council is required under any former Act or any ordinance, be, with the consent of the Commissioners in writing under their seal, but not otherwise, submitted to His Majesty in Council under this Act, and be proceeded on as if it were a statute made by the Commissioners, with the substitution only of the University or the College for the Commissioners in the provisions of this Act in that behalf; and the same, if and as far as it is approved by Order in Council under this Act, shall have effect as if it had been submitted and proceeded on under any former Act or any ordinance.

57. Nothing in this Act shall be construed to repeal any provision of the Universities Tests Act, 1871.

STATUTES

TO 1 OCTOBER 2000

TITLE I

OF INTERPRETATION

(This Title is a 'Queen-in-Council' statute—see Title XIV, Section VII.*)*

1. In these statutes and in all decrees or regulations made under them, unless in any case a contrary intention shall appear,

(*a*) words importing the singular number shall include the plural and vice versa;

(*b*) words importing the masculine gender shall include the feminine and vice versa;

(*c*) 'the University' shall mean 'the University of Oxford';

(*d*) 'Congregation' shall mean 'the Congregation of the University';

(*e*) 'Council' shall mean 'the Council of the University';

(*f*) 'the statutes' shall mean the statutes of the University in force for the time being;

(*g*) 'decrees' shall mean decrees made by Council;

(*h*) 'regulations' shall mean regulations made by other bodies under the authority of the statutes or of Council;

(*i*) 'ordinary degrees' shall mean degrees other than Degrees by Diploma, Honorary Degrees, Degrees by Special Resolution, and Degrees by Incorporation.

2. If any question shall arise on the interpretation of a statute, decree, or regulation, it shall be referred to the Vice-Chancellor. In the case of a question on a decree or regulation, the Vice-Chancellor shall, after consulting such persons as he may wish, give a ruling which shall be binding on all members of the University and shall be published in the *University Gazette*. In the case of a question on a statute, the Vice-Chancellor shall consult the High Steward; if they agree on a ruling, it shall be binding on all members of the University and shall be published in the *University Gazette*; if they fail to agree, they shall refer the question to the Chancellor, or if the Chancellor is unwilling or unable to act to some other person chosen by them, and his ruling shall be binding on all members of the University and shall be published in the *University Gazette*.

TITLE II

OF THE CONGREGATION OF THE UNIVERSITY

Section I. Of the Functions and Powers of Congregation

(This Section is a 'Queen-in-Council' statute—see Title XV, Section VII.)

1. Congregation shall be the legislative body of the University.

2. The functions, powers, and duties of Congregation shall be:

(*a*) to decide upon proposals submitted to it by Council for amending, repealing, or adding to the statutes;

(*b*) to consider resolutions submitted to it by Council or by any twenty or more of its members;

(*c*) to take note of the replies to questions asked by any two or more of its members;

(*d*) to confer degrees;

(*e*) to make such elections as may be laid down in the statutes or in decrees or regulations;

(*f*) to approve the appointment of the Vice-Chancellor;

(*g*) to perform such further duties as are or shall be assigned to it by the statutes.

Section II. Of the Composition of Congregation

(This Section is a 'Queen-in-Council' statute—see Title XV, Section VII.)

1. Subject to such limit on membership by reason of retirement or age as may be prescribed by Congregation by statute, Congregation shall consist of the following persons:

(1) the Chancellor,

(2) the High Steward,

(3) the Vice-Chancellor,

(4) the Proctors,

(5) the members of the faculties,

(6) the holders of such administrative posts in the University as may be approved for this purpose by decree,

(7) the heads of all the colleges and other societies included in Title VII,

(8) the members of the governing bodies of all the colleges and other societies included in Title VII except the Permanent Private Halls,

(9) the principal bursar or treasurer of each of the colleges and other societies included in Title VII except the Permanent Private Halls, if he or she is not a member of its governing body,

(10) such other persons or classes of persons as may be admitted by decree,

(11) every person who was a member of Congregation under the statutes as they stood on the day before this statute was approved by Her Majesty in Council[1] for as long as he or she possesses the qualification which entitled him or her to membership on that date.

2. The Registrar shall keep a register of the persons qualified to be the members of Congregation, and shall publish annually in the *University Gazette* as soon as possible after 1 January the register as it stood at that date. No person shall be admitted to vote or act as a member of Congregation unless that person's name is in the register and he or she is qualified under clause 1 above.

Section III. Of Procedure in Congregation

1. Meetings of Congregation shall be held on the Tuesdays in the first, second, fourth, sixth, and eighth weeks of each Full Term and on the second Tuesday after each Full Term (provided always that a meeting shall be cancelled if there is no business for it) and at such other times as the Chancellor or the Vice-Chancellor may determine.

2. The Chairman of Congregation at the Encaenia, or at any other meeting held for the conferment of Degrees by Diploma or Honorary Degrees, shall be the Chancellor, or, in his or her absence, the Vice-Chancellor or a Pro-Vice-Chancellor; the Chairman on all other occasions shall be the Vice-Chancellor, or, in his or her absence, a Pro-Vice-Chancellor.

3. At any meeting of Congregation the Chairman may adjourn any question, provided always

(*a*) that the Chairman shall not have such power of adjournment if notice of objection to the question is by statute required to be given before the meeting of Congregation;

(*b*) that no question shall be adjourned more than once in total under the provisions of this clause or of clause 4 below.

4. Any twenty members of Congregation may, not later than noon on the eighth day before a meeting of Congregation, give notice in writing to the Vice-Chancellor that they request the adjournment of any question or questions on the agenda for that meeting, provided always

(*a*) that such a request may be submitted only in respect of a question notice of objection to which is by statute required to be given before the meeting of Congregation; and

(*b*) that no question shall be adjourned more than once in total under the provisions of this clause or clause 3 above.

Whenever such a request is received, the Vice-Chancellor shall refer it to the Proctors, who shall decide whether or not it shall be granted. The Proctors' decision shall be published in the *University Gazette* not less than four days

[1] The relevant date is 25 January 1968.

before the meeting of Congregation to which the question or questions concerned was or were originally due to be submitted. If the Proctors decide that the request shall not be granted, any two members of Congregation may, by rising in their places at the meeting, demand that a vote be taken on whether or not the question or any of the questions in respect of which the request was submitted shall nevertheless be adjourned; and, if such a demand is made, the Chairman shall, after any debate on the question of adjournment, put that question to the vote in accordance with the provisions of clause 6 below.

5. Consideration of any question adjourned under the provisions of clause 3 or clause 4 above shall be resumed at the next meeting of Congregation (or at such later meeting as the Chairman may determine), and the Registrar shall give not less than five days' notice in the *University Gazette* that the debate will be resumed.

6. At any meeting of Congregation the Chairman may propose at any time the adjournment of the House. The motion shall be put forthwith, and, if it is carried, the House shall be adjourned. After any meeting has lasted two full hours the Chairman shall have the power of adjourning the House without question put. Any adjournment of the House shall be to the following day, unless the Chairman shall fix another day.

7. Subject to the provisions of clauses 3, 4, and 6 above, every vote in Congregation shall be taken immediately after the close of the debate (if any) on the question. Every question shall be settled by a simple majority (with the Chairman having a second or casting vote in the case of an equality of votes) except where the statutes provide otherwise.

8. When any question has been put to Congregation by the Chairman he or she may direct that a division be taken, or may announce that in his or her opinion the proposal is accepted or rejected, as the case may be. If the Chairman's opinion so declared is challenged by at least six members of Congregation rising in their places, he or she shall direct that a division be taken.

9. Every statute shall be introduced by a member of Council or of the General Board as Council may direct.

10. Before any statute, amendment to a statute, or resolution is submitted to the House, the Chairman shall direct the Registrar to read aloud the preamble in the case of a statute, the amendment, or the resolution as the case may be.

11. When the sole business for a meeting of Congregation comprises one or more questions to which, or to each of which (as the case may be), no opposition or proposed amendment has been notified, and in respect of which, or each of which (as the case may be), no request for an adjournment has been received, the Vice-Chancellor shall have power to declare the item or items to have been approved without holding the meeting, provided always

(*a*) that notice of the cancellation is published in the *University Gazette* not less than four days before the meeting is due to be held;

(*b*) that the Vice-Chancellor shall exercise the power to cancel a meeting only when, in his or her opinion, the business is not of such general concern to the

University as a whole that it would be inappropriate to proceed without an opportunity for further explanation or debate.

12. At any meeting of Congregation the Chairman shall have the right to withdraw a statute at any time before it has been submitted to the vote of the House. Council may resubmit the statute to the House at a subsequent meeting.

13. No member of Congregation shall without leave of the Chairman speak more than once on any item, provided that the mover of an item shall have the right to reply at the close of the debate thereon.

14. The operation of any of the clauses of this section may be suspended by resolution of Congregation, subject to the provisions of Section VI of this Title.

Section IV. Of the Submission of Statutes to Congregation

1. Every statute to be submitted to Congregation shall contain a preamble stating shortly the principle of the measure, and an enacting part carrying out in detail the principle of the statute as stated in the preamble.

2. Notice of the promulgation of a statute shall be published in the *University Gazette* not later than the nineteenth day before the date of promulgation.

3. Any two members of Congregation may, not later than noon on the eighth day before the date of promulgation, give notice in writing to the Registrar that they propose to oppose the motion for the adoption of the preamble. Such notice shall be published by the Registrar in the *University Gazette* not later than the fourth day before the date of promulgation. If such notice has not been given, and unless Council shall determine otherwise, the preamble shall, at the conclusion of proceedings on it, be declared by the Chairman to be carried without question put. If the preamble is carried, further proceedings on the proposed statute shall be adjourned to a date to be fixed by the Chairman not less than fourteen days later, of which notice shall be published by the Registrar in the *University Gazette* not later than the eleventh day before the date so fixed.

4. If the preamble is not rejected, amendments to the statute may be proposed by two or more members of Congregation, provided that such amendments signed by the mover and seconder are delivered in writing to the Registrar not later than noon on the eighth day before the date to which further proceedings on the proposed statute have been adjourned under the provisions of clause 3 above.

5. The Vice-Chancellor shall report to Council all amendments which in his or her judgement are not inconsistent with or irrelevant to the principle of the statute as stated in the preamble, and Council shall forward them to Congregation, together with any amendments which Council itself may propose.

6. If any such amendment shall have been adopted by Congregation, the statute, as amended, shall be published in the *University Gazette* and printed so as to show the amendments made. Further proceedings on the proposed statute shall be adjourned to a date to be fixed by the Chairman not less than fourteen days

later, of which notice shall be published by the Registrar in the *University Gazette* not later than the eleventh day before the date so fixed.

7. Further amendments to the statute as published under the provisions of the last preceding clause may be proposed by six or more members of Congregation, provided that such amendments signed by the proposer and not less than five supporters reach the Registrar not later than noon on the fourth day after that on which the statute as amended was published. Such further amendments, together with any further amendments which Council itself may propose, shall be submitted to Congregation in accordance with the provisions of clause 5 above.

8. At any time before the statute is finally submitted to Congregation Council may propose further amendments or submit to Congregation the choice between contradictory or inconsistent provisions which may have been introduced into the statute; or it may withdraw the statute.

9. If any amendment proposed under clauses 7 or 8 above shall have been adopted by Congregation, the statute, as amended, shall be published in the *University Gazette* and printed so as to show the amendments made. Further proceedings on the proposed statute shall be adjourned to a date to be fixed by the Chairman not less than fourteen days later, of which notice shall be published by the Registrar in the *University Gazette* not later than the eleventh day before the date so fixed.

10. Any amendment which is not moved and seconded in Congregation shall lapse.

11. All amendments forwarded to Congregation under the provisions of clauses 5, 7, and 8 above shall be published by the Registrar in the *University Gazette* not later than the fourth day before the Congregation in which they are to be moved, shall be printed consecutively, and shall be moved in that order unless otherwise determined by the Chairman, who shall give notice of any such change of order at the opening of the Congregation.

12. If amendments have been proposed but either have been rejected or have lapsed under the provisions of clause 10 above, the question that the statute do pass shall be submitted to Congregation not less than fourteen days after the meeting at which the amendments have been rejected or have lapsed. The date shall be fixed by the Chairman and not less than eleven days' notice shall be published by the Registrar in the *University Gazette*.

13. If no proposals to make amendments are forwarded to Congregation under the provisions of clauses 4 and 5 above, the question that the statute do pass shall be submitted to Congregation on the date fixed by the Chairman under the provisions of clause 3 above.

14. Any two members of Congregation may, not later than noon on the eighth day before the date on which voting on the enacting part of a statute is on the agenda for Congregation, give notice in writing to the Registrar that they intend to vote against the enacting part; the Registrar shall report the giving of such

notice to Council and shall publish it in the *University Gazette* not less than four days before the enacting part is to be voted on. If such notice has not been given, and unless Council shall determine otherwise, the statute shall be declared by the Chairman to be passed without question put, and the provisions of Sect. III, cll. 9–10 of this Title shall not apply to the statute.

15. Council shall not be entitled to reintroduce a statute which has been rejected by Congregation earlier than the beginning of the fourth term after the term in which it was rejected.

16. Subject to the provisions of Sect. V, cl. 12 below, at least 125 members must vote in favour of, and constitute a majority in favour of,

(*a*) the rejection of a preamble, or

(*b*) the acceptance of an amendment to the enacting part of a statute (except an amendment proposed by or acceptable to Council), or

(*c*) the rejection of an amendment proposed by or acceptable to Council, or

(*d*) the rejection of the enacting part of a statute

for such an acceptance or rejection to be effective. If fewer than 125 members vote in favour, the preamble under (*a*) or the amendment under (*c*) or the enacting part under (*d*) shall be deemed to have been accepted, or the amendment under (*b*) shall be deemed to have been rejected, as the case may be.

17. The operation of any of the preceding clauses of this section may be suspended by resolution of Congregation, subject to the provisions of Section VI of this Title.

18. A statute shall come into effect on the date on which it is approved by Congregation, subject to the provisions of Sect. X, cl. 2 below.

Section V. Of the Submission of Resolutions to Congregation

1. Either Council, or any twenty or more members of Congregation, may at any time submit a resolution on any topic; provided that, in the case of a resolution submitted by twenty or more members of Congregation, the Vice-Chancellor may rule that resolution inadmissible

(*a*) if it is not, in his or her opinion, on a topic concerning the policy or administration of the University (which terms shall be deemed to include calling upon Council or any other body or any person to annul, amend, or repeal a decree or regulation); or

(*b*) if it relates to a particular college or other society, or (subject to (*a*) above) to a particular person other than the Vice-Chancellor.

2. Notice of a resolution proposed by twenty or more members of Congregation, signed by all the members concerned, shall be delivered to the Registrar not later than noon on the twenty-second day before any stated meeting of Congregation at which they propose to move it.

3. Subject to the provisions of clause 4 below and of Section VI of this Title, notice of a resolution shall be published in the *University Gazette* not later than the nineteenth day before the Congregation at which it is to be moved.

4. A resolution submitted by Council conferring a Degree by Resolution under the provisions of Section VIII of this Title shall be published in the *University Gazette* and shall be deemed to have been approved *nemine contradicente* at noon on the fourth day after the day on which it was published, unless by that time the Registrar has received notice in writing from two or more members of Congregation that they wish the resolution to be put to a meeting of Congregation. If such notice is received, Council may either withdraw the resolution (in which case the Registrar shall publish notice of this withdrawal in the *University Gazette*) or republish the resolution not later than the fourth day before that on which it is to be moved in Congregation.

5. Any two members of Congregation may propose an amendment to a resolution, except a resolution submitted under the provisions of clause 4 above or of Section VI of this Title. Notice of any such amendment, signed by the proposer and seconder, shall be delivered to the Registrar not later than noon on the eighth day, and published in the *University Gazette* not later than the fifth day, before the meeting of Congregation at which the resolution is to be moved. If more than one amendment is received, they shall be printed consecutively and shall be moved in that order unless otherwise determined by the Chairman, who shall give notice of any such change of order at the opening of Congregation.

6. Members of Congregation proposing an amendment under the provisions of clause 5 above shall state whether or not the amendment is in their view hostile to the resolution (that is to say, the amendment is such that if it were not carried the proposers of the amendment would oppose the resolution). If they state that it is not hostile, and if the amendment is acceptable to Council, then Council may decide that proceedings on the resolution and on the proposed amendment thereto shall be adjourned to a meeting of Congregation held not fewer than fourteen days after the meeting at which the resolution was originally to be moved under the provisions of clause 3 above; Council may also, by publication of a notice in the *University Gazette* not later than the twelfth day before the meeting of Congregation to which the proceedings have been adjourned, require that any two members proposing to oppose the amendment shall give notice in writing to the Registrar to that effect not later than the eighth day before the meeting to which the proceedings have been adjourned, and such notice, if given, shall be published by the Registrar in the *University Gazette* not later than the fourth day before that meeting. If such notice of opposition, having been duly required, has not been given, and if Council has not decided by 4 p.m. on the eighth day before the meeting at which the resolution was originally to be moved that the proposed amendment is unacceptable to Council, or, in the event that Council has decided that the proposed amendment is unacceptable to it, if Council has not also caused a notice to that effect to be published in the *University Gazette* not later than the fourth day before the meeting, then the amended resolution shall, at the conclusion of proceedings on the amendment

and the resolution, be declared by the Chairman to be carried without question put, and the provisions of clause 7 below, and of Sect. III, cl. 10 of this Title, shall not apply to the amendment or the resolution; provided always that Council may determine that a division shall be taken on a resolution which would otherwise have been declared carried without question put. Alternatively, if proceedings have not been so adjourned, then, subject to the provisions of clause 7 below, the proposed amendment shall, at the conclusion of proceedings on it, be put to the House; if the amendment is carried, the amended resolution shall subsequently be declared by the Chairman to be carried without question put, while, if the amendment is rejected, the unamended resolution shall subsequently be declared by the Chairman to be carried without question put, and in neither case shall the provisions of clause 7 below, or of Sect. III, cl. 10 of this Title, apply to the resolution; provided always that Council may determine that a division shall be taken on a resolution (whether or not so amended) which would otherwise have been declared carried without question put.

7. Subject to the provisions of clause 9 below, any resolution or amendment thereto which is not moved and seconded in Congregation shall lapse.

8. At the conclusion of the debate and voting on the amendments, the resolution shall be put. If any amendments shall have been accepted, the resolution as amended shall be put, and the proposer of the resolution shall have the right to speak first in the debate thereon.

9. Subject to the provisions of clause 4 above, any two members of Congregation may, not later than noon on the eighth day before the meeting at which the resolution is to be moved, give notice in writing to the Registrar that they propose to oppose the resolution; or Council may, not later than 4 p.m. on that day, instruct the Registrar to give notice that the resolution is unacceptable to Council. Such notice (whether of opposition by members of Congregation or of unacceptability to Council) shall be published by the Registrar in the *University Gazette* not later than the fourth day before the meeting. If such notice has not been given, and unless Council shall determine otherwise, the resolution shall, at the conclusion of proceedings on it, be declared by the Chairman to be carried without question put, and the provisions of clause 7 above, and of Sect. III, cl. 10, of this Title, shall not apply to the resolution.

10. Subject to the provisions of Sect. VI, cl. 3 of this Title, it shall be the duty of Council to give consideration to a vote on a resolution proposed by Council, if the resolution is carried in Congregation, but Council shall not be bound by such a vote. Council shall, however, be bound by the rejection of such a resolution in Congregation, provided that the resolution is either rejected on a division with at least 125 members voting against or rejected on a postal vote held under the provisions of Section X of this Title. In the case of a resolution proposed by twenty or more members of Congregation, provided that

(*a*) the resolution is carried on a division with at least 125 members voting in favour; or (*b*) the resolution is carried *nemine contradicente*, or otherwise without a division, at a meeting at which at least 125 members are present on the floor of the House at the time when the resolution is declared by the Chairman to have been carried; or

(*c*) the resolution is declared by the Vice-Chancellor to have been carried without holding the meeting, under the provisions of Sect. III, cl. 11 above,

Council shall be bound, not later than the eighth week of the Full Term after that in which the resolution was carried, to promulgate a statute, or to make a decree, or to take such other action as it considers appropriate (as the case may be), in order to give effect to the resolution. Pursuant to proviso (*b*) above, the Proctors shall, whenever a resolution is carried *nemine contradicente*, or otherwise without a division, certify the number of members present on the floor of the House at the time when the resolution is declared by the Chairman to have been carried. For the purposes of this clause, the expression 'the floor of the House' shall mean the whole of the Convocation House or the Area and Semicircle of the Sheldonian Theatre, as the case may be.

11. When a statute is promulgated or a decree is made under the provisions of clause 10 above, Council shall, if the passing of the statute or the making of the decree would involve additional expenditure from university funds, publish a certificate stating whether that financial provision can be made without curtailment of existing services or of services for which money has already been allocated.

12. In the event of Council being required, under the provisions of clause 10 above, to promulgate a statute to which it is opposed, the provisions of Sect. IV, cl. 16 above shall not apply.

13. In the event of Council being required, under the provisions of clause 10 above, to make a decree, the decree shall be put to Congregation for approval not later than the eighth week of the Full Term after that in which the resolution was carried. Such a decree shall be published in the *University Gazette* not later than the nineteenth day before that on which it is to be put to Congregation, and amendments may be proposed under the same procedure as that laid down for amendments of resolutions in clauses 5–8 above.

14. The operation of any of the clauses of this section may be suspended by resolution of Congregation, subject to the provisions of Section VI below.

Section VI. Of the Suspension of Statutory Procedures

1. A resolution proposed under the provisions of Section V of this Title may provide for the suspension of the operation of clauses in Sections III–V and Sections X–XII of this Title, or of clauses, other than clause 2, of this section.

2. A resolution under clause 1 above shall be published in the *University Gazette* not later than the fourth day before that on which it is to be moved; provided that if the resolution is so published not later than the nineteenth day before that on which it is to be moved, Council may include in the procedure

for dealing with the resolution the requirement that any member of Congregation who proposes to oppose the resolution must, by noon on the eighth day before the meeting at which the resolution is to be moved, give notice in writing to the Registrar of such opposition. If such notice has been received by that time from at least two members of Congregation in respect of a resolution for opposition to which Council has imposed that requirement, the Registrar shall publish the notice in the *University Gazette* not later than the fourth day before the meeting; if such notice has not been so received, and unless Council shall determine otherwise, the resolution shall, at the conclusion of proceedings on it, be declared by the Chairman to be carried without question put, and the provisions of Sect. III, cl. 10 and Sect. V, cl. 7 of this Title shall not apply to the resolution. A resolution under clause 1 above shall contain not only a reference to the clauses to be suspended but also a statement of the procedure to be followed in the event of the suspension being approved. Unless the resolution is declared carried without question put in accordance with the preceding provisions of this clause, it shall not be moved if twenty or more members signify their objection by rising in their places after the resolution has been read by the Registrar.

3. Council shall be bound by the vote on a resolution under clause 1 above.

Section VII. Of the Asking of Questions in Congregation

1. Any member of Congregation may at a meeting of Congregation in Full Term ask a question relating to any matter concerning the policy or the administration of the University.

2. Written notice of any such question signed by the member of Congregation proposing to put it and by one supporter shall be sent to the Registrar not later than noon on the eighteenth day before it is to be asked. Unless the Vice-Chancellor considers the question to be inadmissible in substance or in form, it shall be published by the Registrar in the *University Gazette*, together with the answer (which shall be drafted by Council), not less than five days before the question is to be asked.

3. Any answer so published shall be read in Congregation either by a member of Council or by such other person as shall be nominated by Council. No debate shall be permitted upon the answer, but at the Chairman's discretion supplementary questions may be asked to elucidate the answer given.

Section VIII. Of the Conferment of Degrees by Congregation

1. The procedure for the conferment of Degrees by Diploma and Honorary Degrees approved by resolution shall be made by Council.

2. In the case of a person in any of the following categories who does not hold, and is not qualified for, any of the Degrees (other than Honorary Degrees) of Doctor of Divinity, Doctor of Civil Law, Doctor of Medicine, Master of Arts, Master of Biochemistry, Master of Chemistry, Master of Earth Sciences, Master

of Engineering, Master of Mathematics, or Master of Physics of the University, Council shall as soon as possible propose to Congregation that a Degree of Master of Arts by Resolution be conferred upon that person without fee, provided in every case that he or she holds both a bachelor's and a doctor's degree (other than an honorary degree) of any university or universities or of any such other institution or institutions as Council may determine by decree from time to time, or that at least twenty terms have lapsed since he or she first became a member of a university or such other institution, or, in the case of a person who is not a member of any university, that he or she is at least 25 years of age:

(1) the Chancellor;

(2) the High Steward;

(3) the Vice-Chancellor;

(4) the Proctors;

(5) the heads of all the colleges and other societies included in Title VII;

(6) the members of the governing bodies of all the colleges and other societies included in Title VII except the Permanent Private Halls;

(7) the principal bursar or treasurer of each of the colleges and other societies included in Title VII except the Permanent Private Halls, if he or she is not a member of its governing body.

In the case of a person excluded because none of the above provisos is met, Council shall proceed as soon as possible after one of them has been met. Nothing in this clause shall restrict the power of Council to propose to Congregation that a Degree by Resolution be conferred without fee upon any person it considers appropriate.

3. A Degree by Resolution shall be deemed to have been conferred as soon after the approval of the resolution by Congregation as the recipient shall have been matriculated.

4. The procedure for the conferment of ordinary degrees and degrees by incorporation shall be laid down by decree.

Section IX. Of the Holding of Elections in Congregation

1. Every election by Congregation shall be held in Full Term, unless Council shall order otherwise. The Registrar shall publish twenty-eight days' notice of every election and shall at the same time give notice of the latest days on which nominations of candidates must be received.

2. Every election in Congregation held for the purpose of filling a vacancy about to be caused by lapse of time in any committee or other body set up by or under the authority of the statutes shall take place in the term before the vacancy will arise, and the person elected shall enter upon office on the first day of the following term.

3. Every election in Congregation held for the purpose of filling a vacancy caused otherwise than by lapse of time shall take place as soon as may be after

the occurrence of the vacancy (subject to the provisions of clause 1 above). The person elected shall enter upon office immediately upon election but shall hold office for the unexpired residue only of the period of office of the person whom he or she succeeds.

4. Save as is provided otherwise by statute or decree, elections shall be subject to the following rules as to the nomination of candidates:

(*a*) No candidate shall have votes reckoned to him or her at any election, unless he or she shall have been nominated in writing not later than 4 p.m. on the twenty-fourth day before that fixed for the election by two members of Congregation other than the candidate or not later than 4 p.m. on the seventeenth day before that fixed for the election by six members of Congregation other than the candidate.

(*b*) All nominations, dated and signed, shall be delivered to the Registrar within the times above prescribed, and in such form as shall be prescribed by the Vice-Chancellor, and shall be published by the Registrar in the *University Gazette* as soon as possible.

(*c*) If at the close of the time prescribed for the nomination of candidates for election in Congregation so many candidates only have been nominated, or being nominated have not withdrawn, as to leave no more than are sufficient to fill the vacancies, the candidates so nominated shall be deemed to be duly elected from the date appointed for the election; and the election shall be published in the *University Gazette*.

(*d*) If at the time of election there shall be a greater number of vacancies than the number of candidates nominated and not having withdrawn, the Vice-Chancellor and Proctors jointly shall have power to nominate a candidate for each vacancy remaining to be filled, and such candidates shall then be declared to be duly elected.

(*e*) If at the time of election in Congregation there shall be a number of candidates nominated greater than the number of vacancies, the procedure of the election shall be as follows:

(i) The Registrar shall dispatch to every member of Congregation at his or her last known place of residence, or at such other place as the member shall in writing direct, not later than the fourth day before the day fixed by the Vice-Chancellor for the election, a voting paper on which shall be specified the latest time by which it must be delivered to the Registrar.

(ii) The form of the voting paper, and the method of recording votes, shall be prescribed by the Vice-Chancellor.

(iii) The voting paper, after being signed by the voter, shall be delivered to the Registrar by post prepaid or by hand.

(iv) An election shall not be deemed to be invalid owing to misdirection or non-receipt of any voting paper.

(v) The Registrar shall be responsible for the counting of the votes, but the Vice-Chancellor and Proctors shall decide on the validity of any vote which, in the opinion of the Registrar, is in doubt.

(vi) The senior in university standing of any candidates for whom an equal number of votes have been given shall be deemed to be duly elected.

(vii) The result of the election shall be published in the *University Gazette*.

(*f*) In any election where vacancies are to be filled for periods of different length, the elected candidates shall hold office so that the tenure of those who receive more votes shall be longer than that of those who receive fewer votes; but if the election is uncontested or if two candidates receive the same number of votes, the candidate senior in academic standing shall hold office for the longer period.

(*g*) An election in Congregation conducted under the procedure laid down in sub-clause (*e*) above shall be deemed to be an election complying with the provisions of Tit. XIV, Sect. III, cl. 2.

Section X. Of the Submission of Decisions of Congregation to a Postal Vote

1. Notwithstanding the other provisions of the statutes but subject to the provisions of this section, a question decided or a resolution carried or rejected at a meeting of Congregation shall be submitted for confirmation or rejection to a postal vote of the members of Congregation if, not later than 4 p.m. on the sixth day after that meeting,

(*a*) Council so decides; or

(*b*) the question has been decided, or the resolution has been carried or rejected, on a division at a meeting at which not fewer than twenty-five members of Congregation were present on the floor of the House at the time when the division was taken and if a requisition for such a postal vote signed by at least fifty members of Congregation is delivered to the Vice-Chancellor.

Pursuant to proviso (*b*) above, the Proctors shall, whenever a division is taken at a meeting of Congregation, certify the number of members present on the floor of the House at the time of the division. For the purposes of this clause, the expression 'the floor of the House' shall mean the whole of the Convocation House or the Area and Semicircle of the Sheldonian Theatre, as the case may be.

2. No decision taken, or resolution carried or rejected, by Congregation on a division otherwise than by such a postal vote shall be deemed to be operative or to have been carried or rejected

(*a*) before 4 p.m. on the sixth day after the meeting of Congregation at which the question was decided or the resolution carried or rejected; or

(*b*) where a postal vote is required to be taken under clause 1, before the decision has been confirmed by such a vote.

3. The Registrar shall publish in the *University Gazette* a verbatim record (or if the Vice-Chancellor shall so decide, a summary record approved by the Vice-Chancellor) of the proceedings of Congregation relating to any question on which a postal vote is to be held under clause 1.

4. Where a question is submitted to a postal vote under clause 1, the Vice-Chancellor may submit any other question decided at the same meeting of Congregation (whether decided on a division or not) to a postal vote at the same time if it appears to him or her that the questions are so related that they should be submitted for confirmation or rejection at the same time.

5. The procedure for the conduct of a postal vote under clause 1 shall be as follows:

(*a*) The Registrar shall dispatch to every member of Congregation at his or her last known place of residence, or at such other place as the member shall in writing direct, not later than the fourth day before the day fixed by the Vice-Chancellor for the vote, a voting paper on which shall be specified the latest time by which it must be delivered to the Registrar: provided that the time so specified shall not be earlier than seven days after the publication of the *University Gazette* referred to in clause 3.

(*b*) The form of the voting paper including the manner in which the question is to be put, and the method of recording votes, shall be prescribed by the Vice-Chancellor.

(*c*) The voting paper, after being signed by the voter, shall be delivered to the Registrar by post prepaid or by hand.

(*d*) No postal vote shall be deemed to be invalid owing to misdirection or non-receipt of any voting paper.

(*e*) The Registrar shall be responsible for the counting of the votes, but the Vice-Chancellor and Proctors shall decide on the validity of any vote which, in the opinion of the Registrar, is in doubt.

(*f*) The result of the vote shall be published in the *University Gazette*.

6. Any question submitted to a postal vote under clause 1 shall be determined by the majority of the votes cast, notwithstanding any provision of the statutes relating to the number of persons required to vote for or against a proposal in order that it may be passed or rejected. In the event of an equality of votes the Vice-Chancellor shall have a second or casting vote.

7. This section shall not apply to:

(*a*) a resolution approving the conferment of a degree of the University (including a Degree by Diploma or an Honorary Degree);

(*b*) anything done under Section IX or Section XII of this Title;

(*c*) any decision of Congregation relating to the adjournment of the House; or

(*d*) elections to the Vice-Chancellorship.

8. The operation of any of the clauses of this section may be suspended by resolution of Congregation, subject to the provisions of Section VI of this Title.

Section XI. Of the Vice-Chancellor's Oration and the Annual Report of the University

1. During each academic year the Vice-Chancellor shall at a meeting of Congregation deliver an Oration in which he or she shall address the House on issues of current concern to the University. In a year in which the holder of the office of Vice-Chancellor changes, the Oration shall be delivered by the outgoing Vice-Chancellor before the installation of the incoming Vice-Chancellor.

2. During each academic year Council shall produce an Annual Report to Congregation on the main items of business which it has conducted, and on the other affairs of the University, in the preceding academic year.

3. Both the Vice-Chancellor's Oration and the Annual Report shall be published in the *University Gazette*. The Annual Report shall subsequently be presented at a meeting of Congregation in accordance with the provisions of clause 5 below.

4. The Vice-Chancellor's Oration shall be placed on the agenda for a meeting of Congregation in Michaelmas Term, at which meeting, at the discretion of the Chairman, discussion shall be permitted and questions may be asked concerning the Oration.

5. The Annual Report shall be presented at a meeting of Congregation. Notice of presentation shall be published in the *University Gazette* not later than the nineteenth day before that meeting. At the meeting at which the Annual Report is presented, the report shall be introduced by a member of Council, after which, at the discretion of the Chairman, discussion shall be permitted and questions may be asked concerning the report; provided that any member of Congregation who wishes to speak or to ask a question concerning the report shall, not later than noon on the eighth day before that meeting, give notice in writing to the Registrar of his or her wish to do so. If such notice has not been given by at least two members of Congregation, the Chairman shall declare the Annual Report to have been presented to Congregation without introduction by a member of Council and without question put; and, unless the meeting of Congregation is required to deal with other business, the Vice-Chancellor shall have power to declare the Annual Report to have been presented without holding the meeting, provided that notice of the cancellation is published in the *University Gazette* not less than four days before the meeting is due to be held.

6. The operation of any of the clauses of this section may be suspended by resolution of Congregation, subject to the provisions of Section VI of this Title.

[*Note.* Under Decree (4) of 1 October 1998 (*Gazette*, Vol. 129, p. 63), notwithstanding the provisions of cll. 2, 3, and 5 above,

(*a*) During each academic year Council shall produce (i) an Annual Review of such of the affairs of the University in the preceding academic year as shall seem to Council to be of particular importance in the national and international context, and (ii) a Year Report containing a detailed survey of the activities of the University's faculties, departments, and other institutions in the preceding academic year.

(*b*) The Annual Review shall be circulated to all members of Congregation. The Year Report shall be made available in university and college libraries in paper form, and so far as possible electronically, and a paper copy of any part or all of it shall be made available to any member of Congregation on request.

(*c*) The Annual Review shall subsequently be presented at a meeting of Congregation in accordance with the same procedure as that prescribed in Tit. II, Sect. XI, cl. 5 for the presentation of the Annual Report, but the Year Report shall not be circulated beyond the arrangements set out at (*b*) above.]

Section XII. Of the Submission of Topics for Discussion in Congregation

1. Either Council, or any twenty or more members of Congregation, may put forward for discussion in Congregation any topic of concern to the University, including any issue on which it would be permissible for it or them to submit a resolution under the provisions of Section V of this Title, provided that, in the case of a topic put forward by twenty or more members of Congregation, the Vice-Chancellor may rule that topic inadmissible

(*a*) if it is not, in his or her opinion, a topic of concern to the University; or

(*b*) if it relates to a particular college or other society, or to a particular person other than the Vice-Chancellor.

2. Notice of a topic put forward by twenty or more members of Congregation, signed by all the members concerned, shall be delivered to the Registrar not later than noon on the twenty-second day before any stated meeting at which they propose that it should be discussed.

3. Notice of a topic shall be published in the *University Gazette* not later than the nineteenth day before the Congregation at which it is to be discussed.

4. In the case of a topic put forward by Council, a member of Council shall be invited by the Chairman to speak first in the discussion, and in the case of a topic put forward by twenty or more members of Congregation, one of those members shall be invited by the Chairman to speak first in the discussion; provided that if such an invitation is declined, the Chairman may nevertheless, at his or her discretion, invite any other members of Congregation to speak on the topic. For the purposes of Sect. III, cl. 13 of this Title, the person invited by the Chairman to speak first in the discussion shall be deemed to be the mover of the item.

5. It shall be the duty of Council to give consideration to the remarks made in the discussion, but Council shall not be bound to take any further action in regard to the topic.

6. The operations of any of the clauses of this section may be suspended by resolution of Congregation, subject to the provisions of Section VI of this Title.

APPENDIX TO TITLE II

GUIDE TO PROCEDURES IN CONGREGATION

Important Note. This guide has been drawn up as a convenient *aide-mémoire* for members of Congregation. It should not be seen as a substitute for the formal legislation contained in Tit. II, Sectt. III–XII, which remains the authority in this matter and to which reference should always be made in any case of doubt or difficulty. A member of Congregation seeking advice on questions relating to procedures in Congregation, other than elections, should contact the Senior Assistant Registrar responsible as indicated in the University's Internal Telephone Directory; questions relating to elections should be addressed to the Head Clerk.

Key to guide

Meetings of Congregation (see Tit. II, Sect. III)

1. The stated dates for meetings of Congregation are the Tuesdays of First, Second, Fourth, Sixth, Eighth, and 'Tenth' Weeks, though entirely straightforward business is deemed to have been approved without holding a meeting (see paras. 6, 12, and 14 below). Meetings begin at 2 p.m. and take place either in the Sheldonian Theatre or in the Convocation House, depending on the number of members expected to attend and the nature of the business. The Vice-Chancellor may, if necessary, summon an additional meeting at any time (see also para. 22 below).

Statutes (see Tit. II, Sectt. III and IV)

2. The most regular items of business before Congregation are statutes promoted by Council. All statutes must be first promulgated, and then (if promulgation is approved) enacted at a later date; some, but not all, statutes subsequently need to be approved by Her Majesty The Queen in Council.

3. A statute proposed for promulgation must be published by Council in the *Gazette* at least nineteen days before the relevant meeting of Congregation (e.g. on the Thursday of First Week if promulgation is proposed at the meeting of Congregation on the Tuesday of Fourth Week). Any two members of Congregation may oppose the promulgation, provided that written notice, signed by each, is delivered to the Registrar by noon on the eighth day before the meeting (in the above example, the Monday of Third Week). If such notice is not received, the promulgation will be declared to have been approved unless Council considers that the opportunity for discussion should still be offered, or the matter is adjourned (see para. 19 below).

4. Once a statute has been promulgated, the enacting part must be submitted to a subsequent meeting of Congregation, not less than two weeks later (in the example in para. 3 above, on the Tuesday of Sixth Week); formal notice of the date must be published in the *Gazette* at least eleven days in advance (e.g. on the Thursday of Fourth Week). Any two members of Congregation may propose an amendment to the statute, provided that written notice of the amendment, signed by the proposer and seconder, is delivered to the Registrar by noon on the eighth day before the date to which further proceedings on the statute have been adjourned. The Vice-Chancellor is empowered to disallow any proposed amendment which is in the Vice-Chancellor's judgement inconsistent with or irrelevant to the principle of the statute as stated in the preamble. Any proposed amendments not so disallowed, and any amendments proposed by Council, must then be published in the *Gazette,* and further proceedings on the statute in Congregation may need to be postponed in order to maintain the minimum notice (e.g. until the Tuesday of Eighth Week). There is then an opportunity for any six members of Congregation to propose *a further* amendment, provided that written notice of the amendment, signed by each, is delivered to the Registrar by noon on the fourth day after the publication of the initial amendments (e.g., if the initial amendments are published on the Thursday of Fifth Week, notice of further amendments must be received by noon on the Monday of Sixth Week); such amendments, and any additional amendments proposed by Council, must then be published in the *Gazette,* and further proceedings on the statute in Congregation may again need to be postponed in order to maintain the minimum notice (e.g. until the Tuesday of 'Tenth' Week).

5. Any two members of Congregation may oppose the enactment of a statute which has previously been promulgated, provided that written notice, signed by each, is delivered to the Registrar by noon on the eighth day before the meeting (e.g. the Monday of Fifth Week in the case of a meeting on the Tuesday of Sixth Week). If such notice is not received and there is no proposed amendment, the enactment will be declared to have been approved unless Council considers that the opportunity for discussion should still be offered, or the matter is adjourned (see. para. 19 below).

6. If no such notice of opposition, no proposed amendment, and no request for an adjournment has been received, the Vice-Chancellor is empowered to declare a statute promulgated or enacted without holding a meeting of Congregation,

provided that notice is published in the *Gazette* the previous week, and provided also that the business concerned is in the Vice-Chancellor's opinion not of such general concern to the University as a whole that it would be inappropriate to proceed without an opportunity for further explanation or debate.

7. If there is a vote at a meeting of Congregation, at least 125 members must vote, and constitute a majority, in favour of

(*a*) the rejection of the promulgation of a statute;

(*b*) the acceptance of an amendment to the enacting part of a statute (except an amendment acceptable to Council);

(*c*) the rejection of an amendment proposed by or acceptable to Council; or

(*d*) the rejection of the enacting part of a statute

for their vote to be effective. It is, however, subsequently possible in certain circumstances either for Council to decide to hold, or for fifty or more members of Congregation to requisition, a postal vote on the matter concerned (see paras. 17–18 below).

Resolutions (see Tit. II, Sectt. V and VI)

8. Resolutions on any topic may be submitted to Congregation either by Council or by twenty (or more) members of Congregation, provided that the Vice-Chancellor may rule a 'twenty member' resolution inadmissible either if it is not, in his or her opinion, on a topic concerning the policy or administration of the University, or if it relates to a particular college or other society, or to a particular person other than the Vice-Chancellor (although such a resolution may always call upon Council or any other body or person to annul, amend, or repeal a decree or regulation).

9. Notice of a 'twenty-member' resolution, in the form of the text of the resolution signed by each of the members of Congregation proposing it, must be delivered to the Registrar by noon on the twenty-second day before the meeting of Congregation at which the members wish to move it (e.g. the Monday of First Week in the case of a meeting on the Tuesday of Fourth Week). Either such a resolution or a resolution submitted by Council must be published in the *Gazette* at least nineteen days in advance of the meeting (e.g. on the Thursday of First Week), except in the case of a resolution suspending statutory procedures (see para. 14 below) or conferring a Degree by Resolution. The latter is normally used to confer the degree of MA on a member of the governing body of a college or other society (see Tit. II, Sect. VIII, cl. 2), and must be published in the *Gazette* (e.g. on the Thursday of First Week); it is then deemed to have been approved *nem. con.* at noon on the fourth day after publication (in the above example, the Monday of Second Week) unless by that time the Registrar has received notice in writing, signed by two (or more) members of Congregation, that they wish the resolution to be put to a meeting of Congregation. If such notice is received, Council may either withdraw the resolution or republish it not later than the fourth day before that on which it is to be moved in Congregation (e.g. on the Thursday of Third Week in the case of a meeting on the Tuesday of Fourth Week).

10. Any two members of Congregation may propose an amendment to a resolution (except a resolution suspending statutory procedures or conferring a Degree by Resolution), provided that written notice of the amendment, signed by the proposer and seconder, is delivered to the Registrar by noon on the eighth day before the meeting (in the example given in para. 9 above, the Monday of Third Week). Members of Congregation proposing an amendment are required to state whether or not the amendment is in their view hostile to the resolution (viz. hostile in the sense that, if it were not carried, they would oppose the resolution). If they state that it is not, and the amendment is acceptable to Council, then Council may *either* adjourn proceedings on the resolution and proposed amendment for at least two weeks (e.g. to the Tuesday of Sixth Week) *or*, if the matter is too urgent for that, decide that the amendment should be dealt with at the meeting at which the resolution was originally to be moved. In both cases the amendment must be published in the *Gazette* not later than the fifth day before that meeting (e.g. the Thursday of Third Week), but if proceedings are adjourned Council may at the same time publish a notice requiring that any two members of Congregation who (despite the view of the amendment's proposers and of Council that the amendment is non-hostile) oppose the amendment should give written notice, signed by each, to the Registrar by noon on the eighth day before the meeting to which proceedings have been adjourned (e.g. the Monday of Fifth Week). If such notice has not been received, the amended resolution will be declared to have been carried, without (when appropriate) holding the meeting (see para. 12 below). Alternatively, if proceedings on an unopposed resolution and on an ostensibly non-hostile amendment are adjourned, the meeting must be held and the proposed amendment must be put to the House. If the amendment is then carried, the *amended* resolution will be declared to have been carried without itself being put to the House; if, on the other hand, the amendment is rejected, the *original* resolution will be declared to have been carried without being put to the House; provided that Council may always determine that a division shall be taken on a resolution (whether or not so amended).

11. Any two members of Congregation may oppose a resolution (except a resolution suspending statutory procedures or conferring a Degree by Resolution), provided that written notice, signed by each, is delivered to the Registrar by noon on the eighth day before the meeting (in the example given in para. 9 above, the Monday of Third Week). If such notice is not received and there is no proposed amendment, and if in the case of a 'twenty-member' resolution that resolution is acceptable to Council, the resolution will be declared to have been carried unless Council considers that the opportunity for discussion should still be offered, or the matter is adjourned (see para. 19 below). (To oppose a resolution suspending statutory procedures, see para. 14 below; to oppose a resolution conferring a Degree by Resolution, see para. 9 above.)

12. If no notice of opposition, no proposed amendment, and no request for an adjournment has been received, and if in the case of a 'twenty-member' resolution that resolution is acceptable to Council, the Vice-Chancellor is empowered to declare the resolution carried without holding a meeting of

Congregation, provided that notice is published in the *Gazette* the previous week, and provided also that the subject of the resolution is in the Vice-Chancellor's opinion not of such general concern to the University as a whole that it would be inappropriate to proceed without an opportunity for further explanation or debate.

13. Council is required to give consideration to, but is not bound by, a vote in Congregation on a resolution which it has itself submitted and which has been carried in Congregation. Council is bound to take action (i.e. by promoting legislation in appropriate cases) if a 'twenty-member' resolution is carried, provided that

(*a*) the resolution is carried on a division with at least 125 members voting in favour; or

(*b*) the resolution is carried *nem. con.*, or otherwise without a division (see para. 27 below), when at least 125 members are present on the floor of the House;[1] or

(*c*) the resolution is declared to have been carried without holding the meeting (see para. 12 above).

It is, however, subsequently possible in certain circumstances either for Council to decide to hold, or for fifty or more members of Congregation to requisition, a postal vote on a resolution (see paras. 17–18 below).

14. A resolution suspending statutory procedures, which is principally used to expedite the normal procedures (e.g. to permit the promulgation and enactment of a statute at the same meeting of Congregation), must be published in the *Gazette* not later than the fourth day before the meeting at which it is to be moved (e.g. the Thursday of Third Week in the case of a meeting on the Tuesday of Fourth Week). If such a resolution is published in the *Gazette* at least nineteen days in advance (e.g. on the Thursday of First Week), Council may require that any member of Congregation who proposes to oppose the resolution should notify the Registrar in writing by noon on the eighth day before the meeting (e.g. on the Monday of Third Week); if so, and in the absence of such notification from at least two members, the resolution shall be declared carried without question put unless Council considers that the opportunity for discussion should still be offered, or the matter is adjourned (see para. 19 below). In such circumstances the meeting of Congregation may be cancelled. If on the other hand the resolution is not published at least nineteen days in advance (or if Council does not require advance notice of opposition), then at the meeting twenty (or more) members of Congregation may, by rising in their places, prevent the moving of the resolution, and the procedures which were to have been suspended accordingly remain in force.

[1] I.e. excluding any members present in the Lower or Upper Gallery of the Sheldonian Theatre.

Questions (see Tit. II, Sect. VII)

15. Any member of Congregation may, if supported by another member, ask at a meeting in Full Term (i.e. not at the meeting in 'Tenth' Week) 'a question relating to any matter concerning the policy or the administration of the University'. Written notice of such a question, signed by the member and the supporter, must be delivered to the Registrar by noon on the eighteenth day before the meeting of Congregation at which the members wish to move it (e.g. the Friday of First Week in the case of a meeting on the Tuesday of Fourth Week). Unless the Vice-Chancellor considers the question inadmissible in substance or in form, it must be published in the *Gazette,* together with the answer drafted by Council, not less than five days before the meeting (in the above example, on the Thursday of Third Week). The published answer is read out at the meeting, after which at the Chairman's discretion supplementary questions may be asked to elucidate the answer; a debate on the answer is not permitted.

Elections (see Tit. II, Sect. IX)

16. Members of a number of university bodies, including ten of the members of Council, are elected by Congregation. Such elections are normally held in Full Term, and notice must be published in the *Gazette* at least twenty-eight days in advance. Except in the case of casual vacancies, which are dealt with *ad hoc,* elections are traditionally held on the Thursday of Fifth Week, so that notice is published not later than the Thursday of First Week. Candidates may be nominated by two members of Congregation (other than the candidate) up to 4 p.m. on the twenty-fourth day before the election (on the above timetable, the Monday of Second Week), and by six members (other than the candidate) up to 4 p.m. on the seventeenth day before the election (e.g. the Monday of Third Week). Nominations must be dated and signed by all the members submitting them, whose names are then published in the *Gazette.* At least one nomination in respect of each candidate must be made on an official nomination form (copies of which are available from the Head Clerk at the University Offices). In the case of a contested election, voting is by postal ballot, and brief biographies of the candidates are published in the *Gazette* of the week before the closing date for the return of completed voting papers (e.g. the *Gazette* of Fourth Week); any vacancy for which no valid nomination is received may be filled by an appointment made by the Vice-Chancellor and Proctors jointly.

Postal Votes (see Tit. II, Sect. X)

17. A decision of Congregation concerning a statute or a resolution (except a resolution approving the conferment of a degree of the University, including a Degree by Diploma or an Honorary Degree), if reached at a meeting of Congregation, remains subject to a subsequent postal vote of all members of Congregation, provided that by 4 p.m. on the sixth day after the meeting (e.g. the Monday of Fifth Week in the case of a meeting on the Tuesday of Fourth Week)

(*a*) Council so decides; or

(*b*) a requisition for a postal vote, signed by at least fifty members of Congregation, is delivered to the Vice-Chancellor—such a requisition may, however, be made *only* if the decision concerned was put to a division, and at least twenty-five members of Congregation were present on the floor of the House[1] at the meeting at the time when the division was taken.

18. If a postal vote is held on any matter, a verbatim record (or, if the Vice-Chancellor so decides, a summary) of the debate in Congregation must be published in the *Gazette*. Voting papers are sent to each member of Congregation for return by a specified time, which must not be either less than seven days after the publication of the record (or summary) or less than four days after the dispatch of the voting papers. Each voter must sign the paper before returning it. In the case of a postal vote, a simple majority decides the question.

Adjournment (see Tit. II, Sect. III)

19. Any twenty members of Congregation may request the adjournment of any item on the agenda for a forthcoming meeting of Congregation *except* a resolution suspending statutory procedures if advance notice of opposition has not been required (see para. 14 above) or conferring a Degree by Resolution, a question, an election, the Vice-Chancellor's Oration and the Annual Report (see paras. 22–3 below), or a Topic for Discussion (see para. 24 below), provided that written notice, signed by each, is delivered to the Registrar by noon on the eighth day before the meeting (e.g. the Monday of Third Week in the case of a meeting on the Tuesday of Fourth Week), and provided also that no item may be adjourned more than once in total in response to a request from members of Congregation or on the proposal of the Chairman at a meeting (see para. 20 below). Any such request will be decided by the Proctors, and their decision must be published in the *Gazette* not less than four days before the meeting (in the above example, on the Thursday of Third Week). If they reject the request, any two members of Congregation may, by rising in their places at the meeting, demand that the question of adjournment be put to a vote.

20. The Chairman has similar powers in respect of the adjournment of an *item* at a meeting. The Chairman may at any time propose the adjournment of a *meeting* by putting the question of the adjournment to a vote. After any meeting has lasted for two hours, the Chairman is empowered to adjourn the House without that question being put.

Flysheets (see Appendix to Ch. I)

21. Any ten or more members of Congregation may arrange for a flysheet (i.e. a single sheet of A4 size, printed on both sides if desired) to be circulated with the *Gazette* (*a*) on matters before Congregation or (*b*) relating to matters of

[1] I.e. excluding any members present in the Lower or Upper Gallery of the Sheldonian Theatre.

general interest to the University. The detailed conditions and arrangements for the circulation of flysheets are set out in the Appendix to Ch. I of the University's Decrees and are also printed from time to time in the *Gazette*. Further information may be obtained from the Senior Assistant Registrar to whom reference is made in the '*Important Note*' at the head of this guide.

The Vice-Chancellor's Oration and the Annual Report (see Tit. II, Sect. XI)

22. At the beginning of each academic year, normally on the Tuesday of the week before, or of the week next but one before, the First Week of Michaelmas Full Term, the Vice-Chancellor delivers to a special meeting of Congregation an Oration on issues of current concern to the University. At this meeting the Pro-Vice-Chancellors for the year, and when there is a change in the office of Vice-Chancellor the new Vice-Chancellor, are installed. The Oration is subsequently published in the *Gazette* and must be placed on the agenda for a meeting of Congregation in Michaelmas Term, when, at the discretion of the Chairman, the Oration may be discussed and questions may be asked about it. If, however, at least two members of Congregation have not, by noon on the eighth day before the meeting (e.g. the Monday of Third Week in the case of a meeting on the Tuesday of Fourth Week), given written notice to the Registrar of their wish to speak or to ask a question, the Vice-Chancellor is empowered to declare the Oration to have been presented without holding the meeting, provided that notice is published in the *Gazette* the previous week.

23. The Annual Report of the University must also be published in the *Gazette* during the academic year next following that in respect of which the report is made. It must then be formally presented at a meeting of Congregation. On that occasion, at the discretion of the Chairman, the Annual Report may be discussed and questions may be asked about it. If, however, at least two members of Congregation have not, by noon on the eighth day before the meeting (e.g. the Monday of Third Week in the case of a meeting on the Tuesday of Fourth Week), given written notice to the Registrar of their wish to speak or to ask a question, the Vice-Chancellor is empowered to declare the Annual Report to have been presented without holding the meeting, provided that notice is published in the *Gazette* the previous week.

[*Note*. Special arrangements apply with effect from 1 October 1998 until further notice: see Decree (4) of that date, reproduced following Tit. II, Sect. XI above.]

Topics for Discussion (see Tit. II, Sect. XII)

24. Under a procedure introduced in 2000, either Council or any twenty (or more) members of Congregation may submit a Topic to Congregation on any issue of concern to the University, including any issue on which it would be permissible for it or them to submit a resolution (see paras. 8–13 above). The procedure is the same as for 'twenty-member' resolutions *except* that a division is not taken (nor can there be a postal vote), and Council, while having a duty

to give consideration to the remarks made in the discussion, is not bound to take any further action in regard to the topic.

Procedure at Meetings of Congregation (see Tit. II, Sect. III)

25. When a meeting of Congregation is held, each item of business (other than the declaration of the promulgation or approval of an unopposed statute, or of the approval of an unopposed resolution, or the introduction of a Topic for Discussion) is formally proposed and, when appropriate, seconded. In cases in which the procedure then provides for debate or discussion, the Chairman invites members of Congregation who indicate their wish to speak to do so. (The procedure also provides in such cases for certain Junior Members to be invited to speak.) At the end of any general speeches, the Chairman normally invites the leader of any opposition to sum up for the opposition, and finally invites the proposer to reply on behalf of those in favour; other members of Congregation are not normally permitted to speak more than once on any item.

26. Any proposed resolution (unless unopposed and declared carried without question put), or any proposed amendment to a statute or resolution, which is not formally moved and seconded at the meeting lapses.

27. At the close of any debate or discussion (except on a Topic), the Chairman puts the item to the vote by asking those in favour to shout 'Aye' and those against to shout 'No'. If there has been no indication of opposition in any previous discussion but there is nevertheless at this point a shout of 'No', the Chairman may offer the opponent(s) a further chance to explain to the House the reasons for so shouting. After such explanation(s), if any, and any response(s), the Chairman will put the item to the vote again. If in the Chairman's opinion the Ayes have it, the Chairman will declare that the item is approved unless at least six members of Congregation, by rising in their places, require that a division be taken. (Unless a division is taken, there cannot subsequently be a postal vote on the item concerned—see para. 17 above.) If at least six members rise, or if it is not the Chairman's opinion that the Ayes have it, a formal division is taken. In the case of a meeting held in the Sheldonian Theatre, members of Congregation are normally invited to go through the door marked 'Aye' or the door marked 'No', where those voting are counted by the Proctors. When the voting is complete, members may return to the floor of the House to hear the result and to conduct any remaining business. In the case of a meeting held in the Convocation House, members remain in their places and their votes are taken individually by the Proctors.

28. For the procedure for voting on the question of an adjournment, see also paras. 19–20 above.

TITLE III

OF CONVOCATION

(This Title is a 'Queen-in-Council' statute—see Title XV, Section VII.)

1. The functions, powers, and duties of Convocation shall be to elect the Chancellor and to perform such other duties as are or shall be assigned to it by the statutes or by decrees.

2. Convocation shall consist of all the holders of the Degrees (other than Honorary Degrees) of Doctor of Divinity, Doctor of Civil Law, Doctor of Medicine, or Master of Arts, and of those not holding such degrees who are members of Congregation; provided always that a member of Convocation may, with the consent of Council for reasons which it shall deem sufficient, resign his membership, provided that he undertakes to continue to observe the statutes, decrees, and regulations of the University as though he had continued to be a member thereof.

3. The holders of the following degrees shall also be eligible to become members of Convocation in or after the twenty-first term from their matriculation under such conditions as shall be laid down by decree:

Doctor of Philosophy
Doctor of Clinical Psychology if a matriculated member of the University[1]
Master of Science
Master of Letters
Master of Philosophy
Master of Studies
Master of Theology if a matriculated member of the University
Magister Juris
Master of Business Administration
Master of Fine Art
Master of Biochemistry
Master of Chemistry
Master of Earth Sciences
Master of Engineering
Master of Mathematics
Master of Physics
Bachelor of Divinity
Bachelor of Civil Law
Bachelor of Medicine
Bachelor of Letters
Bachelor of Science
Bachelor of Philosophy
Bachelor of Theology if a matriculated member of the University.

[1] The insertion of the words in italics is subject to the approval of Her Majesty in Council.

4. The procedure for the holding of elections in Convocation or for the holding of any other proceedings in Convocation shall be laid down by decree.

5. Council shall by decree lay down rules to govern academic precedence and standing.

TITLE IV

OF THE COUNCIL OF THE UNIVERSITY

Section I. Of the Functions and Powers of Council

(This Section is a 'Queen-in-Council' statute—see Title XV, Section VII.)

1. Subject to the provisions of the statutes, Council shall be responsible for the administration of the University and for the management of its finances and property, and shall have all the powers necessary for it to discharge these responsibilities.

2. Subject to the provisions of the statutes, Council, and any other body to which the statutes or decrees may give such power, may make, amend, and repeal decrees, not inconsistent with the statutes, designed to give detailed effect to the provisions of the statutes or to provide for any matter not provided for in the statutes; and such decrees shall bind all members of the University. All such decrees shall be published in the *University Gazette* and shall come into effect from the fifteenth day after the date of their publication (though the decree may contain an earlier or later date from which it shall then be effective), provided always that if notice of a resolution calling upon Council to annul or amend the decree is received by the Registrar by noon on the eleventh day after the day on which it was published, the decree shall not come into effect until the resolution has been put and rejected.

3. Subject to the provisions of the statutes, Council may by decree authorize any other body or person to make, amend, and repeal regulations, not inconsistent with the statutes, dealing with such matters as it shall think fit to delegate. All such regulations, and all regulations made under the authority of the statutes, shall be published in the *University Gazette* and shall come into effect from the fifteenth day after the date of their publication (though the regulation may contain an earlier or later date from which it shall then be effective), provided always that if notice of a resolution calling upon Council to annul or amend the regulation is received by the Registrar by noon on the eleventh day after the day on which it was published, the regulation shall not come into effect until the resolution has been put and rejected. Regulations shall have the same force as decrees, but (whether made under the authority of Council or under powers conferred by the statutes) may at any time be annulled, amended, or repealed by decree except that this shall not apply to regulations made by the Rules Committee unless Council is required to make such a decree by a resolution.

4. Subject to the provisions of the statutes, Council may from time to time delegate responsibility for any matter to any other body or person and may delegate such powers (other than the power to put statutes to Congregation) as it may consider necessary for the discharge of this responsibility, provided always that any such delegations may be withdrawn (either generally or in

respect of a specific item) at any time and that such delegations shall not relieve Council of general responsibility for the matters delegated.

Section II. Of the Composition of Council

(This Section is a 'Queen-in-Council' statute—see Title XV, Section VII.)

1. Council shall consist of:

(1) the Vice-Chancellor;

(2) the Chairman of the Conference of Colleges;

(3), (4) the Proctors;

(5) the Assessor;

(6) a member of Congregation elected by the Conference of Colleges;

(7), (8) two persons, not being members of Congregation and not being resident holders of teaching, research, or administrative posts in the University or in any college or other society, who shall be nominated by Council subject to the approval of Congregation;

(9)–(11) the Heads of the Divisions of Life and Environmental Sciences, of Mathematical and Physical Sciences, and of Medical Sciences;

(12)–(14) three members of Congregation elected by Congregation from members of the faculties in the Divisions of Life and Environmental Sciences, of Mathematical and Physical Sciences, and of Medical Sciences;

(15), (16) the Heads of the Divisions of Humanities and of Social Sciences;

(17)–(20) four members of Congregation elected by Congregation from members of the faculties in the Divisions of Humanities and of Social Sciences;

(21)–(23) three members of Congregation, not necessarily being members of any division and not in any case being nominated in a divisional capacity, who shall be elected by Congregation;

provided always that not more than three of the members elected under (12)–(14), (17)–(20), and (21)–(23) above may be members of the governing body of any one college or other society. If the outcome of any election in Congregation would otherwise result in there being more than three such members, the candidate (or the appropriate number of candidates) receiving the greatest number (or the greater numbers) of votes shall be deemed to have been elected; or, if the election is uncontested or if two candidates receive the same number of votes, the candidate most senior (or the appropriate number of candidates more senior) in academic standing shall be deemed to have been elected. If in such circumstances two or more candidates receive the same number of votes or are equal in academic standing, as the case may be, the election of the successful candidate or candidates shall be decided by lot. If in consequence of these provisions one or more vacancies are left unfilled, that vacancy or those vacancies shall lapse to the Vice-Chancellor and the Proctors jointly under the provisions of Tit. II, Sect. IX, cl. 4 (*d*).

Council may co-opt up to three members of Congregation as additional members of Council.

2. The Vice-Chancellor, or, in his or her absence, a member of Council deputed by the Vice-Chancellor, shall take the chair at all meetings of Council.

3. Elected, nominated, and co-opted members of Council shall serve for four years and shall be re-eligible, provided that casual vacancies shall be filled for the remaining period of office of the member being replaced.

4. If an elected member of Council shall cease to be a member of Congregation, his or her seat shall forthwith be vacated. If a nominated member, having been appointed under the provisions of clause 1 (7), (8) above, shall become a member of Congregation or the resident holder of a teaching, research, or administrative post in the University or in any college or other society, his or her seat shall forthwith be vacated.

5. Council may determine by decree that if an elected, nominated, or co-opted member of Council shall have attended fewer than a prescribed number of meetings in any academic year, his or her seat shall be vacated at the close of such year.

6. Council shall determine by decree arrangements whereby three Junior Members shall be entitled to attend meetings of Council except for such matters of business as may be prescribed by decree.

7. Any member of Council, and the chairman or vice-chairman of any committee of Council who is not a member of Council, may be relieved of such of his or her university duties, without loss of stipend, as Council shall determine; and Council shall be empowered to make such financial provision as it thinks fit for the carrying out of any of the duties of which such person has been relieved either by Council or by his or her college or other society.

Section III. Of the Committees of Council

1. There shall always be the following committees of Council:
   (*a*) the Planning and Resource Allocation Committee;
   (*b*) the Educational Policy and Standards Committee;
   (*c*) the General Purposes Committee;
   (*d*) the Personnel Committee.

2. The composition, terms of reference, powers, and duties of the committees listed in clause 1 above shall be determined by Council by decree.

3. Council may set up such other committees as it may from time to time think fit. Such committees may consist wholly or partly of persons who are not members of Council, and may consist wholly or partly of persons appointed by persons or bodies other than Council.

4. The composition, terms of reference, powers, and duties of committees set up under the provisions of clause 3 above shall be laid down by Council, by decree or otherwise as Council shall think appropriate, subject to the provisions of the statutes.

5. A complete list of all the permanent committees of Council shall be published annually in the *University Gazette* in Michaelmas Term, with the names of their chairmen (and vice-chairmen where appropriate) and other members.

TITLE V

OF THE DIVISIONS

Section I. Of the Number of the Divisions

1. The academic activities of the University in the sciences shall be grouped in the following three divisions:

(1) Life and Environmental Sciences;

(2) Mathematical and Physical Sciences;

(3) Medical Sciences.

2. The academic activities of the University in the arts and humanities shall be grouped in the following two divisions:

(1) Humanities;

(2) Social Sciences.

3. The composition of each division shall be determined by Council by decree.

Section II. Of the Divisional Boards

§ 1. *Functions and Powers of Divisional Boards*

1. There shall be a divisional board with responsibility, under Council and subject to plans, policies, and guidelines set by Council and its committees, for each division. The terms of reference, powers, and duties of each board shall include the following, and such other powers and duties as may be assigned to it by Council by decree or otherwise:

(*a*) the oversight of the organization, development, and delivery of curricula (with an equal focus on graduate and on undergraduate studies) in collaboration with the colleges, and oversight and development of the general context of research, in the broad subject area covered by the division concerned, in close consultation with the units of academic administration in the division (hereinafter referred to as 'sub-units');

(*b*) the development and proposal, in collaboration with the colleges, sub-units, and academic services sector, of comprehensive and detailed strategic five-year plans and one-year operating statements covering academic, financial, information and communications technology, physical resource, and staffing issues, bearing in mind the particular needs of small units and interdisciplinary activities;

(*c*) within the context of approved plans and statements, and of overall university policies, the general oversight of and responsibility for all matters concerning budgets, space, syllabus, and staffing, across the sub-units of the division, in consultation with the colleges as thought appropriate by the board; provided that day-to-day operational responsibility for these matters shall be devolved to the sub-units, in the context of local plans and budgets delegated for that purpose, and that the board shall monitor the work of the sub-units against those plans and budgets;

(*d*) the periodic strategic review of particular sub-units;

(*e*) the approval of appointments and reappointments of academic staff made by the sub-units (but excluding appointments which are made by electoral boards established by statute or decree), and of appointments of heads of department, the consideration of proposals from the sub-units on the payment of salaries within the incremental scale for university lecturers, and the keeping under review of the general terms and conditions of employment of academic staff in the broad subject area;

(*f*) the settling of college associations for new and vacant academic posts, on the recommendation of the sub-units following liaison with colleges;

(*g*) the maintenance of educational quality and standards in the broad subject area;

(*h*) the consideration of reports of examiners, including external examiners, on the advice of the relevant sub-unit or sub-units;

(*i*) the oversight of relationships between the sub-units, and the consideration (for detailed and balanced recommendation to Council) of any proposals to reorganize the sub-units;

(*j*) the division's relations with the colleges at the strategic and the broad subject level, and in cases in which individual problems cannot be resolved between the colleges and the University at the sub-unit level;

(*k*) the division's relations with the other divisions on matters of common interest;

(*l*) the division's relations with the Continuing Education Board on matters of common interest and in all cases in which planned developments relate to part-time provision, outreach, or other continuing education activities;

(*m*) the division's relations with the Committee for Educational Studies on matters of common interest;

(*n*) the division's relations with the academic services sector at the broad subject level;

(*o*) the division's relations with external funding agencies, subject to overall university policies and practice;

(*p*) the oversight of fund raising in the broad subject area, subject to overall university policies and practice;

(*q*) the regular review of the scope for further delegation of authority from the centre to the divisions, and from the divisions to the sub-units.

2. Each board shall make an annual report to Council on the activities of its division in the preceding academic year, measured against the division's agreed operating statement.

3. The composition of each board shall be determined by Council by decree.

4. There shall be a head of each division, who shall chair the divisional board, and the arrangements for whose appointment shall be determined by Council by decree.

§ 2. *Additional Functions and Powers of the Medical Sciences Board*

1. In addition to the functions and powers of divisional boards laid down under sub-section 1 above, the Medical Sciences Board shall

(*a*) consider questions of medical policy affecting the relations of the University with N.H.S. bodies within the region, and make recommendations, where appropriate, to Council and the committees of Council after such consultation as may be necessary with the N.H.S. body concerned;

(*b*) promote work in the field of medical research by the allocation, through a Medical Research Fund Committee, of that part of the annual income of the Nuffield Benefaction for the Advancement of Medicine approved for that purpose by the Trustees of the Benefaction, together with such other funds as may accrue in the General Clinical Fund under the provisions of Ch. VII, Sect. I, § 5. B, cl. 3 (*e*), and any other contributions or donations for general medical research purposes. The Medical Research Fund Committee shall comprise:

(1) the Head of the Medical Sciences Division or his or her nominee (chairman);

(2)–(4) three persons appointed by the Nuffield Benefaction Committee;

(5)–(7) three persons appointed by the Medical Sciences Board from among the members of the Faculty of Clinical Medicine;

provided that at least four of the six persons appointed under (2)–(7) shall be the holders of one of the professorships listed in Ch. VII, Sect. I, § 5, SCHEDULE C, and at least one of those six persons shall be a person engaged in hospital laboratory work.

2. There shall be a standing committee of the Medical Sciences Board for the regulation of arrangements for the validation of the Oxford Doctoral Course in Clinical Psychology. The committee shall consist of two representatives of the Medical Sciences Board and two representatives of the Course Directorate. The committee shall have such powers and duties in respect of the Degree of Doctor of Clinical Psychology as may from time to time be prescribed by the Medical Sciences Board. The representatives of the course shall have the right to attend any meeting of the divisional board for any item concerning the course.

3. The Medical Sciences Board shall be responsible for maintaining a University Medical Students' Register of such members of the University as are engaged in the study of Medicine in Oxford with a view to obtaining a qualification to practise, and shall make such regulations as it shall deem necessary for the discharge of such responsibility. No person shall be admitted to the First Examination for the Degree of Bachelor of Medicine unless his or her name is on the register.

4. The Medical Sciences Board shall also maintain a Clinical Students' Register of students admitted to work in Oxford for the Second Examination for the Degree of Bachelor of Medicine, or other qualifying medical examinations, and is empowered to remove any name from such register (in the case of a matriculated member of the University, after consultation with the student's

society). No person shall be admitted to the Second Examination for the Degree of Bachelor of Medicine unless his or her name is on the register.

5. The Secretary to the Medical Sciences Board shall, when required, sign certificates for medical examinations for students who have completed courses satisfying requirements of the General Medical Council and the examining body concerned.

TITLE VI

OF THE FACULTIES, FACULTY BOARDS, AND DEPARTMENTS

Section I. Of the Faculties

1. There shall be seventeen faculties:

(1) the Faculty of Theology;

(2) the Faculty of Law;

(3) the Faculty of Literae Humaniores;

(4) the Faculty of Modern History;

(5) the Faculty of English Language and Literature;

(6) the Faculty of Medieval and Modern European Languages and Literatures other than English (elsewhere in the statutes referred to as the Faculty of Medieval and Modern Languages);

(7) the Faculty of Oriental Studies;

(8) the Faculty of Physical Sciences;

(9) the Faculty of Biological Sciences;

(10) the Faculty of Social Studies;

(11) the Faculty of Anthropology and Geography;

(12) the Faculty of Music;

(13) the Faculty of Psychological Studies;

(14) the Faculty of Mathematical Sciences;

(15) the Faculty of Clinical Medicine;

(16) the Faculty of Physiological Sciences;

(17) the Faculty of Management.

2. The members of each faculty shall be:

(*a*) the holders of all university posts[1] approved for this purpose by the General Board the duties of which include research or teaching;

(*b*) the holders of all posts in the colleges and other societies of the University the duties of which are certified by the head of the college or society to include research or teaching;

[1] The posts approved under this clause are those of professor, reader, university lecturer (including faculty, C.U.F., special (non-C.U.F.), and junior lecturer), senior research officer, instructor, clinical professor, clinical reader, clinical tutor, clinical lecturer, tutor in General Practice, lector under the aegis of the Board of the Faculty of Medieval and Modern Languages, research officer in the Institute of Economics and Statistics and in the Sub-Department of Particle and Nuclear Physics, and departmental lecturer. In addition, holders of the following titles shall be faculty members: visiting professor, professor, reader, visiting lecturer, university research lecturer, university lecturer (including C.U.F. lecturer and special (non-C.U.F.) lecturer), clinical professor, clinical reader, and clinical lecturer.

(*c*) such persons as may be made members by a faculty board on account of the work being done by them in Oxford in the subjects with which the board is concerned;

provided that

(i) the General Board may, if it think fit, permit non-matriculated persons to be made 'additional members' of faculties under (*c*) above, but such 'additional members' shall not be qualified for membership of Congregation under the provisions of Tit. II, Sect. II, cl. 1 (5);

(ii) no person who has exceeded the age of 70 years shall be made a member of a faculty, provided that a member of a faculty who has attained that age but has not attained the age of 75 years may remain a member under (*a*)–(*c*) above, and provided further that in no case shall any person remain a member of a faculty after attaining the age of 75 years.

3. The General Board shall determine the faculty or faculties of which those qualified under clause 2 (*a*) and (*b*) above shall be members, and shall publish the lists of the members of the faculties annually in the *University Gazette*. These lists shall also show the sub-faculties (if any) to which the members of the faculties belong.

4. The faculties shall elect members of the faculty boards, and shall perform such other functions as are or shall be assigned to them by the statutes, by decrees, by regulations, or by the faculty boards under the provisions of Sect. II, cl. 6 below.

5. Subject to the approval of the General Board, a faculty board may divide its faculty into sub-faculties and may determine that functions normally performed by the whole faculty shall be performed by the sub-faculties severally.

Section II. Of the Faculty Boards

[*Note.* Under the provisions of Decree (3) of 18 May 2000 (*Gazette*, Vol. 130, p. 1199), notwithstanding any provision of any statute, decree, or regulation to the contrary, and pursuant to cll. 13 and 55 of the Statute approved by Congregation on 29 June 1999 (*Gazette,* Vol. 129, pp. 1323, 1482), and subsequently by Her Majesty in Council, references in any statute, decree or regulation to the Bioscience Research Board shall, with effect from the establishment of the divisional boards listed below, be deemed to be references to the Medical Sciences Board, and references in any statute, decree, or regulation to any of the following former faculty boards shall with effect from that date be deemed to be references to the relevant divisional board as follows.

Former faculty board	*Divisional board*
Anthropology and Geography	*Life and Environmental Sciences*[1]
Biological Sciences	Life and Environmental Sciences

[1] The insertion of the words in italics is subject to the approval of Congregation.

Clinical Medicine	Medical Sciences
Mathematical Sciences	Mathematical and Physical Sciences
Physical Sciences	Mathematical and Physical Sciences
Physiological Sciences	Medical Sciences
Psychological Studies	Medical Sciences
Social Studies	*Social Sciences*[1]

1. There shall be a faculty board for each of the following faculties:
[Anthropology and Geography;][2]
(1) English Language and Literature;
(2) Law;
(3) Literae Humaniores;
(4) Management;
(5) Medieval and Modern Languages;
(6) Modern History;
(7) Music;
(8) Oriental Studies;
[Social Studies][3]
(9) Theology.

Unless otherwise prescribed for a particular board by decree, each board shall consist of

(*a*) '*official members*': such number as shall be specified by decree, made on the recommendation of the General Board, of those qualified to be 'official members' of the faculty board (that is, such professors, readers, and other persons in the faculty as shall be determined to be so qualified by decree made on the recommendation of the General Board), elected by the members of the faculty; or all those so qualified, if not more than the number so specified;

(*b*) '*ordinary members*': such number of members of the faculty as shall be specified by decree made on the recommendation of the General Board, elected by the members of the faculty not qualified to be 'official members';

(*c*) '*co-opted members*': up to four co-opted members.

2. The functions and powers of the faculty boards shall be as laid down from time to time in the statutes or by the General Board under the provisions of Tit. V, Sect. I, cl. 4.

3. The arrangements for the election and period of tenure of the members of the faculty boards shall be laid down by regulation of the General Board, provided always that the normal period of tenure shall not be less than two years.

4. Each faculty board shall elect a chairman (whose name shall be published in the *University Gazette*) from among its own members, who shall hold office for

[1] The insertion of the words in italics is subject to the approval of Congregation.
[2] The deletion of the words in square brackets is subject to the approval of Congregation.

one year but shall be re-eligible for as long as he or she remains a member of the board. Any such chairman may be relieved of such of his or her regular university duties as the General Board on the recommendation of the faculty board concerned may determine without loss of stipend; and the General Board shall be empowered to make such financial provision as it thinks fit for the carrying out of any of the duties of which a chairman has been relieved either by the General Board or by his or her college or other society.

5. Each faculty board may set up such committees, with such composition (provided that each committee shall contain at least one member of the board) and terms of reference, as it shall from time to time think fit.

6. Each faculty board may from time to time delegate to any other body or person responsibility for any matter for which responsibility has been laid on it, and may delegate such powers (other than the power to make, amend, or repeal regulations) as it may consider necessary for the discharge of the responsibility, provided always that:

(*a*) any such delegations may be withdrawn (either generally or in respect of a specific item) at any time;

(*b*) such delegations shall not relieve the faculty board of general responsibility for the matters delegated.

Section III. Of Departments and Departmental Committees

1. No department or other unit of academic administration shall be set up except by statute or decree or by regulation of the General Board.

2. The care of each department or unit shall be entrusted to such body or person as may be laid down by statute, decree, or regulation, and the functions and powers of that body or person shall be as laid down by decree or regulation.

3. Where the care of a department or unit is entrusted to a person he or she shall be designated the head of that department or unit.

4. For such of the departments covered by clause 3 above as the General Board shall by regulation determine, there shall be a departmental committee with such constitution as the General Board shall in each particular case approve, provided always that the head of the department shall be chairman *ex officio* (but may from time to time appoint another member of the committee to act for him or her).

5. Subject to the provisions of clause 2 above, the functions and powers of the departmental committees shall be as laid down from time to time by regulation of the General Board.

Section IV. Of Joint Committees with Junior Members

Every faculty board shall make arrangements to the satisfaction of the General Board for the establishment of Joint Committees or other means of consultation with Junior Members about undergraduate and graduate affairs.

TITLE VII

OF THE COLLEGES AND OTHER SOCIETIES OF THE UNIVERSITY

Section I. Of the Colleges

(This Section is a 'Queen-in-Council' statute—see Title XV, Section VII.)

1. The following foundations for academic study shall be recognized as colleges of the University of Oxford:

All Souls College
Balliol College
Brasenose College
Christ Church
Corpus Christi College
Exeter College
Hertford College
Jesus College
Keble College
Lady Margaret Hall
Linacre College
Lincoln College
Magdalen College
Manchester Academy and Harris College
Mansfield College
Merton College
New College
Nuffield College
Oriel College
Pembroke College
Queen's College
St. Anne's College
St. Antony's College
St. Catherine's College
St. Edmund Hall
St. Hilda's College
St. Hugh's College
St. John's College
St. Peter's College
Somerville College
Templeton College
Trinity College
University College
Wadham College
Wolfson College
Worcester College

2. The University may, by statute subject to the approval of Her Majesty in Council, add further foundations to those listed in clause 1, above.

Section II. Of St. Cross College

1. St. Cross College shall be a society through which persons who are graduates of other universities (or in the opinion of the governing body possess comparable qualifications) and who are not members of any college or other society may be admitted as members of the University.

2. The governing body may admit to membership of St. Cross College

(*a*) students desiring to work for research degrees;

(*b*) other graduate students desiring to pursue academic work in Oxford;

(*c*) other persons at the discretion of the governing body.

3. The members of St. Cross College shall have, in relation to the University, the same privileges and obligations as members of colleges.

4. The governing body shall consist of the Master and Official and Pusey Fellows and such other fellows as shall be made members of the governing body in accordance with by-laws determined by the governing body and approved by Council pursuant to the provisions of clause 5 below.

5. The governing body may from time to time make by-laws which, when approved by Council, shall be binding on all Fellows of St. Cross College. The governing body shall also have full powers (subject to the provisions of this statute) to do all that may be necessary to administer St. Cross College as a graduate society for men and women, provided that:

(*a*) it shall submit a report annually to Council;

(*b*) it shall submit estimates to Council in Hilary Term in respect of the ensuing financial year, and shall satisfy Council that no charge will fall on university funds except such as may be provided by Council.

6. The Master of St. Cross College shall be appointed by Council, after it has considered any recommendations which the governing body may submit, on such terms and conditions as Council shall determine. The Master may hold his or her office in conjunction with a professorship, readership, university lecturership, or other university teaching or research post if Council, after consultation with the General Board and any other bodies concerned, shall so decide.

7. The officers of St. Cross College shall be appointed by the governing body on such terms and conditions as it may determine, subject to the approval of Council.

8. The governing body may elect to Official Fellowships at the college, on terms and conditions determined by the governing body and approved by Council, the holders of university appointments who are entitled to fellowships under the provisions of any statute or decree, or who will become so entitled if their university appointments are confirmed to retiring age.

9. A board ('the Nominating Board') composed of not more than two Official Fellows of the college elected for the purpose by the governing body and not more than six of the Governors of the Charity known as Dr. Pusey Memorial Fund shall nominate suitably qualified persons for Pusey Fellowships at the college. The governing body shall admit persons so nominated to Pusey Fellowships at the college and to membership of the governing body as they present themselves for admission, provided that such Pusey Fellowships shall not exceed three in number. Pusey Fellowships shall be on terms and conditions to be determined by the governing body and approved by Council, but to be no less favourable to the Pusey Fellows than those applicable to Official Fellowships. The Nominating Board shall make its own procedural regulations provided that:

(*a*) reasonable notice of all meetings shall be sent to every member of the board;

(*b*) notice having been sent in accordance with the preceding sub-clause, the quorum for meetings of the board shall be any five members.

10. The governing body may elect suitably qualified persons to other categories of fellowships approved by Council, on terms and conditions determined by the governing body and approved by Council.

Section III. Of Green College

1. Green College shall be a society

(*a*) through which persons who are graduates of other universities (or in the opinion of the governing body possess comparable qualifications) and who are not members of any college or other society may be admitted as members of the University, and

(*b*) to which graduates of the University who are members of a college or other society may migrate.

2. Graduate members of any college or hall may be admitted, with the approval of their own college or other society, as junior associate members of Green College.

3. The members of Green College shall have, in relation to the University, the same privileges and obligations as members of colleges.

4. The Governing Body of Green College shall consist of the Warden and Fellows, and shall have full powers (subject to the provisions of this statute) to do what may be necessary to administer Green College as a society for graduate men and women, provided that:

(*a*) it shall submit a report annually to Council;

(*b*) it shall submit estimates to Council in Hilary Term in respect of the ensuing financial year, and shall satisfy Council that no charge will fall on university funds except such as may be provided by Council.

5. Green College shall not be eligible for support from the College Contributions Fund.

6. The governing body may admit to membership of Green College:

(*a*) students who have been admitted to work for the Second Examination for the Degree of Bachelor of Medicine;

(*b*) students desiring to work for research degrees of the University;

(*c*) other graduate students desiring to pursue academic work in Oxford;

(*d*) other persons at the discretion of the governing body.

7. The Warden of Green College shall be appointed by Council, after it has considered any recommendations which the governing body may submit, on such terms and conditions as Council shall determine.

8. The officers of Green College shall be appointed by the governing body on such terms and conditions as it may determine, subject to the approval of Council.

9. The governing body may elect suitably qualified persons as Fellows of Green College, on terms and conditions determined by the governing body and approved by Council, including the holders of university appointments who are

entitled to fellowships under the provision of any statute or decree, or who will become so entitled if their university appointments are confirmed to retiring age.

10. The governing body may elect to Professorial Fellowships at the college, on terms approved by Council, university professors, university readers, and holders of other university offices which are declared by any university statute or decree to qualify the holder for a Professorial Fellowship.

Section IV. Of the Members of St. Catherine's Society

All persons who were matriculated through St. Catherine's Society shall be deemed to have been matriculated through St. Catherine's College, except that those who were matriculated in Michaelmas Term 1961 or later who were not reading for the Degree of Bachelor of Arts shall be deemed to have been matriculated through Linacre College.

Section V. Of Kellogg College

1. Kellogg College shall be a society of the University.

2. Kellogg College may present for matriculation as members of the University the President and any Fellow of Kellogg College, if not a member of any college or other society, together with any person admitted to Kellogg College for the purpose of working for a graduate degree course on a part-time basis or for the Postgraduate Certificate in Education on a full-time basis, provided that in the latter case Council shall have power to determine from time to time by decree the maximum number of such students who may be presented for matriculation.[1] Members of a college or other society may migrate to Kellogg College on assuming the office of President, or on election as Fellow, or on admission as a student as aforesaid.

3. The members of Kellogg College shall have, in relation to the University, the same privileges and obligations as members of colleges.

4. The Director of the Department for Continuing Education shall *ex officio* be President of Kellogg College, and he or she shall make available to the Governing Body of Kellogg College accommodation and other facilities on terms approved from time to time by Council and the General Board. The directorship shall not be held concurrently with the headship or a fellowship (other than an Honorary or Emeritus Fellowship) in any college or in any other society of the University. Council shall be empowered from time to time to designate a member of Congregation as Acting President, with power in the absence or during the sickness of the President, or during a vacancy in the presidency, to undertake all acts which the President is authorized or required to perform.

[1] The number of full-time students studying at any one time for the P.G.C.E. whom Kellogg College may present for matriculation, under these provisions, shall not exceed twenty (Decree (5) of 25 June 1993, as amended by Decree (8) of 14 July 1994).

5. The Governing Body of Kellogg College shall consist of the President and Fellows (other than Emeritus, Honorary, Supernumerary, and Visiting Fellows). The governing body may from time to time make by-laws which, when approved by Council, shall be binding on all Fellows of Kellogg College. The governing body shall have full powers (subject to the provisions of this statute) to do all that may be necessary to administer Kellogg College as a society of the University, provided that:

(*a*) it shall submit a report annually to Council; and

(*b*) it shall submit to Council each Hilary Term estimates of its income and expenditure in respect of the ensuing financial year and shall satisfy Council that no charge will fall on university funds except in so far as may already have been authorized by Council.

6. Kellogg College shall not be eligible for support from the College Contributions Fund.

7. The governing body shall offer to elect to a Fellowship of Kellogg College every full-time University Lecturer in the Department for Continuing Education whose office is tenable to the retiring age, or who has been appointed for a limited period on the basis that he is eligible for reappointment thereafter to the retiring age.

8. The governing body may elect to a Fellowship of Kellogg College

(*a*) any person who is entitled under proviso (*e*) to Tit. X, Sect. I to hold a fellowship in a college or other society, or who, holding an appointment for a limited period with eligibility for reappointment to the retiring age, would be so entitled on reappointment; and

(*b*) any other member of Congregation, provided that the total number of fellows elected under this sub-clause shall not exceed one-quarter of the total number of fellows who constitute the governing body;

provided always that a Fellowship of Kellogg College shall not be held concurrently with the headship of or a fellowship (other than an Honorary or Emeritus Fellowship) in any college or any other society of the University.

9. The governing body may, in accordance with by-laws approved from time to time by Council under the provisions of clause 5 above, elect to Emeritus, Honorary, and Visiting Fellowships of Kellogg College and to not more than twenty Supernumerary Fellowships of Kellogg College.

10. The governing body may elect to Professorial Fellowships at the college, on terms approved by Council, university professors, university readers, and holders of other university offices which are declared by any university statute or decree to qualify the holder for a Professorial Fellowship.

11. Any Fellow of Kellogg College who ceases to hold the post by virtue of which he or she was elected to a Fellowship of Kellogg College shall thereupon vacate that fellowship.

12. The officers of Kellogg College shall be appointed by the governing body. The terms and conditions of such appointments shall be determined by the governing body, subject to the approval of Council.

Section VI. Of the Permanent Private Halls

§ 1. *Of the granting of licences to open Permanent Private Halls*

1. The Vice-Chancellor may grant a licence for the establishment of a Permanent Private Hall, subject to the following conditions:

(*a*) that provision shall have been made for the establishment of the Hall on a permanent footing, and for the government thereof;

(*b*) that the Hall is not to be established for the purposes of profit;

(*c*) that the Master of the Hall be a Master of Arts of the University, and that his or her appointment as Master, by the governing body of the Hall, be subject to the approval of Council;

(*d*) that the buildings of the Hall be situate within two miles and a half of Carfax, and that after inspection by the Proctors they shall have been certified by the Proctors, to the satisfaction of the Vice-Chancellor, to be fit for the residence of students;

(*e*) that the consent of Congregation be given by resolution to the grant of the licence, and to the name by which the Hall is to be called.

2. The Master of the Hall before he or she enters on his or her office shall appear before the Vice-Chancellor and subscribe the following declaration:

'I, A. B., hereby promise that

I will observe the statutes concerning Permanent Private Halls:

I will open my Hall for the inspection of the Vice-Chancellor or other university authorities in any matter relating to the students thereof.

A. B.'

3. If the Vice-Chancellor shall deem that the Master of a Permanent Private Hall or his or her deputy has offended against the statutes, the Vice-Chancellor may, after due inquiry, admonish him or her or suspend the licence of the Hall for a time.

4. If it shall appear to the Vice-Chancellor that it is in the interests of the University that a licence granted for a Permanent Private Hall shall be revoked, it shall be lawful for him or her, after obtaining the consent of Council and of Congregation, to revoke the licence.

5. Students admitted into a duly licensed Permanent Private Hall shall have in relation to the University the same privileges and obligations as if they had been admitted into a college, and all statutes of the University in which mention is made generally and without distinction of colleges and other societies shall be deemed to include and apply to the members of Permanent Private Halls except as shall be determined otherwise by Council by decree.

§ 2. *Of the Office of Master of a Permanent Private Hall*

1. The Master of a Permanent Private Hall shall stand in tutorial relation to all members of his or her Hall who are *in statu pupillari*, and shall exercise supervision over their conduct and studies. In case the disciplinary officers of the University shall have occasion to deal with any of the students of his or her Hall the Master shall support the authority of the University, and see that its judgements are duly carried into effect.

2. The Master of a Permanent Private Hall shall reside in his or her Hall during at least six weeks in each term. The Master shall provide courses of instruction for the undergraduate members of the Hall during at least twenty-four weeks in the academic year, exclusive of the time devoted to any examinations in the Hall.

3. In case of the illness or absence for a sufficient reason of any Master of a Permanent Private Hall the Vice-Chancellor may give him or her leave to nominate a member of Convocation as deputy from time to time for any period not exceeding a year, such nomination to be subject to the approval of the Vice-Chancellor. The deputy so nominated shall be the vicegerent of the Master in all university business or acts, which may concern the Hall, as well as in the tuition of the students and management of the Hall.

§ 3. *Of the students of Permanent Private Halls*

1. Each Master of a Permanent Private Hall shall keep a register wherein shall be inserted the names of all students whom he or she may admit to his or her Hall. The Master shall from time to time, within one month of being requested so to do, transmit to the Registrar of the University a list of all his or her students in residence in the University in such term or terms as shall be specified.

2. Council shall have power to determine from time to time by decree the maximum number of students at each Permanent Private Hall studying for any degree, diploma, or certificate of the University, or of any category of such students.

3. The Master shall undertake to pay all fees, dues, and other moneys which may be payable to the University by any member of his or her Hall.

§ 4. *Of the supervision of Permanent Private Halls*

1. Every Permanent Private Hall shall be under the supervision and control of the Vice-Chancellor and Proctors.

2. Each Master of a Permanent Private Hall shall make available for inspection, at any reasonable time, by the Vice-Chancellor and Proctors, or by any one or more of them, the register of students admitted to his or her Hall.

TITLE VIII

OF OTHER UNIVERSITY BODIES

Section I. Of the Visitatorial Board

(This Section is a 'Queen-in-Council' statute—see Title XV, Section VII.*)*

1. The Visitatorial Board shall be composed of:

(1) a chairman appointed by or on behalf of the High Steward in accordance with the provisions of clause 2 below;

(2)–(5) four persons (who shall be members of Congregation, or other members of the University of the Degree of Master of Arts at the least, of not less than ten years' standing as members of Congregation or as Masters of Arts) selected from a panel of twelve persons elected by Congregation under arrangements which shall be prescribed from time to time by Council by decree.

2. The High Steward shall appoint the chairman of the board, to serve for two years, from amongst members of Congregation who are barristers or solicitors of at least five years' standing or who have judicial experience, provided that if the chairman is unable to attend on any occasion the High Steward, or if he or she is unable to act the Vice-Chancellor, shall appoint a member of Congregation who is a barrister or solicitor of at least five years' standing or who has judicial experience to act for the chairman on that occasion. If a vacancy arises through the chairman dying or resigning or ceasing to be a member of Congregation before the completion of his or her period of office, the person next appointed shall hold office for the remainder of the period of the person whom he or she replaces.

3. The Vice-Chancellor may, and at the request of any member of the board shall, convene a meeting of the board to consider any matter (other than a reference made under Title XVI) which falls within its jurisdiction.

4. The provisions of clauses 7–17 shall not apply in relation to anything done or omitted to be done on or after the date on which Title XVI came into effect.

5. The board shall consider:

(*a*) any reference made by the Vice-Chancellor under Title XVI concerning a person included in the Schedule to this statute; or

(*b*) any other matter which falls within its jurisdiction.

6. Title XVI, Part III, cll. 17 and 18 shall apply to the procedure of the board following a reference made by the Vice-Chancellor under that Part.

7. If the board has reason to suppose that a person included in the Schedule to this statute may have been guilty of misconduct, or wilful disobedience to the statutes, or other enactments of the University relating to his office, or may have failed satisfactorily to perform the duties of his office by reason of neglect or incompetence, the board may hold an inquiry into the circumstances of the case.

8. The board shall make provision by Standing Orders (which shall not be operative until approved by decree but shall when approved be binding on the board) in regard to its own procedure at any such inquiry.

9. Not less than twenty-eight days before the date fixed for the opening of the inquiry, notice shall be given in writing to the person concerned (or sent to his last known place of abode), of the board's intention to hold such an inquiry, of the date fixed for the opening of the inquiry, and of the acts or omissions with which he is charged.

10. The person concerned shall have the right to appear before the board to make his defence, and shall have the right to be represented; provided always that if he fail to appear before the board on the date fixed by the notice under clause 6 above, the board may (unless in its opinion his failure to appear was due to circumstances beyond his control) proceed with the inquiry in his absence.

11. If the board is satisfied that the person concerned has been guilty of misconduct, or wilful disobedience to the statutes or other enactments of the University relating to his office, or has failed satisfactorily to perform the duties of his office by reason of neglect or incompetence, the board may either

(*a*) admonish him; or

(*b*) suspend him from discharging his duties for a period not exceeding one year, and, either in addition or alternatively to such suspension, order any part of the emoluments of his office not exceeding the amount thereof for one year to be withheld; or,

(*c*) deprive him of his office, if in its judgement the gravity of the case shall so require;

provided that the board shall have power to act in cases of unsatisfactory performance by reason of incompetence only if the person concerned was elected or appointed to the office in question on or after 1 July 1986.

For the purposes of this statute the emoluments of an office shall be deemed to include any annual payment or other emolument annexed to it by the statutes of any college, but shall not include the income of a canonry or other ecclesiastical benefice, or any sums applied by the University in paying the premiums on policies under the Federated Superannuation System for Universities.

12. A person who has been sentenced by the board to be deprived of his office, or to be suspended from discharging the duties of it, or to be deprived of emoluments, may appeal against the sentence to the Chancellor, who may confirm, alter, or annul the sentence and whose decision shall be final: provided always

(*a*) that notice of such appeal shall be sent both to the Chancellor and to the Registrar within twenty-eight days of the passing of the sentence;

(*b*) that a written statement of the grounds of the appeal shall be submitted to the Chancellor and one copy sent to the Registrar within twenty-eight days of the giving of notice of appeal;

(*c*) that the Chancellor may, if he is satisfied that the appellant for reasons beyond his own control cannot comply with provisos (*a*) or (*b*), grant such extension of time as he may consider reasonable;

(*d*) that the Chancellor shall determine by whom and in what proportions the costs of the appeal shall be borne;

(*e*) that, in the event of the incapacity or absence abroad of the Chancellor, or during a vacancy in the Chancellorship, the notice of the appeal and the written statement of the grounds of the appeal shall be submitted to the Registrar; the other functions and powers of the Chancellor under this clause shall be exercised by the High Steward or, if he is unable or unwilling to act, by a person nominated by the Vice-Chancellor and the appellant, or, if they fail to agree on a nomination, by a board consisting of one person nominated by the Vice-Chancellor, one person nominated by the appellant, and a third person nominated by the other two nominees, and the Registrar shall be responsible for taking such action as is necessary to ensure that the appeal is brought to a hearing with reasonable expedition.

13. This statute shall be without prejudice to any power given by the statutes of any college to the Visitor of the college or to the governing body thereof to deprive a professor or reader or holder of a Professorial Fellowship who is a fellow of the college of his fellowship or of any part of the emoluments which he is entitled to receive as fellow for any cause for which any other fellow of the college would be liable to be so deprived.

14. If it be proved to the satisfaction of the board that any of the persons included in the Schedule to this statute is by reason of physical or mental infirmity temporarily unable to discharge his duties, the board may determine that provision shall be made for the discharge of such duties during the period of such incapacity by a competent deputy appointed by the persons who would have appointed to the office if it had been vacant; and such deputy shall receive out of the emoluments of the office such remuneration as the board shall determine: provided always

(*a*) that no such appointment of a deputy shall be made for a period exceeding one year without the approval of Council;

(*b*) that nothing in this statute shall be deemed to modify the conditions laid down or to be laid down elsewhere concerning the voluntary or compulsory retirement of persons employed by the University.

15. If it be proved to the satisfaction of the board that any of the persons included in the Schedule to this statute is by reason of physical or mental infirmity permanently unable to discharge his duties, the board may relieve him of his office.

16. The Vice-Chancellor shall have power to suspend any of the persons included in the Schedule to this statute from the discharge of his duties for a continuous period not exceeding a vacation and one calendar month of Full Term, if in his judgement such suspension is necessary in order to protect the

interests of the University. Such suspension may be further prolonged while any inquiry into the circumstances of the case is being conducted by the board.

17. Notwithstanding the provisions of this statute, if any examiner shall in the conduct of the examination for which he is appointed so act as in the judgement of the Vice-Chancellor or of the two Proctors to appear unmindful of the obligations of his office of examiner and the credit of the University, he shall be removed from his office of examiner by the Vice-Chancellor or by the two Proctors, as the case may be.

SCHEDULE

Any person who is employed by the University and who is a member of either the Federated Superannuation System for Universities or the Universities Superannuation Scheme or who would be a member if he had not been exempted under the provisions of Title X, Sect. I, (*g*) (ii).

Section II. Of the Delegates of the University Press

1. There shall be a Delegacy of the University Press which shall have charge of the affairs of the Press. It shall appoint the Secretary to the Delegates, the Deputy Secretary or Secretaries, and any other officer whose appointment shall entitle him or her to a seat on the Finance Committee, and shall have such other powers as shall be laid down by decree.

2. The Delegacy shall consist of:

(1) the Vice-Chancellor;

(2), (3) the Proctors;

(4) the Assessor;

(5) the Chairman of the Finance Committee of the Delegacy if not already a Delegate when elected as chairman;

(6)–(22) seventeen members of Congregation appointed by Council.

3. An appointed Delegate shall hold office for five years, except that in the case of a vacancy arising in the course of an academic year the appointment shall be for five years together with the remainder of that academic year. The Delegate shall then be eligible for reappointment for a second period of five years. Exceptionally any Delegate may be reappointed for a third period of five years, and the Chairman of the Finance Committee may be reappointed for up to three periods of five years from his or her first appointment as a Delegate, but appointment for a third period shall require to be confirmed by Council by decree.

4. Council shall, in making appointments, bear in mind the need to ensure that the composition of the Delegacy as a whole is such as to cover the main branches of academic studies and at the same time to provide a sufficiency of persons competent in matters of organization and finance.

5. If a Delegate appointed by Council shall have attended fewer than nine meetings of the Delegates in the course of any academic year, his or her seat

shall at the close of such year be declared by the Vice-Chancellor to be vacant and shall thereupon be vacated; provided always that

(*a*) a person elected to fill a casual vacancy shall only be required to attend the same proportion of meetings held subsequent to the date of his or her election as nine bears to the total number of meetings held in the academic year, any fraction being reckoned to the nearest unit;

(*b*) the Delegates may waive the requirement in the case of a member absent from Oxford for a purpose approved by them.

6. There shall be a Finance Committee of the Delegacy which, subject to the general authority of the Delegates, shall have the direction of the finance and management of the business. The constitution of the committee shall be determined by decree, and, notwithstanding the provisions of Tit. IX, Sect. III, cl. 2, the decree may provide for a person other than the Vice-Chancellor to be chairman.

7. The Delegates may from time to time delegate to any other body or person responsibility for any matter for which responsibility has been laid on the Delegates, and may delegate such powers as they may consider necessary for the discharge of this responsibility, provided always that any such delegations may be withdrawn (either generally or in respect of a specific item) at any time and that such delegations shall not relieve the Delegates of general responsibility for the matters delegated.

Section III. Of the Curators of the University Libraries

1. There shall be a body called the Curators of the University Libraries consisting of:

(1) the Pro-Vice-Chancellor (Academic Services and University Collections), who shall be chairman;

(2) one of the Proctors or the Assessor as may be agreed between them;

(3)–(6) four persons elected by Council, of whom one shall be a member both of Council and of its Planning and Resource Allocation Committee, and of whom two shall be persons not being resident holders of teaching, research, or administrative posts in the University or in any college or other society;[1]

(7)–(11) one member from each of the five Divisional Boards, elected by their respective boards;

(12)–(15) four persons elected by Congregation from amongst its members;

(16) a person elected by the Conference of Colleges;

(17) a Junior Member elected by the Executive of the Oxford University Student Union;

[1] Council has agreed (*a*) that one of the external members should be someone with experience of managing a major research library, and (*b*) that it should also appoint a person with experience in the application of IT to libraries.

(18) a Junior Member elected by the Graduate Committee of the Oxford University Student Union.

The curators shall have power to co-opt not more than two additional members for such periods as the curators may determine from time to time.

The curators under (3)–(16) shall hold office for four years and shall be re-eligible, and the curators under (17) and (18) shall hold office for one year and shall be re-eligible; provided always that the tenure of office of elected curators shall be subject to their retaining the qualifications in virtue of which they were elected; and provided also that a curator elected to fill a vacancy caused otherwise than by lapse of time shall hold office for the unexpired residue only of the period of office of the curator whom he or she succeeds.

The Director of University Library Services and Bodley's Librarian shall be secretary to the Curators.

No Junior Member shall be present for the discussion of, or receive the papers or minutes relating to, reserved business as defined in Ch. II, Sect. II, cl. 7.

2. The curators shall be responsible to Council for:

(*a*) ensuring that provision is made for the University's library and information requirements for teaching and research;

(*b*) making financial provision, from funds made available to them by Council or from other sources, for such libraries as Council shall from time to time determine;[1]

(*c*) ensuring that the University's major research libraries, including the Bodleian, Sackler, and Taylorian Libraries, are maintained as a national and international scholarly resource;

(*d*) advising as necessary on the University's trusteeship of the collections held in its libraries, including, where appropriate, advising on the need for specialist legal or financial advice;

(*e*) advising on any proposals involving the use of resources in the University for library and information provision for teaching and research;

(*f*) such other responsibilities as may be determined by Council from time to time.

3. The curators shall have authority under Council to make such arrangements as are necessary to fulfil their responsibilities and shall have such other powers as may be laid down by statute, decree, or regulation.

4. The Director of University Library Services and Bodley's Librarian shall be appointed by an electoral board which shall be chaired by the Vice-Chancellor or his or her nominee, and the other members of which shall be appointed by

[1] The libraries which Council has already agreed should be funded through the Curators of the University Libraries are the Bodleian Library and its dependent libraries, the Sackler Library, the Taylor Institution Library, the Cairns Library, the Institute of Health Sciences Library, the English, History, Modern Languages, Music, and Theology Faculty Libraries, and the Social Studies Libraries.

the curators. The electors in making their choice shall have regard to the direction given by Sir Thomas Bodley, that Bodley's Librarian should be 'one that is noted and known for a diligent student, and in all his conversation to be trusty, active, and discreet: a graduate also, and a linguist'.

5. The Director of University Library Services and Bodley's Librarian shall act for the curators and shall be responsible to them in the exercise of their powers.

6. The curators shall approve arrangements for the delegation of appointments within the University Library Services, provided that the appointment of senior library staff at grade 6 shall be subject to the approval of the curators on the recommendation of the Director of University Library Services and Bodley's Librarian.

Section IV. Of the Visitors of the Ashmolean Museum

1. The purpose of the museum is to assemble, preserve, and exhibit such objects of art and antiquity and such printed and other documents as may increase knowledge of history, archaeology, and art, to assist in relevant teaching and research within the University, and, in general, to promote the study of such objects and documents; and the General Board shall, in assessing the grant to be made to the museum from the money available to the General Board, have regard to the obligation of the University to maintain the museum as a national and international as well as a university museum.

2. The expression 'the museum' includes

(*a*) the collections, comprising all objects of art and antiquity, and reproductions, records, and catalogues of such objects, and other study material, which have been or shall have been assigned to the Ashmolean Museum by the University or otherwise acquired;

(*b*) the Griffith Institute;

(*c*) the buildings, or part of buildings, which have been or shall have been assigned by the University for the exhibition and custody of the collections and library or for the use of the staff, and all other premises under the control of the Visitors, together with the precincts and appurtenances thereof.

3. (*a*) The departments of the museum are those parts into which for purposes of custody the collections have been or shall have been divided, together with the rooms in which they are housed;

(*b*) The departments shall be the Department of Antiquities, the Department of Western Art, the Department of Eastern Art, the Heberden Coin Room, and the Cast Gallery.

4. (*a*) The Visitors of the museum shall be:

(1) the Vice-Chancellor;

(2) a chairman who shall be appointed by the Vice-Chancellor;

(3) one of the Proctors or the Assessor as may be agreed between them;

(4)–(6) three persons appointed by Council;

(7)–(9) three persons appointed by the General Board.

(*b*) The Visitors shall have power to co-opt up to four additional members of whom not more than two shall be members of Congregation.

(*c*) The chairman shall hold office for three years and may be reappointed for one further period of up to three years. Elected and co-opted members shall hold office for four years and shall be re-eligible. No person holding office in the museum (other than the office of Curator of the Cast Gallery) shall be eligible to be a Visitor.

5. The Visitors shall be responsible for the safe keeping, preservation, orderly administration, finance, and general policy of the museum. They shall make rules and take all other steps necessary for its maintenance and security, and shall make provision for the lighting, warming, water-supply, and cleaning of the buildings.

6. The Visitors shall appoint a Keeper of each Department of the Museum, except that the Keeper of the Cast Gallery shall be the Lincoln Professor of Classical Archaeology and Art by virtue of his or her office and shall be styled Curator of the Cast Gallery.

In the absence of the Director, the Visitors may appoint one of the Keepers to act in his or her stead.

7. The Visitors shall have such powers as may be laid down by decree.

Section V. Of Other Bodies

1. There shall also be the following bodies:

Committee for Archaeology
Committee for the Archives
Delegates for the Nomination of Candidates for Ecclesiastical Benefices
Curators of the Botanic Garden
Committee for the Careers Service
Committee for the University Club
Committee for Comparative Philology and General Linguistics
Committee for Educational Studies
Curators of the Examination Schools
Advisory Committee for Forestry
Board of Management of the Frere Exhibition for Indian Studies
Board of Management of the Gotch Memorial Prize
Board of Management of the Hall, Hall-Houghton, and Houghton Prizes
Committee for the History of Art
Committee for the History of Science, Medicine, and Technology
Trustees of the Mathematical Prizes
Delegates for Military Instruction
Committee of Management of the Modern Languages Faculty Library
Visitors of the Oxford University Museum of Natural History
Advisory Council for Ornithology
Curators of the University Parks
Committee for the Proctors' Office

Inter-faculty Committee for Queen Elizabeth House
Committee for the Nomination of Select Preachers
Curators of the Sheldonian Theatre
Curators of the Taylor Institution
Joint Undergraduate Admissions Committee

2. The composition and functions of these bodies shall be laid down by decree or regulation.

TITLE IX

OF THE OFFICERS OF THE UNIVERSITY

Section I. Of the Chancellor

1. The Chancellor shall be elected by Convocation and shall hold office during his or her life or until his or her resignation. The Chancellor may from time to time admit major benefactors of the University to membership of the Chancellor's Court of Benefactors, and shall have such other functions and powers as are or shall be assigned to him or her by the statutes or by the law of the land.

2. In the event of the incapacity or absence abroad of the Chancellor, or during a vacancy in the Chancellorship, or on delegation from the Chancellor, the Vice-Chancellor may exercise any of the functions and powers of the Chancellor, except where the statutes provide otherwise.

Section II. Of the High Steward

1. The High Steward shall have such functions and powers as are or shall be assigned to him or her by the statutes, by the Chancellor, or by decree.

2. The High Steward shall be appointed by the Chancellor and shall hold office until he or she reaches the age of 75 or until his or her resignation, whichever is the earlier.

3. If the Chancellor has made no appointment within three months of the office becoming vacant, Council shall make the appointment.

Section III. Of the Vice-Chancellor

1. The Vice-Chancellor shall have such functions and powers as are or shall be assigned to him or her by the statutes or by Council, whether by decree or otherwise, or by the law of the land.

2. The Vice-Chancellor shall be *ex officio* chairman of all committees and other bodies of which he or she is a member, and, notwithstanding any provisions of the statutes concerning the composition of committees and other bodies and the appointment of chairmen and vice-chairmen, the Vice-Chancellor may attend any meeting of any committee or other body set up by or under the authority of the statutes and may take the chair at it if he or she so wishes, or may appoint any member of Congregation (whether a member of the committee or not) to attend any meeting on his or her behalf and to take the chair if he or she so directs, provided only that the Vice-Chancellor shall not have the right to take the chair or to appoint a chairman in the case of a meeting at which the Chancellor is present.

3. Subject to the provisions of the statutes, the Vice-Chancellor may delegate any of his or her functions and powers to any member of Congregation,

provided always that such delegations may be withdrawn (either generally or in respect of a specific item) at any time and that such delegations shall not relieve the Vice-Chancellor of general responsibility for the matters delegated.

4. The Vice-Chancellor shall hold office for five years on initial appointment, which may be extended by reappointment for up to two further years, provided that, when a Vice-Chancellor vacates the office before the expiry of his or her full term of office and at a time other than the end of the academic year, his or her successor's period shall consist of the remainder of that academic year and five further years, which may be extended by reappointment for up to two additional years.

5. Any person shall be eligible for appointment as Vice-Chancellor provided only that he or she can serve the full period permitted under clause 4 above before reaching the retiring age as prescribed by Tit. X, Sect. I.

6. Subject to the provisions of clause 4 above, no person shall be appointed Vice-Chancellor a second time, except that, if a Vice-Chancellor vacates his or her office before the expiry of a full term of office, a person who has previously been Vice-Chancellor may be appointed Vice-Chancellor again for one year (or, if the retiring Vice-Chancellor vacates his or her office at a time other than the end of an academic year, for the remainder of that academic year and one further year). The age-limit in clause 5 above shall not apply to such a second appointment.

7. The Vice-Chancellor shall be appointed or reappointed in accordance with the following procedure:

(*a*) not less than one year before the initial period of office of a Vice-Chancellor is due to come to an end by effluxion of time, a committee consisting of:

(1) the Chancellor, or, if the Chancellor is unable or unwilling to act, one of the members of Council nominated under the provisions of Tit. IV, Sect. II, cl. 1 (7), (8), who shall if possible be appointed by the Chancellor for this purpose, or, if the Chancellor is unable or unwilling to make such an appointment, shall be appointed by Council, and who shall chair the committee;

(2)–(5) four persons, not also being members of Council, appointed by Congregation;

(6)–(8) three persons appointed by Council, of whom, if the Chancellor is to chair the committee personally, one shall be one of the members of Council nominated under the provisions of Tit. IV, Sect. II, cl. 1 (7), (8);

(9)–(13) one person appointed by each of the five divisional boards;

(14) the Chairman of the Conference of Colleges or his or her nominee;

(15) one person, not also being a member of Council, appointed by the Conference of Colleges

shall report to Council with a recommendation either that the current Vice-Chancellor be reappointed for a further period of not more than two years, or that another, named, person be appointed as the next Vice-Chancellor;

(*b*) not less than one year before any period of reappointment to the office of Vice-Chancellor is due to come to an end by effluxion of time, the committee at (*a*) above shall report to Council with a recommendation that a named person be appointed as the next Vice-Chancellor;

(*c*) the appointed members of the committee at (*a*) above shall hold office for five years and shall not be eligible for reappointment until the expiry of five years from the date on which this period of office expires, except that a member appointed for less than a full period in order to fill a casual vacancy may be reappointed for one full period. A member of the committee appointed under (*a*) (2)–(5) or (15) above who becomes a member of Council during his or her period of office shall forthwith vacate his or her office; no person shall be appointed under (*a*) (2)–(13) or (15) above if the result of his or her appointment would be that more than two members of the committee, excluding the chairman, were members of the governing body of any one college or other society. If this rule is broken by reason of persons being appointed simultaneously by different bodies, the person or persons senior in academic standing shall be deemed appointed to the extent permitted by the rule, and the other or others shall be deemed not appointed (in the event of equality in academic standing, appointment being made by lot);

(*d*) when Council has considered the committee's report, and any further report on the appointment or reappointment which it may have requested the committee to make, Council shall submit to Congregation either the name of the person proposed for appointment, or a proposal for the reappointment of the current Vice-Chancellor, as the case may be;

(*e*) Council's proposal for the appointment of a new Vice-Chancellor shall be deemed approved unless it is rejected with at least 125 members voting in favour of rejection. If a proposal for the appointment of a new Vice-Chancellor is rejected, Council shall, after consultation with the committee, within two months nominate two persons to Congregation (of whom one may be the person previously rejected) and offer Congregation the choice between them;

(*f*) Council's proposal for the reappointment of the current Vice-Chancellor shall be deemed approved unless it is rejected with at least 125 members voting in favour of rejection. If a proposal for the reappointment of the current Vice-Chancellor is rejected, Council shall, after consultation with the committee, within two months submit to Congregation the name of another person for appointment as a new Vice-Chancellor, and the same procedure shall apply as at (*e*) above;

(*g*) if for any reason there is no Vice-Chancellor-elect able and willing to take up office on the laying down of office by a Vice-Chancellor, an Acting Vice-Chancellor shall be appointed under the provisions of clause 8 below, until such time as a new Vice-Chancellor shall have been appointed under the procedure laid down in (*a*)–(*f*) above.

8. In the event of the incapacity or absence from Oxford of the Vice-Chancellor, or in the event of a vacancy in the Vice-Chancellorship, one of the

Pro-Vice-Chancellors shall be appointed Acting Vice-Chancellor. The appointment shall be made

(*a*) by the Vice-Chancellor if the incapacity or absence is unlikely to be longer than two months;

(*b*) by the Chancellor if the incapacity or absence is likely to be for longer than two months, or after an appointment under (*a*) has lasted for two months, or in the event of a vacancy in the Vice-Chancellorship;

(*c*) by Council in default of an appointment under (*a*) or (*b*).

9. An Acting Vice-Chancellor shall have all the functions and powers of the Vice-Chancellor.

Section IV. Of the Vice-Chancellor-Elect

1. A person appointed Vice-Chancellor under the provisions of Sect. III, cl. 7 above, shall be known as the Vice-Chancellor-elect until such time as he or she takes up office.

2. The Vice-Chancellor-elect shall be entitled to attend and to speak at meetings of Council and of all committees of Council from the time of the approval by Congregation of his or her appointment to the time at which he or she takes up office, but shall not be entitled to vote at any such meeting. He or she shall have such other functions and powers as are or shall be assigned to him or her in the statutes.

Section V. Of the Pro-Vice-Chancellors

1. The Vice-Chancellor may appoint any members of Congregation as Pro-Vice-Chancellors, subject to such limitation on the number of Pro-Vice-Chancellors and to such other conditions as may be laid down by decree.

2. The Pro-Vice-Chancellors shall have such functions and powers as are or shall be assigned to them by the statutes or by the Vice-Chancellor under the provisions of Sect. III, cll. 2 and 3 above.

Section VI. Of the Proctors, Assessor, and Pro-Proctors

§ 1. *Of the appointment of the Proctors and Assessor*

1. There shall be two Proctors and an Assessor who shall be elected annually on the Wednesday in the eighth week of Hilary Full Term and shall hold office from the Wednesday in the week after the end of Hilary Full Term in the year next following.

2. Any member of Congregation shall be eligible for election as Proctor or Assessor provided that he or she has not held either office before and, on the day on which he or she takes up office,

(*a*) will have passed his or her twenty-ninth, but not fifty-second birthday and

(*b*) will have been a member of Congregation for at least two years.

3. The Proctors and Assessor to be admitted to office in the years from 1998 to 2017 inclusive shall be elected by the colleges and other societies as shown in the following Schedule.

SCHEDULE

Year of admission to office	*Societies electing Proctors*	*Society electing Assessor*
1998	Exeter, St Catherine's	Queen's
1999	Lady Margaret Hall, Pembroke	Nuffield
2000	Wadham, St Edmund Hall	St Peter's
2001	Green, Jesus	Trinity
2002	Merton, Somerville	Linacre
2003	Keble, Lincoln	Kellogg
2004	Corpus Christi, University	St Hugh's
2005	Brasenose, St John's	St Cross
2006	All Souls, St Hilda's	Christ Church
2007	Balliol, Wolfson	Hertford
2008	St Anne's, Worcester	Magdalen
2009	New College, St Antony's	Mansfield
2010	Queen's, St Catherine's	Templeton
2011	Nuffield, Pembroke	Harris Manchester
2012	St Edmund Hall, St Peter's	Oriel
2013	Green, Trinity	Exeter
2014	Linacre, Merton	Lady Margaret Hall
2015	Keble, St Hugh's	Wadham
2016	Corpus Christi, Kellogg	Jesus
2017	Brasenose, St Cross	Somerville

4. All members of the electing college or other society who are members of Congregation (but who are not members of the governing body of another college or other society) together with any members of its governing body who are not members of Congregation shall be entitled to take part in the election of a Proctor or Assessor.

5. The candidate who receives the most votes shall be declared elected. If two or more candidates obtain an equal number of votes the head of the college or other society or, if he or she is absent or the headship is vacant, the vicegerent shall have a casting vote. If the election is not completed in one day and the result announced to the Vice-Chancellor by 9 p.m., the Vice-Chancellor shall within a week appoint as Proctor or Assessor a member of any college or other society who is qualified under clause 2 above.

6. If a Proctor or Assessor dies or resigns before the end of his or her year of office, the head of his or her college or society, or if the head is absent or the headship is vacant, the vicegerent shall within one week appoint a substitute qualified under clause 2 above. If no such appointment is made within a week, the Vice-Chancellor shall appoint a member of any college or other society who is qualified under clause 2 above.

7. The Vice-Chancellor shall have power to settle any question concerning the election of a Proctor or Assessor which is not covered by the preceding clauses in consultation with the head of the college or society entitled to make the election and the head of one other college or society; or, if the Vice-Chancellor is himself or herself the head of the college or society making the election, in consultation with the heads of two other colleges or societies.

8. The Proctor in each year who was first admitted to the Degree of Master of Arts shall be the Senior Proctor, and the other the Junior Proctor.

§ 2. *Of the appointment of Pro-Proctors*

1. Each Proctor shall, at the time of admission to office, appoint two Pro-Proctors, being members of Congregation not less than twenty-nine years of age, each of whom shall act as deputy for the Proctor appointing him or her on such occasions as he or she shall determine.

2. At any time during his or her period of office a Proctor may, subject to the approval of the Vice-Chancellor, appoint additional Pro-Proctors, being members of Congregation not less than twenty-nine years of age. Each such additional Pro-Proctor shall act as deputy to the Proctor appointing him or her on such occasions and for such periods as the Proctor shall determine. He or she shall be admitted to office by the Vice-Chancellor as soon as possible after appointment, and his or her name shall be published in the *University Gazette*. An additional Pro-Proctor shall receive such stipend as Council shall determine, provided that it shall not exceed the annual stipend fixed by Council for Pro-Proctors appointed under the provisions of cl. 1 above.

§ 3. *Of the duties and powers of the Proctors*

1. The Proctors shall have such functions and powers as are or shall be assigned to them by the statutes or by decree.

2. The Proctors shall take an active part in the business of the University. Each Proctor shall have the right to see the papers of, and to attend and speak at any meeting of, any committee or other body set up by or under the authority of the statutes; but he or she shall not have the right to vote (unless a member of the committee), nor shall he or she be sent the papers of any committee of which he or she is not a member unless he or she so requests.

3. The Proctors shall see that examinations are properly conducted and in accordance with the statutes, decrees, and regulations concerning them; and they may make such regulations concerning conduct in examinations as they consider necessary.

4. The Proctors shall attend the Chancellor or his or her deputy at official university ceremonies and presentations for degrees, and on other university and public occasions at the Chancellor's request.

5. The Proctors shall be available for consultation by members of the University and may investigate complaints; and may summon any member of the

University before them to assist in their investigations, any failure to attend without reasonable cause being an offence under Tit. XIII, cl. 2 (*a*). They also shall generally ensure that the statutes, customs, and privileges of the University are observed.

§ **4.** *Of the duties and powers of the Assessor*

1. The Assessor shall take an active part in the business of the University. He or she shall have the right to see the papers of, and to attend and speak at any meeting of, any committee or other body set up by or under the authority of the statutes; but shall not have the right to vote (unless a member of the committee) nor shall the Assessor be sent the papers of any committee of which he or she is not a member unless he or she so requests.

2. The Assessor shall undertake any inquiry or special study of any matter concerning the policy or administration of the University at the request of Council or the General Board.

3. The Assessor shall perform such other duties as may be laid down from time to time by statute or decree.

Section VII. Of the Registrar and Other Officials

1. The Registrar shall be appointed by Council.

2. The Registrar shall act as principal adviser on strategic policy to the Vice-Chancellor and to Council, and shall ensure effective co-ordination of advice from other officers to the Vice-Chancellor, Council, and other university bodies.

3. The Registrar shall be the secretary of Congregation and of Council. He or she shall also be responsible for providing the secretary of any committee or body set up by Congregation or Council under the provisions of any statute or decree, which has no executive officer.

4. The Registrar shall, under the Vice-Chancellor, be the head of the central administrative services of the University, and shall be responsible for the management and professional development of their staff and for the development of other administrative support.

5. The Registrar may delegate any of his or her functions or powers to any of the University's senior administrative officers, provided always that such delegations are not inconsistent with the due performance of the duties set out in clause 10 below, and that they may be withdrawn (either generally or in respect of a specific item) at any time, and that such delegations shall not relieve the Registrar of general responsibility for the matters delegated.

6. The Registrar shall, under the direction of the Vice-Chancellor, be responsible for overseeing the University's external relations and for communications which express the general policy of the University.

7. The Registrar shall have such other functions and powers as are or shall be assigned to him or her by the statutes or by the Vice-Chancellor under the provisions of Sect. III, cl. 3 above.

8. The Registrar shall be entitled to receive the papers of every committee or other body set up by or under the authority of the statutes and decrees, and the Registrar or his or her nominee may attend or speak (though not vote) at any meeting.

9. The Registrar shall be responsible, as specified by Council by decree, for ensuring the maintenance and dissemination of university records and registers, and for furnishing certificates of matriculation, graduation, and the results of university examinations, and for university publications.

10. The University's senior administrative officers shall be under the general direction of the Registrar and shall be responsible to him or her for the due performance of their duties, provided always that they shall have the right to make their views on financial, professional, and technical matters known to the Vice-Chancellor, Council, and the appropriate committees of the University.

11. The University's senior administrative officers shall be appointed by Council, after consultation with the Registrar.

12. In the absence or incapacity of the Registrar, or during a vacancy in the Registrarship until an appointment to the vacant office has been made, the Vice-Chancellor shall designate an Acting Registrar who shall have all the functions, powers, and duties of the Registrar.

13. For the purposes of this Section, the phrase 'the University's senior administrative officers' shall mean officers who are directly responsible to the Registrar and who hold established posts in the highest administrative grade.

TITLE X

OF THE CONDITIONS OF SERVICE OF PERSONS EMPLOYED BY THE UNIVERSITY

Section I. Of General Conditions

The numbers of persons employed by the University, their conditions of service, and their method of appointment shall be determined, subject to the provisions of the statutes, from time to time by Council, in consultation, where appropriate, with the General Board, provided always that:

(*a*) the three main categories of academic staff shall be professors, readers, and lecturers;

(*b*) the holders of all professorships enumerated in Schedules A and B annexed to Ch. VII, Sect. I, § 5, shall be paid the same salary (from which shall be deducted the canonical salary in the case of professorships to which a canonry at Christ Church is annexed), provided that this shall not prevent the payment of additional emoluments, which may be pensionable, (i) in the form of such allowances in respect of administrative responsibilities as may be prescribed by decree, or (ii) in the form of awards in recognition of academic distinction or contribution to academic work of the University in accordance with arrangements to be determined from time to time by Council;

(*c*) the university salaries of non-medical lecturers shall, under arrangements to be approved by Council, be determined by the General Board, which in discharging this function shall have regard to, but shall not be bound by, scales related to age;

(*d*) arrangements shall be made by Council under which all professors, readers, lecturers, and holders of other posts approved for this purpose by Council shall be entitled to apply for one term of leave for every six terms of service;

(*e*) every holder of a full-time professorship or readership, or of any other post approved for this purpose by decree, and every holder of a full-time lecturership who has been appointed to that lecturership until retirement age, shall be entitled to hold a fellowship in a college or other society, provided that the offer of a fellowship to any person who is entitled under this statute, or to any person who would become so entitled on reappointment to the retirement age, shall satisfy any obligation of the University in respect of that person's entitlement to hold a fellowship;

(*f*) every full-time professorship shall be allocated from time to time by Council to a college or other society, and the successive holders of that professorship shall be fellows of that college or other society; the college or society of allocation shall have the right to have two representatives on the board of election for the professorship;

(*g*) all persons employed by the University shall be subject either to the Federated Superannuation System for Universities, or to the Universities

Superannuation Scheme, or (if they are not eligible to become members of either scheme) to a Pension Scheme managed by the University, and shall be entitled to the benefits of any scheme for the supplementation of superannuation benefits that may be applicable to universities generally, provided that:

(i) Council shall determine in any cases of doubt, but having regard to the practice of universities generally, and the rules of the Universities Superannuation Scheme, to which scheme a person shall belong;

(ii) Council shall exempt from the need to be subject to a scheme any person who is excluded from membership of the appropriate scheme by virtue of age or who is already in receipt of pension from one of the schemes or who submits a written request for exemption; and Council may exclude from membership of a scheme any person on account of the short-term or part-time nature of his or her employment or if he or she is subject to an alternative scheme approved by Council;

(*h*) every employee of the University who is subject to the jurisdiction of the Visitatorial Board under the provisions of Tit. VIII, Sect. I, other than the holder of a professorship to which a canonry is annexed who is exempt from membership of the appropriate pension scheme referred to in proviso (*g*) above, shall retire not later than the 30 September immediately preceding his or her 66th birthday, and every employee of the University who is not subject to that jurisdiction shall retire not later than the 31 July immediately preceding his or her 66th birthday, provided always that:

(i) any person may elect to retire on, or at any time after, his or her 60th birthday;

(ii) Council may make arrangements to provide for the continued employment in special cases of a person who wishes to remain in the employment of the University and whose services for the University it desires to retain, provided always that no person shall continue in the regular employment of the University after, if subject to the jurisdiction of the Visitatorial Board, the 30 September or, if not so subject, the 31 July immediately preceding his or her 71st birthday;

(iii) any person who at 1 July 1985 held an appointment (whether or not of the University) with entitlement to hold office at least until his or her 67th birthday (or any person then holding an appointment to which he or she was appointed on the basis that if subsequently reappointed he or she would be entitled to hold office at least until that age), and who continuously thereafter shall have held an appointment or appointments with such entitlement, shall not be required, if subject to the jurisdiction of the Visitatorial Board, to retire before the 30 September immediately preceding his or her 68th birthday; and for the purposes of this proviso, (*a*) in determining whether such appointments have been held continuously, any interval between a successful application for, and the taking up of, an appointment shall be disregarded; and (*b*) appointments accepted by, but not taken up until after, 1 July 1985 shall be deemed to be held at that date;

(*i*) any employee of the University who is not subject to the jurisdiction of the Visitatorial Board under the provisions of Tit. VIII, Sect. I, shall, in the event of dismissal, in a case in which the dismissal arises from disciplinary action, have a right of appeal to a panel consisting of two members of the Staff Committee appointed by the Chairman of the Staff Committee (or his or her deputy) and one member of Council, not being a member of the Staff Committee, appointed by the Vice-Chancellor. Pending the outcome of any appeal, the employee will be regarded as suspended without pay. On the hearing of an appeal, the panel may confirm or revoke the dismissal or may make such order as it may think just, and the Curators of the University Chest shall pay the appellant the sum, if any, ordered by the panel to be paid to him or her.

Section II. Of Authority in relation to Employment

1. No official of the University or any other person employed by the University or working in or in connection with any department of or under the control of the University shall have authority to offer any person employment as a member of the University's academic-related or non-academic staff, or to sign letters of appointment for such academic-related and non-academic staff, or to dismiss such non-academic staff, or to dismiss such academic-related staff in circumstances other than those which fall within the provisions of Title VIII or Title XVII, Parts II–IV, except with the express consent of Council and provided that

(*a*) any offer of employment shall be on the appropriate terms and conditions of employment for the category of staff concerned; and

(*b*) any dismissal shall have complied with the appropriate procedures for the dismissal of the member of staff concerned.

No consent given by Council under the provisions of this clause shall be operative until a copy of the resolution of Council, certified by the Registrar, shall have been delivered to such official or such other person concerned.

2. Council may delegate its powers hereunder to the Staff Committee, or to the chairman or to an officer or officers of that committee, as it may deem appropriate and on such conditions as it may lay down and a consent signed by the chairman of the Staff Committee or by a designated officer shall have the same effect as a certified resolution of Council.

Section III. Of Authority to make Representations on behalf of the University in certain Matters

1. No official of the University or any other person employed by the University or working in or in connection with any department of or under the control of the University shall in connection with any invention, discovery, or patent, or (except under the authority of the Delegates of the Press, in matters falling within their jurisdiction) process, or manufacture have authority to make any representations on behalf of the University or to enter into any contract on behalf of the University or to be concerned in any transaction whatsoever in

connection therewith on behalf of the University except with the express consent of Council. No consent given by Council under the provisions of this clause shall be operative until a copy of the resolution of Council, certified by the Registrar, shall have been delivered to such official or such other person concerned.

2. Council may delegate its powers hereunder to such committee or officer as it may deem appropriate and on such conditions as it may lay down and a consent signed by the chairman of the designated committee or by the designated officer shall have the same effect as a certified resolution of Council.

Section IV. Of Intellectual Property

1. Subject to clause 2 below and to the provisions of the Patents Act 1977, and unless otherwise agreed in writing between the person concerned and the University, the University claims ownership of the following forms of intellectual property; in the case of (*c*), (*d*), (*e*), and (*f*) (and (*g*) as it relates to (*c*)–(*f*)) the claims are to intellectual property devised, made, or created, by staff in the course of their employment by the University, and by persons engaged by the University under contracts for services:

(*a*) works generated by computer hardware or software owned or operated by the University;

(*b*) films, videos, multimedia works, typographical arrangements, and other works created with the aid of university facilities;

(*c*) patentable and non-patentable inventions;

(*d*) registered and unregistered designs, plant varieties, and topographies;

(*e*) university-commissioned works not within (*a*), (*b*), (*c*), (*d*), or (*e*);

(*f*) databases, computer software, firmware, courseware, and related material not within (*a*), (*b*), (*c*), (*d*), or (*e*), but only if they may reasonably be considered to possess commercial potential; and

(*g*) know-how and information associated with the above.

2. Notwithstanding clause 1 above, the University will not assert any claim to the ownership of copyright in:

(*a*) artistic works, books, articles, plays, lyrics, scores, or lectures, apart from those specifically commissioned by the University;

(*b*) audio or visual aids to the giving of lectures; or

(*c*) computer-related works other than those specified in clause 1 above.

3. 'Commissioned works' for the purpose of clauses 1 and 2 above are works which the University has specifically employed or requested the person concerned to produce, whether in return for special payment or not. However, save as separately agreed between the University Press and the person concerned, works commissioned by the University Press in the course of its publishing business shall not be regarded as 'works commissioned by the University'.

4. The provisions of this section shall take effect on 1 October 2000, and shall apply to all intellectual property devised, made, or created on or after 1 October 2000.

5. The policy set out above shall be administered in accordance with procedures which shall be determined from time to time by Council by decree.

TITLE XI

OF MATRICULATION, RESIDENCE, DEGREES, DIPLOMAS, CERTIFICATES, AND EXAMINATIONS

1. No person shall be matriculated as a member of the University unless he or she shall first have been made a member of a college or other society, and no person shall continue to be a member of a college or other society unless he or she is presented for matriculation as a member of the University within a period laid down by decree or regulation.

2. No person shall be matriculated as a member of the University unless he or she has the qualifications which shall be laid down by decree or regulation.

3. Notwithstanding the provisions of clauses 1 and 2 above, (*a*) any person who has been accorded the status of Master of Arts under the provisions of Tit. II, Sect. II, cl. 3, shall be matriculated; (*b*) any person who is appointed a Bedel under the provisions of the decree relating to those offices shall be matriculated, and shall at the time of his or her matriculation be instructed in the statutes, privileges, and customs of the University so far as they affect him or her.

4. The following degrees shall be conferred by the University:

Doctor of Divinity
Doctor of Civil Law
Doctor of Medicine
Doctor of Letters
Doctor of Science
Doctor of Music
Doctor of Philosophy
Doctor of Clinical Psychology
Master of Arts
Master of Surgery
Master of Science
Master of Letters
Master of Philosophy
Master of Studies
Magister Juris
Master of Theology
Master of Education
Master of Business Administration
Master of Fine Art
Master of Biochemistry
Master of Chemistry
Master of Earth Sciences
Master of Engineering
Master of Mathematics
Master of Physics
Bachelor of Divinity
Bachelor of Civil Law
Bachelor of Medicine
Bachelor of Surgery
Bachelor of Music
Bachelor of Philosophy
Bachelor of Arts
Bachelor of Fine Art
Bachelor of Theology
Bachelor of Education

5. Any person on whom the degree of Bachelor of Letters or Bachelor of Philosophy (in a subject other than Philosophy) has been conferred may apply to the Registrar through his or her college or other society for the redesignation of the title of his or her degree to that of Master of Letters or of Master of Philosophy respectively. On receipt of such an application, the Registrar shall issue a revised degree certificate and amend his or her records accordingly.

6. Any person on whom the degree of Bachelor of Science has been conferred may apply to the Registrar through his or her college or other society for the redesignation of the title of his or her degree to that of Master of Science. On receipt of such an application, the Registrar shall issue a revised degree certificate and amend his or her records accordingly. Any person to whom a certificate has been issued or leave to supplicate for the degree of Bachelor of Science has been granted but who has not yet proceeded to the degree, shall be deemed to have been issued a certificate or granted leave to supplicate for the degree of Master of Science.

7. The University shall award such diplomas and certificates as may be provided for by decree or regulation. They may be made open to persons who are not members of the University.

8. The periods of residence and the qualifications to be attained for ordinary degrees and for diplomas and certificates shall be laid down by decree or regulation.

9. Council shall make arrangements by decree under which members of the Universities of Cambridge and of Dublin may be incorporated as members of this University (that is to say, be admitted to the same degree or position in this University as that to which they have attained in their former university), provided always that Council shall have power to determine

(*a*) the members and classes of members of the Universities of Cambridge and of Dublin to which this privilege shall be open;

(*b*) the conditions upon which the privilege shall be granted in each case.

10. Council may make arrangements by decree under which the status of Master of Arts may be given to such persons, under such conditions, as it may determine.

11. A member of the University may, with the consent of Council for reasons which it shall deem sufficient, resign his or her membership, provided that he or she undertakes to continue to observe the statutes, decrees, and regulations of the University as though he or she had continued to be a member thereof.

TITLE XII

OF COLLEGE CONTRIBUTIONS AND PAYMENTS TO COLLEGES

(This Title is a 'Queen-in-Council' statute—see Title XV, Section VII.)

Section I. Of College Contributions and their Distribution

1. In this section and in the Appendix hereto the following expressions have where the context admits the meanings assigned to them respectively in this clause, that is to say:

(*a*) 'the scheme' means the scheme described in clause 2 below;

(*b*) 'the fund' means the College Contributions Fund constituted by the contributions to be paid by the colleges;

(*c*) 'the committee' means the College Contributions Committee;

(*d*) 'college' means

(i) any of the colleges listed in Tit. VII, Sect. I, cl. 1, with the exception of Mansfield College until it attains an initial endowment equivalent in value to £5,500,000 at 31 July 1988, with the exception of Templeton College until it attains an initial endowment equivalent in value to £7,000,000 at 31 July 1992, and with the exception of the Manchester Academy and Harris College until it attains an initial general endowment equivalent in value to £4,000,000 at 31 July 1993, and

(ii) any foundation which Council, after consultation with the colleges listed in Title VII, Sect. I, cl. 1, shall by decree declare to be a college for the purposes of the scheme;

(*e*) 'statutory endowment income' means income calculated in accordance with the rules set out in the Appendix hereto;

(*f*) 'the societies' means

(i) the society known as St. Cross College and

(ii) such other societies as Council, after consultation with the colleges listed in Title VII, Sect. I, cl. 1, shall by decree declare to be societies for the purposes of the scheme;

(*g*) 'year' means a year beginning on 1 August and ending on 31 July following;

(*h*) 'initial endowment' means the sum total of the assets of a college (excluding assets used for the functional purposes of the college, money given to the college specifically for building for the functional purposes of the college and set aside for that purpose, and such other amounts as the committee shall consider should not be regarded as applicable to endowment) valued

(i) in the case of the colleges listed in Title VII, Sect. I, cl. 1, at the time of the passing of this statute, at 31 December 1965 (but any sums paid by decree for the enlargement of the permanent endowment of the college between 1 January 1966 and the date on which the first distribution of endowment grants is made under the provisions of this statute shall be included);

(ii) in the case of any other college, at a date to be determined by decree at the time it becomes a college for the purposes of the scheme;

(*i*) 'land' includes buildings, easements, and sporting rights;

(*j*) 'agricultural land' means land used for agricultural purposes and includes sporting rights, and 'non-agricultural land' means any other land.

2. The purpose of the scheme is to establish the College Contributions Fund, which shall be used

(*a*) to make endowment grants to St. Cross College until such time as the aggregate of the endowment grants made to that society amounts to £1,500,000 or until such earlier time as the society waives its claim to these endowment grants; or until Council, on the recommendation of the committee, decides by decree that the society has received benefactions of such amounts as to make it unreasonable for further endowment grants to be paid to it;

(*b*) to make such other grants and loans to colleges and societies as may from time to time seem desirable;

(*c*) to make loans to the Loan Fund for College Buildings established by Sect. III of this Title;

(*d*) to make supplementary endowment grants until the following additional amounts have been paid to the colleges listed as follows:

	£
Keble College	499,612
Lady Margaret Hall	878,534
St. Anne's College	188,944
St. Catherine's College	875,396
St. Edmund Hall	1,958,323
St. Hilda's College	1,005,250
St. Peter's College	1,534,162
	£6,940,221

or until such earlier time as a college waives its claim to these further endowment grants; or until Council, on the recommendation of the committee, determines by decree that a college has received benefactions of such amounts as to make it unreasonable for further endowment grants to be paid to it; provided always that Council may determine by decree that the amounts listed above for these further endowment grants shall, in order to allow for inflation, be increased by such percentage in respect of 1988–9 and each subsequent year concerned as Council may decide, subject to an upper limit on such percentage increases equal to the percentage increase for the corresponding period in total recurrent university costs as calculated from time to time for the Committee of Vice-Chancellors and Principals of the Universities of the United Kingdom.

3. The College Contributions Committee shall be a committee of Council and shall consist of:

(1) the Vice-Chancellor;

(2) a Curator of the University Chest appointed by Council;

(3) a member of Council appointed by Council;

(4) a person appointed by Council who need not be a member of Council;

(5)–(8) four persons appointed by a special meeting to which each college and other society except the Permanent Private Halls shall be entitled to send two representatives. One of the four shall be a person with financial experience outside the University.

The members under (2)–(8) shall hold office for such periods as the body appointing them shall determine.

4. The committee shall have the duty of

(*a*) administering the scheme;

(*b*) making recommendations to Council not less than once a year as to the allocation of the fund or any part thereof to and between the colleges and societies and the Loan Fund for College Buildings; and

(*c*) keeping the working of the scheme including the rates of contribution under constant review and making recommendations in respect thereof and reporting thereon to Council not less often than once in every five years.

5. The committee shall have power

(*a*) to call for all such accounts, documents, and information as the committee may from time to time think it desirable to have from any college or any of the societies; and

(*b*) to determine conclusively all questions and matters of doubt arising as to the ascertainment of the initial endowment or the statutory endowment income of any college at any time or of the amount payable to the fund by any college in respect of any year or (subject to the provisions of Title I, cl. 2) otherwise howsoever in respect of the scheme.

6. Each college shall as soon as possible after the end of each year and in any case before the 31 January next following pay into the University Chest for the account of the fund a sum calculated as follows:

	Payment to be made in Hilary Term, based on accounts for the immediately preceding financial year:								
	2000	*2001*	*2002*	*2003*	*2004*	*2005*	*2006*	*2007*	*2008*
In respect of the first 8 units of statutory endowment income	Nil	Nil	Nil	Nil	Nil	Nil	Nil	Nil	Nil
In respect of the next unit	2.5	3.0	3.5	4.0	4.5	5.0	5.0	5.0	5.0
In respect of the next unit	5.0	6.0	7.0	8.0	9.0	10.0	10.0	10.0	10.0
In respect of the remainder	7.5	9.0	10.5	12.0	13.5	15.0	15.0	15.0	15.0

The unit of statutory endowment income for a particular financial year being an amount decided by Council by decree on the recommendation of the committee before the end of that year.

7. Distributions from the fund to the colleges and the societies or any of them and to the Loan Fund for College Buildings when appropriate shall be made annually by decree after Council has considered the recommendations made by the committee.

APPENDIX TO SECTION I

Rules for Ascertaining the Statutory Endowment Income of a College

1. *General rule*. All receipts of the nature of income shall be included without any exclusions or deductions except as mentioned below.

2. *Particular instances*

(*a*) Any income-tax recoverable by a college shall be included if it was paid or deducted in respect of income which was itself statutory endowment income.

(*b*) Underwriting commissions earned by a college and royalties payable to a college in respect of any copyright shall be included.

(*c*) The full amount of the rent (excluding any rates paid to the college for onward transmission to the local authority) payable to a college in respect of any tenancy shall be included subject to a deduction for any rent which may be irrecoverable but with no deduction for any rent which may be waived.

(*d*) If a college retains agricultural land unlet and uses it for agriculture, a fair rent shall be notionally attributed to it, but the standard deduction under para. 8 below shall be allowed.

(*e*) If a college allows the head or a fellow of the college or a person employed by it to occupy a rateable hereditament outside the curtilage of the college and owned or leased by the college, the gross value of such a hereditament for rating purposes shall be treated as the rent payable irrespective of any rent paid or reduction made in emoluments, but the standard deduction under para. 8 below shall be allowed.

(*f*) A quarter of the net proceeds of the sale of timber and a third of the gross proceeds of any minerals or mineral rights belonging to a college shall be treated as statutory endowment income.

(*g*) Receipts which under the provisions of the Universities and College Estates Acts of 1925 and 1964 are required to be treated as capital moneys shall not be treated as statutory endowment income.

(*h*) Income of funds established under Section 29 of the Universities and College Estates Act, 1925 (as amended) and approved by the committee shall not be treated as statutory endowment income.

(*i*) Income of any pension fund, whether existing at the time of the passing of this statute or created subsequently, conducted or contributed to by a college and approved by the committee shall not be treated as statutory endowment income.

(*j*) Commissions payable to a college in respect of insurances effected by it on its own behalf shall not be included.

3. *General exclusions.* Statutory endowment income shall not include any money received by a college (*a*) from carrying out its functions as an institution for education and research or (*b*) (except as mentioned below) from the use or letting of land within the curtilage of the college or land used by the college directly in connection with those functions. Under (*a*) there shall be excluded from statutory endowment income all fees, dues, establishment charges, charges for meals paid to the college by its members, and such proportion (if any) of the rent paid to the college by student members for furnished accommodation outside the college as the committee may think reasonable. Under (*b*) there shall normally be excluded payments received by the college for the use of college buildings for conferences or for the use of its sports facilities by outsiders when not required by its own members; but there shall be included payments received by the college for the use of college buildings or of sports facilities under arrangements which in the opinion of the committee give the user virtually exclusive use for a substantial period.

4. *Benefactions.* Benefactions, whether of a single sum or recurring, shall not be treated as statutory endowment income, but any income resulting from the investment of such benefactions shall be so treated. However, where a benefaction takes effect as a legal or equitable assignment of a right to income of an income-producing asset, the income so assigned shall be treated as statutory endowment income.

5. *Income received by a college as sole trustee.* All income of a trust of which a college is sole trustee shall (whether applied or retained or accumulated) be treated as statutory endowment income except as provided in para. 7 below.

6. *Payment or application of money by trustees of trusts other than trusts of which the college is sole trustee.* In the case of a payment by trustees to a college or the application by trustees of money for any purpose of a college the

moneys paid or applied shall not be treated as statutory endowment income in so far as they are paid or applied out of moneys which are capital in the hands of the trustees. Where the moneys are paid or applied out of moneys which are income in the hands of the trustees, then they shall be treated as statutory endowment income if (but only if) the college or some purpose of the college was the named or described beneficiary or (otherwise than solely as being a college of a university or of Oxford University) one of the named or described beneficiaries under the instrument or instruments creating the trust.

7. *Income of trusts applicable for external purposes.* If any income receivable by the college under the terms of any trust must under the trust be applied for some purpose wholly outside the objects of the college, then (whether the college is or is not the trustee of the trust) any income which must be so applied shall be disregarded in calculating statutory endowment income.

8. *Permissible deductions*

(*a*) *Standard deductions*. There shall be allowed a standard deduction of: 25 per cent in respect of the full amount of rents from agricultural land; 40 per cent in respect of the full amount of rents from non-agricultural land which is let on terms that the tenant is not responsible for any structural repairs; 10 per cent in respect of the full amount of rents from non-agricultural land let on other terms (including, at gross value for rating purposes, college houses outside the curtilage occupied by the head, fellows, or employees); 5 per cent in respect of the gross amount of interest and dividends.

(*b*) *Deductions in respect of leaseholds.* In the case of leasehold land held by a college there shall be deductible

(i) any rent paid by the college and,

(ii) any annual sum which is paid or applied by the college for the purpose of recouping the capital moneys applied by the college to the purchase of a lease. Such annual sum shall not be greater than an amount calculated either on the 3½ per cent table for the period which the lease has still to run from the year in which it was purchased by the college or, if the college so decides initially, on the premium on a leasehold redemption policy for the said lease.

(*c*) *Deduction of interest.* Any interest paid by a college shall be deductible.

(*d*) *Exceptional obligations.* If a contributing college makes to the committee a written application on the ground that its endowment income or some part thereof is burdened by some charge or obligation of an exceptional nature in respect of which a deduction ought fairly to be made (whether imposed on the college or accepted voluntarily by the college for reasons which the committee considers reasonable having regard to the interest not necessarily only of the college but if appropriate also of the University and colleges as a whole), the committee shall consider such application and may in its discretion decide what deduction (if any) shall be allowed to the college in respect of such charge or obligation.

Section II. Of the Accounts of the Colleges

1. As soon as may be after 31 July in each year every college shall prepare and submit for examination by an auditor or auditors statements which in respect of the financial year ended on that date.

(*a*) give a true and fair view of

(i) the income of the college from all sources, the expenditure of a revenue nature properly chargeable against such income, and the extent by which in total such income exceeded or fell short of such expenditure;

(ii) the allocation of the aforesaid income and expenditure as between

(A) Endowment

(B) Education and Research

(C) Internal

in accordance with the provisions of this statute, showing the resultant surplus or deficit in each case:

(iii) the nature and extent of all other changes in the balances of the funds, other than invested balances of capital and trust funds, administered by the college (provided that in relation to the revenue transactions of trust funds administered for purposes wholly external to the college it shall suffice to show only the amount by which the income exceeded or fell short of the expenditure);

(iv) the assets and liabilities by which the aforesaid balances were represented at the end of the financial year;

(*b*) show the computation of the statutory endowment income and of the liability for, or as the case may be the exemption from, college contribution.

2. The aforesaid statements

(*a*) shall be prepared so as to conform in all material respects with the specimen statements in the Schedule to this statute;

(*b*) shall contain not less information than is provided for in those specimen statements;

(*c*) shall include for comparison in the statements numbered I, II, III, IV, V, and VII the corresponding amounts relating to the preceding financial year.

3. For the purpose of clause 1 (*a*) (ii) above

(*a*) income and expenditure shall be allocated in accordance with the heads shown in the relevant specimen statements in the Schedule hereto;

(*b*) income and expenditure under heads which are shown in more than one of these statements shall be apportioned between them on such bases as are approved by the College Accounts Committee either generally or in relation to a particular college;

(*c*) the amounts of the respective contributions to the Endowment Account from the Education and Research Account and the Internal Account towards expenditure on college premises shall be computed in such manner as is prescribed by the College Accounts Committee either generally or in relation to a particular college.

4. The auditor or auditors to whom the statements are submitted shall

(*a*) be a member or members, or a firm the majority of whose partners are members, of one or more of the following professional bodies, namely

The Institute of Chartered Accountants in England and Wales
The Institute of Chartered Accountants of Scotland
The Association of Certified Accountants
The Institute of Chartered Accountants in Ireland;

(*b*) certify that in his or their opinion

(i) the statements comply with the provisions of this statute;

(ii) the statutory endowment income and the amount payable as college contribution have been correctly computed.

5. Not later than 31 December in each year, the statements and the certificate of the auditor or auditors thereon shall be presented to the College Accounts Committee, which shall thereupon order their publication within the University.

6. The College Accounts Committee shall have power

(*a*) to call from a college for such explanations, which shall include calling upon a college to obtain if necessary a supplementary certificate from its auditors, of matters contained in the statements presented to it as it may consider necessary;

(*b*) subject only to any general powers of interpretation vested in other persons by the statutes, to determine conclusively all questions and matters of doubt arising out of the operation of this section, except those relating to the ascertainment of the income on which college contribution is to be assessed; and shall have the duty of reporting to Council on the operation of this section not less often than once in every five years.

7. The College Accounts Committee shall consist of:

(1) the Vice-Chancellor;

(2) a Curator of the University Chest nominated by the Vice-Chancellor;

(3) a member of Council appointed by Council;

(4) a person appointed by Council who need not be a member of Council;

(5)–(7) three persons appointed by a special meeting to which each college and other society except the Permanent Private Halls shall be entitled to send two representatives.

The members under (2)–(7) shall hold office for such period as the person or body appointing them shall determine.

SCHEDULE

I. Consolidated Revenue Statement. *Year ended 31 July ....*

	£	£
INCOME		
From endowments and other funds:		
Net income as shown in Statement III	....	
Less: College contribution (Statement III)	....	
		....

From fees, dues, and charges (including room rents)	....	
Less: Collected on behalf of the University	....	
		....
From grants and donations:		
(*Specify under main heads*)	....	
		....
From other sources:		
(*Specify under main heads*)	....	
		....
Total income		£.........

EXPENDITURE	£	£
For the college's own purposes:		
Other than on premises:		
Education and Research (Statement IV)	....	
Internal (Statement V)	....	
On college premises (Statement III):	....	
		....
For other purposes, excluding college contribution (Statement III):		....
Total expenditure		£.........

SURPLUS/(DEFICIT) FOR YEAR carried to Statement VI	£	£
Trust funds of which, under the terms of trusts, there was:		
(*a*) available for the college's general purposes	....	
(*b*) carried forward for the trust purposes	....	
Reserves and special funds	....	
Revenue account	....	
		£.........

Attributable to:		
Endowment (Statement III)	....	
Education and Research (Statement IV)	....	
Internal (Statement V)	....	
	£.........	

II. Statutory Endowment Income and College Contribution. *Year ended 31 July ....*

NOTE. *All terms used in this statement are to be interpreted in accordance with the definitions and provisions contained in Title XII, Sect. I.*

GROSS INCOME	£	£
(*Include under this head all amounts which fall to be brought into account by virtue of paragraphs 1 to 7 of the Appendix to Title XII, Sect. I.*)		
From all relevant sources except trusts of which the college is not sole trustee:		
Rent:		
Agricultural land	....	
Non-agricultural land:		
Let on terms that the tenant is not responsible for any structural repairs	....	
Let on other terms	....	
Gross value for rating purposes of college houses outside the curtilage occupied by the head, fellows, or employees	....	
Income from timber	....	
Income from minerals and mineral rights	....	
Interest and dividends	....	
Underwriting commissions	....	
Copyright royalties	....	
Other income	....	
(*Specify under main heads*)		
	....	
Less: Amount (if any) of income included above which has to be appropriated to funds established, with the approval of the College Contributions Committee, under Section 29 of the Universities and College Estates Act, 1925 (as amended) but not separately invested	....	
Amounts which must be applied by the college as sole trustee for purposes wholly outside the objects of the college out of the income and in compliance with the terms, of trusts of which the income is included above as being in part applicable for the benefit of the college	....	
		....
		....
From trusts of which the college is not sole trustee: Income paid to the college by the trustees or applied by them to any purpose of the college		....
Total of gross income from endowments and other sources as shown in Statement III		....

PERMISSIBLE DEDUCTIONS	£	£
(*a*) Standard deductions:		
In respect of the full amount of rents from agricultural land £.... at 25%	....	

In respect of the full amount of rents from non-agricultural land which is let on terms that the tenant is not responsible for any structural repairs £.... at 40%	....	
In respect of the full amount of rents from non-agricultural land let on other terms (including, at gross value for rating purposes, college houses outside the curtilage occupied by the head, fellows, or employees) £.... at 10%	....	
In respect of the gross amount of interest and dividends £.... at 5%	....	
(*b*) In respect of leaseholds:		
Rent payable	....	
Amortization of lease premium	....	
(*c*) Interest	....	
(*d*) Allowances for exceptional obligations	....	
		....
STATUTORY ENDOWMENT INCOME		£.........
CONTRIBUTION PAYABLE		
On £....		Nil
On £.... at ...%		....
On £.... at ...%		....
On £.... at ...%		....
£.........		£.........

III. Endowment Account. *Year ended 31 July ....*

INCOME	£	£
Gross income from endowment and other sources as shown in Statement II		....
Surplus/(deficit) on home farms and farms, sporting rights, etc., in hand after deducting rental value included in gross income above and any relevant expenses not taken into account below		....
Rents, less rental value included in gross income above, in respect of rateable hereditaments outside the curtilage of the college occupied by the head, a fellow, or an employee of the college		....
		....
Less: Expenses of obtaining that income:		
Rent, rates, taxes and insurance (*less* commission)		....
Provision for major repairs	....	
Other repairs and maintenance	....	
Amortization and depreciation	....	
Agency, management, and administration	....	
Donations and subscription in connection with estates	....	
Other expenses	....	
(*Give details of any material amounts*)	....	
		....
Net income as shown in Statement I		....

AMOUNTS PAYABLE OUT OF ABOVE NET INCOME OTHERWISE THAN FOR THE COLLEGE'S OWN PURPOSES		
College contribution (Statement II)	....	
Donations and subscriptions:		
For university objects	....	
Other	....	
Livings	....	
Maintenance of schools	....	
Other	....	
		....
Net income available for college's own purposes		....
Less: Amount of trust fund income transferred to Statements IV and V equivalent to expenditure from trusts included in those Statements:		
Statement IV	....	
Statement V	....	
		....
BALANCE AVAILABLE FOR THE COLLEGE'S OWN PURPOSES		£.........
EXPENSES OF COLLEGE PREMISES AND AEDES ANNEXAE		
(*Include among these expenses the wages, national insurance etc., of college maintenance staffs and the cost of materials used by them*)		
Repair and maintenance, etc. of fabric and exterior of buildings:		
Provision for major repairs		
Other repairs and maintenance	....	
Amortization and depreciation	....	
	....	
	....	
Upkeep of gardens and grounds	....	
		....
All other building repairs and maintenance (including interior redecoration):		
Provision for major items	....	
Other repairs and maintenance	....	
Rent	....	
Rates and taxes	....	
Insurance (*less* commission)	....	
		....
		....

	£	£
Less: Contribution from Statements IV and V:		
For upkeep of fabric, gardens, and grounds (based on standard formula)	....	
For other expenses	....	
		....
		£.........
SURPLUS/(DEFICIT)		£.........

IV. Education and Research Account. *Year ended 31 July ....*
V. Internal Account

	IV Education and Research £	*V Internal* £	*Total* £
INCOME			
Fees (other than those collected for the University)			
Consolidated	....		....
Tuition	....		....
Dues and establishment charges	....	....	....
Degree	....		....
Library	....		....
Other	....		....
	....	....	....
Charges for accommodation (including notional room rents), meals, and service	....	....	....
Rents from furnished accommodation outside the college occupied by student members	....	....	....
Sales from buttery and stores		....	....
			....
	....	...........*	....
Amount of trust fund income available only for expenditure dealt with in this account (transferred from Statement III)	....	....	....
Research grants:			
From the University	....		
From other Oxford colleges	....		
From outside sources	....		
	....		....
Other grants and contributions:			
From the University	....		
From other Oxford colleges	....		
From outside sources	....		
	....		....
Charges to other accounts:			
Statement III:			
Entertainment of tenants and others		....	
Statement IV:			
Common Table		....	
College hospitality		....	
		....	....

Other income:	....	....	....
	£.........	£.........	£.........
Total income	£.........	£.........	£.........

* NOTE: Charged to	
Members and employees of the college	....
Other colleges	....
Others (conferences etc.)	....
	£.........

	IV Education and Research £	*V Internal* £	*Total* £
EXPENDITURE			
Head of college	....		....
Teaching fellows	....		....
Other fellows	....		....
Stipendiary lecturers	....		....
Outside tuition payments	....		....
Other tuition and research expenses (including research assistants	....		....
Common Table	....		....
Library	....		....
Research studentships, scholarships, exhibitions, prizes, and grants:			
Provided from trust funds	....		
Provided otherwise	....		
	....		....
Examiners and examination expenses (including fees paid to the Oxford Colleges Admissions Office)	....		....
Chaplain and chapel services	....		....
College hospitality	....		....
Junior Clubs	....		....
Subscriptions and donations to the College's own academic objectives	....		....
Catering supplies consumed (less sale of waste)		....	....
Outside caterers' and other colleges' charges		....	....
Services:	....	....	....
Domestic staff			
Heat, light, and water	....	....	....
Laundry and cleaning	....	....	....
Repair, renewal, insurance (*less* commission), and depreciation of furniture and equipment	....	....	....
	....	....	....
Administration:	....	....	....
College officers and others			
Office and clerical staff	....	....	....
Office expenses	....	....	....
Legal and professional charges	....	....	....
	....	....	....

Pensions paid to former members and employees of the college	....	....	....
Other expenses	....	....	....
	....	....	....
College premises:			
Contribution to Statement III for repair and maintenance, rent, rates, taxes, and insurance	....	....	....
Total expenditure	£.........	£.........	£.........
SURPLUS (DEFICIT)	£.........	£.........	£.........

VI. Summary of Transactions affecting Accumulated Balances.

Year ended 31 July

	Trust funds		*Capital account*	*Reserves and special funds*	*Revenue account*	*Total*
	Only for purposes wholly outside the objects of the college	*Other*				
	£	£	£	£	£	£
BALANCES AT BEGINNING OF YEAR (*excluding invested balances of trust fund and capital account*)	£	....	....	....	....	....
ADD:						
Net proceeds of sale of estates	....	....	....			....
Net proceeds of sale and redemption of securities of trust funds and capital account	....	....	....			....
Surplus/(deficit) of income for the year:						
Trust funds only for purposes wholly outside the objects of the college	....	....	....			....
Capital account—income of funds established under Section 29 of the Universities and College Estates Act, 1925 (as amended)			....			....
Other accounts and funds (Statement I)		....		....	....	....
Internal transfers—amounts added:						
As the result of charges made in arriving at amounts of surplus/(deficit) of income for the year			....	....		....
Otherwise	....	....	....	....	....	....
Other receipts (*Specify*)						
	£........	....	....	....	....	....
DEDUCT:						
Cost of purchase and improvement of estates	....	....	....			....
Cost of purchase of securities for trust funds and capital account	....	....	....			....
Cost of additions and improvements to college premises			....	....	....	....
Expenditure out of fund for1						
major repairs to estates,				....		....
major repairs to fabric and exterior of buildings,				....		....
other major repairs and maintenance (including interior redecoration)				....		....
Internal transfers—amounts deducted otherwise than in arriving at surplus/(deficit) of income for the year				....	....	....
Other payments (*Specify*)						
	£........	....	....	....	....	....
BALANCES AT END OF YEAR (*excluding invested balances of trust funds and capital account*)	£........	....	....	....	....	....

Section III. Of Loans to Colleges

The amount standing in the 'Fund earmarked for loans to colleges' in the Common University Fund on 31 July 1968 shall be set aside to form a fund, to be known as the 'Loan Fund for College Buildings', from which loans may be made by Council on the recommendation of the College Contributions Committee to colleges listed in Tit. VII, Sect. I, cl. 1, with the exception of the Manchester Academy and Harris College, Mansfield College, and Templeton College until they respectively attain the initial endowments specified in Tit. XII, Sect. I, cl. 1 (*d*), and to societies as defined in Tit. XII, Sect. I, cl. 1 (*f*), for such building purposes, and on such conditions, as Council shall determine; and all repayments of, and payments of interest on, loans made from the fund before 31 July 1968 shall be paid into this new fund.

TITLE XIII

OF UNIVERSITY DISCIPLINE

(This Title is a 'Queen-in-Council' statute—see Title XV, Section VII.*)*

1. For the purposes of this Title, the following words shall have the following meanings:

(*a*) 'college' shall include any of the societies recognised in Title VII;

(*b*) the term 'Junior Member' shall include both a member of the University who has not been admitted to membership of Convocation, and a member of the University who has been admitted to Convocation but who is registered as a student, or as a candidate, for a degree, diploma, or certificate of the University;

(*c*) 'expulsion' by the University shall mean the permanent loss of membership of the University and college (and where college statutes or by-laws so provide, loss of membership of the University shall also mean loss of membership of the college concerned);

(*d*) 'banning' by the University shall mean a withdrawal of the rights of access to specified premises or facilities for a fixed period or pending the fulfilment of certain conditions;

(*e*) 'rustication' by the University shall mean the withdrawal of the right of access to the premises or facilities of the University for a fixed period or pending the fulfilment of certain conditions;

(*f*) 'suspension' by the University shall mean a withdrawal of the right of access as in (*e*) above where action is taken as an interim measure pending further investigation, or where action is required in a non-disciplinary situation. Such withdrawal may be for a limited period pending the fulfilment of certain conditions, or may be indefinite;

(*g*) 'in a university context' shall mean any of the following:

(i) on university/college premises;

(ii) in the course of university activity in Oxford, be it academic, sporting, cultural, or social;

(iii) in the course of university-based activities outside Oxford, such as field trips, laboratory or library work, or sporting, musical, or theatrical tours;

(*h*) an 'offence' shall be any breach of clause 2 below, breaches of the regulations and rules covering the dress of Junior Members, the use of libraries, or conduct in examinations, breaches of any regulations or rules relating to clubs, publications, and motor vehicles, breaches of any regulations made by the Rules Committee, or breaches of any rule referred to in clause 6 below;

(*i*) 'harassment' shall mean a course of unwarranted behaviour such as to cause and as may reasonably be expected to cause such distress or annoyance as seriously to disrupt the work or substantially to reduce the quality of life of another person.

2. (*a*) No member of the University shall in a university context intentionally or recklessly

(i) disrupt or attempt to disrupt teaching or study or research or the administrative, sporting, social, or other activities of the University, or disrupt or attempt to disrupt the lawful exercise of freedom of speech by members, students, and employees of the University and by visiting speakers, or obstruct or attempt to obstruct any employee or agent of the University in the performance of his or her duties;

(ii) damage or deface any property of the University or of any college or of any member, officer, or employee of the University or of any college, or knowingly misappropriate such property;

(iii) occupy or use or attempt to occupy or use any property or facilities of the University or of any college except as may be expressly or impliedly authorised by the university or college authorities concerned;

(iv) forge or falsify any university certificate or similar document or knowingly make false statements concerning standing or results obtained in examinations;

(v) engage in any activity likely to cause injury or to impair safety;

(vi) engage in violent, indecent, disorderly, threatening, or offensive behaviour or language;

(vii) engage in any dishonest behaviour in relation to the University or the holding of any university office;

(viii) refuse to disclose his or her name and other relevant details to an officer or an employee or agent of the University or of any college in circumstances where it is reasonable to require that that information be given;

(ix) use, offer, sell, or give to any person drugs, the possession or use of which is illegal;

(x) engage in the harassment of any member, visitor, employee, or agent of the University or of any college.

(*b*) Every member of the University shall, to the extent that such provisions may be applicable to that member, comply with the provisions of the Code of Practice on Freedom of Speech issued from time to time by Council pursuant to the duty imposed by Section 43 of the Education (No. 2) Act 1986 and duly published in the *University Gazette*.

3. There shall be a Rules Committee, the constitution and powers of which shall be as set out in Schedule I hereto.

4. Alleged breaches of clause 2 above shall be dealt with in the following manner:

(*a*) In the case of a Senior Member of the University who is an employee of the University, complaints shall be made to the Registrar, who shall invoke the relevant procedures under Title XVII, Part III.

(*b*) In the case of a Senior Member of the University who is not an employee of the University and who is not registered as a student for a degree or diploma of the University, complaints shall be made to the Registrar, who shall notify the relevant authority.

(*c*) In the case of a Junior Member, alleged breaches shall be dealt with by the procedure set out below.

5. A penalty of suspension or rustication imposed by a college shall apply also to university premises and facilities, subject to a right of appeal in writing to the Proctors, who shall have discretion to hear oral representations from the Junior Member concerned. Where the Proctors are satisfied that there are special circumstances, they may permit the Junior Member concerned to continue to have access to university premises and facilities, with or without conditions as to such access.

6. The Proctors shall have power, if they consider the matter urgent, to make rules to cover a matter not covered by clause 2 above or by any other provision. Such rules shall have immediate effect, and shall be published. Any exercise of this power shall be reported at once to the Rules Committee, and the rule shall lapse unless the Rules Committee confirms it by a regulation, in the same or substantially the same terms, made and published in the *University Gazette* within three weeks of Full Term from the day the rule was made by the Proctors. If the rule is not confirmed, it shall none the less have effect from the time at which it was made until the time the Rules Committee decides not to confirm it, or until it lapses, whichever is the earlier.

7. The Proctors shall have the duty of taking such steps as they may consider necessary to enforce and prevent breaches of clause 2 above, the regulations made by the Rules Committee, and the regulations, rules, or other provisions covering the matters referred to in clause 6 above; and to identify those responsible when an offence has been committed. They shall have the power to summon any member of the University before them to assist them in their inquiries, and failure to attend without reasonable cause shall be an offence under clause 2 (*a*) (i) above.

8. If the Proctors believe that there is prima facie evidence that an offence has been committed they shall, if they decide to proceed,

(*a*) if the alleged offender is a Senior Member, inform him or her in writing of the offence alleged against him or her and that the charge will be brought to the attention of the Registrar, who shall invoke the relevant procedures under Title XVII, Part III if the Senior Member is an employee of the University, and who shall in any other case notify the relevant authority;

(*b*) if the alleged offender is a Junior Member, inform him or her in writing of the alleged offence and summon him or her before them. In the event of non-compliance, they may rusticate the Junior Member concerned. In the event that the Junior Member notifies the Proctors in writing that he or she proposes to opt for a hearing before the Disciplinary Court, the Proctors may dispense with his or her personal attendance.

9. (*a*) When a Junior Member attends under clause 8 above, the Proctors shall

(i) if the offence is a minor offence, inform the person charged that the offence will be dealt with by them;

(ii) in any other case, offer the person charged the choice between having the charge dealt with by them and having it dealt with by the Disciplinary Court. If in their opinion the circumstances of the case so warrant, the Proctors may refuse to deal with the charge and may instead refer it for consideration by the Disciplinary Court.

(*b*) An offence shall be treated as a minor offence when the Proctors are satisfied that they should, if the charge were proved, not impose expulsion, rustication, or a monetary penalty exceeding the sum set out in (*c*) below.

(*c*) The maximum financial penalty excluding damages which may be imposed in the case of a minor offence shall be £60, and in any other case shall be £1,000.

(*d*) From 1 October 1998 the maximum penalties shall be fixed every three years by Council by a decree to be published with the University's financial decrees, provided always that any increase in the amount shall not exceed the increase over the preceding three years in the Retail Price Index.

10. The Disciplinary Court shall be constituted in accordance with the provisions of Schedule II hereto.

11. If the alleged offence is one for which the alleged offender is liable to be prosecuted in a court of law, the Proctors shall not proceed, if at all, unless they are satisfied either that any criminal proceedings in respect of that act or conduct have been completed, whether by conviction or acquittal or discontinuance of the proceedings, or that the alleged offender is unlikely to be prosecuted in a court of law in respect of that act or conduct.

12. In the event that criminal proceedings are pending or that the Proctors are of the opinion that action is necessary to safeguard the interests of other members of the University, the Proctors shall be entitled to suspend the alleged offender from some or all of the premises or facilities of the University pending the outcome of such criminal proceedings or hearing before the Proctors or the Disciplinary or Appeal Court. A Junior Member suspended in this way for more than seven days shall have a right of appeal to the Vice-Chancellor or to his of her duly authorised deputy.

13. In the event that a Junior Member has been convicted of a criminal offence of such seriousness that an immediate term of imprisonment might have been imposed (and whether or not such a sentence was in fact imposed on the Junior Member), the Proctors shall have power to expel such Junior Member or to impose such lesser penalty as they think fit, subject to a right of appeal to the Disciplinary Court.

14. If the offence is to be dealt with by the Proctors, the person charged shall have the right to have the proceedings adjourned so that he or she may prepare his or her defence. The Proctors and the person charged may call witnesses (and failure by a member of the University to attend when summoned shall, unless there was reasonable cause for such failure, be an offence under clause 2 (*a*) (i)

above) and may question any witness. The person charged may bring any member of Congregation to help him or her in his or her defence. If the Proctors find the charge proved, they may, subject to the provisions of clause 9 above, impose such penalty as they think fit.

15. There shall be no appeal from decisions taken by the Proctors on minor offences unless the Junior Member concerned is given leave to appeal by the Chairman of the Disciplinary Court.

16. The Disciplinary Court shall hear

(*a*) appeals from decisions taken by the Proctors under clause 14 above, on offences where the person charged elected to have the case dealt with by the Proctors, or from decisions taken on minor offences where leave has been given under clause 15 above;

(*b*) cases of offences where the person charged or the Proctors have elected to have the case dealt with by the Disciplinary Court.

17. Where a case is referred for hearing before the Disciplinary Court, the person charged shall be given the choice of a hearing in public or in private, and with or without two Junior Members sitting on the court under the provisions of clause 1 of Schedule II.

18. Notice of intention to appeal under clause 16 (*a*) above must be lodged with the Proctors within seven days of the Proctors' decision and specify whether the appeal is against verdict or penalty, or both. The appellant must in addition state within fourteen days of the Proctors' decision the grounds for his or her appeal, whether he or she wishes two Junior Members to sit on the Disciplinary Court under the provisions of clause 1 of Schedule II, and whether he or she wishes the Disciplinary Court to sit in public.

19. In the case of appeals under clause 16 (*a*) above, the Proctors and the Chairman of the Disciplinary Court shall have power to suspend the application of a penalty pending the outcome of an appeal against the imposition of that penalty.

20. Subject to the provisions of this statute, the Disciplinary Court shall determine its own procedure and shall be empowered to make interlocutory orders on procedural matters. It shall also have power to strike out an appeal on the grounds of non-prosecution.

21. In any case before the Disciplinary Court, the person charged may be represented by any person he or she chooses (including, if he or she so wishes, a barrister or solicitor engaged in professional practice).

22. The Chairman of the Disciplinary Court shall be empowered to act alone in uncontentious procedural or technical matters.

23. (*a*) In the case of a hearing under clause 16 (*a*) above, the Disciplinary Court, if it finds the case proved, may confirm, reduce, or increase the penalty imposed by the Proctors, and the Disciplinary Court's decision in such cases shall be final.

(*b*) In the case of a hearing under clause 16 (*b*) above, the Disciplinary Court, if it finds the case proved, may impose such penalty as it thinks fit.

24. The Disciplinary Court may reach a decision by a simple majority of members present and voting.

25. The Disciplinary Court shall sit in private unless the person charged asks that the hearing be held in public.

26. In all cases coming before the Disciplinary Court, the onus of proof shall lie on the Proctor bringing the charge, and the burden of proof shall be to the civil standard. He or she and the person charged may call witnesses, may be represented by anyone they choose (including, if they so wish, a barrister or solicitor engaged in professional practice), and may cross-examine any witness. Failure by a member of the University to attend when summoned to appear before the Court as defendant or witness, unless after inquiry the Court is satisfied that there was reasonable cause for such failure, in the case of a Junior Member shall be summarily punishable by the Court by fine, suspension from membership of the University, or rustication, on such terms as the Court may think fit; and in the case of a Senior Member shall be punishable by making a complaint to the Registrar, who shall invoke the relevant procedures under Title XVII, Part III. The person charged shall be given a reasoned decision in writing.

27. In the case of conviction by the Disciplinary Court under clause 16 (*b*) above, the person convicted may appeal, against sentence or conviction or both, to an Appeal Court, which shall be constituted in accordance with the provisions of Schedule III hereto.

28. The Chairman of the Disciplinary Court or of the Appeal Court may suspend the application of a penalty pending the outcome of an appeal against the imposition of that penalty under clause 23 (*b*) above.

29. No witnesses or new evidence shall be allowed (unless the Appeal Court is satisfied that a serious miscarriage of justice might otherwise result, in which event it may either hear and act upon such new evidence or remit the case to be heard again by the Disciplinary Court), but the Proctor bringing the charge and the appellant may be represented by any person they choose (including, if they so wish, a barrister or solicitor engaged in professional practice). The Appeal Court, if it affirms the decision of the Disciplinary Court, may confirm or reduce the penalty imposed by the Disciplinary Court, and its decision shall be final. The appellant shall be given a reasoned decision in writing.

30. The Clerk of the Disciplinary Court shall be responsible in all cases under clause 16 (*b*) above for keeping such records as may be required should there be an appeal under clause 23 (*b*) above. Written notice of an appeal under clause 23 (*b*) above must be lodged with the Clerk within a week of the Disciplinary Court's decision, and when lodging the appeal the appellant must state whether he or she wishes the appeal to be held in public, and whether he or she wishes to be represented by a solicitor or barrister engaged in professional practice. The Clerk shall at once inform the Vice-Chancellor, who shall thereupon appoint

another member of the panel set up under clause 6 of Schedule II below, to make the necessary arrangements for the hearing of the appeal and to act as Clerk of the Appeal Court.

31. The Appeal Court may reach a decision by a simple majority of members present and voting. If any one vacancy shall occur in the Appeal Court after the hearing of a case has begun, the remaining members may, if they think fit, complete that hearing and decide upon it.

32. Subject to the provisions of this statute, the Appeal Court shall determine its own procedure.

33. The Appeal Court shall sit in private unless the appellant asks that the hearing be held in public.

34. In the event of any dispute or uncertainty, and notwithstanding the provisions of Title I, the Appeal Court shall be empowered to interpret Statutes, Decrees, and Regulations as they bear on cases before it.

35. If during a hearing before the Disciplinary Court or the Appeal Court the conduct of any person is disorderly or otherwise in breach of clause 2 above in respect of the Court, the Court shall, if he or she is a Junior Member of the University, have summary power to fine, suspend from membership of the University, or rusticate him or her, on such terms as the Court may think fit, and if he or she is a Senior Member of the University, have power to make a complaint to the Registrar, who shall invoke the relevant procedures under Title XVII, Part III. A Junior Member of the University convicted under this clause shall be given a reasoned decision in writing.

36. (*a*) In the case of conviction by the Disciplinary Court acting in the exercise of the summary powers conferred on it under clauses 26 and 35 above, the person convicted may appeal against conviction or against a monetary penalty exceeding the amount of the maximum penalty which the Proctors may impose for minor offences under clause 9 (*c*) above or against a sentence of rustication or suspension of membership of the University, or against both conviction and such sentence, to an Appeal Court constituted as under Schedule III below. The appellant may be represented by any person he or she chooses (including, if he or she so wishes, a barrister or solicitor engaged in professional practice). Written notice of such an appeal must be lodged with the Clerk of the Disciplinary Court within seven days from such conviction, and when lodging the appeal the appellant must state whether he or she wishes the appeal to be held in public and whether he or she wishes to be represented by a solicitor or barrister engaged in professional practice. The Clerk shall at once inform the Vice-Chancellor, who shall thereupon appoint another member of the panel set up under clause 6 of Schedule II below, to make the necessary arrangements for the hearing of the appeal and to act as Clerk of the Appeal Court, which shall hear the appeal according to whatever procedure the Court shall think fit. If the Appeal Court affirms the conviction, the Court may confirm or reduce the penalty imposed by the Disciplinary Court, and its decision shall be final. The appellant shall be given a reasoned decision in writing. Notwithstanding the right

of appeal hereby conferred, the Disciplinary Court shall (unless satisfied that a serious miscarriage of justice might otherwise result) continue the hearing of the case during which the offence summarily punished was committed.

(*b*) In the case of conviction by the Appeal Court acting in the exercise of the summary powers conferred on it under clause 35 above the person convicted may apply in writing to the High Steward within seven days from such conviction for leave to appeal against conviction or against a monetary penalty exceeding a sum equivalent to twice the amount of the maximum penalty which the Proctors may impose for minor offences under clause 9 (*c*) above or against a sentence of rustication or suspension from membership of the University or against both conviction and such sentence. If he or she allows the application, the High Steward (or any person being a barrister or solicitor of not less than five years' standing, and not being a member of the Appeal Court, whom the High Steward shall nominate as his or her deputy) shall hear the appeal according to whatever procedure the High Steward (or his or her deputy) shall think fit. If the High Steward (or his or her deputy) affirms the conviction, he or she may confirm or reduce the penalty imposed, and his or her decision shall be final. Notwithstanding any application for leave to appeal (whether or not granted), the Appeal Court shall (unless satisfied that a serious miscarriage of justice might otherwise result) continue the hearing of the appeal during which the offence summarily punished was committed.

37. The Proctors shall at the end of Hilary Term in each year make a report to Congregation giving the number and kinds of offences dealt with during the year by them, by the Disciplinary Court, and by the Appeal Court, and giving the number and kinds of penalty imposed.

38. At the conclusion of a hearing before the Disciplinary or the Appeal Court, the court shall be empowered to direct the University to pay costs to the Junior Member; the amount of such costs shall be at the discretion of the Court concerned.

39. (*a*) Where any fine is imposed upon a Junior Member, whether by the Proctors under clause 14 above or by the Disciplinary Court under clauses 23, 26, and 35 above or by the Appeal Court under clause 35 above, it shall be paid within seven days whether or not an appeal is pending, and in the event of non-payment the Proctors or the Disciplinary Court or the Appeal Court, whoever or whichever imposed the fine, may rusticate the Junior Member.

(*b*) Fines or any damages imposed by the Proctors shall be paid through the Clerk to the Proctors and fines or any damages imposed by the Disciplinary Court or the Appeal Court shall be paid through the respective Clerks of the Courts.

SCHEDULE I

Rules Committee

1. There shall be a Rules Committee consisting of:

(1) the Senior Proctor (or in his or her absence the Junior Proctor), who shall act as chairman;

(2), (3) the two persons who will be Proctors in the following year;

(4), (5) two College Deans appointed by a special meeting to which each college or other society included in Title VII except the Permanent Private Halls shall be entitled to send two representatives;

(6) one member of Congregation appointed by Council;

(7), (8) two Junior Members (who must at the time they take up office have been matriculated for at least three terms) elected by the Council of the Oxford University Student Union from among its members;

(9), (10) two Junior Members (who must at the time they take up office have been matriculated for at least three terms) elected by the Executive of the Oxford University Student Union not necessarily from among its members;

(11), (12) two Junior Members elected by the Graduate Committee of the Oxford University Student Union from among its members.

The members under (4)–(6) shall hold office for three years, and shall not be eligible for reappointment until the expiry of three years from the date on which their period of office expires. The members under (7)–(12) shall hold office for one year and shall not be eligible for reappointment under (7)–(12). If a member under (4)–(12) dies or resigns or leaves the University during his or her period of office, his or her place shall either be filled for the remainder of his or her period of office by the body which appointed him or her or (if the appointing body shall so decide) be left vacant. If he or she dies or resigns or leaves the University before the expiry of one-half of his or her period of office, the rules about re-eligibility shall apply to his or her successor as if his or her successor had served for a full period; otherwise the rules shall not apply. Except in the case of casual vacancies, the members under (4)–(12) shall take up office on the Wednesday in the week after the end of Michaelmas Full Term.

2. The Rules Committee shall make regulations for the conduct of Junior Members governing such matters as it shall think fit, except that it shall not make regulations

(*a*) covering matters covered by clause 2 of Title XIII above;

(*b*) covering the dress of Junior Members, the use of libraries, or conduct in examinations.

3. The Rules Committee shall in each Hilary Term review the regulations of the committee in force and shall make any amendments or new regulations it considers necessary before the end of each Hilary Full Term. Any such amendments or new regulations shall be published as having effect from the beginning of the following Michaelmas Full Term. The Proctors shall arrange for all the regulations of the committee to be printed, and for copies to be sent to each college and other society for distribution to all Junior Members on first coming into residence. The committee shall not make or amend regulations at other times except for regulations confirming a rule made by the Proctors under clause 6 of Title XIII above.

4. Any six members shall constitute a quorum for meetings of the Rules Committee. In the case of equality of votes at any meeting at which not all

members are present, the matter shall be adjourned until a further meeting. If at this further meeting the voting is still equal, or if there is an equality of votes at a meeting at which all members are present, the chairman shall have a casting vote.

SCHEDULE II

Disciplinary Court

1. The Disciplinary Court shall consist of three members of Congregation, not being Proctors or persons who will be Proctors in the following year or persons who have been Proctors during the preceding five years, except that two Junior Members appointed in the way laid down in clause 4 below shall also be members of the Court if the person charged so wishes and Junior Members so appointed consent to serve.

2. The three Congregation members of the Disciplinary Court shall hold office for two years. Of the two members of the Court other than the chairman one shall retire at the beginning of each Trinity Term. In the case of these two members the Rules Committee shall in each Hilary Term draw up a list of ten names from which the Registrar shall by lot

(*a*) fill the vacancy that will arise at the beginning of the following Trinity Term;

(*b*) fill any *ad hoc* vacancy that may arise through the inability or refusal of a member to attend any particular hearing;

(*c*) fill any vacancies that may arise through any member dying, resigning, or leaving the University; a person so appointed shall hold office for the remainder of the period of the person whom he or she replaces.

3. The High Steward shall appoint the chairman of the Disciplinary Court, to serve for two years, from amongst members of Congregation who are barristers or solicitors of at least five years' standing or who have judicial experience, provided that if the chairman is unable to attend on any occasion the High Steward, or if he or she is unable to act the Vice-Chancellor, shall appoint a member of Congregation who is a barrister or solicitor of at least five years' standing or who has judicial experience to act for him or her on that occasion. If a vacancy arises through the chairman dying or resigning or ceasing to be a member of Congregation before the completion of his or her period of office, the person next appointed shall hold office for the remainder of the period of the person whom he or she replaces.

4. The Junior Members of the Disciplinary Court under clause 1 above shall hold office for one year from the beginning of Trinity Term. The Rules Committee shall in each Hilary Term draw up a list of ten names from which the Registrar shall by lot

(*a*) fill the vacancies that will arise at the beginning of the following Trinity Term;

(*b*) fill any *ad hoc* vacancy that may arise through the inability or refusal of a member to attend any particular hearing;

(*c*) fill any vacancies that may arise through any member dying, resigning, or leaving the University; a person so appointed shall hold office for the remainder of the period of the person whom he or she replaces.

5. (*a*) If any member of the Disciplinary Court is prevented from attending after a hearing has begun, the remaining members may complete that hearing and reach a decision. If more than one vacancy in a Court originally of three members, or more than two vacancies in a Court originally of four or five members, shall arise, the proceedings shall start afresh.

(*b*) Whenever any case, the hearing of which has already begun, is still outstanding at the beginning of Trinity Term, any member or members of the Disciplinary Court then retiring in accordance with the provisions of clauses 2 and 4 above shall, notwithstanding those provisions, continue to serve as a member or members of the Disciplinary Court for the purpose of such a case until the hearing thereof has been completed, a decision reached, and a reasoned decision given in writing.

6. The Disciplinary Court shall always have a Clerk of the Court, who shall be appointed by the Vice-Chancellor from a panel of four names, consisting of solicitors practising in Oxford or members of Congregation who have practised as barristers or solicitors, drawn up by the Rules Committee in each Hilary Term.

SCHEDULE III

Appeal Court

There shall be an Appeal Court which shall consist of:

(1) the High Steward as chairman, provided that if he or she is unable to attend on any occasion he or she, or, if he or she is unable to act, the Vice-Chancellor, shall appoint a person who is a barrister or solicitor of at least five years' standing to act for him or her;

(2), (3) two persons other than the Vice-Chancellor and Proctors appointed for each occasion by Council, not necessarily from its own number, in the absence of the Proctors and any members of the Disciplinary Court who are at the time members of Council.

TITLE XIV

OF JUNIOR MEMBERS AND MEDICAL INCAPACITY

1. The Regius Professor of Medicine shall be responsible for the appointment of a panel of medical practitioners who shall be available, when called upon, to assist the Proctors in the administration of the procedures prescribed in this Title. In the event that the Regius Professor is not clinically qualified, he or she shall take appropriate medical advice before making the appointments. When a panel member is approached under these procedures he or she shall be known as the University Doctor for the purpose of these procedures.

2. The term 'Junior Member' shall have the same meaning as in Title XIII.

3. In the event that the Proctors believe that a Junior Member is suffering from a serious problem arising from ill-health, whether this has come to light in the course of a disciplinary investigation or otherwise, they may refer the student to the University Doctor. Before any such reference is made, the student shall be given a reasonable opportunity to make representation to the Proctors as to why such a reference should not take place.

4. If disciplinary proceedings have already been commenced, they shall be adjourned pending a determination under these procedures.

5. The University Doctor shall be responsible for seeking medical evidence from the Junior Member's general practitioner and may recommend that the Junior Member submit to an independent medical examination at the University's expense. Any request for a medical report from a Junior Member's general practitioner shall observe the provisions of the Access to Medical Reports Act 1988.

6. In the event that a Junior Member fails to co-operate with the University Doctor's inquiry, or refuses to provide a medical report, or to attend for the purposes of a medical examination, he or she may be liable to suspension by the Proctors.

7. The University Doctor, having considered the evidence available, shall report his or her findings to the Proctors.

8. If the Proctors are of the opinion that further action may be necessary, they shall summon the Junior Member to a hearing to consider all the evidence. The Junior Member may be represented at the hearing by a member of Congregation. Having considered the evidence, the Proctors may proceed in one of the following ways:

(*a*) in any case of such gravity that expulsion might be considered, the Proctors shall refer the matter for consideration by a Medical Board;

(*b*) in any case where disciplinary proceedings have been adjourned, but the Proctors are satisfied that the Junior Member is not suffering from a serious problem relating to ill-health, they may resume those proceedings;

(*c*) in any other case

(i) they may discharge the Junior Member, whether absolutely, or subject to conditions (e.g. as to medical treatment); or

(ii) they may suspend the Junior Member (whether or not subject to certain conditions) for a specified period or for an indefinite period.

9. In the event that the Junior Member fails to attend or to make representations, the Proctors may proceed in his or her absence.

10. Any hearing under these procedures shall be in camera.

11. Where a Junior Member's conduct gives rise to a need for urgent action, the Proctors may suspend him or her forthwith pending investigation, such suspension not to exceed twenty-one days. The Junior Member shall have the right of appeal to the Vice-Chancellor or to his or her duly appointed deputy in respect of such an interim order.

12. A Junior Member who has been suspended on the grounds of his or her state of health under clause 8 above shall be entitled to invite the Proctors to reconsider the case after the expiry of at least fourteen days from the date of the initial decision and on the production of medical evidence in support of his or her claim.

13. The Junior Member shall have a right of appeal in respect of an indefinite suspension, or in respect of the conditions attached to his or her suspension under clause 8 (*c*) (ii) above, to the Medical Board, and shall have a right to be represented at that appeal. The decision of the Medical Board shall be final.

14. If a case has been referred to the Medical Board for consideration under clause 8 (*a*) above, the Junior Member shall be given reasonable notice of any hearing, and shall be entitled to legal or other representation before the board.

15. The Medical Board, having considered the evidence, shall recommend to the Proctors that they

(*a*) discharge the Junior Member, whether or not subject to conditions; or

(*b*) suspend the Junior Member (whether or not subject to certain conditions) for a specified period, or for an indefinite period; or

(*c*) expel the Junior Member.

16. There shall be a right of appeal to the High Steward against expulsion.

17. The Medical Board shall comprise

(1) a person nominated by Council;

(2) a person nominated by Council in consultation with the Junior Member's college;

(3) a medically qualified chairman nominated by the Regius Professor of Medicine.

TITLE XV

OF OTHER MATTERS WHICH REQUIRE TO BE GOVERNED BY STATUTE

Section I. Of the Sites and Buildings of the University, and Access to University Facilities and Services

1. No allocation for university purposes of a site the area of which exceeds 1,000 square metres or of a building the overall floor area of which exceeds 600 square metres shall be made unless approved by resolution of Congregation.

2. Any person or body having charge of any land or building of the University, or of any facilities or services provided by or on behalf of the University, shall have power, subject to any statute, decree, or regulation of general application, to make regulations governing the use of that land or building, or of those facilities or services. Any such person or body may also make rules governing the use of that land or building, or of those facilities or services, provided that

(*a*) the Proctors are satisfied that the rules relate to minor matters, governing the detailed management of the land, building, facilities, or services concerned, of a kind which can appropriately be covered by rule rather than by regulation; and

(*b*) the rules are published in such a way as reasonably to bring them to the notice of the users of the land, building, facilities, or services concerned.

3. Any person or body having charge of any land or building of the University, or of any facilities or services provided by or on behalf of the University, or the authorized agent of any such person or body, may exclude from that land or building, or from access to those facilities or services, any person whose actions are such as to cause or to threaten to cause damage to property or inconvenience to other users. A member of the University who is so excluded for a period exceeding two weeks may apply to the Proctors (in the case of a Junior Member) or to the Visitatorial Board (in the case of a Senior Member) to be readmitted, and shall be readmitted (either unconditionally or under specified conditions) on the recommendation of the Proctors or the Visitatorial Board as the case may be if they are or it is satisfied after full inquiry and consultation that continued exclusion is not necessary for the protection of the property concerned or the convenience of other users. The decision taken on such an application by the Proctors or the Visitatorial Board as the case may be shall be final.

Section II. Of Professorships

1. There shall be the following professorships in the University:

Drue Heinz Professorship of American Literature
Nuffield Professorship of Anaesthetics
Dr. Lee's Professorship of Anatomy

Rawlinson and Bosworth Professorship of Anglo-Saxon
Professorship of Biological Anthropology
Professorship of Social Anthropology
Laudian Professorship of Arabic
Khalid bin Abdullah Al Saud Professorship for the Study of the Contemporary Arab World
Edward Hall Professorship of Archaeological Science
Professorship of the Archaeology of the Roman Empire
Lincoln Professorship of Classical Archaeology and Art
Professorship of European Archaeology
Calouste Gulbenkian Professorship of Armenian Studies
Slade Professorship of Fine Art
Professorship of the History of Art
Savilian Professorship of Astronomy
Whitley Professorship of Biochemistry
Professorship of Clinical Biochemistry
Professorship of Bioinformatics
E. P. Abraham Professorship of Cell Biology
David Phillips Professorship of Molecular Biophysics
Sherardian Professorship of Botany
Field Marshal Alexander Professorship of Cardiovascular Medicine
Jesus Professorship of Celtic
Dr. Lee's Professorship of Chemistry
Waynflete Professorship of Chemistry
Professorship of Inorganic Chemistry
Coulson Professorship of Theoretical Chemistry
Shaw Professorship of Chinese
Professorship of Computing
Professorship of Computing Science
Lady Margaret Professorship of Divinity
Regius Professorship of Divinity
Spalding Professorship of Eastern Religions and Ethics
Professorship of Economics
Edgeworth Professorship of Economics
Sir John Hicks Professorship of Economics
Professorship of Educational Studies
Professorship of Egyptology
Donald Pollock Professorship of Chemical Engineering
Professorship of Civil Engineering
Professorship of Electrical and Electronic Engineering
Professorship of Optoelectronic Engineering
BP Professorship of Information Engineering
Professorship of Mechanical Engineering
Merton Professorship of English Language
Goldsmiths' Professorship of English Literature
Merton Professorship of English Literature

Thomas Warton Professorship of English Literature
J. R. R. Tolkien Professorship of English Literature and Language
Dean Ireland's Professorship of the Exegesis of Holy Scripture
Professorship of French Literature
Marshal Foch Professorship of French Literature
Professorship of General Linguistics
Professorship of General Practice
Professorship of Genetics
Professorship of Geography
Halford Mackinder Professorship of Geography
Professorship of Geology
Savilian Professorship of Geometry
Taylor Professorship of the German Language and Literature
Professorship of German Medieval and Linguistic Studies
Gladstone Professorship of Government
Andrew W. Mellon Professorship of American Government
Regius Professorship of Greek
Bywater and Sotheby Professorship of Byzantine and Modern Greek Language and Literature
Dr. Lee's Professorship of Experimental Philosophy
Regius Professorship of Hebrew
Harold Vyvyan Harmsworth Professorship of American History
Rhodes Professorship of American History
Camden Professorship of Ancient History
Wykeham Professorship of Ancient History
Beit Professorship of the History of the British Commonwealth
Professorship of the History of Latin America
Professorship of the History of Philosophy
Professorship of the History of Science
Chichele Professorship of the History of War
Regius Professorship of Ecclesiastical History
Chichele Professorship of Economic History
Carroll Professorship of Irish History
Chichele Professorship of Medieval History
Professorship of Modern History
Regius Professorship of Modern History
Montague Burton Professorship of International Relations
Lester B. Pearson Professorship of International Relations
Oriel and Laing Professorship of the Interpretation of Holy Scripture
Fiat-Serena Professorship of Italian Studies
Nissan Professorship of Modern Japanese Studies
Professorship of Jurisprudence
Rupert Murdoch Professorship of Language and Communication
Corpus Christi Professorship of Latin
Professorship of Law
Regius Professorship of Civil Law

Norton Rose Professorship of Commercial and Financial Law
Clifford Chance Professorship of Comparative Law
Allen & Overy Professorship of Corporate Law
Professorship of English Law
Vinerian Professorship of English Law
Jacques Delors Professorship of European Community Law
Reuters Professorship of Intellectual Property and Information Technology Law
Chichele Professorship of Public International Law
KPMG Professorship of Taxation Law
Professorship of Socio-Legal Studies
Wykeham Professorship of Logic
Professorship of Mathematical Logic
Professorships (two) of Management Studies
Ernest Butten Professorship of Management Studies
Peter Moores Professorship of Management Studies
The Peninsular and Oriental Steam Navigation Company Professorship of Management Studies
American Standard Companies Professorship of Operations Management
Professorship of Marketing
Cookson Professorship of Materials
Rouse Ball Professorship of Mathematics
Wallis Professorship of Mathematics
Professorship of Mathematics and its Applications
Professorship of Pure Mathematics
Waynflete Professorship of Pure Mathematics
May Professorship of Medicine
Regius Professorship of Medicine
Nuffield Professorship of Clinical Medicine
Professorship of Molecular Medicine
Isaac Wolfson Professorship of Metallurgy
Professorship of Microbiology
Iveagh Professorship of Microbiology
Professorship of the Physics and Chemistry of Minerals
Professorship of Morbid Anatomy
Norman Collisson Professorship of Musculo-skeletal Science
Heather Professorship of Music
Action Research Professorship of Clinical Neurology
Professorship of Numerical Analysis
Nuffield Professorship of Obstetrics and Gynaecology
Imperial Cancer Research Fund Professorship of Clinical Oncology
Nuffield Professorship of Orthopaedic Surgery
Action Research Professorship of Paediatrics
Professorship of Pathology
Nuffield Professorship of Pathology
E. P. Abraham Professorship of Chemical Pathology
Masoumeh and Fereydoon Soudavar Professorship of Persian Studies

Professorship of Pharmacology
Professorship of Comparative Philology
Wilde Professorship of Mental Philosophy
Waynflete Professorship of Metaphysical Philosophy
White's Professorship of Moral Philosophy
Sedleian Professorship of Natural Philosophy
Nolloth Professorship of the Philosophy of the Christian Religion
Halley Professorship of Physics
Wykeham Professorship of Physics
Professorships (three) of Experimental Physics
Waynflete Professorship of Physiology
Sibthorpian Professorship of Plant Science
Professorship of Poetry
Drummond Professorship of Political Economy
Nuffield Professorship of Comparative European Politics
King John II Professorship of Portuguese Studies
W. A. Handley Professorship of Psychiatry
Professorship of Child and Adolescent Psychiatry
Professorship of Psychology
Watts Professorship of Psychology
Professorship of Public Health
Charles Simonyi Professorship of the Public Understanding of Science
Rhodes Professorship of Race Relations
Professorship of Romance Languages
Professorship of Russian
Boden Professorship of Sanskrit
Andreas Idreos Professorship of Science and Religion
Barnett Professorship of Social Policy
Chichele Professorship of Social and Political Theory
Professorship of Sociology
Professorship of Sociology and Social Policy
King Alfonso XIII Professorship of Spanish Studies
Professorship of Applied Statistics
Professorship of Statistical Science
Nuffield Professorship of Surgery
Regius Professorship of Moral and Pastoral Theology
Rhodes Professorship of Therapeutic Sciences and Clinical Pharmacology
Professorship of Transplantation
Donald Schultz Professorship of Turbomachinery
Professorship of Zoology
Linacre Professorship of Zoology
Hope Professorship of Zoology (Entomology)
George Eastman Visiting Professorship
Newton-Abraham Visiting Professorship

2. Under such arrangements as Council may determine by decree from time to time, Council may appoint additional *ad hominem* professors, create

professorships to last for the tenure of one holder or for a fixed period of years not exceeding ten, and confer the title of professor.

Section III. Of the Composition of Committees

1. Throughout this section the term 'committee' shall comprise every body, other than Congregation, Convocation, faculties, and sub-faculties, set up by or under the authority of the statutes.

2. No person appointed or serving as a member of a committee while holding any academic post of the University or any other of the university or college posts specified in Tit. II, Sect. II, cl. 1 (6)–(10) shall continue to serve on that committee after having retired from such post (or, in the case of a person retiring at different dates from such university and college posts previously held by him or her, after the date of the later of such retirements), and no person who has previously retired from any of the university or college posts specified in Tit. II, Sect. II, cl. 1 (6)–(10), and who does not continue to hold another such post, shall be appointed a member of a committee, unless Council, by a vote carried by not less than two-thirds of the members present and voting, shall otherwise determine in an individual case. No other person appointed or serving as a member of a committee while not holding such a university or college post shall continue to serve on that committee, and no such person shall be appointed a member of a committee, after the 30 September immediately preceding his or her 66th birthday, unless Council, by a vote carried by not less than two-thirds of the members present and voting, shall otherwise determine in an individual case. In no case, however, shall any member of a committee continue in office after attaining the age of 75 years.

3. Except as provided in Tit. VIII, Sect. I, cl. 13, and Tit. XIII, cl. 7, the person taking the chair at any committee meeting shall have a second or casting vote in the event of equality of voting.

4. Unless otherwise provided by statute or decree, a vacancy about to be caused by lapse of time in any committee shall be filled by the appointing body in the term before the vacancy will arise, and the person appointed shall enter upon office on the first day of the following term. A vacancy caused otherwise than by lapse of time shall be filled as soon as may be after the occurrence of the vacancy. The person appointed shall enter upon office immediately upon appointment, but shall hold office for the unexpired residue only of the period of office of the person whom he or she replaces.

5. If at any time a vacancy or vacancies arise in any committee through an appointing body having failed to make an appointment or, in the case of an election, through insufficient nominations having been received by the due date or for any other reason, the Vice-Chancellor and Proctors shall appoint a person or persons to the vacancy or vacancies.

6. When a person becomes Vice-Chancellor, he or she shall (unless he or she resigns) remain a member of all committees of which he or she was formerly a member, except for boards of electors of which he or she was formerly an

elected or appointed member; when a person becomes Proctor or Assessor, he or she shall (unless he or she resigns) remain a member of all committees of which he or she was formerly a member. In the case of the Vice-Chancellor or a Proctor or Assessor not resigning his or her former seat on becoming an *ex officio* member of a committee, that seat shall, save in the case of a seat on a board of electors formerly occupied by the Vice-Chancellor as an elected or appointed member, remain vacant until he or she resumes it on laying down office or until his or her normal period of office as a member of the committee comes to an end; in the latter case, he or she may, subject to any rules about re-eligibility, be re-elected. When a person other than the Vice-Chancellor, or a Proctor or Assessor becomes an *ex officio* member of a committee of which he or she was an elected or appointed member, he or she shall be deemed to have resigned from his or her former seat.

Section IV. Of Consultation with Junior Members

§ 1. *Of Consultation with Junior Members*

1. There shall be an Oxford University Student Union, which shall be an association of the generality of Junior Members of the University. Junior Common Rooms and Middle Common Rooms of the colleges and other societies recognized under Title VII may be affiliated to the Oxford University Student Union. Such affiliated Junior Common Rooms and Middle Common Rooms shall severally be the constituent organizations of the Oxford University Student Union.

2. For the purposes of this sub-section Junior Members shall be those persons who, having been admitted to matriculation, are residing to fulfil the requirements of any statute, decree, or regulation of the University or reading for any degree, diploma, or certificate of the University and who have not proceeded to membership of Convocation.

3. Every Junior Member of the University shall have the right to opt out of membership of the Oxford University Student Union.

4. The Oxford University Student Union shall be recognized by the University as the organization representing the generality of Junior Members on university, as distinct from college, matters and shall elect Junior Members to such committees as may be specified by statute, decree, or regulation.

5. The Oxford University Student Union shall have a written constitution. The provisions of this constitution shall be subject to the approval of the Hebdomadal Council and to review by the Hebdomadal Council at intervals of not more than five years.

6. The Hebdomadal Council shall take such steps as are necessary to satisfy itself that elections to major offices of the Oxford University Student Union are fairly and properly conducted.

7. The Oxford University Student Union shall not have as an officer or as a full member, that is a member entitled to vote in any meeting or election, any person who is not a Junior Member of the University.

8. The President and Vice-Presidents may be full-time officers of the Oxford University Student Union. If the President or any of the three Vice-Presidents is a full-time officer, the period of his or her office up to a maximum of one year shall not be counted towards his or her standing for the purposes of any degree, diploma, or certificate of the University other than the Degree of Master of Arts. The President and Vice-Presidents shall be required to reside, in the terms of the relevant decrees governing the residence of Junior Members,[1] for at least six weeks in every Full Term during their term of office. Any prospective candidate for the Presidency or the Vice-Presidencies shall, before his or her name may appear on the ballot paper, obtain the permission of his or her college or other society (and, in the case of a person reading for a postgraduate degree or diploma, of the relevant faculty board) to stand for election, and the permission of his or her college or other society to reside during his or her term of office, if elected. No one shall be eligible to stand for election to the Presidency or the Vice-Presidencies who is not a Junior Member of the University. No person who has held the office of President or Vice-President shall be eligible to stand for re-election or for election to any of the other three posts.

[*Note*. Under the provisions of Decree (6) of 5 March 1998 and Decree (14) of 3 August 2000, the Student Union may, for a period of six years, appoint a Vice-President (Graduates) as an additional full-time officer. Under the provisions of Decree (1) of 30 June 2000, the Student Union may also appoint a Vice-President (Access and Academic Affairs) as an additional full-time officer. In both cases election to and holding of the post shall otherwise be subject to all the provisions of this sub-section as if it were one of the posts of Vice-President of the Student Union therein specified.]

9. The Oxford University Student Union shall submit to the Hebdomadal Council for approval annual estimates in respect of the ensuing financial year and its accounts shall be published by the University and audited by the University Auditor. The Oxford University Student Union shall make available to all students and to the Hebdomadal Council annually a financial report in respect of the last financial year. Such reports shall contain, in particular, a list of external organizations to which the Oxford University Student Union has made donations in the period to which the report relates and details of those donations. The Hebdomadal Council shall take such other steps as are necessary effectively to monitor the expenditure of the Oxford University Student Union.

10. If the Oxford University Student Union decides to affiliate to any external organization, it shall publish notice of its decision stating the name of the organization and details of any subscription or similar fee paid or proposed to

[1] I.e., Ch. V, Sectt. VI and VIII.

be paid, and of any donation made or proposed to be made, to the organization. Such notice shall be made available to the Hebdomadal Council and to all Junior Members.

11. The Oxford University Student Union shall make available annually to the Hebdomadal Council and to all Junior Members a report containing a list of external organizations to which the Union is currently affiliated together with details of subscriptions or similar fees paid or donations made during the past year.

12. The Oxford University Student Union shall annually submit to its members for approval a list of affiliations to external bodies and shall also make provision at any time for a requisition by five per cent of its members that the question of continued affiliation to any particular organization shall be decided by a secret ballot. The result of such a ballot shall be binding for one year.

13. The Oxford University Student Union shall make available an internal complaints procedure to all Junior Members or groups of Junior Members who are dissatisfied in their dealings with the Union or claim to be unfairly disadvantaged by reason of their having exercised the right to opt out of membership of the Union. If having exhausted the internal complaints procedure the complainant remains unsatisfied, he or she may refer his or her complaint to the Hebdomadal Council which shall appoint an independent person to investigate and report on complaints. Where a complaint is upheld at this stage, the Oxford University Student Union shall make an effective remedy.

14. The Hebdomadal Council shall publish a code of practice setting out the manner in which the requirements of the Education Act 1994 with regard to student unions are to be carried into effect. The code of practice shall be brought to the attention of all Junior Members once a year together with any restrictions imposed on the Oxford University Student Union by the law relating to charities and with the provisions of section 43 of the Education (No. 2) Act 1986.

15. Information with regard to the right to opt out of membership of the Oxford University Student Union, and arrangements made to supply student union services to Junior Members who have exercised this right, shall be drawn to the attention of all Junior Members annually and to the attention of persons considering whether to become students at the University.

16. There shall be a committee of Presidents of Junior Common Rooms to which the President (or other chief officer) of the Junior Common Room of every college and other society recognized under Title VII shall be entitled to belong.

17. The committee shall elect from its own number undergraduate Junior Members to such committees as may be specified by statute, decree, or regulation.

§ **2.** *Of Joint Committees with Junior Members*

No recommendation from a Joint Committee with Junior Members, or other body for consultation with Junior Members, established under any statute, decree, or regulation shall be rejected without the Junior Members of the committee or body having been given an opportunity of discussion with the body with which it is a joint committee or consultative body.

Section V. Of Certain Financial and Other Matters

1. No member of the University shall be required to pay any fee or other charge (save one required by way of penalty or fine imposed under the authority of a statute, decree, or regulation) unless it is required by statute, decree, or regulation.

2. Council shall, at its discretion, arrange for the investment of all funds and endowments of the University and capital money held or to be held under the provisions of the Universities and College Estates Acts, 1925 and 1964, which are not required for immediate use upon such securities, shares, stocks, funds, or other investments (including land) in any part of the world and whether involving liability or not as it shall in its absolute discretion think fit, so that it shall be empowered to invest and transpose the investments of such funds in the same unrestricted manner as if it were the beneficial owner thereof. The powers conferred by this clause shall extend to the investment (including the variation of the investment) of the funds of any specific trust administered or to be administered by or for purposes connected with the University, subject to the proviso that, when less than sixty years have elapsed since the instrument creating a trust came into operation, the powers conferred by this clause may not be exercised in the following circumstances:

(*a*) if the terms of that trust expressly provide to the contrary; or

(*b*) in the case of a trust of which the University is not sole trustee, without the consent of the trustees or governing body of that trust.

3. The Common Seal of the University shall not be affixed to any deed or writing except by the Registrar or his or her deputy, in the presence of the Proctors or their respective deputies. The Registrar shall keep a record of all documents to which the Common Seal has been affixed. In all cases in which it shall be necessary or desirable so to do, the Proctors or their deputies present at the sealing shall attest under their hands the due affixing of the Seal. The Vice-Chancellor, or, if he or she is absent from Oxford, a Pro-Vice-Chancellor, may authorize the Common Seal to be affixed to any documents.

4. The Registrar is authorized to affix the Small Seal of the University:

(*a*) to the agreements, notices, assignments, or receipts respecting or relative to policies of assurance effected under the provisions of the Federated Superannuation System for universities;

(*b*) to any notices, assignments, or receipts in connection with the University's Pension Scheme;

(*c*) to degree certificates and any other certificates issued by him or her under the authority of any statute, decree, or regulation, and to the lists, furnished by him or her from time to time, to the Registrar of the General Medical Council of Great Britain and Ireland, of persons admitted to medical and surgical degrees in the University;

(*d*) to such other documents as Council may from time to time determine.

Section VI. Of Intellectual Property generated by Students

1. Subject to clause 2 below and to the provisions of the Patents Act 1977, and unless otherwise agreed in writing between the student concerned and the University, the University claims ownership of the following forms of intellectual property; in the case of (*c*), (*d*), (*e*), and (*f*) (and (*g*) as it relates to (*c*)–(*f*)) the claims are to intellectual property devised, made, or created by students in the course of or incidentally to their studies:

(*a*) works generated by computer hardware or software owned or operated by the University;

(*b*) films, videos, multimedia works, typographical arrangements, and other works created with the aid of university facilities;

(*c*) patentable and non-patentable inventions;

(*d*) registered and unregistered designs, plant varieites, and topographies;

(*e*) university-commissioned works not within (*a*), (*b*), (*c*), or (*d*);

(*f*) databases, computer software, firmware, courseware, and related material not within (*a*), (*b*), (*c*), (*d*), or (*e*), but only if they may reasonably be considered to possess commercial potential; and

(*g*) know-how and information associated with the above.

2. Notwithstanding clause 1 above, the University shall not assert any claim to the ownership of copyright in:

(*a*) artistic works, books, articles, plays, lyrics, scores, or lectures, apart from those specifically commissioned by the University;

(*b*) audio or visual aids to the giving of lectures; or

(*c*) computer-related works other than those specified in clause 1 above.

3. For the purpose of clauses 1 and 2 above:

(*a*) a 'student' is a person reading and registered for a degree, diploma, or certificate of the University;

(*b*) 'commissioned works' are works which the University has specifically requested the student concerned to produce, whether in return for special payment or not. However, save as may be separately agreed between the University Press and the student concerned, works commissioned by the University Press in the course of its publishing business shall not be regarded as 'works commissioned by the University'.

4. Students shall sign any documents necessary in order to give effect to the claim made by the University in clause 1 above; and shall waive any rights in

respect of the subject-matter of the claim which may be conferred on them by Chapter IV of Part 1 of the Copyright, Designs and Patents Act 1988.

5. The provisions of this section shall take effect on 1 October 2000, and shall apply to all intellectual property devised, made, or created on or after 1 October 2000.

6. The policy set out above shall be administered in accordance with procedures which shall be determined from time to time by Council by decree.

Section VII. Of Amendments of Statutes

1. Congregation shall have full power to amend, repeal, or add to the statutes, provided always that none of the statutes in the Schedule to this section shall be amended, repealed, or added to without the approval of Her Majesty in Council.

2. Council may by decree suspend the operation of any statute, other than those in the Schedule to this section, to cover some specific case.

SCHEDULE

Title I
Title II, Sections I and II
Title III
Title IV, Sections I and II
Title VII, Section I
Title VIII, Section I
Title XII
Title XIII
Title XVI
Title XVII

TITLE XVI

OF STATUTES AMENDING TRUSTS

(This Title is a 'Queen-in-Council' statute—see Title XV, Section VII.)

Section I. Of the Bampton Lectures

1. There shall be delivered, annually or biennially, at the Church of St. Mary the Virgin, eight divinity lecture sermons, to be called the Bampton Lectures. The sermon lectures shall be delivered 'upon either of the following subjects: to confirm and establish the Christian Faith, and to confute all heretics and schismatics—upon the divine authority of the Holy Scriptures—upon the authority of the writings of the Primitive Fathers, as to the Faith and Practice of the Primitive Church—upon the Divinity of our Lord and Saviour Jesus Christ—upon the Divinity of the Holy Ghost—upon the Articles of the Christian Faith, as comprehended in the Apostles' and Nicene Creeds'.

2. The Bampton Lectures shall be delivered on such eight days in either or both of Full Hilary and Trinity Terms as the Vice-Chancellor may appoint.

3. The Bampton Lecturer shall be elected by the heads of colleges only, and proceedings for such election shall be initiated after at least six calendar months' public notice, not less than twenty-two nor more than twenty-six calendar months before the day upon which the first of his Bampton Lectures is to be preached.

4. The stipend of the Bampton Lecturer shall be such sum being not less than £300 as the electors shall from time to time determine; but the lecturer shall not be paid, nor be entitled to be paid, before there shall have been printed, within twelve months after they are preached, unless an extension of time is granted by the electors in view of special circumstances, sufficient copies of his or her lecture sermons for one copy to be given to the Chancellor of the University, one to the head of every college, one to the Lord Mayor of the City of Oxford, and one to the Bodleian Library. The expense of printing shall be paid from the fund.

5. No person shall be qualified to preach the Bampton Lectures unless he or she be a university graduate. The same person shall not preach the Bampton Lectures twice.

6. The first charge on the income of the Bampton Fund shall be the stipend of the Bampton Lecturer, and the expense of printing the Bampton Lectures; any balance may, at the discretion of the electors to the Bampton Lecturership, be carried forward for use in a subsequent year or applied in one or more of the following ways:

(*a*) towards the payment of the travelling expenses of the lecturers;
(*b*) towards other costs associated with the Bampton Lectures;

(*c*) in the making of grants for the promotion of studies in the subjects specified in clause 1 above.

Section II. Of the Beit Professor of the History of the British Commonwealth

1. The Beit Professor of the History of the British Commonwealth shall lecture and give instruction in the History of the British Empire and Commonwealth.

2. The professor shall be elected by an electoral board consisting of:

(1) the Vice-Chancellor or, if the head of the college specified in (2) of this clause is Vice-Chancellor, a person appointed by Council on the occurrence of a vacancy to act as an elector on that occasion;

(2) the head of the college to which the professorship shall be for the time being allocated by Council under any statute, or, if the head is unable or unwilling to act, a person appointed by the governing body of the college on the occurrence of a vacancy to act as an elector on that occasion;

(3) a person appointed by the governing body of the college specified in (2) of this clause;

(4) a person appointed by Council;

(5) a person appointed by the General Board;

(6), (7) two persons elected by the Board of the Faculty of Modern History.

3. The Professor shall be subject to any general statutes, decrees, or regulations concerning the duties of professors and to any particular decrees or regulations which are applicable to his chair.

Section III. Of the Slade Professor of Fine Art

1. (*a*) The purpose for which the trust fund and the income thereof are held is the establishment of a professorship to be called 'The Slade Professorship of Fine Art'.

(*b*) In each year there shall be paid out of the income of the trust fund for that year:

(i) to the professor such allowance for his travelling and other expenses as the board of electors (hereinafter mentioned) shall resolve; and

(ii) the proper costs of administering the trust in that year; and

(iii) such sum or sums for the purchase of slides or other illustrative material (which slides or other material shall become the property of the University) as the board shall resolve; and

(iv) to the professor such stipend (not being less than £400 or more than the balance of the income of the fund) as the board shall resolve.

(*c*) Any part of the income of the trust fund in any year which is not applied under the foregoing provisions shall either be invested in augmentation of capital, or carried forward for use in a subsequent year, or applied in such other ways, for the furtherance of the study of the Fine Arts in Oxford, as may be determined by the board.

2. The professorship shall be tenable for one year.

3. The professor shall give during this tenure of the professorship at such place as the Vice-Chancellor shall appoint not less than eight lectures on the History, Theory, and Practice of the Fine Arts or some section or sections of them. The lectures shall be given in Full Term and shall be open to all members of the University.

4. The professor shall be elected by the board of electors, consisting of:

(1) the Vice-Chancellor;

(2) the Director of the National Gallery;

(3) a person appointed by the Governing Body of All Souls College;

(4) a person appointed by Council;

(5) a person appointed by the General Board;

(6) a person appointed by the Committee for the History of Art;

(7) a person appointed by the Visitors of the Ashmolean Museum.

5. The Registrar shall see that not less than one calendar month's notice be given to the electors of any vacancy in the professorship, and of the day, hour, and place proposed for the election of a successor, and of the name or names of the candidate or candidates; and shall also see that not less than a week's notice be given to the electors of the day, hour, place, and purpose of any other meeting of the board.

6. All matters brought before the board shall be decided by a majority of votes. The members of the board shall be entitled to transmit their votes in writing for the election or compulsory retirement of a professor, provided that the election or compulsory retirement of a professor shall not be valid unless a majority of the board shall have voted in favour of the decision. The members of the board shall be entitled to vote on any other business only when personally present at a meeting of the board.

7. Should the professor, either from illness, or from any urgent cause to be approved by the Vice-Chancellor, be temporarily prevented from discharging his duties he shall name a fit and sufficient deputy to be approved by the board; and in case of his declining or neglecting so to do the board shall appoint such deputy. It shall rest with the board to determine what portion of the professor's stipend shall be assigned to the deputy.

8. A professor may at any time retire from office, and may by a unanimous vote of all the electors be compelled so to retire.

9. Upon the death, resignation, or retirement from office, of a professor during his tenure of the professorship:

(*a*) the board shall decide what proportion of the stipend which would have been payable to such professor under the provisions of clause 1 above if he had completed his tenure shall be paid to such professor or his personal representative as the case may be, regard being had to the length of time during which such professor has held office and to the number of lectures which he has given;

(*b*) the board shall decide whether or not to fill the vacancy in the professorship before the next day on which a professor normally assumes office;

(*c*) if the board shall decide to fill the vacancy it may resolve that there shall be paid out of the income of the trust fund to the new professor such stipend (not exceeding the amount of any unapplied balance of the previous professor's stipend) as it may see fit in respect of the period until the next day on which a professor normally assumes office and it may if it sees fit appoint to fill the vacancy the same person as it shall appoint or shall have appointed to be the professor for the next following year and such person shall then hold office continuously until the end of the next following year.

Section IV. Of the Estlin Carpenter Fund

1. The assets of the Estlin Carpenter Trust (established in 1927 by a bequest under the will of the late Dr. Joseph Estlin Carpenter) shall form a fund to be known as the Estlin Carpenter Fund.

2. The fund shall be administered by the Committee on Continuing Education and the income used for the promotion of extension lectures to be known as the Estlin Carpenter Lectures on subjects relating to the place of man in nature, such as the sciences of Astronomy, Geology, Biology, Geography, and kindred studies bearing on human development in Psychology, History, Literature, Art, Social Organization, Economics, and Political Philosophy.

3. Any income of the fund remaining unexpended under the provisions of clause 2 above at the end of any financial year shall be carried forward for expenditure in subsequent years.

Section V. Of the Craven Fellowships and Scholarships

1. The annual income of the foundation of John Lord Craven shall be applied to the maintenance of two or more fellowships and three scholarships for the promotion of classical learning and taste, to be styled the Craven University Fellowships and Craven University Scholarships respectively.

2. The fellowships shall be open to all who shall not have exceeded the twenty-first term from their matriculation. They shall be tenable for two years, and shall be of such value as shall be determined from time to time by the Board of the Faculty of Literae Humaniores. In any particular case the board, after consideration of a report from the committee for the time being constituted under the terms of clause 3 below, may also agree to refund expenses incurred, in its opinion, in the reasonable discharge of the obligations imposed on him by clause 4 below, in so far as such expenses cannot be met from another source.

3. At least one fellow shall be elected annually in Trinity Term or in Michaelmas Term, provided candidates of sufficient merit present themselves, by a committee of five persons appointed for the purpose by the Board of the Faculty of Literae Humaniores. The committee shall have power to elect either

without examination or after such examination in Greek and Latin literature, history, and antiquities, or in some part of these subjects, as it shall think fit.

4. Each fellow shall be deemed to have entered on his fellowship on the first of August in the year in which he was elected. He shall be required as a condition of his becoming entitled to the emoluments of his fellowship to spend at least eight months out of the twenty-six months immediately following his entry upon his fellowship in residence abroad for the purpose of study at some place or places approved by the electing committee. But the electing committee shall have power to allow such residence to be postponed for any period not exceeding six months, or to grant total or partial dispensation from the requirement of residence abroad, and to authorize the payment of such part of the emoluments as they shall think reasonable to a fellow who shall have failed to complete his period of residence. The electing committee may require the fellow to produce such evidence of diligence in the prosecution of his study as it shall think expedient.

5. The scholarships shall be open to all members of the University who shall not have exceeded the twelfth term from their matriculation. The value of the scholarships, which shall be payable on award, shall be as determined from time to time by the Board of the Faculty of Literae Humaniores. The committee constituted under this section shall have power to award part or all of the emoluments of the scholarships as grants for the purchase of books or for foreign travel or both.

6. Three scholars shall be elected annually after an examination held in Michaelmas Term, provided candidates of sufficient merit present themselves. The examiners for the scholarships shall be three persons nominated by the committee which nominates examiners for Honour Moderations in Greek and Latin Literature. No two examiners shall be of the same college or other society; and the same person shall not be nominated as examiner more than twice consecutively.

7. The examination shall be the same as that held for the election to Dean Ireland's Scholarship, and the person elected to be Dean Ireland's Scholar, if he has not already been elected to a Craven Scholarship, shall be elected at the same time to the first Craven Scholarship.

8. No person shall be elected a second time to a Craven Scholarship.

9. The committee appointed to elect to the fellowships shall give notice in the *University Gazette* (at least twenty days in advance) of the time and place at which it will receive the names of candidates; and in case it determines to hold an examination it shall give a further notice of not less than ten days of the time and place thereof. The electors to the scholarships shall give notice in the *University Gazette* (at least twenty days in advance) of the time and place of the examination.

10. Every candidate for the scholarships shall produce to the examiners the written consent of the head or vicegerent of his college or other society, together with proof of his standing, two days at least before the commencement of the

examination. Every candidate for the fellowships shall produce the like consent, together with proof of his standing, on or before the day appointed by the committee for receiving the names of candidates.

11. When an election to a fellowship or to scholarships has been made, the electors shall arrange for the names of the persons elected to be published in the *University Gazette*. In addition they shall publish the names of candidates whom they have mentioned as having distinguished themselves in the examination; and the same record shall be kept of all such names as of the fellows and scholars elected.

12. The Board of the Faculty of Literae Humaniores shall have power to apply so much of the income as they think necessary towards the expense of any examination for the fellowships or the scholarships, including the honorarium of the examiners. The surplus of the annual income shall be carried to a fund, to be called the Craven University Fund, from which grants may be made from time to time by the board for any purpose connected with the advancement of classical learning.

13. Congregation may from time to time alter or dispense with, and Council may by decree dispense from, any of the foregoing provisions, always provided that the main object of the founder be kept in view, namely, the promotion of classical learning and taste.

Section VI. Of the Vinerian Scholarships

1. Any surplus income of the Vinerian Fund which remains after paying the emoluments of the scholars shall be applied towards defraying the stipend of the Vinerian Professor of English Law unless on any occasion Council shall by decree determine otherwise.

2. One Vinerian Scholarship and one award of *proxime accessit* shall be offered for competition in the Trinity Term of each year, and shall be open to any member of the University who is qualified to obtain Honours in the examination for the Degree of Bachelor of Civil Law held in that term. The value of the scholarship and *proxime accessit* award shall be set at such sums, not exceeding one-sixth of the annual income of the fund, as the Board of the Faculty of Law shall from time to time determine, and the scholar and *proxime accessit* award winner shall be paid this sum on their election.

3. The scholarship shall be awarded by the examiners for the Degree of Bachelor of Civil Law to the candidate whose work in the examination for that degree is of the highest merit if in their opinion his or her work renders the candidate worthy of election to the scholarship. The award of *proxime accessit* shall be awarded by the examiners for the Degree of Bachelor of Civil Law to the candidate whose work in the examination for that degree is of the second highest merit if in their opinion his or her work renders the candidate worthy of the award. The examiners shall attach special importance to proficiency in English Law.

4. Congregation may if it thinks fit amend the provisions of this statute concerning the time and content of the examination, the examiners, and the conditions on which the scholarships are held.

Section VII. Of the Kennicott and the Pusey and Ellerton Funds and Awards

1. There shall be a Kennicott Fellowship and Pusey and Ellerton Prizes which shall be managed by a board of management consisting of:

(1) the Regius Professor of Divinity;

(2) the Regius Professor of Hebrew;

(3) the President of Magdalen College, or a member of Congregation appointed by him for three years and capable of reappointment;

(4) the Dean of Christ Church, or a member of Congregation appointed by him for three years and capable of reappointment;

(5) the Warden of Wadham College, or a member of Congregation appointed by him for three years and capable of reappointment;

(6) a representative of the Board of the Faculty of Oriental Studies, to be appointed by the faculty board for three years and capable of reappointment.

2. The board shall appoint for each year not more than three electors, who shall consider the applications of candidates for the fellowship, shall make the elections to the fellowships, shall recommend, if they think fit, the making of grants of money or books to unsuccessful candidates for the fellowship, and shall receive from the Pusey and Ellerton Fund remuneration for their services at rates to be determined for each year by the board.

3. (*a*) The board shall in at least every third year offer, and the electors, if a candidate suitable in their judgement present himself, shall in the Trinity Term of that year, or as soon as possible thereafter, elect to, a Kennicott Fellowship, either without an examination or after such examination, as they may think fit.

(*b*) The fellowship shall be open, with preference to candidates who have not on the first day of the term of the election passed their 25th birthday, to any person who is a member of the University who has obtained a first or second class in an Honour School, or who has, in the opinion of the electors, achieved comparable academic standing in another university. Every candidate must submit with his application both evidence of his knowledge of Hebrew and a statement satisfactory to the electors as to the course of study he intends to pursue in connection with the Hebrew language, literature, history, or archaeology, or the cognate Semitic languages so far as they illustrate Hebrew, and, in the case of a candidate who is already a member of the University, a statement of consent to his candidature from the head of his college or other society.

(*c*) The fellowship shall be tenable for two years from the first day of the Michaelmas Term of the year of election, provided that its assumption may be deferred at the discretion of the board, and shall be renewable for a third year at the discretion of and under conditions to be determined by the board. No person shall be eligible a second time for the fellowship. As a condition of becoming entitled to the emoluments of his fellowship, a fellow must have been admitted to matriculation as a member of the University, must reside within the University for two academic years unless the electors give him leave to pursue his course of study elsewhere, and must satisfy the board in each term that he is diligently prosecuting a course of studies in Hebrew approved by the board.

(*d*) The emoluments of the fellowship, which shall be paid out of the Kennicott Fund (subject to the provisions of clause 5 below), shall be such sum as the board shall determine in the light of any other emoluments accruing to the fellow during his tenure of the fellowship.

4. There shall be Senior and Junior Pusey and Ellerton Prizes offered each year in accordance with the following regulations:

(*a*) One or more senior prizes shall be awarded on the recommendation of the examiners in the Final Honour School of Theology, and one or more on the recommendation of the examiners in the Final Honour School of Oriental Studies, to those candidates whose performance in Biblical Hebrew the examiners judge to be of sufficient merit.

(*b*) Two or more junior prizes shall be awarded on the recommendation of the moderators in the Preliminary Examination for Theology, and two or more on the recommendation of the moderators in the Preliminary Examination in Oriental Studies, to those candidates whose performance in Biblical Hebrew the moderators judge to be of sufficient merit.

(*c*) The senior prize shall be open to any member of the University qualified to obtain Honours in the Honour Schools of Theology or Oriental Studies.

(*d*) The value of the prizes, which shall be paid out of the Pusey and Ellerton Fund (subject to the provisions of clause 5 below), shall be such as the board shall from time to time determine.

5. If in any year the income available in either fund, after defraying all necessary expenses of administration (including the remuneration of the electors and the cost of examinations), shall be insufficient to meet the emoluments of the fellowship or of the prizes as the case may be, the deficiency on that fund shall be made good out of the income of the other.

6. Any surplus income remaining in the funds over and above that required for the foregoing purposes shall at the discretion of the board either be carried forward for expenditure in a subsequent year or be applied in one or more of the following ways:

(*a*) in awarding a second fellowship on the same terms as are set out in clause 3 above;

(*b*) in assisting publications which may forward the objects of the trusts;

(*c*) for the encouragement in other ways of the objects of the trusts;

provided always that the main objects of the founders be kept in view, namely in the case of the Kennicott Fund, the promotion of Hebrew studies, and, in the case of the Pusey and Ellerton Fund, the promotion of sound theology through a solid and critical knowledge of Hebrew.

7. Congregation may from time to time alter or dispense with any of the foregoing provisions, provided always that the main objects of the founders, as set out in clause 6 above, be kept in view.

Section VIII. Of the Boden Fund

1. (*a*) The first charge upon the income of the Boden Fund shall be the payment of a contribution towards the cost of the Boden Professorship of Sanskrit equal to one-half of the total income of the fund, net of such management fee as shall be determined by the Curators of the University Chest, from year to year.

(*b*) In the event of a vacancy in the professorship this contribution shall be paid into the University General Fund.

2. The second charge on the income of the Boden Fund shall be the financing of the Boden Scholarship for the encouragement of the study of, and proficiency in, the Sanskrit Language and Literature tenable on the conditions hereinafter mentioned for two years in the first instance, with an annual stipend to be fixed at the discretion of the Board of the Faculty of Oriental Studies.

3. The Board of the Faculty of Oriental Studies shall be the board of management of the scholarship.

4. The scholar shall be elected in such term as the board may from time to time determine, provided that not less than three months' notice of each election shall have been given in the *University Gazette*. The electors shall be the Boden Professor of Sanskrit or his deputy and one or more others appointed by the board on each occasion not less than one month before the election. The election shall take into account the previous records and declared intentions of the candidates, and they may also, if they think fit, examine them either orally or in writing or in both ways.

5. The scholarship shall be open to all graduate members of the University of Oxford whether men or women who on the first day of the term in which the election is held shall have exceeded the ninth term from their matriculation but not the 30th year of their age. Candidates shall produce to the Boden Professor documentary evidence of their eligibility under this clause, and also a written permission, signed by the heads or vicegerents of their respective colleges or other societies, to offer themselves as candidates, provided always that no person shall be eligible whose vernacular language is any Indian language.

6. The board may, on the recommendation of the electors, permit a scholar to retain his scholarship for a third year but not for longer.

7. The scholar shall keep statutable residence for six weeks in every term of the tenure of his scholarship unless, on the recommendation of the Boden Professor, the board shall grant him leave to reside elsewhere on the ground that he can there pursue his studies more profitably than in Oxford. He shall be required during residence in Oxford to attend such of the Boden Professor's lectures as the professor shall deem best adapted to the scholar's proficiency in Sanskrit.

The board may also dispense with statutory residence on the ground of illness or for other urgent cause.

8. The scholarship shall become *ipso facto* void if the scholar be non-resident in any term (unless his residence shall have been dispensed with under clause 7 above) or fail to comply with any other requirement herein specified.

9. At the end of each term the scholar shall apply to the Boden Professor for a certificate that he is worthy to receive his stipend and shall deliver such a certificate signed by the Boden Professor together with a certificate of residence to the Registrar, and in default of such certificates or either of them (subject nevertheless to any dispensation as to residence granted under clause 7 above) the scholar shall receive no stipend in respect of the following term.

10. Electors other than the Boden Professor may, if the board for good reasons so determines on any occasion, receive an honorarium not exceeding £5. Any such honorarium and all other necessary expenses of administration shall be paid out of the income of the fund.

11. Any surplus income of the fund not required for the purposes aforesaid (including any emoluments forfeited by a scholar and any income accruing during a vacancy and not required to be paid into the University General Fund as aforesaid) shall be applied in the first instance to making a grant to the Library of the Indian Institute of £50 per annum or such less sum as may in any given year be available and subject thereto may at the discretion of the board be applied to any one or more of the following purposes, namely:

(*a*) to the provision of a junior scholarship or prize for the encouragement of the study of and proficiency in the Sanskrit Languages and Literature;

(*b*) to the assistance of publications or any other purpose connected or consistent with the advancement of Sanskrit studies.

12. Any balance of such surplus income not applied to one or more of the objects specified in clause 11 above shall be carried forward for expenditure in subsequent years.

Section IX. Of the Denyer and Johnson Travelling Fellowship and Prize

1. The annual proceeds of the benefaction of Elizabeth Denyer, widow, and of that moiety of the benefaction of John Johnson, D.D., which he appropriated to the promotion of the study of Theology, shall form an endowment fund for a travelling fellowship and a prize for the encouragement of the study of Theology, to be called the Denyer and Johnson Travelling Fellowship and Prize.

2. The Board of the Faculty of Theology shall be the board of management for the fund.

3. There shall be a travelling fellowship of a value to be determined in each case by the board of management, tenable for one year.

4. One travelling fellow shall be elected every other year, if a fit candidate presents himself. Candidates must be members of the University who, on the

first day of October in the academic year in which the election takes place are under 40 years of age, and either

(*a*) have qualified by examination for any degree of the University; or

(*b*) are members of Congregation.

5. The travelling fellowship shall not be awarded to the same person more than twice.

6. Every travelling fellow elected shall, unless he shall have received from the board exemption from the requirement, be required to spend at least three months of his tenure of the fellowship in residence outside the United Kingdom for the purpose of study at some place or places approved by the board. Part of the value of the travelling fellowship as determined by the board shall be applied, at its discretion, to meet expenses necessarily incurred by the travelling fellow under this condition. The board shall have power to authorize the payment of such part of the emoluments of the fellowship as it may deem reasonable to a fellow who shall have failed to complete his period of residence outside the United Kingdom; and the board shall further have power to require a fellow to produce such evidence of diligence in the prosecution of his studies as it may think expedient.

7. Subject to this statute, the board shall have power to make, and to vary from time to time, provisions concerning the mode of election to, and the conditions of tenure and time of payment of the emoluments of, the travelling fellowship, provided that no election to a travelling fellowship shall be made by the board unless notice of not less than twenty days has been given by it of the time and place at which names of the candidates are to be received.

8. There shall be a prize which shall be awarded on the recommendation of the examiners in the Final Honour School of Theology to the candidate whose performance the examiners judge to be the best and of sufficient merit for the prize, provided that it shall not be awarded to a candidate who has been awarded a Senior Pusey and Ellerton Prize in Biblical Hebrew unless there is no other candidate of sufficient merit to be awarded the Denyer and Johnson Prize.

9. The value of the prize shall be such as the board shall from time to time determine.

10. Any income from the benefaction in excess of the sum required in each year for paying the emoluments of the fellowship and prize may be used by the board in one or more of the following ways:

(*a*) for the award of an additional travelling fellowship on the same terms and conditions as the above;

(*b*) for studentships to be awarded to graduates reading for higher degrees under the Board of the Faculty of Theology, on conditions laid down by the board;

(*c*) for grants or any purpose connected with the advancement of theological learning.

11. Congregation may from time to time alter or dispense with, and Council may by decree dispense from, any of the foregoing provisions, always provided that the main object of the founders be kept in view, namely, the encouragement of the study of Theology.

Section X. Of the Paget Toynbee Prizes

1. Paget Toynbee Prizes shall be awarded for proficiency in the study of either (1) the works of Dante or (2) Old French Language and Literature including Provençal Language and Literature. The Board of the Faculty of Medieval and Modern Languages shall be the board of management of the prizes.

2. The board shall have power to make regulations, subject to the approval of the General Board, concerning the number and value of the prizes, the subjects in which they are to be awarded, the form of competition, and the standing of candidates, provided always that:

(*a*) in each of the two fields specified in clause 1 above at least one prize shall be offered at least every other year; and

(*b*) the prizes shall only be open to members of the University of not more than twenty-eight terms' standing.

3. It shall be the duty of the board to appoint examiners for the prizes and to determine their remuneration.

4. No prize shall be awarded unless a candidate of sufficient merit presents himself.

5. Surplus income in any year, however arising, may, as the board shall from time to time determine, either be applied in the promotion or encouragement of the study within the University of the works of Dante, Old French Language and Literature, or Old Provençal Language and Literature or be carried forward for expenditure in subsequent years.

6. This statute may be amended from time to time by Congregation provided that the object of the bequest shall always be kept in view, namely the provision of an annual prize for the encouragement of the study of the works of Dante and Old French Language and Literature including Provençal Language and Literature.

Section XI. Of the Oldham Scholarships in Classical Studies

1. The annual income arising from that moiety of Mr. Charles Oldham's bequest which was set aside for the establishment of a prize in the Ancient Classics shall be applied to the provision of not less than four scholarships a year for travel connected with Greek or Roman studies.

2. The scholarships shall be open to members of the University reading for Honour Moderations in Greek and Latin Literature or for Honour Moderations in Latin Literature with Greek or for any Honour School of which in the judgement of the board of management Classics forms a substantial part. Preference will normally be given to candidates who on the first day of Trinity

Term in the year of their election have not entered upon the twelfth term from their matriculation.

3. No person shall be elected twice to a scholarship.

4. The Board of the Faculty of Literae Humaniores shall be the board of management of the scholarships. It shall have power to fix the number, subject to clause 1 above, value, and tenure of the scholarships and shall elect the scholars, provided candidates of sufficient merit present themselves, either without examination or after such examination as it shall think fit.

5. The board shall have power to appoint a subcommittee of its members to act for it in connection with these scholarships.

6. The board shall have power:

(*a*) to defray from the income of the fund any expenses incidental to the award of the scholarships, including the remuneration of the examiners (if any);

(*b*) to carry forward or to add to capital any income not expended under the above provisions in any year.

Section XII. Of the George Webb Medley Endowment Fund

1. The Board of the Faculty of Social Studies shall be the board of management of the George Webb Medley Endowment Fund.

2. The board shall use the income of the fund for the promotion of the study and advance of the science of Political Economy by giving scholarships, prizes, and grants on such terms as it shall think fit.

3. Any income not spent in any year under the provisions of clause 2 above shall, at the discretion of the board, either be carried forward for expenditure in some future year, or be invested in augmentation of the capital of the fund.

Section XIII. Of the Ellerton Theological Essay Prize

1. The annual income of the benefaction given in 1825 by the Revd. Edward Ellerton, D.D., Fellow of Magdalen College, for the encouragement of theological learning in the University by the establishment of an annual prize for an English Essay shall continue to form the endowment fund for the Ellerton Theological Essay Prize.

2. The prize shall be of a value determined by the board of management and shall be offered annually for the best English Essay on some doctrine or duty of the Christian religion or on any other subject of theology which shall be deemed meet and useful.

3. The prize shall be open to all members of the University who, on the day fixed for the submission of essays, shall not have exceeded thirty terms from their matriculation, provided that any candidate holding a degree of another university at the time of his matriculation shall not have exceeded twenty-one terms from his matriculation.

4. No one to whom the prize shall have been adjudged shall again offer himself as a candidate.

5. The Board of the Faculty of Theology shall be the board of management of the prize. The board shall appoint annually not more than three judges who shall be paid such fee as the board shall provide, and who shall award the prize.

6. A difference of opinion among the judges shall be decided by a majority.

7. Not later than the end of the fourth week in Michaelmas Term candidates shall submit titles for approval by the judges and the essays shall be sent in on or before the first day of the Trinity Term next ensuing. The length of an essay shall not exceed 10,000 words.

8. Any surplus available either because the prize has not been awarded or for any other reason may be employed by the board in any manner it may think desirable for the furtherance of the study of Theology in the University.

9. Congregation may alter, and Council may by decree suspend, any of the foregoing provisions, provided always that the object of the founder be kept in view, namely the encouragement of theological learning in the University by the establishment of an annual prize for an English Essay.

Section XIV. Of the John Locke Prize

1. The endowment given by the late Mr. Henry Wilde to found a prize in Mental Philosophy shall be administered and managed by the Board of the Faculty of Literae Humaniores.

2. The first charge on the income of the endowment shall be the emoluments of the prize, which shall always be called, in honour and memory of John Locke, the John Locke Prize.

3. The prize shall be awarded, provided that a candidate of sufficient merit presents himself, after an examination in Mental Philosophy. The prize shall be open to:

(*a*) members of the University who have passed all the examinations requisite for the Degree of Bachelor of Arts, provided that they shall not take the examination later than the tenth term from that in which they completed the said examinations;

(*b*) members of the University working for or having obtained postgraduate degrees of the University who are not included under (*a*) provided that they shall not take the examination later than the tenth term from their matriculation.

4. The value of the prize, payable on award, shall be £300 or such greater sum from the income of the endowment as the faculty board shall determine subject to clause 2 above.

5. The prize shall not be awarded twice to the same person.

6. The examiners for this prize shall be as follows:

(1) and (2) In 1971 and thereafter in every second year the Wykeham Professor of Logic and the Professor of the History of Philosophy; in 1972 and

thereafter in every second year White's Professor of Moral Philosophy and the Waynflete Professor of Metaphysical Philosophy; (3) the Wilde Professor in Mental Philosophy; provided (*a*) that each of these officers if he thinks fit, may appoint some other person, of the Degree of Master of Arts at least and approved by the board, to act in his place; (*b*) that the Professor of Psychology (or his deputy) shall act as assessor for such part of the examination as involves a technical knowledge of psychology; (*c*) in case of an equality of votes, the senior examiner shall have a casting vote.

7. The examiners shall have power to award the sum of £100 or such greater sum from the income of the endowment as the faculty board shall determine subject to clause 2 above to the *proxime accessit* if and only if they would have judged him worthy of the prize had there not been a better candidate.

8. The board shall fix the remunerations of the examiners and assessor and shall defray any other expenses arising in connection with the prize from the income of the endowment.

9. Any surplus income arising in any year may at the discretion of the board be:

(*a*) carried forward for expenditure in a subsequent year;

(*b*) invested in augmentation of the capital;

(*c*) applied in any other way which the board shall think conducive to the promotion of the study of Mental Philosophy among the junior members of the University of Oxford.

10. Congregation shall have full power to alter this statute from time to time, provided always that the main object of the foundation shall be kept in view, namely, the promotion of the study of Mental Philosophy among the junior members of the University of Oxford.

Section XV. Of the Squire and Marriott Endowment Fund

1. The Board of the Faculty of Theology shall be the board of management of the Squire and Marriott Endowment Fund.

2. The board shall use the income of the endowment for the making of grants at its discretion to any member of the University who declares at the time of application that he or she sincerely desires and intends to seek, when qualified, ordination in the Church of England or any church in communion therewith and who requires financial assistance in connection with his or her studies at the University.

3. The board shall have discretion to make additional bursaries available, after Anglican candidates have been considered, to matriculated students of the University intending ministry in churches with which the Church of England has ecumenical relations, or who as lay men or women intend to serve their church as theologians.

4. Of the grants made under the provisions of clause 2 above one-half (as near as may be) shall be called 'Rebecca Flower Squire Bursaries' and the others

'James William Squire Bursaries' provided that from time to time and in any case not less than once in five years a grant to a student of theology shall be called a 'Marriott Bursary'. Grants shall normally be paid in termly instalments subject to such conditions as the board shall determine.

5. Income in any year not used for the making of grants under the provisions of clause 2 above (or on any expenses incurred by the board in the making of them) shall be carried forward for expenditure in future years.

6. The board may appoint a committee to exercise any or all of the powers given to it by this statute. If such a committee is appointed, it shall report on its activities to the board at least once in each year.

7. Congregation shall have power from time to time to alter this statute, provided that the main object for which the endowment fund was established, as defined in clause 2 above, is always kept in view.

Section XVI. Of the Shute Fund

1. The income of the Shute Fund shall be applied in such manner as Council shall from time to time determine by decree to the assistance of members of the University who are not members of any of the colleges listed in Tit. VII, Sect. I, cl. 1, and who are in need of pecuniary assistance for their support at the University.

2. Income not expended in any year shall be carried forward for expenditure in a subsequent year.

3. All income in hand on the day on which this statute becomes effective shall be available for use under the provisions of this statute.

Section XVII. Of the Randall-MacIver Benefaction

1. The income of the Randall-MacIver Benefaction shall be applied towards the maintenance of junior research fellowships, to be known as the Joanna Randall-MacIver Junior Research Fellowships, tenable at Lady Margaret Hall, Somerville College, St. Hugh's College, St. Hilda's College, and St. Anne's College, and at such other colleges as Congregation may from time to time by statute determine. The fellowships shall be open only to women candidates.

2. The fellowships shall be tenable for a maximum period of two years and shall not be renewable. The subjects in which they may be held shall be the fine art, or music, or literature of any nation in any period.

3. The annual value of each fellowship shall be such sum as Council shall from time to time determine; and in addition such sum as Council may from time to time determine shall be paid to each fellow's college towards the cost of working accommodation and other expenses incurred by the college in connection with the fellowship.

4. In Michaelmas Term in each year Council shall consider how many, if any, new fellowships can be offered with effect from the Michaelmas Term following

and, after consultation with the colleges named in this section, shall allocate any such fellowships to such of those colleges wishing to receive them as it thinks fit. The colleges of allocation shall then be entirely responsible for arranging for the selection and appointment of the fellows. The colleges of allocation shall also be responsible for fixing the conditions on which the fellowship shall be held, provided always that provision is made for the granting of leave of absence to any fellow whose work requires it.

5. Any income not required in any financial year for the maintenance of fellowships shall, at the discretion of Council, be carried forward for expenditure on fellowships in a subsequent year.

6. Congregation shall have full power to alter this statute from time to time, provided always that the main object of the benefaction, namely, the support of junior research fellowships tenable by women, is always kept in view.

Section XVIII. Of the Heath Harrison Fund

1. The benefaction of £25,000 accepted by Decree (3) of Convocation on 17 June 1919 (as subsequently amended) from Sir Heath Harrison, Bart., of Brasenose College, shall continue to be known as the Heath Harrison Fund.

2. The income of the fund shall be applied

(*a*) as to not more than one-fourth of the annual income, in providing instruction within the University in French and other Modern European languages;

(*b*) in the institution of senior and junior travelling scholarships;

(*c*) as to any surplus income not required under (*a*) and (*b*) above, in any other manner which the board of management shall consider will promote the study by junior members of the University of Modern European languages.

3. The senior and junior travelling scholarships shall be held exclusively by persons who are either

(*a*) by birth or by descent

(i) Citizens of the United Kingdom and Colonies, or

(ii) Commonwealth Citizens within the meaning of Section 1 of the British Nationality Act, 1948, or

(iii) Citizens of the Republic of Ireland; or

(*b*) persons born before 1 January 1949 who were deemed to have been natural-born British subjects prior to that date; and who are members of the University, while studying French and other modern European languages in foreign countries.

4. The junior travelling scholarships shall be open for competition to undergraduate members of the University otherwise qualified as in clause 3 above.

5. The scholarships shall be awarded by a board of management consisting of the Vice-Chancellor or a member of Congregation nominated by him from year

to year, the Marshal Foch Professor of French Literature, and three members of Congregation elected, two by the Board of the Faculty of Medieval and Modern Languages, and one by the Board of the Faculty of Modern History.

6. The elected members of the board shall hold office for three years, and shall be eligible for re-election at the end of that period, but no elected member who has held office for six years consecutively shall be immediately re-eligible. When an elected member vacates his seat otherwise than by expiration of his period of office, the body which elected him shall elect another member of Congregation for the unexpired residue of his term of office.

7. The board shall have power

(*a*) to fix the amount to be paid in each year for providing instruction in Modern European languages and to determine the allocation thereof;

(*b*) to make regulations as to the award and tenure of the travelling scholarships;

(*c*) to defray from the income of the fund any expenses incidental to the carrying out of the provisions of this statute, including the remuneration of examiners, if any;

(*d*) to promote by the award of grants or in any other way at its discretion the study by junior members of the University of Modern European languages.

8. The board shall have power to carry forward or to order the temporary or permanent investment of any income not expended under the conditions of this statute in any year.

9. This statute may be altered from time to time by Congregation provided that the main objects of the fund as expressed in clauses 2 and 3 above shall always be kept in view.

Section XIX. Of the Sadler, Churton Collins, Smith, Cartwright, and Pickstock Fund

1. The assets of the Sadler Scholarship Fund, the Churton Collins Memorial Fund, the A. L. Smith Memorial Fund, the E. S. Cartwright Testimonial Fund, and the F. V. Pickstock Testimonial Fund shall form one fund to be known as the Sadler, Churton Collins, Smith, Cartwright, and Pickstock Fund.

2. The fund shall be administered by the Committee on Continuing Education and the income used to award grants to enable students to attend residential courses for which grants would not normally be available from other sources.

3. Income in any year not used for the making of grants under the provisions of clause 2 above (or on any expenses incurred by the committee in the making of them) shall be carried forward for expenditure in subsequent years.

Section XX. Of the Marquis of Lothian's Studentship in Modern History

1. The Lothian Fund, accepted by the University in 1870 from William Schomberg Robert, eighth Marquis of Lothian, shall, after payment of any

charges for administration, be used to maintain a studentship, to be called the Marquis of Lothian's Studentship in Modern History.

2. The Board of Management of the Bryce Research Studentship in History shall be the board of management of the studentship.

3. Any member of the University engaged on research in Modern History for the Degree of Doctor of Philosophy shall be eligible for election to the studentship.

4. The board of management shall elect to the studentship on such other terms as it shall see fit.

5. Congregation may from time to time alter, and Council may by decree dispense from, any of the foregoing provisions, provided that the fund shall always be employed for the encouragement of the study of Modern History and in memory of the founder. Previous notice of any such alteration shall be given to the person or persons entitled to the estate charged with the annuity granted by the founder (being of full age and of sound mind and within the United Kingdom) but the consent of such person or persons to such alteration shall not be necessary.

Section XXI. Of the Dean Ireland's Scholarship

1. There shall be a scholarship of such value as shall be determined from time to time by the Board of the Faculty of Literae Humaniores, to be known as the Dean Ireland's Scholarship, for the promotion of classical learning and taste, no regard being had to the place of birth, school, parentage, or pecuniary circumstances of the candidates.

2. The candidates shall be undergraduate members of the University who shall not have exceeded their twelfth term from their matriculation inclusively.

3. No person shall be received as a candidate without the consent of the head of his college or other society, or the consent of the vicegerent in the absence of the said head, and such consent, as well as the standing of the candidate, shall be expressed in writing, and signed by the said head or vicegerent.

4. The scholarships shall be managed by the Board of the Faculty of Literae Humaniores.

5. Any surplus income which remains after paying the emoluments of the scholar and the expenses incidental to the trust shall be carried to a fund to be called the Ireland University Fund.

6. The board shall have power

(*a*) to make grants from the Ireland University Fund for any purpose connected with the promotion of classical learning and taste;

(*b*) to direct the temporary investment of such part of the Ireland University Fund as it may think fit, and to add to the Ireland University Fund the interest accruing from such investments; provided that it shall always be within the power of the board to use the sums so invested for the purpose set out under (*a*) above.

7. The election of the scholar shall take place annually after an examination held in Michaelmas Term, provided a candidate of sufficient merit presents himself. The money accumulated in consequence of vacancies shall be employed as directed by clause 6 above.

8. The examiners shall be the three persons appointed as electors to the Craven Scholarships, and the examination shall be the same as that held for the election of the Craven Scholars. The examiners shall receive such remuneration as the board may determine.

9. Every candidate shall deliver to the examiners the certificate of standing, and of the consent of the head or vicegerent, as required by clause 3 above, two days at least before the commencement of the examination; and without such certificates the examiners shall not proceed to examine any candidate.

10. All the three examiners shall act in the examination and vote at the election. In other respects the examination shall be left entirely to the discretion of the examiners.

11. When the examiners have elected a scholar, they shall arrange for the name of the person elected to be published in the *University Gazette* and for the emoluments of the scholarship to be paid to him.

12. Congregation shall have full power to alter this statute from time to time, with the exception of clauses 1 and 2 above which contain the original intention of the Founder and may not be altered except with the approval of Her Majesty in Council.

Section XXII. Of the James Mew Scholarships in Arabic and Rabbinical Hebrew

1. There shall be two scholarships, called the James Mew Arabic Scholarship and the James Mew Rabbinical Hebrew Scholarship respectively, each tenable for one year from the day of election.

2. The scholarships shall be awarded solely for proficiency in the linguistic study of either Arabic or Rabbinical Hebrew.

3. In each year an election shall be made either to a James Mew Arabic Scholarship or to a James Mew Rabbinical Hebrew Scholarship or to both, provided that candidates of sufficient merit present themselves.

4. The scholarships shall be open to those who have qualified for a degree of this or another university and who have not exceeded the twenty-sixth year from the date of their birth on the day appointed for the examination, provided that those who have qualified for a degree at another university shall become matriculated members of this University before entering into tenure of a scholarship. No candidate shall be eligible for election to an Arabic Scholarship

whose vernacular language is Arabic, or to a Rabbinical Hebrew Scholarship whose vernacular language is Hebrew.

5. There shall be a board of management consisting of the Vice-Chancellor, the Regius Professor of Hebrew, the Laudian Professor of Arabic, and two persons appointed by the Board of the Faculty of Oriental Studies, and holding office for two years and being re-eligible.

6. The board shall every year appoint not more than four examiners, who shall examine candidates and elect the scholar or the scholars. Each examiner shall be paid out of the income of the fund for his services such sum as the board shall from time to time determine; provided that the aggregate of the payments made on any one occasion to the examiners in each language shall not exceed one-twelfth of the annual income of the fund for the time being.

7. The examination shall be conducted, after not less than one month's notice, at such place and time as the examiners, with the approval of the Vice-Chancellor, may from time to time determine. It shall be wholly in writing, and shall be occupied exclusively with the linguistic study of Arabic or Rabbinical Hebrew as the case may be and not with questions of history, Biblical or other.

8. Every scholar during his tenure of the scholarship shall pursue such a course of study or research as the Laudian Professor of Arabic or the Regius Professor of Hebrew, as the case may be, shall approve, and shall for this purpose reside for eight weeks within the University in each of the three university terms, unless he desires to study elsewhere with the permission of the board.

9. Each scholar shall receive a total emolument of £100 or such larger sum, not exceeding the value of one year's income of the fund after the expenses of management and the examiner's fees have been deducted, as the board may, having regard to any other emoluments accruing to the scholar and to the state of the fund, determine. The total emolument of each scholar shall be payable in such instalments as the board may determine, provided always that the scholar shall conform to the requirements of clause 8 above.

10. Neither of the two scholarships shall be awarded to the same person a second time.

11. Any surplus income arising in any year may at the discretion of the board either be carried forward for expenditure in a subsequent year or be applied in one or more of the following ways:

(*a*) for the award, on the recommendation of the examiners for the scholarship, of James Mew exhibitions in Arabic or Rabbinical Hebrew to candidates for the scholarship (provided they are qualified under clause 4 above) whose work, though not of merit sufficient for the award of a scholarship, is of a standard sufficient to justify an award from the fund; the value and tenure of such exhibitions to be determined by the board;

(*b*) for the award from time to time, under regulations to be made by the board, of one or more James Mew Prizes for essays on subjects concerned exclusively with the literature of Arabic or Rabbinical Hebrew;

(*c*) for the award, on the recommendation of the examiners in the Honour School of Oriental Studies, of one or more James Mew Senior Prizes, and on the recommendation of the moderators in the First Public Examination in Oriental Studies, of one or more James Mew Junior Prizes, to those candidates whose performance in Arabic or in Rabbinical Hebrew the examiners or moderators judge to be of special merit;

(*d*) for making grants at the discretion of the board, subject to the consent of the Board of the Faculty of Oriental Studies, for any purpose concerned with the encouragement of the linguistic study of Arabic or Rabbinical Hebrew.

12. The provisions of this statute shall apply to women members of the University as well as to men.

13. The board shall have power to make from time to time subordinate regulations for carrying any of the provisions of this statute into effect; and Congregation shall have power to alter the provisions of this statute from time to time provided that the main object of the founder, namely, the encouragement of the linguistic study of Arabic and Rabbinical Hebrew, is always kept in view, and that the limitation of the subjects for which the scholarships or exhibitions or prizes are awarded is maintained.

Section XXIII. Of the Gibbs Prizes

1. The awards established under the will of Mr. Charles Day Dowling Gibbs shall be called, in memory of the founder, the Gibbs Prizes.

2. Prizes shall be offered annually for proficiency in Modern History, Chemistry, Law, Biochemistry, Zoology, Politics, and Geography. The number, value, and conditions of award of the prizes shall be fixed at the discretion of the board of management.

3. Candidates for the prizes shall be members of the University who at the beginning of the examination have not exceeded the twelfth term from their matriculation, and are reading for a final honour school, provided that Council may grant dispensation, on grounds of protracted illness or other good reason, to a candidate who has exceeded the twelfth term from his or her matriculation.

4. The prizes shall be administered by a board of management consisting of the Vice-Chancellor, and one member appointed by each of the Boards of the Faculties of Modern History, Physical Sciences, Law, Social Studies, Biological Sciences, and Anthropology and Geography, and holding office for five years and being re-eligible.

5. The board shall every year appoint examiners, not fewer than two in number for each subject in which a prize is to be awarded, who shall examine the candidates and award the prize or prizes if candidates of sufficient merit offer themselves, provided that the board may arrange for the prize or some or all of the prizes in any subject to be awarded on the results of a Public Examination of the University by the examiners in that subject. Examiners shall receive such remuneration as the board shall from time to time determine.

6. Where a special examination is held for a Gibbs Prize it shall be conducted, after due notice, at such time and place as the examiners may appoint. All expenses connected with the examination, including the remuneration of the examiners and the printing of examination papers, shall be paid out of the Gibbs Trust Fund.

7. The board shall have power to make provision for the award of grants to unsuccessful candidates for a prize who have done meritorious work in the examination in which they have offered themselves as candidates.

8. In the event of there being unspent income in the fund, this shall be spent, at the discretion of the board, on additional prizes in such subjects as the board shall from time to time determine.

9. Congregation shall have power to alter this statute from time to time, provided that the main object of the foundation, namely, the endowment and maintenance of awards to be established in Classics, Mathematics, Law, Science, History, Divinity, or other subjects as the University shall determine and to be given to undergraduates, is always kept in view.

Section XXIV. Of the Gerrans Fund

1. The income of the Gerrans Fund (established in 1922 by a bequest under the will of the late Henry Tresawna Gerrans) shall be employed by the Curators of the Taylor Institution at their sole discretion for the promotion of the study of the German Language and Literature in the University.

2. Any income of the fund remaining unexpended at the end of each financial year shall be, at the discretion of the curators, either carried forward for expenditure in any subsequent year or added to the capital of the fund.

Section XXV. Of Certain Trusts Affecting the Indian Institute Library

A statute made for the University of Oxford in the matter of the two indentures made respectively the one between Sir Monier Monier-Williams of the one part and the Chancellor, Masters, and Scholars of the University of Oxford of the other part and the other between the Reverend Solomon Caesar Malan of the one part and the said Chancellor, Masters, and Scholars of the other part.

I. The trusts declared in the indenture made the twenty-sixth day of May one thousand eight hundred and ninety-five between Sir Monier Monier-Williams, Knight Commander of the Order of the Indian Empire, Master of Arts, Doctor of Civil Law, Boden Professor of Sanskrit in the University of Oxford of the one part and the Chancellor, Masters, and Scholars of the University of Oxford of the other part are varied as hereafter in this statute provided.

As from the date on which this statute comes into operation, clauses 1, 2, 3, and 4 of the said indenture and every part of the said clauses are hereby repealed and shall cease to have any force or effect.

As from the date on which this statute comes into operation, the said indenture shall be read and have effect as if the following clauses had been originally therein in lieu of the said clauses 1, 2, 3, and 4, that is to say:

(1) The said books and manuscripts shall be placed in the Indian Institute or elsewhere under the charge of the Curators of the Bodleian Library and shall be kept and used in accordance with the rules and regulations of the Bodleian Library.

(2) An inscription commemorating the benefaction of Sir Monier Monier-Williams shall be placed in the Library of the Indian Institute.

II. The trusts declared in the indenture made the thirtieth day of March one thousand eight hundred and eighty-five between the Reverend Solomon Caesar Malan of Balliol College, Doctor of Divinity, Vicar of Broadwindsor in the County of Dorset of the one part and the Chancellor, Masters, and Scholars of the University of Oxford of the other part are varied as hereinafter in this statute provided.

As from the date on which this statute comes into operation, clause 1 of the said indenture shall be read and have effect as if the words 'upon the trusts' had been originally inserted therein in lieu of the words 'upon trust for the purpose of the Indian Institute within the University of Oxford'.

As from the date on which this statute comes into operation clause 2, including sub-clauses (i), (ii), (iii), (iv), (v), (vi), and (vii) of clause 2, of the said indenture and every part of the said clause and subclauses are hereby repealed and shall cease to have any force or effect.

As from the date on which this statute comes into operation, the said indenture shall be read and have effect as if the following clause had been originally inserted therein in lieu of the said clause 2.

(2) The said Chancellor, Masters, and Scholars, hereby covenant and agree with the said Solomon Caesar Malan that they the said Chancellor, Masters, and Scholars will hold the said library of books and all other books that may be hereafter added thereto by the said Solomon Caesar Malan upon trust subject to the following conditions:

(i) The said books shall be placed in the Indian Institute or elsewhere under the charge of the Curators of the Bodleian Library and shall be kept and used in accordance with the rules and regulations of the Bodleian Library.

(ii) An inscription commemorating the benefaction of the Reverend Solomon Caesar Malan shall be placed in the Library of the Indian Institute.

Section XXVI. Of the King Charles I Foundation

The assets of the King Charles I Foundation shall be distributed equally between Exeter, Jesus, and Pembroke Colleges for them to hold and to apply the income arising therefrom in the same ways as they have hitherto applied the income received by them from the University.

Section XXVII. Of the Rawnsley Studentships

1. The studentships established under the bequest of the late Miss Hilda Mary Virtue-Tebbs shall be named 'Rawnsley Studentships' after the late Flight-Lieutenant Derek Rawnsley, R.A.F., who died in February 1942.

2. The studentships shall be tenable at St. Hugh's College for the study of the Czech or the Polish language and literature by Czech or Polish nationals or, should a suitable Czech or Polish national not be available, by some other person whose qualifications are considered suitable, or for the study of the English language and literature by Czech or Polish nationals.

3. The studentships shall be tenable at St. Hugh's College and shall be administered by the governing body of that college under the general control of the University.

4. The Governing Body of St. Hugh's College shall make regulations for the award of the studentships and shall have power from time to time to amend the regulations provided that the conditions prescribed by the testatrix in her will are always adhered to (save only that the studentships may also be held by Czech or Polish nationals wishing to study the English language and literature).

5. The Curators of the University Chest shall have control of the investments of the trust fund and shall place the income at the disposal of the Governing Body of St. Hugh's College.

6. The term 'Czech national' shall include any national of either the Czech Republic or the Slovak Republic and the term 'Czech language and literature' shall include all the languages and literatures of the Czech Republic and the Slovak Republic.

7. Congregation shall have power from time to time to alter this statute, subject to the consent of the Governing Body of St Hugh's College and provided that the main object of the founder (namely the establishment of Rawnsley Studentships, tenable at St Hugh's College, for the purposes defined in clause 2 above) is always kept in view.

Section XXVIII. Of the Eldon Law Scholarship Fund

1. The Eldon Law Scholarship Fund shall be administered by the Board of the Faculty of Law.

2. After payment of any expenses of administration the net income of the Eldon Law Scholarship Fund, shall be applied by the board in maintaining scholarships, to be called 'Eldon Law Scholarships', which may consist of single payments, or of not more than three annual payments, which may be of varying amounts, as the board shall determine in each case.

3. The following persons only shall be eligible to receive Eldon Law Scholarships, namely those members of the University of Oxford who:

(*a*) shall have passed their examination for the Degree of Bachelor of Arts or for the Degree of Bachelor of Civil Law or for the Degree of Magister Juris in European and Comparative Law; and

(*b*) shall have been placed in the First Class in one or other of the said examinations or in Honour Moderations or shall have gained one of the Chancellor's Prizes; and

(*c*) shall intend to follow the profession of the law; and

(*d*) shall have applied for one of the said scholarships either before, or within two years next following, the date of their call to the Bar.

Provided that in awarding the said scholarships the board shall take into account the financial circumstances of the applicants.

4. Within the limits prescribed by this statute, the board shall have full power to make rules for the award of the said scholarships, including rules as to the value and period of tenure of the awards, and the qualifications, and method of ascertainment and selection, of beneficiaries.

Section XXIX. Of the Reader in Transport Studies

1. The sums generously contributed between 1958 and 1968 by the Chartered Institute of Transport acting on behalf of the contributors shall be applied to the establishment and maintenance of a Readership in Transport Studies and the promotion of transport studies in the University under the arrangements set out below.

2. The first charge on the income of the endowment shall be the cost of the readership. Such part of the income of the endowment in any year which shall exceed the cost of the readership shall be carried to a separate fund which shall be known as the Transport Studies Fund and which shall be applied under such conditions as may be laid down by decree for the support of the work of the reader and for the encouragement and advancement of Transport Studies in the University. During any vacancy in the readership the whole of the income of the endowment shall be paid into the fund.

3. The duties of the reader, provided always that these shall be consistent with the primary purpose of the endowment to promote the study of transport in the University, and the manner of his election shall be determined by decree.

Section XXX. Of the Johnson University Prizeman

That moiety of the proceeds arising from Dr. Johnson's bequest which is appropriated to the promotion of mathematical studies shall be given annually in money to the Senior University Mathematical Prizeman (which prize shall be awarded under conditions laid down by decree), who shall be called 'The Johnson University Prizeman'.

Section XXXI. Of the John Wilfred Jenkinson Memorial Lecturership

1. A lecturership shall be established and maintained in the University of Oxford to be called the John Wilfred Jenkinson Memorial Lecturership.

2. One or more lecturers shall be appointed in each year. Each lecturer shall hold office for one year and shall be re-eligible. He shall deliver one or more lectures or lecture demonstrations on comparative or experimental embryology.

3. Lectures given by the lecturers shall be open to all members of the University without fee.

4. The lecturers shall receive such stipend as the board of management shall from time to time determine.

5. The lecturers shall be elected by an electoral board consisting of:

(1) the Vice-Chancellor;

(2) the Rector of Exeter College;

(3) the Regius Professor of Medicine;

(4) the Linacre Professor of Zoology;

(5) the Waynflete Professor of Physiology;

(6) Dr. Lee's Professor of Anatomy;

(7) a member of the Board of the Faculty of Biological Sciences elected by that board to hold office for five years.

6. The board of electors shall be the board of management for the revenues arising from the bequest. Any income in excess of the sum required in each year for the payment of the stipend of the lecturers, and after the payment of the necessary costs of administration, may be applied by the board in one or more of the following ways:

(*a*) for the payment of travelling expenses incurred by the lecturers;

(*b*) towards the cost of the publication of the lectures;

(*c*) towards the making of grants for research, or for the maintenance of those engaged on research, on comparative or experimental embryology of animals to be carried out in the Department of Zoology under the direction of the Linacre Professor of Zoology;

(*d*) carried forward for use in a subsequent year;

(*e*) invested in augmentation of capital.

Section XXXII. Of the Newdigate Prize

1. The examiners for the Newdigate Prize shall be the Professor of Poetry and the two members of Convocation appointed by the Vice-Chancellor and Proctors as examiners for the Chancellor's English Essay Prize. If in any year the office of Professor of Poetry is vacant or if the Professor is unable to act, the Vice-Chancellor and Proctors shall appoint another member of Convocation to act as examiner in his place. No examiner shall vote on any candidate's merits except at a meeting of the examiners.

2. The prize shall be open to women on the same terms as to men.

3. A copy of the winning entry shall be deposited in the Bodleian Library.

4. The income of the Newdigate Fund shall be divided equally between the prize and the Master of University College, who shall use his share towards the maintenance of the Master's Lodgings. In any year in which the prize is not awarded, the half of the income due to the prize shall be placed into a Reserve Fund, and the income of the Reserve Fund in that year shall be added to the Reserve Fund. The winner of the prize in each year shall receive half of the income of the main fund in that year together with the income of the Reserve Fund in that year.

Section XXXIII. Ford's Lecturer in British History

1. Ford's Lecturer in British History shall hold office for one year, and no lecturer shall be re-eligible until four years have elapsed from his or her appointment.

2. The lecturer shall deliver not less than six lectures on British History, and these lectures shall be delivered either in Michaelmas or in Hilary Term, or partly in the one and partly in the other.

3. The lecturer shall be elected by a board of seven electors, consisting of:

(1) the Vice-Chancellor;

(2)–(4) three persons appointed by Council;

(5)–(7) three persons appointed by the Board of the Faculty of Modern History.

Each of the appointed electors shall hold office for three years, and shall be re-eligible; and one elector in each division shall vacate office every year.

4. The lecturer shall receive from the revenues of the Ford Bequest, on completion of his or her course of lectures, £600 or such larger sum as the board of electors, with the approval of Council, shall determine.

5. The board of electors shall make an election to the lecturership at any time up to three years before the lecturer shall take up office.

6. Candidates for election to the office of lecturer shall send in their names, together with the subject of the lectures which they propose to deliver, and with any further explanation which they may think fit to offer, to the Registrar not later than the first day of November in each year; and the Registrar shall forward the applications without delay to the Vice-Chancellor. But the choice of the electors shall not be necessarily limited to such candidates.

7. No member of the board of electors shall be eligible for the office of lecturer. On the occurrence of a vacancy on the board of electors the Registrar shall notify the vacancy to Council or to the Board of the Faculty of Modern History, as the case shall be; and Council or the board shall fill up the vacancy as soon as may be.

8. The board of electors aforesaid shall be the board of management for the revenues arising from the Ford Bequest. Any income in excess of the sum required in each year for the payment of the stipend of the lecturer may be used by the board at its discretion in one or more of the following ways:

(i) for the payment of travelling expenses incurred by the lecturer for that or for any subsequent year;

(ii) for the payment of expenses incidental to the delivery of the lectures;

(iii) for the payment of expenses incurred in connection with the entertainment of the lecturer;

(iv) for the payment in any year of one or more James Ford Special Lecturers, each to deliver a single lecture on some aspect of British History, for which he or she shall receive a fee of up to £100, or such larger sum as the board of electors, with the approval of Council, shall determine, together with reimbursement of the travelling and other incidental expenses incurred in connection with the delivery of the lecture, and the payment of expenses incurred in connection with the entertainment of the Special Lecturer;

(v) for such other means of support for the teaching of British History in the University as the board of electors shall from time to time determine.

9. Any income not expended in accordance with the provisions of the preceding clauses of this section shall be carried forward for expenditure in a subsequent year.

Section XXXIV. Winter Williams Prizes and Studentships

1. The fund for the Winter Williams University Law Prize for Undergraduates and the fund for the Winter Williams Law Prize for Women Undergraduates, established by Ivy Williams, B.C.L., M.A., Society of Oxford Home-Students (now St. Anne's College), to found awards in Jurisprudence in memory of Winter Williams, late of Corpus Christi College, shall be combined to form a single fund, to be called the Winter Williams Fund. The fund shall be administered by the Board of the Faculty of Law.

2. There shall be two prizes, the First Winter Williams Law Prize and the Second Winter Williams Law Prize. The value of each prize shall be such sum as the board shall previously determine, provided that

(*a*) the value of the second prize shall always be less than the value of the first prize; and

(*b*) the combined value of the two prizes shall not exceed the income of the fund (after meeting all expenses of administration and examination) in the financial year immediately preceding the award.

3. The board may at its discretion award grants to unsuccessful candidates who have done meritorious work, provided that the total value of such grants made in any year shall not exceed £100, or the balance of income as defined in clause 2 (*b*) after payment of the prizes, whichever shall be less.

4. Candidates for the prizes shall be undergraduate members of the University who have not exceeded (at the time fixed for the submission of entries) the tenth term from matriculation and who are reading for the Honour School of Jurisprudence.

5. The prizes shall be awarded by the board, on the recommendation of the examiners, the First Prize to the candidate who shall be adjudged to have submitted the best and the Second Prize to the candidate who shall be adjudged to have submitted the second-best essay, of not more than 5,000 words, on any one among the topics which the board shall have selected for the purpose. The board shall make such selection at its second meeting in each Michaelmas Term for competition in the following year. Candidates shall send their essays to the Registrar in time to be received by the last day of September. No prize shall be awarded unless there shall be a candidate of sufficient merit.

6. The board shall appoint examiners in such number and on such terms as it shall see fit.

7. The board may from time to time use surplus income for either or both of the following purposes:

(*a*) to award a studentship, to be called the Winter Williams Studentship, tenable by any graduate citizen of any Commonwealth country overseas while reading in the University for a degree in Law of the University, other than the Degree of Bachelor of Arts;

(*b*) to make grants to students who are reading in the University for a degree in Law of the University, other than the Degree of Bachelor of Arts, and who are in need of financial assistance.

In this clause 'surplus income' shall mean income unexpended in any financial year after payment of any prizes and grants as defined in clauses 2 and 3 and all expenses of administration and examination, together with any such income carried forward from previous years.

8. This statute may be amended from time to time by Congregation, provided that the main object, namely encouragement of the study of law at the University, is always kept in view.

Section XXXV. Of the Charles Oldham Shakespeare Prize

1. The prize shall be awarded, if a suitable candidate presents himself, after an examination in the knowledge of Shakespeare, on such conditions as the Board of the Faculty of English Language and Literature may determine.

2. The Board of the Faculty of English Language and Literature shall be the Board of Management of the prize.

3. All expenses incurred in connection with the award of the prize, including examiners' fees and expenses of administration, shall be met from the annual income arising from that moiety of Mr. Charles Oldham's bequest which was set aside for the establishment of a prize in the knowledge of Shakespeare's works.

4. The board shall from time to time determine how many examiners are required and shall appoint examiners each year. The examiners shall receive such remuneration as the board shall direct.

5. The examination shall be conducted, after not less than one month's notice, at such time and place as the board may determine. The subjects of examination shall be fixed from time to time by the board.

6. The value of the prize shall be fixed from time to time by the board and shall be announced at the same time as the subjects of examination.

7. The prize shall in no case be awarded to the same person a second time.

8. Any income of the fund not required for the prize or for meeting the expenses of the examination shall be applied by the board for any of the following purposes:

(i) the augmentation of the capital of the fund;

(ii) the award in any year, on the recommendation of the examiners, of an additional prize or additional prizes, of a value to be determined by the board when making the award;

(iii) any other purpose consistent with the main object of the bequest as defined in cl. 10.

9. All income in hand on the day on which this statute is passed (including that now in the Accumulations Fund) may be spent in accordance with the terms of this statute.

10. In any change of statute the main object of the bequest shall always be kept in view, namely the encouragement and promotion of the knowledge of William Shakespeare's works among members of the University.

Section XXXVI. Of the Matthew Arnold Memorial Prize

1. The prize shall be called the Matthew Arnold Memorial Prize, and shall be awarded annually, if a candidate of sufficient merit presents himself, for an English essay upon some subject connected with English Literature.

2. The Board of the Faculty of English Language and Literature shall be the Board of Management of the prize.

3. All expenses incurred in connection with the award of the prize, including examiners' fees and any expenses of administration, shall be met from the annual income from the trust.

4. The examiner or examiners shall be appointed by the board, and shall receive such remuneration as the board shall direct.

5. The value of the prize shall be fixed from time to time by the board and shall be announced at the same time as the subject of the essay.

6. The subject of the essay shall be set by the board and shall be announced not later than the last day of Trinity Full Term, and the competing essays shall be sent in to the Registrar on or before the first day of the following March.

7. The candidates must be members of the University, whether men or women, who, on the day appointed for sending in the essay, have qualified by examination for the degree of B.A. and have not exceeded seven years from their matriculation, or have qualified by examination for any other degree of the University and have not exceeded four years from their matriculation, or, not being graduates of the University, are pursuing a course of study leading to a postgraduate degree of the University and have not exceeded three years from their matriculation.

8. The prize shall in no case be awarded to the same person a second time.

9. Surplus income arising from vacancies or from any other cause may at the discretion of the board be applied for any of the following purposes:

(i) the augmentation of the capital of the fund;

(ii) the award in any year, on the recommendation of the examiner or examiners, of an additional prize or additional prizes, of a value to be determined by the board when making the award;

(iii) any other purpose consistent with the main object of the bequest as defined in cl. 10.

10. In any change of statute the main object of the bequest shall always be kept in view, namely the encouragement and promotion of the study of English Literature among members of the University.

Section XXXVII. Of the Fortnum Trusts and Parker's Benefaction

1. The whole of the income of the Fortnum Trusts and of Parker's Benefaction shall be put at the disposal of the Visitors of the Ashmolean Museum to be applied towards the maintenance and increase of the Ashmolean collections.

2. This statute shall first have effect in the financial year ending 31 July 1972.

Section XXXVIII. Of the Egerton Coghill Landscape Prize

1. The prize shall be called 'The Egerton Coghill Landscape Prize' in memory of the donor's father.

2. The prize shall be competed for annually by members of the University who are reading for any degree, diploma, or certificate of the University and by students of the Ruskin School of Drawing and of Fine Art.

3. Only landscape paintings in oils painted during the preceding twelve months of some four square feet in area shall be admissible as entries. No competitor shall submit more than one entry for any one competition. The winner of the prize in any one year shall not be eligible to compete in any subsequent year.

4. The competition shall be announced according to University custom in the *Calendar* and *Gazette*, and shall be judged by the Ruskin Master of Drawing (or a deputy appointed by him) and the Keeper of the Department of Western Art (or a deputy appointed by him) for the time being.

5. The annual income from the prize fund shall be divided as to one-fifth for each of the judges for the year in question as their fees for judging the competition and as to three-fifths for the winner, provided nevertheless that if in any year in the opinion of the judges no competitor shall submit an entry of sufficient quality to win the competition they shall declare that no competitor shall have won the competition, and the three-fifths share of the income which would have been paid to a winner in that year shall be added to the capital of the prize fund. If in any year there are no entries for the prize, the whole of the income for that year shall be added to the capital of the prize fund.

6. The winning entry shall be displayed in some prominent position during Commemoration Week or any other suitable occasion.

7. Provided that the main intention of the donor (namely, the establishment of a landscape painting prize for members of the University reading for any degree, diploma, or certificate and for students of the Ruskin School of Drawing and of Fine Art) is kept in view, Congregation may from time to time make such modifications of this statute as may in its opinion be necessary or desirable.

Section XXXIX. Rhodes Readership in the Laws of the British Commonwealth and the United States

1. There shall be a Rhodes Readership in the Laws of the British Commonwealth and the United States.

2. The reader shall lecture and give instruction in those laws on such conditions as the General Board shall from time to time determine.

3. The reader shall be elected by a board consisting of:

(1) the Vice-Chancellor;

(2) a person appointed by Council;

(3) a person appointed by the General Board;

(4)–(7) four persons appointed by the Board of the Faculty of Law.

4. The Rhodes Fund for the study of Roman-Dutch Law shall be transferred to the support of the Readership in the Laws of the British Commonwealth and the United States. The income of the fund shall be applied towards the cost of the readership, provided that any balance of the travel fund established by Decree (16) of 11 March 1958, including accrued interest, may be paid to the reader as a contribution to his expenses on visiting any part of the British Commonwealth or of the United States in connection with his duties under this statute.

5. This statute may be amended from time to time by Congregation provided that the main object, namely the encouragement of the study of the laws of the British Commonwealth and the United States, is always kept in view.

Section XL. The Gaisford Fund

1. The income of the fund established in memory of the late Dr. Thomas Gaisford, Dean of Christ Church and Regius Professor of Greek, shall be applied for the advancement of classical learning in the University of Oxford.

2. There shall be a board of management for the fund consisting of

(1) the Regius Professor of Greek

(2) and (3) two members of the Sub-faculty of Classical Languages and Literature elected by the Board of the Faculty of Literae Humaniores to hold office for a period of three years.

3. The board of management shall elect annually a lecturer, to be known as the Gaisford Lecturer, to hold office for one academic year in the course of which he shall deliver one lecture on a subject of his own choosing in the field of Greek or Latin Literature. The lecture shall normally be delivered in Trinity Term unless the board of management decides otherwise.

4. The board of management shall determine the emoluments of the lecturer, and provision for his travelling expenses, for payment from the Gaisford Fund.

5. The board of management shall offer the following annual prizes of such value and on such terms and conditions as it shall from time to time determine:

(*a*) a Gaisford Essay Prize for Greek Language and Literature (for which only undergraduates shall be eligible);

(*b*) a Gaisford Dissertation Prize for Greek or Latin Language and Literature (for which only graduates shall be eligible).

6. Any income not used to pay either the emoluments and expenses of the Gaisford Lecturer or the cost of the Gaisford Prizes and the remuneration of judges may at the discretion of the board of management:

(*a*) be carried forward for use in a subsequent year; or

(*b*) be applied in any other way which the board of management shall think conducive to the promotion of classical learning in the University of Oxford.

7. This statute may be amended from time to time by Congregation on the recommendation of the Board of the Faculty of Literae Humaniores provided that the main object of the fund, namely the encouragement of classical learning, is always kept in view.

Section XLI. Of the English Poem on a Sacred Subject

1. The prize for an English poem on a sacred subject shall be offered for competition once in every three years.

2. The candidates shall be members of the University who, not later than the closing date for entries for the competition, which shall be specified when the subject is announced, shall have qualified by examination for a degree of the University, or shall hold the Degree of Master of Arts by incorporation or by

decree or resolution or shall hold the status of Master of Arts, or shall have qualified by examination for a degree of any other university.

3. No person to whom the prize has been twice awarded shall be a candidate.

4. The judges shall be the Professor of Poetry, the Public Orator, and a third judge, who shall be appointed by them, and who shall be a Master of Arts, or Bachelor of Civil Law, or Bachelor of Medicine, or a graduate of superior rank.

5. The subject or subjects for the poems for a particular competition shall be selected by the judges who adjudicated the last preceding competition, and shall be announced by them, together with the kind of poem prescribed and any other conditions prescribed by them, at least two years before the closing date for the competition. No composition for the prize shall be less than sixty, nor more than three hundred, lines in length.

6. The judges shall award the prize to the candidate whose composition they adjudge the best, provided they adjudge it of sufficient merit, and the prize shall consist of three years' income after the deduction of the judges' honoraria, the value of any award made under clause 7 below, and all other proper expenses.

7. The judges are empowered to nominate a candidate as *proxime accessit* who, at the judges' discretion, may be awarded such sum, not exceeding one-sixth of the three years' income available for that year's prize, as they shall determine. Such a nomination may only be made if the candidate's entry is of a quality which would have qualified it for the award of the main prize had not a better entry been received.

8. Copies of the successful composition shall be sent by the author to the Chancellor, heads of colleges and other societies, the two Proctors, the Assessor, the judges of the compositions, the professors in the Faculties of English Language and Literature and of Theology, the Secretary of Faculties (ten copies), and the Bodleian Library.

9. The judges shall receive honoraria, together with all proper expenses, to be paid out of the income of the fund, of such amounts as the General Board shall from time to time determine.

10. Any surplus income shall be applied towards such purpose or purposes for the encouragement of religion or literature among members of the University as the General Board shall determine after consultation with the Boards of the Faculties of English Language and Literature, and of Theology.

11. This statute may be amended from time to time by Congregation provided that the main object of the fund, the maintenance of a prize competition for an English poem on a sacred subject, is always kept in view.

Section XLII. Of the E. K. Chambers Studentships

1. The fund derived from the bequest of the residue of the estate of the late Lady Chambers shall continue to be invested and the income used for the maintenance of studentships in English Literature known as the E. K. Chambers

Studentships, which shall be tenable either concurrently or alternatively as funds may permit at Corpus Christi College and Somerville College by persons of good classical attainments who have graduated from a university in the British Isles with an honours degree in a subject other than ('single honours') English.

2. The fund shall be administered by a board of management consisting of:

(1) the Vice-Chancellor;

(2) the Regius Professor of Greek;

(3) the Merton Professor of English Literature;

(4) the President of Corpus Christi College;

(5) the Principal of Somerville College;

(6) a person nominated by the Governing Body of Corpus Christi College;

(7) a person nominated by the Governing Body of Somerville College.

3. Congregation shall have power from time to time to amend the provisions of clause 2 above.

Section XLIII. Of the Horatio Symonds Studentship in Surgery

1. The studentship founded under the terms of the bequest of Miss Anne Harrison Symonds shall be called 'The Horatio Symonds Studentship in Surgery'.

2. The electors to the studentship shall be:

(1) the Regius Professor of Medicine;

(2) the Nuffield Professor of Surgery;

(3) Dr. Lee's Professor of Anatomy.

3. Candidates for the studentship must be suitably qualified graduates who intend to reside in the University and to undertake postgraduate study in the science and art of Surgery.

4. The studentship shall be offered from time to time as the electors may determine (provided that it shall be offered at least once in any period of two years during which there is a vacancy in the studentship) and shall be awarded, unless no candidates of sufficient merit present themselves, either after examination or upon consideration of the past records of the candidates and of the programmes of work proposed by them. The studentship shall be tenable for such period not exceeding five years, and shall be of such value, as the electors may determine.

5. The electors shall have power to deprive any student of his studentship or of any part of the emoluments thereof on account of his idleness, misconduct, or failure to comply with this statute.

6. The first charge on the annual income of the fund shall be the necessary expenses of its administration, and the payment of any examiners who may be appointed under clause 4 above. The remainder of such income shall be applied to the emoluments of the studentship, provided that any surplus income shall be carried forward for use in subsequent years.

7. This statute may be amended from time to time by Congregation on the recommendation of the electors provided that the main object of the fund, namely the maintenance of a postgraduate studentship in Surgery, is always kept in view.

Section XLIV. Of the Thomas Whitcombe Greene Bequest

1. The annual income of the Thomas Whitcombe Greene Bequest shall be applied, in the first instance, to the maintenance of a prize and one or more postgraduate scholarships for Classical Art and Archaeology.

2. The prize and scholarships shall be awarded by a committee (hereinafter termed 'the committee') consisting of the Lincoln Professor of Classical Archaeology and Art together with five persons appointed by the Board of the Faculty of Literae Humaniores.

3. The prize shall be called the Thomas Whitcombe Greene Prize and shall be open to members of the University who are reading for an honour school in the University. The value of the prize shall be determined by the Board of the Faculty of Literae Humaniores, and the prize shall be offered annually. If there is no candidate of sufficient merit it shall not be awarded. The prize shall not be awarded a second time to the same person.

4. The scholarships shall be called the Thomas Whitcombe Greene Scholarships and shall be open to members of the University who are engaged in advanced research, subject to any further conditions which the Board of the Faculty of Literae Humaniores may prescribe, provided always that if an undergraduate is elected to a scholarship the election shall be conditional on his proceeding to a degree in the University before he receives any part of the emoluments. The value of the scholarships shall be determined by the Board of the Faculty of Literae Humaniores.

5. The committee shall determine the conditions of award of the prize and scholarship, and of the tenure of the scholarship, and there shall be defrayed from the income of the bequest any expenses incidental to the carrying out of its purposes, including the remuneration of examiners (if any).

6. Any balance of income, so far as not required for the purposes aforesaid, may either be carried forward for expenditure in subsequent years, or, if the committee so determines, be applied to one or more of the following:

(*a*) to the provision of occasional additional prizes or scholarships; or

(*b*) to the maintenance of a foundation to be known as the 'Thomas Whitcombe Greene Reserve Fund', which shall be applied by the committee to furnish grants to members of the University for the furtherance of the study of Classical Art and Archaeology, or to institutions connected with those subjects; or

(*c*) to the foundation of an additional scholarship or scholarships.

7. This statute may be amended from time to time by Congregation on the recommendation of the Board of the Faculty of Literae Humaniores provided

that the main object of the founder shall always be kept in view, namely, the foundation of a prize for Classical Art and Archaeology and the foundation of postgraduate scholarships for advanced research.

Section XLV. Of the Prendergast Fund

1. The bequest of the residue of the estate of the late Dr. J. S. Prendergast shall be used:

(*a*) for the creation of two bursaries to be held by members of the Order of St. Benedict belonging to Glenstal Abbey, Murroe, County Limerick, while they pursue their studies at St. Benet's Hall, the maximum value of such bursaries to be set by the board of management for the bequest at its discretion, and

(*b*) to assist persons born in the Republic of Ireland whose parents are citizens of the Republic of Ireland to proceed to the University of Oxford for the purpose of either taking their degrees or undergoing postgraduate courses.

2. The bequest shall be administered by a board of management of which the constitution shall be determined by Council.

Section XLVI. Of the Stanhope Studentship in Modern History

1. The Stanhope Fund, accepted by the University in 1855 from Philip Henry, fifth Earl of Stanhope, shall, after payment of any charges for administration, be used to maintain a studentship, to be called the Stanhope Studentship in Modern History.

2. The studentship shall be subject to the same administration and terms as the Marquis of Lothian's Studentship in Modern History, as laid down in Tit. XV, Sect. XX, cll. 2–4.

3. Congregation may from time to time alter, and Council may by decree dispense from, any of the foregoing provisions, provided that the fund shall always be employed for the encouragement of the study of Modern History and in memory of the founder.

Section XLVII. Of the Abbott Fund

1. The assets from time to time representing Mr. John Abbott's bequest, accepted by the University in 1871, shall constitute a fund known as the Abbott Fund.

2. The fund shall be administered by a board of management of which the constitution shall be determined by Council.

3. The board shall from time to time apply the income of the fund in making awards, to be known as Abbott's Bursaries, for the support of members of the University who are children (including orphan children) of the clergy of the Church of England, and who are:

(*a*) reading for (i) a first degree, or (ii) the Degree of Bachelor of Medicine or an equivalent degree, or (iii) a second Honour School, of the University; and (*b*) standing in need of financial assistance to enable them to obtain the full benefit of a university education.

4. The board shall, subject to the approval of Council, determine from time to time the conditions of award of the bursaries, and their several value and tenure, and the eligibility of candidates, provided that:

(*a*) the bursaries shall be awarded in such a way as to give encouragement to learning, and

(*b*) if two or more candidates show equal proficiency, preference shall be given to candidates who establish that they were born in the area of the former West Riding of Yorkshire.

Section XLVIII. Of the Montague Burton Professorship of International Relations

1. The Montague Burton Professor of International Relations shall lecture and give instruction on the theory and practice of International Relations.

2. The professor shall be elected by an electoral board consisting of:

(1) the Vice-Chancellor, or, if the Master of Balliol College is Vice-Chancellor, a person appointed by Council on the occurrence of a vacancy to act as an elector on that occasion;

(2) the Master of Balliol College, or, if he is unable or unwilling to act, a person appointed by the Governing Body of Balliol College on the occurrence of a vacancy to act as an elector on that occasion;

(3) a person appointed by the Governing Body of Balliol College;

(4) a person appointed by Council;

(5) a person appointed by the General Board;

(6), (7) two persons elected by the Board of the Faculty of Social Studies;

(8) a person elected by the Board of the Faculty of Modern History.

3. The professor shall be subject to the General Provisions of the decree concerning the duties of professors and to those Particular Provisions of the same decree which are applicable to his chair.

4. The income of the endowment received by the University from the late Sir Montague Burton shall be applied, in proportions and on conditions to be determined from time to time by the General Board of the Faculties, in consultation with the Board of the Faculty of Social Studies, primarily towards the costs (including support costs) of the professorship, and, subject to this, to the general advancement of the study of International Relations.

5. This statute may be amended from time to time by Congregation provided that the main object of the benefactor, namely the maintenance of the professorship, is always kept in view.

Section XLIX. Of the Hensley Henson Fund

1. The income of the bequest by the late Bishop Herbert Hensley Henson, D.D., Honorary Fellow of All Souls College, shall be used to support an annual lecturership for the delivery by an Ordained Minister of the Episcopal Church of England, the Presbyterian Church of Scotland, or the Church of Sweden, of not less than four or more than six lectures in the University of Oxford, under arrangements to be determined by the Board of the Faculty of Theology, upon the subject of 'The Appeal to History as an integral part of Christian apologetics'.

2. Any balance of income not required for the lecturership may at the discretion of the Board of the Faculty of Theology be applied in furtherance of the study of Theology in the University.

Section L. Of the Sibthorpian Professorship of Plant Science

1. The Sibthorpian Professor of Plant Science shall lecture and give instruction in Plant Science.

2. The professor shall be elected by an electoral board consisting of:

(1) the Vice-Chancellor, or, if the President of St. John's College is Vice-Chancellor, a person appointed by Council on the occurrence of a vacancy to act as an elector on that occasion;

(2) the President of St. John's College, or, if he is unable or unwilling to act, a person appointed by the Governing Body of St. John's College on the occurrence of a vacancy to act as an elector on that occasion.

(3) a person appointed by the Governing Body of St. John's College;

(4) a person appointed by Council;

(5) a person appointed by the General Board;

(6), (7) two persons appointed by the Board of the Faculty of Biological Sciences.

3. The professor shall be subject to the General Provisions of the decree concerning the duties of professors and to those Particular Provisions of the same decree which are applicable to his chair.

4. Accommodation shall be assigned for the use of the Sibthorpian Professor of Plant Science, as the place in which the books now belonging to the Sibthorpian Library, or hereafter to be purchased out of the Sibthorpian Benefaction, shall be preserved, provided that such of the books, belonging to the Sibthorpian Library and now being in the Library of the Department of Plant Sciences, as the Sibthorpian Professor shall think fit shall continue to be preserved in such last-mentioned library until Council shall make further order by decree.

5. Congregation shall have power from time to time to amend the provisions of cll. 2 and 3 above.

Section LI. Of the Glasstone Benefaction

1. The assets of the trust established by Professor Samuel Glasstone, the trusteeship of which was accepted by the University in 1971, together with the accumulated income thereof and the further assets added thereto in accordance with the provisions of Professor Glasstone's Will, shall constitute the Glasstone Benefaction.

2. The benefaction shall be divided into two equal funds which shall be known respectively as the Glasstone Fund for Men and the Glasstone Fund for Women. The net income arising from each fund shall be used for the establishment of fellowships for research in the University in the fields of Botany, Chemistry (Inorganic, Organic, or Physical), Engineering, Mathematics, Metallurgy, and Physics. The fund for men shall support fellowships open only to men candidates, and the fund for women shall support fellowships open only to women candidates.

3. The fellowships shall be in memory of Professor Glasstone and his wife, Violette Glasstone, and shall be named the Violette and Samuel Glasstone Research Fellowships in Science; and the recipients of the fellowships shall be given a statement describing the identities and interests of the said Violette and Samuel Glasstone.

4. The fellowships shall not be restricted to graduates of the University, nor shall there be any age limit for recipients of the fellowships.

5. The fellowships shall be awarded from time to time by the University in accordance with arrangements approved by Council, and shall be tenable at the University. They shall be awarded for a period of one year, but with the possibility of annual renewal for up to two further years at the absolute discretion of the body or persons responsible for the award of the fellowship or fellowships in question.

6. Income not used in any year in support of current fellowships shall be carried forward for use in a subsequent year.

Section LII. Of the Mike Soper Bursary Fund

1. The Mike Soper Bursary Fund, established to commemorate on his retirement the services of Mr M. H. R. Soper to the University and to Agriculture, and including a gift from Messrs Heygate and Sons Ltd, shall be applied in the award of travel bursaries to members of the University who, at the time of making application, are studying biological sciences within the University, preference being given to those whose studies relate to agriculture, forestry, or some other use of rural land.

2. The first charge on the net income of the fund shall be the award of bursaries to undergraduates to enable them to pursue their studies outside Oxford in a scientific, economic, or practical context.

3. The fund shall be administered in accordance with arrangements determined by Council.

4. Congregation may from time to time amend this statute, provided that the main object of the fund, as defined in clause 1 above, is always maintained.

Section LIII. Of the Travel Fund for the Economics of Developing Countries

1. The fund which was created by the benefaction for the study of Colonial Affairs accepted by the University in 1943 from the United Africa Company, and held as an earmarked part of the Higher Studies Fund, shall be used to support travel for the purposes of the study of the economics of developing countries (broadly conceived) through grants awarded to the holders of established academic posts within the University.

2. Subject always to the agreement of the Trustees of the Higher Studies Fund,[1] the travel fund shall be administered under such arrangements as shall be approved from time to time by Council by decree.

Section LIV. Of the Bagby Bequest

1. The bequest by Mr. Philip H. Bagby of the residue of his estate shall be used, as to either income or principal, in such manner as shall seem to the authorised officers of the University best to encourage within the appropriate department or departments of the University the comparative study of the development of urban, literate cultures in accordance with anthropological principles and methods.

2. The authorised officers for the purpose of administering the bequest shall be the Board of the Faculty of Anthropology and Geography on the recommendation of the Professor of Social Anthropology.

3. The appropriate department of the University for the purpose of study under the terms of the bequest shall be the Institute of Social and Cultural Anthropology.

4. Congregation may from time to time amend this statute, provided that the main object of the bequest, as defined in clause 1 above, is always maintained.

Section LV. Of the Levens Travel Bursary

1. The award established under a gift under covenant from R.G.C. Levens, M.A., Fellow of Merton College, of £150 a year net for seven years together with other contributions from relatives and friends shall be used to maintain, in memory of his son Andrew Levens, a travel bursary to assist members of the University whose course of study includes Russian (whether in the Honour School of Modern Languages or otherwise) to visit an area which is predominantly Russian-speaking and which was formerly included in the Soviet

[1] See Special Resolution of Congregation of 28 January 1992 (*Gazette*, Vol. 122, p. 648).

Union (or, if travel to such an area is impracticable, to assist students of two languages, of which Russian is one, to travel to a country in which the other language is spoken), which shall be called the Andrew Levens Travel Bursary.

2. The bursary shall be administered by the Board of the Faculty of Medieval and Modern Languages, which shall have power, subject to the conditions of this statute, to make regulations as to the award and the tenure of the bursary.

3. Surplus income arising from whatever cause shall be carried forward for expenditure in future years.

4. Congregation may from time to time amend this statute, provided that the main intention of the founder is always kept in view.

Section LVI. Of the Osgood Memorial Prize

1. The prize established from a benefaction by Mrs. June Osgood, with a view to encouraging composition in some form of Chamber Music, and research in the history and aesthetics of Music, shall be called the John Lowell Osgood Memorial Prize, and shall be offered every year; it shall be offered alternately for a composition in some form of Chamber Music and for a dissertation involving serious research on some subject, approved by the Heather Professor of Music, dealing with Music from the historical or the aesthetic aspect, provided that such dissertation as a whole has not yet been, nor is about to be, submitted for a degree of this or any other university.

2. The prize shall be administered by the Board of the Faculty of Music, which shall have power, subject to the conditions of this statute, to make regulations as to the award of the prize and as to the appointment and remuneration of the judges.

3. Any surplus income may be used, at the discretion of the Board of the Faculty of Music, either to assist successful candidates in publishing their dissertations or compositions or for any other purpose connected with the advancement of the study of Music at Oxford approved by the board and not inconsistent with the encouragement of composition in some form of Chamber Music or research in the history and aesthetics of Music.

4. This statute may be amended from time to time by Congregation, provided that the main object of the benefactor, the encouragement of composition in some form of Chamber Music, and research in the history and aesthetics of Music, is always kept in view.

Section LVII. Of the Marjory Wardrop Fund

1. The fund shall be called the 'Marjory Wardrop Fund'.

2. There shall be a board of management, which shall be charged with the application of the income arising from the fund and from the investment of any gifts or bequests in augmentation of that fund which may hereafter be made for

the encouragement of the study of the language, literature, and history of Georgia, in Transcaucasia.

3. The board of management shall consist of the following five persons:

(1) a person appointed by the Curators of the University Libraries;

(2) a person appointed by the Board of the Faculty of Medieval and Modern Languages;

(3) a person appointed by the Curators of the Oriental Institute;

(4) a person appointed by Council;

(5) a person being a member of Convocation and of Balliol College, appointed by the Master and Fellows of Balliol College.

4. Each appointed member of the board of management shall hold office for five years and shall be re-eligible. If any member of the board of management shall die, or shall resign his or her office, the person appointed in his or her place shall hold office only for the unexpired residue of the period for which the said member was appointed. The board shall have power to co-opt up to two additional members for periods of five years.

5. The board of management shall apply the interest of the fund to one or more of the following purposes at its discretion, in such manner and at such times as it may judge most expedient:

(*a*) the improvement and increase of the Georgian section of the Bodleian Library;

(*b*) the publishing, or assisting in the publication of, Georgian and English works on the language, literature, or history of Georgia;

(*c*) the assistance of carefully selected British students to study the language, literature, and history of Georgia;

(*d*) the public teaching, and encouragement of the study, in Oxford of the language, literature, and history of Georgia.

6. If in any year the income from the fund be not wholly expended, the balance left at the end of the year may, at the discretion of the board of management, be subsequently applied by the board to any of the purposes specified in clause 5 above.

7. Congregation shall have power from time to time to alter this statute, provided always that the main objects for which the fund was founded, as expressed in clauses 1 and 5 above, are kept in view.

Section LVIII. Of the Calouste Gulbenkian Professorship of Armenian Studies

1. The first charge on the net income of the fund for the endowment of the Calouste Gulbenkian Professorship of Armenian Studies shall be the costs (including support costs) of the professorship.

2. Any balance of income not required for the professorship may be applied, under such arrangements as may be approved from time to time by the General

Board, towards the travel and other research expenses of the Calouste Gulbenkian Professor. Subject thereto, income not used in any year shall be carried forward for use in subsequent years.

3. This statute may be amended from time to time by Congregation, provided that the main object of the benefactor, namely the maintenance of the professorship, is always kept in view.

Section LIX. Of the Welch Scholarships

1. The income from the fund derived from the bequest to the University from Christopher Welch, MA, Wadham College, the Founder of the Welch Scholarships, shall be applied for the promotion of the study of Biology within the University by:

(*a*) the support of scholarships, to be called the Welch Scholarships, to be awarded to persons who are, or who have been accepted for admission as, members of the University and who have not exceeded the sixteenth term from their matriculation, and therein more especially for the encouragement of such as give proof of capacity for original observation and research;

(*b*) the discharge of all expenses incidental to the purposes of the fund, including the payment of honoraria to examiners;

and by all or any of the following:

(*c*) the purchase of books or instruments such as microscopes to be awarded to deserving but unsuccessful candidates for the scholarships;

(*d*) the award of prizes or exhibitions; and

(*e*) such other way or ways as shall be thought fit by the board of management of the fund.

2. Surplus income arising in any year shall be carried forward for expenditure in subsequent years.

3. The fund shall be administered by a board of management the membership of which shall be determined by Council by decree, provided that the Warden of Wadham College, or the Warden's representative, shall always be a member.

4. The board shall determine from time to time the terms and conditions on which the scholarships shall be awarded, including their tenure and annual value, provided that no person shall hold a scholarship for more than four years.

5. Congregation may from time to time amend this statute, provided that the main objects of the fund, as defined in clause 1 above, are always kept in view.

Section LX. Of the Bequest for the Lyell Reader in Bibliography

Any part of the income from the bequest accepted by the University in 1948 for the election of the James P.R. Lyell Reader in Bibliography which is not required for the furtherance of the purposes specified in Ch. VII, Sect. III, § 24, cl. 8 shall be applied by the electors with the consent of the General Board to the furtherance of teaching or research (or both) in one or more of the subjects specified in clause 1 of that sub-section.

Section LXI. Of the Macbride Sermon

The income from the fund derived from an anonymous benefaction accepted by the University in 1848, now known as the Macbride Fund after J.D. Macbride, D.C.L., Principal of Magdalen Hall, shall be paid to the preacher of the annual sermon known as the Macbride Sermon. The Macbride Sermon shall be preached upon 'the application of the prophecies in Holy Scripture respecting the Messiah to our Lord and Saviour Jesus Christ'.

Section LXII. Of the Hope Fund

1. The assets from time to time representing the benefactions accepted by the University from The Reverend Frederick William Hope in 1849 and 1860 and from Ellen Hope in 1862, together with the gift of Dr. George Blunsdell Longstaff in 1909, shall constitute a fund to be known as the Hope Fund.

2. The collections donated by the said Frederick William Hope shall be known respectively as the Hope Entomological Collection, the Hope Library, and the Hope Collection of Engraved Portraits.

3. The income from the fund shall be used for the support of the collections and library.

4. A sum representing three-thirteenths of the income of the fund shall be applied to the support of the Keeper of Western Art in the Ashmolean Museum, who shall be the Keeper of the Hope Collection of Engraved Portraits.

5. In addition to any sums that may be allocated under clause 6 below, a sum representing one-thirteenth of the income of the fund shall be applied to the support of the Hope Entomological Collection (including the related part of the Hope Library), and an equal sum of one-thirteenth of the income shall be applied to the support of the Hope Collection of Engraved Portraits (including the related part of the Hope Library).

6. The balance of the income of the fund shall be administered by the Board of the Faculty of Biological Sciences and shall be applied to the furtherance of the study of Entomology with particular reference to the purposes of the Hope Entomological Collection.

7. The purposes for which the income shall be used under clause 6 above may include:

(*a*) the support of a Professorship of Zoology (Entomology), to be called the Hope Professorship of Zoology, the holder of which shall lecture and give instruction in Zoology with special reference to the articulata;

(*b*) the support of studentships, which shall be called the Hope Studentships, to be awarded to persons who are, or have been accepted for admission as, members of the University and who intend to undertake graduate study under the Board of the Faculty of Biological Sciences in association with the Hope Entomological Collection;

(*c*) the purchase of books or equipment for, or the provision of grants towards research expenses incurred in support of, the Hope Entomological Collection;

(*d*) the support of research fellowships or curatorial services in connection with the Hope Entomological Collection;

(*e*) such other support of the Hope Entomological Collection as the Board of the Faculty of Biological Sciences shall think fit.

8. Surplus income arising in any year shall be carried forward for expenditure in subsequent years.

9. Congregation may from time to time amend this statute, provided that the main object of the fund, as defined in clauses 3 and 6 above, is always kept in view.

Section LXIII. Of the Michael Daly Memorial Fund

1. The net income of the fund established by the gift made to the University in 1992 by Mr and Mrs Allen Daly as a memorial to their son, Michael, shall be applied in awards, to be known as Michael Daly Awards, to members of staff of the Bodleian Library or, in default of suitable applicants in any year, to members of staff of other libraries of the University. The awards shall be used by the recipients to enable them to study the languages or cultures of the Turkic-speaking world; the Caucasus; the Slavonic and East European worlds; the Middle East; the Far East; or South and South-East Asia; with preference given whenever possible to applicants studying some aspect of the Turkic-speaking world and the Caucasus.

2. The fund shall be administered by a board of management comprising Bodley's Librarian and the Keeper of Oriental Books, or their respective nominees or deputies, one of the Curators of the University Libraries to be chosen from time to time by the curators, and a person to be chosen from time to time by the Board of the Faculty of Oriental Studies from among the holders of academic posts in Turkish. The board shall determine which of the eligible candidates shall receive the awards, their several value, and any conditions governing their use.

3. Congregation shall have power from time to time to alter clause 2 of this statute.

TITLE XVII

OF ACADEMIC STAFF

(This Title is a 'Queen-in-Council' statute—see Title XV, Section VII.)

PART I. OF CONSTRUCTION, APPLICATION, AND INTERPRETATION

1. This statute and any decree or regulation made under this statute shall be construed in every case to give effect to the following guiding principles, that is to say:

(*a*) to ensure that academic staff have freedom within the law to question and test received wisdom, and to put forward new ideas and controversial or unpopular opinions, without placing themselves in jeopardy of losing their jobs or privileges;

(*b*) to enable the University to provide education, promote learning, and engage in research efficiently and economically; and

(*c*) to apply the principles of justice and fairness.

2. No provision in Part II, Part III, Part IV or Part VII shall enable any member of the academic staff to be dismissed unless the reason for the dismissal may in the circumstances (including the size and administrative resources of the University) reasonably be treated as a sufficient reason for dismissal.

3. (1) This statute shall apply

(*a*) to professors, readers, and lecturers;

(*b*) to employees of the University who are subject to the jurisdiction of the Visitatorial Board under the provisions of Tit. VIII, Sect. I; and

(*c*) to the Vice-Chancellor to the extent and in the manner set out in Part VII.

(2) In this statute any reference to 'a member of the academic staff' is a reference to a person to whom this statute applies.

4. In this statute 'dismiss' and 'dismissal' mean dismissal of a member of the academic staff and

(*a*) include remove or, as the case may be, removal from office; and

(*b*) in relation to employment under a contract, shall be construed in accordance with section 55 of the Employment Protection (Consolidation) Act 1978.

5. (1) For the purposes of this statute 'good cause' in relation to the dismissal or removal from office or place of a member of the academic staff, being in any case a reason which is related to conduct or to capability or qualifications for performing work of the kind which the member of the academic staff concerned was appointed or employed to do, means:

(*a*) conviction for an offence which may be deemed by the Visitatorial Board in the exercise of its powers under Part III to be such as to render the person convicted unfit for the performance of the duties of the office or employment as a member of the academic staff; or

(*b*) conduct of an immoral, scandalous, or disgraceful nature incompatible with the duties of the office or employment; or

(*c*) conduct constituting failure or persistent refusal or neglect or inability to perform the duties or comply with the conditions of office or employment; or

(*d*) physical or mental incapacity established under Part IV.

(2) In this clause:

(*a*) 'capability', in relation to such a member, means capability assessed by reference to skill, aptitude, health, or any other physical or mental quality; and

(*b*) 'qualifications', in relation to such a member, means any degree, diploma or other academic, technical, or professional qualification relevant to the office or position held by that member.

6. For the purposes of this statute dismissal shall be taken to be a dismissal by reason of redundancy if it is attributable wholly or mainly to

(*a*) the fact that the University has ceased, or intends to cease, to carry on the activity for the purposes of which the person concerned was appointed or employed by the University, or has ceased, or intends to cease, to carry on that activity in the place in which the person concerned worked; or

(*b*) the fact that the requirements of that activity for members of the academic staff to carry out work of a particular kind, or to carry out work of a particular kind in that place, have ceased or diminished or are expected to cease or diminish.

7. (1) In any case of conflict, the provisions of this statute shall prevail over those of any other of the statutes and over those of the decrees and regulations and the provisions of any decree made under this statute shall prevail over those of any other decree; provided that Part III and Part VII shall not apply in relation to anything done or omitted to be done before the date on which the instrument making this statute was approved under subsection (9) of section 204 of the Education Reform Act 1988;[1] and provided also that disciplinary proceedings in relation to anything done or omitted to be done before that date may continue or be instituted after that date under the relevant statutes in force immediately before that date.

(2) Nothing in any appointment made, or contract entered into, shall be construed as overriding or excluding any provision made by this statute concerning the dismissal of a member of the academic staff by reason of redundancy or for good cause; provided that this shall not invalidate any waiver made under section 142 of the Employment Protection (Consolidation) Act 1978.

[1] 27 October 1993 (The University Commissioners (Statute Modifications) (The University of Oxford) Order 1993 — SI 1993 No. 2674).

(3) In any case where an officer of the University or any other person is designated to perform any duties or exercise any powers under this statute, and that officer or other person is involved in the matter in question, an alternate may be appointed to act in his or her place under procedures prescribed by decrees made under this statute.

(4) Nothing in any other of the statutes or in any decree or regulation made thereunder shall authorise or require any officer of the University to sit as a member of any committee, tribunal, or body appointed under this statute or to be present when any such committee, tribunal, or body is meeting to arrive at its decision or for the purpose of discussing any point of procedure.

(5) This statute shall be without prejudice to any power given by the statutes of any college to the governing body thereof to deprive a member of the academic staff who is a fellow of the college of his or her fellowship or of any part of the emoluments which he or she is entitled to receive as fellow for any cause (including redundancy) for which any other Fellow of the college would be liable to be so deprived.

(6) In this statute references to numbered Parts, clauses, and sub-clauses are references to Parts, clauses, and sub-clauses so numbered in this statute.

PART II. OF REDUNDANCY

8. This Part enables Council, as the appropriate body, to dismiss any member of the academic staff by reason of redundancy.

9. (1) Nothing in this Part shall prejudice, alter, or affect any rights, powers, or duties of the University or apply in relation to a person unless:

(*a*) his or her appointment is made, or his or her contract of employment is entered into, on or after 20 November 1987; or

(*b*) he or she is promoted on or after that date.

(2) For the purposes of this clause in relation to a person, a reference to an appointment made or a contract entered into on or after 20 November 1987 or to promotion on or after that date shall be construed in accordance with subsections (3) to (6) of section 204 of the Education Reform Act 1988.

10. (1) Council shall be the appropriate body for the purposes of this Part.

(2) This Part applies only where Congregation has decided that it is desirable that there should be a reduction in the academic staff

(*a*) of the University as a whole; or

(*b*) of any faculty, school, department, or other similar area of the University by way of redundancy.

11. (1) Where Congregation has reached a decision under clause 10 (2), the appropriate body shall appoint a Redundancy Committee (to be constituted in accordance with sub-clause (3) of this clause) to give effect to that decision by such date as the appropriate body may specify, and for that purpose

(*a*) to select and recommend the requisite members of the academic staff for dismissal by reason of redundancy; and (*b*) to report its recommendations to the appropriate body.

(2) The appropriate body shall either approve any selection recommendation made under sub-clause (1), or shall remit it to the Redundancy Committee for further consideration in accordance with its further directions.

(3) A Redundancy Committee appointed by the appropriate body shall comprise:

(*a*) a Chairman; and

(*b*) two members of Congregation nominated by Council; and

(*c*) two members of the academic staff nominated by the General Board.

12. (1) Where the appropriate body has approved a selection recommendation made under clause 11 (1), it may authorise an officer of the University as its delegate to dismiss any member of the academic staff so selected.

(2) Each member of the academic staff selected shall be given separate notice of the selection approved by the appropriate body.

(3) Each separate notice shall sufficiently identify the circumstances which have satisfied the appropriate body that the intended dismissal is reasonable and in particular shall include:

(*a*) a summary of the action taken by Congregation and the appropriate body under this Part;

(*b*) an account of the selection processes used by the Redundancy Committee;

(*c*) a reference to the rights of the person notified to appeal against the notice and to the time within which any such appeal is to be lodged under Part V; and

(*d*) a statement as to when the intended dismissal is to take effect.

PART III. OF DISCIPLINE, DISMISSAL, AND REMOVAL FROM OFFICE

13. (1) Minor faults shall be dealt with informally.

(2) Where the matter is more serious but falls short of constituting possible good cause for dismissal, the following procedure shall be used:

Stage 1—Oral Warning

If conduct or performance does not meet acceptable standards the member of the academic staff will normally be given a formal oral warning by the head of department (which for the purposes of this statute means the head of the relevant department or other institution of the University or, in the absence of such an entity, the chairman of the relevant faculty board or similar university body). The member will be advised of the reason for the warning, that it is the first stage of the disciplinary procedure, and of the right of appeal under this clause. A brief note of the oral warning will be kept but it will be spent after twelve months, subject to satisfactory conduct and performance.

Stage 2—Written Warning

If the offence is a serious one, or if a further offence occurs, a written warning will be given to the member of the academic staff by the head of department. This will give details of the complaint, the improvement required, and the time scale. It will warn that a complaint may be made to the Registrar seeking the institution of charges to be heard under this Part by the Visitatorial Board if there is no satisfactory improvement and will advise of the right of appeal under this clause. A copy of this written warning will be kept by the head of department, but it will be disregarded for disciplinary purposes after two years subject to satisfactory conduct and performance.

Stage 3—Appeals

A member of the academic staff who wishes to appeal against a disciplinary warning shall inform the Registrar within two weeks. A Pro-Vice-Chancellor shall hear all such appeals and his or her decision shall be final.

14. (1) If there has been no satisfactory improvement following a written warning given under Stage 2 of the procedure in clause 13, or in any case where it is alleged that the conduct or performance of a member of the academic staff may constitute good cause for dismissal or removal from office, a complaint, seeking the institution of charges to be heard by the Visitatorial Board, may be made to the Registrar who shall bring it to the attention of the Vice-Chancellor.

(2) To enable the Vice-Chancellor to deal fairly with any complaint brought to his or her attention under sub-clause (1), such investigations or inquiries (if any) shall be instituted as appear to the Vice-Chancellor to be necessary.

(3) If it appears to the Vice-Chancellor that a complaint brought to his or her attention under sub-clause (1) relates to conduct or performance which does not meet acceptable standards but for which no written warning has been given under clause 13 or which relates to a particular alleged infringement of decrees or regulations for which a standard penalty is normally imposed in the University or within the faculty, school, department, or other relevant area, or is trivial or invalid, he or she may dismiss it summarily, or decide not to proceed further under this Part.

(4) If the Vice-Chancellor does not dispose of a complaint under sub-clause (3), he or she shall treat the complaint as disclosing a sufficient reason for proceeding further under this Part and, if he or she sees fit, the Vice-Chancellor may suspend the member on full pay pending a final decision, the said power of suspension being exercisable either at this stage or at any time prior to the final decision.

(5) Where the Vice-Chancellor proceeds further under this Part, he or she shall write to the member of the academic staff concerned, inviting comment in writing.

(6) As soon as may be following receipt of the member's comments (if any) the Vice-Chancellor shall consider the matter in the light of all the material then available and may

(*a*) dismiss it; or

(*b*) refer it for consideration under clause 13; or

(*c*) deal with it informally, if it appears to the Vice-Chancellor appropriate to do so and if the member of the academic staff agrees in writing that the matter should be dealt with by the Vice-Chancellor in that way; or

(*d*) direct that a charge or charges be preferred under clause 15 for consideration by the Visitatorial Board under this Part.

(7) If no comment is received within twenty-eight days, the Vice-Chancellor may proceed as aforesaid as if the member concerned had denied the substance and validity of the alleged case in its entirety.

15. (1) In any case where the Vice-Chancellor has directed that a charge or charges be preferred under clause 14 (6) (*d*), he or she shall refer the case to the Visitatorial Board to hear the charge or charges under this Part and to determine whether the conduct or performance of the member of the academic staff concerned constitutes good cause for dismissal or otherwise constitutes a serious complaint relating to the member's appointment or employment.

(2) Where the Visitatorial Board has been requested to hear the charge or charges under this Part, the Registrar or a solicitor or other suitable person appointed by the Vice-Chancellor shall be instructed to formulate, or arrange for the formulation of, the charge or charges and to present, or arrange for the presentation of, the charge or charges before the board.

(3) It shall be the duty of the person formulating the charge or charges

(*a*) to forward the charge or charges to the board and to the member of the academic staff concerned, together with the other documents therein specified; and

(*b*) to make any necessary administrative arrangements for the summoning of witnesses, the production of documents, and generally for the proper presentation before the board of the case against the member concerned.

16. The Visitatorial Board shall be constituted in accordance with Tit. VIII, Sect. I; provided that no member of the board who has been involved in or associated with the making of the complaint or any part of it, or who has been involved in any preliminary hearing or investigation, shall take part in the hearing of the complaint.

17. (1) The procedure to be followed in respect of the preparation, hearing, and determination of charges by the Visitatorial Board under this Part shall be that set out in decrees made under this clause.

(2) Without prejudice to the generality of the foregoing, such decrees shall ensure

(*a*) that the person charged is entitled to be represented by another person, whether such person be legally qualified or not, in connection with and at any hearing of charges by the board;

(*b*) that a charge shall not be determined without an oral hearing at which the person charged and any person appointed to represent that person are entitled to be present;

(*c*) that witnesses may be called, both on behalf of the person charged and by the person presenting the charge and may be questioned concerning any relevant evidence; and

(*d*) that full and sufficient provision is made:

(i) for postponements, adjournments, dismissal of the charge or charges for want of prosecution, and remission of the charge or charges to the Vice-Chancellor for further consideration and for the correction of accidental errors; and

(ii) for appropriate time limits for each stage (including the hearing) to the intent that any charge shall be heard and determined by the board as expeditiously as reasonably practicable.

18. (1) The Visitatorial Board shall send its decision on any charge referred to it (together with a statement of its findings of fact and the reasons for its decision regarding that charge, and its recommendations, if any, as to the appropriate penalty) to the Vice-Chancellor and to each party to the proceedings, namely the person presenting the charge, the person charged, and any person added as a party at the direction of the board.

(2) The board shall draw attention to the period of time within which any appeal should be made, by ensuring that a copy of Part V accompanies each copy of its decision sent to a party to the proceedings in accordance with sub clause (1).

19. (1) Where any charge is upheld and the Visitatorial Board finds good cause and recommends dismissal or removal from office, but in no other case, the appropriate officer shall decide whether or not to dismiss the person concerned. If the appropriate officer decides to accept the recommendation, he or she may dismiss that person forthwith.

(2) In any case where a charge is upheld, other than a case where the appropriate officer has decided under sub-clause (1) to dismiss the person concerned, the action available to the appropriate officer (not comprising a greater penalty than that recommended by the board) may be:

(*a*) to discuss the issues raised with the person concerned; or

(*b*) to advise the person concerned about his or her future conduct; or

(*c*) to warn the person concerned; or

(*d*) to suspend the person concerned with or without pay for such period as the appropriate officer shall think fair and reasonable, not to exceed three months after the board's decision; or

(*e*) to take such further or other action under the contract of employment or terms of appointment of the person concerned as appears fair and reasonable in all the circumstances of the case; or

(*f*) any combination of any of the above.

20. (1) The Vice-Chancellor shall be the appropriate officer to exercise the powers conferred by clause 19, but he or she may appoint a delegate to exercise those powers, and any reference to the appropriate officer includes a reference to any such delegate.

(2) Any action taken by the appropriate officer shall be confirmed in writing.

PART IV. OF REMOVAL FOR INCAPACITY ON MEDICAL GROUNDS

21. (1) This Part makes separate provision for the assessment of incapacity on medical grounds as a good cause for dismissal or removal from office.

(2) In this Part references to medical grounds are references to capability assessed by reference to health or any other physical or mental quality.

(3) In this Part references to the appropriate officer are references to the Vice-Chancellor or an officer acting as his or her delegate to perform the relevant act.

(4) References to the member of the academic staff include, in cases where the nature of the alleged disability so requires, a responsible relative or friend or other person with authority to act on behalf of that member, in addition to (or instead of) that member.

22. (1) Where it appears to the appropriate officer that the dismissal or removal from office of a member of the academic staff on medical grounds would be justified, the appropriate officer:

(*a*) shall inform the member accordingly;

(*b*) may suspend the member from duty without loss of pay; and

(*c*) shall notify the member in writing that it is proposed to make an application to the member's medical practitioner for a medical report and shall seek the member's consent in writing in accordance with the requirements of the Access to Medical Reports Act 1988.

(2) If the member elects to retire voluntarily on medical grounds, he or she shall be allowed to do so, and the University shall meet the reasonable costs of any medical opinion required.

(3) If the member does not elect to retire voluntarily on medical grounds, the appropriate officer shall refer the case in confidence, with any supporting medical and other evidence (including any medical evidence submitted by the member), to a board (hereinafter referred to as the 'Medical Board') comprising:

(*a*) one person nominated by Council;

(*b*) one person nominated by the member concerned or, in default of the latter nomination, by the General Board; and

(*c*) a medically qualified chairman jointly agreed by Council and the member or, in default of agreement, nominated by the President of the Royal College of Physicians.

(4) The Medical Board appointed under this clause may require the member concerned to undergo medical examination at the University's expense.

(5) The procedure to be followed in respect of the preparation, hearing, and determination of a case by a Medical Board shall be prescribed by decrees made under this sub-clause. Such decrees shall ensure:

(*a*) that the member concerned is entitled to be represented by another person, whether such person is legally qualified or not, in connection with and at any hearing of the board;

(*b*) that a case shall not be determined without an oral hearing at which the member concerned, and any person appointed to represent that member, are entitled to be present;

(*c*) that witnesses may be called and may be questioned concerning any relevant evidence; and

(*d*) that the case is heard and determined as expeditiously as is reasonably practicable.

23. If the Medical Board appointed under clause 22 determines that the member shall be required to retire on medical grounds, the appropriate officer shall forthwith terminate the employment of the member concerned on those medical grounds.

PART V. OF APPEALS

24. This Part establishes procedures for hearing and determining appeals by members of the academic staff who are dismissed or under notice of dismissal or who are otherwise disciplined.

25. (1) This Part applies:

(*a*) to any appeal against a decision of Council as the appropriate body (or of a delegate of that body) to dismiss in the exercise of its powers under Part II;

(*b*) to any appeal arising in any proceedings, or out of any decision reached, under Part III other than appeals against disciplinary warnings under clause 13;

(*c*) to any appeal against dismissal otherwise than in pursuance of Part II, III, IV, or VII;

(*d*) to any appeal against a disciplinary decision otherwise than in pursuance of Part III;

(*e*) to any appeal against a decision reached under Part IV; and

(*f*) to any appeal against a decision reached by a Tribunal under Part VII; and 'appeal' and 'appellant' shall be construed accordingly.

(2) No appeal shall however lie against:

(*a*) a decision of Congregation under clause 10 (2);

(*b*) any finding of fact of the Visitatorial Board under clause 18 (1) save where, with the consent of the person or persons hearing the appeal, new evidence is called on behalf of the appellant at that hearing;

(*c*) any medical finding by a board set up under clause 22 (3), save where, with the consent of the person appointed, new evidence is called on behalf of the appellant at that hearing.

(3) In this Part references to 'the person appointed' are references to the person appointed by Council under clause 28 to hear and determine the relevant appeal.

(4) The parties to an appeal shall be the appellant, the Registrar or a solicitor or other suitable person appointed by the Vice-Chancellor, and any other person added as a party at the direction of the person appointed.

26. A member of the academic staff shall institute an appeal by serving on the Registrar, within the time allowed under clause 27, notice in writing setting out the grounds of the appeal.

27. (1) A notice of appeal shall be served within twenty-eight days of the date on which the document recording the decision appealed from was sent to the appellant or such longer period, if any, as the person appointed may determine under sub-clause (3).

(2) The Registrar shall bring any notice of appeal received (and the date when it was served) to the attention of Council and shall inform the appellant that he or she has done so.

(3) Where the notice of appeal was served on the Registrar outside the twenty-eight-day period the person appointed under clause 28 shall not permit the appeal to proceed unless he or she considers that justice and fairness so require in the circumstances of the case.

28. (1) Where an appeal is instituted under this Part, Council shall appoint a person described in sub-clause (2) to hear and determine that appeal.

(2) The persons described in this sub-clause are:

(*a*) the High Steward; or

(*b*) a person not employed by the University holding, or having held, judicial office or being a barrister or solicitor of at least ten years' standing.

(3) The person appointed shall sit alone unless he or she considers that justice and fairness will best be served by sitting with two other persons.

(4) The other persons who may sit with the person appointed shall be:

(*a*) one member of Congregation nominated by Council; and

(*b*) one member of the academic staff nominated by the General Board.

29. (1) The procedure to be followed in respect of the preparation, consolidation, hearing, and determination of appeals shall be that set out in decrees made under this clause.

(2) Without prejudice to the generality of the foregoing, such decrees shall ensure:

(*a*) that an appellant is entitled to be represented by another person, whether such person be legally qualified or not, in connection with and at any hearing of the appeal;

(*b*) that an appeal shall not be determined without an oral hearing at which the appellant and any person appointed to represent the appellant are entitled to be present and, with the consent of the person or persons hearing the appeal, to call witnesses;

(*c*) that full and sufficient provision is made for postponements, adjournments, dismissal of the appeal for want of prosecution, and for the correction of accidental errors; and (*d*) that the person appointed may set appropriate time limits for each stage (including the hearing itself), to the intent that any appeal shall be heard and determined as expeditiously as reasonably practicable.

(3) The person or persons hearing the appeal may allow or dismiss an appeal in whole or in part and, without prejudice to the foregoing, may:

(*a*) remit an appeal from a decision under Part II (or any issue arising in the course of such an appeal) to Council as the appropriate body for further consideration as the person or persons hearing the appeal may direct; or

(*b*) remit an appeal arising under Part III for rehearing or reconsideration by the Visitatorial Board as the person or persons hearing the appeal may direct; or

(*c*) remit an appeal from a decision of the appropriate officer under Part IV for further consideration as the person or persons hearing the appeal may direct; or

(*d*) remit an appeal by the Vice-Chancellor arising under Part VII for rehearing or reconsideration by the same or by a differently constituted tribunal to be appointed under that Part; or

(*e*) substitute any lesser alternative penalty that would under Part III have been open to the appropriate officer following a finding by the Visitatorial Board on the original charge or charges.

30. The person appointed shall send a reasoned decision, including any decision reached in exercise of his or her powers under clause 29 (3) (*a*), (*b*), (*c*), or (*d*), on any appeal together with a statement of any findings of fact different from those of Council as the appropriate body under Part II, or of the Visitatorial Board under Part III, or of the Medical Board under Part IV, or of the tribunal appointed under Part VII, as the case may be, to the Vice-Chancellor (or, where the Vice-Chancellor is a party to the appeal, to the Chancellor) and to the parties to the appeal.

PART VI. OF GRIEVANCE PROCEDURES

31. The aim of this Part is to settle or redress individual grievances promptly, fairly, and so far as may be, within the faculty, school, department, or other relevant area by methods acceptable to all parties.

32. The grievances to which this Part applies are ones by members of the academic staff concerning their appointments or employment where those grievances relate:

(*a*) to matters affecting themselves as individuals; or

(*b*) to matters affecting their personal dealings or relationships with other staff of the University,

not being matters for which express provision is made elsewhere in this statute.

33. (1) If other remedies within the faculty, school, department, or other relevant area have been exhausted, the member of the academic staff may raise the matter with the head of department (as defined in clause 13 (2)).

(2) If the member of the academic staff is dissatisfied with the result of an approach under sub-clause (1) or if the grievance directly concerns the head of department, the member may apply in writing to the Vice-Chancellor for redress of the grievance.

(3) If it appears to the Vice-Chancellor that the matter has been finally determined under Part III, IV, or V, or that the grievance is trivial or invalid, he or she may dismiss it summarily or take no action upon it. If it so appears to the Vice-Chancellor, he or she shall inform the member accordingly.

(4) If the Vice-Chancellor is satisfied that the subject matter of the grievance could properly be considered with (or form the whole or any part of):

(*a*) a complaint under Part III,

(*b*) a determination under Part IV, or

(*c*) an appeal under Part V,

he or she shall defer action upon it under this Part until the relevant complaint, determination, or appeal has been heard or the time for instituting it has passed, and he or she shall notify the member accordingly.

(5) If the Vice-Chancellor does not reject the complaint under sub-clause (3), or if he or she does not defer action upon it under sub-clause (4), the Vice-Chancellor shall decide whether it would be appropriate, having regard to the interests of justice and fairness, to seek to dispose of it informally. If the Vice-Chancellor so decides, he or she shall notify the member and proceed accordingly.

34. If the grievance has not been disposed of informally under clause 33 (5), the Vice-Chancellor shall refer the matter to the Grievance Committee for consideration.

35. There shall be a Grievance Committee appointed by Council, which shall comprise:

(*a*) a Chairman; and

(*b*) one member of Congregation; and

(*c*) one member of the academic staff nominated by the General Board.

36. The procedure in connection with the consideration and determination of grievances shall be determined in decrees in such a way as to ensure that the aggrieved person, and any person against whom the grievance lies, shall have the right to be heard at a hearing and to be accompanied by a friend or representative.

37. The committee shall inform Council whether the grievance is or is not well-found, and if it is well-found the committee shall make such proposals to Council for the redress of the grievance as it sees fit, and Council shall take such action as it deems fit.

PART VII. OF REMOVAL OF THE VICE-CHANCELLOR FROM OFFICE

38. The Chancellor may be requested to remove the Vice-Chancellor from office for good cause in accordance with the procedure described in this Part.

(1) A complaint seeking the removal from office of the Vice-Chancellor for good cause may be made by not less than eight members of Council to the Chancellor.

(2) If it appears to the Chancellor, on the available material, that the complaint raises a prima facie case and that this could, if proved, constitute good cause for removal from office, he or she shall require Council to appoint a tribunal to hear and determine the matter.

(3) If it appears to the Chancellor that a complaint made under sub-clause (1) does not raise a prima facie case or is trivial or invalid, he or she may recommend to Council that no further action be taken upon it.

(4) When Council has appointed a tribunal under sub-clause (2), the Chancellor shall instruct the Registrar to appoint a solicitor or other suitable person to formulate a charge or charges and to present, or arrange for the presentation of, the charges before the tribunal. It shall be the duty of the person formulating the charge or charges:

(*a*) to forward the charge or charges to the tribunal and to the Vice-Chancellor, together with the other documents therein specified; and

(*b*) to make any necessary administrative arrangements for the summoning of witnesses, the production of documents, and generally for the proper presentation before the tribunal of the case against the Vice-Chancellor.

(5) A tribunal appointed by Council shall comprise:

(*a*) a person not employed by the University holding, or having held, judicial office or being a barrister or solicitor of at least ten years' standing, who shall act as Chairman; and

(*b*) one member of Congregation selected by Council; and

(*c*) one member of the academic staff selected by the General Board.

(6) A charge referred to the tribunal shall be dealt with in accordance with the procedure prescribed in clause 17, provided (*a*) that the Chancellor shall perform any duty, and exercise any power, there assigned to the Vice-Chancellor; and (*b*) that the only recommendation that the tribunal may make is whether or not the Vice-Chancellor should be removed from office.

(7) The tribunal shall send its reasoned decision on any charge referred to it, together with a statement of its findings of fact regarding the charge and its recommendation on the question of removal from office, to the Chancellor and to the Vice-Chancellor, drawing attention to the period of time within which any appeal under Part V should be made.

(8) Where a charge or charges have been upheld by the tribunal and not dismissed on appeal, the Chancellor shall decide whether or not to remove the Vice-Chancellor from office. If the Chancellor decides to accept the recommendation for removal, he or she may remove the Vice-Chancellor from office forthwith.

39. Where a complaint is to be referred to a tribunal under clause 38, the Chancellor may suspend the Vice-Chancellor from his or her duties and may

exclude the Vice-Chancellor from the precincts of the University or any part thereof without loss of salary.

40. For the purpose of the removal of the Vice-Chancellor for incapacity on medical grounds, Part IV shall have effect subject to the following modifications:

(*a*) for references to a member of the academic staff there shall be substituted references to the Vice-Chancellor;

(*b*) for any reference to the office of Vice-Chancellor there shall be substituted a reference to the office of Chancellor; and

(*c*) for clause 23 there shall be substituted:

'23. If the Medical Board determines that the Vice-Chancellor should be required to retire on medical grounds, it shall ask the Chancellor, as the appropriate officer, to decide whether or not to terminate the appointment of the Vice-Chancellor on those grounds. If the Chancellor accepts the board's determination, he or she may remove the Vice-Chancellor from office forthwith.'

DECREES AND REGULATIONS

TO 1 OCTOBER 2000

NOTE

In numbering certain portions of the decrees and regulations, in each group of ten the last few units have been left vacant, so that the alphabetical order can conveniently be preserved when new items are added.

CHAPTER I

CONGREGATION AND CONVOCATION

Section I. Admission to Degrees

§ 1. *Conditions to be fulfilled for admission*

1. No person shall be presented for a degree unless

(*a*) he or she has paid all the sums due from him or her to the University;

(*b*) he or she has fulfilled the academic requirements for the degree, except in so far as dispensed from them;

(*c*) he or she has completed the periods of residence required for the degree, except in so far as dispensed from them;

(*d*) he or she has a grace from his or her college or other society in the form given in the First Schedule to this section; each Dean or other appropriate officer shall give the Registrar before the ceremony a list signed by him or her of the candidates to whom the college or other society has given a grace.

2. The names of candidates for degrees shall be entered at the University Offices, not later than noon of the tenth day before the degree day, by some person deputed by the college or other society to which they belong: provided always

(*a*) that the Vice-Chancellor shall have power for some reasonable cause to dispense with such entry;

(*b*) that candidates who being qualified at the time have nevertheless failed to have their names so entered on the tenth day before the degree day shall be at liberty to have them entered in the manner hereinbefore prescribed not later than 5 p.m. on the day preceding the degree day on payment of a fee of £17·00 in addition to the degree fee;

(*c*) that candidates who have become qualified for their degree by passing an examination on any of the ten days preceding the degree day may have their names entered in the manner hereinbefore prescribed not later than 5 p.m. on the day preceding the degree day, but that such candidates shall not pay any additional fee.

The Registrar shall ascertain whether each candidate has passed such examinations and in such a manner as to entitle the candidate to supplicate for the degree.

3. Each candidate for a degree shall be presented by a Master of Arts of his or her own college or other society (unless the Vice-Chancellor shall have given leave otherwise), except that

(*a*) candidates for the Degrees of Bachelor of Divinity and Doctor of Divinity shall be presented by the Regius Professor of Divinity;

(*b*) candidates for the Degrees of Magister Juris, Bachelor of Civil Law, and Doctor of Civil Law shall be presented by the Regius Professor of Civil Law;

(*c*) candidates for the Degrees of Bachelor of Medicine, Master of Surgery, and Doctor of Medicine shall be presented by the Regius Professor of Medicine;

(*d*) candidates for the Degree of Doctor of Letters shall be presented by the Regius Professor of Greek;

(*e*) candidates for the Degree of Doctor of Science shall be presented by the Sedleian Professor of Natural Philosophy;

(*f*) candidates for the Degree of Doctor of Music shall be presented by the Heather Professor of Music;

(*g*) candidates for the Degrees of Master of Education and Bachelor of Education shall be presented by the Principal of Westminster College or the Principal's deputy;

(*h*) candidates for the Degrees of Master of Theology and Bachelor of Theology shall be presented by the head of their society or his or her deputy; provided that in each case the professor may appoint a Master of Arts to deputize for him or her. If the Master of Arts or other person presenting a candidate on behalf of his or her college or other society or as deputy to a professor is not a member of Congregation, that Master of Arts or other person shall be deemed to be such a member for the purposes, and only for the purposes, of the meeting of Congregation at which the candidate is presented by him or her;

(*i*) candidates for the Degree of Doctor of Clinical Psychology shall be presented by the Principal of Harris Manchester College or the Principal's deputy.

4. The Vice-Chancellor and Proctors may direct that the name of any candidate be removed from the list, provided always

(*a*) that the reason for the removal shall be stated in writing to the candidate and to his or her college or other society;

(*b*) that if the name is removed from a list on more than one occasion, the candidate's college or other society may require that the name be put to Congregation at a subsequent ordinary meeting by a Proctor with the reasons which led the Vice-Chancellor and Proctors to remove it and that, after a representative of the college or other society has had the opportunity to speak, the name be put to the vote. Notice of the putting of a name to Congregation in this way shall be given by the Registrar in the *University Gazette* not less than fourteen days before the meeting at which the name is to be put.

5. Notwithstanding the provisions of Ch. VI, no person may supplicate more than once for the same degree. Any person who, under the provisions of Ch. VI, has satisfied the examiners or is granted permission to supplicate for a degree which has already been conferred upon him or her, and has satisfied all other necessary requirements laid down by statute, decree, or regulation for the award of the degree, shall, if he or she so requests, be issued with a certificate to the effect that he or she has satisfied the requirements for the award of the degree in question.

6. For the purposes of this section Westminster College shall be treated as a society in the case of candidates who have been following courses of instruction there for the Degrees of Master of Theology, Master of Education, Bachelor of Theology, and Bachelor of Education.

7. For the purposes of this section the institutions specified below shall be treated as societies in the case of candidates who have been following courses of instruction there for the Degrees of Master of Theology and Bachelor of Theology: Ripon College, Cuddesdon; and St. Stephen's House.

§ 2. *Order of ceremonies*

1. At the beginning of the ceremony the Registrar shall testify that graces have been given for all candidates and that he or she is satisfied that they are qualified for the degree for which they are supplicating. The Registrar shall also testify, if a college shall so request and shall provide a grace, that a deceased member of that college, whom he or she shall name, having fulfilled all the requirements for admission to a degree, would, but for death, have been admitted to that degree at that ceremony.

2. One or other of the Proctors shall read out (in the form given in the Second Schedule to this section) the names of those supplicating for the various degrees, except that the names of those supplicating for degrees in absence, which have been published by the Registrar at the entrance to the Sheldonian Theatre, shall not be read out, and the supplications of those persons shall be presented to Congregation in the formula set out in the final clause of the Second Schedule to this section.

3. After the names have been read out, the Proctors shall seek the approval of Congregation, and if this is given shall announce the fact with the words: '*Hae gratiae concessae sunt, et sic pronuntiamus concessas*.'

4. The candidates shall be presented to the Vice-Chancellor with the appropriate formula set out in the Third Schedule to this section.

5. One of the Proctors shall say to those supplicating for the Degrees of Doctor of Divinity, Doctor of Civil Law, Doctor of Medicine, Master of Surgery, or Master of Arts:

'(*Domini Doctores, Magistri,* or *Domini,*) *vos dabitis fidem ad observandum statuta, privilegia, consuetudines, et libertates istius Universitatis.*

'*Item quod quum admissi fueritis in domum Congregationis et in domum Convocationis, in iisdem bene et fideliter, ad honorem et profectum Universitatis, vos geretis. Et specialiter quod in negotiis quae ad gratias et gradus spectant non impedietis dignos, nec indignos promovebitis.*

'*Item quod in electionibus habendis unum tantum semel et non amplius in singulis scrutiniis scribetis et nominabitis; et quod neminem nominabitis nisi quem habilem et idoneum certo sciveritis vel firmiter credideritis.*'

and the candidates shall reply: '*Do fidem.*'

6. To those supplicating for any other degree, one of the Proctors shall say:

'*Vos tenemini ad observandum omnia statuta, privilegia, consuetudines, et libertates istius Universitatis, quatenus ad vos spectent.*'

7. The Vice-Chancellor shall admit the candidates with the appropriate formula set out in the Fourth Schedule to this section.

8. After admission the candidates shall depart, and shall subsequently return wearing the academic dress of the degree to which they have been admitted.

9. The precise ordering of the ceremony within the framework laid down in this section shall be determined by the Vice-Chancellor and Proctors.

10. Notwithstanding the provisions both of the preceding clauses of this subsection and of Ch. V, Sect. II, cl. 1, a degree day shall be deemed to have been held on the Saturday of the first week of each Hilary Full Term for the purpose of the conferment of degrees in absence. The names of candidates for such a degree day shall be entered in accordance with the provisions of § 1 of this section, and the list of those supplicating for degrees shall be published on that Saturday by the Registrar at the entrance to the University Offices. The Vice-Chancellor shall then have power to declare the degrees conferred without holding the meeting of Congregation.

§ **3.** *Ceremonies for persons who have not been matriculated by the University*

1. Notwithstanding the provisions of Sect. I, §§ 1, 2, and 4 and Sect. II of this chapter, when appropriately qualified candidates who have not been matriculated by the University are admitted to degrees of the University, their admissions (whether in person or in absence) shall take place at special ceremonies arranged for this purpose.

2. The dates of such ceremonies shall be as determined from time to time by the Vice-Chancellor and when determined shall forthwith be published in the *University Gazette*.

3. The precise ordering of such ceremonies shall be as determined from time to time by the Vice-Chancellor and Proctors, provided always that the graces, forms of supplication, forms of presentation, and forms of admission used in the ceremonies, shall *mutatis mutandis,* be as prescribed in the Schedules to this section.

§ **4.** *Deprivation*

1. Congregation shall have the power to deprive any graduate of the University of his or her degree or degrees for any reason it thinks fit.

2. The procedure for de-gradation shall be laid down by decree on each occasion.

FIRST SCHEDULE
Graces

1. *Bachelor of Arts*

Ego A. B. decanus (*or* censor) collegii (*or* aulae *or* societatis) C. D. (*or* decani *or* censoris vicem-gerens) testor E. F. (*or, if more than one*, X, Y, etc.), e collegio (*or* aula *or* societate) C. D., quem (*or* quos) per integrum tempus ad gradum Baccalaurei in Artibus per statuta requisitum intra academiam, prout statuta requirunt, cubile et victum continue sumpsisse scio, quatenus examen publicum subierit (*or* subierint) et reliqua compleverit (*or* compleverint) omnia quae per statuta Universitatis requiruntur (nisi quatenus cum eo dispensatum fuerit), gratiam (*or* gratias) a collegio suo (*or* aula sua *or* societate sua) pro gradu Baccalaurei in Artibus concessam (*or* concessas) fuisse; fide mea data huic Universitati.

A. B. decanus Coll. C. *or* censor, etc.

2. *Master of Arts*

Ego A. B. decanus (*or* censor) collegii (*or* aulae *or* societatis) C. D. (*or* decani *or* censoris vicem-gerens) testor E. F. (*or, if more than one*, X, Y, etc.) e collegio *or* aula *or* societate C. D. quatenus terminum vicesimum primum a matriculatione attigerit (*or* attigerint), bonarum literarum studio incubuerit (*or* incubuerint), et reliqua compleverit (*or* compleverint) omnia quae per statuta Universitatis requiruntur, gratiam (*or* gratias) a collegio suo (*or* aula sua *or* societate sua) pro gradu Inceptoris in Artibus concessam (*or* concessas) fuisse; fide mea data huic Universitati.

A. B. dec. Coll. C.

3. *Bachelor of Music*

Ego A. B. etc. testor E. F. scholari in Musica, e collegio (*or* aula *or* societate) C. D. quatenus examen pro gradu Baccalaurei in Musica subierit, unum canticum in Schola Musicae ediderit, et reliqua praestiterit quae per statuta Universitatis requiruntur, gratiam a collegio suo (*or* aula sua *or* societate sua) pro gradu Baccalaurei in Musica concessam fuisse; fide mea data huic Universitati.

A. B. dec. Coll. C.

4. *Bachelor of Philosophy*

Ego A. B. etc. testor E. F. e collegio (*or* aula *or* societate) C. D. quem per sex terminos intra academiam prout statuta requirunt cubile et victum sumpsisse scio quatenus studio speciali sive investigationi incubuerit et reliqua omnia praestiterit quae per statuta Universitatis requiruntur (nisi quatenus, etc.), gratiam a collegio suo (*or* aula sua *or* societate sua) pro gradu Baccalaurei in Philosophia concessam fuisse; fide mea data huic Universitati.

A. B. dec. Coll. C.

5. *Bachelor of Medicine*

Ego A. B. etc. testor E. F. Magistro (*or* Baccalaureo facultatis Artium *or* Baccalaureo in Jure Civili) e collegio (*or* aula *or* societate) C. D. quatenus examen pro gradu Baccalaurei in Medicina subierit, et reliqua omnia praestiterit quae per statuta Universitatis requiruntur (nisi quatenus, etc.), gratiam a collegio suo (*or* aula sua *or* societate sua) pro gradu Baccalaurei in Medicina concessam fuisse; fide mea data huic Universitati.

A. B. dec. Coll. C.

6. *Bachelor of Civil Law*

Ego A. B. etc. testor E. F. Magistro facultatis Artium (*or* Baccalaureo in Artibus) e collegio (*or* aula *or* societate) C. D. quatenus examen pro gradu Baccalaurei in Jure Civili subierit, et reliqua praestiterit omnia quae per statuta Universitatis requiruntur (nisi quatenus, etc.), gratiam a collegio suo (*or* aula sua *or* societate sua) pro gradu Baccalaurei in Jure Civili concessam fuisse; fide mea data huic Universitati.

A. B. dec. Coll. C.

7. *Bachelor of Divinity*

Ego A. B. etc. testor E. F. Magistro facultatis Artium e collegio (*or* aula *or* societate) C. D. quatenus examen pro gradu Baccalaurei in S. Theologia subierit, et reliqua praestiterit omnia quae per statuta Universitatis requiruntur (nisi quatenus, etc.), gratiam a collegio suo (*or* aula sua *or* societate sua) pro gradu Baccalaurei in S. Theologia concessam fuisse; fide mea data huic Universitati.

A. B. dec. Coll. C.

8. *Doctor of Music*

Ego A. B. etc. testor E. F. Baccalaureo in Musica e collegio (*or* aula *or* societate) C. D. quatenus a tempore suscepti gradus Baccalaureatus sui novem terminos in studio vel praxi Musicae posuerit, examen pro gradu Inceptoris in Musica subierit, unum saltem canticum in schola Musicae ediderit, et reliqua praestiterit omnia quae per statuta Universitatis requiruntur, gratiam a collegio suo (*or* aula sua *or* societate sua) pro gradu Inceptoris in Musica concessam fuisse; fide mea data huic Universitati.

A. B. dec. Coll. C.

9. *Doctor of Philosophy*

Ego A. B. etc. testor E. F. e collegio (*or* aula *or* societate) C. D. quem per novem (*or* sex) terminos intra academiam prout statuta requirunt cubile et victum sumpsisse scio, quatenus studio speciali sive investigationi incubuerit et reliqua omnia praestiterit quae per statuta Universitatis requiruntur (nisi quatenus, etc.), gratiam a collegio suo (*or* aula sua *or* societate sua) pro gradu Doctoris in Philosophia concessam fuisse; fide mea data huic Universitati.

A. B. dec. Coll. C.

10. *Doctor of Letters; Doctor of Science*

Ego A. B. etc. testor E. F. Artium Magistro (*or* Baccalaureo in Litteris *or* in Scientia) e collegio (*or* aula *or* societate) C. D. quatenus terminum ... a matriculatione (apud Cantabrigienses *or* Dublinenses) attigerit (*or* nomen suum in promptuarii libro domus suae per viginti terminos habuerit inscriptum) et reliqua compleverit omnia quae per statuta Universitatis requiruntur, gratiam a collegio suo (*or* aula sua *or* societate sua) pro gradu Doctoris in Litteris (*or* Scientia) concessam fuisse; fide mea data huic Universitati.

A. B. dec. Coll. C.

11. *Master of Surgery*

Ego A. B. etc. testor E. F. Chirurgiae Baccalaureo e collegio (*or* aula *or* societate) C. D. quatenus examen subierit, et reliqua omnia praestiterit quae per statuta Universitatis requiruntur, gratiam a collegio suo (*or* aula sua *or* societate sua) pro gradu Inceptoris in Chirurgia concessam fuisse; fide mea data huic Universitati.

A. B. dec. Coll. C.

12. *Doctor of Medicine*

Ego A. B. etc. testor E. F. Medicinae Baccalaureo e collegio (*or* aula *or* societate) C. D. quatenus post susceptum gradum Baccalaurei in Medicina dissertationem scripserit, et reliqua omnia praestiterit quae per statuta Universitatis requiruntur, gratiam a collegio suo (*or* aula sua *or* societate sua) pro gradu Inceptoris in Medicina concessam fuisse; fide mea data huic Universitati.

A. B. dec. Coll. C.

13. *Doctor of Civil Law*

Ego A. B. etc. testor E. F. Juris Civilis Baccalaureo e collegio (*or* aula *or* societate) C. D. quatenus post susceptum Baccalaureatus gradum quinque annos in studio Juris Civilis posuerit, dissertationem scripserit, et coram Professore recitaverit, et reliqua compleverit omnia quae per statuta Universitatis requiruntur (nisi quatenus, etc.), gratiam a collegio suo (*or* aula sua *or* societate sua) pro gradu Inceptoris in Jure Civili concessam fuisse; fide mea data huic Universitati.

A. B. dec. Coll. C.

14. *Doctor of Divinity*

Ego A. B. etc. testor E. F. Magistro (*or* Baccalaureo *or* scholari) facultatis Artium (*or* Doctori in Philosophia *or* Magistro *or* Baccalaureo in Litteris *or* in Scientia) e collegio (*or* aula *or* societate) C. D. quatenus terminum tricesimum (*or* nonum *or* vicesimum primum) attigerit, et reliqua compleverit omnia quae per statuta Universitatis requiruntur (nisi quatenus, etc.), gratiam a collegio suo (*or* aula sua *or* societate sua) pro gradu Inceptoris in S. Theologia concessam fuisse; fide mea data huic Universitati.

A. B. dec. Coll. C.

15. *Master of Science*

Ego A. B. etc. testor E. F. e collegio (*or* aula *or* societate) C. D. quem per tres terminos intra academiam prout statuta requirunt cubile et victum sumpsisse scio quatenus studio speciali sive investigationi incubuerit et reliqua omnia praestiterit quae per statuta Universitatis requiruntur (nisi quatenus, etc.), gratiam a collegio suo (*or* aula sua *or* societate sua) pro gradu Magistri in Scientia concessam fuisse; fide mea data huic Universitati.

A. B. dec. Coll. C.

16. *Bachelor of Fine Art*

Ego A. B. etc. testor E. F. (*or, if more than one*, X, Y, etc.), e collegio (*or* aula *or* societate) C. D., quem (*or* quos) per integrum tempus ad gradum Baccalaurei in Bellis Artibus per statuta requisitum intra academiam, prout statuta requirunt, cubile et victum continue sumpsisse scio, quatenus examen publicum subierit (*or* subierint) et reliqua compleverit (*or* compleverint) omnia quae per statuta Universitatis requiruntur (nisi quatenus, etc.), gratiam (*or* gratias) a collegio suo (*or* aula sua *or* societate sua) pro gradu Baccalaurei in Bellis Artibus concessam (*or* concessas) fuisse; fide mea data huic Universitati.

A. B. dec. Coll. C.

17. *Master of Letters, Philosophy*

Ego A. B. etc. testor E. F. e collegio (*or* aula *or* societate) C. D. quem per sex terminos inter academiam prout statuta requirunt cubile et victum sumpsisse scio quatenus studio speciali sive investigationi incubuerit et reliqua omnia praestiterit quae per statuta Universitatis requiruntur (nisi quatenus, etc.), gratiam a collegio suo (*or* aula sua *or* societate sua) pro gradu Magistri in Litteris (*or* in Philosophia) concessam fuisse; fide mea date huic Universitati.

A. B. dec. Coll. C.

18. *Master of Studies*

Ego A. B. etc. testor E. F. e collegio (*or* aula *or* societate) C. D. quem per tres terminos intra academiam prout statuta requirunt cubile et victum sumpsisse scio quatenus studio speciali sive investigationi incubuerit et reliqua omnia praestiterit quae per statuta Universitatis requiruntur (nisi quatenus, etc.), gratiam a collegio suo (*or* aula sua *or* societate sua) pro gradu Magistri in Studiis concessam fuisse; fide mea data huic Universitati.

A. B. dec. Coll. C.

19. *Magister Juris*

Ego A. B. etc. testor E. F. e collegio (*or* aula *or* societate) C. D. quem per tres terminos intra academiam prout statuta requirunt cubile et victum sumpsisse scio quatenus studio speciali sive investigationi incubuerit et reliqua omnia praestiterit quae per statuta Universitatis requiruntur (nisi quatenus, etc.), gratiam a collegio suo (*or* aula sua *or* societate sua) pro gradu Magistri Juris concessam fuisse; fide mea data huic Universitati.

A. B. dec. Coll. C.

20. *Master of Theology*

Ego A. B. etc. testor E. F. e collegio (*or* aula *or* societate) C. D. quatenus examen pro gradu Magistri in Theologia subierit, et reliqua compleverit omnia quae per statuta Universitatis requiruntur (nisi quatenus, etc.) gratiam a collegio suo (*or* aula sua *or* societate sua) pro gradu Magistri in Theologia concessam fuisse; fide mea data huic Universitati.

A. B. Princ. *or* dec. Coll. C.

21. *Master of Education*

Ego A. B. etc. testor E. F. e Collegio Westmonasterii quatenus examen pro gradu Magistri in Educatione subierit, et reliqua compleverit omnia quae per statuta Universitatis requiruntur (nisi quatenus, etc.) gratiam a societate illa pro gradu Magistri in Educatione concessam fuisse; fide mea data huic Universitati.

A. B. Princ. Coll. Westmonasterii

22. *Bachelor of Theology*

Ego A. B. etc. testor E. F. e collegio (*or* aula *or* societate) C. D. quatenus examen pro gradu Baccalaurei in Theologia subierit, et reliqua compleverit omnia quae per statuta Universitatis requiruntur (nisi quatenus, etc.) gratiam a societate illa pro gradu Baccalaurei in Theologia concessam fuisse; fide mea data huic Universitati.

A. B. Princ *or* dec. Coll. C.

23. *Bachelor of Education*

Ego A. B. etc. testor E. F. e Collegio Westmonasterii quatenus examen pro gradu Baccalaurei in Educatione subierit, et reliqua compleverit omnia quae per statuta Universitatis requiruntur (nisi quatenus, etc.) gratiam a societate illa pro gradu Baccalaurei in Educatione concessam fuisse; fide mea data huic Universitati.

A. B. Princ. Coll. Westmonasterii

24. *Master of Biochemistry*

Ego A. B. etc. testor E. F. (*or, if more than one*, X, Y, etc.), e collegio (*or* aula *or* societate) C. D., quem (*or* quos) per integrum tempus ad gradum Magistri in Biochimia per statuta requisitum intra academiam, prout statuta requirunt, cubile et victum continue sumpsisse scio, quatenus examen publicum subierit (*or* subierint) et reliqua compleverit (*or* compleverint) omnia quae per statuta Universitatis requiruntur (nisi quatenus cum eo dispensatum fuerit), gratiam (*or* gratias) a collegio suo (*or* aula sua *or* societate sua) pro gradu Magistri in Biochimia concessam (*or* concessas) fuisse; fide mea data huic Universitati.

A. B. dec. Coll. C.

25. *Master of Chemistry*

Ego A. B. etc. testor E. F. (*or, if more than one*, X, Y, etc.), e collegio (*or* aula *or* societate) C. D., quem (*or* quos) per integrum tempus ad gradum Magistri in Chimia per statuta requisitum intra academiam, prout statuta requirunt, cubile et victum continue sumpsisse scio, quatenus examen publicum subierit (*or* subierint) et reliqua compleverit (*or* compleverint) omnia quae per statuta Universitatis requiruntur (nisi quatenus cum eo dispensatum fuerit), gratiam (*or* gratias) a collegio suo (*or* aula sua *or* societate sua) pro gradu Magistri in Chimia concessam (*or* concessas) fuisse; fide mea data huic Universitati.

A. B. dec. Coll. C.

26. *Master of Earth Sciences*

Ego A. B. etc. testor E. F. (*or, if more than one,* X, Y, etc.), e collegio (*or* aula *or* societate) C. D., quem (*or* quos) per integrum tempus ad gradum Magistri in Scientiis Terrenis per statuta requisitum intra academiam, prout statuta requirunt, cubile et victum continue sumpsisse scio, quatenus examen publicum subierit (*or* subierint) et reliqua compleverit (*or* compleverint) omnia quae per statuta Universitatis requiruntur (nisi quatenus cum eo dispensatum fuerit), gratiam (*or* gratias) a collegio suo (*or* aula sua *or* societate sua) pro gradu Magistri in Scientiis Terrenis concessam (or concessas) fuisse; fide mea data huic Universitati.

A. B. dec. Coll. C.

27. *Master of Engineering*

Ego A. B. etc. testor E. F. (*or, if more than one,* X, Y, etc.), e collegio (*or* aula *or* societate) C. D., quem (*or* quos) per integrum tempus ad gradum Magistri in Ingeniaria per statuta requisitum intra academiam, prout statuta requirunt, cubile et victum continue sumpsisse scio, quatenus examen publicum subierit (*or* subierint) et reliqua compleverit (*or* compleverint) omnia quae per statuta Universitatis requiruntur (nisi quatenus cum eo dispensatum fuerit), gratiam (*or* gratias) a collegio suo (*or* aula sua *or* societate sua) pro gradu Magistri in Ingeniaria concessam (*or* concessas) fuisse; fide mea data huic Universitati.

A. B. dec. Coll. C.

28. *Master of Mathematics*

Ego A. B. etc. testor E. F. (*or, if more than one*, X, Y, etc.), e collegio (*or* aula *or* societate) C. D., quem (*or* quos) per integrum tempus ad gradum Magistri in Mathematicis per statuta requisitum intra academiam, prout statuta requirunt, cubile et victum continue sumpsisse scio, quatenus examen publicum subierit (*or* subierint) et reliqua compleverit (*or* compleverint) omnia quae per statuta Universitatis requiruntur (nisi quatenus cum eo dispensatum fuerit), gratiam (*or* gratias) a collegio suo (*or* aula sua *or* societate sua) pro gradu Magistri in Mathematicis concessam (*or* concessas) fuisse; fide mea data huic Universitati.

A. B. dec. Coll. C.

29. *Master of Physics*

Ego A. B. etc. testor E. F. (*or, if more than one*, X, Y, etc.), e collegio (*or* aula *or* societate) C. D., quem (*or* quos) per integrum tempus ad gradum Magistri in Physica per statuta requisitum intra academiam, prout statuta requirunt, cubile et victum continue sumpsisse scio, quatenus examen publicum subierit (*or* subierint) et reliqua compleverit (*or* compleverint) omnia quae per statuta Universitatis requiruntur (nisi quatenus cum eo dispensatum fuerit), gratiam (*or* gratias) a collegio suo (*or* aula sua *or* societate sua) pro gradu Magistri in Physica concessam (*or* concessas) fuisse; fide mea data huic Universitati.

A. B. dec. Coll. C.

30. *Master of Business Administration*

Ego A. B. etc. testor E. F. (*or, if more than one*, X, Y, etc.), e collegio (*or* aula *or* societate) C. D., quem (*or* quos) per tres terminos intra academiam prout statuta requirunt cubile et victum sumpsisse scio quatenus studio speciali sive investigationi incubuerit (*or* incubuerint) et reliqua omnia praestiterit (*or* praestiterint) quae per statuta Universitatis requiruntur (nisi quatenus, etc.), gratiam a collegio suo (*or* aula sua *or* societate sua) pro gradu Magistri in Negotiis Administrandis concessam fuisse; fide mea data huic Universitati.

A. B. dec. Coll. C.

31. *Master of Fine Art*

Ego A. B. etc. testor E. F. (*or, if more than one,* X, Y, etc.) e collegio (*or* aula *or* societate) C. D., quem (*or* quos) per tres terminos intra academiam prout statuta requirunt cubile et victum sumpsisse scio quatenus studio speciali sive investigationi incubuerit (*or* incubuerint) et reliqua omnia praestiterit (*or* praestiterint) quae per statuta Universitatis requiruntur (nisi quatenus, etc.), gratiam (*or* gratias) a collegio suo (*or* aula sua *or* societate sua) pro gradu Magistri in Bellis Artibus concessam (*or* concessas) fuisse; fide mea data huic Universitati.

A. B. dec. Coll. C.

32. *Doctor of Clinical Psychology*

Ego A. B. etc. testor E. F. (*or, if more than one*, X, Y, etc.), e collegio de Harris et Manchester quatenus studio speciali sive investigationi incubuerit et reliqua omnia praestiterit quae per statuta Universitatis requiruntur (nisi quatenus, etc.) gratiam a collegio suo pro gradu Doctoris in Psychologia Medica concessam fuisse; fide mea data huic Universitati.

A.B. Princ. Coll. de Harris et Manchester.

SECOND SCHEDULE
Forms of Supplication

1. *Degrees in person*

Supplicant venerabili Congregationi Doctorum et Magistrorum regentium hi Studiosi (*or* hae Studiosae) qui compleverunt omnia quae per statuta requiruntur (nisi quatenus cum eo dispensatum fuerit); ut haec sufficiant, quo admittantur ad gradum enumeratum.

Doctoris in Sacra Theologia

A. B. e collegio C.
D. E. e collegio F.
[etc.]

Baccalaurei in Iure Civili et Doctoris in eadem facultate

A. B. e collegio C.

Doctoris in Iure Civili

A. B. e collegio C.

Doctoris in Medicina

A. B. e collegio C.

Doctoris in Litteris

A. B. e collegio C.

Doctoris in Scientia

A. B. e collegio C.

Doctoris in Musica

A. B. e collegio C.

Doctoris in Philosophia

A. B. e collegio C.

Doctoris in Psychologia Medica

A. B. e collegio de Harris et Manchester.

Magistri in Chirurgia

A. B. e collegio C.

Magistri in Scientia

A. B. e collegio C.

Magistri in Litteris

A. B. e collegio C.

Magistri in Philosophia

A. B. e collegio C.

Magistri in Studiis

A. B. e collegio C.

Magistri in Theologia

A. B. e collegio C.

Magistri in Educatione

A. B. e collegio C.

Magistri in Negotiis Administrandis

A. B. e collegio C.

Magistri in Bellis Artibus

A. B. e Collegio C.

Magistri in Artibus

A. B. e collegio C.

Magistri in Biochimia, vel Chimia, vel Scientiis Terrenis, vel Ingeniaria, vel Mathematicis, vel Physica

A. B. e collegio C.
D. E. e collegio F.
[etc.]

Baccalaurei in Sacra Theologia

A. B. e collegio C.

Baccalaurei in Iure Civili

A. B. e collegio C.

Magistri Iuris

A. B. e collegio C.

Baccalaurei in Medicina

A. B. e collegio C.

Baccalaurei in Musica

A. B. e collegio C.

Baccalaurei in Philosophia

A. B. e collegio C.

Baccalaurei in Artibus

A. B. e collegio C.

Baccalaurei in Bellis Artibus

A. B. e collegio C.

Baccalaurei in Theologia

A. B. e collegio C.

Baccalaurei in Educatione

A. B. e collegio C.

2. *Degrees in absence*

Supplicant in absentia venerabili Congregationi Doctorum et Magistrorum regentium omnes quorum nomina in schedulis rite a Registrario publicata sunt, qui omnia praestiterunt quae per statuta requiruntur (nisi quatenus cum eis dispensatum fuerit); ut haec sufficiant, quo admittantur ad eum gradum quem quisque petat.

THIRD SCHEDULE
Forms of Presentation

1. *Bachelor of Arts*

Insignissime Vice-Cancellarie, vosque egregii Procuratores, praesento vobis hunc meum scholarem (*or* hos meos scholares) in facultate Artium, ut admittatur (*or* admittantur) ad gradum Baccalaurei in Artibus.

2. *Master of Arts*

Insignissime, etc., praesento vobis hunc Baccalaureum (*or* hos Baccalaureos) in facultate Artium, ut admittatur (*or* admittantur) ad incipiendum in eadem facultate.

3. *Bachelor of Music*

Insignissime, etc., praesento vobis hunc scholarem in facultate Musicae, ut admittatur ad gradum Baccalaurei in eadem facultate; ad quam admissionem eum aptum, habilem et idoneum esse, sub chirographis hominum in arte musica peritissimorum abunde testatum accepistis.

4. *Doctor of Music*

Insignissime, etc., praesento vobis hunc Baccalaureum in facultate Musicae, ut admittatur ad incipiendum in eadem facultate: ad quam admissionem, etc. (as above).

5. *Bachelor of Philosophy*

Insignissime, etc., praesento vobis hunc meum scholarem (*or* hunc Baccalaureum *or* Magistrum) in facultate Artium ut admittatur ad gradum Baccalaurei in Philosophia.

6. *Doctor of Philosophy*

Insignissime, etc., praesento vobis hunc meum scholarem (*or* hunc Baccalaureum *or* Magistrum) in facultate Artium ut admittatur ad gradum Doctoris in Philosophia.

7. *Doctor of Letters; Doctor of Science*

Insignissime, etc., praesento vobis hunc Magistrum in facultate Artium (*or* Baccalaureum in Litteris *or* Scientia) ut admittatur ad gradum Doctoris in Litteris (*or* Scientia).

8. *Bachelor of Medicine*

Insignissime, etc., praesento vobis hunc Studiosum in Medicina ut admittatur ad gradum Baccalaurei in eadem facultate.

9. *Master of Surgery*

Insignissime, etc., praesento vobis hunc Baccalaureum Chirurgiae, ut admittatur ad incipiendum in eadem facultate.

10. *Doctor of Medicine*

Insignissime, etc., praesento vobis hunc Baccalaureum in Medicina, ut admittatur ad incipiendum in eadem facultate.

11. *Bachelor of Civil Law*

Insignissime, etc., praesento vobis hunc Studiosum in Jure Civili, ut admittatur ad gradum Baccalaurei in eadem facultate.

12. *Doctor of Civil Law*

Insignissime, etc., praesento vobis hunc Baccalaureum in Jure Civili, ut admittatur ad incipiendum in eadem facultate.

13. *Bachelor of Divinity*

Insignissime, etc., praesento vobis hunc Studiosum in S. Theologia, ut admittatur ad gradum Baccalaurei in eadem facultate.

14. *Doctor of Divinity*

Insignissime, etc., praesento vobis hunc Magistrum (*or* Baccalaureum *or* scholarem) facultatis Artium (*or* Doctorem in Philosophia *or* Magistrum *or* Baccalaureum in Litteris *or* in Scientia), ut admittatur ad incipiendum in facultate S. Theologiae.

15. *Master of Science*

Insignissime, etc., praesento vobis hunc meum scholarem (*or* hunc Baccalaureum *or* Magistrum) in facultate Artium ut admittatur ad gradum Magistri in Scientia.

16. *Bachelor of Fine Art*

Insignissime, etc., praesento vobis hunc meum scholarem, ut admittatur ad gradum Baccalaurei in Bellis Artibus.

17. *Master of Letters, Philosophy*

Insignissime, etc., praesento vobis hunc meum scholarem (*or* hunc Baccalaureum *or* Magistrum) in facultate Artium ut admittatur ad gradum Magistri in Litteris (*or* in Philosophia).

18. *Master of Studies*

Insignissime, etc., praesento vobis hunc meum scholarem (*or* hunc Baccalaureum *or* Magistrum) in facultate Artium ut admittatur ad gradum Magistri in Studiis.

19. *Magister Juris*

Insignissime, etc., praesento vobis hunc meum scholarem (*or* hunc Baccalaureum *or* Magistrum) in facultate Artium ut admittatur ad gradum Magistri Juris.

20. *Master of Theology, Education; Bachelor of Theology, Education*

Insignissime, etc., praesento vobis hunc meum scholarem in Theologia (*or* Educatione *or* hunc Baccalaureum *or* Magistrum in facultate Artium), ut admittatur ad gradum Magistri (*or* Baccalaurei) in Theologia (*or* Educatione).

21. *Master of Biochemistry, Chemistry, Earth Sciences, Engineering, Mathematics, Physics*

Insignissime, etc., praesento vobis hos meos scholares in facultate Artium, ut admittantur ad gradum Magistri in Biochimia, vel Chimia, vel Scientiis Terrenis, vel Ingeniaria, vel Mathematicis, vel Physica prout in schedula a Registrario publicata scriptum est.

22. *Master of Business Administration*

Insignissime, etc., praesento vobis hunc meum scholarem (*or* hunc Baccalaureum *or* Magistrum) in facultate Artium ut admittatur ad gradum Magistri in Negotiis Administrandis.

23. *Master of Fine Art*

Insignissime, etc., praesento vobis hunc meum scholarem (*or* hunc Baccalaureum *or* Magistrum) in facultate Artium ut admittatur ad gradum Magistri in Bellis Artibus.

24. *Doctor of Clinical Psychology*

Insignissime, etc., praesento vobis hunc meum scholarem in Psychologia Medica (*or* hunc Baccalaureum *or* Magistrum) ut admittatur ad gradum Doctoris in Psychologia Medica.

FOURTH SCHEDULE
Forms of Admission

1. *Bachelor of Music*

Domine (*or* Domini, *if more than one*), ego admitto te (*or* vos) ad gradum Baccalaurei in Musica.

2. *Doctor of Music*

Domine *or* Magister (*or* Domini *or* Magistri), ego auctoritate mea et totius Universitatis do tibi (*or* vobis) licentiam incipiendi in facultate Musicae.

3. *Bachelor of Arts*

Domine (*or* Domini), ego admitto te (*or* vos) ad gradum Baccalaurei in Artibus; insuper auctoritate mea et totius Universitatis, do tibi (*or* vobis) potestatem legendi, et reliqua omnia faciendi quae ad eundem gradum spectant.

4. *Bachelor of Philosophy*

Domine *or* Magister, etc., ego admitto te (*or* vos) ad gradum Baccalaurei in Philosophia.

5. *Bachelor of Medicine*

Domine *or* Magister (*or* Domini *or* Magistri), ego admitto te (*or* vos) ad gradum Baccalaurei in Medicina.

6. *Bachelor of Civil Law*

Domine *or* Magister (*or* Domini *or* Magistri), ego admitto te (*or* vos) ad gradum Baccalaurei in Jure Civili.

7. *Bachelor of Divinity*

Domine *or* Magister (*or* Domini *or* Magistri), ego admitto te (*or* vos) ad gradum Baccalaurei in S. Theologia.

8. *Doctor of Philosophy*

Domine *or* Magister (*or* Domini *or* Magistri), ego admitto te (*or* vos) ad gradum Doctoris in Philosophia.

9. *Doctor of Letters; Doctor of Science*

Domine *or* Magister (*or* Domini *or* Magistri), ego admitto te (*or* vos) ad gradum Doctoris in Litteris *or* Scientia.

10. *Master of Science*

Domine *or* Magister (*or* Domini *or* Magistri), ego admitto te (*or* vos) ad gradum Magistri in Scientia.

11. *Bachelor of Fine Art*

Domine (*or* Domini), ego admitto te (*or* vos) ad gradum Baccalaurei in Bellis Artibus.

12. *Master of Letters, Philosophy*

Domine *or* Magister (*or* Domini *or* Magistri), ego admitto te (*or* vos) ad gradum Magistri in Litteris (*or* in Philosophia).

13. *Master of Studies*

Domine *or* Magister (*or* Domini *or* Magistri), ego admitto te (*or* vos) ad gradum Magistri in Studiis.

14. *Magister Juris*

Domine *or* Magister (*or* Domini *or* Magistri), ego admitto te (*or* vos) ad gradum Magistri Juris.

15. *Master of Theology, Education; Bachelor of Theology, Education*

Domine (*or* Magister) (*or* Domini *or* Magistri) ego admitto te (*or* vos) ad gradum Magistri (*or* Baccalaurei) in Theologia (*or* Educatione).

16. *Master of Biochemistry, Chemistry, Earth Sciences, Engineering, Mathematics, Physics*

Domini, ego admitto vos ad gradum Magistri in Biochimia, vel Chimia, vel Scientiis Terrenis, vel Ingeniaria, vel Mathematicis, vel Physica prout in schedula a Registrario publicata scriptum est; insuper auctoritate mea et totius Universitatis, do vobis potestatem legendi, et reliqua omnia faciendi quae ad eundem gradum spectant.

17. *Master of Business Administration*

Domine *or* Magister (*or* Domini *or* Magistri), ego admitto te (*or* vos) ad gradum Magistri in Negotiis Administrandis.

18. *Master of Fine Art*

Domine *or* Magister (*or* Domini *or* Magistri), ego admitto te (*or* vos) ad gradum Magistri in Bellis Artibus.

19. *Doctor of Clinical Psychology*

Domine *or* Magister (*or* Domini *or* Magistri), ego admitto te (*or* vos) ad gradum Doctoris in Psychologia Medica.

20. *Other degrees*

'Ad honorem Domini nostri Jesu Christi, et ad profectum sacrosanctae matris ecclesiae et studii, ego auctoritate mea et totius Universitatis do tibi (*or* vobis) licentiam incipiendi in facultate Artium (*or* facultate Chirurgiae, Medicinae, Juris, S. Theologiae) legendi, disputandi, et caetera omnia faciendi quae ad statum Doctoris (*or* Magistri) in eadem facultate pertinent, cum ea completa sint quae per statuta requiruntur: in nomine Domini, Patris, Filii, et Spiritus Sancti.' (*When saying these last words, the Vice-Chancellor shall reverently bare his or her head.*) *The Vice-Chancellor shall omit the words* 'Ad honorem Domini nostri Jesu Christi, et ad profectum sacrosanctae matris ecclesiae et studii' *and* 'in nomine Domini, Patris, Filii, et Spiritus Sancti' *in appropriate cases on application by the Dean or other appropriate officer of the candidate's college or other society.*

Section II. Conferring Degrees in Absence

1. It shall be lawful to confer any degree of the University upon a person who is not present to receive the degree under the conditions prescribed by this decree, provided that the candidate, having satisfied all statutory conditions precedent to the degree for which he or she desires to supplicate and having obtained the grace of his or her college or other society, supplicates for the grace of Congregation.

2. When the conditions above mentioned are satisfied, if Congregation is willing, the degree shall be conferred in the following form which shall be recited by the Vice-Chancellor after all the candidates for the degree of Bachelor of Arts have been admitted:

'*Ego Vice-Cancellarius, auctoritate mea et totius Universitatis, admitto ad eum gradum quem quisque petat eos quibus etiam in absentia supplicare licuit ut per schedulas rite a Registrario publicatas satis apparet.*'

3. Persons so admitted to degrees in absence shall pay such fees as are set forth in Ch. VIII.

Section III. Incorporation

1. The incorporation of any person under the provisions of this decree shall mean his or her admission to the same degree or position in this University as that to which he or she has attained in his or her former university. The board of a faculty shall have power to determine whether the particular qualifications by examination which a person incorporated has obtained at his or her former university may be accepted, for the purpose of any statute, decree, or regulation concerning an examination under the supervision of that board, as the equivalent of any particular qualifications obtained at this University.

2. (*a*) The privileges of incorporation shall be limited to Bachelors of Arts, Masters of Arts, Bachelors of Divinity, and Doctors of Divinity of the University of Cambridge or the University of Dublin, and Masters of

Engineering, Masters of Natural Sciences, Bachelors of Law, Doctors of Law, Bachelors of Medicine, Doctors of Medicine, and Masters of Surgery of the University of Cambridge; provided that a person who has been awarded both the Degree of Bachelor or Master of Arts and the Degree of Master of Engineering or Natural Sciences by that university shall not be admitted to either of the first- or second-named degrees of this University as well as to the Degree of Master of Biochemistry, Chemistry, Earth Sciences, Engineering, Mathematics, or Physics; and provided also that Council shall determine from time to time the subjects studied for the Degree of Master of Natural Sciences of the University of Cambridge which shall respectively qualify an eligible holder of that degree to be admitted to the Degree of Master of Biochemistry, Chemistry, Earth Sciences, Mathematics, or Physics of this University.

(*b*) Doctors of Science and Doctors of Music of the University of Cambridge or the University of Dublin, Doctors of Letters and Doctors of Philosophy of the University of Cambridge, and Doctors of Literature and Doctors of Philosophy of the University of Dublin may apply for incorporation if at the same time, being qualified, they apply for incorporation as Masters of Arts;

provided that such persons, though not qualified for incorporation as Masters of Arts, may be incorporated as doctors if they would be qualified under Tit. II, Sect. II, cl. 1 to become members of Congregation should the degree or status of Master of Arts be conferred upon them under Tit. II, Sect. II, cl. 3.

Bachelors of Law and Doctors of Law of the University of Cambridge shall, when incorporated, become Bachelors of Civil Law and Doctors of Civil Law respectively of this University, and Doctors of Literature of the University of Dublin shall, when incorporated, become Doctors of Letters of this University.

3. Every person who desires to be incorporated as a graduate must obtain the permission of Council. For this purpose he or she must make an application to Council through the head or vicegerent of a college or other society.

The application must be supported by a written statement showing that there are adequate reasons for granting the permission for which the person applies, and by evidence showing that he or she has kept by residence at Cambridge or Dublin, before taking the degree, the same number of terms that he or she would have been required to keep by residence at Oxford before admission to the corresponding degree at this University; provided always

(*a*) that permission for the incorporation of a Bachelor of Arts or a Master of Engineering or a Master of Natural Sciences shall not be granted unless Council receive from the society which submits the application an assurance that the candidate has obtained the consent of all the authorities necessary before taking up a definite course of study in Oxford, and that he or she proposes to pursue that course of study and is stated by proper authorities of Cambridge or

Dublin to be of good character or has obtained some educational position in the University;[1]

(*b*) that permission to incorporate as a Master of Arts shall not be granted unless the candidate either fulfil the conditions laid down in proviso (*a*) for the incorporation of a Bachelor of Arts, or have obtained some educational position in Oxford, or have rendered valuable services to the University or to its members.

4. If a person desires to be incorporated as an undergraduate, the permission of Council shall not be required. Evidence of admission to the University of Cambridge or of Dublin shall qualify the person for registration for matriculation at Oxford; and any person so incorporated, who is qualified to enter at Cambridge or Dublin for any final examination leading to a degree, shall be exempt from the First Public Examination and, subject to the provisions of Ch. VI, Sect. I. C, § I, shall be qualified for admission to the Second Public Examination.

5. Incorporations shall take place at a meeting of Congregation. The name of a person who desires to be incorporated at any such meeting shall be entered at the University Offices by some officer of a college or other society, not later than noon on the tenth day before that on which the meeting is to be held.

6. The name of any person who desires to be incorporated as an undergraduate must be entered within twenty-one days of his or her matriculation or provisional matriculation.

7. At the time of entering a name the following certificates, signed by the proper authorities at Cambridge or at Dublin, must be produced to the Registrar:

(1) a certificate of the date of matriculation;

(2) a certificate showing the number of terms during which the candidate's name has been on the books of the college or society of which he or she has been a member;

(3) a certificate showing all the terms kept by residence;

(4) if the candidate is an undergraduate, a certificate showing the university examinations which he or she had passed at Cambridge or Dublin;

(5) if the candidate is a graduate, a certificate of admission to the degree;

(6) if the candidate is a Master of Natural Sciences of the University of Cambridge, a certificate showing the Part III Natural Sciences Tripos examination passed.

8. In every case of incorporation, the Registrar shall certify in Congregation that the conditions of clauses 3, 6, and 7 above have been fulfilled.

[1] Council has decided that graduates reading for a Final Honour School should not normally be allowed to incorporate, and that candidates for those diplomas open to non-members of the University should, in general, not be allowed to incorporate but that applications submitted on behalf of candidates for such diplomas could nevertheless be considered.

9. Before supplicating in Congregation for incorporation, whether as a graduate or an undergraduate, every person who desires to be incorporated must be matriculated as a member of this University or have been provisionally matriculated, and must pay the fees prescribed in Ch. VIII, Sect. I, §§ 1 and 4, provided that

(*a*) persons who are to be incorporated into the Degree of Master of Arts and into some other degree shall be required to pay only the fee for one degree, whichever fee is the higher;

(*b*) persons who incorporate by virtue of having obtained some educational position in the University shall not be required to pay any of the fees prescribed in Ch. VIII, Sect. I, §§ 1 and 4.

10. For a graduate above the degree of Bachelor of Arts or Master of Engineering or Master of Natural Sciences the form of supplicating shall be as follows: *Supplicat A. B. e Collegio* (or *ex Aula* or *e Societate*) *C., Magister in Artibus* (or *Baccalaureus* or *Doctor in S. Theologia* or *Doctor in Litteris* or *Doctor in Scientia*, or *Baccalaureus* or *Doctor in Jure* or *Baccalaureus* or *Doctor in Medicina or Magister in Chirurgia*, or *Doctor in Philosophia*) *in Academia Cantabrigiensi* (or *Dubliniensi*) *creatus, cui licentia incorporandi per Concilium Hebdomadale data est, ut bona vestra cum venia admittatur ad eundem gradum statum dignitatem et privilegia apud Oxonienses, quibus ornatus est apud suos Cantabrigienses* (or *Dublinienses*). For a Bachelor of Arts or Master of Engineering or Master of Natural Sciences the form shall be as follows: *Supplicat A. B. e Collegio* (or *ex Aula* or *e Societate*) *C., Baccalaureus in Artibus* (or *Magister in Ingeniaria* or *in Scientiis Naturalibus*) *in Academia Cantabrigiensi* (or *Dubliniensi*) *creatus, cui licentia incorporandi per Concilium Hebdomadale data est, ut bona vestra cum venia admittatur ad eundem gradum statum et dignitatem apud Oxonienses, quibus ornatus est apud suos Cantabrigienses* (or *Dublinienses*); *necnon ut* [duodecim] *terminos in eadem Academia completos hic secundum rationem Oxoniensem sibi reputatos habeat*.

11. When the granting of the grace has been declared, the presentation shall be made in the following form: *Insignissime, etc., praesento vobis hunc Baccalaureum* (or *Magistrum*) *in Artibus (or Baccalaureum* or *Doctorem in S. Theologia* or *Doctorem in Litteris* or *Doctorem in Scientia* or *Baccalaureum* or *Doctorem in Jure* or *Baccalaureum* or *Doctorem in Medicina* or *Magistrum in Chirurgia* or *Doctorem in Philosophia* or *Magistrum in Ingeniaria* or *in Scientiis Naturalibus*) *in Academia Cantabrigiensi* (or *Dubliniensi*) *creatum, ut sit eodem gradu statu dignitate et privilegiis apud nos Oxonienses, quibus ornatus est apud suos Cantabrigienses* (or *Dublinienses*).

12. After presentation one of the Proctors shall say to each person who is being incorporated as a graduate above the Degree of Bachelor of Arts: '*Magister* (or *Domine* or *Domine Doctor*), *tu dabis fidem ad observandum statuta privilegia consuetudines et libertates istius Universitatis*'; and each shall make answer: '*Do fidem.*'

13. Then the Vice-Chancellor shall admit each graduate in the following form: '*Domine* (or *Magister* or *Domine Doctor*), *ego admitto te ad eundem gradum statum dignitatem et privilegia hic apud nos Oxonienses, quibus ornatus es apud tuos Cantabrigienses* (or *Dublinienses*).' To which form, in the case of a Bachelor of Arts or a Master of Engineering or a Master of Natural Sciences, he or she shall add: '*Insuper* [duodecim] *termini, quos in Academia Cantabrigiensi* (or *Dubliniensi*) *complevisti, hic tibi secundum rationem nostram reputentur*.'

14. For an undergraduate the form of supplicating shall be as follows: '*Supplicat A. B. e Collegio* (or *ex Aula* or *e Societate*) *C., qui olim in matriculam Universitatis Cantabrigiensis* (or *Dubliniensis*) *relatus est, ut bona vestra cum venia* [tres] *terminos in Universitate praedicta per residentiam a se completos hic secundum rationem Oxoniensem sibi reputatos habeat*.' Then, so soon as the granting of the grace has been declared, the Vice-Chancellor shall pronounce as follows: '[Tres] *termini, quos A. B. in Universitate Cantabrigiensi* (or *Dubliniensi*) *per residentiam complevit, hic ei secundum rationem nostram reputentur*.'

15. A person incorporated shall be permitted to reckon as terms kept by residence those terms during each of which he or she was actually resident in his or her university for forty-two days.

16. The standing of a person incorporated as an undergraduate or a Bachelor of Arts or a Master of Biochemistry, Chemistry, Earth Sciences, Engineering, Mathematics, or Physics shall be reckoned from the date of his or her matriculation at Cambridge or at Dublin; the standing of all other persons incorporated shall be reckoned from the day of their incorporation.

17. A person incorporated as a Doctor of Divinity, Medicine, or Civil Law, or as a Master of Arts shall acquire the right of voting in Convocation on incorporation.

Section IV. Admission of Holders of Certain Degrees to Membership of Convocation

1. Any person holding one of the following degrees may be admitted to membership of Convocation under the provisions of this decree in or after the twenty-first term from his or her matriculation:

Bachelor of Divinity
Bachelor of Civil Law
Bachelor of Medicine
Bachelor of Letters
Bachelor of Science
Bachelor of Philosophy
Bachelor of Theology if a matriculated member of the University
Master of Biochemistry
Master of Chemistry
Master of Earth Sciences

Master of Engineering
Master of Mathematics
Master of Physics
Master of Business Administration
Master of Fine Art
Magister Juris
Master of Science
Master of Studies
Master of Letters
Master of Philosophy
Master of Theology if a matriculated member of the University
Doctor of Philosophy
Doctor of Clinical Psychology if a matriculated member of the University

2. Any person who desires to be admitted to the privileges of membership of Convocation under the provisions of this decree shall apply, through an officer of a college or other society, to the Registrar. The application shall be accompanied by

(*a*) a statement by the officer of the college or other society that the application has the approval of that college, or other society;

(*b*) a completed form of application for admission to membership of Convocation, and

(*c*) a registration fee of the same amount as shall be determined from time to time by Council by decree as the fee normally payable on supplication for the Degree of Master of Arts, under the provisions of Ch. VIII, Sect. I, § 4, cl. 1.

3. Any person admitted to membership of Convocation under the provisions of this decree shall thereafter be entitled to enjoy all the privileges of a Master of Arts of the University, provided that he or she shall be entitled neither to describe himself or herself as a Master of Arts nor (unless so entitled as the holder of the Degree of Master of Biochemistry or Master of Chemistry or Master of Earth Sciences or Master of Engineering or Master of Mathematics or Master of Physics) to wear the academic dress appropriate to a Master of Arts, and that membership of Convocation under the provisions of this section shall not qualify a person to be a member of Congregation for the purposes of the proviso to Tit. II, Sect. II, cl. 1.

Section V. Language at University Ceremonies

The proceedings of Congregation and Convocation (except for the conferment of Degrees by Diploma and Honorary Degrees and the admission to office of university officers) shall be in English. Degree ceremonies of Congregation, the proceedings at Encaenia (except for the Creweian Oration, which shall be delivered in English), the conferment of Degrees by Diploma and Honorary Degrees at any other times, the installation of the Chancellor and the admission to office of other university officers, and the Matriculation ceremony shall be in Latin.

Section VI. Elections in Convocation

1. An election in Convocation shall be held in Full Term, unless Council shall order otherwise, on a date fixed by Council. The Registrar shall publish at least twenty-one days' notice of every election and shall at the same time give notice of the latest days on which nominations of candidates must be received by him or her.

2. In the case of vacancy which will be caused through lapse of time, the election shall take place in the term before the vacancy will arise; in other cases the election shall take place as soon as may be after the occurrence of the vacancy (subject to the provisions of clause 1 above).

3. Elections shall be subject to the following rules as to the nomination of candidates:

(*a*) No candidate shall have votes reckoned to him or her at any election, unless the candidate shall have been nominated in writing not later than 4 p.m. on the seventeenth day before that fixed for the election by not fewer than the minimum number of members of Convocation prescribed by clause 4 below.

(*b*) All nominations, dated and signed, and accompanied by a statement signed by the person nominated consenting to the nomination, shall be delivered to the Registrar within the times above prescribed, and shall be published by him or her in the *University Gazette* as soon as possible.

(*c*) If at the close of the time prescribed for the nomination of candidates for election in Convocation only one candidate has been nominated, or remains after other nominated candidates have withdrawn, the candidate so nominated shall be deemed to be duly elected from the date appointed for the election; and the election shall be published in the *University Gazette*.

(*d*) If at the time of election no candidate has been nominated, or having been nominated has withdrawn, the Vice-Chancellor and Proctors jointly shall have power to nominate a candidate, and such a candidate shall then be declared to be duly elected; and the election shall be published in the *University Gazette*.

(*e*) If at the time of election there shall be more than one candidate nominated for each vacancy and not having withdrawn, the procedure of the election shall be as follows:

(i) The Vice-Chancellor and Proctors shall attend during the day fixed for the election during such times as the Vice-Chancellor shall determine (these times having been published in the *University Gazette* when the notice of the election was given), except that in the case of an election of the Chancellor voting shall take place on two days, both of which shall be within one week and one of which shall be the Saturday in that week.

(ii) The form of the voting-paper, and the method of casting votes, shall be prescribed by the Vice-Chancellor.

(iii) The Proctors shall be responsible for the counting of the votes, but the Vice-Chancellor shall decide on the validity of any vote which is, in their opinion, doubtful.

(iv) In the case of an equality of votes, the Vice-Chancellor shall decide between the candidates.

(v) The result of the election shall be published in the *University Gazette*.

(*f*) An election in Convocation conducted under the procedure laid down in sub-clause (*c*) above shall be deemed to be an election complying with the provisions of Tit. XIV, Sect. III, cl. 2.

4. The minimum number of members of Convocation other than the candidate required as signatories of the nomination of a candidate for the office of Chancellor of the University shall be fifty. The minimum number of members of Convocation other than the candidate required as signatories of the nomination of a candidate for the office of Professor of Poetry shall be twelve.

Section VII. Submission of Business to Convocation

1. Any item of business for Convocation other than an election shall be published as an agendum for Convocation in the *University Gazette*, and shall be deemed to have been approved *nemine contradicente* at noon on the eleventh day after the day on which it was published, unless by that time the Registrar has received notice in writing from twelve or more members of Convocation that they wish the item put to a meeting of Convocation.

2. If such a notice is received, the item shall be put to a meeting of Convocation to be held immediately before a stated meeting of Congregation, of which notice shall be published in the *University Gazette* not later than the eleventh day before the day on which the meeting is to be held.

3. Procedure at any meeting of Convocation shall be governed by the provisions of Tit. II, Sect. III, cll. 2–7 and cl. 13, concerning procedure in Congregation, with the substitution of 'Convocation' for 'Congregation' in those clauses.

Section VIII. Academic Precedence and Standing

The rules of academic precedence and standing shall be:

1. The holders of the following degrees shall rank in the order shown:
Doctor of Divinity
Doctor of Civil Law
Doctor of Medicine if also a Master of Arts
Doctor of Letters if also a Master of Arts
Doctor of Science if also a Master of Arts
Doctor of Music if also a Master of Arts
Doctor of Philosophy if also a Master of Arts
Doctor of Clinical Psychology if also a Master of Arts
Master of Surgery if also a Master of Arts
Master of Science if also a Master of Arts
Master of Letters if also a Master of Arts
Master of Philosophy if also a Master of Arts

Master of Studies if also a Master of Arts
Master of Theology if also a Master of Arts
Master of Education if also a Master of Arts
Master of Business Administration if also a Master of Arts
Master of Fine Art if also a Master of Arts
Master of Arts or Master of Biochemistry or Chemistry or Earth Sciences or Engineering or Mathematics or Physics if a member of Convocation[1]
Doctor of Medicine if not also a Master of Arts
Doctor of Letters if not also a Master of Arts
Doctor of Science if not also a Master of Arts
Doctor of Music if not also a Master of Arts
Doctor of Philosophy if not also a Master of Arts
Doctor of Clinical Psychology if not also a Master of Arts
Master of Surgery if not also a Master of Arts
Master of Science if not also a Master of Arts
Master of Letters if not also a Master of Arts
Master of Philosophy if not also a Master of Arts
Master of Studies if not also a Master of Arts
Master of Theology if not also a Master of Arts
Master of Education if not also a Master of Arts
Master of Business Administration if not also a Master of Arts
Master of Fine Art if not also a Master of Arts
Bachelor of Divinity
Bachelor of Civil Law
Magister Juris
Bachelor of Medicine
Bachelor of Surgery
Bachelor of Letters
Bachelor of Science
Bachelor of Music
Bachelor of Philosophy
Bachelor of Arts or Master of Biochemistry or Chemistry or Earth Sciences or Engineering or Mathematics or Physics if not a member of Convocation
Bachelor of Fine Art
Bachelor of Theology
Bachelor of Education.

2. Within each degree the order shall be determined by the date on which the holder was admitted to the degree; and in the case of persons admitted on the same day, by the alphabetical order of their names.

[1] If the Degree of Master of Biochemistry or Chemistry or Earth Sciences or Engineering or Mathematics or Physics is held together with a higher degree, the holder will rank in precedence equally with a person who holds the same higher degree together with the Degree of Master of Arts.

Section IX. Membership of Congregation

The following persons and classes of person shall be qualified for membership of Congregation under the provisions of Tit. II, Sect. II, cl. 1 (6) and (10):

(1) the Deputy Steward;
(2) the Public Orator;
(3) the Keeper of the Archives;
(4) the Warden of Rhodes House;
(5) the Director of the Maison Française;
(6) the Secretary to the Delegates of the University Press;
(7) the Deputy Secretaries to the Delegates of the University Press;
(8) the Tutors in Fine Art at the Ruskin School of Drawing and Fine Art;
(9) the Emeritus Professors who are under the age of 75 years;
(10) all persons working in any university department or institution who hold posts on Administrative, Senior Library and Museum, and Computer Staff Grades 3 and above, on Research Staff Grades II and above, and on any equivalent grades for academic-related staff;
(11) such other persons as Council shall determine;
(12) every person who was a member of Congregation under the provisions of this section as they stood on 1 June 1977 for as long as he or she continues to hold a post which entitled him or her to membership under those provisions.

Section X. Speaking by Junior Members in Congregation

Any junior member, as defined in Tit. XIV, Sect. IV, § 1, cl. 2, may speak at a meeting of Congregation, if called upon to do so by the Chairman at the Chairman's discretion, provided that the Chairman may at any time terminate a debate on the floor of the House and proceed to the final speeches and the taking of a vote.

Note: The Vice-Chancellor has, with the agreement of Council, approved the following arrangements for junior members to speak in Congregation under the terms of the above decree. The Chairman of Congregation will normally expect to call upon nominated representatives of the Oxford University Student Union if they wish to speak in debate, and will normally expect to call upon junior members to speak only from among those who have given advance notice of their wish to be called. Should the Chairman consider that the number of junior members who have given such notice is excessive, he or she will have to be selective in calling upon them. The Chairman will try to ensure a balanced debate in relation to the apparent spread and strength of views held by junior members. If informed selection is to be possible it is desirable that when giving notice of the wish to be called a junior member should indicate (*a*) whether he or she intends to support or oppose the motion before the House, (*b*) whether he or she would speak on behalf of any club, committee, group, or association, (*c*) whether he or she is supported by other junior members (up to twelve of whom might sign his or her notice).

If the number giving notice is small they will all be admitted to the floor of the House although this does not ensure their being called. In other cases some selection may be necessary at the stage of both admission and calling of speakers. If there is to be time to tell applicants whether they will be admitted notice will have to be received in good time. Junior members should therefore send in such notice, in writing, to the Registrar to be received by him or her at the University Offices not later than 10 a.m. on the Monday preceding the debate in question. The name of any representative nominated by O.U.S.U. should also be communicated to the Registrar, in writing, through the President by that time. A notice will then be posted in the University Offices and on the gate of the Clarendon Building not later than 10 a.m. on the morning of the debate, indicating whether all applicants will be admitted to the floor of the House or, if selection has had to take place, the names of those selected for admission to the floor.

Junior members not admitted to the floor of the House will normally be permitted to listen to the debate from the gallery. Junior members on the floor of the House will be asked to remain in their places while a vote is being taken.

APPENDIX TO CHAPTER I

Circulation of Flysheets

Ten or more members of Congregation may arrange to have a flysheet circulated with the *Gazette* (*a*) on matters before Congregation, or Convocation in regard to the election of the Professor of Poetry, or (*b*) relating to matters of general interest to the University, subject to the following general conditions:

(i) no flysheet will be circulated which in the opinion of the Vice-Chancellor and Proctors might be defamatory or otherwise illegal;

(ii) the right is reserved on behalf of the University and its employees, without prior consultation with the signatories, to publish an apology in respect of any statement in a flysheet which is complained of as defamatory or otherwise illegal (whether or not the statement can be shown to be true);

(iii) the signatories shall jointly and severally indemnify the University and its employees against any costs or damages payable in respect of their flysheet and, unless a Queen's Counsel (to be mutually agreed on by the signatories and the University) shall advise within four months of the making of any claim in respect of a flysheet that any proceedings could be contested with the probability of success, such damages shall include any sum paid by the University in settlement of any claim arising out of the flysheet;

(iv) the flysheet shall consist of one leaf only (though text may appear on both sides of the leaf); the text shall include the name and college or department of each of the signatories;

(v) a copy of the text of the flysheet shall be delivered to the Registrar before 10 a.m. on the Monday of the week in which circulation is desired; it shall be accompanied by an indemnity in accordance with condition (iii) above drawn up on a form obtainable from the Registrar and signed by each of the signatories of the flysheet; the Registrar shall be informed at the same time which of the signatories is to be notified whether the Vice-Chancellor and Proctors have authorized circulation;

(vi) the Registrar shall arrange for the production by the University Press of copies of a flysheet the circulation of which has been duly authorized.

Though every effort will be made to circulate on the day desired flysheets so received, it must be understood that this cannot be guaranteed.

(*a*) *Matters before Congregation or Convocation*

If the flysheet deals with a matter that is a formal agendum for Congregation, or for Convocation in regard to the election of the Professor of Poetry, or the subject of a report published in the *Gazette*, the production costs will be met from university funds.

(*b*) *Matters of general interest to the University*

If the flysheet deals with a matter that is not a formal agendum for Congregation, or for Convocation in regard to the election of the Professor of Poetry, or the subject of a report published in the *Gazette*, the Vice-Chancellor will decide whether it is of sufficient general interest to warrant circulation with the *Gazette*; the production costs for such a flysheet will be the responsibility of the signatories.

Oxford University Student Union

The Executive and the Graduate Committee of the Oxford University Student Union may have flysheets circulated with the *Gazette* under the arrangements and subject to the conditions set out above, provided that:

(1) the number of names to be included on the flysheet under condition (iv) shall be not less than a majority of the total number of members of the Executive or the Graduate Committee of O.U.S.U., as the case may be, and each of the persons named shall sign the indemnity required under condition (v);

(2) the maximum number of flysheets to be circulated as of right, whether on matters before Congregation (to be paid for by the University) or on matters of general interest to the University (to be paid for by O.U.S.U. and to be subject to the Vice-Chancellor's decision as prescribed under (*b*) above) shall be three per term for each of these bodies, save that the Vice-Chancellor shall have discretion to permit further flysheets.

Subject to proviso (1) above, the Executive and the Graduate Committee of O.U.S.U. may also support flysheets signed by not less than ten members of Congregation.

CHAPTER II

COUNCIL, DIVISIONAL BOARDS, FACULTY BOARDS, AND FACULTIES

Section I. Committees of Council and attendance at meetings of Council

§ 1. *Educational Policy and Standards Committee*

1. The Educational Policy and Standards Committee shall consist of:

(1) the Vice-Chancellor;

(2) the Pro-Vice-Chancellor (Academic), who shall normally chair the committee;

(3)–(5) the Proctors and the Assessor;

(6) the Chairman of the Academic Subcommittee of the Conference of Colleges;

(7) the Chairman of the Committee of Tutors for Graduates;

(8)–(11) four persons elected by Council from among the members of Council specified in Tit. IV, Sect. II, cl. 1 (12)–(14), (17)–(20), and (21)–(23);

(12) a member of the Joint Undergraduate Admissions Committee elected by that committee;

(13), (14) two Junior Members elected by the Council of the Oxford University Student Union, of whom one shall be a representative of undergraduates and one a representative of graduate students.

Subject to the approval of Council on each occasion, the committee may co-opt up to two additional members.

The members under (8)–(12) and co-opted members shall serve for three years and shall be re-eligible, provided that casual vacancies shall be filled for the remaining period of office of the member being replaced. The members under (13) and (14) shall serve for one year and shall be re-eligible.

2. The participation by Junior Members in the business of the committee shall be subject to the same conditions, *mutatis mutandis*, as are prescribed for the junior member representatives at meetings of Council under the provisions of Sect. II, cll. 4, 5, and 7–9 of this chapter.

3. The committee shall be responsible under Council for the following matters, in liaison with colleges as appropriate and necessary:

(*a*) the definition and keeping under review in the context of the University's Mission Statement of the educational philosophy, policy, and standards of the collegiate University in respect of

(i) access and admissions,

(ii) curriculum design and course structure,

(iii) teaching, learning, and assessment (including all aspects of the practical arrangements for examination, in consultation with the Proctors),

(iv) academic and pastoral support and guidance,

(v) provision and use of learning resources,

bearing in mind in particular

(vi) the arrangements for the pursuit of graduate studies,

(vii) the arrangements for part-time study;

(*b*) the establishment and keeping under review of structures and mechanisms for assuring the implementation of these policies, the maintenance of standards, and the enhancement of good practice;

(*c*) the administration of a programme for the regular review of divisions[1] and their sub-units by reference to criteria which explicitly seek comparisons by international standards of excellence in matters referred to in (*a*) above;

(*d*) the oversight and co-ordination of activities associated with external agencies involved in quality assurance;

(*e*) in the light of all the above and on the basis of divisional five- and ten-year plans, the consideration of the overall balance of activity and provision of resources between graduate studies, undergraduate studies, and continuing education respectively, and the making of recommendations to Council through its Planning and Resource Allocation Committee.

4. The committee shall make reports and recommendations to Council as appropriate.

§ **2.** *General Purposes Committee*

1. The General Purposes Committee shall consist of:

(1) the Vice-Chancellor;

(2)–(4) the Proctors and the Assessor;

(5) the Chairman of the Conference of Colleges;

(6)–(10) the heads of each of the five divisions;

(11)–(13) three persons elected by Council from among the members of Council specified in Tit. IV, Sect. II, cl. 1 (12)–(14), (17)–(20), and (21)–(23).

Elected members shall serve for three years and shall be re-eligible, provided that casual vacancies shall be filled for the remaining period of office of the member being replaced. In electing the members at (11)–(13) above, Council shall always ensure that there is within the total membership of the committee as appropriate a balance between the sciences divisions, the humanities and social sciences divisions, and the non-divisional constituency as is reasonably practicable.

2. The committee shall keep under review the following matters and shall advise Council, and make recommendations to it, as appropriate:

(*a*) the long-term strategic development of the University, in terms both of its national and of its international roles;

(*b*) relations with local, regional, and national government;

(*c*) relations with other external bodies;

[1] In this context, including the Continuing Education Board.

(*d*) policy in respect of issues or activities which are university-wide and transcend the remit of the other main committees of Council or other specialist committees (making proposals as appropriate and necessary to the Planning and Resource Allocation Committee as part of the latter's annual planning exercise);

(*e*) advice and recommendations on *ad hoc* matters as they arise;

(*f*) monitoring the University's new governance arrangements;

(*g*) recommendations on appointments by Council to other committees.

§ 3. *Personnel Committee*

1. The Personnel Committee shall consist of:

(1), (2) two members of Council elected by Council, of whom one shall be appointed by Council to chair the committee;

(3)–(5) the Proctors and the Assessor;

(6) the Chairman of the Academic Subcommittee of the Conference of Colleges;

(7)–(11) the heads of each of the five divisions;

(12)–(16) one person elected by each of the five Divisional Boards.

The committee may co-opt up to seven additional members, provided that the committee shall always ensure by the use of its power of co-optation that the range of interests and concerns in the faculties, departments, and academic services of the University, and in the colleges of the University, is as fully reflected within the total membership of the committee as is reasonably practicable.

Elected and co-opted members shall serve for three years and shall be re-eligible, provided that casual vacancies shall be filled for the remaining period of office of the person being replaced.

2. The committee shall be responsible, under Council, in the light of employment legislation and other relevant requirements, and in liaison with the colleges of the University as appropriate, for the development and review of comprehensive policies on the employment of all university staff, including policies on recruitment and selection, staff development and training, equality of opportunity, and salaries and other conditions of service.

3. The committee shall

(*a*) oversee any centrally organized exercises relating to personnel matters, such as the conferment of the title of professor or reader and the making of distinction awards for professors;

(*b*) be responsible for, and make recommendations to Council on, the policy in respect of joint appointments between the University and the colleges, exercising this responsibility through a subcommittee on which there shall be balanced college and university representation;

(*c*) monitor the implementation and effectiveness of the University's policies;

(*d*) oversee the relations between the University and its employees through recognised employee representatives.

4. The committee shall make recommendations to Council as appropriate.

§ 4. *Planning and Resource Allocation Committee*

1. The Planning and Resource Allocation Committee shall consist of:

(1) the Vice-Chancellor;

(2) the Pro-Vice-Chancellor (Planning and Resource Allocation), who shall be vice-chairman of the committee;

(3) the Pro-Vice-Chancellor (Academic Services and University Collections);

(4)–(6) the Proctors and the Assessor;

(7) the Chairman of the Finance and General Purposes Committee of the Conference of Colleges;

(8)–(12) the heads of each of the five divisions;

(13)–(17) five persons elected by Council from among the members of Council specified in Tit. IV, Sect. II, cl. 1 (12)–(14), (17)–(20), and (21)–(23);

(18) a person elected by Council from among the members of Council specified in Tit. IV, Sect. II, cl. 1 (7), (8).

In electing the members at (13)–(17) above, Council shall always ensure that there is within the total membership of the committee as appropriate a balance between the sciences divisions, the humanities and social sciences divisions, and the non-divisional constituency as is reasonably practicable.

Subject to the approval of Council on each occasion, the committee may co-opt one additional member, provided that the committee shall always ensure by the use of its power of co-optation that the range of interests in the collegiate University is as fully reflected within the total membership of the committee as is reasonably practicable.

Elected and co-opted members shall serve for three years and shall be re-eligible, provided that casual vacancies shall be filled for the remaining period of office of the member being replaced.

2. The committee shall be responsible, under Council, for the following matters, making recommendations to Council as appropriate:

(*a*) the preparation and annual updating of a five-year rolling plan for all aspects of the academic, academic services, and other activities of the University (in the light of plans prepared by the Divisional Boards, the academic services sector, and any other spending sectors);

(*b*) the consideration of the financial resources available to the University, and the making of recommendations to Council on an annual budget in the light of the overall plan, the annual operating statements from the academic divisions, and other relevant information;

(*c*) the development, implementation, refinement, and monitoring of resource allocation procedures to enable annual budgets to be set, and the making of recommendations to Council as appropriate;

(*d*) the keeping under review of, and the making of recommendations to Council as necessary on, student numbers, the distribution of students between various categories, and levels of student fee;

(*e*) the monitoring of the work of the academic divisions and academic services sector against their approved plans and budgets;

(*f*) the oversight of the University's research policy, in the light of the views of the academic divisions, and the consideration of, and the taking of action as necessary on, all aspects of the relationship between HEFCE funding and research funding from other sources;

(*g*) the oversight of, and the making of recommendations to Council on, the financial arrangements between the University and the colleges arising from the college fee settlement;

(*h*) the oversight of, and the making of recommendations to Council on, the work of the University Development Programme;

(*i*) the giving of advice to Council on the needs of the University as established by its plans, and in order that Council can take these views into account when establishing investment policy;

(*j*) the consideration of, and the giving of advice to Council on, the use of any resources which are not delegated or allocated to the academic divisions, academic services sector, or other bodies (whether trust funds, university reserves, unearmarked benefactions, capital funds, or reserves of any other description);

(*k*) as appropriate, the consideration of, and the giving of advice to Council on, all aspects of the financial relationships between the University, HEFCE, and other external funding bodies.

§ **5.** *Committee on Animal Care*

1. The Committee on Animal Care shall consist of:

(1) the Pro-Vice-Chancellor (Academic Services and University Collections) or a deputy appointed by him or her, who shall be a person not being engaged in work governed by the Animals (Scientific Procedures) Act 1986 and who shall be chairman;

(2), (3) two persons appointed by Council, of whom one shall be and one shall not be a member of a department in which work regulated under the Animals (Scientific Procedures) Act 1986 is undertaken;

(4) the holder of the Certificate of Designation for the Medical and Scientific Departments of the University of Oxford or a person appointed by the Certificate-holder;

(5) the chairman of the Ethics Panel if not otherwise a member;

(6) one of the Proctors or the Assessor as may be agreed between them;

(7)–(9) three persons appointed by the Medical Sciences Board;

(10) a person appointed by the Life and Environmental Sciences Board.

The committee shall have power to co-opt up to two additional members, who shall hold office for one year and shall be re-eligible.

Appointed members of the committee shall hold office for three years and shall be re-eligible. Casual vacancies shall be filled for the unexpired residue of the period of office of the member demitting office. The Director of Biomedical

Services and the Supervisor of Veterinary Services shall normally attend meetings of the committee.

2. The committee shall meet at least once a term. It shall promote best practice and a culture of care for all animals held within or on behalf of the University and, to this end, shall:

(*a*) advise Council, the Pro-Vice-Chancellor (Academic Services and University Collections), and other university bodies, as may be required, on the provision and development of services, facilities, and supporting staff in furtherance of the University's aims and objectives and in accordance with the Animals (Scientific Procedures) Act 1986 and other relevant enactments;

(*b*) keep under review the general maintenance, breeding, supply, and condition of animals held within the University (and external research units operating under the University's Certificate of Designation);

(*c*) keep under review and advise Council and the medical and scientific departments (and external research units operating under the University's Certificate of Designation) on questions concerning the application of the Animals (Scientific Procedures) Act 1986, on the Codes of Practice, conditions, and guidance set out thereunder, and on other relevant legislation;

(*d*) advise Council on matters relating to the use of animals in teaching and research and on public relations aspects of animal experimentation;

(*e*) make arrangements for the holding of regular meetings of representatives of all departments and external research units engaged in work under the Animals (Scientific Procedures) Act 1986 for consultation on the development of best practice, on questions concerning Biomedical Services, on veterinary reports, and, as required, on other matters within the committee's terms of reference;

(*f*) receive forecasts, annual budgets, and reports for Biomedical Services, and report thereon to the Pro-Vice-Chancellor (Academic Services and University Collections) and, as necessary, to Council;

(*g*) receive a termly report from the Supervisor of Veterinary Services on the condition of the animals held within the University, together with any comments thereon by the Ethics Panel and the departmental representative group established under (*e*) above; the committee shall forward each report to Council, under such conditions as Council shall determine, with its recommendations for action if required;

(*h*) have general oversight of Biomedical Services and Veterinary Services; including the provision of supporting staff and their career-development, and the provision of resources to enable the services to discharge their functions effectively.

3. The Supervisor of Veterinary Services and the Director of Biomedical Services shall be appointed by Council, with the approval of the Certificate-holder and after consultation with the committee. The terms and conditions of service of the supervisor and the director shall be determined by Council, with the approval of the Certificate-holder and after consultation with the committee,

and the supervisor and the director shall be responsible to the committee and to the Certificate-holder for the performance of their duties.

4. The committee shall have power to establish by standing order such subcommittees as it may deem appropriate, provided that these shall always include:

(*a*) an Ethics Panel (and associated subcommittees) whose composition and terms of reference may not be amended otherwise than with the approval of the Secretary of State, under the terms of conditions of the Certificate of Designation;

(*b*) a Biomedical Services Committee, which shall, in consultation with the Director of Biomedical Services, have oversight of the provision of biomedical services, of the forecasts, budgets, and performance of the Department of Biomedical Services, and of ensuring a consistent and transparent approach to cost recovery. The committee shall arrange appropriate consultation with users on matters relating to the service and shall report termly to the Committee on Animal Care.

§ **6.** *Buildings and Estates Subcommittee*

1. There shall be a Buildings and Estates Subcommittee of the Planning and Resource Allocation Committee consisting of:

(1) one of the members of Council serving on the Planning and Resource Allocation Committee, appointed by that committee, who shall be chairman of the subcommittee;

(2) the Pro-Vice-Chancellor (Planning and Resource Allocation);

(3)–(7) five persons of whom one shall be elected by each of the Divisional Boards;

(8) the Director of University Library Services and Bodley's Librarian or a person nominated by the Director;

(9) a person elected by the Committee for the Museums and Scientific Collections from amongst the Directors of the University's museums;

(10), (11) two persons elected by Congregation.

The subcommittee may co-opt up to two additional members from within or outside the University to advise it on architectural, planning, and environmental matters.

Elected and co-opted members shall serve for three years and shall be re-eligible, provided that casual vacancies shall be filled for the remaining period of office of the person being replaced.

2. The subcommittee shall consider, and shall make recommendations to the Planning and Research Allocation Committee on:

(*a*) strategic proposals for the development of the University's functional estate, taking account of institutional plans and environmental, aesthetic, architectural, and heritage issues;

(*b*) the acquisition, leasing, disposal, and allocation of functional land and property which neither form part of the University's investment portfolio nor are the responsibility of the Property Management Subcommittee of the Planning and Resource Allocation Committee;

(*c*) all proposals for capital spending on the University's functional estate, including the initiation and management of major building projects.

3. The subcommittee shall oversee the security of the University's functional estate, the provision of telecommunications (excluding issues of telecommunications strategy), environmental issues, and arrangements for car parking and transport policy.

§ 7. *Audit Committee*

1. The Audit Committee shall consist of:

(1) a person appointed by Council who shall not be the holder of a teaching or administrative post in the University, or in any college or other society, and who shall serve as chairman;

(2)–(4) three persons appointed by Council who shall not be members of Council or of any other committee which in the view of Council has main-line executive authority within the University.

Members shall serve for three years and shall be re-eligible. Casual vacancies shall be filled for the unexpired residue of the period of office of the member demitting office.

2. The committee shall, except in so far as concerns the financial business of the Delegates of the University Press:

(*a*) review the effectiveness of the financial and other internal control systems of the University;

(*b*) review the scope and effectiveness of the work of the Internal Audit Office, including planning and operation of the work and the results of the six-monthly reports from the Internal Auditor;

(*c*) report on the audit of the accounts;

(*d*) receive and subsequently report on the External Auditor's management letters and have direct access to the External Auditor;

(*e*) call for any investigations that it considers necessary;

(*f*) receive any comments or recommendations from the Internal or External Audit;

(*g*) report to Council as appropriate on any of the foregoing matters;

(*h*) advise Council on the criteria for the selection and appointment of the Internal Auditor;

(*i*) advise Council on the criteria for the appointment of the External Auditor and the scope of his or her work;

(*j*) meet not less than twice yearly to discharge these functions.

§ 8. *Finance Committee*

1. There shall be a Finance Committee consisting of:

(1) the Vice-Chancellor;

(2)–(4) three persons elected by Council of whom at least one shall be a member of Council and one shall be a member of the Audit Committee.

Elected members shall serve for three years and shall be re-eligible, provided that casual vacancies shall be filled for the remaining period of office of the person being replaced.

2. The committee shall be responsible to Council for:

(*a*) the review and approval of the University's annual financial statements, in liaison with the Audit Committee;

(*b*) the examination and consideration of, and report to Council on, the annual report and accounts of the Delegates of the University Press;

(*c*) the review of the University's financial regulations and consideration of any necessary changes in those regulations;

(*d*) the approval of the University's banking arrangements;

(*e*) such other action on behalf of Council in relation to the University's financial business as may be required from time to time.

§ **9.** *Health and Safety Management Committee*

1. There shall be a Health and Safety Management Committee consisting of:

(1) a member of Congregation appointed by the Vice-Chancellor as chairman of the committee;

(2) a member of Council appointed by Council;

(3) the Head of the Life and Environmental Sciences Division;

(4) the Head of the Mathematical and Physical Sciences Division;

(5) the Head of the Medical Sciences Division;

(6) the Head of the Humanities Division or the Head of the Social Sciences Division, as may be agreed between them from time to time.

2. The committee shall be responsible, under Council, for the following:

(*a*) the determination of the health and safety management strategy and policies necessary for the University to discharge its legal obligations in that regard;

(*b*) the recommendation of appropriate action necessary to implement the University's Safety Policy, as designed to promote the safety of staff, students, authorised visitors, and members of the public lawfully on university property;

(*c*) the taking of action on all management matters of health and safety and within other areas of the committee's remit, including the control of such funds as may be allocated to it.

3. The committee's remit shall include all matters covered by legislation on health and safety, fire safety, food safety, and the transport of dangerous goods, and by environmental protection legislation relating to the disposal of all hazardous wastes, radioactive substances, and genetic modification.

4. The committee may set up such subcommittees and specialist advisory groups as it shall consider desirable, and shall determine their membership and terms of reference.

5. The committee shall meet at least once a term, and following each meeting shall report to Council on the main matters which it has discussed. The committee shall also make an annual report to Council.

§ 10. *Committee on Honorary Degrees*

The Committee on Honorary Degrees (which will consist of the Vice-Chancellor, the Assessor, and not more than six members of Council) shall report on proposals to confer Degrees by Diploma and Honorary Degrees.

§ 11. *Information and Communications Technology (I.C.T.) Committee*

1. The Information and Communications Technology (I.C.T.) Committee shall consist of:

(1) the Pro-Vice-Chancellor (Academic Services and University Collections);

(2) a vice-chairman appointed by Council;

(3), (4) two persons appointed by Council, of whom one shall not be the holder of a teaching, research, or administrative post in the University or in any college or other society;

(5)–(9) five persons of whom one shall be appointed by each of the Divisional Boards, normally from amongst the members of the board;

(10) a person appointed by the Continuing Education Board;

(11) a person appointed by the Curators of the University Libraries;

(12) a person appointed by the Committee for the Museums and Scientific Collections;

(13) a person appointed by the Conference of Colleges;

(14) a person appointed by the Colleges' I.T. Group;

(15) a person appointed by the I.T. Users' Group;

(16) one of the Proctors or the Assessor as may be agreed between them;

(17), (18) two Junior Members appointed by the Oxford University Student Union, of whom one shall be a Junior Member who is a graduate.

The committee shall have power to co-opt up to four additional members for such periods as it thinks fit, of whom one shall normally be a departmental administrator.

The Director of the Computing Services shall be the technical secretary to the committee. The Director of Management Information Services, the Telecommunications Director, and the chairman of the I.T. Support Staff Group shall normally be invited to attend meetings of the committee.

The appointed members of the committee shall hold office for three years, except that the members appointed by the Oxford University Student Union shall hold office for one year, and shall be re-eligible. Casual vacancies shall be filled for the remainder of the period of office of the person being replaced.

The members appointed by the Oxford University Student Union shall not take part in any reserved business of the committee, as defined in Ch. II, Sect. II, cl. 7.

2. The committee shall be responsible under Council for:

(*a*) the formulation and continued development of a strategy for information and communications technology in furtherance of the University's aims and objectives;

(*b*) the strategic planning of the University's I.T. and telecommunications networks;

(*c*) considering and advising Council and its committees, the Divisional Boards, extra-divisional departments, and the central and departmental administrations on all matters relating to information and communications technology, and co-ordinating on these matters with colleges;

(*d*) in furtherance of the strategic development and co-ordination of I.C.T. throughout the collegiate University and in the context of the University's I.C.T. strategies, receiving and keeping under review the I.C.T. elements of the strategic plans of the Divisional Boards, extra-divisional departments, and the central and departmental administrations, and co-ordinating on these matters with colleges, and commenting on them as appropriate; reviewing the planning statements and budgets of the Divisional Boards and other university bodies in so far as they concern developments relating to I.C.T., and commenting on them to Council and the Divisional Boards and other university bodies as part of the planning process and at other times as the committee shall think appropriate; and keeping under review the implementation of these plans in so far as they affect matters relating to I.C.T.;

(*e*) the strategic oversight of the operations and budgets of the Computing Services and Educational Technology Resources Centre, which shall include:

(i) advising and instructing the Director of the Computing Services and the Director of the Educational Technology Resources Centre as required in order for the Directors to fulfil their functions;

(ii) subject to the provisions of any statute, decree, or regulation of general application, the appointment and determination of the duties and conditions of service of the Director of the Computing Services and the Director of the Educational Technology Resources Centre, and the determination of the terms and conditions of appointment and level of salary scales which shall be applied to staff of the Computing Services and Educational Technology Resources Centre other than the Directors;

(*f*) making, amending, and publishing rules, subject to approval by Council, for the regulation and security of the use of the University's I.T. facilities;

(*g*) applying, on the University's behalf, to outside bodies for funds for I.C.T., and encouraging, and in so far as is necessary in the particular circumstances, co-ordinating and approving, such bids from other bodies within the University in response to external funding opportunities for I.C.T. developments.

3. The committee shall consider, and advise Council on, the strategic development of management information systems in the collegiate University. The committee shall approve the I.T. components of projects involving the development of management information systems, and associated budgetary proposals, and forward its comments on them to Council. The committee shall monitor the framework for the delivery of such projects, and their progress, commenting to Council as appropriate. The committee shall keep under review the performance of the I.T. components of the collegiate University's management information systems, and shall advise Council and other bodies in the collegiate University accordingly. The committee shall also advise the Divisional Boards, extra-divisional departments, and the central and departmental administrations, and co-ordinate with colleges, on these matters.

§ **12.** *Investment Committee*

1. There shall be an Investment Committee consisting of at least four persons elected by Council of whom at least one shall not be the holder of a teaching or administrative post in the University or in any college or other society, and at least one shall be a person active in business and with experience of investment matters.

2. The committee shall be responsible to Council for:

(*a*) the management of the endowed funds of the University, both general and those for specific purposes, and the review and monitoring of investment policy and performance in respect of all such funds;

(*b*) the establishment and review of guidelines for the investment of the University's cash deposits and reserve funds;

(*c*) the management of any funds placed with the University by external bodies;

(*d*) making recommendations to Council as appropriate concerning investment policies for the funds under the committee's management, taking due account of the University's financial strategy and cash needs as determined from time to time by Council on the recommendation of the Planning and Resource Allocation Committee.

3. The committee shall report to Council at least twice a year on its activities and the performance of the funds under its management.

§ **13.** *Joint Committee with Junior Members*

1. The Joint Committee with Junior Members shall consist of:

(1) a chairman (who shall be the Vice-Chancellor or a member of Council appointed by the Vice-Chancellor);

(2) one of the Proctors or the Assessor as may be agreed between them;

(3)–(7) five members of Congregation appointed by Council, of whom at least two shall be members of Council;

(8) the President of the Oxford University Student Union;

(9), (10) two Junior Members elected by the Executive of the Oxford University Student Union from amongst their own number;

(11)–(14) four Junior Members elected by the Council of the Oxford University Student Union, of whom two shall be Junior Members who are graduates.[1]

2. The committee shall receive on behalf of Council all reports, budget estimates, constitutional amendments, and other business under Tit. XV, Sect. IV and shall make recommendations to Council. Only those members elected under (1)–(7) may vote on business under Tit. XV, Sect. IV.

3. The committee shall consider and advise Council on any university matter which affects Junior Members other than matters which fall within the scope of the joint committees of the General Board, or of any faculty, sub-faculty, or departmental joint committee, or of the Curators of the University Libraries, or of the Rules Committee. The committee shall have power to consider matters which fall within the terms of reference of any joint committee other than the foregoing or of any committee which contains representatives of Junior Members, but only if they have first been considered by that committee.

§ 14. *Risk Management Committee*

1. There shall be a Risk Management Committee consisting of a Pro-Vice-Chancellor appointed by the Vice-Chancellor as chairman, and such other persons as the Vice-Chancellor may determine from time to time after consultation with the chairman of the committee.

2. The committee shall be responsible to Council for identifying risks across the whole range of the University's activities, for prioritization of those risks, and for the development of a risk management strategy.

3. The committee shall report to Council at least once in each term.

§ 15. *Committee to Review the Salaries of Senior University Officers*

1. There shall be a Committee to Review the Salaries of Senior University Officers, which shall consist of:

(1) a person appointed by Council as chairman of the committee, who shall be a former Vice-Chancellor of the University;

(2) the Senior Proctor;

(3) the Chairman of the University's Audit Committee;

(4), (5) two persons appointed by Council, one of whom shall be the head of one of the colleges or other societies included in Title VII, and the other of whom shall be the head of another university or equivalent institution of higher education.

[1] Under the provisions of Decree (6) of 5 March 1998 (*Gazette*, Vol. 128, p. 865), one of these representatives shall be the Vice-President (Graduates) of the Student Union.

Appointed members of the committee shall serve for three years, or for as long as they hold the office by virtue of which they were eligible for appointment to the committee (whichever period shall be the shorter), except that casual vacancies shall be filled for the unexpired period of the member demitting office, and they shall be re-eligible provided always that no person shall serve on the committee for more than six years in total.

2. The committee shall in the calendar year 1996 and every three years thereafter review, and then make recommendations to Council on, the salaries to be paid to the Vice-Chancellor, the Chairman of the General Board, the Registrar, and such other senior officers of the University as Council may from time to time determine. The committee shall also carry out such reviews at any other time if requested by Council to do so.

3. In carrying out such reviews the committee shall consider whether there have been any significant changes in the duties of, or any significant developments associated with, the offices concerned since the salaries of the holders of the offices were last determined.

§ 16. *Committee on Statutes before the Privy Council*

1. The Committee on Statutes before the Privy Council (which will consist of not more than five members appointed by Council) shall report whether statutes made by colleges under the Universities of Oxford and Cambridge Act, 1923, directly affect the University within the meaning of s. 46 of the Schedule to the Act, or constitute alterations of statutes which affect the University within the meaning of s. 7 (2) of the Act. It shall also draw attention to the implications, if any, which alterations to college statutes may have for the University and colleges as a whole.

2. Each report of the Committee on Statutes before the Privy Council shall state the effect of the Statute reported on. Every such statement shall be printed in the *University Gazette*, and Council shall determine whether (*a*) the Statute itself, (*b*) the rest of the report or any part of it, shall be printed in the *Gazette* in addition to such statement.

§ 17. *Committee on Value for Money*

1. There shall be a Committee on Value for Money (V.F.M.), which shall consist of:

(1) a person appointed by the Vice-Chancellor as chairman of the committee;

(2)–(6) five persons elected by Council of whom at least one shall be a member of Council;

(7) the Chairman of the Domestic Bursars' Committee;

(8) the Director of Finance and Secretary of the University Chest;

(9) the University Purchasing Officer.

The committee may co-opt up to two additional members. The members of the committee shall hold office for three years, except that casual vacancies shall be filled for the unexpired period of the member demitting office, and shall be re-eligible provided always that no person shall serve on the committee for more than six years in total. The persons appointed or co-opted need not be members of the University.

2. The committee shall be responsible to Council for:

(*a*) matters of policy and strategy in regard to obtaining V.F.M. for the University;

(*b*) keeping an overview of detailed work by the officers on V.F.M. initiatives;

(*c*) addressing any V.F.M. questions not relating to purchasing.

3. The committee shall submit reports on its activities, and shall make recommendations, to Council as appropriate.

§ 18. *Attendance at meetings of Council*

1. If a member of Council elected under the provisions of Tit. IV, Sect. II, cl. 1 (6), (12)–(14), or (17)–(23), or co-opted under the provisions of cl. 1 para. 2 of that section, shall have attended fewer meetings than eight less the number of any meetings which have been cancelled in the course of any academic year, his or her seat shall at the close of such year be declared by the Vice-Chancellor to be vacant and shall thereupon be vacated; provided always

(*a*) that a person elected or co-opted to fill a casual vacancy shall only be required to attend the same proportion of meetings due to be held subsequent to the date of his or her election or co-optation as eight bears to the total number of meetings due to be held in the academic year, any fraction being reckoned to the nearest unit, and the resulting number then being reduced by the number of any meetings cancelled which were due to be held subsequent to the date of his or her election or co-optation;

(*b*) that if a member of Council has been dispensed from his or her prescribed university or college duties for not less than one term in any year, he or she shall be deemed to have satisfied the requirements of this sub-section if he or she has attended in that year at least six meetings less the number of any meetings which have been cancelled, or in the case of a person elected or co-opted to fill a casual vacancy has attended such lesser number as shall have been calculated in proportion to six by the method (*mutatis mutandis*) prescribed in proviso (*a*) above;

(*c*) that a member of Council whose minimum attendance requirement has not been reduced under proviso (*b*) above may, at the discretion of the Vice-Chancellor, be deemed to have satisfied the requirements of this sub-section if in any year he or she has attended, but for good reason has been prevented from attending more than, six meetings less the number of any meetings which have been cancelled, or in the case of a person elected or co-opted to fill a casual vacancy has attended, but for good reason has been prevented from attending more than, such lesser number as shall have been calculated in proportion to six by the method (*mutatis mutandis*) prescribed in proviso (*a*) above.

2. If a member of Council nominated under the provisions of Tit. V, Sect. II, cl. 1 (7), (8) shall have attended fewer meetings than eight less the number of any meetings which have been cancelled in the course of any academic year, his or her seat shall at the close of such year be declared by the Vice-Chancellor to be vacant and shall thereupon be vacated; provided always

(*a*) that a person nominated to fill a casual vacancy shall only be required to attend the same proportion of meetings due to be held subsequent to the date of the approval by Congregation of his or her nomination as eight bears to the total number of meetings due to be held in the academic year, any fraction being reckoned to the nearest unit, and the resulting number then being reduced by the number of any meetings cancelled which were due to be held subsequent to the date of such approval;

(*b*) that such a member may, at the discretion of the Vice-Chancellor, be deemed to have satisfied the requirements of this sub-section if in any year he or she has attended, but for good reason has been prevented from attending more than, six meetings less the number of any meetings which have been cancelled, or in the case of a person nominated to fill a casual vacancy has attended, but for good reason has been prevented from attending more than, such lesser number as shall have been calculated in proportion to six by the method (*mutatis mutandis*) prescribed in proviso (*a*) above.

Section II. Junior Member Attendance at Council

1. Junior members shall have the right to be represented at meetings of Council under the arrangements set out below.

2. The junior members shall be represented by:

(*a*) the President of the Oxford University Student Union, *ex officio*;

(*b*) one member of the Council of the Oxford University Student Union chosen by that council;

(*c*) one member of the Graduate Committee of the Oxford University Student Union chosen by that union.[1]

3. The President of the Student Union shall serve for one year from the Tuesday after Trinity Full Term. The member of the Council of the Student Union shall serve for one year from Saturday of the first week of Hilary Full Term. The member of the Graduate Committee of the Oxford University Student Union shall serve for one year from the first day of Hilary Term.[1] The members appointed under cl. 2 (*b*)–(*c*) shall be re-eligible.

4. If a casual vacancy occurs among the members appointed under cl. 2 (*b*)–(*c*), another member shall be appointed to serve for the remainder of the period of office of the vacating member; provided always that not more than one such replacement appointment may be made during any one period of office.

[1] Under the provisions of Decree (6) of 5 March 1998 (*Gazette*, Vol. 128, p. 865), the representative of the Graduate Committee shall be the Vice-President (Graduates) of the Student Union.

5. If the representative of the Graduate Committee of the Oxford University Student Union is or shall become during his or her period of office a senior member, he or she shall nevertheless be regarded as a junior member for the purposes of this section.

6. The junior members shall be entitled to speak at meetings of Council but not to vote.

7. No junior member shall be present for the discussion of reserved business. The following matters shall be reserved:

(*a*) decisions on appointments, promotions, and other matters concerning the personal position of members of the staff of the University;

(*b*) the admission of individuals and their academic assessment and personal affairs;

(*c*) proposals for honorary degrees and degrees by diploma;

(*d*) all items referring to terms and conditions of employment of all categories of staff;

(*e*) any other matter at the discretion of the chairman.

In any case of doubt, the chairman shall decide whether an item of business falls under one of the categories listed above, and his or her decision shall be final.

8. The junior members shall receive the full Council agenda paper but not the papers or minutes relating to reserved business.

9. The junior members shall respect the conventions of Council as set out in its standing orders.

10. For the period covered by this decree, the provisions of Tit. XV, Sect. IV, § 2, concerning access by junior members on a joint committee to the parent body, shall not apply to the Joint Committee of Council with Junior Members.

Section III. Divisions

1. The Life and Environmental Sciences Division shall comprise the following sub-faculties and departments:

(1) Anthropology;

(2) Archaeology [*Note*. Holders of posts in Archaeology who are on the establishment of faculties or sub-faculties under the auspices of the Humanities Division will remain on those establishments.];

(3) Biochemistry;

(4) Geography;

(5) Plant Sciences;

(6) Zoology.

2. The Mathematical and Physical Sciences Division shall comprise the following faculties:

(1) Mathematical Sciences;

(2) Physical Sciences.

3. The Medical Sciences Division shall comprise the following faculty, sub-faculty, and departments:

(1) Clinical Medicine;
(2) Human Anatomy;
(3) Pathology;
(4) Pharmacology;
(5) Physiology;
(6) Psychology.

4. The Humanities Division shall comprise the following faculties, sub-faculties, departments, and subjects:

(1) Ancient History;
(2) Chinese Studies;
(3) Classical Languages and Literature;
(4) Comparative Philology and General Linguistics;
(5) Drawing and Fine Art (Ruskin School);
(6) English Language and Literature;
(7) Medieval and Modern Languages;
(8) Modern History;
(9) Modern Middle Eastern Studies;
(10) Music;
(11) Oriental Studies;
(12) Philosophy;
(13) Theology.

5. The Social Sciences Division shall comprise the following faculties, sub-faculties, departments, and subjects:

(1) African Studies;
(2) Brazilian Studies;
(3) Development Studies (Queen Elizabeth House);
(4) Economics;
(5) Educational Studies;
(6) Japanese Studies;
(7) Latin American Studies;
(8) Law;
(9) Management;
(10) Politics and International Relations;
(11) Slavonic and East European Studies;
(12) Social Policy and Social Work;
(13) Sociology;
(14) South Asian Studies.

Section IV. Divisional Boards

§ 1. *Membership*

1. The Life and Environmental Sciences Board shall consist of:

(1) the Head of the Life and Environmental Sciences Division, who shall be chairman;

(2), (3) two persons elected by and from among the members of the Sub-faculty of Anthropology;

(4), (5) two persons elected by and from among the members of the Sub-faculty of Geography;

(6), (7) two persons elected by and from among the members of a faculty or sub-faculty who at the time of the election are working in the Department of Biochemistry;

(8), (9) two persons elected by and from among the members of a faculty or sub-faculty who at the time of the election are working in the Department of Plant Sciences;

(10), (11) two persons elected by and from among the members of a faculty or sub-faculty who at the time of the election are working in the Department of Zoology;

(12) a person elected by the Conference of Colleges from among the members of the sub-faculties in the Life and Environmental Sciences Division and from among the other members of a faculty or sub-faculty who at the time of the election are working in the departments in that division.

The board may co-opt up to two additional members, provided that, if there is no member of the Sub-faculty of Archaeology among the persons at (2)–(12) above, the board shall always ensure by the use of its power of co-optation that there is a member of that sub-faculty serving on the board in a capacity other than that of chairman; and provided also that the board shall always ensure by the use of that power that the overall range of other activities and concerns in the division is as fully represented within the total membership of the board as is reasonably practicable.

2. The Mathematical and Physical Sciences Board shall consist of:

(1) the Head of the Mathematical and Physical Sciences Division, who shall be chairman;

(2)–(4) three persons elected by and from among the members of the Sub-faculty of Chemistry;

(5)–(7) three persons elected by and from among the members of the Sub-faculty of Engineering;

(8)–(10) three persons elected by and from among the members of the Sub-faculty of Physics;

(11)–(13) three persons elected by and from among the members of the Faculty of Mathematical Sciences who at the time of the election are working in the Mathematical Institute;

(14), (15) two persons elected by and from among the members of the Sub-faculty of Earth Sciences;

(16), (17) two persons elected by and from among the members of the Sub-faculty of Materials;

(18), (19) two persons elected by and from among the members of the Faculty of Mathematical Sciences who at the time of the election are working in the Computing Laboratory;

(20) a person elected by and from among the members of the Faculty of Mathematical Sciences who at the time of the election are working in the Department of Statistics;

(21) a person elected by the Conference of Colleges from among the members of the faculties in the Mathematical and Physical Sciences Division.

The board may co-opt up to two additional members, provided that the board shall always ensure by the use of its power of co-optation that the overall range of activities and concerns in the division is as fully represented within the total membership of the board as is reasonably practicable.

3. The Medical Sciences Board shall consist of:

(1) the Head of the Medical Sciences Division, who shall be chairman;

(2) the Regius Professor of Medicine;

(3) the Chairman of the Oxfordshire Health Authority, or his or her nominee;

(4)–(8) five persons elected by and from among the members of the Faculty of Clinical Medicine;

(9)–(13) five persons elected jointly by and from among the members of the Faculty of Physiological Sciences and the Sub-faculty of Psychology, of whom one shall be from the Department of Human Anatomy and Genetics, one from the Sir William Dunn School of Pathology, one from the Department of Pharmacology, one from the Department of Physiology, and one from the Department of Experimental Psychology;

(14) a person elected by the Conference of Colleges from among the members of the faculties and sub-faculty in the Medical Sciences Division and from among the other members of a faculty or sub-faculty who at the time of the election are working in the departments in that division.

The board may co-opt up to four additional members, provided that the board shall always ensure by the use of its power of co-optation that the overall range of activities and concerns in the division is as fully represented within the total membership of the board as is reasonably practicable.

4. The Humanities Board shall consist of:

(1) the Head of the Humanities Division, who shall be chairman;

(2)–(4) three persons elected by and from among the members of the Faculty of English Language and Literature;

(5)–(7) three persons elected by and from among the members of the Faculty of Literae Humaniores;

(8)–(10) three persons elected by and from among the members of the Faculty of Medieval and Modern Languages;

(11)–(13) three persons elected by and from among the members of the Faculty of Modern History;

(14) a person elected by and from among the members of the Faculty of Music;

(15) a person elected by and from among the members of the Faculty of Oriental Studies;

(16) a person elected by and from among the members of the Faculty of Theology;

(17) a person elected by the Conference of Colleges from among the members of the faculties and sub-faculties in the Humanities Division and from among the other members of a faculty or sub-faculty who at the time of the election are working in the departments and subjects in that division.

The board may co-opt up to three additional members, provided that the board shall always ensure by the use of its power of co-optation that the overall range of activities and concerns in the division is as fully represented within the total membership of the board as is reasonably practicable.

5. The Social Sciences Board shall consist of:

(1) the Head of the Social Sciences Division, who shall be chairman;

(2)–(5) four persons elected by and from among the members of the Faculty of Social Studies;

(6)–(8) three persons elected by and from among the members of the Faculty of Law;

(9), (10) two persons elected by and from among the members of the Faculty of Management;

(11), (12) two persons elected by and from among the members of the academic staff holding established posts in the Department of Educational Studies;

(13) a person elected by and from among the academic post-holders in Queen Elizabeth House and the Senior Members of the University formally affiliated to that department;

(14) a person elected jointly by the chairmen of the inter-faculty committees and the directors of the area studies centres for the subjects specified in Sect. IV, cl. 5 (1), (2), (6), (7), (11), and (14) of this chapter;

(15) a person elected by the Conference of Colleges from among the members of the faculties and sub-faculties in the Social Sciences Division and from among the other members of a faculty or sub-faculty who at the time of the election are working in the departments and subjects in that division.

The board may co-opt up to two additional members, provided that the board shall always ensure by the use of its power of co-optation that the overall range of activities and concerns in the division is as fully represented within the total membership of the board as is reasonably practicable.

6. Elected and co-opted members of the Divisional Boards shall serve for four years and shall be re-eligible, provided that casual vacancies shall be filled for the remaining period of office of the member being replaced.

7. If an elected or co-opted member shall cease to belong to the category of persons from among whom he or she was elected, his or her seat shall forthwith be vacated.

§ **2.** *Manner of holding elections*

1. The elections to the Divisional Boards, other than the elections by the Conference of Colleges and the elections under the provisions of § 1, cl. 5 (14) and § 4 of this section, shall be held annually in Trinity Term, and on such other occasions as may be necessary to fill casual vacancies, on days to be fixed by the Vice-Chancellor. The Secretary of Faculties and Academic Registrar shall give, in the *University Gazette*, at least twenty-eight days' notice of the day of election, and shall at the same time give notice of the constituencies by and from among which the members are to be elected, of the number of vacancies in each constituency, and of the latest days on which nominations of candidates must be delivered at the University Offices.

2. No candidate shall have votes reckoned to him or her at any election, unless he or she shall have been nominated in writing not later than 4 p.m. on the twenty-fourth day before that fixed for the election by two persons, other than the candidate, qualified under the provisions of sub-section 1 of this section to vote for his or her election, or not later than the seventeenth day before that fixed for the election by six such persons other than the candidate.

3. All nominations, dated and signed, shall be delivered to the Secretary of Faculties and Academic Registrar within the times above prescribed, and in such form as shall be prescribed by the Vice-Chancellor, and shall be published by the Secretary of Faculties and Academic Registrar in the *University Gazette* as soon as possible.

4. If the number of candidates duly nominated for election as members of any board shall not exceed the number of places to be filled on that board, or if a candidate withdraws or candidates withdraw after having been duly nominated so as to leave such number, the Secretary of Faculties and Academic Registrar on the day appointed for the election shall declare the candidates nominated, and not having withdrawn, to be duly elected as members of the board.

5. If the number of candidates duly nominated for election to any board, and not having withdrawn, shall exceed the number of places to be filled on that board, the procedure of the election shall be as follows.

(1) The Secretary of Faculties and Academic Registrar shall send to every elector, not later than the fourth day before the day fixed for the election, a voting paper which shall list the names of those nominated and on which shall be specified the latest time by which, after having been signed by the voter, it may be received at the University Offices.

(2) An election shall not be deemed to be invalid owing to misdirection or non-receipt of any voting paper.

(3) The Secretary of Faculties and Academic Registrar shall be responsible for the counting of the votes, but the Vice-Chancellor shall decide on the validity of any vote which, in the opinion of the Secretary of Faculties and Academic Registrar, is in doubt.

(4) If two or more candidates have received an equal number of votes they shall be placed in order of seniority in academic standing.

(5) The result of the election shall be published in the *University Gazette*.

6. If at the time of election there shall be a greater number of vacancies than the number of candidates nominated, and not having withdrawn, the Vice-Chancellor and Proctors jointly shall have power to nominate a candidate for each vacancy remaining to be filled, and such candidates shall then be declared to be duly elected.

7. In any election in which vacancies are to be filled for periods of different length, the elected candidates shall hold office so that the tenure of those who receive more votes shall be longer than that of those who receive fewer votes; but if the election is uncontested or if two candidates receive the same number of votes, the candidate senior in academic standing shall hold office for the longer period.

8. If in any election a person is simultaneously elected to fill more than one vacancy, that person shall select the vacancy which he or she shall be deemed to have been elected to fill, and the other vacancy shall be filled by the candidate for that vacancy who has received the next highest number of votes. If there is no such other candidate, the provisions of clause 6 above shall be applied to the filling of the other vacancy.

9. The elections to the Divisional Boards by the Conference of Colleges shall be held in such manner as the Conference shall determine.

10. The elections to the Social Sciences Board under the provisions of § 1, cl. 5 (14) of this section shall be held in such manner as the electors shall jointly determine.

§ 3. *Co-opted members of Divisional Boards*

1. Subject to the provisions of sub-section 1 of this section, any Divisional Board may at any meeting, by a majority of votes, fill a vacant place for a co-opted member of that board, provided that notice of the intention to propose such a co-optation and the name of the person to be proposed shall have been sent through the secretary to all the members of the board fourteen days at least before the day of the meeting.

2. If a co-opted member of a Divisional Board shall become an *ex officio* or elected member of that board, he or she shall thereupon vacate his or her seat as a co-opted member.

§ **4.** *Junior Member attendance at Divisional Boards*

1. Junior Members shall have the right to be represented at meetings of each of the Divisional Boards under the arrangements set out below.

2. The Junior Members shall be represented at each board by two members of the Oxford University Student Union who are working in the subject area of the division concerned, and of whom one in each case shall be a member who is registered as a graduate student. The representatives shall be elected by the appropriate body of the Student Union, as shall be determined by the Council of that union, provided that each such election shall be subject to ratification by the Council of the union.

3. The representatives shall serve for one year, and shall be eligible for re-election if they remain members of the Student Union who are working in the subject area of the division concerned.

4. If a casual vacancy occurs among the representatives, another person shall be elected under the provisions of clause 2 above to serve for the remainder of the period of office of the vacating representative; provided always that not more than one such replacement election may be made during any one period of office.

5. If a graduate representative is or shall become during his or her period of office a Senior Member, he or she shall nevertheless be regarded as a Junior Member for the purposes of this section.

6. The Junior Members shall be entitled to speak at meetings of Divisional Boards but not to vote.

7. No Junior Member shall be present for the discussion of reserved business as defined in Ch. II, Sect. II, cl. 7.

8. The Junior Members shall receive the full agenda paper for the relevant Divisional Board but not the papers or minutes relating to reserved business.

9. The Junior Members shall respect the conventions of the relevant Divisional Board as set out in its standing orders.

§ **5.** *Attendance by other persons at Divisional Boards*

Such officers of the University, including officers of university committees, as Council may from time to time determine shall receive all the papers circulated to each Divisional Board, and each may attend, or may nominate a deputy to attend on his or her behalf, for the discussion of any item or items at any meeting of any Divisional Board. They shall be entitled to speak during any such discussion but not to vote on any item.

Section V. Heads of Division

1. The head of each division shall be appointed, subject to the approval of Council, by a selection committee consisting of:

(1) the Vice-Chancellor;

(2), (3) two persons appointed by Council;

(4), (5) two persons appointed by the Divisional Board;

provided always that Council may appoint an additional member of a selection committee if such an appointment seems to Council to be desirable.

A selection committee shall be appointed on, or in anticipation of, each vacancy in the headship to act on that occasion.

2. A member of a selection committee may resign from that committee in order to offer himself or herself as a candidate for the headship, provided that he or she does so before the published closing date for the receipt of applications, or that he or she is invited after that date by the other members to do so. If a member resigns in such circumstances, Council shall nominate a person to act in his or her place for the remainder of the proceedings to fill the vacancy.

3. The head of each division shall have such functions and powers as are or shall be assigned to him or her by the statutes, decrees, and regulations, or by Council.

4. Subject to the provisions of the statutes, decrees, and regulations, the head of each division shall be appointed for a period of five years on each occasion. A person who holds, or has previously held, the headship shall be eligible for consideration for a further such appointment.

5. The salary and other terms and conditions of appointment of each head of division shall be as determined from time to time by Council.

Section VI. Membership of Faculty Boards

§ 1. *Official members of faculty boards*

The persons qualified to be official members of the boards of the faculties listed in Tit. VI, Sect. II, cl. 1 (other than the Boards of the Faculties of Management, of Medieval and Modern Languages, and of Music) shall be:

(1) the persons enumerated in the annexed schedule; and

(2) the holders of posts in the following categories:

(*a*) the single-tenure and fixed-term professorships (including *ad hominem* professorships, but excluding titular professorships conferred under the provisions of Ch. VII, Sect. I, § 10 and visiting professorships) which are on the establishment of the faculty board concerned;

(*b*) the readerships to which appointments are made by the General Board (but excluding titular readerships conferred under the provisions of Ch. VII, Sect. I, § 10) and which are on the establishment of the faculty board concerned; and

(*c*) the headships of the departments, and the directorships of the groups or units with the standing of full departments, which are under the aegis of the faculty board concerned.

SCHEDULE OF PROFESSORS AND READERS

ENGLISH

American Literature, Drue Heinz
Anglo-Saxon, Rawlinson and Bosworth
English Language, Merton
English Literature, Goldsmiths'
English Literature, Merton
English Literature, Thomas Warton
English Literature and Language, J. R. R. Tolkien
Language and Communication, Rupert Murdoch
Poetry
Bibliography and Textual Criticism, Reader in
Icelandic Literature and Antiquities, Ancient, Vigfusson Rausing Reader in

LAW

Jurisprudence
Law
Law, Civil, Regius
Law, Commercial and Financial, Norton Rose
Law, Comparative, Clifford Chance
Law, Corporate, Allen & Overy
Law, English
Law, English, Vinerian
Law, European Community, Jacques Delors
Law, Intellectual Property and Information Technology, Reuters
Law, Public International, Chichele
Law, Taxation, KPMG
Law, Reader in
Law, All Souls Reader in
Laws of the British Commonwealth and United States, Rhodes Reader in

LITERAE HUMANIORES

Archaeology and Art, Lincoln
Archaeology of the Roman Empire
Greek, Regius
Byzantine and Modern Greek Language and Literature, Bywater and Sotheby
History, Ancient, Camden
History, Ancient, Wykeham
History of Philosophy
Latin Language and Literature, Corpus Christi
Logic, Mathematical
Logic, Wykeham
Philology, Comparative
Philosophy, Mental, Wilde
Philosophy, Metaphysical, Waynflete
Philosophy, Moral, White's

MODERN HISTORY

Archaeology, European
Archaeology of the Roman Empire
Economy, Political, Drummond
Geography
Government, Gladstone
History, American, Harold Vyvyan Harmsworth
History, American, Rhodes
History, Ancient, Camden
History, Ancient, Wykeham
History, Ecclesiastical, Regius
History, Economic, Chichele
History, Irish, Carroll
History, Medieval, Chichele
History, Modern
History, Modern, Regius
History of Art
History of the British Commonwealth, Beit
History of Latin America
History of Science
History of War, Chichele
International Relations, Montague Burton
Japanese Studies, Modern, Nissan
Jurisprudence
Law, English, Vinerian
Law, Public International, Chichele
Race Relations, Rhodes
Social and Political Theory, Chichele
History, Economic, Reader in
History, Modern South Asian, Reader in
History, Recent Social and Economic, Reader in
History of Medicine, Reader in
Diplomatic, Lecturer (or Reader) in

ORIENTAL STUDIES

Arab World, Contemporary, Study of the, Khalid bin Abdullah Al Saud
Arabic, Laudian
Armenian Studies, Calouste Gulbenkian
Chinese, Shaw
Egyptology
Hebrew, Regius
Japanese Studies, Modern, Nissan
Persian Studies, Masoumeh and Fereydoon Soudavar
Religions and Ethics, Eastern, Spalding
Sanskrit, Boden
Holy Scripture, Interpretation of, Oriel and Laing
History, Modern South Asian, Reader in
Jewish Studies, Reader in

THEOLOGY

Divinity, Lady Margaret
Divinity, Regius
Hebrew, Regius
Ecclesiastical History, Regius
Philosophy of the Christian Religion, Nolloth
Science and Religion, Andreas Idreos
Scripture, Holy, Exegesis of, Dean Ireland's
Scripture, Holy, Interpretation of, Oriel and Laing
Theology, Moral and Pastoral, Regius

§ **2.** *Ordinary members of boards of faculties*

The ordinary members of the several boards of faculties shall be members of the several faculties chosen from time to time in the manner hereinafter provided. A person shall be eligible as an ordinary member notwithstanding that he or she is qualified to be an official member.

§ **3.** *Electors*

1. Subject to the special provisions of Sectt. VIII–X of this chapter, the electors to the board of each faculty shall be (*a*) in the election of an official member all the members of the faculty; (*b*) in the election of an ordinary member the members of the faculty, exclusive of the persons qualified to be official members.

2. If a question shall arise as to the right of any person to take part in the election of members of the board of any faculty, it shall be decided by the Vice-Chancellor.

§ **4.** *Number and tenure of members*

1. The number of official and ordinary members of boards of faculties (except those of Management, of Medieval and Modern Languages, and of Music, as to which see Sectt. VIII–X of this chapter) shall be as follows:

	Official members	*Ordinary members*
English Language and Literature	8	12
Law	8	17[1]
Literae Humaniores	8	15[2]
Modern History	8	12
Oriental Studies	8	12
Theology	6	10

Provided that, if in the case of any board the number of persons qualified under the provisions of § 1 of this section to be official members of the board is less than the number specified above, then the number of official members of the board shall be such smaller number.

2. The number of members of boards of faculties to be elected at each annual election shall be as follows:

[1] Of whom two shall be the faculty board's Directors of Graduate Studies, and one the chair of the faculty, *ex officio*.

[2] Of whom three shall be the faculty board's Directors of Graduate Studies *ex officio*.

	Official members[1]	*Ordinary members*
English Language and Literature	4	6
Law	4	7
Literae Humaniores	4	6
Modern History	4	6
Oriental Studies	4	6
Theology	3	5

3. Every elected member of a board of a faculty shall commence office on the first day of the Michaelmas Term next following the date of his or her election, and shall hold office for two years from that day.

4. When an elected member vacates his or her seat otherwise than by lapse of time, the vacancy shall, as soon as possible, be filled up by the electors by whom he or she was elected. If the vacancy shall be filled up before the expiration of the period for which the member so vacating his or her seat was elected, the person elected to fill the vacancy shall hold office for the unexpired residue only of such period.

5. The persons qualified to elect the ordinary members of the board of any faculty may, if they think fit, direct by by-law that no ordinary member shall serve for more than three successive periods of two years each. A meeting of such electors may be summoned at any time by the chairman of the faculty, or, if the faculty has been divided into sub-faculties, by the chairman of the board, for the purpose of making or rescinding such by-law, and shall be so summoned by him or her on the requisition of not less than one-half of the total number of such electors, or if the number of such electors shall exceed thirty, on the requisition of not less than fifteen. Not less than seven clear days' notice shall be given of any such meeting. The chairman of the faculty or the chairman of the board shall (unless some other chairman be appointed by the meeting) preside at the meeting, but shall not (unless he or she be an elector) vote thereat. The chairman of the meeting shall forthwith notify to the Secretary of Faculties the decision of the meeting, which shall be published in the *University Gazette*.

6. If an ordinary member of a board of any faculty shall become an official member of the board, he or she shall thereupon vacate his or her seat as an ordinary member.

§ 5. *Manner of holding elections*

1. The elections to the boards of faculties shall be held annually in Trinity Term on days to be fixed by the Vice-Chancellor. The Secretary of Faculties shall give, in the *University Gazette*, at least twenty-eight days' notice of the day of election, and shall at the same time give notice of the number of official members, if any, and the number of ordinary members to be elected, and of the

[1] Where an election is required.

latest days on which nominations of candidates must be delivered at the University Offices.

2. No candidate shall have votes reckoned to him or her at any election, unless he or she shall have been nominated in writing not later than 4 p.m. on the twenty-fourth day before that fixed for the election by two persons, other than the candidate, qualified under the provisions of § 3, cl. 1 of this section to vote for his or her election, or not later than the seventeenth day before that fixed for the election by six such persons other than the candidate.

3. All nominations, dated and signed, shall be delivered to the Secretary of Faculties and Academic Registrar within the times above prescribed, and in such form as shall be prescribed by the Vice-Chancellor, and shall be published by the Secretary of Faculties and Academic Registrar in the *University Gazette* as soon as possible.

4. If the number of candidates duly nominated for election either as official or as ordinary members of any board shall not exceed respectively the number of official or ordinary places to be filled on that board, or if a candidate or candidates withdraw after having been duly nominated so as to leave such a number in either class as shall not exceed the number of places to be filled in that class, the Secretary of Faculties on the day appointed for the election shall declare the candidates nominated and not having withdrawn to be duly elected as members of the board.

5. If the number of candidates of either class duly nominated for election to any board, and not having withdrawn, shall exceed the number of places of that class to be filled on that board, the procedure of the election shall be as follows:

(1) The Secretary of Faculties shall send to every elector at his or her last known place of residence, or at such other place as the elector shall in writing direct, not later than the fourth day before the day fixed for the election, a voting-paper which shall list the names of those nominated and of the nominators and on which shall be specified the latest time by which it may be received at the University Offices.

(2) The voting-paper, after being signed by the voter shall be delivered at the University Offices by post prepaid or by hand.

(3) An election shall not be deemed to be invalid owing to misdirection or non-receipt of any voting-paper.

(4) The Secretary of Faculties shall be responsible for the counting of the votes, but the Vice-Chancellor shall decide on the validity of any vote which, in the opinion of the Secretary of Faculties, is in doubt.

(5) If two or more candidates have received an equal number of votes they shall be placed in order of seniority in academic standing.

(6) The result of the election shall be published in the *University Gazette*.

6. If at the time of election there shall be a greater number of vacancies than the number of candidates nominated and not having withdrawn, the Vice-Chancellor and Proctors jointly shall have power to nominate a candidate for

each vacancy remaining to be filled up, and such candidates shall then be declared to be duly elected.

7. In any election where vacancies are to be filled for periods of different length, the elected candidates shall hold office so that the tenure of those who receive more votes shall be longer than that of those who receive less votes; but if the election is uncontested or if two candidates receive the same number of votes, the candidate senior in academic standing shall hold office for the longer period.

§ 6. *Co-opted members of boards of faculties*

1. The Board of any Faculty may at any meeting, by a majority of votes, co-opt an additional member or members; provided that notice of the intention to propose such a co-optation and of the name of the person to be proposed shall have been sent through the Secretary to all the members of the board fourteen days at least before the day of meeting, and that the number of co-opted members shall never exceed four. A person who is not a member of Convocation shall not be thereby disqualified for co-optation as a member of a board.

2. Every person added by co-optation to the board of a faculty shall hold office for two years, but shall be re-eligible.

3. If a co-opted member of the board of any faculty shall become an official or ordinary member of the board, he or she shall thereupon vacate his or her seat as a co-opted member.

Section VII. Functions and Powers of Faculty Boards

§ 1. *Functions and powers of boards of faculties in general*

The functions and powers of each board of a faculty shall be:

1. To exercise supervision over such parts of the studies and examinations of the University as are or may be allotted to it by statute or otherwise.

2. To prepare, whenever it appears desirable, and to present to the General Board a report upon any matter relevant to such supervision, and generally to advise the General Board on all such matters.

3. To frame lists of lectures in accordance with the provisions of § 3 of this section.

4. To receive and consider reports and representations from the faculty, sub-faculties, departments, and boards of examiners.

5. To make recommendations to the General Board for appointments of such readers as are not elected by special boards.

6. To appoint university lecturers in accordance with the provisions of Ch. VII.

7. To make recommendations to the General Board for

(*a*) the payment of the stipends of university lecturers appointed by it;

(*b*) the provision of senior university studentships for the encouragement of advanced study or research;

(*c*) the provision and equipment of faculty rooms and libraries;

(*d*) other purposes of the faculty.

Recommendations made by a board of faculty under sub-clauses (*a*), (*b*), (*c*), and normally under sub-clause (*d*) of this clause shall be made in Hilary Term.

8. To appoint members of the boards of electors to certain professorships under the provisions of Ch. VII.

9. To perform the duties assigned to it under the provisions of Ch. VI.

10. To perform such other duties as are or may be assigned to it by statute or regulation.

§ 2. *Special functions and powers belonging to the Board of the Faculty of English Language and Literature*

1. The Board of the Faculty of English Language and Literature shall be responsible for the administration of the English Library.

2. The balance standing to the credit of the English Fund constituted under Statt. Tit. V, Sect. XIV, as the Section stood in Hilary Term 1926, shall be invested by the Curators of the University Chest to form a fund for the endowment of the English Library, and the income of this fund shall be used at the discretion of the Board of the Faculty of English Language and Literature for the benefit of the Library.

§ 3. *Special functions and powers belonging to the Board of the Faculty of Theology*

There shall be a standing committee of the Board of the Faculty of Theology for the regulation of arrangements to validate courses in Theology at Westminster College. The committee shall consist of two representatives of the Board of the Faculty of Theology, and two representatives of Westminster College. It shall have such powers and duties in respect of the Degrees of Master and Bachelor of Theology, the Postgraduate Diploma in Applied Theology, and the Diploma of Higher Education (Theology) as may from time to time be prescribed by the Board of the Faculty of Theology. The representatives of the college shall have the right to attend any meeting of the Board of the Faculty of Theology for any item concerning the college.

§ 4. *Lectures and instruction to be given under the authority of the boards of faculties*

1. Every professor and reader shall, on or before a day to be fixed by the Vice-Chancellor in each term, send to the Secretary of Faculties a Schedule of the lectures and courses of instruction intended to be given by him or her, or by his or her deputy, or departmental lecturer, or assistant, during the ensuing term in the subjects of his or her faculty; and every university lecturer shall do the same

in regard to the lectures intended to be given by him or her during the ensuing term in discharge of the obligations attached to his or her appointment by the board of his or her faculty.

2. The head of every society shall, on or before the above-mentioned day, send to the Secretary of Faculties a like Schedule of the inter-collegiate lectures (if any) which are intended to be given during the ensuing term under the authority of such society.

3. Every Schedule shall state the places, days, hours, and subjects of the lectures mentioned therein.

4. The chairman of the board of each faculty shall, with all convenient speed after the expiration of the time appointed for sending in the Schedules, call a meeting of the board for the consideration of the Schedules of lectures in the subjects of the faculty.

5. If a faculty is divided into sub-faculties, a draft of the list to be framed by the board of the lectures in the subjects of each sub-faculty shall be submitted for consideration to the sub-faculty; and in other cases a draft of the list to be framed by the board of the lectures in the subjects of the faculty shall be submitted for consideration to the faculty.

6. The board of each faculty shall revise the days and hours proposed in the several Schedules in such manner as it may deem advisable for making the lectures more accessible to students. It may also, if it thinks fit, require an alteration of the subjects proposed, if it is satisfied that such an alteration is desirable for the proper teaching of subjects in which instruction ought to be given.

7. It shall be the duty of every professor, reader, university lecturer, and inter-collegiate lecturer, in arranging their lectures, to have due and reasonable regard to the recommendations of the board of the faculty to which they belong.

8. The board of each faculty shall, out of the Schedules as revised, frame a list or lists of the lectures to be delivered under the authority of the board during the ensuing term in the subjects of the faculty. The board shall not alter any Schedule without the consent of the person named in it. But if a recommendation made by the board be not acceded to, the board may, if it thinks fit, exclude the Schedule or the part of it affected by such recommendation from the list. But any professor, reader, university lecturer, or inter-collegiate lecturer, whose lecture has been excluded, may appeal to the General Board, whose decision shall be final.

9. The board of each faculty shall have power to include in the list or lists framed by it such other lectures to be given within the University in the subjects of the faculty as it shall think fit.

10. The board of each faculty shall also have power to frame a scheme of lectures for the whole academical year, and such information as may be necessary to enable it to do so shall, so far as possible, be given to the board, in the manner prescribed in clauses 1 and 2, regarding the lectures to be given

during the ensuing academical year by any professor, reader, university lecturer, or inter-collegiate lecturer.

Section VIII. Board of the Faculty of Management

The Board of the Faculty of Management shall be constituted as follows:

(1)–(3) three persons elected by the Council for the Saïd Business School from industry, government, public service, and the sponsors of the school, such persons not normally being members of Congregation;

(4) a person appointed by the Benefactor of the Saïd Business School in pursuance of Ch. III, Sect. LIII, cll. 15 and 16;

(5) the Peter Moores Director of the Saïd Business School;

(6)–(9) the Deputy Directors of the Saïd Business School;

(10) a person elected by the General Board;

(11) the President of Templeton College;

(12)–(15) four persons elected by members of the Faculty of Management in accordance with Sect. VI, § 5;

(16) the Chairman of the Faculty of Management.

Section IX. Board of the Faculty of Medieval and Modern Languages

The Board of the Faculty of Medieval and Modern Languages shall be constituted as follows:

(1)–(5) the chairmen of each of the Sub-faculties of French, German, Italian, Russian and Other Slavonic Languages, and Spanish;

(6)–(11) six persons of whom one shall be elected by and from among the members of each of the following sub-faculties holding posts on the establishment or under the aegis of the faculty board;

(*a*) the Sub-faculty of Italian;

(*b*) the Sub-faculty of Linguistics;

(*c*) the Sub-faculty of Modern Greek;

(*d*) the Sub-faculty of Portuguese;

(*e*) the Sub-faculty of Russian and other Slavonic Languages;

(*f*) the Sub-faculty of Spanish;

(12)–(14) three persons elected by and from among the members of the Sub-faculty of French holding posts on the establishment or under the aegis of the faculty board;

(15)–(16) two persons elected by and from among the members of the Sub-faculty of German holding posts on the establishment or under the aegis of the faculty board;

(17) the Jesus Professor of Celtic or his or her nominee.

The board may co-opt not more than four additional members in accordance with Sect. VI, § 6.

Elected members of the Modern Languages Board: Regulations of the General Board

1. The period of office of elected members of the Modern Languages Board shall be three years, provided that no elected member shall serve for more than two successive periods of three years each.

2. The arrangements for the election of members shall be laid down by standing order of the faculty board.

Section X. Board of the Faculty of Music

The Board of the Faculty of Music shall be constituted as follows:

(1) Two official members, elected from among the following in the manner prescribed in Sect. VI, § 5:

The Heather Professor of Music.

The Choragus.

Such other persons as shall from time to time be qualified for official membership by virtue of holding posts on the establishment or under the aegis of the faculty board in any of the categories prescribed in Sect. VI, § 1, cl. 1 (2).

(2) The remaining members of the faculty if not more than six in number, or, if the remaining members of the faculty are more than six in number, then six of them elected in the manner prescribed in Sect. VI, § 5. The official members shall not nominate or vote at such election.

(3) Not more than four persons co-opted in accordance with Sect. VI, § 6.

Section XI. Faculties

1. Meetings shall be held, once at least in every term, in accordance with the provisions of Sect. VII, § 4, cl. 5, of the members of each faculty or sub-faculty, to consider the proposed lecture lists for each ensuing term or year, as the case may be, before these are submitted to the board of the faculty for ratification and issue.

2. Each faculty, or where a faculty has been divided into sub-faculties each sub-faculty, shall elect a chairman annually. The chairman thus elected may, when he or she judges it expedient, summon meetings of the faculty or sub-faculty of which he or she is chairman, and shall do so on the requisition of not less than one-half of the members of the body to be summoned, or, if the number of members of such body shall exceed thirty, on the requisition of not less than fifteen members. Each faculty or sub-faculty shall have power to regulate its proceedings by by-laws. The chairman of the meeting of any faculty or sub-faculty shall notify its decisions to the Secretary of Faculties, who shall preserve a record thereof.

3. The chairman of the board of any faculty which has been divided into sub-faculties may, if he or she judges it expedient, summon a meeting of the faculty, and shall do so on the requisition of not less than one-half of the members of the

faculty, or, if the number of members of the faculty shall exceed thirty, on the requisition of not less than fifteen members.

Section XII. Departments and Departmental Committees

Regulations of the General Board

§ 1. *Units of Academic Administration*

The following units of academic administration not otherwise provided for by statute or decree shall be recognized:

Department of the History of Art;
Nuffield Laboratory of Ophthalmology;
Ruskin School of Drawing and Fine Art;
Nissan Institute of Japanese Studies.

§ 2. *Constitution and terms of reference of departmental committees*

1. The membership of a departmental committee shall be confined to faculty members working in the department and to academic-related staff of grade RSII and above, or of grade ALC3 and above, who work in the department and have more than three years' service in the employment of the University of Oxford in RS or ALC grades.

2. Subject to the provisions of cl. 1 above, the number of members of which a departmental committee is to consist, the balance between elected and *ex officio* members (and the method of election of the former and the definition of the latter), and the provision (if any) for co-opted members, shall be matters for settlement *ad hoc* within the department concerned in the light of the circumstances in that department, subject always to the approval of the General Board, which shall have the right to modify a particular provision touching these matters if it shall think fit on grounds of general university policy.

3. If the General Board shall by regulation prescribe that there shall be a departmental committee for any department the initial constitution of that committee shall be determined as follows. All the faculty members working in that department shall at a meeting (or meetings) to be summoned by the head of the department draw up for submission to the General Board agreed proposals touching the matters specified in cl. 2 above. After the General Board has approved these proposals (or such modification of them as it may think fit) these shall become the constitution for that department, and a committee constituted in accordance therewith shall be set up forthwith.

4. Subject always to the approval of the General Board, a departmental committee may at any time amend its constitution.

5. The functions of a departmental committee shall be to advise the head of the department on all matters affecting the department, with particular reference to (*a*) annual estimates; (*b*) allocation of resources and accommodation; (*c*) junior academic appointments.

6. Subject to the provisions of cl. 5 above, a departmental committee shall make such rules regulating its proceedings as it shall think fit, provided always that

(*a*) meetings shall be held not less often than once a term;
(*b*) minutes shall be kept of each meeting.

Departments in which departmental committees shall be established

7. There shall be a departmental committee in each of the following departments:[1]

Biochemistry, Biological Anthropology, Saïd Business School, Computing, Continuing Education, Earth Sciences, Engineering Science, Geography, Human Anatomy and Genetics, Materials, Mathematical Institute, Pathology, Pharmacology, Physiology, Plant Sciences, Experimental Psychology, Queen Elizabeth House,[2] Ruskin School of Drawing and Fine Art,[3] Social and Cultural Anthropology, Statistics, Zoology.

8. Committees shall also be established in the three sub-departments of the Department of Chemistry and in the six sub-departments of the Department of Physics. Each committee shall advise the head of the sub-department on all matters affecting the sub-department. Its constitution and terms of reference shall otherwise be in accordance with clauses 1–4 and 6 of this subsection.

[1] For the departmental committee for the Ashmolean Museum, see Ch. III, Sect. XI, § 1, cl. 5.

[2] Members of the academic and academic-related staff working in Queen Elizabeth House who are eligible under the provisions of Ch. III, Sect. LXVII, § 2, cl. 2 (8)–(10) to elect from their own number members of the Inter-faculty Committee for Queen Elizabeth House, shall be deemed to be 'faculty members' working in the department for the purposes of cll. 1 and 3 of this sub-section.

[3] Persons appointed to teaching posts in the Ruskin School of Drawing and Fine Art in accordance with the provisions of Ch. III, Sect. LXVIII, cl. 4 shall be deemed to be 'faculty members' working in the school for the purposes of cll. 1 and 3 of this sub-section.

CHAPTER III

OTHER UNIVERSITY BODIES

Section I. Elections, Nominations, and Appointments to be made by the Vice-Chancellor and Proctors

Except where otherwise provided by statute, every election, nomination, or appointment to be made by the Vice-Chancellor and Proctors for the purpose of filling a vacancy caused or about to be caused by lapse of time in any Board of Delegates, Curators, or Visitors shall take place in Trinity Term or not later than the first Saturday in the Michaelmas Full Term next ensuing, and the person elected, nominated, or appointed shall enter or be deemed to have entered upon office on the first day of the said Michaelmas Term.

Section II. African Studies, Inter-faculty Committee for

1. There shall be an Inter-faculty Committee for African Studies, consisting of:

(1), (2) two persons appointed by the Board of the Faculty of Anthropology and Geography;

(3), (4) two persons appointed by the Board of the Faculty of Biological Sciences;

(5), (6) two persons appointed by the Board of the Faculty of Modern History;

(7), (8) two persons appointed by the Board of the Faculty of Social Studies;

(9) one person appointed by the Board of the Faculty of Oriental Studies;

(10) one person appointed by the Inter-faculty Committee for Queen Elizabeth House;

(11) one person appointed by the Curators of the University Libraries;

(12) one person appointed by the General Board.

The members of the committee shall hold office for four years from the date of election (except that casual vacancies shall be filled for the unexpired residue of the period of the person demitting office), and shall be re-eligible. The committee shall have power to co-opt up to three additional members for periods of two years. The committee shall elect its own chairman.

2. The functions of the committee shall be to consider questions concerning the organization of the studies and examinations of the University in the field of African Studies which may be referred to it by the board of any faculty, and generally to advise the faculty boards concerned on all such matters.

Section IV. Anthropology and Museum Ethnography, School of

§ 1. *School of Anthropology and Museum Ethnography and its Management Committee*

1. There shall be a School of Anthropology and Museum Ethnography consisting of the Institute of Biological Anthropology, the Institute of Social and Cultural Anthropology, and the Pitt Rivers Museum.

2. There shall be a management committee for the school consisting of:

(1) the Professor of Social Anthropology;

(2) the Professor of Biological Anthropology;

(3) the Director of the Pitt Rivers Museum;

(4)–(7) four persons appointed by the Board of the Faculty of Anthropology and Geography, who shall represent the range of disciplines covered by the school.

3. Appointed members of the committee shall hold office for three years and shall be re-eligible. Casual vacancies shall be filled for the period of office of the person demitting office.

4. There shall be a chairman of the committee who shall also be the head of the school and who shall be appointed by the faculty board from among the heads of the three constituent units. The chairman shall serve for a period of three years and shall not normally be reappointed for a second consecutive term.

5. The functions of the committee shall be the co-ordination of teaching, the rationalization of library resources, responsibility for such documentation of teaching and research as may be required from time to time, the consideration of academic and academic-related staffing matters within the school as a whole, and any other matters of management and administration of common concern to the constituent units which may be referred to it from time to time by one of the units or by the faculty board or by the General Board.

§ 2. *Institute of Biological Anthropology*

1. The premises allocated for the purposes of lecturing, instruction, advanced study, and research in Biological Anthropology shall be called the Institute of Biological Anthropology.

2. The institute shall be under the general supervision of the head of the institute appointed from time to time by the General Board under the provisions of Ch. VII, Sect. I, § 5. B, who shall make provision for the lighting, warming, water supply, and cleansing of those premises.

3. The premises allocated for the Pauling Human Sciences Centre shall also be under the general supervision of the Head of the Institute of Biological Anthropology, subject to the proviso that the allocation of accommodation within the centre shall be the responsibility of the Standing Committee for Human Sciences. The head of the institute shall make provision for the lighting, warming, water supply, and cleansing of those premises.

4. The staff of the institute and of the Pauling Centre shall be appointed, and their duties and conditions of service shall be prescribed, by the head of the institute, subject to:

(*a*) the provisions of any statute, decree, or regulation of general application;

(*b*) the approval by the Board of the Faculty of Anthropology and Geography and the General Board of any appointment which carries a stipend of more than the maximum prescribed in Ch. VII, Sect. IV, § 1, cl. 2 (ii), such approval to cover the person appointed, stipend payable, period of office, duties, and any other conditions.

§ 3. *Institute of Social and Cultural Anthropology*

1. The premises allocated for the purposes of lecturing, instruction, advanced study, and research in Social and Cultural Anthropology shall be called the Institute of Social and Cultural Anthropology.

2. The institute, including the Tylor Library of Social and Cultural Anthropology, shall be under the general supervision of the director of the institute appointed from time to time by the General Board under the provisions of Ch. VII, Sect. I, § 5. B, cl. 5, who shall make provision for the lighting, warming, water supply, and cleansing of those premises, except in so far as is otherwise provided in § 5, cl. 7 below.

3. The staff of the institute shall be appointed, and their duties and conditions of service shall be prescribed, by the director of the institute, subject to:

(*a*) the provisions of any statute, decree, or regulation of general application:

(*b*) the approval by the Board of the Faculty of Anthropology and Geography and the General Board of any appointment which carries a stipend of more than the maximum prescribed in Ch. VII, Sect. IV, § 1, cl. 2 (ii), such approval to cover the person appointed, stipend payable, period of office, duties, and any other conditions.

§ 4. *Pitt Rivers Museum*

1. The Pitt Rivers Museum shall house the Pitt Rivers Collection, and any other items of material assigned to the care of the Director by the University.

2. The Pitt Rivers Collection shall consist of:

(1) the Anthropological Collection presented by the late Lieutenant-General Augustus Henry Lane Fox Pitt Rivers, F.R.S., under an Indenture dated 20 May 1884 and accepted by Decree of Convocation of 7 March 1883;

(2) additions to the collection made subsequently in accordance with the provisions of clause 1 of the said Indenture;

(3) records, reproductions, and catalogues of or concerning items in the collection;

(4) the Balfour Library and the Archive Collections.

3. The purpose of the collection and of the museum shall be to examine, assemble, preserve, and exhibit such objects as may increase knowledge of

Ethnography and Prehistory and promote the study of Man and his Ecology in general, and to facilitate and assist such studies.

4. There shall be a Committee for the Pitt Rivers Museum consisting of:

(1) the Vice-Chancellor;

(2), (3) the Proctors;

(4) the Assessor;

(5) the Director of the Pitt Rivers Museum;

(6) the Director of the Oxford University Museum of Natural History;

(7) a person elected by Council;

(8) a person elected by the General Board of the Faculties;

(9) a person elected by the Visitors of the Ashmolean Museum;

(10)–(15) six persons elected by the Board of the Faculty of Anthropology and Geography;

(16) a person elected by the Curators of the Pitt Rivers Museum from amongst their own number.

The committee may co-opt up to four other members. Elected and co-opted members shall hold office for a period of three years, and shall be eligible for further periods of office. Casual vacancies shall be filled for the remainder of the period of office of the person being replaced.

5. The committee shall be responsible for the general supervision of the museum, and shall prepare annually for submission to Congregation a report on the activities of the museum.

6. The Director of the museum shall act as secretary to the committee, provided, however, that the committee may require him or her to withdraw from part or all of any meeting.

7. The appointment or reappointment of university lecturers who are also Curators at the museum shall be made by the Board of the Faculty of Anthropology and Geography, on the recommendation of a committee consisting of the chairman of the faculty board and an equal number of persons appointed by the faculty board and by the committee.

§ 5. *Director of the Pitt Rivers Museum*

1. The Director of the Pitt Rivers Museum shall be the first officer of the museum and shall act for and be generally responsible to the Committee for the Pitt Rivers Museum.

2. The Director shall give sixteen lectures or classes in each academic year in Ethnology or Prehistory under the direction of the Board of the Faculty of Anthropology and Geography.

3. The Director shall give attendance on at least 200 weekdays in each year.

4. The Director shall be appointed by a board of electors composed of:

(1) the Vice-Chancellor;

(2) the head of the college with which Council shall for the time being have associated the directorship, or, if the head is unable or unwilling to act, a person appointed by the governing body of the college;

(3) a person appointed by the governing body of the college specified in (2) of this clause;

(4) a person appointed by Council;

(5), (6) two persons appointed by the General Board;

(7), (8) two persons appointed by the Board of the Faculty of Anthropology and Geography;

(9) a person appointed by the Committee for Archaeology.

5. The provisions of Ch. VII, Sect. I, § 2 shall apply to elections to the directorship as if such elections were elections to a professorship to which those clauses applied.

6. The Director shall have power, subject to the concurrence of the Committee for the Pitt Rivers Museum, to delete from the registers of the museum and to remove permanently from the collection:

(1) any object deemed to be or to have become, by material degradation or otherwise, devoid of artistic, historical, ethnographic, or archaeological value, or otherwise irrelevant to the purposes of the museum;

(2) any object the transfer of which to another museum or similar institution will tend, in his or her opinion, to increase knowledge;

(3) any object the transfer of which to an institution or individual is, in his or her opinion, desirable in order to effect an exchange.

7. The museum (including those premises of the Institute of Social and Cultural Anthropology which are allocated for the museum and for the Donald Baden-Powell Quaternary Research Centre) shall be assigned to the Director. He or she shall make provision for the lighting, warming, water supply, and cleansing of those premises.

8. The staff of the museum shall be appointed, and their duties and conditions of service shall be determined by, the Director, subject to:

(*a*) the provisions of any statute, decree, or regulation of general application;

(*b*) the approval by the committee for the museum and the General Board of any appointment which carries a stipend of more than the maximum prescribed in Ch. VII, Sect. IV, § 1, cl. 2 (ii), such approval to cover the person appointed, stipend payable, period of office, duties, and any other conditions.

Section V. Archaeology, Committee for, and Sub-faculty of

1. There shall be a Committee for Archaeology, consisting of:

(1) the Edward Hall Professor of Archaeological Science;

(2) the Professor of the Archaeology of the Roman Empire;

(3) the Lincoln Professor of Classical Archaeology and Art;

(4) the Professor of European Archaeology;

(5) the Director of the Pitt Rivers Museum (or a person nominated by the Director);

(6) the Keeper of the Department of Antiquities in the Ashmolean Museum;

(7) the Keeper of the Heberden Coin Room in the Ashmolean Museum;

(8) the Director of Graduate Studies in Archaeology;

(9) the Chairman of the Archaeology Information Technology Subcommittee;

(10), (11) two persons appointed by the Board of the Faculty of Literae Humaniores;

(12)–(14) one person appointed by each of the following faculty boards: Anthropology and Geography, Modern History, Oriental Studies;

(15)–(17) three persons appointed by the Sub-faculty of Archaeology;

(18) one person appointed by the Committee of Heads of Science Departments.

Appointed members of the committee shall hold office for three years and shall be re-eligible. Casual vacancies shall be filled for the period of office of the person demitting office. The committee shall have power to co-opt not more than two additional members, who shall hold office for three years and shall be re-eligible. The committee shall elect its own chairman from among its members.

2. The committee shall have charge of the Institute of Archaeology. The committee shall make provision for the lighting, warming, water-supply, and cleansing of the premises allocated to the institute.

3. The staff of the institute shall be appointed, and their duties and conditions of service shall be prescribed, by the committee, subject to

(*a*) the provisions of any statute, decree, or regulation of general application;

(*b*) the approval by the General Board of any appointment carrying with it a stipend of more than the maximum prescribed in Ch. VII, Sect. IV, § 1, cl. 2 (ii), such approval to cover the person appointed, his or her stipend, period of office, duties, and any other conditions.

4. The committee shall submit annually to the General Board estimates of receipts and expenditure in respect of the institute.

5. The main function of the Institute of Archaeology shall be to provide for teaching and research in Archaeology.

6. There shall be an Edward Hall Professor of Archaeological Science. The professor shall lecture and give instruction in Archaeological Science.

7. The professor shall be subject to the General Provisions of the decree concerning the duties of professors and to those Particular Provisions of the same decree which are applicable to this chair.

8. The professor shall be elected by an electoral board consisting of:

(1) the Vice-Chancellor, or, if the Principal of Linacre College is Vice-Chancellor, a person appointed by Council on the occurrence of a vacancy to act as an elector on that occasion;

(2) the Principal of Linacre College, or, if the Principal is unable or unwilling to act, a person appointed by the governing body of the college on the occurrence of a vacancy to act as an elector on that occasion;

(3) a person appointed by the Governing Body of Linacre College;

(4) a person appointed by Council;

(5) a person appointed by the General Board;

(6), (7) two persons appointed by the Committee for Archaeology;

(8) a person appointed by the Board of the Faculty of Physical Sciences.

(9) a person appointed by the Board of the Faculty of Biological Sciences.

9. The committee shall have general supervision of the Research Laboratory for Archaeology and the History of Art and shall appoint a subcommittee to advise it about the laboratory. The subcommittee (which may include those who are not members of the Committee for Archaeology) shall include the Edward Hall Professor of Archaeological Science, the Director of the Research Laboratory for Archaeology and the History of Art, and representatives of both the humanities and the natural sciences. It shall have power to co-opt.

10. The work of the Research Laboratory for Archaeology and the History of Art shall be to carry out advanced study and research into the devising of such methods, especially of the physical and biological sciences, for the examination of archaeologically and historically significant material as may cause knowledge of the history of human activity to be advanced; to apply such methods to the same ends; and to set out the results from time to time in a manner suitable for publication.

11. The committee shall, in consultation with the departments and institutions concerned, keep under review and co-ordinate the services associated with Archaeology and the research done in Science-based Archaeology in the University as a whole.

12. The committee shall co-ordinate arrangements for lectures and courses of instruction in Archaeology given within the University, shall consider questions concerning the organization of the studies and examinations of the University in this field referred to it by the board of any faculty or by any committee, and shall generally advise the boards and committees concerned on all such matters.

13. The committee shall have the powers of a board of a faculty in respect of courses and examinations for such degrees or diplomas in Archaeology as may be established by decree.

14. The committee shall be recognized as having an interest in the appointment of university lecturers and any other academic staff whose duties include teaching in archaeological subjects; the faculty boards and other bodies responsible for such appointments shall ensure that in each case the selection committee, if not already including a member of the Committee for Archaeology, shall be afforced so as to include such a member.

15. The committee may act as publisher in accordance with arrangements approved from time to time by Council for works of research on subjects related to Archaeology undertaken under the auspices of the University.

16. The committee shall make an annual report of its proceedings to the General Board.

17. There shall be a Sub-faculty of Archaeology, and the Committee for Archaeology shall have the powers of a faculty board to determine the membership of that sub-faculty in accordance with Tit. VI, Sect. I, cll. 2 and 3, and Ch. II, Sect. XII. The members of the sub-faculty shall be deemed to be members of a faculty for the purposes of Tit. II, Sect. II, cl. 1. The sub-faculty shall report to the Committee for Archaeology.

Section VI. Archives, Committee for the

1. There shall be a Committee for the Archives which shall have entrusted to it, under Council, the general control of the affairs of the University Archives.

2. The committee shall consist of:

(1) the Vice-Chancellor, or a person appointed by the Vice-Chancellor who shall chair the committee;

(2) one of the Proctors or the Assessor as may be agreed between them;

(3) the Registrar, or a person appointed by the Registrar;

(4) Bodley's Librarian, or a person appointed by Bodley's Librarian;

(5)–(9) five persons appointed by Council of whom at least three shall be members of Congregation.

The members appointed under (5)–(9) shall hold office for three years and shall be re-eligible.

3. The Keeper of the Archives shall be appointed by the committee on terms and conditions which shall be subject to approval by Council.

4. The Keeper shall take charge, subject to the general direction of the committee, of the administration of the Archives and shall be responsible to the committee for the same and shall report to it as required.

5. The Archives shall comprise the following materials:

(*a*) (i) charters, grants, signed Orders in Council, title deeds, trust documents, and other similar;

(ii) records of the Chancellor's Court;

(iii) the Registers referred to in Tit. IX, Sect. VII, cll. 5 and 6;

(iv) any other material from the official files of the University, including its departments and units, whose preservation is in the opinion of the committee desirable;

(v) any other material similar in character to the above whose preservation is in the opinion of the committee desirable;

in so far as any of the above are not in current use;

(*b*) collections of statutes and decrees, of the proceedings of Council, the Curators of the University Chest, the General Board, and faculty boards, and the signed minutes of the same; the Registers of Estates and Investments, the *University Calendar*, and the *University Gazette*.

6. The Keeper shall make the archives available for their administrative purposes to, or to the order of, the heads of those university departments or offices which have transferred them and to such other persons or classes of person as the committee shall determine.

7. The committee shall determine the conditions, including payment, under which archives may be inspected or removed from the Archive Rooms.

8. The Keeper upon taking office shall give an undertaking in words recited to him or her by the Senior Proctor as follows:

'*Magister* (or *Magistra* or *Doctor*), *tu dabis fidem quod Chartas omnes Munimenta Registra et alia quaecunque ad Universitatem spectantia, tuae fidei concredita salva et in tuto custodies; quodque secreta Universitatis non revelabis*.'

and the Keeper shall reply '*Do fidem*'.

Section XI. Ashmolean Museum of Art and Archaeology

§ 1. *Visitors of the Ashmolean Museum*

1. The Visitors of the Ashmolean Museum shall be appointed as provided in Tit. VIII, Sect. V.

2. The Visitors may appoint Assistant Keepers and Departmental Assistants on the recommendation of committees set up by them on each occasion a vacancy arises, consisting of the Director, the Keeper of the Department concerned, one or more Visitors appointed by the Visitors, one representative appointed by the faculty board, or each of the faculty boards, concerned, and, if the Visitors so desire in any particular case, one or more persons with experience in the field in question appointed by them. Every Assistant Keeper shall be appointed in the first instance for a term of five years, at the end of which he or she shall be eligible for reappointment and, if reappointed, shall hold office until he or she reaches the retiring age, subject to the provisions of § 4, cl. 3, below, provided that the Visitors may, with the concurrence of the General Board, in a special case (*a*) appoint an Assistant Keeper for a shorter initial term than five years or (*b*) reappoint an Assistant Keeper who has completed his or her initial term of appointment for a further limited period, after which if reappointed he or she shall hold office as aforesaid. All appointments and reappointments of Assistant Keepers shall be subject to the approval of the General Board.

3. The Visitors shall, in consultation with the Director, appoint the Administrator of the Museum.

4. The Visitors shall exercise a general control over the purchasing policy of the Museum and shall establish a central purchasing fund. They shall also establish central funds for publications and for travel grants.

5. The Visitors shall set up a departmental committee, the membership of which shall be confined to academic staff working in the museum. The balance between elected and *ex officio* members (and the method of election of the former and the definition of the latter), and the provision (if any) for co-opted members, shall be subject to the approval of the General Board, which may modify a particular provision touching these matters if it shall think fit on grounds of general university policy. The functions of the committee shall be to advise the director on all matters affecting the museum, with particular reference to annual estimates, allocation of resources and accommodation, and appointments of academic-related staff. Meetings shall be held not less often than once a term and minutes shall be kept of each meeting.

6. The Visitors may, subject to any powers vested in the Committee of Management of the Griffith Institute, assign the use of rooms in the Museum among the different Departments and Library, and may sanction the transfer of objects in any one Department to any other Department. They may also assign the use of rooms in any other building under their control for such purposes as they may think fit.

7. The Visitors may authorize and make rules for the use of the Museum by professors, readers, and lecturers in History, Archaeology, Oriental Studies, and the Fine Arts, and by such other persons as may be authorized to teach or study therein.

8. The Visitors may make rules and arrangements for the admission of members of the University, students, and members of the public to the Museum at such hours and on such conditions as they may think fit.

9. The Visitors may enter into agreements with the Governing Bodies of the Griffith Institute and Oriental Institute, with the Ruskin Trustees, and with any other body or any faculty board in the University, for the organization of and payment for common services, and for the transfer of any parts of the Collections to the premises of those institutes or bodies, or conversely for the receipt in the Museum of books or objects which are the property of such institutes or bodies, and for the custody and administration of the same in the places to which they are transferred; provided that any such agreement which affects objects or books or rooms which have been assigned to a Department of the Museum shall be made in consultation with the Keeper of that Department.

10. The Visitors shall have power, on the recommendation of the Keeper of a Department but subject to the unanimous vote of those present, to delete from the registers of the Museum and permanently remove from the Collections:

(*a*) any object deemed to be or to have become, by material degradation or otherwise, devoid of artistic, historical, or archaeological value, or otherwise irrelevant to the purposes of the Museum;

(*b*) any object whose transfer to another museum or similar institution will tend, in their opinion, to increase knowledge;

(*c*) any object whose transfer to an institution or individual is desirable, in their opinion, in order to effect an exchange.

11. The Visitors shall have power, on the recommendation of the Keeper of a Department, to transfer on loan to another institution, subject to any conditions or limitations that they may think fit, any object whose transfer shall, in their opinion, tend to the increase of knowledge or otherwise promote the purposes of the Museum.

12. The Visitors shall hold two Stated Meetings in each term on such days as they shall determine.

13. The Visitors shall lay before Congregation annually a printed report on the general state and activities of the Museum.

§ 2. *Director of the Ashmolean Museum*

1. The Director of the Ashmolean Museum shall be the first officer and representative of the Museum as a whole.

2. The Director shall act for and be responsible to the Visitors in the exercise of their powers. He or she shall appoint the clerical, technical, and maintenance staffs, and other non-academic staff employed in the Museum (provided that he or she may delegate to the Keeper of a Department the appointment of clerical and technical staff required for duties special to that Department). The Director shall assist the Visitors in all matters for which they have general responsibility.

3. The Director shall be the Secretary to the Visitors, provided, however, that the Visitors, at their discretion, may require him or her to withdraw from any meeting.

4. The Director shall give attendance on at least 200 week days in each year, provided that the Visitors may dispense with his or her attendance for such period or periods as they may think fit.

5. The Director shall be elected by an electoral board consisting of:

(1) the Vice-Chancellor, or, if the head of the college with which the directorship is on that occasion associated is Vice-Chancellor, a person appointed by Council;

(2) the head of the college with which the directorship is on that occasion associated, or, if the head is unable or unwilling to act, a person appointed by the governing body of the college;

(3) a person appointed by the governing body of the college specified in (2) of this clause;

(4) a person appointed by Council;

(5), (6) two persons appointed by the General Board;

(7)–(9) three persons appointed by the Visitors of the Ashmolean Museum.

§ 3. *Keepers of Departments*

1. The Keepers of Departments and the Curator of the Cast Gallery shall be responsible to the Director for the charge of the rooms and collections of their respective Departments and shall undertake the personal and regular supervision thereof.

2. The Keepers and the Curator of the Cast Gallery may attend, without voting, any meeting of the Visitors, and speak on any matter affecting their Departments, provided, however, that the Visitors, at their discretion, may require them to withdraw.

3. The Keeper of each Department (but not the Curator of the Cast Gallery) shall give attendance on at least 200 week-days in each year; provided that the Visitors, after consultation with the Director, may dispense with his or her attendance for such period or periods as they may think fit. A Keeper shall have the right to teach but shall not hold office in the University or elsewhere without leave of the Visitors, nor shall he or she undertake any work which, in the opinion of the Visitors, is incompatible with the due discharge of his or her duties as a Keeper.

4. The Keeper of a Department shall have power, subject to such rules as the Visitors from time to time prescribe, to expend all sums assigned by gift, legacy, or other benefaction specifically to the maintenance, improvement, or increase of his or her Department, all sums received by the Visitors for the sole purposes of his or her Department, and any sums allocated to his or her Department by the Visitors.

5. The Keeper of a Department shall have power, subject to such rules as the Visitors may from time to time prescribe, to acquire by purchase or to receive by gift, legacy, exchange, or loan, and to add to the collections entrusted to him or her any object of art or antiquity, or any reproduction or copy of such object, or any manuscript or printed matter or other document which will in the Keeper's opinion increase the artistic or historical or archaeological value of the collections; provided that a description of any object of art or antiquity so acquired shall be inscribed in a register maintained for that purpose.

6. The Keeper of a Department may at his or her own discretion temporarily remove any object from the collections for purposes of study, repair, cleaning, or security, provided that all objects removed from the building shall be recorded in a register kept by the Director.

7. The Keeper of a Department may, subject to any rules made by the Visitors or the Director from time to time, give permission and prescribe conditions for copying or photographing any object or other property of the Museum.

8. It shall be the duty of the Keeper of a Department by all means at his or her disposal, including the arrangement of exhibitions, demonstrations, or lectures, and the preparation of printed catalogues and guides, to facilitate the study and inspection of the collections.

9. The Keeper of a Department may, with the consent of the Director, appoint clerical and technical staff required for duties special to his or her Department and, after consultation with the Administrator, fix their hours of work and pay.

10. In the event of the absence of a Keeper, the Director shall, after consultation with the Keeper if he or she is available, nominate an officer of the

Department to act for him or her in the discharge of his or her duties and powers.

§ **4.** *Assistant Keepers*

1. Assistant Keepers shall assist the Keeper of their Department in the care and supervision of the rooms and collections that have been assigned to him or her, and in the discharge of the duties laid down in § 3 of this section.

2. They shall not be required to teach, but they shall have the right to do so, subject to the Visitors being satisfied in each case that the interests of the Museum are safeguarded.

3. Their services may be terminated by the Visitors, subject to the provisions of any statute or decree in force at the time, for reasons of grave misconduct, neglect of duty, incompetence, or physical or mental infirmity.

4. The Visitors may, with the approval of the General Board, in appropriate cases give the title 'Senior Assistant Keeper' to any of the Assistant Keepers.

§ **5.** *Administrator*

1. The Administrator shall be responsible to the Director for the expenditure of all sums received by the Visitors for the maintenance, security, lighting, warming, cleaning, and invigilating of the Museum, and for all services common to two or more of the Departments.

2. The Administrator shall be responsible to the Director for the appointment and supervision of all clerical, technical, and maintenance staff other than those appointed under § 3, cl. 9, of this section, and for determining their conditions of service and pay. He or she shall assist the Keepers in the engagement of staff appointed under § 3, cl. 9. He or she shall be responsible for the payment of all clerical, technical, and maintenance staff.

3. The Administrator shall be responsible to the Director for all the administrative work in connection with the appointment of staff under § 1, cl. 2, of this section.

4. The Administrator shall be responsible to the Director for the preparation of the annual estimates of the administration account and shall give assistance in the preparation of departmental estimates; and he or she shall be responsible to the Director for the preparation of a consolidated Museum account and estimates for presentation to the Visitors.

5. The Administrator shall be responsible to the Director for forwarding all communications with the University Offices concerning matters relating to any of the Museum Administration or Departmental accounts, clerical, technical, and maintenance staff salaries and wages and conditions of service.

6. The Administrator shall, in accordance with the Director's instructions, supervise the interior structure, plant, equipment, and decoration of the Museum, and shall take all steps necessary for the security, invigilation, and

authorized use of the Museum and its premises. He or she shall be the channel for all communications concerning security and maintenance.

7. The Administrator shall be responsible to the Director for the purchase, supervision, and distribution of all supplies in common use throughout the Museum.

8. The Administrator shall be responsible to the Director for the contracts, sale, distribution, and accountancy of all Ashmolean publications (including photographs and slides) and for supervising the work of the Publications Officer.

9. The Administrator shall be responsible to the Director for the custody of the files and records of the matters referred to above and of all matters affecting the Museum generally.

10. The Administrator shall be responsible to the Director for any other business that the Director may delegate to him or her.

11. The Administrator's services may be terminated by the Visitors, subject to the provisions of any statute or decree in force at the time, for reasons of grave misconduct, neglect of duty, incompetence, or physical or mental infirmity.

§ 6. *Admission to the Museum*

1. Subject to any rules made under § 1, cl. 7 of this section, members of the University and members of the public may enter the exhibition galleries of the Museum during such hours and subject to such conditions as the Visitors shall from time to time prescribe; provided that the Keeper of a Department may, subject to the approval of the Director if he or she is available, close any room or part of any room temporarily.

2. Any person who shall steal, mark, mutilate, deface, or damage any object or other property of the Museum, or behave in a disorderly manner within its precincts, shall forthwith be excluded from the Museum and shall not be readmitted except by authorization of the Visitors. It shall be the duty of any member of the staff to apprehend any person detected in wilfully abstracting any object or other property of the Museum or otherwise committing a felony in the Museum.

§ 7. *Library*

1. The purpose of the Library is to assemble, preserve, and make available to members of the University, to the staff of the Ashmolean Museum, and to persons authorized to study in the Museum or Griffith Institute such books, manuscripts, or other documents as pertain to the study of history, archaeology, art, and Greek or Latin languages and literature.

2. There shall be a Committee for the Ashmolean Library composed of the following persons:

(1) a chairman, appointed by the Vice-Chancellor;

(2) the Director of the Ashmolean Museum;

(3)–(6) the Keepers of the Ashmolean Departments;

(7) the Curator of the Cast Gallery;

(8), (9) two persons elected by the Sub-faculty of Ancient History;

(10), (11) two persons elected by the Sub-faculty of Classical Languages and Literature;

(12) one person elected by the Board of the Faculty of Modern History;

(13), (14) two persons elected by the Committee for Archaeology;

(15) one person elected by the Libraries Board;

(16), (17) two persons elected by the Committee of Management of the Griffith Institute;

(18) one person elected by the Committee for the History of Art.

The Librarian shall be the secretary of the committee.

3. The members of the committee shall hold office for six years and shall be re-eligible, provided that a member elected to fill a vacancy caused otherwise than by lapse of time shall initially hold office only for the residue of the period of office of the member whom he or she succeeds. The committee shall have power to co-opt not more than two additional members for such periods as it shall determine.

4. The committee shall exercise general control of the affairs of the library, and, having regard to the role of the Library as an essential complement of the collections in the Ashmolean Museum and as an essential working instrument of its departments, shall so administer it as to safeguard and promote the interests and efficiency of the Museum and its staff.

5. The committee shall have general responsibility for the receipt and expenditure of all funds made available for the purposes of the Library, provided that responsibility for the safekeeping, maintenance, heating, and lighting of such rooms and premises in the Museum as may be assigned for the use of the Library and its staff lie with the Visitors of the Ashmolean Museum.

6. The committee may make rules and arrangements for the admission of readers and use of the Library, and in consultation with the Visitors may determine its hours of opening and means of access.

7. The committee shall appoint a Librarian, who shall have powers to acquire by purchase, or to receive by legacy, gift, loan, or otherwise, any such books and other documents as are relevant to the purposes of the Library, and shall be responsible for their maintenance and binding. He or she shall also be responsible for the appointment of Library staff, and shall perform such other duties as the committee may from time to time determine.

APPENDIX TO SECTION XI

Ashmolean and Taylorian Site

Decree (1) of Congregation of 24 November 1931

The site of nos. 68 and 69 St. Giles', Oxford, after providing space sufficient for a roadway on the north side shall be assigned as to the frontage to a depth of 30 feet to the future extension of the Taylor Institution and as to the remaining portion thereof, together with such portion of the Taylorian site as may be required to ensure a width of 34 feet, to the future extension of the Ashmolean Museum, a space of 10 feet between the two allocations being reserved as a passage-way to give access to the rear of both buildings.

Section XII. Benefices Delegacy

1. There shall be a Benefices Delegacy consisting of:

(1) the Vice-Chancellor;

(2), (3) the Proctors;

(4) the Assessor;

(5) the Regius Professor of Divinity;

(6) the Lady Margaret Professor of Divinity;

(7)–(10) four members of Convocation, who shall be elected by Congregation and shall hold office for six years.

Of the elected members, two shall vacate office every three years. When an elected member vacates office otherwise than by lapse of time, Congregation shall elect another person to fill the vacancy for the unexpired residue of the term of appointment. No person who has been an elected member for the full period shall be re-eligible until after the expiration of two years.

2. Whenever the University becomes entitled to exercise the right of presentation to a vacant benefice, the delegacy is empowered, subject to the approval of Council, to select the priest to be offered presentation.

3. The delegacy shall advise the Vice-Chancellor from time to time on the appointment of suitable persons to act as representatives of the University in connection with the exercise of rights of presentation, as required by Section 8 of the Patronage (Benefices) Measure 1986. After taking into account the advice of the delegacy, the Vice-Chancellor is empowered to appoint, or to authorize the appointment of, such representatives when required. After accepting appointment in respect of a particular vacancy in a benefice, the University's representative shall, in connection with the exercise of the right of presentation to the benefice concerned, discharge on the University's behalf the functions of a registered patron so far as is required by the Measure. The delegacy shall offer to such representatives such guidance as it judges appropriate on the discharge of the functions assigned to them.

4. The Vice-Chancellor is empowered, whenever the consent or concurrence of the University is required as patron of a benefice, to give such consent or express such concurrence on behalf of, or in the name of, the University.

Section XIII. Bodleian Library

§ 1. *Bodley's Librarian*

1. When a vacancy in the office of Librarian occurs or is known to be imminent the Curators of the University Libraries shall give public notice of the same one month at least before they proceed to an election.

2. Before entering upon the duties of his or her office, the Librarian shall make a declaration before the Vice-Chancellor in the following manner. The Senior Proctor shall say to the Librarian:

'*Tu dabis fidem te ea omnia fideliter executurum quae ad officium Bibliothecarii spectant.*'

And the Librarian shall answer, '*Do fidem.*'

3. The Librarian shall not hold any office in the University or elsewhere without leave of the curators, nor shall he or she undertake any work which, in the opinion of the curators, is incompatible with the due discharge of his or her duties as Librarian.

4. The term of office of the Librarian shall not be extended under proviso (*h*) (ii) to Tit. X, Sect. I, except on the recommendation of the curators after a ballot taken not less than eight months before the day on which his or her tenure of office would terminate. If the Librarian shall at any time in the judgement of the majority of the whole number of the curators be so far unable, by reason of physical or mental infirmity, to discharge his or her duties, that it is in the interest of the Library that the Librarian should cease to hold his or her office, and if he or she be unable or unwilling to resign the same, the curators shall make a representation on the matter to the Visitatorial Board with a view to his or her removal from office under the provisions of Tit. VIII, Sect. I.

5. In the event of the negligence or maladministration by the Librarian in the affairs of the Library, it shall be lawful for the Vice-Chancellor, with the assent of the curators, to admonish him or her.

§ 2. *The Officers of the Library*

1. Every Officer of the Library shall before entering upon the duties of his or her office make a declaration in the same manner and form as that set forth in § 1, cl. 2 above, with the necessary alteration of title.

2. No Officer of the Library shall hold any office in the University or elsewhere without leave of the Curators of the University Libraries, nor shall he or she undertake any work which, in the opinion of the curators, is incompatible with the due discharge of his or her library duties.

3. The term of office of an Officer of the Library shall not be extended under proviso (*h*) (ii) to Tit. X, Sect. I, except on the recommendation of the curators after a ballot taken not less than eight months before the day on which his or her tenure of office would terminate.

4. The Officers of the Library shall assist the Librarian in the discharge of his or her duties; direct and supervise, in accordance with the Librarian's instructions, the work of the staff of their departments; assist readers; and take such share in the work of the Library as the Librarian may assign to them.

5. If any Officer of the Library should be guilty of grave misconduct, neglect of the duties of his or her office, or wilful disobedience to the statutes of the University relating to it, or if by reason of physical or mental infirmity he or she should not be able to perform satisfactorily the duties of his or her office, the curators may, on the recommendation of the Librarian, make a representation to the Visitatorial Board with a view to his or her removal from office under the provisions of Tit. VIII, Sect. I, provided that such a representation shall be made only with the assent of the majority of the whole number of the curators.

§ 3. *Attendance of the Librarian and of the Officers of the Library*

1. The Librarian and the Officers of the Library shall reside within the University and, except as hereinafter provided, give attendance at the Library on all days on which it is open to readers; and during the hours at which the Old Library is open one at least of their number, or a senior member of the staff approved for the purpose by the Librarian, or a Curator of the University Libraries, shall be there present.

2. If the Librarian or an Officer of the Library be absent on the business of the Library the time of such absence shall not be reckoned as part of the leave of absence allowed to him or her under cl. 3 below, but if such absence exceed three days it shall be reported to the curators at their next meeting.

3. The Librarian shall be allowed seventy days, and each of the Officers of the Library sixty days, leave of absence in each year, exclusive of those days on which the staff is not normally required to attend. The curators may also allow to the Librarian or to any Officer of the Library, on account of ill health or for purposes of study or for other reason deemed by them to be sufficient, additional leave of absence not exceeding an aggregate period of ninety days in two consecutive years.

4. Council may if it think fit grant by decree to the Librarian or to an Officer of the Library, on account of ill health or for other reason judged by it to be sufficient, leave of absence for any period not exceeding one year, provided that the power thus given to Council shall be exercised only after a report made to it by the curators.

5. The Librarian shall so arrange the period of absence allowed under cl. 3 above that he or she or one at least of the Officers of the Library shall always be in residence and shall give daily attendance at the Library.

§ 4. *The Staff*

1. No member of the staff who would, unless exempted or excluded under the provisions of Title X, Sect. I (*g*) (ii), be eligible to be a member of the Federated Superannuation System for Universities or the Universities Superannuation Scheme shall be permitted to retain office after 30 September next following his or her 67th birthday, or if his or her birthday falls on 30 September, then after his or her 67th birthday, unless the Librarian with the approval of not less than two-thirds of the Curators of the University Libraries present and voting at a stated meeting, and with the concurrence of the Visitatorial Board under proviso (*h*) (ii) to Tit. X, Sect. I shall permit him or her to retain office for a further term which shall in no case exceed three years.

2. No other member of the staff shall be permitted to retain office after 31 July next following his or her 65th birthday, or if his or her birthday falls on 31 July then after his or her 65th birthday unless the Librarian with the approval of not less than two-thirds of the curators present and voting at a stated meeting and, in the case of those who are participants in the Employees' Pension Scheme, with the concurrence of the Curators of the Chest, shall permit him or her to retain office for a further period.

§ 5. *Admission of readers*

1. The Librarian may at any time require in respect of any undergraduate reading or proposing to read in any part of the Library a recommendation from a member of his or her society being a member of Congregation.

2. All recommendations or credentials submitted by other persons must be submitted to the Librarian or to an Officer of the Library who may, if he or she sees fit, refuse to accept them or restrict the privileges granted. The Librarian may, if he or she sees fit, refuse to accept a recommendation under cl. 1 above and an undergraduate thus excluded may not be admitted to read in the Library except by authorization of the Curators of the University Libraries.

§ 6. *The use and care of books and other objects*

1. The access of readers to books in the Library and the conditions under which books are issued to readers, or transferred for their use from one reading room to another, shall be governed by the regulations and rules of the Library in force for the time being. It shall be the duty of the Librarian and the Officers to see that these rules are duly observed, to exercise discretion in allowing the use of books of special value, and to take all reasonable precaution for the safety of such books when in use.

2. Every reader shall observe the general regulations and rules of the Library concerning the use of books, and any special instructions which may be given with regard to particular volumes or other objects given out for his or her use.

3. Books requiring binding or repair and other objects requiring special treatment for their preservation or improvement may be sent out of the Library for this purpose under such conditions as the Librarian may prescribe.

4. Such paintings, drawings, and other objects as have been deposited in the Ashmolean Museum shall be distinguished as the property of the Library and if acquired by gift shall be distinguished also by the name of the donor. They shall not be removed from the precincts of the Museum without the consent of the Curators of the University Libraries; but the Visitors of the Ashmolean Museum may, under the rules approved by themselves and the curators, allow any article deposited in the Museum which is in need of mounting, repair, or other treatment to be sent temporarily outside its precincts.

5. If it be ascertained that the Library possesses more than one copy of the same edition of any printed book, the Librarian may, with the concurrence of a committee of the curators appointed for such purposes, determine that the best only of such copies shall be retained, and may dispose of the other copy or copies by gift or for the benefit of the Library by deposit, sale, or exchange. But no book which has been acquired by legacy or gift shall be alienated under the provisions of this clause if the terms of the legacy or gift forbid this to be done. No book printed before the year 1800 shall be alienated under the provisions of this clause unless ten of the curators concur in a resolution to that effect.

6. The curators may on the Librarian's recommendation eliminate material of no literary, historical, or artistic value or of an ephemeral nature which it is not in the interests of the Library to include in the general catalogue or preserve on the shelves.

7. The authority to give permission and to prescribe the conditions for the copying or photographing of any book or other property of the Library shall rest with the Librarian subject to any conditions which may be imposed by the curators from time to time.

§ 7. *The Radcliffe Science Library*

1. The Curators of the University Libraries shall be advised on the administration of the collections and on other matters pertaining to the Radcliffe Science Library by a Science Libraries Committee whose composition and terms of reference shall be as agreed from time to time by the Curators and the Committee of Heads of Science Departments.

2. The following persons, in addition to those for whom provision is made in the Scheme approved by an Order of the Chancery Division of the High Court of Justice dated the 9th day of March 1927,[1] shall be allowed, on application to the Keeper of Scientific Books or his or her deputy, to take books out of the Radcliffe Science Library for their own use in the department, hospital, or institution to which they are attached, subject to the conditions laid down in the said clause of the statute:

(*a*) professors in, and heads of, medical departments;

(*b*) any persons working in a scientific or medical department or institution within the City of Oxford or working in a hospital associated with the

[1] See *Statutes*, 1997, p. 62.

University, who are recommended by a professor or head of a department being a member of any of the Faculties of Biological Sciences, Clinical Medicine, Mathematical Sciences, Physical Sciences, and Physiological Sciences, and are approved by the Science Libraries Committees.

§ 8. *Indian Institute Library*

1. The Indian Institute Library shall be a department of the Bodleian Library and, except as hereinafter provided, shall be controlled and administered by the Curators of the University Libraries under the provisions of Tit. VIII, Sect. III.

2. The Indian Institute Library shall consist of the stock of books and manuscripts held by the Indian Institute in 1927 and additions to that stock made from funds made specially available for that purpose (referred to below as the Indian Institute Collection), together with such holdings of the Bodleian Library as have or shall have been deposited in it in accordance with cl. 4 below.

3. The Library shall deal with topics relevant to India, Pakistan, Burma, Afghanistan, Nepal, Sri Lanka (formerly Ceylon), Thailand, and Tibet, exclusive of the history of Sri Lanka since 1795.

4. The curators shall transfer to the Library, and shall continue in future to deposit in it, such printed books not belonging to special collections as they may determine which bear primarily on the subjects above mentioned. They shall have the right to recall books if it seems desirable.

5. There shall be a committee for the Indian Institute Library consisting of:

(1) Bodley's Librarian, who shall be chairman;

(2) the Boden Professor of Sanskrit;

(3) the Spalding Professor of Eastern Religions and Ethics;

(4) the Reader in Modern South Asian History;

(5) the Keeper of Oriental Books;

(6), (7) two persons elected by the Curators of the University Libraries;

(8) one person elected by the Visitors of the Ashmolean Museum;

(9) one person elected by the Board of the Faculty of Oriental Studies;

(10), (11) two persons elected by the Board of the Faculty of Anthropology and Geography;

(12) one person elected by the Board of the Faculty of Modern History;

(13) one person elected by the Board of the Faculty of Social Studies.

The elected members of the committee shall hold office for five years and shall be re-eligible. The committee shall have power to co-opt not more than two additional members.

6. The committee shall advise the curators on the administration of the Indian Institute Library and on the purchase of books for it.

7. The committee shall act as custodians for the Indian Institute Collection, from which books may be borrowed by members of Congregation and other persons approved on behalf of the curators by the Committee for the Indian

Institute Library. The committee shall have the right to dispose of Indian Institute Collection books which are no longer required provided that they are duplicates of Bodleian books.

8. The committee shall expend such money as shall be placed at its disposal for this purpose by the University on the purchase for the Indian Institute Collection of duplicates of Bodleian books.

§ 9. *Rhodes House Library*

The Curators of the University Libraries shall have power to enter into agreements with the Rhodes Trustees for the administration of such portions of the library as shall be housed at Rhodes House. Such agreements and any amendments thereto which may be made from time to time shall be published in the *University Gazette*.[1]

§ 10. *Bodleian Law Library*

1. There shall be a committee for the Bodleian Law Library consisting of:

(1) Bodley's Librarian, who shall be chairman;

(2), (3) two persons elected by the Curators of the University Libraries;

(4), (5) two persons elected by the Board of the Faculty of Law.

The elected members of the committee shall hold office for five years and shall be re-eligible. The committee shall have power to co-opt not more than two additional members.

2. The committee shall advise the curators on the administration of the Bodleian Law Library and on the purchase of books for it.

§ 11. *The Hooke Library*

The Hooke Library shall be a lending library for the natural sciences. The curators shall be responsible for its administration and maintenance and shall apply thereto such funds as the University may make specially available for this purpose.

§ 12. *Divinity School*

Responsibility for the Divinity School and the Convocation House shall be vested in the Curators of the University Libraries, on the understanding that both buildings will be available whenever required by Council or the Curators of the Sheldonian Theatre.

[1] The agreement between the Curators of the Bodleian Library and the Rhodes Trustees was published in the *University Gazette* of 28 November 1938. Revised agreements were published in the *University Gazette* of 11 January 1950, 13 February 1958, 28 June 1968, and 26 July 1984.

§ 13. *Bodleian Japanese Library at the Nissan Institute*

1. The Bodleian Japanese Library at the Nissan Institute shall be a dependent library of the Bodleian Library and, except as provided in clause 6 below, shall be controlled and administered by the Curators of the University Libraries under the provisions of Tit. VIII, Sect. III.

2. The Bodleian Japanese Library at the Nissan Institute shall consist of:

(*a*) such holdings of the Bodleian as shall be deposited in the former library in accordance with clause 4 below;

(*b*) the collection held in 1992 in the Nissan Institute Library and such other books as may be bought to augment that collection (to be known as 'the Nissan Collection');

(*c*) holdings belonging to St Antony's College and on loan to the Bodleian Japanese Library, provided that these holdings shall be returned to the college if the Nissan Collection is ever disbanded.

3. The library shall deal with material on Japan.

4. The curators shall transfer to the library, and shall continue to deposit in it, such printed books as they may determine as bearing primarily on the subject specified in clause 3 above, provided that they shall have the right to recall books if it seems to them to be desirable to do so.

5. There shall be a Committee for the Bodleian Japanese Library at the Nissan Institute consisting of:

(1) Bodley's Librarian, or his or her deputy, who shall be chairman;

(2) the Director of the Nissan Institute;

(3) the Keeper of Oriental Books;

(4), (5) two persons elected by the Curators of the University Libraries;

(6), (7) two persons elected by the Board of the Faculty of Oriental Studies;

(8) one person elected by the Board of the Faculty of Modern History;

(9) one person elected by the Board of the Faculty of Social Studies;

(10) one person elected by the Board of the Faculty of Anthropology and Geography;

(11) one person elected by St Antony's College.

The elected members of the committee shall hold office for five years and shall be re-eligible. The faculty boards shall elect their representatives in consultation with the Inter-faculty Committee for Japanese Studies. The committee shall have power to co-opt not more than two additional members. The senior librarian in immediate charge of the running of the Bodleian Japanese Library shall serve as secretary to the committee.

6. The functions of the committee shall be:

(*a*) to advise the Curators of the University Libraries on the administration of the Bodleian Japanese Library and on the purchase of books for it;

(*b*) to act as custodian for the Nissan Collection, from which books may be borrowed by members of the University and other persons approved on behalf of the curators by the committee. The committee shall have the right to supplement that collection.

(*c*) to advise on the expenditure of such funds as may be placed at its disposal by the General Board, from the Nissan Benefaction, for the purposes of the library. The committee shall submit annually for information to the Inter-faculty Committee for Japanese Studies reports and estimates of expenditure for the following year.

§ 14. *Other dependent libraries*

Under the provisions of Tit. VIII, Sect. III, the Curators of the University Libraries shall also control and administer the following dependent library collections in accordance with such regulations as may be made from time to time by the curators after consultation with the other relevant institutions, faculties, or sub-faculties and subject to approval by the General Board:

Library of the Oriental Institute,

Library of the Institute for Chinese Studies,

Eastern Art Library;

Philosophy Library.

§ 15. *Regulations of the Curators of the University Libraries*

Library of the Oriental Institute, Library of the Institute for Chinese Studies, Eastern Art Library

1. The Curators of the University Libraries shall be advised on the administration of the collections and on the purchase of books for them by committees for, severally, Chinese, Islamic, and Ancient Near Eastern and Jewish Studies, whose composition shall be subject to approval by the curators.

2. The Keeper of Oriental Books shall submit annually for information to the Board of the Faculty of Oriental Studies reports on, and estimates of, expenditure for the following year.

3. The curators shall have general responsibility for the receipt and expenditure of all funds made available for the purposes of the Eastern Art Library in the Ashmolean Museum, provided that responsibility for the safe keeping, maintenance, heating, and lighting of such rooms and premises in the museum as may be assigned for the use of this library and its staff shall lie with the Visitors of the Ashmolean Museum, in accordance with the provisions of Tit. VIII, Sect. IV, cl. 5. The curators shall exercise general control of the affairs of the Eastern Art Library and shall so administer it as to safeguard and promote the interests and efficiency of the Ashmolean Museum and its staff.

The Philosophy Library

1. The Philosophy Library shall consist of the stock of books and other library material held by the Library of the Sub-faculty of Philosophy in 1994, and such additions to that stock as shall be made from funds specifically made available for purchase of library material by the Curators of the University Libraries.

2. The Philosophy Library shall provide a lending facility for use by junior members of the University, members of Congregation, and such other scholars as may be admitted at the discretion of the Library Committee.

3. The curators may transfer to the Philosophy Library such printed books on philosophy or matters relating to it as they may determine, under such conditions of use as the curators may lay down in consultation with the Library Committee. The curators shall have the right to recall such books if it seems desirable to them to do so.

4. There shall be a Committee of the Philosophy Library consisting of:

(1) Bodley's Librarian, or the Deputy Librarian, who shall be chairman;

(2), (3) two representatives appointed by the Curators of the University Libraries;

(4)–(9) six members of the Sub-faculty of Philosophy, one of whom shall chair the Book Selection Committee and shall be vice-chairman of the Library Committee.

The elected members of the committee shall hold office for three years and shall be re-eligible. The committee shall appoint a standing subcommittee for book selection which shall make recommendations to the Library Committee on the purchase of books and other library materials. The Philosophy Librarian shall serve as secretary to the Library Committee and the Book Selection Committee.

5. The committee shall advise the curators on the administration of the Philosophy Library and on the purchase of books and library material for it.

6. The committee shall meet at least once in every term.

APPENDIX TO SECTION XIV

Special Resolution (2) of Congregation of 4 June 1974

That with effect from the time at which the Clarendon Building ceases to be required for use by the University Offices, it shall be allocated to the Curators of the Bodleian Library[1] on the understanding that arrangements shall be made

(*a*) to provide the necessary facilities in connection with university ceremonial occasions;

(*b*) to provide for the requirements of the University Police in the central area;

(*c*) to provide for the requirements of the Faculty of Modern History for seminar space; and

(*d*) to safeguard the interest of the Delegates of the Press in the Delegates' Room;

such arrangements to be approved by Council and the General Board.

[1] Now the Curators of the University Libraries.

Section XIV. Botanic Garden, Curators of the

1. Seven members of Convocation; of whom

(1)–(3) three elected by Council;

(4)–(6) three elected by Congregation;

(7) the Sherardian Professor of Botany for the time being *ex officio*

shall be the Curators of the Botanic Garden. The elected curators shall hold office for six years and shall be re-eligible. Any casual vacancy occurring by death, resignation, or otherwise among the appointed or elected curators shall be filled by an appointment or election for the remainder of the period for which the vacating curator would have held office.

2. The Curators of the University Chest shall pay annually to the Curators of the Botanic Garden the sum of £150 and such further sum as Council shall from time to time determine to be necessary for keeping the Garden in proper order and for the provision and equipment necessary for raising and preserving rare plants in accordance with the usual practice in such gardens.

3. The direction and control of the Garden shall be exercised by the curators. The Sherardian Professor of Botany for the time being shall have charge and supervision of the Garden, and shall be called the Keeper of the Botanic Garden, provided always that the curators at the request of the professor may assign such charge and supervision to some other person.

4. The professor shall not later than the second week of each Hilary Term submit to the curators an estimate of the necessary expenditure on the upkeep of the Garden together with a programme of work for the ensuing financial year. The curators may amend the estimates before submitting them to the Curators of the University Chest and shall approve the programme with or without amendment.

5. The curators

(*a*) shall appoint, and may dismiss, a head gardener, who shall be called the Superintendent of the Botanic Garden, and shall, subject to the approval of Council, determine his or her terms and conditions of service;

(*b*) shall determine what additional employees are required and their terms and conditions of service. Such employees shall be appointed by the professor and may be dismissed by him or her.

6. It shall be the duty of the curators to prepare and lay before Congregation annually a printed report.

7. If the University shall at any time cease to maintain a library in which the bequest of books, dried plants, fruits, and seeds received by it under the will of Dr. William Sherard, who died in 1728, are kept under the custody of the Sherardian Professor of Botany, this decree shall become null and void and the provisions of the decree of the Court of Chancery of 11 June 1734 as modified by the Order of the same Court dated 13 November 1886 shall again become operative.

8. This decree shall not be amended without the consent of the Royal College of Physicians of London.

Section XV. Brazilian Studies, Centre for

1. Following the provision of support from donors in Brazil, there shall be within the University a Centre for Brazilian Studies.

2. The functions of the centre shall be to co-ordinate and develop graduate teaching and research on Brazil and through its programme of lectures, seminars, conferences, and publications to act as a focus for the study of Brazil and for the promotion of a greater understanding of Brazil and its place in the world, in the United Kingdom, and in Europe. The aim of the centre shall be to promote a greater understanding of the history and culture of Brazil, its society, its economic and political development, and its place in the world.

3. There shall be an advisory council for the centre which shall contribute to promoting the centre in Brazil and internationally, and to raising funds for the continuation of the centre after the initial five years from the date of its establishment.

4. The centre shall be under the general supervision of the Inter-faculty Committee for Latin American Studies.

5. There shall be a director of the centre who shall hold the title of Director of the Centre for Brazilian Studies. The post shall be on the establishment of the Inter-faculty Committee for Latin American Studies. The director shall be appointed for such periods as Council may from time to time determine. The director shall be elected by an electoral board consisting of:

(1) the Vice-Chancellor, or, if the head of the college specified in (2) of this clause is Vice-Chancellor, a person appointed by Council;

(2) the head of the college with which the directorship shall be for the time being associated, or, if the head is unable or unwilling to act, a person appointed by the governing body of the college;

(3) a person appointed by the governing body of the college specified in (2) of this clause;

(4)–(6) three persons appointed by the Inter-faculty Committee for Latin American Studies;

(7) a person appointed by Council;

(8), (9) two persons appointed by the General Board;

6. The director shall have charge of the premises allocated for the centre and shall make provision for the lighting, warming, water supply, and cleansing of the premises.

7. The director shall be a member *ex officio* of the Inter-faculty Committee for Latin American Studies and of the Latin American Centre Committee.

8. The director shall submit to the General Board an annual report on the work of the centre.

9. The director shall be subject to the General Provisions of the decree concerning the duties of professors and shall reside within the University during six months at least in each academical year, between the first day of October and the ensuing first day of August.

10. There shall be a management committee for the centre consisting of the director, the chairman and two nominees of the Inter-faculty Committee for Latin American Studies, and a nominee of St Antony's College. The director shall be chairman of the management committee. The management committee shall supervise the academic activities of the centre, including the selection of its visitors.

11. The staff of the centre shall be appointed, and their duties and conditions of service shall be determined, by the director, subject to:

(*a*) the provisions of any statute, decree, or regulation of general application;

(*b*) the approval by the Inter-faculty Committee for Latin American Studies, on the recommendation of a committee appointed by the inter-faculty committee (of which the director shall be a member and which may include other persons not being members of the inter-faculty committee), and by the General Board of any appointment which carries a stipend of more than the maximum prescribed in Ch. VII, Sect. IV, § 1, cl. 2 (ii), such approval to cover the person appointed, stipend payable, period of office, duties, and any other conditions.

Section XVI. Byzantine Studies, Committee for

1. There shall be a Committee for Byzantine Studies which shall consist of:

(1) the Bywater and Sotheby Professor of Byzantine and Modern Greek Language and Literature;

(2)–(4) three persons appointed by the Board of the Faculty of Literae Humaniores;

(5)–(7) three persons appointed by the Board of the Faculty of Modern History;

(8)–(9) two persons appointed by the Board of the Faculty of Oriental Studies;

(10) one person appointed by the Board of the Faculty of Medieval and Modern Languages;

(11) one person appointed by the Board of the Faculty of Theology;

(12) one person appointed by the Visitors of the Ashmolean Museum.

The members of the committee shall hold office for four years from the date of appointment (except that casual vacancies shall be filled for the unexpired residue of the period of office) and shall be re-eligible.

The committee shall have power to co-opt up to three additional members who shall hold office for two years and shall be re-eligible. The committee shall elect its own chairman.

2. The functions of the committee shall be to promote Byzantine Studies within the University, to consider such questions concerning the organization of the

studies and examinations of the University in that field as may be referred to it by the board of any faculty, and generally to advise the faculty boards concerned on all such matters.

Section XXI. Careers Service, Committee for

1. There shall be a Committee for the Careers Service consisting of:

(i) the Vice-Chancellor;

(ii) the Proctors;

(iii) the Assessor;

(iv) five persons who shall be appointed by Council of whom one at least shall be appointed from among its own members;

(v) one person who may be appointed by each of the colleges and other societies (hereinafter referred to as 'societies');

(vi) one resident Junior Member appointed by the Graduate Committee of the Oxford University Student Union;

(vii) two resident Junior Members appointed by the Oxford University Student Union;

(viii) not more than sixteen other persons co-opted by the committee who need not be members of the University, and of whom not less than two shall be representatives of professions and careers of particular interest to women.

2. Members of the committee shall hold office for such period as may be specified at the time of their appointment, but in the case of (*a*) members appointed by Council not exceeding three years, provided always that the periods of office of the members appointed by Council shall not be fixed so as to expire simultaneously; (*b*) members appointed by the societies and co-opted members, not exceeding two years; (*c*) members appointed by the Graduate Committee of the Oxford University Student Union and the Oxford University Student Union not exceeding one year. Members of the committee shall be eligible for reappointment.

3. The committee shall assist members of the University by giving advice on careers and by seeking and receiving information of openings for employment and by supplying such information to them and also by supporting the applications of suitable candidates.

4. The financial arrangements for the support of the work of the Careers Service shall be such as Council may approve.

5. The committee may appoint a Director and Deputy Director of the Careers Service, other academic-related staff, and clerical and other assistants and, subject to the concurrence of Council, determine their conditions of service.

6. The committee may

(*a*) constitute an Executive Committee, of which the Vice-Chancellor or the Vice-Chancellor's deputy shall be chairman, consisting of one of the Proctors and not less than seven other members of the committee, of whom not less than half the total number minus one shall be members of the committee appointed under the provisions of clause 1 (v) above, and one a member of the committee appointed under the provisions of clause 1 (iv) above;

(*b*) give the Executive Committee such powers in regard to the performance of the duties of the committee as it may deem expedient.

7. The committee shall invite each society to appoint a member of its body, who may be the member of the committee appointed by the society, to act as a representative and correspondent of the committee in the society concerned. Such persons shall hold office for two years and shall be re-eligible.

8. The committee may appoint from its own members a special subcommittee (which may co-opt such other persons competent to give advice as it may from time to time require) to organize, on such terms and conditions as the committee may deem expedient, vacation schools for business executives.

Section XXII. Chemistry, Department of

§ 1. *Department of Chemistry and Chairman of Chemistry*

1. The Department of Chemistry shall be assigned by the General Board from time to time for a specified period not exceeding five years in the first instance to a person holding an established academic post in the department, normally with the title of professor or reader, after consultation with the Board of the Faculty of Physical Sciences, the heads of the sub-departments of the Department of Chemistry, and the other holders of established academic posts in those sub-departments. The person to whom the headship of the department is assigned shall have the title of Chairman of Chemistry.

2. The Chairman shall be eligible for reappointment, provided that no one person shall hold the post for a total of more than ten years in aggregate.

3. The Chairman shall receive a stipend equivalent to that of a professor holding a special allowance under Ch. VII, Sect. I, § 7, Schedule I.

4. The Chairman, advised and assisted by the Chemistry Management Committee, shall have the powers and responsibilities set out in clause 2 of the Particular Provisions applicable to professors enumerated in Ch. VII, Sect. I, § 5. B, Schedule B, provided that:

(*a*) the Chairman's duties related to teaching shall be as specified in clause 5 below; and

(*b*) the Chairman may delegate to the heads of sub-departments responsibilities in relation to their sub-departments as set out in clause 2 of the said Particular Provisions applicable to professors enumerated in Schedule B.

5. The Chairman may undertake teaching and research in accordance with such arrangements as may be made from time to time with the Board of the Faculty of Physical Sciences, and may undertake examining and graduate supervision, but the provisions of Ch. VII, Sect. I, § 5. A, cll. 6 and 7 imposing examining and supervision as duties shall not apply to this office.

6. The Chairman shall be eligible to apply to the General Board for sabbatical leave in accordance with the regulations made by the Board under the provisions of Ch. VII, Sect. I, § 5. A, cl. 14. During a period of leave, a deputy shall be appointed by the General Board on the advice of the Board of the Faculty of Physical Sciences. The deputy shall receive an appropriate proportion of a Schedule I allowance, in accordance with the arrangements which apply when a head of department is on sabbatical leave.

§ **2.** *Chemistry Management Committee*

1. There shall be a Chemistry Management Committee consisting of:

(1) the Chairman of Chemistry;

(2) the Head of the Sub-department of Inorganic Chemistry;

(3) the Head of the Sub-department of Organic Chemistry;

(4) the Head of the Sub-department of Physical and Theoretical Chemistry;

(5) the Director of the Oxford Centre for Molecular Sciences;

(6) a member of the Academic Committee of the Department of Chemistry appointed by that committee;

(7)–(9) three members, one from each of the Sub-departments of Inorganic, Organic, and Physical and Theoretical Chemistry, elected by the holders of established academic posts in the Department of Chemistry.

The committee shall have the power to co-opt up to two additional members.

The election of the members under (7)–(9) shall be conducted by the Chairman of Chemistry. The members under (6)–(9) shall each hold office for a period of three years and shall be re-eligible. The Chairman of Chemistry shall be chairman of the committee.

2. The Chemistry Management Committee shall advise and assist the Chairman of Chemistry in carrying out the duties of the office.

§ **3.** *The Heads of the Sub-departments of the Department of Chemistry*

1. There shall be three sub-departments of the Department of Chemistry: the Sub-department of Inorganic Chemistry, the Sub-department of Organic Chemistry, and the Sub-department of Physical and Theoretical Chemistry.

2. The head of each sub-department shall be responsible for academic work in the subject area of that sub-department, including overseeing research, and for collaborating with other sub-departments and with the Sub-faculty of Chemistry and the Chemistry Management Committee in arranging for the teaching of Chemistry. The head shall also have responsibility for the allocation and expenditure of the budget assigned by the Chairman of Chemistry to that sub-department.

3. The head of each sub-department shall be appointed for a specified period of not less than five years from among those holding established academic posts in that sub-department, normally from amongst those with the title of professor or reader, by the General Board after consultation with the Board of the Faculty

of Physical Sciences, the Chemistry Management Committee, and the holders of established academic posts in that sub-department.

4. The head for the time being of each sub-department shall undertake teaching in accordance with such arrangements as shall be made from time to time with the Board of the Faculty of Physical Sciences. When the head of a sub-department is a professor, his or her teaching duties shall normally be those laid down in Ch. VII, Sect. I, § 5. B, cl. 2 (*b*).

5. The head of each sub-department shall receive a special allowance of the amount receivable by certain professors in accordance with Ch. VII, Sect. I, § 7, as follows:

Inorganic Chemistry	Schedule III
Organic Chemistry	Schedule III
Physical and Theoretical Chemistry	Schedule III

Section XXIII. Chinese Studies, Institute for

1. There shall be within the University an Institute for Chinese Studies.

2. The Institute for Chinese Studies shall provide a focus for teaching about and research on the Chinese world, particularly for those studies which are based upon primary materials. It shall also act as a centre both for the Oxford scholarly community working in the field and for scholars from the Chinese world.

3. The Curators of the Oriental Institute shall make provision for the lighting, heating, water supply, and cleansing of the parts of the Clarendon Press Institute allocated to the Institute for Chinese Studies and for such other parts of the Clarendon Press Institute as may be allocated to them.

4. The Curators of the Oriental Institute shall have power to appoint such staff (excluding library staff) as may be required to carry out their functions under clause 3 above and to determine their duties and conditions of service, subject to the provisions of any statute, decree, or regulation of general application and to the approval by the General Board of any appointment carrying with it a stipend of more than the maximum prescribed in Ch. VII, Sect. IV, § 1, cl. 2 (ii), such approval to cover the person appointed, his or her stipend, period of office, and duties, and any other conditions.

5. The Curators of the Oriental Institute shall be responsible for the safe keeping, maintenance, heating, and lighting of such rooms and premises in the Clarendon Press Institute as may be allocated for housing library collections administered by the Curators of the Bodleian Library.

6. The Inter-faculty Committee for Chinese Studies shall act as the committee of management of the Institute for Chinese Studies.

7. The Institute for Chinese Studies shall include a library which shall be a dependent library of the Bodleian Library and shall be controlled and

administered by the Curators of the University Libraries under the provisions of Tit. VIII, Sect. III.

8. There shall be a Director of the Institute, who shall be appointed by the General Board from time to time for a specified period of not less than five years. The directorship shall be held by a person holding an established academic post in the field, normally with the title of professor or reader.

Section XXIV. Chinese Studies, Inter-faculty Committee for

1. There shall be an Inter-faculty Committee for Chinese Studies consisting of:

(1) the Vice-Chancellor;

(2) the Shaw Professor of Chinese;

(3) the Director of the Institute for Chinese Studies, if not otherwise a member;

(4) one person elected by the General Board of the Faculties;

(5), (6) two persons elected by the Board of the Faculty of Anthropology and Geography;

(7), (8) two persons elected by the Board of the Faculty of Modern History;

(9), (10) two persons elected by the Board of the Faculty of Oriental Studies;

(11), (12) two persons elected by the Board of the Faculty of Social Studies;

(13), (14) two persons elected by the Governing Body of Wolfson College.

The elected members of the committee shall hold office for four years from the date of election (except that casual vacancies shall be filled for the unexpired residue of the period of office of the member demitting office) and shall be re-eligible. The committee shall have power to co-opt up to three additional members for periods of two years.

2. The functions of the committee shall be:

(*a*) to keep under review, and to advise the General Board and other bodies concerned generally on, the provision and organization of studies at both graduate and undergraduate level and examinations in the field of Chinese Studies, and the co-ordination and balance of such studies, and to promote co-operation between the bodies concerned with Chinese Studies in the University, including the Institute for Chinese Studies;

(*b*) to allocate such funds as may be placed at its disposal by the General Board or other bodies for specific or general purposes connected with Chinese Studies;

(*c*) to act as committee of management of the Institute for Chinese Studies.

Section XXV. Clubs Committee

§ 1. *Clubs Committee*

1. There shall be a Clubs Committee which shall comprise:

(1) the Assessor (or if the Assessor and the Proctors shall so agree one of the Proctors) who shall be the chairman;

(2)–(4) three members of Congregation appointed by Council;

(5), (6) two members of Congregation appointed by a special meeting to which each college and other society except the permanent private halls shall be entitled to send two representatives. One of the two appointed shall be a Senior Treasurer of Amalgamated Clubs;

(7) one resident Junior Member appointed by the Graduate Committee of the Oxford University Student Union;

(8)–(10) three resident Junior Members appointed by the Oxford University Student Union;

(11), (12) two persons co-opted from the members of the sub-committee provided for in § 2, cl. 1 below.

The members appointed under (2)–(6) above shall hold office for three years and the members appointed under (7)–(12) shall hold office for one year, and shall be re-eligible. Casual vacancies shall be filled for the remainder of the period of office of the person being replaced.

The committee may co-opt not more than two other persons who shall hold office for periods to be fixed by the committee, and shall be re-eligible.

2. The committee shall

(*a*) operate a scheme to provide assistance for university clubs, societies, and publications and in particular to receive and decide applications for financial assistance from university clubs, societies, and publications;

(*b*) have the power to require such clubs, societies, and publications to satisfy such conditions as it may from time to time determine as a precondition of any assistance granted under (*a*) above, and further have the power to take such steps as may be necessary to satisfy itself that any grants so made have been applied in accordance with any conditions laid down;

(*c*) have power to provide and administer a Clubs Central Office, and appoint secretarial and clerical staff, and, subject to the concurrence of Council, determine their conditions of service;

(*d*) be responsible for the expenditure of all moneys allocated to the committee, except that it may delegate to the subcommittee provided for in § 2, cl. 1 below the power to decide applications for grants for non-recurrent expenditure from clubs, societies, and publications;

(*e*) consider questions concerning clubs, societies, and publications referred to it by any university body and generally advise on all such matters.

3. The Curators of the University Chest may receive contributions from the colleges and other societies and, subject to the consent of Council, from any other persons, or bodies of persons, these funds to be applied for the purposes of the committee; and the committee may charge such fees to members of the University using the services provided under its auspices as it shall think fit.

4. The committee shall annually prepare and publish accounts which shall be audited by the University Auditor.

5. The Committee shall make a report of its proceedings every year to Congregation, which shall be published in the *Gazette*.

§ 2. *Subcommittee of the Clubs Committee*

1. There shall be a subcommittee of the Clubs Committee which shall comprise

(1) (as chairman) the chairman of the Clubs Committee;

(2) a Senior Member appointed by the Clubs Committee being a member of that committee;

(3), (4) two Junior Members appointed by the Clubs Committee being members of that committee appointed by the Oxford University Student Union;

(5) the Junior Member appointed by the Graduate Committee of the Oxford University Student Union to the Clubs Committee;

(6)–(15) ten resident Junior Members appointed by ten university clubs, societies, and publications registered with the Proctors and nominated for this purpose by the Clubs Committee at the end of the preceding academic year.

The member appointed under (2) shall hold office for three years and those under (3), (4), and (5) for one year (provided they remain members of the Clubs Committee). The members appointed under (6)–(15) shall hold office for one year. All shall be re-eligible. Casual vacancies shall be filled for the remainder of the period of office of the person being replaced.

2. The subcommittee shall have such powers and duties as the Clubs Committee may from time to time determine.

Section XXVI. Comparative Philology and General Linguistics, Committee for

1. There shall be a Committee for Comparative Philology and General Linguistics, consisting of:

(1) a person nominated by the General Board who shall be chairman;

(2) the Professor of Comparative Philology;

(3) the Professor of General Linguistics;

(4) the Director of Graduate Studies appointed for the time being by the committee;

(5)–(10) two persons nominated by each of the following faculty boards: English Language and Literature, Literae Humaniores, and Medieval and Modern Languages;

(11)–(12) one person nominated by each of the following faculty boards: Oriental Studies, Psychological Studies;

(13)–(15) up to three co-opted members.

Elected members of the committee shall serve for periods of four years and shall be re-eligible. Vacancies occurring at any time before the proper period among the elected members of the committee shall be filled for the residue only of the period.

2. The committee shall have power to make arrangements for lectures and courses of instruction in Comparative Philology and General Linguistics to be given within the University and to consider questions concerning the organization of the studies and examinations of the University in these fields referred to it by the board of any faculty or committee and generally to advise boards and committees concerned on all such matters.

3. The committee shall have the powers of a board of a faculty in respect of courses and examinations for such degrees or diplomas in these fields as may be established by decree and for the admission and examination of students for advanced degrees in these fields.

4. The committee shall have power to allocate such funds as may be placed at its disposal by the General Board for purposes connected with Philology and Linguistics.

Section XXVII. Computing in the Arts, Committee on

There shall be a Committee on Computing in the Arts, the composition and terms of reference of which shall be laid down from time to time by the Information and Communications Technology Committee.

Section XXVIII. Computing Laboratory

1. The work of the Computing Laboratory shall be:

(*a*) to encourage and develop the use of electronic and other types of computing machines in scientific and other research work done in the University;

(*b*) to advise on both specific and general problems of computation;

(*c*) to provide lectures and instruction on computation and related topics and to carry out research in these fields.

2. The Board of the Faculty of Mathematical Sciences shall exercise general supervision over the work of the laboratory and for this purpose shall set up a Sub-faculty of Computation.

3. Subject to the provisions of this section, the Director of the laboratory shall supervise the work of the laboratory. He or she shall also lecture and give instruction, and engage in research, in some field related to that of the laboratory.

4. The staff of the laboratory shall be appointed, and their duties and conditions of service shall be prescribed, by the Director, provided that

(*a*) any appointment to a teaching or research post carrying a stipend of more than the maximum prescribed in Ch. VII, Sect. IV, § 1, cl. 2 (ii) shall be made by the Board of the Faculty of Mathematical Sciences on the recommendation of a committee appointed by the board (of which the director shall be a member and which may include other persons not being members of the board), and the duties and conditions of service shall be prescribed by the board. Such appointments shall also require approval by the General Board, such approval to cover the person appointed, his or her stipend, period of office, and duties, and any other conditions as determined by the board;

(*b*) all appointments shall be subject to the provisions of any statute, decree, or regulation of general application.

5. The Director of the laboratory shall be appointed under such arrangements as the University shall from time to time prescribe by statute or decree.

Section XXIX. Computing Services and Educational Technology Resources Centre

1. The Computing Services shall:

(*a*) provide a computing service and advisory services on computing and related matters for academic bodies, departments, and institutions, and other organizations within the University and (on conditions to be approved by the Information and Communications Technology Committee) for organizations not part of the University; and

(*b*) provide instruction in computing and related matters, including the application of computers to teaching, to members and staff of the University and (on conditions to be approved by the Information and Communications Technology Committee) to organizations not part of the University.

2. The Educational Technology Resources Centre shall provide educational technology resources, in particular audio-visual technology services, for academic bodies, departments, and institutions and other individuals and organizations within the University, and (on conditions to be approved by the Information and Communications Technology Committee) for organizations not part of the University.

3. The Computing Services and the Educational Technology Resources Centre shall be responsible to the I.C.T. Committee under the provisions of Ch. II, Sect. I, § 11.

Section XXXI. Continuing Education Board

1. There shall be a Continuing Education Board consisting of:

(1), (2) one or two members elected by Council from amongst its own members (as determined from time to time by Council, bearing in mind the desirability of there being strong representation of the board on Council and its committees, particularly the Educational Policy and Standards and Planning and Resource Allocation Committees), of whom one shall be designated chairman of the board by the Vice-Chancellor after consultation with the Director of the Department for Continuing Education;

(3)–(7) five persons of whom one shall be elected by each Divisional Board;

(8), (9) two persons elected by the Advisory Council on Continuing Education;

(10) the Director of the Department for Educational Studies or the Director's nominee;

(11)–(15) the Director, Deputy Directors, and Academic Dean of the Department for Continuing Education;

(16)–(18) three other members of the Department for Continuing Education elected by the members of the department from amongst their number.

The board may co-opt up to four additional members, who shall not be members of the Department for Continuing Education.

Elected and co-opted members shall serve for three years and shall be re-eligible, provided that casual vacancies shall be filled for the remaining period of office of the member being replaced.

2. The board shall be responsible, under Council and subject to the plans, policies, and guidelines set by Council and its committees, for continuing education. The functions and powers of the board shall include the following, and such other functions and powers as may be assigned to it by Council by decree or otherwise.

(*a*) The board shall, in collaboration with the Divisional Boards under the provisions of Tit. V, Sect. II, cl. 1 (*l*), promote the provision of continuing education opportunities across the University, with the exception of the postgraduate medical education for which the Director of Postgraduate Medical and Dental Education and Training has specific responsibility, and for this purpose shall promote co-operation between the University and other agencies. Continuing education shall be defined in this context as all education taken up after a substantial break following initial education, except for the education of mature students on courses leading to postgraduate qualifications under the aegis of the divisions.

(*b*) The board shall consider and advise Council on the funding requirements of continuing education across the University, with particular reference to the preparation of bids under HEFCE or any subsequent public funding system.

(*c*) The board shall exercise general supervision over the Department for Continuing Education.

(*d*) The board shall have the powers of a Divisional Board in respect of continuing education courses and examinations conducted within the University except where otherwise specifically provided, and for the admission and examination of students for such advanced degrees as may be established under its aegis from time to time.

3. The board shall make an annual report to Council on the activities of the board and of the Department for Continuing Education in the preceding academic year, measured against the board's agreed operating statement.

Section XXXII. Economics, Department of

1. The Board of the Faculty of Social Studies shall exercise general supervision over the department.

2. The department shall be assigned by the General Board for a specified period not exceeding three years in the first instance to a person holding an established academic post in the University or an equivalent appointment in a college or

other society, after consultation with the Board of the Faculty of Social Studies. The person to whom the headship of the department is assigned from time to time shall have the title of Head of the Department of Economics. The head of department shall be eligible for reappointment for a maximum of one further period of office not exceeding three years.

3. The duties of the head of department shall include the general supervision, under the Board of the Faculty of Social Studies, of research, advanced study, and teaching in the department. The head of department shall engage in advanced study or research and shall give such number of lectures and hold such number of classes as are required by the terms of appointment of his or her normal university post, except that the Board of the Faculty of Social Studies may recommend to the General Board that he or she be given remission from such specified duties attached to that post as shall be considered appropriate in view of his or her additional responsibilities as head of department. The head of department shall have charge of the department subject to clause 1 of this decree and to Ch. III, Sect. LXIX, concerning the St Cross Building Management Committee. The head of department shall receive a special allowance as set out in Ch. VII, Sect. I, § 7, Schedule V.

4. The staff of the department shall be appointed, and their duties and conditions of service shall be prescribed, by the head of department, provided that

(*a*) any appointment to a teaching or research post carrying a stipend of more than the maximum prescribed in Ch. VII, Sect. IV, § 1, cl. 2 (ii) shall be made by the faculty board on the recommendation of a committee appointed by the board (of which the head of department shall be a member, and which may include other persons not being members of the board), and the duties and conditions of service of any such appointment shall be prescribed by the faculty board. Such appointments shall also require approval by the General Board, such approval to cover the person appointed, his or her stipend, period of office, and duties, and any other conditions as determined by the faculty board;

(*b*) all appointments shall be subject to the provisions of any statute, decree, or regulation of general application.

5. The constitution of the department, which shall in all respects be subject to the conditions of this decree, shall be determined by the Board of the Faculty of Social Studies and shall be incorporated in the board's Standing Orders.

Section XXXIII. Educational Studies, Committee for

1. There shall be a Committee for Educational Studies to promote the study of and research in education and to make provision within the University for courses of training for teachers, and for these purposes to promote co-operation between the University and other educational agencies, in particular on educational matters of common concern between the University and Westminster College. The committee shall exercise general oversight of the validation of courses in Educational Studies offered by Westminster College.

2. The committee shall consist of:

(1) one of the Proctors or the Assessor;

(2) the Professor of Educational Studies;

(3) the Reader in Education;

(4) a member of the General Board, appointed by the board;

(5) a member of the Board of the Faculty of Literae Humaniores, being a member of the Sub-faculty of Philosophy, appointed by the faculty board;

(6) a member of the Board of the Faculty of Psychological Studies appointed by the faculty board;

(7) a member of the Board of the Faculty of Social Studies appointed by the faculty board;

(8)–(13) six members of the academic staff of the Department of Educational Studies elected by the academic staff of the department under arrangements to be approved by the Vice-Chancellor and Proctors;

(14) the Director of the Department for Continuing Education;

(15)-(16) two representatives of Westminster College;

(17)–(22) six members of faculties appointed by the General Board.

The committee shall have power to co-opt not more than two additional members, who need not be members of Congregation. The committee shall appoint its own chairman.

3. Appointed, elected, and co-opted members shall serve for three years, provided that they shall serve only for as long as they continue to hold the offices by virtue of which they were appointed to the committee, and shall be re-eligible; casual vacancies shall be filled for the remaining period of office of the person being replaced.

4. The committee shall, in association as appropriate with educational agencies in the Oxford area, make provision for a professional committee which shall satisfy the regulations of the Secretary of State for Education for the training of teachers. All matters of teacher training within, or concerning external teaching qualifications validated by, the University which require professional recognition, approval, or advice, shall be referred to the professional committee. The professional committee shall appoint its own chairman.

5. The Committee for Educational Studies shall have the powers of a board of a faculty in respect of courses and examinations for such degrees, diplomas, and certificates in educational studies as may be established by decree and for the admission and examination of students for advanced degrees in that field.

6. The committee shall exercise general supervision over the Department of Educational Studies.

7. There shall be a Professor of Educational Studies who shall also be the Director of the Department of Educational Studies. He or she shall lecture and give instruction in Educational Studies. The professor shall be subject to the General Provisions of the decree concerning the duties of professors and to those Particular Provisions of the same decree which are applicable to this chair.

8. The professor shall be elected by an electoral board consisting of:

(1) the Vice-Chancellor, or, if the head of the college specified in (2) of this clause is Vice-Chancellor, a person appointed by Council on the occurrence of a vacancy to act as an elector on that occasion;

(2) the head of the college to which the professorship shall be for the time being allocated by Council under any decree in that behalf, or, if the head is unable or unwilling to act, a person appointed by the governing body of the college on the occurrence of a vacancy to act as an elector on that occasion;

(3) a person appointed by the governing body of the college specified in (2) of this clause;

(4) the Secretary of State for Education, or a person appointed by him or her to act as an elector on each occasion;

(5) a person appointed by Council;

(6) a person appointed by the General Board;

(7), (8) two persons appointed by the Committee for Educational Studies (at least one of whom shall be a University Lecturer in Educational Studies);

(9) a person appointed by the Board of the Faculty of Social Studies.

9. The staff of the department shall be appointed, and their duties and conditions of service shall be prescribed, by the Professor of Educational Studies, provided that:

(*a*) any appointment to a teaching or research post carrying a stipend of more than the maximum prescribed in Ch. VII, Sect. IV, § 1, cl. 2 (ii), shall be made by the Committee for Educational Studies on the recommendation of a subcommittee (of which the professor shall be a member and which may include other persons not being members of the committee), and the duties and conditions of service of any such appointment shall be prescribed by the committee; such appointments shall also be approved by the General Board, the approval to cover the person appointed, his or her stipend, period of office, and duties, and any other conditions as determined by the committee;

(*b*) all appointments shall be subject to the provisions of any statute, decree, or regulation of general application.

Section XXXIV. Edward Grey Institute of Field Ornithology

1. The Edward Grey Institute of Field Ornithology, established in 1938 by statute as a memorial to the first Viscount Grey of Fallodon, at one time Chancellor of the University, shall form part of the Department of Zoology and shall be under the charge of the Head of the Department of Zoology.

2. The Edward Grey Institute shall contain the Alexander Library: it shall have a Director (appointed under clause 3 below) and a Librarian, and any members of the staff of, or persons attached to, the Department of Zoology who are engaged in ornithological studies under the Director shall be assigned to the Institute.

3. The Director (who shall be regarded as a reader for the purpose of any statute or decree) shall be elected by a board consisting of:

(1) the Vice-Chancellor;

(2) the Head of the Department of Zoology;

(3) a person appointed by Council;

(4) a person appointed by the General Board;

(5) a person appointed by the Advisory Council for Ornithology;

(6), (7) two persons appointed by the Board of the Faculty of Biological Sciences.

4. The Director shall be responsible, under the Head of the Department of Zoology, for the work of the institute and the maintenance and improvement of the Alexander Library and for the application of such funds, including the interest of the Edward Grey Memorial Fund, as may be allocated for the purposes of the library. The library shall continue to be available for reference (but not borrowing) by members of the British Trust for Ornithology, the British Ornithologists' Union, and the Oxford Ornithological Society, in addition to members of the University.

5. There shall be an Advisory Council for Ornithology which shall meet at least once a year, and may be consulted by the Head of the Department of Zoology in matters concerning the ornithological studies of the Department of Zoology. The Advisory Council shall be composed as follows:

(1) the Head of the Department of Zoology;

(2) the Director of the Edward Grey Institute of Field Ornithology;

(3)–(5) three members appointed by the British Trust for Ornithology;

(6) one member appointed by the British Ornithologists' Union;

(7)–(10) four members appointed by the Board of the Faculty of Biological Sciences.

The appointed members shall hold office for three years and shall be re-eligible. The Director of the Edward Grey Institute of Field Ornithology shall act as Secretary of the Advisory Council.

6. The Head of the Department of Zoology shall have power to nominate the holder of an established academic post in the department with the title of professor or reader, subject to that person's consent, to act as his or her deputy, when desirable, under clauses 1, 4, and 5 above.

7. The bequests of the late W. B. Alexander of certain articles of furniture and paintings for the Edward Grey Institute of Field Ornithology and of the residue of his estate for the purposes of the Alexander Library, in the aforesaid Institute, shall be administered by the Board of the Faculty of Biological Sciences, on the recommendation of the Advisory Council of the Edward Grey Institute of Field Ornithology.

Section XXXV. Environmental Change Institute

1. Following the provision of support from I.B.M. United Kingdom Limited and from a number of other sources, there shall be within the University an Institute for Environmental Change.

2. The functions of the institute shall be to organize and promote collaborative interdisciplinary research on the nature, causes, and impact of environmental change and to contribute to the development of management strategies for coping with future environmental change.

3. The institute shall be under the general supervision of the Board of the Faculty of Anthropology and Geography, in co-operation with the Board of the Faculty of Biological Sciences and the Bioscience Research Board.

4. There shall be a director of the institute who shall hold the title of IBM Director of the Environmental Change Institute and who shall also be Professor of Environmental Studies. The director and professor shall be appointed for such period or periods as Council may from time to time determine. The director and professor shall be elected by an electoral board consisting of:

(1) the Vice-Chancellor or, if the head of the college specified in (2) of this clause is Vice-Chancellor, a person appointed by Council on the occurrence of a vacancy to act as an elector on that occasion;

(2) the head of the college to which the directorship shall be for the time being allocated by Council under any decree in that behalf, or, if the head is unable or unwilling to act, a person appointed by the governing body of the college on the occurrence of a vacancy to act as an elector on that occasion;

(3) a person appointed by the governing body of the college specified in (2) of this clause;

(4), (5) two persons appointed by the Board of the Faculty of Anthropology and Geography, one of whom shall be appointed in consultation with the Board of the Faculty of Biological Sciences;

(6) a person appointed by Council;

(7), (8) two persons appointed by the General Board;

(9) a person appointed by the Board of the Faculty of Biological Sciences.

5. The director and professor shall have charge of the premises allocated for the institute and shall make provision for the lighting, warming, water supply, and cleansing of the premises.

6. The director and professor shall submit to the Boards of the Faculties of Anthropology and Geography and of Biological Sciences an annual report on the work of the institute.

7. The director and professor shall be subject to the General Provisions of the decree concerning the duties of professors and shall reside within the University during six months at least in each academical year, between the first day of October and the ensuing first day of August.

8. There shall be a management committee for the institute consisting of the director and professor, the Professor of Geography, a person appointed by the

Board of the Faculty of Anthropology and Geography, the Director of the Oxford Forestry Institute, and the Linacre Professor of Zoology, who may each appoint deputies to attend meetings in their places. The committee shall elect its chairman from among its members.

9. The staff of the institute shall be appointed, and their duties and conditions of service shall be determined, by the director and professor, subject to:

(*a*) the provisions of any statute, decree, or regulation of general application;

(*b*) the approval by the Board of the Faculty of Anthropology and Geography, on the recommendation of a committee appointed by the board (of which the director and professor shall be a member and which may include other persons not being members of the board), and by the General Board of any appointment which carries a stipend of more than the maximum prescribed in Ch. VII, Sect. IV, § 1, cl. 2 (ii), such approval to cover the person appointed, his or her stipend, period of office, and duties, and any other conditions.

Section XXXVI. European Studies, Institute for

1. There shall be within the University an Institute for European Studies. The institute shall consist of such centres undertaking teaching and research in aspects of European Studies as the General Board shall from time to time determine.

2. The functions of the institute shall be to encourage the co-ordination of the work of the different centres within the University concerned with European Studies and to co-operate with other Institutes of European Studies in other countries of Europe within the Europaeum.

3. The institute shall be under the general supervision of the Committee for European Studies.

4. There shall be a director of the institute who shall be appointed by the General Board, for a fixed period of five years. The directorship shall normally rotate among the directors of the constituent centres of the institute which the General Board has determined shall form part of the institute under clause 1 above.

5. The director of the institute shall co-ordinate and promote the work undertaken by its constituent centres, and shall assist in the creation and development of the Europaeum.

6. The director shall submit to the European Studies Committee and to the Committee for the Europaeum an annual report of the work of the institute.

7. The director shall be a member of the Committee for the Europaeum and of the European Studies Committee.

8. In so far as premises are allocated to the institute itself (as distinct from the individual centres) the director shall have general charge of the premises and shall make provision for their lighting, warming, water supply, and cleansing.

9. At such time as staff are appointed to the institute (as distinct from specific centres within the institute) the director shall be responsible for their appointment and shall determine their duties and conditions of service, subject to the provisions of any statute, decree, or regulation of general application.

Section XXXVII. Examination Schools, Curators of the

1. There shall be seven Curators of the Examination Schools, namely:

(1) a member of Congregation appointed by Council, who shall be chairman;

(2) the Junior Proctor;

(3) the immediately preceding Junior Proctor;

(4) the Chairman of the Undergraduate Studies Committee of the General Board or his or her nominee;

(5)–(7) three members of Congregation elected by Congregation.

The chairman and the elected curators shall hold office for three years (except that casual vacancies shall be filled for the unexpired residue of the period of office of the member demitting office) and shall be re-eligible. In case of an equality of votes at any meeting of the curators the chairman shall have a casting vote.

2. The curators shall be responsible to Council and the General Board

(*a*) for the supervision of the Examination Schools and their precincts and shall make provision for the lighting, warming, water supply, and cleansing of the building;

(*b*) for the provision and management of the facilities therein for examinations, lectures, and all other purposes;

(*c*) for matters relating to the organisation of examinations within the Schools and associated premises, as referred to below; and

(*d*) for the supervision and monitoring of all funds made available to the curators.

The curators shall have power to make such charges for the use of rooms in the Schools as they shall deem reasonable, provided that no charge may be made for the use of rooms by the Vice-Chancellor or Council, or by professors, readers, or university lecturers, in discharge of their official duties. In the event of lack of space in the Schools for the holding of examinations, the curators shall have power to make arrangements for the use of rooms elsewhere.

3. Notwithstanding the provisions of clause 2 above, that area of the basement of the Examination Schools allocated to the Committee for the Archives shall be excluded from the charge of the curators for so long as the said area remains so allocated, provided always that the curators and the Clerk of the Schools shall have the right of access to the area at any reasonable time in order to satisfy themselves that the safety of the building is not being jeopardized.

4. The Clerk of the Schools shall be appointed by the Registrar in consultation with the curators.

Section XLI. Forestry, Institute and Advisory Committee for

§ 1. *Oxford Forestry Institute*

1. There shall be an Oxford Forestry Institute, the primary purpose of which shall be to promote research into all aspects of Forestry. The staff of the Institute shall carry out this research and make it the subject of printed papers, lectures, or informal instruction.

2. The Institute shall be headed by a Director who shall be responsible to the head of the Department of Plant Sciences or to his or her deputy. The Director of the Forestry Institute shall have charge of that area of the Department of Plant Sciences allocated from time to time for the use of the Forestry Institute by the head of the Department of Plant Sciences. He or she shall lecture and give instruction in Forestry.

3. Subject to the approval of the head of department, the staff of the Institute shall be appointed and their duties and conditions of service shall be prescribed by the Director, provided that:

(*a*) any appointment to a teaching or research post carrying a stipend of more than the maximum prescribed in Ch. VII, Sect. IV, § 1, cl. 2 (ii) shall be made by the Board of the Faculty of Biological Sciences on the recommendation of a committee appointed by the board of which the director shall be a member and which may include other persons not being members of the board, and the duties and conditions of service shall be prescribed by the faculty board. Such appointments shall also require approval by the General Board, such approval to cover the person appointed, his or her stipend, period of office, and duties, and any other conditions determined by the faculty board;

(*b*) all appointments shall be subject to the provisions of any statute, decree, or regulation of general application.

4. The Director shall be elected by an electoral board consisting of:

(1) the Vice-Chancellor;

(2) the Sibthorpian Professor of Plant Science;

(3) the Sherardian Professor of Botany;

(4) one person appointed by Council;

(5) one person appointed by the General Board;

(6), (7) two persons appointed by the Board of the Faculty of Biological Sciences.

5. The Director shall be subject to the General Provisions of the decree concerning the duties of professors.

§ 2. *Advisory Committee for Forestry*

1. There shall be an Advisory Committee for Forestry consisting of:

(1) the Vice-Chancellor, or his or her deputy;

(2) the Director of the Forestry Institute;

(3) one person appointed by Council who is not a person engaged in teaching or research in forestry subjects;

(4) one person appointed by the Secretary of State for International Development who is not a forester;

(5) the Forestry Adviser in the Department for International Development;

(6), (7) two persons appointed by Council on the recommendation of the Advisory Committee who are professionally qualified foresters and who, in so far as suitable persons are available, have special knowledge of and practising experience of forestry in (*a*) temperate regions and (*b*) tropical and sub-tropical regions of the world;

(8) one person appointed by the Forestry Commission who is a professionally qualified forester and who, in so far as a suitable person is available, has special knowledge of and practising experience of forestry in the United Kingdom.

Appointed members shall hold office for three years and shall be re-eligible. The Director of the Forestry Institute shall act as Secretary of the committee.

2. The committee may co-opt not more than three persons who shall hold office for three years and shall be re-eligible.

3. The committee shall meet at least once a year and may initiate discussions and make recommendations to the Director of the Forestry Institute or the Board of the Faculty of Biological Sciences on any subject considered to be of importance for forestry teaching and research, but the committee shall especially promote continuous contact between the Oxford Forestry Institute and forestry developments, needs, and thought overseas.

Section XLII. Health and Safety, Consultative Committee for

1. There shall be a Consultative Committee for Health and Safety consisting of:

(1) the Chairman of the Health and Safety Management Committee, who shall chair the Consultative Committee;

(2), (3) two persons employed in the University's technician grades, who shall be appointed by the university branch of the Manufacturing, Science and Finance Union;

(4), (5) two persons employed in the University's clerical and library grades, who shall be appointed by the university branch of UNISON;

(6), (7) two persons employed in the University's academic or academic-related grades, who shall be appointed by the university branch of the Association of University Teachers;

(8) a departmental administrator, who shall be appointed by the Health and Safety Management Committee;

(9)–(11) three departmental safety officers, one each from a clinical department, a science department, and a department in the Humanities or Social Sciences Division, who shall be appointed by the Health and Safety Management Committee;

(12) a member of the Committee of Heads of Science Departments, who shall be appointed by that committee;

(13) a member of the Personnel Committee, who shall be appointed by that committee;

(14)–(16) three persons, each of whom shall be the chairman of a different specialist advisory group set up by the Health and Safety Management Committee, and who shall be appointed by that committee.

The committee may co-opt up to two additional members.

Appointed and co-opted members shall serve for such periods as may be determined by the body appointing or co-opting them.

2. The committee shall constitute the consultative forum on health and safety required by the Safety Representatives and Safety Committee Regulations 1977, or any subsequent legislation. It shall consider and, as appropriate, comment on the following:

(*a*) questions of health and safety policy;

(*b*) the implementation of health and safety policy;

(*c*) administrative matters relating to health and safety;

(*d*) health and safety training within the University;

(*e*) significant accidents and incidents occurring within the University;

(*f*) the minutes of each of the specialist advisory groups set up by the Health and Safety Management Committee;

(*g*) matters brought to the University's attention by trade union safety representatives.

3. The committee shall be invited to consider and comment on all proposed new and revised health and safety policies before they are submitted to the Health and Safety Management Committee.

4. The committee shall meet at least three times a year, and on such additional occasions as the chairman may decide to be appropriate. The minutes of each meeting shall be forwarded to the Health and Safety Management Committee.

Section XLIII. History of Art, Committee for, and Sub-faculty of

1. There shall be a Committee for the History of Art, consisting of:

(1) the Lincoln Professor of Classical Archaeology and Art;

(2) the Professor of the History of Art;

(3) the Ruskin Master of Drawing;

(4) the Director of the Ashmolean Museum;

(5) the Keeper of the Department of Western Art;

(6) the Keeper of the Department of Eastern Art;

(7) one person appointed by the General Board;

(8), (9) two persons appointed by the Board of the Faculty of Modern History;

(10) one person appointed by the Board of the Faculty of English Language and Literature;

(11) one person appointed by the Board of the Faculty of Medieval and Modern Languages;

(12) one person appointed by the Board of the Faculty of Oriental Studies;

(13), (14) two persons appointed by the Sub-faculty of the History of Art.

2. Appointed members of the committee shall hold office for three years and shall be re-eligible. Casual vacancies shall be filled for the period of office of the person demitting office. The committee shall have the power to co-opt not more than two additional members who shall hold office for three years and shall be re-eligible. The committee shall elect its chairman from amongst its own members. The chairman shall normally hold office for two years and shall be re-eligible.

3. The committee shall co-ordinate arrangements for lectures and courses of instruction in the History of Art given within the University, shall consider questions concerning the organization of the studies and examinations of the University in this field referred to it by the board of any faculty or by any committee, and shall generally advise the boards and committees concerned on all such matters.

4. The committee shall have the powers of a board of a faculty in respect of courses and examinations for such degrees or diplomas in the History of Art as may be established by decree.

5. The committee shall have the powers of a board of a faculty in respect of the appointment of university lecturers whose duties lie solely in the area of the History of Art. The committee shall be recognized as having an interest in the appointment of university lecturers, and any other academic staff whose duties include teaching, in the History of Art; the faculty boards and other bodies responsible for such appointments shall ensure that in each case the selection committee, if not already including a member of the Committee for the History of Art, shall be afforced so as to include such a member.

6. The committee shall submit annually to the General Board estimates of receipts and expenditure in respect of the Department of the History of Art, which shall be prepared for the committee's consideration by the head of the department.

7. The committee shall make an annual report of its proceedings to the General Board.

8. There shall be a Sub-faculty of the History of Art, and the Committee for the History of Art shall have the powers of a faculty board to determine the membership of that sub-faculty in accordance with Tit. VI, Sect. I, cll. 2 and 3, and Ch. II, Sect. XII. The members of the sub-faculty shall be deemed to be members of a faculty for the purposes of Tit. II, Sect. II, cl. 1. The sub-faculty shall report to the Committee for the History of Art.

Section XLIV. History of Medicine, Unit for the

1. Following the provision of support by the Wellcome Trust, there shall be within the University a Unit for and a Readership in the History of Medicine.

2. The function of the Unit shall be, under the general supervision of the Board of the Faculty of Modern History and in co-operation with the Boards of the Faculties of Clinical Medicine and Physiological Sciences, to promote teaching and research in the field of the History of Medicine.

3. The Unit shall be under the direction of the Reader in the History of Medicine who shall be elected by an electoral board consisting of:

(1) the Vice-Chancellor;

(2) the head of the college with which the readership shall be for the time being associated, or, if the head is unable or unwilling to act, a person appointed by the governing body of the college;

(3) a person appointed by the governing body of the college specified in (2) of this clause;

(4) a person appointed by Council after consultation with the Wellcome Trust;

(5) a person appointed by the General Board;

(6) a person appointed by the Board of the Faculty of Clinical Medicine;

(7) a person appointed by the Board of the Faculty of Physiological Sciences;

(8), (9) two persons appointed by the Board of the Faculty of Modern History.

4. The Reader shall engage in advanced study or research and shall, under the direction of the Board of the Faculty of Modern History and on such conditions as the board shall from time to time determine, lecture and give instruction in the History of Medicine.

5. The Reader shall make provision for the lighting, warming, water-supply, and cleansing of the premises assigned to the Unit.

6. The staff of the Unit shall be appointed and their conditions of service shall be prescribed by the Reader, provided that

(*a*) any appointment to a teaching or research post carrying a stipend of more than the maximum prescribed in Ch. VII, Sect. IV, § 1, cl. 2 (ii) shall be made by the Board of the Faculty of Modern History on the recommendation of a committee appointed by the board (of which the Reader shall be a member and which shall include a representative of Boards of the Faculties of Clinical Medicine and Physiological Sciences, and the duties and conditions of service shall be prescribed by the Board of the Faculty of Modern History in consultation, as that board may deem necessary, with the Boards of the Faculties of Clinical Medicine and Physiological Sciences. Such appointments shall also require approval by the General Board, such approval to cover the person appointed, his or her stipend, period of office, and duties, and any other conditions of appointment;

(*b*) all appointments shall be subject to the provisions of any statute, decree, or regulation of general application.

7. An annual report on the work of the Unit shall be presented by the Reader to the Boards of the Faculties of Clinical Medicine, Physiological Sciences, and Modern History, for submission to the General Board.

Section XLV. History of Science, Medicine, and Technology

§ 1. *Committee for the History of Science, Medicine and Technology*

1. There shall be a Committee for the History of Science, Medicine, and Technology consisting of:

(1) the Professor of the History of Science, who shall be chairman;

(2) the Reader in the History of Medicine;

(3) one of the Proctors or the Assessor, as agreed between them from time to time;

(4), (5) two persons appointed by Council from among the directors and curators of the university museums other than the Museum of the History of Science;

(6), (7) two persons appointed by the Board of the Faculty of Modern History;

(8) one person appointed by the Sub-faculty of Philosophy;

(9) one person appointed by the Board of the Faculty of Oriental Studies;

(10) one person appointed by the Board of the Faculty of Physical Sciences;

(11) one person appointed by the Boards of the Faculties of Biological Sciences, Clinical Medicine, and Physiological Sciences acting together;

(12) Bodley's Librarian or the Librarian's nominee.

The committee shall have power to co-opt not more than three members with expertise in the field of the History of Science, Medicine, and Technology, at least two of whom should preferably be from outside the University, for such periods as it shall think fit.

The appointed members shall hold office for six years, and shall be re-eligible, provided that members appointed to fill vacancies caused otherwise than by lapse of time shall hold office for the unexpired residue only of the periods of office of the members whom they succeed, and shall be re-eligible.

The Keeper of the museum shall attend meetings of the committee, provided that the committee may require him or her to withdraw for all or part of any meeting.

2. The functions of the committee shall be:

(*a*) to further teaching and research in the History of Science, Medicine, and Technology within the University;

(*b*) to have oversight of the Modern History Board's teaching in the History of Medicine, and to report on this to the Modern History Board;

(*c*) to collaborate with the Wellcome Unit for the History of Medicine;

(*d*) to be responsible for the orderly administration, finance, and general policy of the Museum of the History of Science;

(*e*) to promote the purposes of the museum as defined by decree;

(*f*) to have regard for the Museum of the History of Science as a national and international as well as a university resource;

(*g*) to receive the advice of the Keeper of the museum on the care, development, presentation, promotion, and publication of the museum's collections;

(*h*) to appoint the Keeper and Assistant Keepers of the museum subject to the approval of the General Board, and, if the committee so determines, on the recommendation of a selection committee set up on each occasion, provided that such a committee shall always include the Chairman and at least one member of the Committee for the History of Science, Medicine, and Technology, and (in the case of appointments of Assistant Keepers) the Keeper;

(*i*) to be responsible for devising and monitoring a coherent policy relating to the disposition of material on twentieth-century science, and especially to redundant artefacts from the Oxford Science Area;

(*j*) to submit an annual report to the General Board through the Modern History Board.

§ 2. *Museum of the History of Science*

The purposes of the Museum of the History of Science shall be:

(*a*) to assemble and preserve objects illustrating the History of Science, and especially early scientific instruments, together with related books and manuscripts. These shall include the collection of Lewis Evans accepted by Decree (4) of 4 March 1924, and such further additions of objects and books as have been or may be accepted or acquired by the University;

(*b*) to document the collections of both instruments and books and to promote the publication of catalogues;

(*c*) to afford ready access to the collections for the purposes of academic study and research;

(*d*) to deploy the resources of the collections to best effect in teaching in the University the History of Science;

(*e*) to display the collections of instruments, or some part of them, with a view to stimulating public interest in and understanding of the History of Science;

(*f*) to add to the collections objects and books which enhance or throw fresh light on the collections already held.

§ 3. *Keeper of the Museum of the History of Science*

1. The Keeper of the Museum of the History of Science shall act for and be responsible to the Committee for the History of Science, Medicine, and Technology in the exercise of its powers relating to the museum. The Keeper shall appoint the clerical, technical, and maintenance staffs and other non-

academic staff employed in the museum (provided that he or she may delegate to an Assistant Keeper the appointment of clerical and technical staff). The Keeper shall assist the committee in all matters for which it has general responsibility.

2. The Keeper shall advise the Committee for the History of Science, Medicine, and Technology on the care, development, presentation, promotion, and publication of the museum's collections.

3. The Keeper shall encourage the use of the collections of the museum for the purposes of research and teaching.

4. The Keeper shall offer sixteen lectures or classes in each academic year under the direction of the Committee for the History of Science, Medicine, and Technology in consultation with the faculty board concerned.

§ 4. *Assistant Keepers*

1. The Assistant Keepers shall assist the Keeper in the care and supervision of the rooms and collections of the museum and in the discharge of the duties laid down in § 3, cll. 1-3 of this section.

2. They shall normally be expected to give up to four classes or lectures a year (or their equivalent in other forms of teaching) under the direction of the Committee for the History of Science, Medicine, and Technology in consultation with the faculty board concerned. The Committee for the History of Science, Medicine, and Technology in consultation with the faculty board concerned may exceptionally permit more than four hours of teaching to be given in each year.

Section XLVI. History of the University, Committee on the

1. There shall be a Committee on the History of the University, consisting of:

(1)–(3) three persons appointed by Council;

(4)–(6) three persons appointed by the General Board.

The members of the committee shall hold office for three years (though the initial periods of office of the first members shall be fixed by the appointing bodies so as to ensure that one of the members from each group retires each year) and shall be re-eligible; casual vacancies shall be filled for the remainder of the period of the person being replaced. The committee shall have power to co-opt up to four additional members for periods of two years. The committee shall elect its own chairman.

2. The committee shall be empowered to receive grants and donations, and, subject to the provisions of this decree, to take any action it considers necessary to further the work on the History.

3. The History of the University shall be under the direction of a Director of Research and General Editor, who shall be responsible to the committee, and shall be paid on the readers' scale. The Director may, subject to the approval of the committee, and within the limits of the funds available, appoint additional

staff on such conditions (though subject to any rules of general application) as he or she shall determine.

4. A vacancy in the post of Director and General Editor shall be filled by the committee, subject to the approval of Council.

Section XLVII. Japanese Studies, Inter-faculty Committee for

1. There shall be an Inter-faculty Committee for Japanese Studies consisting of:

(1) the Nissan Professor of Modern Japanese Studies;

(2) one member elected by the General Board of the Faculties;

(3), (4) two members elected by the Board of the Faculty of Anthropology and Geography;

(5), (6) two members elected by the Board of the Faculty of Modern History;

(7), (8) two members elected by the Board of the Faculty of Oriental Studies;

(9), (10) two members elected by the Board of the Faculty of Social Studies;

(11), (12) two members elected by the Governing Body of St. Antony's College.

The elected members of the committee shall hold office for four years from the date of election (except that casual vacancies shall be filled for the unexpired residue of the period), and shall be re-eligible. The committee shall have power to co-opt up to three additional members for periods of two years. The committee shall elect its own chairman from among the elected and co-opted members.

2. The functions of the committee shall be:

(*a*) to keep under review, and to advise the General Board and other bodies concerned generally on, the provision and organization of studies at both graduate and undergraduate level and examinations in the field of Japanese Studies and the co-ordination and balance of such studies, and to promote co-operation between the bodies concerned with Japanese Studies in the University, including the Nissan Institute;

(*b*) to allocate such funds as may be placed at its disposal by the General Board or other bodies for specific or general purposes connected with Japanese Studies;

(*c*) to act as Committee of Management of the Nissan Institute.

Section LI. Language Centre, Committee of Management for

1. There shall be a Committee of Management for the Language Centre, consisting of:

(1) the Pro-Vice-Chancellor (Academic Services and University Collections), or his or her nominee, who shall chair the committee;

(2)–(4) one person appointed by each of the Life and Environmental Sciences, Mathematical and Physical Sciences, and Medical Sciences Boards;

(5) a person appointed by the Humanities Board, not being a member of either the Faculty of Medieval and Modern Languages or the Faculty of Oriental Studies;

(6) a person appointed by the Social Sciences Board, not being a member of the Department of Educational Studies;

(7) a person appointed by the Continuing Education Board;

(8) a person appointed by the Board of the Faculty of Medieval and Modern Languages;

(9) a person appointed by the Board of the Faculty of Oriental Studies;

(10) a person appointed by the Committee for Educational Studies;

(11) the Director of the Language Centre;

(12), (13) two resident Junior Members, one appointed by the Graduate Committee of the Oxford University Student Union, and one appointed by the Academic Affairs Committee of the Oxford University Student Union.

The members under (2)–(10) shall hold office for four years, and members under (12) and (13) shall hold office for one year, and they shall be re-eligible.

The committee shall have power to co-opt up to four additional members, who shall hold office for periods to be fixed by the committee and shall be re-eligible.

2. The committee shall elect its own chairman.

3. The duties of the committee shall be:

(*a*) to determine the policy of the centre, and to exercise general supervision over its work;

(*b*) to appoint the director and assistant director of the centre, and to prescribe their duties and conditions of service, subject to the approval of Council;

(*c*) to submit an annual report to Council.

4. Subject to report to the committee, the director shall:

(*a*) appoint the supporting staff of the centre (other than the assistant director) and prescribe their duties and conditions of service subject to the provisions of any statute, decree, or regulation of general application;

(*b*) make provision for the lighting, warming, water supply, and cleansing of the premises allocated to the centre.

5. The member appointed by the Graduate Committee of the Oxford University Student Union shall not take part in any reserved business of the committee, as defined in Ch. II, Sect. II, cl. 7.

Section LII. Latin American Studies, Inter-faculty Committee for

1. There shall be an Inter-faculty Committee for Latin American Studies consisting of:

(1) the Director of the Centre for Brazilian Studies;

(2)–(9) two persons elected by each of the Boards of the Faculties of Anthropology and Geography, Medieval and Modern Languages, Modern History, and Social Studies;

(10) one person elected by the Board of the Faculty of Biological Sciences;

(11), (12) two persons elected by the Governing Body of St Antony's College.

The elected members of the committee shall hold office for four years from the date of election (except that casual vacancies shall be filled for the unexpired residue of the period) and shall be re-eligible. The committee shall have power to co-opt up to three additional members for periods of two years. The committee shall elect its own chairman.

2. The functions of the committee shall be:

(*a*) to consider questions concerning the organization of the studies and examinations of the University in the field of Latin American Studies which may be referred to it by the board of any faculty, and generally to advise the faculty boards concerned on all such matters;

(*b*) to allocate such funds as may be placed at its disposal by the General Board for general purposes connected with Latin American Studies.

Section LIII. Management Studies

§ 1. *Saïd Business School*

1. In the light of the munificent benefaction of £20 million by Mr Wafic Rida Saïd for the University's School of Management Studies, the School shall be renamed the Saïd Business School. £18 million of this benefaction shall be used towards the construction of a building for the School, and the remaining £2 million for the purchase of a site (the 'adjacent site') adjacent to the site for the School which will be held by the Foundation for the future expansion requirements of the School. The School shall promote study and research within the field of Management Studies.

2. Notwithstanding any provisions of this decree the academic direction and day-to-day management of the School shall be entirely and exclusively the responsibility of the University.

3. For the purposes of a deed of trust to be executed there shall be a Body of Trustees of the Saïd Business School Foundation and such Trustees shall consist of

(1) the Vice-Chancellor of the University for the time being;

(2) the Benefactor or his successor in title;

(3) a distinguished representative from the worlds of business or finance who shall be nominated by the President of the Confederation of British Industry, or by the President or Chairman of such other eminent business- or finance-related successor body as the Trustees may decide;

(4) a distinguished representative from the worlds of business or finance who shall be nominated by an eminent business- or finance-related body or its

President or Chairman, the nominating body or nominating person to be decided by the Trustees and to remain constant as far as circumstances permit;

(5)–(7) three representatives of the University to be appointed by the Vice-Chancellor after consultation with Council;

(8)–(10) three representatives to be appointed by the Benefactor.

The Chairman of the Trustees, who shall have no casting vote, shall be elected by the Trustees from among their number to serve for two years and shall be eligible for re-election.

4. With the exception of the Benefactor no person shall become or remain a Trustee after reaching the age of 75 years. The person or body appointing any Trustee (or his, her, or its successor in title) shall have power from time to time to revoke the appointment with immediate effect and shall have power to make new appointments of Trustees, subject to the provisions of clause 3, in place of Trustees who were appointed by him, her, or it and who have died, retired, or whose appointment has been revoked. Any Trustee who desires to retire may do so two months after giving to the other Trustees notice in writing of such desire.

5. The quorum for meetings of the Trustees shall be six Trustees, including at least two of the Trustees referred to in cl. 3 (1), (5)–(7) and at least two of the Trustees referred to in cl. 3 (2), (8)–(10).

6. The Trustees shall be responsible for the construction of a building for the School. They shall acquire and hold the adjacent site as Trustees of the Foundation and shall fulfil their responsibilities under the trust deed of the Foundation.

7. There shall be a Buildings Committee of the Board of Trustees which shall supervise generally and shall oversee the construction of the building of the School on the site. The Buildings Committee shall be composed as follows:

(1) the Vice-Chancellor;

(2) the Benefactor;

(3) one member to be appointed by the Vice-Chancellor after consultation with Council, with the approval of the Benefactor, such approval not to be unreasonably withheld or delayed; and

(4) one member to be appointed by the Benefactor with the approval of the Vice-Chancellor after consultation with Council, such approval not to be unreasonably withheld or delayed.

The quorum for meetings of the Buildings Committee shall be all four members.

8. The University shall grant the Saïd Business School Foundation a 299-year lease of the site for the building for the School and of the building to be erected on the site. For as long as the building is used for the School or such other use as may be agreed between the University and the Foundation the University will charge the Foundation a peppercorn rent for the lease.

9. If during the period of the lease for any reason after the construction and furnishing of the building have been completed the building shall cease for a

continuous period of twelve months to be used exclusively as the School, then either

(*a*) the University and the Saïd Business School Foundation will agree an alternative use for the building; or, if this is not possible,

(*b*) the Foundation will offer the University the option to buy the lease for a consideration equal to the open market value at that time of the lease, less the proportion to the original cost of the building and the site represented by funding raised from sources other than the Foundation or the Benefactor, plus V.A.T. if applicable.

The open market value assumes

(i) a willing seller;

(ii) a willing buyer;

(iii) that there had been a reasonable period for the proper marketing of the lease;

(iv) that no account is taken of any additional bid by a purchaser with a special interest;

(v) that there is no restriction on the assignment of the lease;

(vi) that the use of the site and building is not limited to the use as a Business School.

The open market value shall be determined by agreement between a valuer appointed by the University and a valuer appointed by the Foundation within six months from the date of cessation and if not so agreed within that time shall be determined by an arbitrator, such arbitrator to be nominated (in the absence of agreement) by the President for the time being of the Royal Institution of Chartered Surveyors and the arbitration to be conducted in accordance with the Arbitration Acts 1950 and 1979 or any statutory modification or re-enactment thereof for the time being in force.

If neither (*a*) nor (*b*) above is agreed within one year, then the Foundation will be free for the remainder of the lease to use the building for whatever purpose it wishes, including an assignment of the lease, at such rent, if any, as may be agreed between the University and the Foundation.

10. The benefaction is conditional on planning permission for the building on the main site being granted, vacant possession of the entire site being obtained, and the problem of the routing of services away from the site being resolved to the satisfaction of the Foundation. If these conditions are not met within one year of the date of this decree, then the Foundation will sell, and the University will buy, the adjacent site for the amount for which the Foundation purchased it plus V.A.T. if applicable.

11. If it ever transpires that the School will not need the adjacent site for expansion purposes and the Foundation decides to sell the adjacent site, the University will be given the right of first refusal on the purchase of this land.

12. For as long as the building is used for the School or such other use as may be agreed between the University and the Foundation the University will be responsible for

(*a*) insuring the building on behalf of the Foundation on a full reinstatement basis;

(*b*) maintaining the structure, repair, and decoration of the building to a standard consistent with its use as a pre-eminent world-class business school;

(*c*) the operation and use of the building according to current Health and Safety legislation and the University's policies for such buildings;

(*d*) upgrading the building to meet changes in legislation.

13. The Directorship of the School, which shall be called the Peter Moores Directorship, shall be held for a period of five years, or such other period as Council may determine from time to time, and may be renewed for such periods thereafter. The appointment of the Director shall be made by Council, on the recommendation of the General Board, after consultation with the Peter Moores Foundation and with the approval of the Saïd Business School Foundation, such approval not to be unreasonably withheld.

14. The income from non-publicly funded courses offered by the School will be paid into the School budget for the support of its activities. Income from research grants and contracts will be treated in the same way. The income so received by the School will be used exclusively for the support of the School's activities except that the University may deduct in any year up to 22 per cent (or such other percentage as may be agreed from time to time between the University and the Foundation, such agreement not to be unreasonably withheld) of the income so paid into the School's budget to meet the reasonable costs of support provided from the central facilities of the University to the School in respect of services used by the School such as are illustrated in (*a*)–(*d*) below:

(*a*) use of central academic facilities such as the Bodleian Library, the faculty libraries, computing services and the Language Centre, and any other relevant facilities;

(*b*) the use of the central services for the payment of bills, the operation of the payroll, and the organization of superannuation accounting and of personnel services;

(*c*) the use of central administrative services such as committee servicing, examination arrangements, and the award of degrees; and

(*d*) the use of building and maintenance services.

15. Notwithstanding the provisions of any statute, decree, or regulation to the contrary, not more than one-third or less than one-fourth of the members of the Board of the Faculty of Management will be elected by the Council for the Saïd Business School ('the Council') from amongst persons from industry, finance, government, public service, and sponsors of the School, such persons not generally being members of Congregation.

16. The Benefactor shall be entitled to appoint, to one of the places identified in clause 15, one member of the Committee for the School.

17. The Benefactor shall be entitled to appoint one member to the Council.

18. This decree may be modified and/or replaced in whole or in part by further decrees or statutes, provided that the Trustees of the Saïd Business School Foundation shall first have approved the modification or replacement,

(*a*) in the case of cll. 1–14 and cll. 16–18 by a four-fifths majority; and

(*b*) in the case of cl. 15 by a simple majority.

§ 2. *Council for the Saïd Business School*

1. There shall be a Council for the Saïd Business School consisting of:

(1) the Vice-Chancellor;

(2) the Peter Moores Director of the Saïd Business School;

(3) the Deputy Director (Research) of the Saïd Business School;

(4) the Deputy Director (Undergraduate Courses) of the Saïd Business School;

(5) the Deputy Director (Graduate Courses) of the Saïd Business School;

(6) the Deputy Director (Corporate Affairs) of the Saïd Business School;

(7)–(10) four persons elected by the Board of the Faculty of Management;

and not less than fifteen persons from industry, finance, government, and sponsors of the school elected by the Hebdomadal Council after consultation with the director of the school and the President of Templeton College.

The council shall have power to co-opt up to four additional members, who need not be members of Congregation.

Members of the council shall hold office for three years from the date of election (except that casual vacancies shall be filled for the unexpired residue of the period of office of the member demitting office) and shall be re-eligible.

2. The functions of the council shall be to advise on the formulation of policy for the school, the design of courses, and the financing of the school, and to foster the relationship of the school to commerce and industry. The council may request the Board of the Faculty of Management to give further consideration to any proposals for major developments which the council considers may not be in the long-term interests of Management Studies in the University.

3. There shall be four Deputy Directors of the Saïd Business School, who shall be responsible for the areas of Research, Undergraduate Courses, Graduate Courses, and Corporate Affairs respectively. Each Deputy Director shall be appointed by the General Board for a period of up to three years and may thereafter be reappointed for a further consecutive period of up to two years. No person shall be eligible for reappointment as a Deputy Director after serving for a total period of five years unless an interval of at least two years has elapsed since the end of the last period of such service. The duties and stipend of each Deputy Director shall be as determined by the General Board from time to time.

Section LIV. Mathematical Institute

1. There shall be a Mathematical Institute for the purposes of research, advanced study, lecturing, and instruction in Mathematics.

2. The Mathematical Institute shall be assigned by the General Board from time to time for a specified period not exceeding five years in the first instance to a person (normally a professor or reader) holding an established academic post under the Board of the Faculty of Mathematical Sciences, other than a post in the Computing Laboratory or the Department of Statistics, after consultation with the Mathematical Sciences Board, and he or she shall be designated Chairman of Mathematics.

3. The Chairman shall be eligible for reappointment, provided that no one person shall hold the post for a total period of more than ten years.

4. The Chairman shall

(*a*) promote research in Mathematics in the University;

(*b*) support and keep under review the research of those holding established academic posts under the Mathematical Sciences Board other than those in the Computing Laboratory or the Department of Statistics.

5. The Chairman shall make provision for the lighting, warming, water-supply, and cleansing of the Mathematical Institute's premises.

6. The Chairman shall

(*a*) appoint and prescribe the conditions of service of the staff required for the Mathematical Institute's premises, subject to

(i) the provisions of any statute, decree, or regulation of general application;

(ii) the approval by the Board of the Faculty of Mathematical Sciences and the General Board of the Faculties of any appointment carrying with it a stipend of more than the maximum prescribed in Ch. VII, Sect. IV, § 1, cl. 2 (ii), such approval to cover the person appointed, his or her stipend, period of office, and duties, and any other conditions;

(*b*) have charge of the allocation of accommodation and the provision of secretarial and other facilities;

(*c*) be responsible for the application of funds made available for the purposes of the Institute;

(*d*) make all necessary arrangements with students wishing to engage in advanced study or research in the Institute.

7. The Chairman shall undertake teaching in accordance with such arrangements as shall be made from time to time with the Board of the Faculty of Mathematical Sciences. When the Chairman is a professor, his or her teaching duties shall normally be those laid down in Ch. VII, Sect. I, § 5. B, cl. 2 (*b*).

8. There shall be a Vice-Chairman of Mathematics, who shall be appointed from time to time for a period not exceeding five years in the first instance by

the General Board after consultation with the Mathematical Sciences Board. The Vice-Chairman shall assist and advise the Chairman in carrying out the Chairman's duties and shall be a member of the departmental committee (as established by regulation of the General Board).

Section LV. Military Instruction, Delegates for

1. For the purpose of this decree there shall be a delegacy consisting of;

(1) the Vice-Chancellor;

(2), (3) the Proctors;

(4) the Assessor;

(5), (6) the Officer Commanding the Oxford University Officers' Training Corps (or his or her representative), and one other officer nominated by him or her;

(7), (8) the Officer Commanding the University Air Squadron (or his or her representative), and one other officer nominated by him or her;

(9), (10) the Officer Commanding the University Royal Naval Unit (or his or her representative) and one other officer nominated by him or her;

(11) the Chichele Professor of the History of War;

(12) a person appointed by the Admiralty Board of the Defence Council;

(13) a person appointed by the Army Board of the Defence Council;

(14) a person appointed by the Air Force Board of the Defence Council;

(15)–(18) four members of Convocation elected as hereinafter provided.

The delegacy shall have power to co-opt not more than five persons as additional members of the delegacy. Such co-opted members shall hold office for two years, and shall be re-eligible.

2. Of the four elected members of Convocation one shall be elected by Congregation, one by Council, one by the Board of the Faculty of Modern History, and one by the Board of the Faculty of Social Studies. They shall hold office for four years, and one shall vacate office every year. Casual vacancies shall be filled for the remainder of the period of office of the vacating delegate.

3. The duties of the delegates shall be:

(*a*) to co-operate with the staff of the Oxford University Officers' Training Corps and of the University Air Squadron in providing instruction in Military Subjects for members of the University;

(*b*) to superintend the instruction of University Candidates for regular Commissions in Her Majesty's Forces;

(*c*) to act as a board for the nomination of such qualified candidates as they may deem fit to receive Her Majesty's Commission;

(*d*) to appoint as Secretary one of the members of the delegacy.

4. The delegates shall have power:

(*a*) to appoint and pay lecturers on Military Subjects and to define their duties;

(*b*) to determine and receive the fees which shall be paid by all persons attending the lectures given by such lecturers;

(*c*) to receive and administer sums contributed for the promotion of military studies in the University;

(*d*) to form a Register of Candidates for regular Commissions in Her Majesty's Forces, and to charge a fee on registration;

(*e*) to make and to vary from time to time regulations for carrying out the provisions of this decree.

5. All expenses incurred by the delegates shall be defrayed out of payments made by or on behalf of candidates for regular Commissions in Her Majesty's Forces, or from funds otherwise provided, and shall not be charged upon the general fund of the University.

Section LVI. Modern Middle Eastern Studies, Committee for

1. There shall be a Committee for Modern Middle Eastern Studies consisting of two members each elected by the Boards of the Faculties of:

(1), (2) Oriental Studies;

(3), (4) Social Studies;

(5), (6) Anthropology and Geography; and

(7), (8) two members elected by the Governing Body of St. Antony's College;

one member each elected by the Boards of the Faculties of:

(9) Modern History;

(10) Medieval and Modern Languages; and

(11) the co-ordinator of the M.Phil. in Oriental Studies (Modern Middle Eastern Studies).

The members of the committee shall hold office for four years from the date of election (except that casual vacancies shall be filled for the unexpired residue of the period), and shall be re-eligible. The committee shall have power to co-opt up to three additional members for periods of two years. The committee shall elect its own chairman.

2. The functions of the committee shall be:

(*a*) to consider questions concerning the organization of the studies and examinations of the University in the field of Modern Middle Eastern Studies which may be referred to it by the board of any faculty, and generally to advise the faculty boards concerned on all such matters;

(*b*) to allocate such funds as may be placed at its disposal by the General Board for general purposes connected with Middle Eastern Studies.

Section LVII. Committee for the Museums and Scientific Collections

1. The Committee for the Museums and Scientific Collections shall consist of:

(1) the Pro-Vice-Chancellor (Academic Services and University Collections), who shall be chairman;

(2), (3) the Director and the Administrator of the Ashmolean Museum;

(4), (5) the Director and the Administrator of the Pitt Rivers Museum;

(6), (7) the Director and the Administrator of the Oxford University Museum of Natural History;

(8), (9) the Keeper of the Museum of the History of Science and the person responsible for the administration of the museum;

(10) the Sherardian Professor of Botany and Keeper of the Botanic Garden;

(11) the Superintendent of the Botanic Garden;

(12) the Curator of the Bate Collection;

(13)–(17) five persons of whom one shall be appointed by each of the Divisional Boards;

(18) a person appointed by the Conference of Colleges;

(19) a person, not being the resident holder of a teaching, research, or administrative post in the University or in any college or other society, appointed by Council;

(20) one of the Proctors and Assessor as may be agreed between them;

(21)–(23) three persons appointed by the committee from among the members of the staff of the museums and scientific collections, who shall have expertise respectively in I.T., conservation, and education.

The members appointed under (13)–(19) and (21)–(23) shall hold office for three years and shall be re-eligible, provided that casual vacancies shall be filled for the remainder of the period of office of the person being replaced.

2. The committee shall advise Council as appropriate on any matters connected with the University's museums and scientific collections.

3. The committee shall facilitate co-ordination between the University's museums and scientific collections, particularly with respect to planning, allocation and use of resources, and the development, care, and promotion of the collections as national and international resources both for teaching and research and for public access.

4. The committee shall liaise as appropriate with local, national, and international bodies set up to co-ordinate museum and collections policy.

Section LVIII. Music, Premises Allocated to the Faculty of

1. The Board of the Faculty of Music shall have charge of the premises allocated to the Faculty of Music for the purpose of lecturing, instruction, and research, and shall make provision for the lighting, warming, water-supply, and cleansing of them.

2. The staff required for the premises shall be appointed and their duties and conditions of service shall be prescribed by the Board of the Faculty of Music subject to

(*a*) the provisions of any statute, decree, or regulation of general or specific application;

(*b*) the approval by the General Board of any appointment carrying with it a stipend of more than the maximum prescribed in Ch. VII, Sect. IV, § 1, cl. 2 (ii), such approval to cover the person appointed, his or her stipend, period of office, and duties, and any other conditions.

Section LXI. Oriental Institute

1. The premises allocated to the Faculty of Oriental Studies for the purposes of lecturing, instruction, advanced study, and research, shall be called the Oriental Institute.[1]

2. The Oriental Institute shall be under the general supervision of the Board of the Faculty of Oriental Studies, which shall appoint a committee of curators to have charge of the Institute.

3. The curators shall make provision for the lighting, heating, water-supply and cleansing of the Oriental Institute and shall be responsible for the care of its contents.

4. The curators shall make provision for the lighting, heating, water supply, and cleansing of such parts of the Clarendon Press Institute as may be allocated to them.

5. The curators shall be responsible for the safe keeping, maintenance, heating, and lighting of such rooms and premises in the Oriental Institute and the Institute for Chinese Studies as may be assigned for housing library collections administered by the Curators of the Bodleian Library.

6. The curators shall have power to appoint such staff as may be required at the Oriental Institute and the Clarendon Press Institute, and to determine their duties and conditions of service, subject to the provisions of any statute, decree, or regulation of general application, and to the approval by the Board of the Faculty of Oriental Studies and by the General Board of any appointment carrying with it a stipend of more than the maximum prescribed in Ch. VII, Sect. IV, § 1, cl. 2 (ii), such approval to cover the person appointed, his or her stipend, period of office, and duties, and any other conditions.

7. The curators shall submit annually to the General Board estimates of receipts and expenditure for the following year.

[1] For the Resolution of Congregation of 31 May 1955 and an extract from the High Court Order dated 19 July 1956, relating to the Oriental Institute and the Indian Institute, see *Statutes*, 1987, p. 250.

Section LXII. Palaeography and related Manuscript and Textual Studies, Joint Standing Committee for

1. There shall be a Committee for Palaeography and related Manuscript and Textual Studies which shall consist of:

(1) a person appointed by the Board of the Faculty of English Language and Literature;

(2) a person appointed by the Board of the Faculty of Literae Humaniores;

(3) a person appointed by the Board of the Faculty of Medieval and Modern Languages;

(4) a person appointed by the Board of the Faculty of Modern History;

(5) a person appointed by the Board of the Faculty of Music;

(6) a person appointed by the Board of the Faculty of Oriental Studies;

(7) the Keeper of Western Manuscripts in the Bodleian Library.

The appointed members of the committee shall hold office for four years from the date of appointment (except that casual vacancies shall be filled for the unexpired residue of the period of the member demitting office) and shall be re-eligible.

The committee shall have power to co-opt up to four additional members who shall hold office for two years and shall be re-eligible. The committee shall elect its own chairman.

2. The functions of the committee shall be to promote Palaeography and related Manuscript and Textual Studies within the University, to encourage the best use of existing collections and expertise, to consider such questions concerning the organization of the studies and examinations of the University in this field as may be referred to it by the board of any faculty or by the General Board, and generally to advise the faculty boards and the General Board on matters relating to this field.

Section LXIII. Physics, Department of

§ 1. *Department of Physics and Chairman of Physics*

1. The Department of Physics shall be assigned by the General Board from time to time for a specified period not exceeding five years in the first instance to a person holding an established academic post in the department, normally to a professor or reader, after consultation with the Board of the Faculty of Physical Sciences, the heads of the sub-departments within the Department of Physics, and the other holders of established academic posts in those sub-departments. The person to whom the headship of the department is assigned shall have the title of Chairman of Physics.

2. The Chairman shall be eligible for reappointment, provided that no one person shall hold the post for a total period of more than ten years in aggregate.

3. The Chairman shall receive a stipend equivalent to that of a professor holding a special allowance under Ch. VII, Sect. I, § 7, Schedule I.

4. The Chairman, advised and assisted by the Physics Management Committee, shall have the powers and responsibilities set out in cl. 2 of the Particular Provisions applicable to professors enumerated in Ch. VII, Sect. I, § 5. B, Schedule B, provided that:

(*a*) the Chairman's duties related to teaching shall be as specified in cl. 5 below; and

(*b*) the Chairman may delegate to the heads of sub-departments the responsibility for supervision of departmental staff under the provisions of cl. 2 (*d*) of the said Particular Provisions.

5. The Chairman may undertake teaching and research in accordance with such arrangements as may be made from time to time with the Board of the Faculty of Physical Sciences, and may undertake examining and graduate supervision, but the provisions of Ch. VII, Sect. I, § 5. A, cll. 6 and 7 imposing examining and supervision as duties shall not apply to this office.

6. The Chairman shall be eligible to apply to the General Board for sabbatical leave in accordance with the regulations made by the Board under the provisions of Ch. VII, Sect. I, § 5. A, cl. 14. During a period of leave, a deputy shall be appointed by the General Board on the advice of the Board of the Faculty of Physical Sciences. The deputy shall receive an appropriate proportion of a Schedule I allowance, in accordance with the arrangements which apply when a head of department is on sabbatical leave.

§ 2. *Physics Management Committee*

1. There shall be a Physics Management Committee consisting of:

(1) the Chairman of Physics;

(2) the Head of Astrophysics;

(3) the Head of Atmospheric, Oceanic, and Planetary Physics;

(4) the Head of Atomic and Laser Physics;

(5) the Head of Condensed Matter Physics;

(6) the Head of Particle and Nuclear Physics;

(7) the Head of Theoretical Physics;

(8) the Chairman of the Sub-faculty of Physics;

(9), (10) two members elected by the permanent academic staff of the Department of Physics from among their number.

The election of the members under (9) and (10) above shall be conducted by the Chairman of Physics; these members shall each hold office for a period of three years and shall be re-eligible. The Chairman of Physics shall be the chairman of the committee.

2. The Physics Management Committee shall advise and assist the Chairman of Physics in carrying out the duties of the office.

§ 3. *Associate Chairman of Physics*

The Chairman of Physics may, after consultation with Physics Management Committee, appoint an Associate Chairman for a specified period of up to five years in the first instance from among the holders of established academic posts in the Department of Physics. The Associate Chairman shall assist and advise the Chairman in carrying out the Chairman's duties and shall be a member of the Physics Management Committee. The Associate Chairman may undertake teaching and research in accordance with such arrangements as may be made from time to time with the Board of the Faculty of Physical Sciences, and may undertake examining and graduate supervision, but the provisions of Ch. VII, Sect. I, § 5. A, cll. 6 and 7 imposing examining and supervision as duties shall not apply to the holder of this office.

§ 4. *The Heads of the Sub-departments of the Department of Physics*

1. The head of each sub-department of the Department of Physics shall be responsible for academic work in the subject area of that sub-department, including overseeing research, and for collaborating with other sub-departments and with the Sub-faculty of Physics and the Physics Management Committee in arranging for the teaching of Physics. The head shall also have responsibility for the allocation and expenditure of the budget assigned by the Chairman of Physics to that sub-department.

2. The head of each sub-department shall be appointed by the General Board from time to time for a specified period of not less than five years from among those holding permanent academic posts in the respective sub-department, normally from among those with the title of professor or reader, after consultation with the Board of the Faculty of Physical Sciences, the Physics Management Committee, and the permanent academic staff of the respective sub-departments, provided that the first appointments to the headships of the sub-departments may be made for periods of less than five years.

3. The head for the time being of each sub-department shall undertake teaching in accordance with such arrangements as shall be made from time to time with the Board of the Faculty of Physical Sciences. When the head of a sub-department is a professor, his or her teaching duties shall normally be those laid down in Ch. VII, Sect. I, § 5. B, cl. 2 (*b*).

4. The head of each sub-department shall receive a special allowance of the amount receivable by certain professors in accordance with Ch. VII, Sect. I, § 7, as follows:

Astrophysics	Schedule V
Atmospheric, Oceanic, and Planetary Physics	Schedule V
Atomic and Laser Physics	Schedule IV
Condensed Matter Physics	Schedule III
Particle and Nuclear Physics	Schedule III
Theoretical Physics	Schedule V.

Section LXIV. Politics and International Relations, Department of

1. There shall be a Department of Politics and International Relations, over which the Board of the Faculty of Social Studies shall exercise general supervision.

2. The department shall be assigned by the General Board for a specified period not exceeding three years in the first instance to a person holding an established academic post in the University or an equivalent appointment in a college or other society, on the recommendation of the Board of the Faculty of Social Studies. The person to whom the headship of the department is assigned shall have the title of Head of the Department of Politics and International Relations. The head of department shall be eligible for reappointment for a maximum of one further period of office not exceeding three years.

3. The duties of the head of department shall include the general supervision, under the Board of the Faculty of Social Studies, of research, advanced study, and teaching in the department. The head of department shall engage in advanced study or research and shall give or hold such number of lectures or classes as are required by the terms of his or her normal university post, except that the Board of the Faculty of Social Studies may recommend to the General Board that he or she be given remission from such specified duties attached to that post as shall be considered appropriate in view of his or her additional responsibilities as head of department. The head of department shall have charge of the department, subject to clause 1 of this decree, and shall receive a special allowance as set out in Ch. VII, Sect. I, § 7, Schedule V.

4. (*a*) The departmental general purposes committee shall appoint all non-academic and academic-related staff and prescribe their duties and conditions of service, provided that the terms of appointment shall be subject to approval by or on behalf of the Personnel Committee.

(*b*) Appointments to academic posts in the department shall be made by the faculty board on the recommendation of a committee appointed by the board (of which the head of department or his or her nominee shall be a member, and which may include other persons not being members of the board), and the duties and conditions of service of any such appointment shall be prescribed by the faculty board. Such appointments shall also require approval by the General Board, such approval to cover the person appointed, his or her stipend, period of office, and duties, and any other conditions as determined by the faculty board.

(*c*) All appointments shall be subject to the provisions of any statute, decree, or regulation of general application.

5. The constitution of the department, which shall in all respects be subject to the conditions of this decree, shall be determined by the Board of the Faculty of Social Studies and shall be incorporated in the board's Standing Orders.

Section LXV. Proctors' Office, Committee for the

1. There shall be a Committee for the Proctors' Office, which shall comprise:

(1) the Vice-Chancellor or his or her nominee, who shall be chairman;

(2), (3) the Proctors;

(4) the Assessor;

(5) the Chairman of the University Security Committee;

(6), (7) two members appointed by Council, at least one of whom shall be a former Proctor.

Those elected under (6)–(7) shall hold office for a period of five years and shall be eligible for re-election, provided that a casual vacancy shall be filled for the remainder of the period of office of the person being replaced.

2. The committee shall meet as frequently as business dictates.

3. The committee shall be responsible for ensuring that the Proctors' Office is organized and operates in a way which provides adequate support for the Proctors and the Assessor, and shall represent the interests of the Proctors' Office on a continuing basis within the University.

4. The committee shall, under Council, have control of any moneys placed at its disposal by Council for the staffing and running of the Proctors' Office and shall have responsibility for any staff appointed against such moneys, including such persons as the Vice-Chancellor may think fit to appoint as Constables under the powers reserved to the Chancellor or Vice-Chancellor in section 23 of the Oxford Police Act, 1881. The committee shall also be responsible for meeting the expenses of Special Constables appointed by the Chancellor and Vice-Chancellor and expenses incurred by the Proctors in connection with their duties.

5. The committee shall be responsible for the appointment, induction, appraisal, and career development of the Clerk to the Proctors, who shall have the general responsibility under the Proctors for the supervision and the direction of the staff of the office except for those members of staff, including the Constables, for whom responsibility is allocated by the Proctors to the University Marshal.

6. The committee shall be available for consultation on an informal basis by the Proctors.

Section LXVI. Committees for the Representation of Non-Academic Staff

1. There shall be a joint committee with the University in respect of each group of non-academic staff in respect of whom there exists a recognition and procedure agreement or terms of reference approved by Council.

2. The composition and operation of each joint committee shall be in accordance with the relevant recognition and procedure agreement or terms of reference.

3. Each recognition and procedure agreement or terms of reference shall be printed in the *Handbook for Non-academic Staff* published by the University from time to time and issued to all non-academic staff.

4. Regulations for the election of staff representatives where applicable and for the conduct of ballots shall be made by each joint committee as appropriate.

Section LXVII. Queen Elizabeth House

§ 1. *Queen Elizabeth House*

There shall be a department called Queen Elizabeth House, the purposes of which shall be:

(*a*) to carry out teaching and research in Development Studies, including administrative, agricultural, economic, historical, legal, political, social, and other matters affecting the peoples of the Commonwealth and other overseas countries;

(*b*) to encourage and foster academic co-operation in the field of Development Studies between the University on the one hand and officials, academics, and others in the Commonwealth and elsewhere on the other, and to that end to provide such persons with a centre for study and research in Oxford;

(*c*) to assist such persons to obtain access to the academic resources of other institutions in the University and elsewhere, and generally to offer its services for the purpose of maintaining contact between such persons and institutions and other organizations as are concerned with the purposes of the House.

§ 2. *Advisory Council for Queen Elizabeth House*

1. There shall be an Advisory Council for Queen Elizabeth House, the duties of which shall be:

(*a*) to assist the Inter-faculty Committee for Queen Elizabeth House and the Director of Queen Elizabeth House in achieving the purposes of Queen Elizabeth House, as defined in sub-section 1 of this section, with particular reference to purposes (*b*) and (*c*) therein;

(*b*) to provide guidance on general directions for research in the department, in light of the needs of developing countries and the relations between developed and developing countries;

(*c*) to assist in fund-raising activities.

2. The Advisory Council shall consist of ten appointed members who shall be persons having special knowledge of developing countries. No member of the Advisory Council, unless appointed by the Hebdomadal Council or co-opted as provided below, shall be the holder of a post in the University or in a college or other society. The members shall be:

(1) one person appointed by Her Majesty's Government;

(2) one person appointed by an academic institution, other than the University, specializing in the study of developing countries and of issues relating to them, in the United Kingdom or another developed country;

(3), (4) two persons appointed by international organizations specializing in work relating to developing countries;

(5) one person appointed by a non-governmental organization specializing in work relating to developing countries;

(6), (7) two persons appointed by the Hebdomadal Council;

(8)–(10) three persons elected by the Director and the academic post-holders in the department, the senior members of the University formally affiliated to the department, and senior members of the research or teaching groups formally associated with the department, of which three persons at least one shall be selected from the business community, and at least one from among the staff of an academic institution in a developing country.

The Advisory Council shall have power to co-opt up to four additional members, of whom at least half shall not be holders of posts in the University or in a college or other society. The specific appointing bodies under (1)–(5) above shall be determined by the Inter-faculty Committee for Queen Elizabeth House from time to time, in consultation with the Director of Queen Elizabeth House. Members shall hold office for a period of three years and shall be re-eligible for one further period of office after their initial period. The Advisory Council shall choose from among its members the person who is to chair it. It shall normally meet once a year. Some of its functions may be carried out by means of correspondence and visits by individual members to Queen Elizabeth House. The agenda for the meetings shall be set by the person chairing the Advisory Council, in consultation with the Director.

The Director of Queen Elizabeth House and those members of the Inter-faculty Committee for Queen Elizabeth House who shall have been elected under the provisions of § 3, cl. 1 (8)–(10) below shall be invited to attend the meetings of the Advisory Council.

§ 3. *Inter-faculty Committee for Queen Elizabeth House*

1. There shall be an Inter-faculty Committee for Queen Elizabeth House, which shall consist of:

(1) the Vice-Chancellor or the Chairman of the General Board or their nominee (as agreed between them from time to time), who shall chair the committee;

(2) the Director of Queen Elizabeth House;

(3)–(7) five persons appointed by the Board of the Faculty of Social Studies;

(8)–(10) three persons elected by and from among the established university academic post-holders in the department, the senior members of the University formally affiliated to the department under the provisions of clause 2 (*d*) below, and senior members of the research or teaching groups formally associated with the department under the provisions of clause 2 (*e*) below;

(11), (12) two persons appointed by the Board of the Faculty of Anthropology and Geography (of whom one shall be a member of the Sub-faculty of Anthropology and the other a member of the Sub-faculty of Geography);

(13) a person appointed by the Board of the Faculty of Modern History;

(14), (15) two persons appointed by the Advisory Council for Queen Elizabeth House.

Elected members shall hold office for three years and shall be re-eligible, provided that a person elected to fill a vacancy caused otherwise than by lapse of time shall initially hold office only for the residue of the period of office of the member whom he or she succeeds. If an elected member shall have been absent from more than two consecutive meetings of the committee his or her seat may forthwith be declared by the chairman to be vacant and shall thereupon be vacated.

2. The duties of the committee shall be:

(*a*) to determine the academic policy of the department, consistently with the purposes set out in the schedule to this section;

(*b*) to exercise general supervision over the department, including overseeing accounts, staffing, space, and library policy, and approving such consultancies and project proposals as shall be referred to it;

(*c*) to exercise as appropriate the functions and powers of a faculty board in accordance with the provisions of Ch. II, Sect. VII, § 1;

(*d*) to appoint affiliated staff and visitors;

(*e*) to consider, and at its discretion to approve, the association of research or teaching groups with the department;

(*f*) to arrange courses of study at the request of overseas governments and to issue certificates in connection with such courses;

(*g*) to give advice to the General Board on the needs of the subjects being studied in the department;

(*h*) to report annually both to each of the constituencies which appoint or elect persons to membership of the committee, and to the General Board, on the work of the department;

(*i*) to consider the organization of studies and examinations of the University in the field of Development Studies, including such questions as may be referred to it by the board of any faculty, and to advise the faculty boards concerned on such matters. The committee shall have the powers of a faculty board in respect of courses and examinations for such degrees or diplomas in these fields as may be established by decree, and for the admission and examination of students for advanced degrees in these fields.

§ 4. *Director of Queen Elizabeth House*

1. Queen Elizabeth House shall be assigned by the General Board for a specified period not exceeding five years in the first instance to a person holding an established academic post in the University or a permanent appointment in a college or other society, after consultation with the Inter-faculty Committee for Queen Elizabeth House. The person to whom the headship of the department is assigned shall have the title of Director of Queen Elizabeth House. The director shall be eligible for reappointment.

2. The director's duties shall include the general supervision, under the Inter-faculty Committee for Queen Elizabeth House, of research, advanced study, and teaching in the department, and the promotion of its wider purposes as set out in sub-section 1 of this section. The director shall engage in advanced study or research and shall give or hold such number of lectures or classes as are required by the terms of his or her normal university post, except that the Inter-faculty Committee for Queen Elizabeth House may recommend to the General Board that he or she be given remission from such specified duties attached to that post as shall be considered appropriate in view of his or her additional responsibilities as director. The director shall reside within the University during six months at least in each academical year, between the first day of October and the ensuing first day of August, and in particular during not less than six weeks of each term. The director shall make provision for the lighting, warming, water-supply, and cleansing of the premises assigned to the department, including any residential accommodation. The director shall receive each year, in addition to a Schedule III allowance, such enhancement of salary as is required to bring his or her stipend to the level of that of a Schedule A professorship, provided that he or she shall undertake not to receive any direct or indirect payment from any funds of, or at the disposal of, the department.

3. The director shall appoint the staff of the department and shall prescribe their duties and conditions of service, provided that:

(*a*) any appointment to a teaching or research post carrying a stipend of more than the maximum prescribed in Ch. VII, Sect. IV, § 1, cl. 2 (ii) shall be made by the Inter-faculty Committee for Queen Elizabeth House on the recommendation of a subcommittee appointed by the committee (of which the director shall be a member and which may include other persons not being members of the committee), and the duties and conditions of service of any such appointment shall be prescribed by the committee; such appointments shall also require approval by the General Board, such approval to cover the person appointed, his or her stipend, period of office, and duties, and any other conditions as determined by the committee;

(*b*) all appointments shall be subject to the provisions of any statute, decree, or regulation of general application.

Section LXVIII. Committee for the Ruskin School of Drawing and Fine Art

1. There shall be a Committee for the Ruskin School of Drawing and Fine Art consisting of:

(1), (2) two persons appointed by the Humanities Board (at least one from among its own members), one of whom shall be the chairman;

(3) the Ruskin Master of Drawing;

(4), (5) two other persons holding full-time teaching posts in the Ruskin School of Drawing and Fine Art, to be elected by all those holding such posts except the Ruskin Master of Drawing under arrangements to be approved by the Vice-Chancellor and Proctors;

(6) one person appointed by the Committee for the History of Art;

(7) the Director of the Ashmolean Museum;

(8) one person appointed by the Visitors of the Ashmolean Museum;

(9) one person appointed by the Committee of Senior Tutors.

Appointed and elected members shall hold office for three years and shall be re-eligible.

2. The committee may co-opt not more than five persons who shall hold office for up to three years and shall be re-eligible.

3. The committee shall have general oversight of the teaching and other necessary arrangements for the Degree of Bachelor of Fine Art, of the general instruction in Fine Art of members of the University, and of the overall working of the Ruskin School.

4. The committee shall appoint the staff of the Ruskin School of Drawing and Fine Art holding posts carrying a stipend of more than the maximum prescribed in Ch. VII, Sect. IV, § 1, cl. 2 (ii), other than the Ruskin Master of Drawing, and prescribe their duties and conditions of service, on the recommendation of a subcommittee appointed by the committee, which shall include among its members at least one of the two persons appointed to the committee by the Humanities Board, the Ruskin Master of Drawing or his or her deputy, and not less than three persons holding academic posts in Fine Art either in the University or at another university or similar institution, provided that in the case of part-time appointments the committee may make such *ad hoc* arrangements as it thinks fit; such appointments shall also require approval by the General Board, such approval to cover the person appointed, his or her stipend, period of office, and duties, and any other conditions as determined by the committee. All appointments shall be subject to the provisions of any statute, decree, or regulation of general application.

5. The committee shall make an annual report to the Humanities Board.

Section LXIX. St. Cross Building Management Committee

1. There shall be a Committee for the Management of St. Cross Building consisting of:

(1) a chairman appointed by the General Board;

(2) the Chairman of the Board of the Faculty of English Language and Literature;

(3) the Chairman of the Board of the Faculty of Law;

(4) the Director of the Institute of Economics and Statistics;

(5) the Librarian of the Bodleian Law Library;

(6) the Librarian of the Institute of Economics and Statistics Library;

(7) the Librarian of the English Faculty Library.

The chairman of the committee shall hold office for four years and shall be re-eligible. The committee may also co-opt up to two additional members who shall hold office for two years and shall be re-eligible.

2. The administrator of the St Cross Building shall act as secretary to the committee.

3. The functions of the management committee shall be:

(*a*) to appoint a secretary and such janitorial and other staff as may be required for common services, and, subject to the provisions of any statute, decree, or regulation of general application, to prescribe their duties and conditions of service;

(*b*) to be responsible for the maintenance, repair, and decoration of the premises, except in so far as this is the responsibility of the Buildings and Estates Subcommittee under Ch. II, Sect. I, § 6, and for the heating, lighting, water-supply, and cleansing of the building, for the supervision and maintenance of common services, and for the allocation of space within such areas of the building and site as are devoted to common use, and to meet the cost of providing such services out of such sums as may be placed at its disposal from time to time by statute or decree.

Section LXXI. Oxford University Museum of Natural History

1. The Visitors of the Oxford University Museum of Natural History shall comprise:

(1) a chairman who shall be appointed by the Vice-Chancellor;

(2) one of the Proctors or the Assessor as may be agreed between them;

(3), (4) two persons appointed by the General Board, of whom one shall be a person who is not a resident holder of a teaching, research, or administrative post in the University or in any college or other society;

(5), (6) two persons appointed by Council, of whom one shall be a person who is not a resident holder of a teaching, research, or administrative post in the University or in any college or other society;

(7) the Linacre Professor of Zoology or his or her nominee;

(8) the Professor of Zoology or his or her nominee;

(9) the Professor of Geology or his or her nominee;

(10) the Professor of the Physics and Chemistry of Minerals or his or her nominee.

The Visitors may co-opt up to three other members, who need not be members of Congregation. Members shall hold office for a period of three years, and shall be re-eligible. Any or all of the Curators of the four Collections may be invited by the Visitors to attend meetings, or parts thereof, but shall not have voting rights.

The director of the museum shall act as secretary to the Visitors provided always that the Visitors at their discretion may require the director to withdraw from part or all of any meeting.

2. The duties of the Visitors shall be

(*a*) to establish, maintain, and as necessary modify the general policy framework governing the museum's operations;

(*b*) to exercise responsibility for the care and maintenance of the collections in the museum, including the acquisition and disposal of collections and specimens;

(*c*) to have general oversight of the museum's finances, and to present annually to the General Board an estimate of receipts and expenditure for the ensuing financial year;

(*d*) to appoint staff for the museum, in particular staff to assist the curators appointed under clause 3 below in the maintenance of the collections, and, subject to the provisions of any statute, decree, or regulation of general application, to determine their duties and conditions of service;

(*e*) to co-ordinate activities to raise additional funds for the museum;

(*f*) to prepare annually for submission to Congregation a printed report of the activities of the Visitors.

3. There shall be in the Department of Zoology two university lecturers appointed under the provisions of Ch. VII, Sect. IV, § 3, one entitled the Curator of the Zoological Collections and the other the Curator of the Entomological Collections, who shall be responsible to the head of that department for the custody and care of the collections in his or her charge, in consultation in the former case with the Linacre Professor of Zoology when not the head of that department. There shall be in the Department of Earth Sciences two university lecturers similarly appointed, entitled respectively the Curator of the Geological Collections and the Curator of the Mineralogical Collections, who shall be responsible to the head of that department for the custody and care of the collections in his or her charge, in consultation respectively with the Professor of Geology and the Professor of the Physics and Chemistry of Minerals when not the head of that department.

4. There shall be a Director of the Oxford University Museum of Natural History, who shall be appointed by a board of electors consisting of:

(1) the Vice-Chancellor, or, if the head of the college specified in (2) of this clause is Vice-Chancellor, a person appointed by Council;

(2) the head of the college with which the directorship is on that occasion associated, or, if the head is unable or unwilling to act, a person appointed by the governing body of the college;

(3) a person appointed by the governing body of the college specified in (2) of this clause;

(4) a person appointed by Council;

(5), (6) two persons appointed by the General Board;

(7)–(9) three persons appointed by the Visitors of the Oxford University Museum of Natural History.

5. The duties of the director shall be:

(*a*) to be the first officer of the museum, to act for and be generally responsible to the Visitors of the Oxford University Museum of Natural History in the exercise of their powers, and to assist the Visitors in all matters for which they have general responsibility;

(*b*) to act as secretary to the Visitors provided always that the Visitors at their discretion may require the director to withdraw from part or all of any meeting;

(*c*) to give attendance on at least 200 week-days in each year, provided that the Visitors may dispense with the director's attendance for such period or periods as they may think fit;

(*d*) to give twenty-eight lectures or classes in each academic year under the direction of the Visitors in consultation with the faculty board concerned;

(*e*) to carry out research in areas relevant to the museum's collections, and to develop the museum as a major centre of research in those fields;

(*f*) to be responsible for the administrative duties and functions which are normal for a head of department, including the operation of the museum's budget and the disposition of space within the museum's precincts;

(*g*) to direct and co-ordinate curatorial, display, and public outreach functions of the museum and its collections;

(*h*) to arrange for the appropriate deployment of the museum's staffing, technical, and other resources.

Section LXXII. Sheldonian Theatre

1. The Curators of the Sheldonian Theatre shall consist of:

(1) the Vice-Chancellor;

(2), (3) the Proctors;

(4) the Assessor;

(5)–(7) three members of Convocation elected by Congregation, holding office for six years and re-eligible.

2. The curators shall have charge of the Theatre and its precincts and shall make provision for the lighting, warming, water-supply, and cleansing thereof; shall make arrangements for the conduct of the business at the Encaenia; and shall have power to appoint and remove all persons whose services may in their judgement be required, whether for a time or continuously, for any purpose connected with the Theatre.

3. The Vice-Chancellor shall have power to hold Congregations and Convocations in the Theatre, when he or she shall think fit, and to grant the use of the building for any academical purposes. Applications for its use for other purposes shall be referred to the curators.

4. All members of the University attending academical meetings in the Theatre shall wear their proper academical dress.

5. The day for holding the Encaenia in any year shall be appointed by Council before the end of the fourth week of Trinity Full Term in the preceding year.

6. The Vice-Chancellor shall have power before the end of Hilary Term in any year, with the consent of Council, to appoint a place other than the Theatre for holding the Encaenia for that year.

7. The estates of the Theatre shall be managed by the Curators of the University Chest. The Curators of the Chest after payment of repairs and charges incidental to the management of the estates shall pay the residue of the income to the Curators of the Theatre. The Buildings and Estates Subcommittee shall be responsible for the maintenance of the fabric of the Theatre. The Curators of the Sheldonian Theatre shall pay to the Curators of the University Chest for this purpose the income from Wills' Benefaction appropriated to the benefit of the Theatre.

8. Except as is otherwise provided in this decree, the expenditure of all moneys appropriated to the uses of the Theatre shall be committed to the care of the Curators of the Theatre, who shall submit their accounts annually to the Auditors of Accounts.

Section LXXIII. Slavonic and East European Studies, Inter-faculty Committee for

1. There shall be an inter-faculty committee for Slavonic and East European Studies consisting of two members each elected by the boards of the faculties of

(1), (2) Modern History;

(3), (4) Medieval and Modern Languages;

(5), (6) Social Studies;

and one member each elected by the boards of the faculties of

(7) Law;

(8) Anthropology and Geography;

(9) the Director of the Graduate Studies appointed for the time being by the committee;

(10) the Director of the Institute of Slavonic Studies.

The members of the committee shall hold office for four years from the date of election (except that casual vacancies shall be filled for the unexpired residue of the period), and shall be re-eligible. The committee shall have power to co-opt up to four additional members for periods of two years. The committee shall elect its own chairman.

2. The functions of the committee shall be:

(*a*) to consider questions concerning the organization of the studies and examinations of the University in the field of Slavonic and East European Studies which may be referred to it by the board of any faculty, and generally to advise the faculty boards concerned on all such matters:

(*b*) to allocate such funds as may be placed at its disposal by the General Board for general purposes connected with Slavonic and East European Studies.

Section LXXIV. Social Policy and Social Work, Department of

1. There shall be a Department of Social Policy and Social Work, over which the Board of the Faculty of Social Studies shall exercise general supervision.

2. The headship of the department shall be assigned by the General Board for a specified period not exceeding three years in the first instance to a person holding an academic post in the University or an equivalent appointment in a college or other society, after consultation with the Board of the Faculty of Social Studies. The person to whom the headship of the department is assigned from time to time shall have the title of Head of the Department of Social Policy and Social Work. The head of department shall be eligible for reappointment for a maximum of one further period of office not exceeding five years.

3. The duties of the head of department shall include the general supervision, under the Board of the Faculty of Social Studies, of research, advanced study, and teaching in the department (with the exception of such activities as are under the direction of the board). The head of department shall engage in advanced study or research and shall give such number of lectures and hold such number of classes as are required by the terms of appointment of his or her normal university post, except that the Board of the Faculty of Social Studies may recommend to the General Board that he or she be given remission from such specified duties attached to that post as shall be considered appropriate in view of his or her additional responsibilities as head of department. The head of department shall have charge of the department, subject to clause 1 of this decree, and shall receive a special allowance as set out in Ch. VII, Sect. I, § 7, Schedule VI.

4. (*a*) The departmental committee shall appoint all non-academic and academic-related staff and prescribe their duties and conditions of service, provided that the terms of appointment shall be subject to approval by or on behalf of the Personnel Committee.

(*b*) Appointments to academic posts in the department shall be made by the faculty board on the recommendation of a committee appointed by the board (of which the head of department shall be a member, and which may include other persons not being members of the board), and the duties and conditions of service of any such appointment shall be prescribed by the faculty board. Such appointments shall also require approval by the General Board, such approval to cover the person appointed, his or her stipend, period of office, and duties, and any other conditions as determined by the faculty board.

(*c*) All appointments shall be subject to the provisions of any statute, decree, or regulation of general application.

5. The constitution of the department, which shall in all respects be subject to the conditions of this decree, shall be determined by the Board of the Faculty of Social Studies and shall be incorporated in the board's Standing Orders.

Section LXXV. Sociology, Department of

1. There shall be a Department of Sociology, over which the Board of the Faculty of Social Studies shall exercise general supervision.

2. The headship of the department shall be assigned by the General Board for a specified period not exceeding three years in the first instance to a person

holding an established academic post in the University or an equivalent appointment in a college or other society, after consultation with the Board of the Faculty of Social Studies. The person to whom the headship of the department is assigned from time to time shall have the title of Head of the Department of Sociology. The head of department shall be eligible for reappointment for a maximum of one further period of office not exceeding three years.

3. The duties of the head of department shall include the general supervision, under the Board of the Faculty of Social Studies, of research, advanced study, and teaching in the department (with the exception of such activities as are under the direction of the board). The head of department shall engage in advanced study or research and shall give such number of lectures and hold such number of classes as are required by the terms of appointment of his or her normal university post, except that the Board of the Faculty of Social Studies may recommend to the General Board that he or she be given remission from such specified duties attached to that post as shall be considered appropriate in view of his or her additional responsibilities as head of department. The head of department shall have charge of the department, subject to clause 1 of this decree, and shall receive a special allowance as set out in Ch. VII, Sect. I, § 7, Schedule VI.

4. (*a*) The departmental committee shall appoint all non-academic and academic-related staff and prescribe their duties and conditions of service, provided that the terms of appointment shall be subject to approval by or on behalf of the Personnel Committee.

(*b*) Appointments to academic posts in the department shall be made by the faculty board on the recommendation of a committee appointed by the board (of which the head of department shall be a member, and which may include other persons not being members of the board), and the duties and conditions of service of any such appointment shall be prescribed by the faculty board. Such appointments shall also require approval by the General Board, such approval to cover the person appointed, his or her stipend, period of office, and duties, and any other conditions as determined by the faculty board.

(*c*) All appointments shall be subject to the provisions of any statute, decree, or regulation of general application.

5. The constitution of the department, which shall in all respects be subject to the conditions of this decree, shall be determined by the Board of the Faculty of Social Studies and shall be incorporated in the board's Standing Orders.

Section LXXVI. South Asian Studies, Inter-faculty Committee for

1. There shall be an Inter-faculty Committee for South Asian Studies consisting of two members each elected by the Boards of the Faculties of

(1), (2) Modern History;
(3), (4) Oriental Studies;
(5), (6) Social Studies;

(7), (8) Anthropology and Geography;
and one member elected by
(9) the General Board.

The members of the committee shall hold office for four years from the date of election (except that casual vacancies shall be filled for the unexpired residue of the period), and shall be re-eligible. The committee shall have power to co-opt up to four additional members for periods of two years. The committee shall elect its own chairman.

2. The functions of the committee shall be to consider questions concerning the organization of the studies and examinations of the University in the field of South Asian Studies which may be referred to it by the board of any faculty, and generally to advise the faculty boards concerned on all such matters.

Section LXXVII. Sports Strategy Committee

1. There shall be a Sports Strategy Committee consisting of:

(1), (2) a chairman and a vice-chairman, appointed by Council, of whom one shall be a man and one a woman;

(3) one of the Proctors or the Assessor as may be agreed between them;

(4), (5) two persons who are Senior Members of foundation sports, appointed by the Senior Members of the clubs concerned;

(6), (7) two persons who are Senior Members of development sports, appointed by the Senior Members of the clubs concerned;

(8) a person who is the Senior Member of an established sport, appointed by the Senior Members of the clubs concerned;

(9), (10) the President of the Sports Federation *ex officio* and another member of the Sports Federation appointed by that federation, of whom one shall be a man and one a woman, and who shall represent the interests of recognized sports;

(11), (12) two persons appointed by the Conference of Colleges, of whom one shall be a man and one a woman, and who shall have an interest in one of the recognized sports or the organization of college sport (or both).

The members appointed under (1) and (2) above shall hold office for four years. The members appointed under (4)–(8) and (11) and (12) above shall hold office for three years. The member appointed under (10) above shall hold office for one year. Members appointed to fill vacancies caused otherwise than by lapse of time shall hold office for the unexpired residue only of the periods of office of the members whom they succeed. All members shall be eligible for reappointment.

The committee shall have power to co-opt up to three additional members for such periods as it shall see fit.

The Director of Sport and the Development Executive (Sport) shall be entitled to attend meetings, but shall not be voting members, of the committee, provided that the committee may require either or both to withdraw for all or part of any meeting.

2. The committee shall be responsible to Council for the governance of university sport, and shall submit annual reports to Council setting out its medium-term plans and the progress made towards achieving those plans.

3. The committee shall receive an annual grant, of an amount determined by the Committee on the Council Departments, towards the costs of the staff of the Sports Department and the running and upkeep of its facilities. The committee shall have oversight of the use of the grant and any other income and funds for university sport received by the department, provided that the day-to-day running of the department shall be the responsibility of the Director of Sport in line with guidelines set from time to time by the Buildings and Estates Subcommittee in relation to buildings, and in accordance with agreements with the Curators of the University Parks for the use of facilities in the University Parks and with the Property Investment Committee for the use of the Marston Field.

Section LXXVIII. Student Health, Committee on (including University Counselling Service)

§ 1. *Committee on Student Health*

1. There shall be a Committee on Student Health consisting of:

(1) a person, who shall be the chairman of the committee, appointed by the Vice-Chancellor after consultation with the Chairman of the Conference of Colleges;

(2) the W. A. Handley Professor of Psychiatry or a person appointed by him or her;

(3) the University Occupational Health Physician;

(4) the Assessor;

(5) a member of Council appointed by Council;

(6)–(10) five persons appointed by the Conference of Colleges;

(11) a person appointed by the Association of Oxford College Medical Officers;

(12) a person appointed by the Oxford University Student Union;

(13) a person appointed by the Graduate Committee of the Oxford University Student Union.

2. The periods of office of the members of the committee appointed by Council, the Conference of Colleges, and the Association of Oxford College Medical Officers shall be three years in the first instance, renewable for a further period of three years but not normally renewable beyond a total period of six years; provided always that casual vacancies shall be filled for the unexpired period of office of the person being replaced. The periods of office of the remaining appointed members of the committee shall be determined at the time of their appointment by the bodies appointing them.

3. The committee shall have power to co-opt up to three additional members, who shall hold office for one year and shall be re-eligible.

4. The committee shall meet at least once in each term.

5. The committee shall have oversight of the provision of arrangements for the health of students based on the college doctor system.

6. The committee shall also be responsible for the management of a University Counselling Service to assist members of the University. In this connection it shall in particular

(*a*) appoint and have charge of such staff as may in its opinion be required, and determine their duties, remuneration, and conditions of service subject to any statute, decree, or regulation of general application and to Council's approval;

(*b*) have charge of, and make provision for the lighting, warming, water-supply, and cleansing of, any premises made available for the service.

7. The committee shall defray the cost of carrying out the functions of the Counselling Service from such sums as may be placed at its disposal by the University or as may be accepted by Council on its behalf. It shall in Hilary Term in each year submit to Council estimates of receipts and payments in respect of the ensuing financial year.

8. The committee shall report both to Council and to the Conference of Colleges.

§ 2. *Executive Subcommittee for the Management of the University Counselling Service*

There shall be an Executive Subcommittee for the Management of the University Counselling Service consisting of:

(1) a member of the Committee on Student Health appointed by the committee to act as chairman of the subcommittee;

(2) the member of the Committee on Student Health appointed by the Association of Oxford College Medical Officers;

(3), (4) two other members of the Committee on Student Health appointed by the committee;

(5), (6) two persons appointed by, but not necessarily being members of, the Committee on Student Health who hold, or have held, tutorial or pastoral responsibilities in a college of the University.

The chairman of the subcommittee shall hold office for an initial period of three years, renewable for one further and final period of three years, and the periods of office of the appointed members of the subcommittee shall be three years, renewable for a further period of three years but not normally renewable beyond a total of six years; provided always that casual vacancies shall be filled for the unexpired period of office of the person being replaced.

The Committee on Student Health shall, at the beginning of each academic year, set policy objectives for the subcommittee, including those relating to the operation, staffing, and finances of the University Counselling Service, and shall delegate responsibility for executive decisions to the subcommittee, save those which involve a requirement for additional funding. The subcommittee shall report in writing to the Committee on Student Health immediately after each meeting; meetings shall be held at least once in each term.

Section LXXXI. Taylor Institution

§ 1. *General*

1. The Curators of the Taylor Institution shall be:

(1) one of the Proctors as may be agreed between them, who shall be chairman;

(2) the Head of the Humanities Division;

(3) the Pro-Vice-Chancellor (Academic Services and University Collections);

(4) the Chairman of the Board of the Faculty of Medieval and Modern Languages;

(5) the Chairman of the Committee for Library Provision in Modern Languages;

(6)–(8) three persons elected by the Board of the Faculty of Medieval and Modern Languages;

(9) one person elected by the Board of the Faculty of Modern History.

The elected curators shall each hold office for five years and shall be re-eligible, provided that casual vacancies shall be filled for the remainder of the period of office of the person being replaced.

2. The curators shall have care of the Taylor Institution and its annexes and shall provide therein accommodation for the Taylor Institution Library and the Modern Languages Faculty Library.

3. The Taylorian Accumulated Fund, as set forth in the 'Register of Estates and other properties of the University of Oxford administered by the Curators of the University Chest', as made up to 31 July 1925, together with any accretions to that fund, shall be at the disposal of the Curators of the Taylor Institution for extraordinary repairs, unforeseen expenses, and for extension of the Institution.

§ 2. *Ilchester endowment for the encouragement of the study of the Slavonic Languages, Literature, and History*

1. The Curators of the Taylor Institution shall be charged with the application of the proceeds of the fund arising from the bequest of the Right Honourable William Thomas Horner, Earl of Ilchester (for the encouragement of the study of the Slavonic Languages, Literature, and History).

2. The curators shall apply the interest of the fund to one or more of the following purposes at their discretion, and in such manner, and at such times, as they may judge most expedient:

(*a*) the delivery of lectures on subjects connected with the Slavonic Languages or Literature, or the History of the Slavonic Nations;

(*b*) the bestowal of prizes or exhibitions for encouraging the study of those subjects;

(*c*) the making of grants for travel for the purposes of study and research in those subjects;

(*d*) the publishing, or assisting in the publication, of works in one or other of those subjects.

3. The balance (if any) of the income of the fund shall, with all other moneys (if any) which may be added to the fund, be invested in augmentation of the capital; provided that any income for the time being not required for the purposes described in clause 2 above, may be applied in any other way which the curators shall think conducive to the object of the fund.

4. The curators may at any time report in writing to Council that the purposes of this decree cannot in their judgement be satisfactorily carried into effect under the foregoing provisions; and such report shall be published as Council may direct; and the powers hereby vested in the curators shall thereupon cease and determine.

Section LXXXII. University Club

1. The University Club shall be a sports and social centre and residence for which the University shall provide such accommodation as Council shall approve.

2. The direction and control of the club, and of the expenditure of any moneys placed at its disposal by Council, shall be exercised, under Council, by a committee comprising:

(1) the Vice-Chancellor;

(2), (3) two persons appointed by Council, one of whom shall be the chairman;

(4) one person appointed by the Curators of the University Chest from amongst their own number;

(5)–(12) eight persons appointed by the members of the club from amongst their own number.

Others may be invited to attend meetings at the discretion of the committee.

The members appointed under (2)–(12) above shall hold office for a period of three years and shall be eligible for re-election. Casual vacancies shall be filled for the remainder of the period of office of the person being replaced.

3. The committee shall have charge of and shall make provision for the lighting, warming, water supply, and cleansing of the buildings allocated to the club under the provisions of clause 1 above.

4. Admission to membership of the club shall be at the discretion of the committee from the following classes of persons:

(*a*) senior members of the University engaged in advanced study or research or teaching or administration within the University;

(*b*) employees of the University and those of certain associated institutions;

(*c*) visitors from overseas, whether members of the University or not, who are temporarily in residence at Oxford for the purpose of advanced study or research;

(*d*) persons registered as graduate students of the University;

(*e*) other persons at the discretion of the committee.

5. The committee shall submit a report annually to Council.

Section LXXXIII. University Parks, Curators of the

1. There shall be nine Curators of the University Parks:

(1) the Vice-Chancellor, or some member of Convocation appointed by the Vice-Chancellor to act in his or her stead;

(2), (3) the Proctors;

(4) the Assessor;

(5) the person appointed by the Planning and Resource Allocation Committee to act as chairman of the Buildings and Estates Subcommittee (or another member of the subcommittee nominated by the chairman);

(6), (7) two elected by Congregation;

(8), (9) two elected by Council.

Those elected under (6)–(9) shall be members of Convocation, each holding office for six years, and re-eligible. Any vacancy occurring before the end of the proper period shall be supplied only to the end of such period.

The curators shall have power to co-opt not more than two persons as additional members for such periods as they shall think fit.

2. The curators, under Council, shall have charge of the Parks, of the Fishery in the Cherwell, of the former Bathing-place and of any other land the care of which may be entrusted to them from time to time by decree, and of all Walks repaired by the University. For these purposes they shall receive and apply the rents and profits of the premises and such other sums as may be determined from time to time by decree. They shall submit their accounts annually to the Curators of the University Chest.

3. It shall be the duty of the curators to prepare and submit annually to Council a report on their current activities.

Section LXXXIV. University Press, Delegacy of the

1. The Delegacy of the University Press shall consist of up to twenty-two Delegates and shall have charge of the affairs of the Press as provided in Tit. VIII, Sect. II.

2. The Finance Committee of the Delegacy required by Tit. VIII, Sect. II, cl. 6, shall consist of:

(1) a Chairman elected by the Delegacy;

(2) the Vice-Chancellor;

(3) the Senior Proctor;

(4)–(9) six members elected by the Delegacy from among the appointed Delegates;

(10)–(12) three persons possessing high qualifications in business or finance and appointed by Council after consultation with the Delegates;

(13) the Secretary to the Delegates;

(14) the Finance Director;

(15)–(19) not more than five senior officers of the Press appointed by the Delegacy.

3. The Chairman shall be elected either from among the appointed Delegates or from among persons who have previously served as a Delegate and who have recently served as a member of the Finance Committee. The Chairman and the six members elected from among the appointed Delegates shall hold office for a period not exceeding five years and, so long as they continue to be Delegates, shall be eligible for re-election for successive further periods not exceeding five years; provided that a Chairman who is not elected from among the appointed Delegates shall serve in that capacity for only one period of five years. If any Delegate-member of the Finance Committee shall cease to be a Delegate, his or her membership of the committee shall forthwith be terminated.

4. The members appointed by Council shall hold office for four years and shall be eligible for reappointment.

5. The senior officers of the Press appointed by the Delegacy shall hold office for such periods as the Delegacy may determine.

6. (*a*) The Delegates shall determine the emoluments and allowances to be paid by the Press to the Chairman of the Finance Committee in respect of his or her tenure of that office.

(*b*) At the request of the Delegates, the General Board may relieve him or her of such of his or her regular university duties, and on such terms, as it may determine.

7. (*a*) The Finance Committee shall submit the minutes of its meetings to the next ensuing meeting of the Delegacy and shall keep the Delegacy informed regarding matters dealt with or under consideration by the Finance Committee.

(*b*) The Finance Committee may set up such subcommittees as it may from time to time think fit. Such subcommittees may include persons who are not members of the Finance Committee.

8. (*a*) The annual accounts of the Delegacy shall be audited according to instructions received from the Delegates by an auditor who shall be appointed annually by Council and shall be paid by the Delegates. The auditor shall transmit to Council a certificate as to the correctness of the accounts.

(*b*) The annual accounts shall be presented to the Delegacy by the Finance Committee at a stated meeting fixed for the purpose, and shall be accompanied by a report on the accounts submitted by the Finance Committee.

9. (*a*) The audited accounts of the Delegacy, together with the Finance Committee's report and an abstract of the accounts, shall be submitted to Council under arrangements approved by Council.

(*b*) The Chairman of the Finance Committee (or his or her deputy), the Secretary to the Delegates (or his or her deputy), and the Auditor of the Press Accounts shall make themselves available in person to supply, and shall supply, such further explanations of the accounts and of the report as may be required in accordance with arrangements prescribed under (*a*) above.

10. The abstract of the accounts and the Auditor's certificate provided for in clauses 8 (*a*) and 9 (*a*) above shall be published in the *University Gazette* as part of the report referred to in clause 11 below.

11. The Delegates shall submit to Council annually a report on the general state and activities of the University Press which shall, subject to the authorization of Council, be published in the *University Gazette*.

12. The Delegates may establish a small Seal of the University to be employed exclusively in the transaction of the business of the Press. They shall provide for the safe custody of the Seal, which may be used only on the authority of the Finance Committee or the Delegacy or the Vice-Chancellor. Any deed or instrument to which the Seal is affixed shall be signed by the Chairman, or by another Delegate-member, of the Finance Committee, and countersigned by the Secretary to the Delegates or by another senior officer of the Press authorized by him or her for the purpose.

CHAPTER IV

OFFICERS OF THE UNIVERSITY

Section I. Admission of the Chancellor, Vice-Chancellor, Proctors, and Assessor

§ 1. *Admission of the Chancellor*

1. As soon as can conveniently be arranged after the election, the newly elected Chancellor shall be admitted at a meeting of Convocation at which the instrument of his or her election under the Common Seal of the University shall be handed to him or her by the Vice-Chancellor and Senior Proctor, together with the insignia of the office of Chancellor, that is, the statute book, the keys, the seal of office, and the staves of the bedels.

2. At the installation of the Chancellor, the Vice-Chancellor shall say:

'*Insignissime et Honoratissime etc. Tu dabis fidem, quod omnia et singula Statuta, Libertates, Consuetudines, Jura, et Privilegia istius Universitatis, quacunque partialitate remota, indifferenter, bene, et fideliter, quantum in te fuerit, et ad tuam notitiam devenerint, durante Officio tuo, tueberis et conservabis. Item quod ea omnia fideliter exequeris quae ad Officium summi Universitatis Cancellarii spectant.*'

and the Chancellor shall reply: '*Do fidem.*'

§ 2. *Admission of the Vice-Chancellor*

1. As nearly as possible at the beginning of the academic year in which he or she takes up office, the Vice-Chancellor shall be admitted at a meeting of Congregation. The retiring Vice-Chancellor shall address the House briefly concerning his or her period of office, hand to the Proctors the statute book, the keys, and the seal of office, and leave his or her place to his or her successor.

2. The new Vice-Chancellor shall then give the following undertaking, to be recited by the Senior Proctor:

'*Insignissime etc. Tu dabis fidem ad observandum Statuta, Privilegia, Libertates, et Consuetudines istius Universitatis.*

'*Item tu dabis fidem, quod ea omnia fideliter exequeris quae ad Officium Vice-Cancellarii spectant.*'

and the Vice-Chancellor shall reply: '*Do fidem.*'

3. The new Vice-Chancellor shall then receive the insignia of office from the Proctors, take his or her seat as Vice-Chancellor, and hand to the Senior Proctor a list of the persons whom he or she has selected to act for the time being as Pro-Vice-Chancellors and perform such of his or her functions as he or she shall depute to them. If the Pro-Vice-Chancellors so nominated are present, they shall thereupon, at the request of the Senior Proctor, give the same undertaking as the Vice-Chancellor. Any that are not there shall take the oath at the next convenient meeting of Congregation.

4. The Vice-Chancellor shall then dismiss Congregation, and, accompanied by the Doctors and Masters, shall escort the retiring Vice-Chancellor to his or her college or other society. The Doctors and Masters shall then escort the new Vice-Chancellor to his or her college or other society.

§ **3.** *Admission of the Proctors and the Assessor*

1. The admission of the Proctors and the Assessor shall take place at a Congregation to be held on Wednesday in the week after the end of Hilary Full Term. The Proctors of the previous year having taken their seats, the Senior Proctor shall address the House briefly concerning the events of the year. Then both Proctors shall give up the insignia of their office, that is, the statute book and the keys.

2. The new Proctors, having been escorted from their colleges or societies (except when the Vice-Chancellor and Proctors shall otherwise determine at the request of the college or society concerned) by the heads and other members of their colleges or societies, preceded by one of the Bedels, and wearing the academic dress appropriate to a Master of Arts, shall be presented to the Vice-Chancellor by the head or vicegerent of their college or society with the following formula:

'*Insignissime Domine Vice-Cancellerie, praesento tibi hunc egregium virum* (or *hanc egregiam feminam) A. B. in Artibus Magistrum* (or *Magistram* or *in superiore aliqua Facultate Baccalaureum* or *Baccalauream* or *Doctorem) e Collegio N. secundum statuta in alterum Procuratorum hujus Universitatis electum (or electam), ut ad munus Procuratorium istius Universitatis in annum sequentem obeundum admittatur.*'

3. The Vice-Chancellor shall then say to each Proctor:

'*Magister (or Magistra), tu dabis fidem, quod ea omnia et singula quae ad officium (senioris* or *junioris) Procuratoris istius Universitatis spectant, bene et fideliter, et indifferenter, quatenus te et officium tuum concernunt, omnimoda partialitate seposita, durante tuo officio, exequeris; et executionem eorundem per deputatos tuos, quantum in te est, procurabis.*'

and each Proctor shall reply: '*Do fidem.*'

4. The Vice-Chancellor shall then hand to each of them the insignia of his or her office, that is, the statute book and the keys, and shall admit them to office with the following formula:

'*Egregie Magister* (or *Egregia Magistra), ego auctoritate mea et totius Universitatis admitto te ad officium Procuratoris istius Universitatis in annum sequentem; necnon ad reliqua omnia praestanda et peragenda, quae ad munus vel officium Procuratoris spectant.*'

5. They shall then take the seats of the Proctors.

6. The head or vice-gerent of the college or other society of the new Assessor shall then present the new Assessor to the Vice-Chancellor with the following formula:

'Insignissime Domine Vice-Cancellarie, praesento tibi hunc egregium virum (or hanc egregiam feminam) A. B. in Artibus Magistrum (or *Magistram* or *in superiore aliqua Facultate Baccalaureum* or *Baccalauream* or *Doctorem), e Collegio N. secundum statuta in Assessorem hujus Universitatis electum* (or *electam), ut ad munus Assessoris istius Universitatis in annum sequentem obeundum admittatur.'*

7. The Vice-Chancellor shall then say to the Assessor:

'Magister (or *Magistra) tu dabis fidem quod ea omnia et singula quae ad officium Assessoris istius Universitatis spectant, bene et fideliter, durante tuo officio, exequeris.'*

and the Assessor shall reply: *'Do fidem.'*

8. The Vice-Chancellor shall then admit the Assessor with the following formula:

'Egregie Magister (or *Egregia Magistra), ego auctoritate mea et totius Universitatis admitto te ad officium Assessoris istius Universitatis in annum sequentem; necnon ad reliqua omnia praestanda et peragenda, quae ad munus vel officium Assessoris spectant.'*

9. Each Proctor shall then nominate his or her deputies. These deputies shall, if they are present, bind themselves, at the request of the Vice-Chancellor, by the same undertaking as the Proctors. If they are not present they shall give this undertaking at the next convenient meeting of Congregation.

10. The Vice-Chancellor shall then dismiss Congregation.

Section II. Number of Pro-Vice-Chancellors

The maximum number of members of Congregation whom the Vice-Chancellor may appoint as Pro-Vice-Chancellors under the provisions of Tit. IX, Sect. V, cl. 3, shall be nine, of whom one shall be the President for the time being of the University Development Programme.

Section III. Deputy Steward and Clerks of the Market

The Chancellor may appoint a Deputy Steward and a Clerk of the Market; and the Vice-Chancellor may appoint a Clerk of the Market. All appointments shall be reported to Congregation.

Section IV. The Registrar

1. The Registrar shall be responsible for the maintenance of the following Registers:

(*a*) a Register of matriculations, which shall contain such particulars concerning all matriculated persons as are prescribed from time to time by decree;

(*b*) a Register of all members of the University in which shall be entered

(i) their matriculation;

(ii) the passing of any university examination;

(iii) any qualification which exempts a candidate from a university examination or from any part thereof or from any requirement as to residence or standing;

(iv) any qualification which entitles a candidate to supplicate for a degree;

(v) the conferment of any degree;

(*c*) a Register of members of Permanent Private Halls;

(*d*) a Register of members of Congregation;

(*e*) a Register of persons holding the status of Master of Arts;

(*f*) a Register of persons who are not members of the University but who are studying with a view to obtaining a diploma or certificate open to persons who are not members of the University, which shall contain the particulars of those persons prescribed from time to time by decree;

(*g*) a Register of all appointments of examiners.

2. The Registrar shall also take charge of the books kept for the registration of Class Lists and of the names of candidates who have satisfied the examiners in any examination.

3. The Registrar shall furnish from the Registers certificates of matriculation, of graduation, and of the results of examinations, on payment of such fees as may be prescribed from time to time by decree. He or she shall also issue to every undergraduate who has been incorporated a certificate showing his or her standing and privileges.

4. The Registrar shall receive the names of candidates for university examinations unless in the case of any particular examination Council shall by decree direct that the names be received by some other person.

5. The Registrar shall receive the names of candidates for degrees, and shall ascertain by reference to the Registers in his or her charge whether the candidates are duly qualified, so far as relates to passing examinations and to standing, to receive their degrees.

6. It shall be the duty of the Registrar to see that the conditions under which the names of candidates for university examinations may be given in to him or her have been satisfied.

7. The Registrar shall be responsible for the publication of

(*a*) the *Oxford University Calendar*, which shall be published each year and shall contain such information as Council shall from time to time determine;

(*b*) the *Examination Decrees*, which shall be published each year and shall contain the decrees and regulations in force concerning examinations and related matters;

(*c*) the *Statutes, Decrees, and Regulations of the University of Oxford*, which shall be published from time to time as occasion requires and shall contain all the statutes in force together with such decrees and regulations in force as are not included in (*b*).

Section V. The Public Orator

1. The Public Orator shall be elected by Congregation from among the members of Convocation.

2. After his or her election the Public Orator shall be admitted to office by the Proctors and shall say: '*Spondeo quod ea omnia et singula fideliter exequar, quae ad Publici Oratoris officium spectant.*'

3. The Public Orator's duties shall be to present those who are to be admitted to an Honorary Degree and to deliver an oration about each one; to compose letters and addresses at the direction of Council; to make speeches at the reception of members of royal families, and on other important occasions, at the direction of the Vice-Chancellor; to deliver the Creweian Oration when required by the Vice-Chancellor; and to perform any other functions that may be laid down by statute or decree.

4. If the Public Orator is on any occasion prevented from performing the duties of his or her office, he or she may appoint a member of Congregation, subject to the approval of the Vice-Chancellor, to act as deputy on that occasion; or if he or she is unable to appoint a deputy, the Vice-Chancellor shall appoint one.

Section VI. Director of Pre-clinical Studies

1. The Director of Pre-clinical Studies shall be appointed by the Board of the Faculty of Physiological Sciences on such conditions as to duties and tenure as the board may determine; provided that

(*a*) the director shall normally be appointed in the first instance for a period of three years, at the end of which he or she may be reappointed for one further period which shall normally not exceed two years;

(*b*) the appointment or reappointment of the director and the conditions determined by the faculty board shall be subject to the approval of the General Board;

(*c*) the appointment or reappointment of the director shall be made on the recommendation of a committee appointed by the faculty board, of which the Regius Professor of Medicine shall be a member and which may include other persons not being members of the board.

2. The duties of the Director of Pre-clinical Studies shall include:

(*a*) to act as an officer of the Medical School under the Regius Professor of Medicine and to perform such administrative duties as the Board of the Faculty of Physiological Sciences may from time to time determine;

(*b*) to take strategic responsibility for the organization and development of the First B.M. and of the other undergraduate courses under the aegis of the Physiological Sciences Board;

(*c*) to advise the Secretary to the Board of the Faculty of Physiological Sciences on matters concerning the Pre-clinical School;

(*d*) to advise prospective medical students, or undergraduates wishing to study Medicine, on matters concerning the pre-clinical medical course and their admission as medical students.

3. The Director of Pre-clinical Studies shall receive an allowance as shall be determined from time to time by the General Board.

Section VII. Director of Clinical Studies

1. The Director of Clinical Studies shall be appointed by the Board of the Faculty of Clinical Medicine on such conditions as to duties and tenure as the board may determine; provided that

(*a*) the director shall normally be appointed in the first instance for a period of three years, and shall normally be eligible for reappointment for a further and final period of two years;

(*b*) the appointment or reappointment of the director and the conditions determined by the faculty board shall be subject to the approval of the General Board.

2. The duties of the Director of Clinical Studies shall include:

(*a*) to act as an officer of the Medical School under the Regius Professor of Medicine and perform such administrative duties as the Board of the Faculty of Clinical Medicine may from time to time determine;

(*b*) to organize the undergraduate clinical course in the hospitals associated with the University;

(*c*) to represent the Clinical Medical School at meetings of Deans of Medical Schools.

3. The Deputy Director of Clinical Studies shall be appointed and may be reappointed by the Board of the Faculty of Clinical Medicine on such conditions as to duties and tenure as the board may determine in consultation with the Director of Clinical Studies, provided that the appointment and reappointment of the deputy director and the conditions determined by the faculty board shall be subject to the approval of the General Board.

4. The directorship shall normally be non-stipendiary, provided that if the director holds a full-time appointment with the National Health Service, the General Board shall determine in consultation with the Board of the Faculty of Clinical Medicine and the N.H.S. Trust concerned the amount to be paid to the trust in compensation for the time taken by the director in pursuance of his or her duties. The deputy director may receive an honorarium determined by the General Board after consultation with the Board of the Faculty of Clinical Medicine, provided that if the deputy director holds a full-time appointment with the National Health Service, the General Board shall determine in consultation with the Board of the Faculty of Clinical Medicine and the N.H.S. Trust concerned the amount to be paid to the trust in compensation for the time taken by the deputy director in pursuance of his or her duties.

Section VIII. Deanship of Clinical Medicine

1. The Dean of Clinical Medicine shall be appointed by the Board of the Faculty of Clinical Medicine on such conditions as to duties and tenure as the board may determine, provided that

(*a*) the appointment or reappointment of the Dean and the conditions determined by the faculty board shall be subject to the approval of the General Board;

(*b*) the appointment or reappointment of the Dean shall be made on the recommendation of a committee appointed by the faculty board which may include persons not being members of the board.

2. The duties of the Dean shall be to act as an officer of the Medical School responsible to the Board of the Faculty of Clinical Medicine and to perform such administrative duties as the board may from time to time determine.

Section IX. Director of Postgraduate Medical Education and Training

1. There shall be a Director of Postgraduate Medical Education and Training who shall be elected by an electoral board consisting of:

(1) the Vice-Chancellor;

(2) a person appointed by the Hebdomadal Council;

(3) a person appointed by the General Board of the Faculties;

(4), (5) two persons appointed by the Board of the Faculty of Clinical Medicine;

(6) a person appointed by the Oxfordshire Health Authority;

(7) a person appointed by the Oxford Regional Health Authority.

2. The duties of the Director shall be as set out at (i)–(xi) below. The Director shall also perform such other duties as the University may from time to time require.

(i) To promote and keep under review postgraduate medical education and training throughout the Oxford Region;

(ii) to advise the University, the Oxfordshire Health Authority, and the Oxford Regional Health Authority on conditions of work and study facilities of doctors in training, study leave, training rotations and secondments, and library and research facilities;

(iii) to administer on behalf of the University the scheme for pre-registration experience for medical practitioners required by the Medical Act 1956, in particular:

(*a*) to approve posts in hospitals or institutions in the United Kingdom or overseas, for the purpose of registration under the provisions of section 15 of the Act, and to forward to the Registrar of the University from time to time, as may be required, lists of the posts to be approved for submission to the General Medical Council, (*b*) to verify for signature by the Registrar or his or her deputy the certificate required, under section 15 of the Act, by members of the University applying for registration;

(iv) to fulfil on behalf of the University any duties arising under section 63 of the Health Services and Public Health Act 1968;

(v) in association with his or her specialist adviser to promote and co-ordinate training schemes and teaching facilities for doctors in the post-registration period, including, where necessary, teaching in pre-clinical subjects;

(vi) to provide a comprehensive information service on medical training facilities and personnel throughout the region, and careers guidance for those who need it;

(vii) to support and co-ordinate the work of the District Medical Centres in the region, and to recommend appointments of District Clinical Tutors to the Board of the Faculty of Clinical Medicine after a proposal for appointment from the appropriate medical staff committee of the district;

(viii) to supervise and co-ordinate as required procedures for progress reports and assessment in connection with specialist training and registration;

(ix) to prepare and submit to the University, the Oxfordshire Health Authority, and the Oxford Regional Health Authority at such times as may be required financial estimates, and to determine fees in appropriate cases;

(x) to appoint such staff as may be required for the discharge of these duties;

(xi) to delegate to a deputy or other person, or a committee, such functions as may from time to time be appropriate for the discharge of these duties.

3. The salary of the Director shall be as determined by the University from time to time.

4. The Director shall report annually to the University, the Oxfordshire Health Authority, and the Oxford Regional Health Authority.

Section X. The Bedels

1. There shall be ordinarily four bedels.

2. The bedels shall be appointed by the Vice-Chancellor and Proctors, and shall be called the Bedels of Divinity, Law, Medicine, and Arts respectively. They shall be in attendance, as required by the Vice-Chancellor, at University Sermons, at meetings of Congregation and Convocation, at the admission of Proctors, on all state occasions, and whenever summoned by the Vice-Chancellor. One shall be from time to time selected by the Vice-Chancellor to be the Bedel of Divinity; of the other three, the senior in order of appointment shall be the Bedel of Law, the next the Bedel of Medicine, and the junior the Bedel of Arts.

3. The Bedel of Divinity shall conduct each preacher from his or her college or other society to church and to the pulpit and back.

4. The three senior bedels carrying gold staves, the junior carrying a silver staff, and all wearing the usual gowns and round caps, shall walk in the customary order before the Chancellor or Vice-Chancellor.

5. All four bedels shall without reference to their respective special designations, and in addition to the special duties which may be imposed upon each of them, perform, by direction of the Vice-Chancellor, all the statutable and customary duties of bedels.

6. The bedels shall be constantly resident in the University, and shall not be absent from Oxford without special leave from the Vice-Chancellor. They may be dismissed at any time by the Vice-Chancellor and Proctors for incapacity, for inattention to their duty, or for any scandalous or immoral conduct.

7. At the Encaenia and on special occasions the Vice-Chancellor may appoint two extraordinary bedels, and may order such payment to be made for their services as he or she shall think proper.

Section XI. Verger of the University

1. The Verger of the University shall be nominated by the Vice-Chancellor and Proctors, and subject to dismissal by them at any time for incapacity, for inattention to his or her duties, or for any scandalous or immoral conduct.

2. His or her duties shall be:

(*a*) to attend at all Sermons preached before the University and all meetings of Congregation and Convocation;

(*b*) to provide for the ringing of the Bell on the occasion of all such sermons or meetings;

(*c*) to provide for the cleaning of and the arrangement of books and furniture in the University Church, and to have the custody of such books and furniture;

(*d*) to perform such other reasonable duties connected with his or her office as may be required by the Vice-Chancellor and Proctors.

Section XII. Custody of Seals

1. The Common Seal of the University shall be kept by the Proctors for use under the provisions of Tit. XV, Sect. V, cl. 3.

2. The Great Seal (or Chancellor's Seal) shall be kept by the Vice-Chancellor for use as the Chancellor or Vice-Chancellor may direct.

3. The Small Seal of the University shall be kept by the Registrar for use under the provisions of Tit. XV, Sect. V, cl. 4.

4. The Minuscule Seal of the University shall be kept by the Registrar.

5. Any seal established by the Delegates of the University Press under the provisions of Ch. III, Sect. LXXXIV, cl. 12, shall be kept in accordance with arrangements made by the Delegates.

CHAPTER V

MATRICULATION AND RESIDENCE

Section I. Number and Length of Terms

For this Section, see *Examination Decrees*.

Section II. Degree Days

For this Section, see *Examination Decrees*.

Section III. Conditions of Residence and Matriculation

§ 1. *General*

For this Sub-section, see *Examination Decrees*.

§ 2. *Arrangements made by Council for provisional matriculation*

1. Any person who is qualified for matriculation may be provisionally matriculated as a member of the University. The matriculation fee, if payable, the candidate's completed matriculation form (i.e. the form he or she is required to complete under the provisions of § 1, cl. 3), and (unless the candidate has previously been registered as qualified for matriculation) evidence that the candidate is qualified for matriculation, must be sent by the authorities of the candidate's society to the Registrar with a request that the candidate be provisionally matriculated.

2. Each person who is so provisionally matriculated shall be given a copy of the *Examination Decrees* and of the Proctors' Memorandum on the Conduct and Discipline of Junior Members of the University.

3. The Registrar shall, not later than the third day before each matriculation ceremony, send to each society a certificate showing those members of the society who have been provisionally matriculated and who are still eligible to be matriculated with effect from the date of their provisional matriculation. (Under the provisions of § 1, cl. 5, but subject to the exception in clause 6 thereof, those provisionally matriculated must be matriculated not later than a matriculation ceremony in the term following their provisional matriculation.) These certificates must be brought by the college officers to the matriculation ceremony (see § 3, cl. 5 below).

§ **3.** *Arrangements made by Council for matriculation ceremonies*

1. Matriculation ceremonies will be held at the beginning and end of each Michaelmas Full Term and at the end of each Hilary and Trinity Full Term. The dates will be fixed by the Vice-Chancellor and published in the *University Gazette*.

2. The time and place for the attendance of each society will be fixed by the Vice-Chancellor's Secretary, who will inform the college officers not later than the Friday before the beginning of Full Term or the Friday in the seventh week of Full Term, as the case may be.

3. The college authorities will send to the Registrar not later than 10 a.m. on the third day previous to the ceremony:

(*a*) duplicate lists of candidates (excluding those who have already been provisionally matriculated), one copy of which will be signed by the Registrar and returned to the college certifying that the candidates are qualified;

(*b*) a completed matriculation form for each candidate (i.e. the form required under the provisions of § 1, cl. 3);

(*c*) evidence that each candidate (other than those previously registered as qualified for matriculation) is qualified for matriculation.

4. The Registrar will remove from such lists the name of any candidate for whom

(*a*) no qualifications for matriculation have been received, or

(*b*) the matriculation form has not been received.

5. At the ceremony the signed Registrar's lists and the Registrar's certificates relating to candidates who have previously been provisionally matriculated will be handed by the college officer to an official of the University Offices, who will receive the assurance of the college officers that all the candidates named on the lists and the certificates are present.

6. Candidates will be presented to the Vice-Chancellor in groups of colleges (the grouping to be determined by the Vice-Chancellor) by the college officer of the college senior in foundation in the group, with the following formula:

'*Insignissime Vice-Cancellarie, praesentamus tibi hos nostros scholares ut referantur in Matriculam Universitatis.*'

The Vice-Chancellor will admit the candidate(s) with the following formula:

'*Scitote vos* (or *Scito te*) *in Matriculam Universitatis hodie relatos* (or *relatum* or *relatam*) *esse, et ad observandum omnia Statuta istius Universitatis, quantum ad vos* (or *ad te*) *spectent, teneri.*'

7. Payment of the matriculation fees, where payable, will be made by each college to the Curators of the University Chest not later than 10 a.m. on the second day after the ceremony.

8. The Curators of the University Chest will send to the Registrar the signed Registrar's lists and the Registrar's certificates relating to candidates who have previously been provisionally matriculated.

9. The Registrar will issue to each candidate after the ceremony a certificate of matriculation stamped with a facsimile of the Vice-Chancellor's signature and initialled by a responsible officer.

The matriculation certificates of those who have been provisionally matriculated and who are matriculated within the period prescribed by statute will be endorsed as follows:

'This candidate was provisionally matriculated under the provisions of Ch. V, Sect. III, § 1, cl. 5, on [*such a date*], and his or her matriculation counts from that date.

A. B.

Registrar (or deputy).'

Section IV. Senior Students

For this Section, see *Examination Decrees*.

Section V. The Special Status of Master of Arts

1. Council shall, as provided in Tit. II, Sect. II, cl. 3, accord the status of Master of Arts to any person who would be qualified for membership of Congregation under the provisions of Tit. II, Sect. II, cl. 1 (5), (6), and (10) if he or she held the Degree of Master of Arts of the University for so long as he or she is so qualified.

2. Council may also accord the status of Master of Arts for limited periods, which shall in no case exceed three years, to distinguished persons temporarily resident in Oxford.

3. Any person accorded the status of Master of Arts under the provisions of clause 1 of this section who has retired from the post by virtue of the holding of which the status was so accorded shall retain the status after his or her retirement notwithstanding his or her ceasing to be a member of Congregation.

4. Any person accorded the status of Master of Arts under the provisions of this section shall, on matriculation or provisional matriculation, enjoy all the rights and privileges attached to that degree except that he or she shall not thereby

(*a*) acquire membership of Convocation if the status is accorded under clause 2 of this section;

(*b*) retain membership of Convocation after ceasing to be a member of Congregation if thereupon retaining the status under clause 3 of this section;

(*c*) be permitted to offer himself or herself as a candidate in any university examination or for any university scholarship, studentship or prize, or for any university diploma or certificate, or to supplicate for any degree in the University.

5. The Registrar shall report the names of those entitled to the status of M.A. under the provisions of clause 1 of this section to Council, and their names shall thereafter be reported by the Vice-Chancellor in the *University Gazette*.

6. Any application for the status of Master of Arts under the provisions of clause 2 of this section shall be made to Council by the authorities of a college or other society and, if granted, the name of the person accorded the status shall be reported by the Vice-Chancellor in the *University Gazette*.

7. The provisions of clause 2 of this section shall not apply to any person who has at any previous time been matriculated as a member of the University unless Council shall on any occasion otherwise determine.

Section VI. Residence of Junior Members

1. A Junior Member who is required to fulfil requirements for residence within the University under the provisions of any statute, decree, or regulation may fulfil such requirements

(*a*) in his or her college or other society;

(*b*) with the consent of his or her college or other society, in other accommodation not being part of any college or other society.

2. A candidate for a degree, who has kept terms by residence as a matriculated member of the University of Cambridge, shall be allowed to reckon not more than three such terms towards the number required to be kept by him or her if

(*a*) he or she has before keeping each of such terms obtained the permission of the Vice-Chancellor and Proctors to absent himself or herself from Oxford for that purpose;

(*b*) after he or she has kept each of such terms, the Vice-Chancellor and Proctors shall, after receipt of such report as they may deem expedient, have confirmed such permission;

(*c*) he or she shall have satisfied the Vice-Chancellor and Proctors that in each of such terms he or she has resided in the University of Cambridge for not less than the number of days of term required to keep that term's residence in that university and under that university's conditions of residence.

Section VII. Readmission and Migration

1. If the name of any person has been removed from the books of any college or other society that person shall not be readmitted to the said society without the written permission of the Proctors if either (1) such removal has taken place while he or she was still subject to any penalty inflicted by the Proctors or the Disciplinary Court or the Appeal Court, or (2) the Proctors have given specific notice in writing to the said society that the consent of the Proctors will be required.

2. If any person *in statu pupillari* shall desire to migrate from any such society to any other, the following conditions shall be observed:

(*a*) If he or she shall be in residence, or shall have been absent from the University for less than one year, he or she shall obtain

(1) a written permission for such migration from the society to which he or she belongs or last belonged;

(2) a written testimonial from the same stating that he or she is of good character;

(3) a certificate signed by the two Proctors that they have seen such permission and testimonial, and that they know of no reason why such person should not be allowed to migrate.

(*b*) If he or she shall have been absent from the University for more than one year, he or she shall obtain

(1) a written permission for such migration from the society to which he or she belongs or last belonged;

(2) a certificate signed by the two Proctors that they have seen such permission and do not oppose his or her migration.

No name which has previously been on the books of any such society within the University shall be placed on the books of any other without the production of the proper certificates.

3. In granting a certificate of migration, the Proctors, with the consent of the Vice-Chancellor, may append thereto such conditions as to residence during the next three terms as may appear to them desirable.

4. If any permission or testimonial required under the provisions of clause 2 above is refused, the Chancellor of the University may nevertheless, if he or she think fit, grant consent in writing for the migration.

5. A record of all such migrations shall be kept by the Senior Proctor, and notice of them shall be sent by him or her on each occasion to the Registrar, who shall enter the same in the Register of persons *in statu pupillari*.

6. If any person *in statu pupillari* shall have been expelled by the authorities of any college or other society, such person shall not be readmitted to membership of the University unless the Chancellor of the University shall have heard the case and given consent in writing for the readmission of the said person. And it shall be the duty of the authorities of colleges and other societies to satisfy themselves that any person applying to them for admission has not previously been so expelled.

7. Any person *in statu pupillari* migrating or having been readmitted to membership of the University except under the conditions hereinbefore laid down shall forfeit all the privileges of the University from the date of such migration or readmission; provided that the two Proctors, if they are satisfied that there was no reason why such person should not have been allowed to migrate or to be readmitted, may exempt him or her from the penalties imposed by this section, and that any person so exempted shall pay to the University Chest through the Registrar a further sum of £5.

8. Nothing in this section shall be taken to apply to any person

(i) who becomes a member of another society in virtue of his or her election to any office or emolument;

(ii) who, being a graduate of the University, becomes a member of another society in order to pursue a further course of study (other than one which continues the academic programme for which he or she has already been admitted as a Probationer Research Student);

provided always that it shall be the responsibility of the head or bursar of the society of which a person becomes a member under (i) or (ii) to include the name of such a person in the Schedule mentioned in Ch. VIII, Sect. I, § 6, unless that person's name is included in the Schedule prepared by the head or bursar of any other society of which the person is already a member.

Section VIII. Persons who are required to Reside within the University and the Limits within which such Residence must be Kept

1. The following shall be required to reside within twenty-five miles of Carfax:

The Vice-Chancellor
The Proctors
Bodley's Librarian and the Officers of the Bodleian Library
The Director and the Departmental Keepers of the Ashmolean Museum
The Keeper of the Archives
The Registrar of the University
The University Land Agent
The Librarian of the Taylor Institution

The holder of any other office or appointment who by any statute or decree or regulation or by the terms of his or her particular appointment is required to reside within the University.

[For clauses 2–8 of this Section, see *Examination Decrees*.]

Section IX. Residence at Oxford by Members of the University of Cambridge

1. Notwithstanding the provisions of Ch. VIII, Sect. I, § 1, no fee shall be payable on matriculation by a matriculated member of the University of Cambridge, who, for the purposes of special study, has obtained the permission of the Council of the Senate to keep not more than three terms by residence at Oxford; provided always that no such person shall count any term as having been kept for any Oxford purpose without subsequent payment of the matriculation fee specified in Ch. VIII, Sect. I, § 1.

2. Notwithstanding the provisions of Ch. VIII, Sect. I, § 6, cl. 1, no composition fees shall be payable by a member of the University who is a matriculated member of the University of Cambridge, and who, for the purposes of special study, has obtained the permission of the Council of the Senate to keep not more than three terms by residence at Oxford; provided always that no such person shall count any such term or terms as having been kept for any Oxford purpose without subsequent payment of the composition fees for such term or terms as specified in Ch. VIII, Sect. I, § 6, cl. 1.

3. A graduate of the University of Cambridge, who, with the permission of Council, is residing in Oxford for the purposes of special study shall not be required to pay a fee on matriculation and shall, during such residence, be entitled to the privileges of a Bachelor of Arts, except that he or she shall not be permitted to offer himself or herself as a candidate in any part of the First or the Second Public Examination, or in any Examination of the University for the Degree of Bachelor of Civil Law, Bachelor of Medicine, or Bachelor of Music, or for any university scholarship, or prize, or to supplicate for any degree in the University.

Section X. Matriculation for Theological Courses of Members of Certain Institutions in Oxford

1. Notwithstanding the provisions of the statutes, and subject to the conditions laid down in cll. 2–3 hereof, in each academic year up to and including 2000–1 St. Stephen's House, and Ripon College, Cuddesdon, shall be permitted between them to present for matriculation by the University

(*a*) not more than thirty-six full-time-equivalent qualified candidates to offer themselves for the qualifications listed in clause 4 below other than the M.Th. in Applied Theology; and

(*b*) not more than twenty four qualified candidates to offer themselves for the M.Th. in Applied Theology.

2. No person may be matriculated under the authority of this decree unless the institution presenting that person for matriculation can certify that he or she is a minister of religion or a bona fide candidate for the ministry.

3. Before presenting any candidate for matriculation under the authority of this decree, the institution presenting him or her shall consult the Board of the Faculty of Theology or such nominee or nominees as the board may appoint to act for it.

4. Persons matriculated under the authority of this decree shall have in relation to the University the same privileges and obligations as if they had been matriculated through a college, except that they may not (unless they migrate to a college or other society listed in Title VII) offer themselves for any university degree, diploma, or certificate examinations other than those for:

(*a*) the Honour School of Theology or any joint Honour School which includes Theology;

(*b*) the Diploma in Theology or a Certificate in Theology or the Degree of Bachelor of Theology;

(*c*) the Degree of Master of Studies or Master of Philosophy in Theology, or Master of Studies or Master of Philosophy in Philosophical Theology, or Master of Theology in Applied Theology;

(*d*) the Degree of Bachelor of Divinity or Doctor of Divinity.

5. A graduate of the University who is a minister of religion or a candidate for the ministry may migrate to one of the institutions listed in cl. 1 in order to read for the Honour School of Theology, for any joint Honour School which includes Theology, for the Diploma in Theology, for the Certificate in Theology, or for the Degree of Bachelor of Theology, provided that he or she shall obtain:

(1) written permission for such migration from the society to which he or she belongs; and

(2) a certificate signed by the two Proctors that they have seen such permission and do not oppose his or her migration.

CHAPTER VI

EXAMINATIONS

See *Examination Decrees.*

CHAPTER VII

ACADEMIC AND OTHER POSTS

Section I. Professorships, etc.—General

§ 1. *Electoral Boards*

1. Wherever it is provided that the election to a professorship shall be vested in a board of electors, the board shall be composed of not fewer than seven nor, unless Council shall determine otherwise by decree, more than nine persons.

2. Every board of electors shall contain not fewer than two persons who at the time the board meets are not resident holders of teaching, research, or administrative posts in the University or in any college or other society.

3. Save as is provided in clause 5 below, elected members of the board of electors to any professorship shall be appointed to hold office from the date authorized by Council under § 2 below for the start of proceedings to fill a vacancy or impending vacancy in the professorship until either an election has been made and the person appointed has entered on his or her duties or a statute or decree abolishing or suspending the filling of the professorship has been made under the provisions of § 2, cll. 8–11 below.

4. An elected member of a board of electors to a post listed in § 2, cl. 16 (*b*) hereof shall, unless otherwise provided, hold office for five years and shall be eligible for re-election.

5. If any elected member of a board of electors shall die or resign, or otherwise vacate his or her place, the body which elected that elector shall as soon as may be elect in his or her place another person to hold office for the unexpired residue of the demitting member's period of office.

6. An elector may resign from an electoral board in order to offer himself or herself as a candidate for the vacant office, provided either that he or she does so before the published closing date for the receipt of applications, or that he or she is invited after that date by the other electors to do so. If an elector resigns in such circumstances, Council shall nominate a person to act in his or her place for the remainder of the proceedings to fill the vacancy.

7. If an election requires to be made by an electoral board which includes the holder of an office *ex officio* and the office is vacant, Council may, if it thinks fit, appoint a substitute elector to act for the occasion.

8. Save as is specifically provided to the contrary in any statute or decree, in this sub-section the word 'professorship' shall include any readership, lecturership, or directorship which is established by statute or decree and to which election is made by an electoral board.

[*Note*. Under the provisions of Decree (11) of 30 June 2000 (*Gazette*, Vol. 130, p. 1403), notwithstanding the terms of any statute or decree which provide that a member or members of an electoral board shall be appointed by the General Board, such appointments shall, with effect from 1 October 2000, be made in accordance with the following scheme.

1. Wherever there is provision for the General Board to appoint one elector, that elector shall be appointed by Council.

2. Wherever there is provision for the General Board to appoint two electors, one shall be appointed by Council and one by the appropriate Divisional Board.

3. At least one elector appointed by either a faculty board or a Divisional Board shall be (in partial fulfilment of the requirement in Ch. VII, Sect. I, § 1, cl. 2) a person who at the time of the meetings of the electoral board is not the resident holder of a teaching, research, or administrative post in the University or in any college or other society.

4. The appointed or elected members of each electoral board shall include the head of the relevant division (or his or her nominee) unless the head waives this right on any particular occasion.

5. To the extent that the constitution of any electoral board as laid down by statute or decree prevents the application of the above principles, the Vice-Chancellor shall have power to approve appropriate changes in that case after consultation, including consultation with the appropriate Divisional Board.]

§ **2.** *Elections to professorships*

1. The Registrar shall give notice to Council of any vacancy in a professorship occurring by the effluxion of time not less than four years before it occurs. Council shall thereupon consider whether the professorship should be altered or abolished and shall invite the General Board and the Board of the Faculty (or Boards of the Faculties) concerned, and, where appropriate, any other university body which appoints an elector to the professorship, in consultation, in the case of a professorship to the holder of which the headship of a department is or may be assigned, with the relevant sub-faculty (or sub-faculties) and department, to comment on this question and on any particular qualifications which they would desire to see in the next holder of it. The boards of faculties and other university bodies concerned shall, unless they wish to recommend the abolition of the post, thereupon consider the appointment of electors and shall prepare, for

consideration by the General Board and Council, a draft of a memorandum of guidance for candidates and electors.

2. The Registrar shall give notice of vacancies occurring by resignation or death at the next meeting of Council after the information of the vacancy or impending vacancy reaches him or her. Council shall forthwith either

(*a*) authorize the immediate start of proceedings to fill the vacancy and invite the comments of the General Board and the Board of the Faculty (or Boards of the Faculties) concerned, and, where appropriate, any other university body which appoints an elector to the professorship, in consultation, in the case of a professorship to the holder of which the headship of a department is or may be assigned, with the relevant sub-faculty (or sub-faculties) and department, on any particular qualifications which they would desire to see in the next holder of the professorship; or

(*b*) consider whether the professorship should be altered or abolished and invite the General Board and the Board of the Faculty (or Boards of the Faculties) concerned, and, where appropriate, any other university body which appoints an elector to the professorship, in consultation, in the case of a professorship to the holder of which the headship of a department is or may be assigned, with the relevant sub-faculty (or sub-faculties) and department, to comment on this question, and on any particular qualifications which they would desire to see in the next holder, if an election is required.

The boards of faculties and other university bodies concerned shall, unless they wish to recommend the abolition of the post, consider the appointment of electors and shall prepare, for consideration by the General Board and Council, a memorandum of guidance for candidates and electors.

3. On consideration of the reports submitted by the boards of faculties and other university bodies concerned, under clauses 1 and 2 above, and after consultation with the General Board, Council may promote a statute or make a decree altering or abolishing the professorship and, where proceedings to fill the post are required, shall either

(*a*) authorize the immediate start of proceedings to fill the vacancy; or

(*b*) fix a date for the start of proceedings to fill the vacancy; or

(*c*) adjourn the start of proceedings until a later date to be determined in due course by Council after consultation with the General Board.

4. Notwithstanding the provisions of Sect. III, § 1 (1), a statute or decree promoted under clause 3 hereof shall not require the consent of a retiring holder of the professorship concerned provided that the statute or decree shall not come into operation until after his or her retirement.

5. On the due date for the start of proceedings to fill the vacancy:

(*a*) the Registrar shall forthwith arrange for the publication of a notice that the electors intend to proceed to an election and invite applications by such date, specified in the notice, as may be determined by the Vice-Chancellor. The notice shall be otherwise in a common form to be determined by Council;

(*b*) those appointed as electors may meet at or before the start of proceedings, to consider their prospective proceedings under the terms of clause 14 below, and they shall thereafter meet on a day to be fixed by the Vice-Chancellor not less than three or more than fourteen weeks after the date fixed for the receipt of applications to consider the applications and any other names which may be suggested by or to the electors together with any representations with regard to the filling of the post, as specified in the memorandum, which may have been submitted to Council by the General Board and the Board of the Faculty (or Boards of the Faculties) concerned, and any comments by Council thereon.

6. If the professorship is allocated to a college the governing body of which is restricted to women, Council shall, on notification of a vacancy or impending vacancy in the professorship, determine to which college open to men it shall be allocated if a man is appointed. The governing body of that college shall then be entitled to appoint two electors to the professorship. All the college electors may take part in the discussions of the electors, but the voting arrangements shall be that, for so long as candidates of both sexes, or women candidates alone, are under consideration, each pair of electors from each college shall have only one vote between them and shall count as one member of the board for the purposes of clauses 7 and 13 below. If during the course of the election only men candidates remain under consideration, the electors from the college open to men and women shall have one vote each and the electors from the women's college shall not be entitled to vote.

7. At any meeting the electors may (and if two electors so request shall) adjourn for a period or periods not exceeding one year in all from the date of their first meeting: provided always that Council, after consultation with the General Board, may for any reason which it judges to be sufficient grant permission for adjournments beyond this period to dates which it shall determine.

8. Before the end of the year or, if Council shall have authorized an adjournment under clause 7 above, at the end of the period of adjournment, the electors shall either

(*a*) make an election; or

(*b*) recommend to Council that the filling of the vacancy be suspended for a period not exceeding two years from the date of the recommendation; or

(*c*) report to the Chancellor of the University that in the opinion of each one of them no suitable person is available for appointment to the vacant professorship.

9. If at the end of the authorized period no action has been taken under clause 8 above or if a recommendation having been made to Council under clause 8 (*b*) Council has not agreed to any suspension, the Chancellor shall appoint to the vacant professorship such person as he or she may deem most fit.

10. If under the provisions of clause 8 (*b*) above a recommendation has been made to and accepted by Council, Council shall make a decree suspending the

filling of the vacancy for a period not exceeding two years from the date of the recommendation, and if such decree be annulled, the Chancellor shall appoint to the vacant professorship such person as he or she may deem most fit.

11. If under the provisions of clause 8 (*c*) above a report has been made to the Chancellor, Council shall either promote a statute or make a decree abolishing the professorship or make a decree suspending the filling of it for a period named in the decree. And if such statute be not approved or such decree annulled, then the Chancellor shall appoint to the vacant professorship such person as he or she may deem most fit.

12. If under the provisions of clauses 10 or 11 above a decree shall have been made suspending the filling of the professorship for a set period, at the end of that period the procedure for filling the vacancy shall be resumed from the point described in clause 5 above.

13. An election may be held even if for any reason there is a vacancy on the electoral board, but no election shall be valid unless a number of electors equal to a majority of the full board shall have been present and voted for the same candidate, provided that when a vacancy in any of the posts in the schedule to clause 16 (*b*) below is caused by the expiry of the period of office of the holder of a post who is eligible for re-election, the electors, having held such meetings as they may themselves determine (or, if they are unanimously in agreement, without a meeting) may re-elect the holder.

14. Subject to this decree, every Board of Electors may regulate its own proceedings.

15. The date on which any professor elected under this decree is to enter upon his or her duties shall be determined by the Vice-Chancellor and shall, wherever possible, be settled before the election is announced. If it is necessary later to consider postponing the announced date by three months or more, this may be authorized by Council. A professor shall receive the emoluments of his or her professorship from the date upon which he or she enters upon the duties of his or her office.

16. (*a*) Save as is specifically provided hereinafter, or in any statute or other decree, in this sub-section the word 'professorship' shall include any readership, lecturership, or directorship which is established by statute or decree and to which election is made by an electoral board.

(*b*) The provisions of Ch. VII, Sect. I, § 1, cll. 1–3, and § 2, cll. 1–12 shall not apply to any of the posts in the following Schedule:

Regius Professorships
Professorships to which a canonry is annexed
Aldrichian Professorship of Medicine
Harold Vyvyan Harmsworth Professorship of American History
George Eastman Visiting Professorship
Newton-Abraham Visiting Professorship
Professorship of Poetry on the Foundation of Henry Birkhead
Slade Professor of Fine Art
University Lecturership in Spanish

James P. R. Lyell Readership in Bibliography
John Locke Lecturership in Philosophy
Ford's Lecturership in British History
Grinfield Lecturership on the Septuagint
Romanes Lecturership
Herbert Spencer Lecturership
Speaker's Lecturership in Biblical Studies
Wilde Lecturership in Natural and Comparative Religion
Halley Lecturership
Ratanbai Katrak Lecturership
John Wilfred Jenkinson Memorial Lecturership
Bampton Lecturership
Sidney Ball Lecturership
O'Donnell Lecturership in Celtic Studies
Litchfield Lecturerships
Cherwell-Simon Lecturership
Cyril Foster Lecturership
Estlin Carpenter Lecturership
Hensley Henson Lecturership
J. M. Gibson Lecturership
Maurice Lubbock Lecturership
Myres Memorial Lecturership
Sir Basil Zaharoff Lecturership
Taylorian Lecturership
William Cohn Memorial Lecturership
G. E. Blackman Lecturership
Nellie Wallace Lecturership
John French Memorial Lecturership.

§ 3. *Discharge of the duties of a professorship during a vacancy or during the absence of a newly elected professor*

1. In case of vacancy in any professorship, or during any interval which may elapse between the election of a professor and his or her entering upon the duties of the professorship, the General Board may, if it thinks fit, appoint a suitable person or persons to carry on the duties of the professorship or such part of them as the board may deem advisable.

2. Every such appointment shall take effect for such period as the General Board shall determine at the time of appointment, and may be renewed for a further period or periods, but every such appointment shall determine upon the appointment of a professor to the vacant professorship or the entrance by the newly elected professor upon the duties of his or her professorship, as the case may be.

3. The remuneration to be paid to any person so appointed shall be fixed by the General Board, and shall be paid out of the emoluments assigned to the professorship.

4. In this decree the word 'professorship' shall include any readership, lecturership, or directorship which is established by statute or decree and to which election is made by an electoral board and Keepers of Departments of the Ashmolean Museum.

§ 4. *Tenure of professorships*

1. Subject to the provisions of Tit. VIII, Sect. I, every professorship shall be tenable in accordance with the provisions of Tit. X, Sect. I (*h*).

2. (*a*) Except as is provided in sub-clause (*b*) below, for the purposes of clause 1 above the word 'professorship' shall include every professorship, readership, and lecturership, any teaching or research post to which the appointment is made or approved by the General Board of the Faculties, and any other university teaching or research post including teaching or research posts the holders of which are regularly employed in any department of the University.

(*b*) Clause 1 above shall not apply to any of the offices specified in the Schedule appended to this clause, but every such office shall be deemed to be tenable for the period for which the holder was appointed, subject to his or her liability to vacate it by deprivation for sufficient cause.

SCHEDULE

Grinfield Lecturership on the Septuagint
Harold Vyvyan Harmsworth Professorship of American History
George Eastman Visiting Professorship
Newton-Abraham Visiting Professorship
Slade Professorship of Fine Art
Ford's Lecturership in British History
Professorship of Poetry
Wilde Lecturership in Natural and Comparative Religion
Speaker's Lecturership in Biblical Studies
John Locke Lecturership in Philosophy
James P. R. Lyell Readership in Bibliography
O'Donnell Lecturership in Celtic Studies.

3. No professorship shall, unless by virtue of express provision in any statute or instrument of foundation relating to it and in force for the time being, be tenable with another professorship within the University, nor with a university readership.

4. Women shall be eligible to any professorship, readership, or other university teachership, on the same conditions as men.

§ 5. *Duties, and dispensation from duties of professors, readers, lecturers, etc.*

The General Provisions of this decree shall apply unless the context requires otherwise (1) to all professors enumerated in the three Schedules annexed to it, (2) to any professors not therein mentioned to whom they shall by any decree be declared to be applicable, and (3) to readers, lecturers (other than C.U.F. Lecturers), and persons holding appointments under the provisions of Ch. VII, Sect. IV, § 1, except that clause 9 shall apply only to the professors enumerated in the three Schedules annexed to this decree.

The Particular Provisions shall apply only to the professors to whom they are by this decree declared to be applicable respectively.

The Particular Provisions of this decree shall be subject to the power to make by decree from time to time other Provisions for any professorship included in the Schedules for which, in consequence of an alteration of the tenure or a material augmentation or diminution of the emoluments of it, new Provisions shall in the judgement of the University be required.

Council may from time to time alter the Schedules annexed to this decree, either by the addition of a professor to any Schedule, or by the transference of a professor from one Schedule to another, provided that no such transference shall be made, if the chair is not vacant, except with the consent of the professor.

Council may also from time to time by decree make further Provisions for regulating the duties of professors in general or of the holder of any particular professorship, the time, place, or manner of delivering lectures, or the matter of such lectures, or the informal instruction or other assistance to be given to students, and also for increasing (should it be deemed expedient) the number of lectures to be delivered, and instruction to be given, or the period of residence required, and for further defining the time of residence or for determining what shall constitute residence.

Every professor shall be subject to any decrees which may be made from time to time for any of the foregoing purposes, or for securing the due performance of the duties of professors, or concerning any other matter relating to professors in general or to the holder of his or her own chair in particular which it is expedient to regulate by decree.

A. GENERAL PROVISIONS

1. The duties of every professor shall include original work by the professor himself or herself and the general supervision of research and advanced work in his or her subject and department.

2. Every professor shall conform to the Particular Provisions applicable to his or her chair.

3. It shall be the professor's duty to give to students assistance in their studies by advice, by informal instruction, by occasional or periodic examination, or otherwise, as he or she may judge to be expedient. For receiving students who desire such assistance he or she shall appoint stated times.

4. At the request of any student who has regularly attended any course of lectures the professor shall certify in writing the fact of such attendance, provided that he or she has been notified at the beginning of the course that a certificate will be required.

5. The ordinary lectures and instruction given by every professor shall be open to all members of the University without payment of any fee, unless the University shall otherwise determine.

Examining[1]

6. It shall be the duty of every professor, reader, university lecturer or holder of any other office the duties of which include teaching or research and appointment to which is made by, or is subject to the approval of, the General Board to act as an examiner or assessor as and when requested to do so by a competent body under the provisions of Ch. VI, Sect. II. A and B, unless he or she can show reasonable cause, to the satisfaction of the Vice-Chancellor and Proctors, why on a particular occasion he or she should not do so; provided always that the provisions of this clause shall not apply to any holder of the title of university lecturer, faculty lecturer, or C.U.F. lecturer who is in the first three years of his or her non-stipendiary office or to the holder of any other non-stipendiary office in the University.

Supervision[2]

7. It shall be the duty of every professor, reader, or holder of any stipendiary academic office the duties of which include teaching or research and appointment to which is made by, or is subject to the approval of, the General Board (other than instructors and lectors), of every holder of the title of clinical lecturer, and, with effect from the beginning of the fourth year of his or her non-stipendiary office, of every holder of the title of university lecturer, faculty lecturer, or C.U.F. lecturer to act as the supervisor of a graduate student as and when requested to do so by a faculty board or other competent body under the various provisions concerning such supervision laid down in Ch. VI unless he or she can show reasonable cause, to the satisfaction of the faculty board or other competent body concerned, why on a particular occasion he or she should not do so.

Headship of departments[3]

8. Every professor or reader who is employed by the University (including those holding *ad hominem* appointments or the title of professor or reader) unless individually exempted shall have the obligation to accept the headship of the department in which his or her post is held if requested to do so by the General Board under the provisions of clause 5 of § 5. B of this section.

[1] This clause shall be effective from 1 October 1972, provided that it shall not apply to the holder of any relevant stipendiary office in the University who was appointed (with tenure to the retiring age) to such office before that date, or to the holder of any non-stipendiary office on whom the relevant university title was conferred before 1 April 1988.

[2] This clause shall be effective from 21 March 1986 provided that (unless specified in the contract of employment and agreed by the appointee) it shall not apply to the holder of any relevant stipendiary office in the University whose appointment was made or advertised before 1 April 1986, or to the holder of the title of clinical lecturer on whom such title was conferred before that date, or to the holder of any other non-stipendiary office in the University on whom the relevant title was conferred before 1 April 1988.

[3] This clause shall not apply to the holder of any professorship or readership who accepted appointment to such office before 1 October 1994 and whose contract of employment did not contain such an obligation.

Restriction on the acceptance of fees

9. Except when they are earned by a professor as the supervisor of graduate students, as an academic adviser under the regulations for Recognized Students, or (subject to the approval of the faculty board or boards concerned and the General Board, including approval as to the length of time for which the permission shall be given) in respect of tutorial teaching for up to four hours per week (exceptionally up to six hours per week), any fees received for other lectures or instruction given by any of the professors enumerated in the three Schedules annexed to this decree in the University shall be applied towards meeting the expenses of the Department of which he or she is in charge, or, if he or she is not in charge of a Department, shall be paid to the Curators of the University Chest for the credit of the University General Fund.

Holding of other appointments

10. Except as provided in the following clause, no professor, reader, lecturer (other than a C.U.F. lecturer), or person holding any office appointment to which is made by, or is subject to the approval of, the General Board may hold any other appointment, whether in the University or not, without leave of the board of the appropriate faculty and of the General Board; and the General Board shall determine what reduction, if any, shall be made in his or her stipend; provided that in the case of the holder of an office whose emoluments are partly or wholly derived from a trust fund appropriated to that office, the reduction shall not reduce his or her income from the trust fund.

11. The provisions of the preceding clause shall not apply in the following cases:

(*a*) the holding of the office of Proctor or Assessor;

(*b*) the holding of the office of examiner in any examination which is part of a degree course at any university;

(*c*) the holding of a commemorative lecturership or similar post in any university with the duty to give not more than eight lectures in any year of office;

(*d*) activities or responsibilities normally associated with, or arising from, scholarly work which do not involve a formal and continuing contract;

provided always that the posts or activities under (*b*)–(*d*) above do not involve dispensation from any prescribed duties.

Dispensation from prescribed duties

12. Complete or partial dispensation from the obligation to reside or to lecture or to give instruction or to perform other prescribed duties (other than the duty prescribed by clauses 6 and 7 hereof) may be granted by the General Board to professors, readers, lecturers, or the holders of other offices appointment to which is made by, or is subject to the approval of, the Board, in accordance with Tit. X, Sect. I, proviso (*d*) or on account of ill health or for any other reason which it judges to be sufficient.

13. Whenever any such dispensation is granted, the General Board shall determine what part of his or her stipend may be retained by, or what other arrangements shall be made in respect of the stipend of, the person to whom dispensation has been granted, and provision may be made for the complete or partial performance of his or her prescribed duties either

(*a*) by a competent deputy approved by the General Board who shall receive such remuneration, if any, from any funds allocated to the board, as it shall determine, or

(*b*) in such other manner as the board may approve.

Notice of the appointment of a deputy shall be published in the *University Gazette*.

14. The General Board shall have power to make regulations from time to time governing the exercise of its powers under the provisions of clauses 12–13 above.

15. Holders of offices the holders of which are required (unless exempted or excluded under the provisions of Tit. X, Sect. I (*g*) (ii)) to be members of the Federated Superannuation System for Universities or the Universities Superannuation Scheme but which are not mentioned in clauses 10 or 12 above may not hold any other appointment without leave of Council; they may be granted complete or partial dispensation from the obligation to perform their duties

(*a*) by the Vice-Chancellor on account of ill health or other urgent cause for a period or periods not exceeding four weeks in all in any two consecutive years; such dispensation shall be reported by the Vice-Chancellor to Council at its next ensuing meeting but shall not count against any periods of dispensation which may be granted by Council under subclause (*b*);

(*b*) by Council for any reason which it judges to be sufficient; provided always

(i) that dispensation for any period beyond one year for any reason other than ill health shall be confirmed by decree;

(ii) that Council shall consult the body with which the officer is principally associated before granting any leave or dispensation;

(iii) that this clause shall not override any special arrangements that may be made in particular cases.

16. Whenever such dispensation is granted by Council under clause 15 above, Council shall determine what part of his or her stipend may be retained by the person to whom dispensation has been granted, and may require provision to be made for the complete or partial performance of his or her prescribed duties either

(*a*) by a competent deputy approved by Council who shall be paid such remuneration, if any, as Council may direct out of the emoluments of the person to whom dispensation has been granted, or out of the University General Fund, or

(*b*) in such other manner as Council may approve.

Notice of the appointment of a deputy shall be published in the *University Gazette*.

17. In considering the grant of dispensation from prescribed duties for reasons of ill health and consequential stipendiary arrangements under clauses 12–13 and 15–16 above, the relevant body shall have regard to the following guidelines which relate the length of time for which university sick pay should be given to length of service with the University:

Service	*Full pay*	*Half pay*
	(inclusive of any university sick pay given in the twelve months preceding the latest period of such leave)	
First three months	2 weeks	2 weeks
Remaining nine months of first year	2 months	2 months
Second and third years	3 months	3 months
Fourth and fifth years	5 months	5 months
After fifth year	6 months	6 months

Sabbatical Leave or Dispensation from Lecturing Obligations: Regulations of the General Board

1. The General Board may dispense any professor, reader, university lecturer (except C.U.F. or special (non-C.U.F.) lecturers, as to which see cll. 4–8 below), senior research officer, Keeper and Assistant Keeper in the Ashmolean Museum, clinical tutor, or clinical lecturer from discharging the duties of his or her office during one term (hereinafter referred to as a term of sabbatical leave) for every six terms of qualifying service (as defined in cl. 2 below), provided that

(i) qualifying service shall normally (otherwise than in the circumstances specified in cl. 3 below) accumulate up to a maximum of eighteen terms, from which six terms are deducted whenever a term of leave is granted;

(ii) not more than three terms of sabbatical leave shall be granted in any one period of three years;

(iii) persons appointed to academic posts in clinical departments under the provisions of Sect. V

(*a*) shall not normally be permitted to take sabbatical leave during the first three years of service; and

(*b*) subject to the general application of these regulations *mutatis mutandis*, the period of leave shall be reckoned in calendar months on the basis of up to one month's leave for six months' qualifying service;

(iv) subject to the general application of these regulations *mutatis mutandis*, the period of leave for Keepers and Assistant Keepers in the Ashmolean Museum shall be reckoned in calendar months on the basis of one month's leave for six months' qualifying service.

2. A term of qualifying service shall be a term during which the applicant has without intermission held and discharged the duties of any of the offices enumerated in cl. 1 above, provided that the General Board shall reckon as a term of qualifying service a term during which an applicant has been dispensed from the whole or part of the duties of his or her office on the grounds of ill health and the board may at its discretion so reckon a term during which an applicant has been granted dispensation on other grounds and otherwise than under these regulations.

3. In exceptional circumstances, leave which is granted in respect of a given period may be deemed to have been granted for an earlier period, provided that

(i) the applicant would have been qualified under cll. 1 and 2 above for leave in that earlier period;

(ii) the faculty board concerned has certified to the General Board that the applicant's absence in that earlier period for which he or she was qualified would be seriously damaging to the work of the faculty;

(iii) the application is made before the beginning of that earlier period.

4. A C.U.F. or special (non-C.U.F.) lecturer who is granted leave of absence by his or her college for one or more terms in any academic year may apply to the General Board for partial or complete dispensation from prescribed university duties for that year, provided that no one shall be dispensed from more than four courses of lectures or classes in any period of fourteen years or more than two courses in any period of three years.

5. The board will normally expect that the holder of an office referred to in cl. 1 above intends to serve for at least one subsequent term in respect of each term of sabbatical leave granted, before resignation or retirement, and that the holder of an office referred to in cl. 4 above intends to deliver at least one course of lectures in the year before resignation or retirement.

6. An applicant shall normally be allowed to retain his or her full stipend during any term of sabbatical leave or period of dispensation from lecturing obligations, provided that

(*a*) he or she will spend a considerable portion of his or her leave in advanced study or research;

(*b*) he or she will give up all teaching and administrative duties in Oxford, other than examining and graduate supervision, in any term of leave or, in the case of the holder of an office referred to in cl. 4 above, in those terms in which leave has been granted by the college;

(*c*) if the holder of an office referred to in cl. 1 or cl. 4 above, after taking account of (1) any loss of normal sources of income (but assuming for the calculation that the holder is in receipt of his or her full university salary and the regular college tutorial salary, if any, that he or she would normally receive) and (2) any gain of income from any new sources (less any additional expenses associated with new activities), is in a better financial position than if the applicant had not taken leave, then he or she shall decide what sum would have to be deducted from his or her income so as to leave him or her approximately in the same financial state as if leave had not been taken, and will forgo from his or her normal pensionable stipend and family allowance in respect of the period of leave or dispensation such proportion of that sum as his or her university salary is (at the date of commencement of leave) of his or her combined university and college salary. Any person granted leave or dispensation under these regulations shall at the conclusion of the leave or period of dispensation inform the Secretary of Faculties whether or not he or she is to forgo any part of his or her normal stipend as aforesaid and, if so, how much.

7. The board shall not grant dispensation under these regulations unless arrangements can be made to its satisfaction for the discharge of the applicant's duties.

8. The board shall receive each application for dispensation under these regulations from the faculty board or other authority concerned; the application shall be accompanied by a statement setting out

(*a*) the grounds on which the application is made;

(*b*) the recommendation of the faculty board or other authority concerned;

(*c*) the means of providing the additional teaching, if any, required in the event of leave being granted;

(*d*) in the case of joint university and college appointments whether the college has concurred.

9. Those to whom the University has granted sabbatical leave or dispensation will be asked at the end of the period of such leave (college leave in the case of C.U.F. lecturers) to submit a report on activities undertaken during the leave.

10. These regulations may be applied to holders of academic offices not enumerated in cll. 1 and 4 above; provided that if any application is made by the holder of an academic office not included in cll. 1 and 4, the board shall decide whether the office or the applicant concerned shall be eligible for dispensation under these regulations.

B. PARTICULAR PROVISIONS

1. The Particular Provisions next following shall be applicable to each of the professors enumerated in Schedule A annexed to this decree:

(*a*) The professor shall reside within the University during six months at least in each academical year, between the first day of October and the ensuing first day of August, and in particular during not less than six weeks of each term.

(*b*) He or she shall lecture or hold classes in two at least of the three university terms. He or she shall give at least thirty-six lectures or classes in all (subject to such regulations as to the number of these which must be lectures as may have been made under (*c*) hereof by the board of the faculty concerned) and not less than twelve in each of two terms.

(*c*) The board of a faculty may with the approval of the General Board make a regulation, applicable to all or some of the Schedule A professorships in the subjects with which that board is principally concerned, prescribing the minimum number of lectures (as distinct from classes) which their holders must give in the discharge of their lecturing obligations as defined in (*b*) hereof

provided that

no Schedule A professor who was appointed before 1 October 1970 may be required to give more than twenty-eight lectures (as distinct from classes).

Regulations of Faculty Boards

Literae Humaniores

Ancient History:

Lincoln Professor of Classical Archaeology and Art	Sixteen
Professor of the Archaeology of the Roman Empire	Sixteen
Camden Professor of Ancient History	Twenty-eight
Wykeham Professor of Ancient History	Twenty-eight

Philosophy: Sixteen (by way of not less than one lecture a week in each of two terms, or two lectures a week in one term).

Modern History: Twenty

Physical Sciences

Chemistry: Sixteen

Engineering Science: Twenty-four

Materials: Twenty-four

Physics: Twenty-four

Social Studies: Twenty

Theology: Twenty-four.

2. The Particular Provisions next following shall be applicable to each of the professors enumerated in Schedule B annexed to this decree:

(*a*) The professor shall reside within the University during six months at least in each academical year, between the first day of October and the ensuing first day of August.

(*b*) He or she shall lecture, or hold classes, in two at least of the three university terms. He or she shall give at least twenty-eight lectures or classes in all and not less than twelve in each of two terms.

(*c*) The Laboratory or Department under the charge of each professor shall be open for at least eight weeks in each term, and at such other times, and for such hours, as the professor shall think fit.

Students shall be admitted to the Laboratory or Department under the charge of each professor, upon such conditions as Council shall from time to time by decree determine, and upon the terms of paying such fees, not exceeding such amount as may be fixed by any decree in force for the time being, as the professor may from time to time require.

(*d*) The professor shall have the charge of such laboratory or department and of such collections as may be assigned to him or her by decree, and shall make provision for the lighting, warming, water-supply, and cleansing of the buildings assigned to him or her. The professor shall undertake the personal and regular supervision of his or her Laboratory or Department, and of any departmental demonstrators and other assistants employed therein. When the professor is in charge of any collection belonging to the University it shall be part of his or her duty to make such collection accessible to, and available for the instruction of, students attending his or her lectures.

(*e*) The professor shall, for seven weeks in each term, be ready to give instruction in the subject of his or her chair to such students as shall have been admitted to the Laboratory or Department under his or her charge; and such instruction shall be given in the Laboratory or Department or in some class room connected therewith.

(*f*) The professor shall also, at the close of each term, inform any society which may request him or her to do so, as to the regularity of attendance and the proficiency of the students belonging to such society who have been admitted into the Laboratory or Department under his or her charge.

(*g*) Any professor in Schedule B may apply through the Board of the Faculty concerned to the General Board for leave to keep a register regulating the number of students who may be admitted to the practical classes in his or her Department. The General Board shall have power to accept or refuse the application and, if it accepts it, to determine, in consultation with the professor concerned, the number of students whose names may be on the register at any one time and the method of their selection.

3. The Particular Provisions next following shall be applicable to each of the professors enumerated in Schedule C annexed to this decree:

(*a*) The professor shall, except as is herein otherwise provided, reside within the University during forty weeks in each academic year.

(*b*) He or she shall give or hold such number of lectures or classes as the Board of the Faculty of Clinical Medicine shall determine. These lectures or classes shall be given or held in each Full Term or such extension of it as the said board may approve.

(*c*) He or she shall, under conditions agreed upon between the Board of the Faculty of Clinical Medicine and the appropriate agents of the National Health Service, perform such clinical, administrative, and other duties in the hospitals or general practices associated with the University as the faculty board may determine or approve.

(*d*) He or she may be granted by the General Board on the recommendation of the Board of the Faculty of Clinical Medicine without loss of emolument such leave of absence for purposes of study as the General Board may determine.

(*e*) He or she shall be permitted to engage in private practice in the said hospitals or in other hospitals in Oxford on such terms as the General Board may from time to time determine, provided that

(i) the proportion of gross salary which may be retained shall not exceed the proportion which may be retained by full-time consultants in the National Health Service;

(ii) any private practice fee which is not claimed by the individual concerned or which remains after payments have been made up to the annual limit specified above shall be made payable to the University Chest and shall be divided by the Chest so that three-quarters is allocated to the relevant university departmental fund and one-quarter to a General Clinical Fund which shall be available to the whole Clinical Medical School for general research purposes under the direction of the Medical Research Fund Committee of the Board of the Faculty of Clinical Medicine.

4. The University Laboratories or Departments and the collections in connection therewith shall be assigned to the professors enumerated in Schedule B in accordance with the following scheme or with such modifications of it as Council may make from time to time by decree:

Department or Laboratory	*Professor*
Department of Human Anatomy and Genetics	Dr. Lee's Professor of Anatomy
Sub-department of Organic Chemistry	Waynflete Professor of Chemistry [1]
Department of Educational Studies	Professor of Educational Studies
Sir William Dunn School of Pathology	Professor of Pathology
Department of Pharmacology	Professor of Pharmacology
Centre for Socio-Legal Studies	Professor of Socio-Legal Studies.

5. The remaining departments shall each be assigned by the General Board from time to time for a specified period of five years, or such other period as the Board may determine from time to time, to a person holding an established academic post in the department, normally with the title of professor or reader, after consultation with the faculty board concerned, and the person to whom for the time being the headship is assigned shall exercise the responsibilities in relation to the department set out in clause 2 of the Particular Provisions applicable to professors enumerated in Schedule B and shall receive a special allowance as set out in § 7 of this section.

6. The Sherardian Professor of Botany shall have the charge and supervision of the Botanic Garden (and shall be called the Keeper of the Botanic Garden) subject to such authority as by any decree in force for the time being or otherwise shall be vested in the Curators of the Garden. He or she shall also have the charge of the Botanical Collections belonging to the University including the Fielding Herbarium, and the Claridge Druce Herbarium and Library, subject to the rights of the Sibthorpian Professor of Plant Science in respect of any books belonging to the Sibthorpian Library.

7. The Sibthorpian Professor of Plant Science shall always have the responsibilities in respect of the Sibthorpian Library laid down in Tit. XVI, Sect. L, cl. 4.

[1] Until such time as Professor Sir Jack Baldwin shall cease to hold the Waynflete Professorship of Chemistry (Decree (3) of 31 July 1997).

8. The Head of the Department of Zoology shall have charge of the University Field Laboratory at Wytham.

9. The Lincoln Professor of Classical Archaeology and Art shall undertake the charge of the University Collection of Casts from the Antique, and of any museum or collection connected with the subject of his or her chair which may from time to time be assigned to him or her by decree. Such charge, so far as it extends to collections in the Ashmolean Museum, shall be exercised subject to the direction and control of the Visitors of the Ashmolean Museum.

10. The following university clinical departments shall be assigned to the professors enumerated in Schedule C in accordance with the scheme set out below or with such modification of it as Council may make from time to time by decree. The heads of these departments shall receive a special allowance as set out in § 7 of this section.

Department	Professor
Nuffield Department of Anaesthetics	Nuffield Professor of Anaesthetics
Department of Cardiovascular Medicine	Field Marshal Alexander Professor of Cardiovascular Medicine
Nuffield Department of Clinical Medicine	Nuffield Professor of Clinical Medicine
Department of Clinical Neurology	Action Research Professor of Clinical Neurology
Department of Primary Health Care	Professor of General Practice
Nuffield Department of Obstetrics and Gynaecology	Nuffield Professor of Obstetrics and Gynaecology
Nuffield Department of Orthopaedic Surgery	Nuffield Professor of Orthopaedic Surgery
Department of Paediatrics	Action Research Professor of Paediatrics
Department of Psychiatry	W. A. Handley Professor of Psychiatry
Department of Public Health	Professor of Public Health
Nuffield Department of Surgery	Nuffield Professor of Surgery

SCHEDULE A

Drue Heinz Professor of American Literature
Rawlinson and Bosworth Professor of Anglo-Saxon
Professor of Biological Anthropology
Professor of Social Anthropology
Laudian Professor of Arabic
Khalid bin Abdullah Al Saud Professor for the Study of the Contemporary Arab World
Edward Hall Professor of Archaeological Science
Professor of the Archaeology of the Roman Empire
Lincoln Professor of Classical Archaeology and Art
Professor of European Archaeology

Calouste Gulbenkian Professor of Armenian Studies
Slade Professor of Fine Art
Professor of the History of Art
Savilian Professor of Astronomy
Whitley Professor of Biochemistry
Professor of Bioinformatics
E.P. Abraham Professor of Cell Biology
David Phillips Professor of Molecular Biophysics
Sherardian Professor of Botany
Jesus Professor of Celtic
Dr. Lee's Professor of Chemistry
Professor of Inorganic Chemistry
Coulson Professor of Theoretical Chemistry
Shaw Professor of Chinese
Professor of Computing
Professor of Computing Science
Regius Professor of Divinity
Lady Margaret Professor of Divinity
Spalding Professor of Eastern Religions and Ethics
Professor of Economics
Edgeworth Professor of Economics
Sir John Hicks Professor of Economics
Professor of Egyptology
Donald Pollock Professor of Chemical Engineering
Professor of Civil Engineering
Professor of Electrical and Electronic Engineering
Professor of Optoelectronic Engineering
BP Professor of Information Engineering
Professor of Mechanical Engineering
Merton Professor of English Language
Goldsmiths' Professor of English Literature
Merton Professor of English Literature
Thomas Warton Professor of English Literature
J. R. R. Tolkien Professor of English Literature and Language
Professor of French Literature
Marshal Foch Professor of French Literature
Professor of General Linguistics
Professor of Genetics
Professor of Geography
Halford Mackinder Professor of Geography
Professor of Geology
Savilian Professor of Geometry
Taylor Professor of the German Language and Literature
Professor of German Medieval and Linguistic Studies
Gladstone Professor of Government
Andrew W. Mellon Professor of American Government

Regius Professor of Greek
Bywater and Sotheby Professor of Byzantine and Modern Greek Language and Literature
Regius Professor of Hebrew
Harold Vyvyan Harmsworth Professor of American History
Rhodes Professor of American History
Camden Professor of Ancient History
Wykeham Professor of Ancient History
Beit Professor of the History of the British Commonwealth
Regius Professor of Ecclesiastical History
Chichele Professor of Economic History
Carroll Professor of Irish History
Professor of the History of Latin America
Chichele Professor of Medieval History
Regius Professor of Modern History
Professor of Modern History
Professor of the History of Philosophy
Professor of the History of Science
Chichele Professor of the History of War
Montague Burton Professor of International Relations
Lester B. Pearson Professor of International Relations
Fiat-Serena Professor of Italian Studies
Nissan Professor of Modern Japanese Studies
Professor of Jurisprudence
Rupert Murdoch Professor of Language and Communication
Corpus Christi Professor of Latin
Professor of Law
Regius Professor of Civil Law
Norton Rose Professor of Commercial and Financial Law
Clifford Chance Professor of Comparative Law
Allen & Overy Professor of Corporate Law
Professor of English Law
Vinerian Professor of English Law
Jacques Delors Professor of European Community Law
Reuters Professor of Intellectual Property and Information Technology Law
Chichele Professor of Public International Law
KPMG Professor of Taxation Law
Wykeham Professor of Logic
Professor of Mathematical Logic
Professors (two) of Management Studies
Ernest Butten Professor of Management Studies
Peter Moores Professor of Management Studies
The Peninsular and Oriental Steam Navigation Company Professor of Management Studies
American Standard Companies Professor of Operations Management
Professor of Marketing

Cookson Professor of Materials
Rouse Ball Professor of Mathematics
Wallis Professor of Mathematics
Professor of Mathematics and its Applications
Professor of Pure Mathematics
Waynflete Professor of Pure Mathematics
Isaac Wolfson Professor of Metallurgy
Professor of Microbiology
Iveagh Professor of Microbiology
Professor of the Physics and Chemistry of Minerals
Heather Professor of Music
Professor of Numerical Analysis
E. P. Abraham Professor of Chemical Pathology
Masoumeh and Fereydoon Soudavar Professor of Persian Studies
Professor of Comparative Philology
Dr Lee's Professor of Experimental Philosophy
Wilde Professor of Mental Philosophy
Waynflete Professor of Metaphysical Philosophy
White's Professor of Moral Philosophy
Sedleian Professor of Natural Philosophy
Nolloth Professor of the Philosophy of the Christian Religion
Halley Professor of Physics
Wykeham Professor of Physics
Professors (three) of Experimental Physics
Waynflete Professor of Physiology
Sibthorpian Professor of Plant Science
Professor of Poetry
Drummond Professor of Political Economy
King John II Professor of Portuguese Studies
Professor of Psychology
Watts Professor of Psychology
Charles Simonyi Professor of the Public Understanding of Science
Rhodes Professor of Race Relations
Professor of the Romance Languages
Professor of Russian
Boden Professor of Sanskrit
Andreas Idreos Professor of Science and Religion
Dean Ireland's Professor of the Exegesis of Holy Scripture
Oriel and Laing Professor of the Interpretation of Holy Scripture
Barnett Professor of Social Policy
Chichele Professor of Social and Political Theory
Professor of Sociology
Professor of Sociology and Social Policy
King Alfonso XIII Professor of Spanish Studies
Professor of Applied Statistics
Professor of Statistical Science

Regius Professor of Moral and Pastoral Theology
Donald Schultz Professor of Turbomachinery
Professor of Zoology
Linacre Professor of Zoology
Hope Professor of Zoology (Entomology)
George Eastman Visiting Professor
Newton-Abraham Visiting Professor

SCHEDULE B

Dr. Lee's Professor of Anatomy
Waynflete Professor of Chemistry
Professor of Educational Studies
Professor of Pathology
Professor of Pharmacology
Professor of Socio-Legal Studies

SCHEDULE C

Nuffield Professor of Anaesthetics
Professor of Morbid Anatomy
Professor of Clinical Biochemistry
Professor of General Practice
Regius Professor of Medicine
May Professor of Medicine
Field Marshal Alexander Professor of Cardiovascular Medicine
Nuffield Professor of Clinical Medicine
Professor of Molecular Medicine
Norman Collisson Professor of Musculo-skeletal Science
Action Research Professor of Clinical Neurology
Nuffield Professor of Obstetrics and Gynaecology
Imperial Cancer Research Fund Professor of Clinical Oncology
Action Research Professor of Paediatrics
Nuffield Professor of Pathology
W. A. Handley Professor of Psychiatry
Professor of Child and Adolescent Psychiatry
Professor of Public Health
Nuffield Professor of Surgery
Nuffield Professor of Orthopaedic Surgery
Rhodes Professor of Therapeutic Sciences and Clinical Pharmacology
Professor of Transplantation

§ **6.** *Stipends of professors*

1. Every professor shall be entitled to receive the income assigned to his or her professorship from any trust funds, Crown Benefactions or the emoluments, if any, appropriated to it under any university or college statute, or decree, and shall receive in addition such sums as will make up the emoluments of his or her

chair (excluding college allowances) to the annual stipend as determined for it by Council from time to time; provided that the sums receivable by the Regius Professor of Divinity and the Lady Margaret Professor of Divinity from the Regius Professor of Divinity Trust and the Crown Benefaction respectively be paid to them in addition to the annual stipend as determined by Council from time to time.

2. Except for the Nuffield Professors of Clinical Medicine, Surgery, Obstetrics and Gynaecology, and Anaesthetics, whose incomes may not be reduced below £2,000 per annum as prescribed by the Deed of Covenant and Trust between Viscount Nuffield and the University executed on 24 November 1936, the income specified for any professorship shall be subject to alteration by Council upon the occurrence of a vacancy in that professorship, and shall not be altered during any tenure of the chair except with the consent of the holder.

3. Any allowance made by the Governing Body of Christ Church to the Regius Professor of Medicine under the provisions of the will of Lady Osler or any benefit accruing thereunder shall be treated as part of the emoluments of his or her chair for the purposes of this sub-section; but fees received under the provisions of Ch. VIII, Sect. II, § 4, shall not be so treated.

§ 7. *Special allowances to certain Heads of Departments*

In addition to the emoluments provided under the previous decree each professor or head of department in the Schedules annexed to this decree shall receive each year the sum specified by Council by way of special allowance in respect of his or her duties as Head of the Department of which he or she is in charge, provided that he or she shall undertake not to receive any direct or indirect payment from any funds of, or at the disposal of, his or her department or laboratory.[1] No such allowance shall be paid to any head of department while he or she is on leave.[2]

SCHEDULE I

Chairman of Chemistry
Head of the Nuffield Department of Clinical Medicine
Chairman of Physics

SCHEDULE II

Head of the Department of Biochemistry
Head of the Department of Engineering Science

[1] The allocation to the appropriate schedule or schedules of the person or persons holding responsibilities related to the Departments of Primary Health Care and of Public Health shall be determined by the General Board.

[2] Subject to the transitional provisions of clause 7 of Decree (2) of 16 July 1998 (*Gazette*, Vol. 128, p. 1475).

SCHEDULE III

Head of the Nuffield Department of Clinical Laboratory Sciences
Head of the Department of Earth Sciences
Head of the Department of Materials
Head of the Department of Paediatrics
Professor of Pathology
Professor of Pharmacology
Head of the Department of Physiology
Head of the Department of Plant Sciences
Head of the Department of Psychiatry
Head of the Department of Experimental Psychology
Head of the Nuffield Department of Surgery
Head of the Department of Zoology

SCHEDULE IV

Dr Lee's Professor of Anatomy
Director of the Computing Laboratory
Deputy Directors of the Saïd Business School
Head of the Department of Clinical Neurology
Head of the Nuffield Department of Obstetrics and Gynaecology

SCHEDULE V

Head of the Department of Cardiovascular Medicine
Head of the Department of Economics
Professor of Educational Studies
Head of the School of Geography
Chairman of Mathematics
Head of the Nuffield Department of Orthopaedic Surgery
Head of the Department of Clinical Pharmacology
Head of the Department of Politics and International Relations
Director of Queen Elizabeth House

SCHEDULE VI

Head of the Nuffield Department of Anaesthetics
Head of the Institute of Biological Anthropology
Head of the Institute of Social and Cultural Anthropology
Director of the Institute of Archaeology
Director of the Research Laboratory for Archaeology and the History of Art
Director of the Centre for Criminological Research
Ruskin Master of Drawing
Chairman of the Board of the Faculty of Music
Head of the Nuffield Laboratory of Ophthalmology
Head of the Department of Social Policy and Social Work
Head of the Department of Sociology
Head of the Department of Statistics

§ **8.** Ad hominem *professorships*

1. Council, on the recommendation of the General Board, may appoint to an *ad hominem* professorship a member of the academic staff of the University in recognition of his or her academic distinction, and may determine the title to be attached to such a professorship.

2. The stipend and duties of an *ad hominem* professor shall be as determined by Council, on the recommendation of the General Board.

§ **9.** *Single-tenure and fixed-term professorships*

1. Council, on the recommendation of the General Board, may create, and make appointment to, a professorship to last for the tenure of one holder or for a fixed period of years not exceeding ten, and may determine the title to be attached to such a professorship.

2. The stipend and duties of the holder of such a professorship shall be as determined by Council, on the recommendation of the General Board, in each case.

§ **10.** *Conferment of title of professor or reader*

1. Subject to report to Council and the General Board, the Distinctions Committee of the General Board may confer as appropriate the title of professor or reader, without stipend, in recognition of personal academic distinction, on either

(*a*) employees of the University or

(*b*) persons not employed by the University but who are making a significant and sustained contribution to it in an academic capacity.

2. Persons on whom one of the titles is conferred shall continue to hold it for as long as they hold the appointment in respect of which the title was conferred, or another appointment regarded by Council and the General Board as at the same level.

§ **11.** *Visiting Professors*

The General Board may, following consideration of a proposal by a faculty board responsible for the field of study concerned, confer the title of Visiting Professor without stipend on a member of the staff of a government research establishment or comparable industrial or other institution outside the University, or on an individual not on the establishment of another academic institution who is deemed suitably qualified, who regularly participates in lecturing or any other form of teaching in the University and/or in the research activities of the department or faculty in question. The title shall be conferred for a period not exceeding three years in the first instance, but may be renewed thereafter on the recommendation of the faculty board for a further period or periods not exceeding five years at a time.

§ 12. *The title Professor Emeritus*

The title of Professor Emeritus shall be borne by the following:

(1) any person who has retired over the age of 60 from a professorship (including an *ad hominem* or titular professorship);

(2) any person who has retired from a professorship to which a canonry is annexed at or after the date on which he would be required by statute to retire if no canonry were annexed to the professorship;

(3) any person who has retired from a professorship and on whom the title has been conferred by decree.

§ 13. *The title Reader Emeritus*

The title of Reader Emeritus shall be borne by the following:

(1) any person who has retired over the age of 60 from a readership (including an *ad hominem* or titular readership);

(2) any person who has retired from a readership and on whom the title has been conferred by decree.

Section II. Allocation of Professorships to Colleges and Societies

1. This section shall apply to the colleges and other societies included in Title VII, except the permanent private halls; and the term 'college' in this section shall include such other societies. The term 'women's college' shall mean a college the governing body of which is restricted to women only.

2. Every professorship shall, subject to the provisions of clauses 3 and 4 below, be allocated by Council, as and when occasion may arise, to a college.

3. Council shall not allocate a professorship to any college, except with the consent of that college, if the result of the allocation of such a professorship would be that the professors holding professorships in that college under the provisions of this section would exceed one-third of the total number of fellows on the governing body of that college, exclusive of professors holding fellowships by virtue of their office and of other persons holding professorial fellowships under the provisions of Sect. VII, § 2, and in the case of Christ Church of the Archdeacon of Oxford.

4. At the end of the year 1988 and of every tenth year thereafter Council shall review and, if it thinks fit, alter the allocation of any professorship, subject to the consent of the college to which it was last allocated; provided always

(i) that in the case of a professorship of which by virtue of his or her office the holder is, under the provisions of its statutes, a fellow of any college, the consent of that college shall be confirmed by an alteration of its statutes;

(ii) that unless the proposal to alter the allocation of any professorship is due to a reduction in the number of professorships which, under the provisions of clause 3 above, can be allocated to the college, or is to be brought into effect only after the retirement of the present holder of the professorship, no alteration shall be made without the consent of the professor concerned.

5. If the appointment to a professorship is vested in a board of electors, the governing body of the college to which the professorship is allocated shall be entitled to appoint one member of such board and the head of that college shall be an *ex officio* member.

6. In the event of a man being elected or appointed to a professorship allocated or to be allocated under the provisions of this decree to a women's college, the professorship shall forthwith by virtue of this decree become, and during his tenure thereof remain, allocated to such one of the colleges open to men as Council shall upon each occasion determine; but the professorship shall count during his tenure thereof as though it were held by a fellow of the women's college to which it was allocated immediately before the election or appointment thereto for the purpose of reckoning the proportion of professorships to fellows in accordance with clause 3 above; and from and after the termination of his tenure, the professorships shall forthwith, by virtue of this decree, again be allocated to the women's college to which it was allocated immediately before his election or appointment thereto.

7. In the event of a woman being elected or appointed to a professorship allocated or to be allocated under the provisions of this decree to a women's college but desiring to hold the professorship at the college specified under clause 6 above, Council shall allocate the professorship to that college for the period of her tenure thereof; and from and after the termination of her tenure, the professorship shall forthwith, by virtue of this decree, again be allocated to the college to which it was allocated immediately before her election or appointment thereto.

8. In the event of a fellow of a women's college being elected to a professorship allocated to another college but desiring to remain a fellow of her present college, Council may, with the consent of the governing body of the college to which the professorship is allocated, allocate the professorship to the women's college concerned for the period of her tenure thereof; the professorship shall count during her tenure thereof as though it were held by a fellow of the college to which it was allocated immediately before the election or appointment thereto for the purpose of reckoning the proportion of professorships to fellows in accordance with clause 3 above; and from and after the termination of her tenure, the professorship shall forthwith, by virtue of this decree, again be allocated to the college to which it was allocated immediately before her election or appointment thereto.

9. In the construction of this decree the word 'professorship' shall mean

(*a*) all the professorships established by Tit. XIV, Sect. II, except the Slade Professorship of Fine Art, the Professorship of Poetry, and the Newton-Abraham and George Eastman Visiting Professorships;

(*b*) such other professorships established by decree to which appointment is made by a board of electors as Council may determine.

Section III. Particular Professorships, Readerships, Lecturerships, etc.

§ 1. *Power of Council to alter Decrees*

Subject to the following provisions Council shall have power from time to time to alter any of the decrees contained in this section:

(1) except in regard to the constitution of the electorate to a chair no alteration shall be made in any of the decrees contained in this section unless either the chair shall be vacant or the holder of the chair shall consent to the proposed alteration;

(2) where a college is represented upon the Board of Electors to a chair no alteration shall be made in the representation of the college and no addition shall be made to the number of the electors without the consent of the governing body of the college;

(3) before proposing any alteration in any of the decrees contained in this section, Council shall consult any Board or Boards of Faculties concerned.

§ 2. *John G. Winant Lecturer in American Foreign Policy*

1. The University accepts with gratitude an anonymous benefaction for the purpose of establishing a John G. Winant Lecturership in American Foreign Policy.

2. The John G. Winant Lecturer shall lecture and give instruction in American Foreign Policy. The lecturer shall be elected, and shall hold the appointment, on such conditions as the Department of Politics and International Relations shall from time to time determine.

3. Any part of the income of the endowment of the lecturership which is not required to meet the costs thereof may be expended, under conditions to be determined from time to time by the Department of Politics and International Relations, on the promotion of teaching and research in American Foreign Policy.

4. Council shall have power to alter this decree from time to time, provided that the main object of the benefaction, as defined in clause 1 above, is always kept in view.

§ 3. *Drue Heinz Professor of American Literature*

1. The University accepts with gratitude the moneys offered for the establishment of a Drue Heinz Professorship of American Literature.

2. The Drue Heinz Professor of American Literature shall lecture and give instruction in American Literature.

3. The professor shall be elected by an electoral board consisting of:

(1) the Vice-Chancellor, or, if the President of St John's College is Vice-Chancellor, a person appointed by Council;

(2) the President of St John's College, or, if the President is unable or unwilling to act, a person appointed by the governing body of the college;

(3) a person appointed by the Governing Body of St John's College;

(4), (5) two persons appointed by Council, one of whom shall be appointed after consultation with the benefactor during her lifetime;

(6), (7) two persons appointed by the General Board;

(8), (9) two persons appointed by the Board of the Faculty of English Language and Literature.

4. Such part of the income of the benefaction as the General Board may determine (after consultation with the benefactor during her lifetime) not to be required to meet the costs, including support costs, of the professorship shall be used to fund visits to Oxford from American writers and academics, to give lectures and seminars in the field of the professorship. This portion of the income shall be managed by a committee under the Board of the Faculty of English Language and Literature, which shall comprise the professor, the benefactor during her lifetime, and two members nominated by the board one of whom shall chair the committee.

5. The professor shall be subject to the General Provisions of the decree concerning the duties of professors and to those Particular Provisions of the same decree which are applicable to this chair.

§ 4. *Nuffield Professor of Anaesthetics*

1. The Nuffield Professor of Anaesthetics shall lecture and give instruction in Anaesthetics.

2. The professor shall be elected by an electoral board consisting of:

(1) the Vice-Chancellor, or, if the Master of Pembroke College is Vice-Chancellor, a person appointed by Council on the occurrence of a vacancy to act as an elector on that occasion;

(2) the Master of Pembroke College, or, if the Master is unable or unwilling to act, a person appointed by the governing body of the college on the occurrence of a vacancy to act as an elector on that occasion;

(3) a person appointed by the Governing Body of Pembroke College;

(4), (5) two persons appointed by Council;

(6) a person appointed by the General Board;

(7), (8) two persons appointed by the Board of the Faculty of Clinical Medicine;

(9) a person holding a clinical appointment appointed by the Oxfordshire Health Authority after consultation with the Oxford Regional Health Authority.

At least three members of the board, of whom one shall be a professor, shall hold clinical appointments.

3. The professor shall be subject to the General Provisions of the decree concerning the duties of professors and to those Particular Provisions of the same decree which are applicable to this chair.

§ **5.** *Dr. Lee's Professor of Anatomy*

1. Dr. Lee's Professor of Anatomy shall lecture and give instruction in Anatomy and shall have charge of the Anatomical Collections deposited in the Department of Human Anatomy and Genetics.

2. The professor shall be elected by an electoral board consisting of:

(1) the Vice-Chancellor, or, if the head of the college specified in (2) of this clause is Vice-Chancellor, a person appointed by Council on the occurrence of a vacancy to act as an elector on that occasion;

(2) the head of the college to which the professorship shall be for the time being allocated by Council under any decree in that behalf, or, if the head is unable or unwilling to act, a person appointed by the governing body of the college on the occurrence of a vacancy to act as an elector on that occasion;

(3) a person appointed by the governing body of the college specified in (2) of this clause;

(4) a person appointed by Council;

(5) a person appointed by the General Board;

(6)–(8) three persons elected by the Board of the Faculty of Physiological Sciences;

(9) a person elected by the Board of the Faculty of Biological Sciences.

3. The professor shall not be allowed to engage in private medical or surgical practice. He or she shall be subject to the General Provisions of the decree concerning the duties of professors and to those Particular Provisions of the same decree which are applicable to this chair.

§ **6.** *Professor of Morbid Anatomy*

1. The Professor of Morbid Anatomy shall lecture and give instruction in pathology for clinical students.

2. The professor shall be elected by a board of electors consisting of:

(1) the Vice-Chancellor, or, if the Principal of Linacre College is Vice-Chancellor, a person appointed by Council on the occurrence of a vacancy to act as an elector on that occasion;

(2) the Principal of Linacre College, or, if the Principal is unable or unwilling to act, a person appointed by the Governing Body of Linacre College on the occurrence of a vacancy to act as an elector on that occasion;

(3) a person appointed by the Governing Body of Linacre College;

(4) a person appointed by Council;

(5) a person appointed by the General Board;

(6), (7) two persons appointed by the Board of the Faculty of Clinical Medicine;

(8) a person appointed by the Board of the Faculty of Physiological Sciences;

(9) a person holding a clinical appointment appointed by the Oxfordshire Health Authority after consultation with the Oxford Regional Health Authority.

At least three members of the board, of whom one shall be a professor, shall hold clinical appointments.

3. The professor shall be subject to the General Provisions of the decree concerning the duties of professors and to those Particular Provisions of the same decree which are applicable to this chair.

§ 7. *Rawlinson and Bosworth Professor of Anglo-Saxon*

1. The Rawlinson and Bosworth Professor of Anglo-Saxon shall lecture and give instruction in the Anglo-Saxon Language and Literature, and may from time to time lecture and give instruction in the other Old Germanic Languages, especially Icelandic.

2. The professor shall be elected by an electoral board consisting of:

(1) the Vice-Chancellor, or, if the head of the college specified in (2) of this clause is Vice-Chancellor, a person appointed by Council on the occurrence of a vacancy to act as an elector on that occasion;

(2) the head of the college to which the professorship shall be for the time being allocated by Council under any decree in that behalf, or, if the head is unable or unwilling to act, a person appointed by the governing body of the college on the occurrence of a vacancy to act as an elector on that occasion;

(3) a person appointed by the governing body of the college specified in (2) of this clause;

(4) a person appointed by Council;

(5), (6) two persons elected by the Board of the Faculty of English Language and Literature;

(7) a person elected by the Board of the Faculty of Medieval and Modern Languages.

3. The professor shall be subject to the General Provisions of the decree concerning the duties of professors and to those Particular Provisions of the same decree which are applicable to this chair.

§ 8. *Professor of Biological Anthropology*

1. The Professor of Biological Anthropology shall lecture and give instruction in Biological Anthropology.

2. The professor shall be elected by a board consisting of:

(1) the Vice-Chancellor, or, if the Principal of Linacre College is Vice-Chancellor, a person appointed by Council;

(2) the Principal of Linacre College, or, if the Principal is unable or unwilling to act, a person appointed by the governing body of the college;

(3) a person appointed by the Governing Body of Linacre College;

(4) a person appointed by Council;

(5) a person appointed by the General Board of the Faculties;

(6) a person appointed by the Board of the Faculty of Biological Sciences;

(7), (8) two persons appointed by the Board of the Faculty of Anthropology and Geography;

(9) a person appointed by the Standing Committee for Human Sciences.

3. The professor shall be subject to the General Provisions of the decree concerning the duties of professors and to those Particular Provisions of the same decree which are applicable to this chair.

§ 9. *Professor of Social Anthropology*

1. The Professor of Social Anthropology shall lecture and give instruction in Social Anthropology.

2. The professor shall be elected by an electoral board consisting of:

(1) the Vice-Chancellor, or, if the Warden of All Souls College is Vice-Chancellor, a person appointed by Council on the occurrence of a vacancy to act as an elector on that occasion;

(2) the Warden of All Souls College, or, if the Warden is unable or unwilling to act, a person appointed by the Governing Body of All Souls College on the occurrence of a vacancy to act as an elector on that occasion;

(3) a person appointed by the Governing Body of All Souls College;

(4) a person appointed by Council;

(5), (6) two persons appointed by the General Board;

(7)–(9) three persons appointed by the Board of the Faculty of Anthropology and Geography.

3. The professor shall be subject to the General Provisions of the decree concerning the duties of professors and to those Particular Provisions of the same decree which are applicable to this chair.

§ 10. *Laudian Professor of Arabic*

1. The Laudian Professor of Arabic shall lecture and give instruction in Arabic language and literature.

2. The professor shall be elected by an electoral board consisting of:

(1) the Vice-Chancellor, or, if the President of St. John's College is Vice-Chancellor, a person appointed by Council on the occurrence of a vacancy to act as an elector on that occasion;

(2) the President of St. John's College, or, if the President is unable or unwilling to act, a person appointed by the Governing Body of St. John's College on the occurrence of a vacancy to act as an elector on that occasion;

(3) a person appointed by the Governing Body of St. John's College;

(4) a person appointed by Council;

(5), (6) two persons appointed by the General Board;

(7)–(9) three persons elected by the Board of the Faculty of Oriental Studies.

3. The professor shall be subject to the General Provisions of the decree concerning the duties of professors and to those Particular Provisions of the same decree which are applicable to this chair.

§ 11. *Al Saud Professor for the Study of the Contemporary Arab World*

1. The Khalid bin Abdullah Al Saud Professor for the Study of the Contemporary Arab World shall lecture and give instruction in one or more aspects of the politics, international relations, economics, sociology, or recent history of the contemporary Arab world.

2. The professor shall be elected by an electoral board consisting of:

(1) the Vice-Chancellor, or, if the President of Magdalen College is Vice-Chancellor, a person appointed by Council on the occurrence of a vacancy to act as an elector on that occasion;

(2) the President of Magdalen College, or, if the President is unable or unwilling to act, a person appointed by the Governing Body of Magdalen College on the occurrence of a vacancy to act as an elector on that occasion;

(3) a person appointed by the Governing Body of Magdalen College;

(4) a person appointed by Council;

(5), (6) two persons appointed by the General Board, one of whom shall be appointed after consultation with the Committee for Modern Middle Eastern Studies;

(7) a person appointed by the Board of the Faculty of Social Studies;

(8) a person appointed by the Board of the Faculty of Anthropology and Geography;

(9) a person appointed by the Board of the Faculty of Oriental Studies.

3. The professor shall be subject to the General Provisions of the decree concerning the duties of professors and to the Particular Provisions of the same decree which are applicable to this chair.

4. Any part of the income of the endowment of the professorship which is not required to meet the costs thereof may be expended, under conditions to be determined from time to time by the General Board, on the provision of grants to the professor for travelling and other expenses incurred in the pursuance of his or her studies.

§ 12. *Lincoln Professor of Classical Archaeology and Art*

1. The Lincoln Professor of Classical Archaeology and Art shall lecture and give instruction on the arts and monuments of classical antiquity.

2. The professor shall be elected by an electoral board consisting of:

(1) the Vice-Chancellor, or, if the Rector of Lincoln College is Vice-Chancellor, a person appointed by Council on the occurrence of a vacancy to act as an elector on that occasion;

(2) the Keeper of Greek and Roman Antiquities in the British Museum;

(3) the Rector of Lincoln College, or, if the Rector is unable or unwilling to act, a person appointed by the Governing Body of Lincoln College on the occurrence of a vacancy to act as an elector on that occasion;

(4) a person appointed by the Governing Body of Lincoln College;

(5) a person appointed by Council;

(6) a person elected by the Board of the Faculty of Literae Humaniores;

(7) a person elected by the Committee for Archaeology.

3. The professor shall be subject to the General Provisions of the decree concerning the duties of professors and to those Particular Provisions of the same decree which are applicable to this chair.

§ 13. *Professor of European Archaeology*

1. The Professor of European Archaeology shall lecture and give instruction in European Archaeology with special reference to the period beginning with the introduction of agriculture and ending with the death of Charlemagne.

2. The professor shall be elected by an electoral board consisting of:

(1) the Vice-Chancellor, or, if the head of the college specified in (2) of this clause is Vice-Chancellor, a person appointed by Council on the occurrence of a vacancy to act as an elector on that occasion;

(2) the head of the college to which the professorship shall be for the time being allocated by Council under any decree in that behalf, or, if the head is unable or unwilling to act, a person appointed by the governing body of the college on the occurrence of a vacancy to act as an elector on that occasion;

(3) a person appointed by the governing body of the college specified in (2) of this clause;

(4) a person appointed by Council;

(5) a person appointed by the General Board;

(6) a person elected by the Board of the Faculty of Literae Humaniores;

(7) a person elected by the Board of the Faculty of Modern History;

(8) a person elected by the Committee for Archaeology;

(9) a person elected by the Board of the Faculty of Anthropology and Geography.

3. The professor shall be subject to the General Provisions of the decree concerning the duties of professors and to those Particular Provisions of the same decree which are applicable to this chair.

§ 14. *Professor of the Archaeology of the Roman Empire*

1. The Professor of the Archaeology of the Roman Empire shall lecture and give instruction in that subject.

2. The professor shall be elected by an electoral board consisting of:

(1) the Vice-Chancellor, or, if the head of the college specified in (2) of this clause is Vice-Chancellor, a person appointed by Council on the occurrence of a vacancy to act as an elector on that occasion;

(2) the head of the college to which the professorship shall be for the time being allocated by Council under any decree, any University Statute in that behalf, or, if the head is unable or unwilling to act, a person appointed by the governing body of the college on the occurrence of a vacancy to act as an elector on that occasion;

(3) a person appointed by the governing body of the college specified in (2) of this clause;

(4) a person appointed by Council;

(5) a person appointed by the General Board;

(6) a person elected by the Board of the Faculty of Literae Humaniores;

(7) a person elected by the Sub-faculty of Ancient History;

(8) a person elected by the Committee for Archaeology;

(9) a person elected by the Board of the Faculty of Modern History.

3. The professor shall be subject to the General Provisions of the decree concerning the duties of professors and to those Particular Provisions of the same decree which are applicable to this chair.

§ 15. *Calouste Gulbenkian Professor of Armenian Studies*

1. The Calouste Gulbenkian Professor of Armenian Studies shall lecture and give instruction in Armenian Studies.

2. The professor shall be elected by an electoral board consisting of:

(1) the Vice-Chancellor, or, if the Master of Pembroke College is Vice-Chancellor, a person appointed by Council on the occurrence of a vacancy to act as an elector on that occasion;

(2) the Master of Pembroke College, or, if the Master is unable or unwilling to act, a person appointed by the Governing Body of Pembroke College on the occurrence of a vacancy to act as an elector on that occasion;

(3) a person appointed by the Governing Body of Pembroke College;

(4) a person appointed by Council;

(5) a person appointed by the General Board;

(6) a person elected by the Board of the Faculty of Theology and the Board of the Faculty of Literae Humaniores;

(7) a person elected by the Board of the Faculty of Modern History;

(8), (9) two persons elected by the Board of the Faculty of Oriental Studies.

3. The professor shall be subject to the General Provisions of the decree concerning the duties of professors and to those Particular Provisions of the same decree which are applicable to this chair.

§ **16.** *Savilian Professor of Astronomy*

1. The Savilian Professor of Astronomy shall lecture and give instruction in theoretical or practical astronomy and shall be responsible for general instruction in astronomy.

2. The professor shall be elected by an electoral board consisting of:

(1) the Vice-Chancellor, or, if the Warden of New College is Vice-Chancellor, a person appointed by Council on the occurrence of a vacancy to act as an elector on that occasion;

(2) the Warden of New College, or, if the Warden is unable or unwilling to act, a person appointed by the Governing Body of New College on the occurrence of a vacancy to act as an elector on that occasion;

(3) a person appointed by the Governing Body of New College;

(4) a person appointed by Council;

(5) a person appointed by the General Board;

(6)–(9) four persons elected by the Board of the Faculty of the Physical Sciences.

3. The professor shall be subject to the General Provisions of the decree concerning the duties of professors and to those Particular Provisions of the same decree which are applicable to this chair.

§ **17.** *Halley Lecturer on Astronomy and Terrestrial Magnetism*

1. The lecture shall be called the Halley Lecture on Astronomy and Terrestrial Magnetism, in honour and memory of Edmond Halley (sometime Savilian Professor of Geometry in the University and Astronomer Royal), in connection with his important contributions to Cometary Astronomy and to our knowledge of the Magnetism of the earth.

2. For the purposes of this lecture Astronomy shall include Astrophysics, and Terrestrial Magnetism shall include the physics of the external and internal parts of the terrestrial globe.

3. The lecturer shall be appointed by a board of electors consisting of:

(1) the Vice-Chancellor;

(2)–(5) four persons elected by the Board of the Faculty of Physical Sciences;

(6), (7) two persons elected by the Board of the Faculty of Mathematical Sciences.

The elected members of the board shall be the same persons as those elected by the aforesaid faculty boards to serve as Trustees of the Johnson Memorial Prizes; they shall hold office for five years and be re-eligible.

4. The lecturer, who may be of any nationality, shall be appointed annually in Trinity Term, and in the academic year next following it shall be his or her duty to deliver a public lecture in Oxford, on a day and at a place to be fixed by the Vice-Chancellor, on some subject relating to Astronomy or Terrestrial Magnetism.

5. No lecturer shall be again eligible for election until the Trinity Term of the third year after that in which he or she was last elected.

6. No person who is a member of the board of electors shall be deemed on that ground to be ineligible as lecturer.

7. The lecturer shall, upon delivery of the lecture, receive such stipend from the income of the endowment fund as the board of electors shall decide. All expenses incurred by the University in the execution of the trust or in defraying any expenses incidental to the delivery of a lecture shall be paid from the income of the endowment fund.

8. Surplus income in any year may either be applied in augmentation of the capital or be reserved for expenditure in future years on the costs of the annual lecture, at the discretion of the board of electors, except that in case of any failure to deliver the lecture, or of the return of his or her stipend by any lecturer, the amount accruing therefrom shall be invested in augmentation of the endowment fund.

9. Council shall have full power to alter this decree from time to time, provided always that the main object of the endowment, namely, the delivery in the University once a year of a lecture on Astronomy and Terrestrial Magnetism—to be called the Halley Lecture—shall be observed and maintained.

§ 21. *Ball Foundation and Lecturer*

1. A lecture, or course of lectures, or a colloquium, carrying the name of Sidney Ball and dealing with modern social, economic, or political questions shall be established in the University of Oxford.

2. The sum of £500 5% War Loan Stock (1929–47), and the stocks, funds, and securities for the time being representing the same, shall form a fund, to be called the 'Sidney Ball Lecture Fund'.

3. The capital of the fund shall be invested in the name of the Chancellor, Masters, and Scholars of the University of Oxford in government securities or in other securities in which trustees are by law allowed to invest trust money, with power for the University from time to time to vary such securities for others of a like nature.

4. There shall be a board of management, which shall consist of such persons as the Board of the Faculty of Social Studies shall determine. The board of management shall from time to time as it shall see fit arrange lectures and colloquia, as defined in clause 1 above, and may make payments to the speakers from the income of the fund.

5. The first charge on the income of the fund shall be the payment of such speakers' fees and expenses. The board of management may apply any income not required for that purpose in any other way for the further advancement in the University of social, economic, and political studies.

6. This decree may be altered by Council, provided that the foundation shall always bear the title of the Sidney Ball Foundation, and that its main objects,

namely, the perpetuation of the memory of Sidney Ball, and the encouragement of Social and Economic Studies, shall be kept in view.

§ 22. *Speaker's Lecturer in Biblical Studies*

1. The lecturership founded by virtue of this scheme shall be called the Speaker's Lecturership in Biblical Studies.

2. The annual income of the fund constituting the endowment of the lecturership shall, after payment of any expenses incurred in the administration of the fund, be applied by the Chancellor, Masters, and Scholars of the University of Oxford in providing a stipend for a Lecturer in Biblical Studies to be elected in manner hereinafter provided.

3. The lecturer shall be elected by a board of seven electors consisting of:

(1) the Vice-Chancellor;

(2)–(4) three persons appointed by Council;

(5)–(7) three persons appointed by the Board of the Faculty of Theology.

Appointed electors shall hold office for three years, and shall be re-eligible; casual vacancies shall be filled for the remainder of the period of the person being replaced.

4. The lecturer shall enter upon office on the first day of Michaelmas Term, and the electors may make an appointment at any time during the preceding year.

5. The electors shall invite candidates for election to the office of lecturer to submit a subject or subjects for the proposed lectures, or shall themselves define and prescribe such subject or subjects. The choice of the electors shall not necessarily be limited to such candidates.

6. [The lecturer shall hold office for a period of two years, which may be extended at the electors' discretion by a further one or two years.] *The lecturer shall hold office for a period of one year, which may be extended at the electors' discretion by a further year.*[1] No person having held the lecturership shall again be eligible for election until at least two years have elapsed from the date of termination of the preceding period of office.

7. The lecturer shall deliver such number of lectures (not being less than six [in each year of his or her lecturership][1]) as the electors may upon making or extending the appointment prescribe. The lectures shall deal with such subject or subjects in connection with Biblical study as shall be approved or prescribed by the electors, and shall be delivered at such times and place as the Board of the Faculty of Theology may determine.

8. The lecturer shall be entitled to receive by way of stipend the net income accruing from time to time during his or her tenure of the lecturership, from the fund constituting the endowment.

[1] The deletion of the words in square brackets and the insertion of the words in italics take effect from 1 October 2001.

9. No member of the board of electors shall be eligible for the office of lecturer.

10. On the occurrence of any casual vacancy on the board of electors, the Registrar shall notify the vacancy to Council or to the Board of the Faculty of Theology as the case may be, and Council or the board shall fill up the vacancy as soon as may be.

11. In case of any accidental vacancy in the lecturership, the net income accruing during the vacancy shall be applied by Council in such manner as it shall judge to be most suitable for furtherance of the purposes of the lecturership.

§ 23. *Lyell Reader in Bibliography*

1. The James P. R. Lyell Reader in Bibliography shall lecture on any of the subjects of bibliography, palaeography, typography, book illustration and old bookbinding, the science of books and manuscripts and, in particular, the class of manuscripts contained in the Lyell bequest of manuscripts to the Bodleian Library, or other manuscripts in the Bodleian Library or in College Libraries in Oxford.

2. The reader shall be elected by an electoral board consisting of:

(1) the Vice-Chancellor;

(2) Bodley's Librarian;

(3) a person appointed by the Board of the Faculty of Literae Humaniores;

(4) a person appointed by the Board of the Faculty of Modern History;

(5) a person appointed by the Board of the Faculty of English Language and Literature;

(6), (7) two persons appointed by the Council of the Oxford Bibliographical Society.

3. Each of the appointed electors shall hold office for five years and shall be re-eligible.

4. The reader shall hold office for one year.

5. A reader shall be elected annually, provided that the electors shall be empowered to make a biennial election if they desire to accumulate funds for the travelling expenses of a reader from overseas.

6. The reader shall deliver not less than five lectures during his or her year of office.

7. The reader shall receive from the revenues of the Lyell bequest such stipend as the board of electors shall decide, one-half of it to be paid as soon as possible after the delivery of the lectures, and the remaining half on submission of the manuscript of the lecture in a form fit, in the judgement of the electors, for publication.

8. The board of electors aforesaid shall be a board of management for the revenues arising from the Lyell bequest, and shall apply them,

(*a*) to the stipend of the reader,

(*b*) towards the cost of the publication with or without illustrations of the reader's lectures, including the provision of a number of copies not exceeding one hundred for distribution at the discretion of the board, and

(*c*) to meeting any expense incidental to the carrying out of these purposes.

§ **24.** *Whitley Professor of Biochemistry*

1. The Whitley Professor of Biochemistry shall lecture and give instruction in Biochemistry and Physiological Chemistry.

2. The professor shall be elected by an electoral board consisting of:

(1) the Vice-Chancellor, or, if the head of the college specified in (3) of this clause is Vice-Chancellor, a person appointed by Council on the occurrence of a vacancy to act as an elector on that occasion;

(2) the Waynflete Professor of Physiology;

(3) the head of the college to which the professorship shall be for the time being allocated by Council under any decree in that behalf, or, if the head is unable or unwilling to act, a person appointed by the governing body of the college on the occurrence of a vacancy to act as an elector on that occasion;

(4) a person appointed by Council;

(5) a person elected by the Board of the Faculty of Physiological Sciences;

(6) a person elected by the Board of the Faculty of Biological Sciences;

(7) a person appointed by the governing body of the college specified in (3) of this clause.

3. The professor shall not be allowed to engage in private medical or surgical practice. He or she shall be subject to the General Provisions of the decree concerning the duties of professors and to those Particular Provisions of the same decree which are applicable to this chair.

§ **25.** *Professor of Clinical Biochemistry*

1. The Professor of Clinical Biochemistry shall lecture and give instruction in Biochemistry for Medical students.

2. The professor shall be elected by a board of electors consisting of

(1) the Vice-Chancellor, or, if the Principal of Hertford College is Vice-Chancellor, a person appointed by Council on the occurrence of a vacancy to act as an elector on that occasion;

(2) the Principal of Hertford College, or, if the Principal is unable or unwilling to act, a person appointed by the Governing Body of Hertford College on the occurrence of a vacancy to act as an elector on that occasion;

(3) a person appointed by the Governing Body of Hertford College;

(4) a person appointed by Council;

(5) a person appointed by the General Board;

(6), (7) two persons appointed by the Board of the Faculty of Clinical Medicine;

(8) a person appointed by the Board of the Faculty of Physiological Sciences;

(9) a person holding a clinical appointment appointed by the Oxfordshire Health Authority after consultation with the Oxford Regional Health Authority. At least three members of the board, of whom one shall be a professor, shall hold clinical appointments.

3. The professor shall be subject to the General Provisions of the decree concerning the duties of professors and to those Particular Provisions of the same decree which are applicable to this chair.

§ 26. *Professor of Bioinformatics*

1. The Professor of Bioinformatics shall lecture and give instruction in Bioinformatics.

2. The professor shall be elected by an electoral board consisting of:

(1) the Vice-Chancellor, or, if the head of the college specified in (2) of this clause is Vice-Chancellor, a person appointed by Council;

(2) the head of the college to which the professorship shall be for the time being allocated by Council under any decree in that behalf, or, if the head is unable or unwilling to act, a person appointed by the governing body of the college;

(3) a person appointed by the governing body of the college specified in (2) of this clause;

(4), (5) two persons appointed by Council;

(6), (7) two persons appointed by the Mathematical and Physical Sciences Board;

(8) a person appointed by the Life and Environmental Sciences Board;

(9) a person appointed by the Medical Sciences Board.

3. The professor shall be subject to the General Provisions of the decree concerning the duties of professors and to those Particular Provisions of the same decree which are applicable to this chair.

§ 27. *Abraham Professor of Cell Biology*

1. The E.P. Abraham Professor of Cell Biology shall undertake research in Cell Biology and shall lecture and give instruction in that subject.

2. The professor shall be elected by an electoral board consisting of:

(1) the Vice-Chancellor, or, if the head of the college specified in (2) of this clause is Vice-Chancellor, a person appointed by Council;

(2) the head of the college to which the professorship shall be for the time being allocated by Council under any decree in that behalf, or, if the head is unable or unwilling to act, a person appointed by the governing body of the college;

(3) a person appointed by the governing body of the college specified in (2) of this clause;

(4) a person appointed by Council;

(5), (6) two persons appointed by the General Board;

(7), (8) two persons appointed by the Board of the Faculty of Physiological Sciences;

(9) a person appointed by the Board of the Faculty of Clinical Medicine.

3. The professor shall be subject to the General Provisions of the decree concerning the duties of professors and to those Particular Provisions of the same decree which are applicable to this chair.

4. Such part of the income of the endowment as the Medical Sciences Board shall determine not to be required to meet the costs of the professorship shall be expended on support for the professor in such manner as the Divisional Board shall direct.

§ **28.** *Phillips Professor of Molecular Biophysics*

1. The University has accepted with deep gratitude the sum of £1,000,000 from the Trustees of the Edward Penley Abraham Research Fund for the endowment of a David Phillips Professorship of Molecular Biophysics and for the provision of supporting costs for the professorship, and a further £250,000 from the Trustees of the E.P.A. Cephalosporin Fund for the support of research and education in the Medical, Biological, and Chemical Sciences.

2. The David Phillips Professor of Molecular Biophysics shall lecture and give instruction in Molecular Biophysics.

3. The professor shall be elected by an electoral board consisting of:

(1) the Vice-Chancellor, or, if the head of the college specified in (2) of this clause is Vice-Chancellor, a person appointed by Council on the occurrence of a vacancy to act as an elector on that occasion;

(2) the head of the college to which the professorship shall be for the time being allocated by Council under any decree in that behalf, or, if the head is unable or unwilling to act, a person appointed by the governing body of the college on the occurrence of a vacancy to act as an elector on that occasion;

(3) a person appointed by the governing body of the college specified in (2) of this clause;

(4) a person appointed by Council;

(5) a person appointed by the General Board;

(6), (7) two persons appointed by the Board of the Faculty of Biological Sciences;

(8), (9) two persons appointed by the Board of the Faculty of Physical Sciences;

4. The professor shall be subject to the General Provisions of the decree concerning the duties of professors and to those Particular Provisions of the same decree which are applicable to this chair.

5. Such part of the income of the endowment as is not required to meet the costs of the professorship shall be expended on supporting expenditure for the professor in such manner as the General Board shall approve.

§ **29.** *Sherardian Professor of Botany*

1. The Sherardian Professor of Botany shall lecture and give instruction in Botany.

2. The professor shall be elected by an electoral board consisting of:

(1) the Vice-Chancellor, or, if the President of Magdalen College is Vice-Chancellor, a person appointed by Council on the occurrence of a vacancy to act as an elector on that occasion;

(2) the President of Magdalen College, or, if the President is unable or unwilling to act, a person appointed by the Governing Body of Magdalen College on the occurrence of a vacancy to act as an elector on that occasion;

(3) a person appointed by the Governing Body of Magdalen College;

(4) a person appointed by Council;

(5) a person appointed by the General Board;

(6), (7) two persons elected by the Board of the Faculty of Biological Sciences.

3. The professor shall be subject to the General Provisions of the decree concerning the duties of professors and to those Particular Provisions of the same decree which are applicable to this chair.

§ **31.** *Imperial Cancer Research Fund Reader in Cancer Studies*

1. The University accepts with deep gratitude the endowment provided by the Imperial Cancer Research Fund for the establishment of an Imperial Cancer Research Fund Readership in Cancer Studies and for the provision of supporting expenditure for the readership.

2. The reader shall be elected by an electoral board consisting of

(1) the Vice-Chancellor;

(2) a person appointed by Council;

(3) a person appointed by the General Board;

(4) the professor designated under the provisions of cl. 3 hereof;

(5), (6) two persons appointed by the Board of the Faculty of Clinical Medicine;

(7) a person appointed by the Board of the Faculty of Physiological Sciences.

3. The reader shall engage in advanced study or research in the epidemiology of cancer or such other field of cancer studies as the Board of the Faculty of Clinical Medicine, after consultation with the Council of the Imperial Cancer Research Fund, shall determine, under the direction of a professor to be designated from time to time by the Board of the Faculty of Clinical Medicine. The reader shall give or hold such number of lectures or classes as the Board of the Faculty of Clinical Medicine shall determine.

4. Such part of the endowment as the General Board shall determine is not required to meet the costs of the readership shall be applied to the provision of supporting expenditure for the reader in such manner as the General Board and

Council, after consultation with the Board of the Faculty of Clinical Medicine, shall direct.

5. Council shall have power, subject to the consent of the Council of the Imperial Cancer Research Fund, to amend this decree, provided that the main object of the endowment, namely the establishment of a senior post in Cancer Studies and the provision of supporting expenditure, is always kept in view.

§ 32. *Carlyle Fund and Lecturer*

1. The University accepts with gratitude the residue of the estate of the late Miss Mary Monteith Carlyle in trust to form a fund to be known as the A. J. Carlyle Fund, the income of which shall be used to finance a lecture or series of lectures on political theory, with a preference for medieval political theory if a suitable medieval scholar is available for this purpose.

2. The income from the fund shall be expended on the objects of the trust by the Boards of the Faculties of Modern History and Social Studies under arrangements to be approved by the General Board and Council.

3. The name of Carlyle shall be associated with any appointment made under the provisions of this decree.

§ 33. *Jesus Professor of Celtic*

1. The Jesus Professor of Celtic shall lecture and give instruction in the Celtic Languages and Literature.

2. The professor shall be elected by an electoral board consisting of:

(1) the Vice-Chancellor, or, if the Principal of Jesus College is Vice-Chancellor, a person appointed by Council on the occurrence of a vacancy to act as an elector on that occasion;

(2) the Principal of Jesus College, or, if the Principal is unable or unwilling to act, a person appointed by the Governing Body of Jesus College on the occurrence of a vacancy to act as an elector on that occasion;

(3) a person appointed by the Governing Body of Jesus College;

(4) a person appointed by Council;

(5) a person appointed by the General Board;

(6), (7) two persons elected by the Board of the Faculty of Medieval and Modern Languages;

(8) a person elected by the Board of the Faculty of English Language and Literature;

(9) a person appointed by the Court of the University of Wales.

3. The professor shall be subject to the General Provisions of the decree concerning the duties of professors and to those Particular Provisions of the same decree which are applicable to this chair.

§ 34. *O'Donnell Lecturer in Celtic Studies*[1]

1. The O'Donnell Lectures shall be in connection with one or other of the following subjects, namely

(*a*) the British or Celtic elements in the English language and the dialects of English counties and the special terms and words used in agriculture and handicrafts,

(*b*) the British or Celtic elements in the existing population of England.

2. The lecturer shall be called the O'Donnell Lecturer in Celtic Studies and shall be elected by an electoral board consisting of:

(1) the Vice-Chancellor;

(2) a person appointed by Council;

(3) a person appointed by the General Board;

(4) a person appointed by the Board of the Faculty of English Language and Literature;

(5) a person appointed by the Board of the Faculty of Medieval and Modern Languages.

3. The lecturer shall hold office for one year but shall be re-eligible and shall be required to give not less than one or more than three lectures, the number of lectures within these limits being left to the lecturer's discretion.

4. The lecturer shall receive from the O'Donnell Fund such stipend and expenses as the board of management shall from time to time determine.

5. Each lecturer shall deliver to the Registrar a copy of his or her lecture or lectures.

6. The board of management may apply any surplus in the fund towards meeting the cost of publication of the lectures or, failing publication, towards increasing the emoluments of the lecturer.

7. The Board of the Faculty of English Language and Literature shall be the board of management of the fund.

§ 35. *Aldrichian Praelector and Reader in Chemistry*

1. The Aldrichian Praelector and Reader in Chemistry shall be appointed by the Board of the Faculty of Physical Sciences from among the University Lecturers in Chemistry. The terms and conditions of the appointment shall be the same as for readers appointed by the General Board.

2. The stipend of the praelector and reader shall be on the readers' scale, and shall include one-third of the income arising from the bequest of George Aldrich, Doctor of Medicine.

[1] See also Ch. IX, Sect. I, § 43.

§ **36.** *Dr. Lee's Professor of Chemistry*

1. Dr. Lee's Professor of Chemistry shall lecture and give instruction in Physical Chemistry.

2. The professor shall be elected by an electoral board consisting of:

(1) the Vice-Chancellor, or, if the head of the college specified in (2) of this clause is Vice-Chancellor, a person appointed by Council on the occurrence of a vacancy to act as an elector on that occasion;

(2) the head of the college to which the professorship shall be for the time being allocated by Council under any decree in that behalf, or, if the head is unable or unwilling to act, a person appointed by the governing body of the college on the occurrence of a vacancy to act as an elector on that occasion;

(3) a person appointed by the governing body of the college specified in (2) of this clause;

(4) a person appointed by Council;

(5), (6) two persons appointed by the General Board;

(7)–(9) three persons appointed by the Board of the Faculty of the Physical Sciences.

3. The professor shall be subject to the General Provisions of the decree concerning the duties of professors and to those Particular Provisions of the same decree which are applicable to this chair.

§ **37.** *Waynflete Professor of Chemistry*

1. The Waynflete Professor of Chemistry shall lecture and give instruction in theoretical and practical Chemistry, especially Organic Chemistry.

2. The professor shall be elected, by an electoral board consisting of:

(1) the Vice-Chancellor, or, if the President of Magdalen College is Vice-Chancellor, a person appointed by Council on the occurrence of a vacancy to act as an elector on that occasion;

(2) the President of Magdalen College, or, if the President is unable or unwilling to act, a person appointed by the Governing Body of Magdalen College on the occurrence of a vacancy to act as an elector on that occasion;

(3) a person appointed by the Governing Body of Magdalen College;

(4) a person appointed by Council;

(5) a person appointed by the General Board;

(6)–(8) three persons elected by the Board of the Faculty of the Physical Sciences.

(9) a person elected by the Board of the Faculty of the Biological Sciences.

3. The professor shall be subject to the General Provisions of the decree concerning the duties of professors and to those Particular Provisions of the same decree which are applicable to this chair.

§ **38.** *Professor of Inorganic Chemistry*

1. The Professor of Inorganic Chemistry shall lecture and give instruction in Inorganic Chemistry.

2. The professor shall be elected by a board consisting of:

(1) the Vice-Chancellor, or, if the head of the college specified in (2) of this clause is Vice-Chancellor, a person appointed by Council on the occurrence of a vacancy to act as an elector on that occasion;

(2) the head of the college to which the professorship shall be for the time being allocated by Council under any decree in that behalf, or, if the head is unable or unwilling to act, a person appointed by the governing body of the college on the occurrence of a vacancy to act as an elector on that occasion;

(3) a person appointed by the governing body of the college specified in (2) of this clause;

(4) a person appointed by Council;

(5) a person appointed by the General Board;

(6)–(9) four persons appointed by the Board of the Faculty of Physical Sciences.

3. The professor shall be subject to the General Provisions of the decree concerning the duties of professors and to those Particular Provisions of the same decree which are applicable to this chair.

§ **39.** *Coulson Professor of Theoretical Chemistry*

1. The Coulson Professor of Theoretical Chemistry shall lecture and give instruction in Theoretical Chemistry.

2. The professor shall be elected by an electoral board consisting of:

(1) the Vice-Chancellor, or, if the Master of University College is Vice-Chancellor, a person appointed by Council on the occurrence of a vacancy to act as an elector on that occasion;

(2) the Master of University College, or, if the Master is unable or unwilling to act, a person appointed by the Governing Body of University College on the occurrence of a vacancy to act as an elector on that occasion;

(3) a person appointed by the Governing Body of University College;

(4) a person appointed by Council;

(5) a person appointed by the General Board;

(6)–(9) four persons elected by the Board of the Faculty of Physical Sciences.

3. The professor shall be subject to the General Provisions of the decree concerning the duties of professors and to the Particular Provisions of the same decree applicable to the professors enumerated in Schedule A annexed thereto.

§ **40.** *Cherwell-Simon Memorial Lecturer*

1. An annual lecture shall be maintained in the University of Oxford to be called the Cherwell-Simon Memorial Lecture, and the lecturer appointed shall be called the Cherwell-Simon Memorial Lecturer.

2. The lecture shall be delivered on a subject in some branch of physics of general interest.

3. The sum of £2,190·49 and the stocks, funds, and securities for the time being representing the same, and any addition made thereto by accumulation or otherwise, shall form a fund to be called the Cherwell-Simon Memorial Fund.

4. There shall be a board of management consisting of:

(1) the Vice-Chancellor;

(2) the Dean of Christ Church;

(3) the Warden of Wadham College;

(4) Dr. Lee's Professor of Experimental Philosophy;

(5) the Wykeham Professor of Physics;

(6) the person to whom for the time being the Sub-Department of Particle and Nuclear Physics is assigned under Ch. III, Sect. LXII, § 4, cl. 2;

(7) the person to whom for the time being the Sub-Department of Atomic and Laser Physics is assigned under Ch. III, Sect. LXII, § 4, cl. 2.

5. The board of management shall appoint the lecturer in every year and fix his or her stipend and the date of the lecture.

6. The stipend of the lecturer shall be the first charge on the income of the fund. Any surplus income shall, at the discretion of the board of management, be applied in one or more of the following ways:

(*a*) applied towards the necessary expenses of the lecturer;

(*b*) carried forward for use in a subsequent year;

(*c*) applied in any other way which the board shall think conducive to the object of the fund.

7. This decree shall be subject to alteration by Council provided that the main object, namely the delivery in the University from time to time of a lecture to be called the Cherwell-Simon Memorial Lecture, shall be observed and maintained.

§ **41.** *Shaw Professor of Chinese* [1]

1. The Shaw Professor of Chinese shall lecture and give instruction within the field of Chinese language and literature.

2. The professor shall be elected by an electoral board consisting of:

(1) the Vice-Chancellor, or, if the Master of University College is Vice-Chancellor, a person appointed by Council on the occurrence of a vacancy to act as an elector on that occasion;

(2) the Master of University College, or, if the Master is unable or unwilling to act, a person appointed by the Governing Body of University College on the occurrence of a vacancy to act as an elector on that occasion;

(3) a person appointed by the Governing Body of University College;

(4) a person appointed by Council;

(5) a person appointed by the General Board;

(6), (7) two persons elected by the Board of the Faculty of Oriental Studies.

3. The professor may be permitted by the General Board to take a period of absence exceptionally for travel and research without loss of income.

4. The professor shall be subject to the General Provisions of the decree concerning the duties of professors and to those Particular Provisions of the same decree which are applicable to this chair.

[2]

Conditions upon which an endowment of a Professorship of Chinese was accepted by Convocation on 5 December 1879

Whereas James Macandrew, William Walkinshaw, Alfred Howell, and James Banks Taylor, Esquires, Trustees of a sum of £3,003 which has been subscribed by persons interested in promoting the study of Chinese, have offered forthwith to invest the same in £3 per cent Government annuities in the name of the Chancellor, Masters, and Scholars of the University of Oxford, upon the following terms and conditions.

1. The said sum of £3,003, and the stocks, funds, and securities in or upon which the same shall for the time being be invested, shall be regarded as a capital fund specifically appropriated towards the endowment of a Professorship of the Chinese Language and Literature in the University of Oxford.

2. The dividends on the said capital fund, and on any additions which may hereafter be made thereto, shall be paid to the person who, whether under the provisions of any existing statute of the University in that behalf or of any statute or decree to be made hereafter, shall hold for the time being the office of Professor of the Chinese Language and Literature in the University.

3. If, on any vacancy occurring in the office of such professor, it shall seem expedient to Council that the appointment of a new professor should be suspended, the dividends accruing during the period for which such appointment shall be suspended shall be invested in augmentation of the capital fund.

§ **42.** *Litchfield Trust for Clinical Instruction*

1. The trust fund created by the will of George Henry, Earl of Litchfield, shall be transferred to, and henceforth stand in the corporate name of the University. The income from this trust fund, together with any accumulations thereof, shall be applied in or towards providing Clinical Instruction in Oxford for members of the University, such instruction to be given by a clinical professor, or by one or more clinical lecturer or lecturers. The qualifications and mode of appointment of any clinical professor or lecturer, the tenure and duties of the

office, the conditions on which instruction shall be given, and all other matters respecting the office which it may be expedient to regulate by decree, may be regulated by or under decrees of the University made from time to time.

2. (*a*) The annual income of the Litchfield Endowment shall be applied to the provision of clinical lectures for members of the University and the instruction given in these lectures shall be such as will be of profit to clinical students as well as to advanced students in that field.

(*b*) The Board of the Faculty of Clinical Medicine shall appoint one or more lecturers annually who shall be persons of distinction in some branch of clinical medicine and shall be known as Litchfield Lecturers.

(*c*) The board shall specify at the time of appointment the number of lectures which it requires from each lecturer.

(*d*) A Litchfield lecturer shall receive a fee and expenses which shall be determined in each case by the Board of the Faculty of Clinical Medicine, having regard to the income of the endowment for the time being.

(*e*) The Nuffield Professor of Surgery[1] shall hold the title of Litchfield Lecturer in Surgery, but shall not receive any emoluments as Litchfield Lecturer in addition to the stipend he or she receives as Nuffield Professor of Surgery, or be required to deliver any lectures in addition to those he or she is required to deliver as Nuffield Professor of Surgery.

(*f*) The Board of the Faculty of Clinical Medicine shall apply any surplus in the fund either to provide, on such terms as the board may think fit, clinical lectures other than those given by the Litchfield Lecturers or to augment the capital of the fund.

§ 43. *Rhodes Lecturer in Commonwealth Studies*

The Rhodes Lecturer in Commonwealth Studies shall lecture and give instruction in Commonwealth Studies. The lecturer shall be elected, and shall hold the appointment, on such conditions and with such duties as the General Board shall from time to time determine.

§ 44. *Professor of Computing*

1. The Professor of Computing shall lecture and give instruction in Computation.

2. The professor shall be elected by an electoral board consisting of:

(1) the Vice-Chancellor, or, if the President of Wolfson College is Vice-Chancellor, a person appointed by Council on the occurrence of a vacancy to act as an elector on that occasion;

(2) the President of Wolfson College, or, if the President is unable or unwilling to act, a person appointed by the Governing Body of Wolfson College on the occurrence of a vacancy to act as an elector on that occasion;

[1] See § 303, below.

(3) a person appointed by the Governing Body of Wolfson College;

(4) a person appointed by Council;

(5), (6) two persons appointed by the General Board;

(7)–(9) three persons elected by the Board of the Faculty of Mathematical Sciences, in consultation with the Sub-faculty of Computation.

3. The professor shall be subject to the General Provisions of the decree concerning the duties of professors and to those Particular Provisions of the same decree which are applicable to this chair.

§ **45.** *Professor of Computing Science*

1. The Professor of Computing Science shall lecture and give instruction in Computing Science.

2. The professor shall be elected by an electoral board consisting of:

(1) the Vice-Chancellor, or, if the Principal of St Hilda's College is Vice-Chancellor, a person appointed by Council on the occurrence of a vacancy to act as an elector on that occasion;

(2) the Principal of St Hilda's College, or, if the Principal is unable or unwilling to act, a person appointed by the Governing Body of St Hilda's College on the occurrence of a vacancy to act as an elector on that occasion;

(3) a person appointed by the Governing Body of St Hilda's College;

(4) a person appointed by Council;

(5), (6) two persons appointed by the General Board;

(7), (8) two persons appointed by the Board of the Faculty of Mathematical Sciences;

(9) one person appointed by the Board of the Faculty of Physical Sciences.

3. The professor shall be subject to the General Provisions of the decree concerning the duties of professors and to those Particular Provisions of the same decree which are applicable to this chair.

§ **46.** *Reader in Chemical Crystallography*[1]

1. There shall be a Reader in Chemical Crystallography who shall be elected by a board consisting of:

(1) the Vice-Chancellor;

(2) the Professor of Inorganic Chemistry;

(3) a person appointed by Council;

(4) a person appointed by the General Board;

(5)–(7) three persons appointed by the Board of the Faculty of Physical Sciences.

[1] See Appendix B to Ch. VII, below.

2. The Reader shall engage in advanced study or research and shall, under the general direction of the Professor of Inorganic Chemistry lecture and give instruction in Chemical Crystallography in every term.

§ 51. *Lecturer (or Reader) in Diplomatic*

1. There shall be a Lecturer in Diplomatic who shall be elected by a board consisting of:

(1) the Vice-Chancellor;

(2) the Regius Professor of Modern History;

(3) the Chichele Professor of Medieval History;

(4) the Regius Professor of Ecclesiastical History;

(5)–(7) three persons appointed by the Board of the Faculty of Modern History.

2. The General Board may from time to time determine, on the recommendation of the Board of the Faculty of Modern History, that the lecturer shall be designated Reader in Diplomatic.

3. The lecturer (or reader) shall lecture and give instruction on such conditions and with such duties as the General Board shall from time to time determine.

§ 52. *Lady Margaret Professor of Divinity*

1. The Lady Margaret Professor of Divinity, who must be in Priest's Orders in the Church of England or in an Episcopal Church in communion with the Church of England, shall either expound some portion of the Holy Scriptures or discuss questions pertaining to the study of Theology.

2. The professor shall be elected by an electoral board consisting of:

(1) the Vice-Chancellor, or, if the Dean of Christ Church is Vice-Chancellor, a person appointed by Council on the occurrence of a vacancy to act as an elector on that occasion;

(2) the Dean of Christ Church, or, if the Dean is unable or unwilling to act, a person appointed by the Governing Body of Christ Church on the occurrence of a vacancy to act as an elector on that occasion;

(3) a person appointed by the Governing Body of Christ Church;

(4), (5) two persons appointed by Council, one of whom shall be appointed after consultation with Christ Church;

(6) a person appointed by the General Board;

(7)–(9) three persons elected by the Board of the Faculty of Theology.

3. The professor shall be subject to the General Provisions of the decree concerning the duties of professors and to those Particular Provisions of the same decree which are applicable to this chair.

§ 53. *Regius Professor of Divinity*

1. The Regius Professor of Divinity shall either expound some portion of the Holy Scriptures or discuss questions pertaining to the study of Theology.

2. The professor shall be subject to the General Provisions of the decree concerning the duties of professors and to those Particular Provisions of the same decree which are applicable to this chair.

§ 54. *Ruskin Master of Drawing*

1. The Ruskin Master of Drawing (who shall be regarded as a reader for the purposes of any statute or decree) shall have charge of the premises assigned to the Ruskin School of Drawing and Fine Art, and shall make provision for the lighting, warming, water supply, and cleansing of the premises and, subject to the supervision of the Committee for the Ruskin School of Drawing and Fine Art, shall be responsible for ensuring the efficient working of the Ruskin School in term and vacation.

2. The Ruskin Master shall appoint the staff of the Ruskin School of Drawing and Fine Art, and prescribe their duties and conditions of service, other than those appointed under the provisions of Ch. III, Sect. LXV, cl. 4, provided that all appointments shall be subject to the provisions of any statute, decree, or regulation of general application

3. The Ruskin Master shall lecture and give instruction in drawing and other aspects of Fine Art on such conditions and with such other duties as the General Board shall from time to time determine. Subject to the supervision of the Committee for the Ruskin School of Drawing and Fine Art, he or she shall be responsible for the teaching and other necessary arrangements for the Degree of Bachelor of Fine Art, and for the general instruction in Fine Art of members of the University.

4. The Ruskin Master shall be appointed by an electoral board consisting of:

(1) the Vice-Chancellor;

(2) one person appointed by Council;

(3) one person appointed by the General Board;

(4), (5) two persons appointed by the Committee for the Ruskin School of Drawing and Fine Art;

(6) one person appointed by the Visitors of the Ashmolean Museum;

(7) one person appointed by the Committee for the History of Art.

5. The interest on the capital sum accepted by the University from the late John Ruskin under the Deed of Declaration of Trust 1875 for the endowment of a Mastership of Drawing shall be used towards defraying the stipend of the Ruskin Master.

§ 61. *Professor of Economics*

1. The Professor of Economics shall lecture and give instruction in economics.

2. The professor shall be elected by an electoral board consisting of:

(1) the Vice-Chancellor, or if the Warden of Nuffield College is Vice-Chancellor, a person appointed by Council on the occurrence of a vacancy to act as an elector on that occasion;

(2) the Warden of Nuffield College, or, if the Warden is unable or unwilling to act, a person appointed by the Governing Body of Nuffield College on the occurrence of a vacancy to act as an elector on that occasion;

(3) a person appointed by the Governing Body of Nuffield College;

(4) a person appointed by Council;

(5) a person appointed by the General Board;

(6), (7) two persons appointed by the Board of the Faculty of Social Studies.

3. The professor shall be subject to the General Provisions of the decree concerning the duties of professors and to those Particular Provisions of the same decree which are applicable to this chair.

§ 62. *Edgeworth Professor of Economics*

1. The Edgeworth Professor of Economics shall lecture and give instruction in economics with special reference to economic theory.

2. The professor shall be elected by an electoral board consisting of:

(1) the Vice-Chancellor, or, if the Warden of Nuffield College is Vice-Chancellor, a person appointed by Council on the occurrence of a vacancy to act as an elector on that occasion;

(2) the Warden of Nuffield College, or, if the Warden is unable or unwilling to act, a person appointed by the Governing Body of Nuffield College, on the occurrence of a vacancy to act as an elector on that occasion;

(3) a person appointed by the Governing Body of Nuffield College;

(4) a person appointed by Council;

(5), (6) two persons appointed by the General Board;

(7)–(9) three persons appointed by the Board of the Faculty of Social Studies.

3. The professor shall be subject to the General Provisions of the decree concerning the duties of professors and to those Particular Provisions of the same decree which are applicable to this chair.

§ 63. *Hicks Professor of Economics*

1. The Sir John Hicks Professor of Economics shall lecture and give instruction in economics.

2. The professor shall be elected by an electoral board consisting of:

(1) the Vice-Chancellor, or, if the head of the college specified in (2) of this clause is Vice-Chancellor, a person appointed by Council;

(2) the head of the college to which the professorship shall be for the time being allocated by Council under any decree in that behalf, or, if the head is unable or unwilling to act, a person appointed by the governing body of the college;

(3) a person appointed by the governing body of the college specified in (2) of this clause;

(4) a person appointed by Council;

(5), (6) two persons appointed by the General Board;

(7)–(9) three persons appointed by the Board of the Faculty of Social Studies.

3. The professor shall be subject to the General Provisions of the decree concerning the duties of professors and to those Particular Provisions of the same decree which are applicable to this chair.

§ 64. *Nuffield Reader in International Economics*

1. The Nuffield Reader in International Economics shall lecture and give instruction in International Economics on such conditions and with such duties as the General Board shall from time to time determine.

2. The reader shall be elected by a board consisting of:

(1) the Vice-Chancellor, or, if the Warden of Nuffield College is Vice-Chancellor, a person appointed by Council on the occurrence of a vacancy to act as an elector on that occasion;

(2) the Drummond Professor of Political Economy;

(3) the Warden of Nuffield College, or, if the Warden is unable or unwilling to act, a person appointed by the governing body on the occurrence of a vacancy to act as an elector on that occasion;

(4) a person appointed by the Governing Body of Nuffield College;

(5) a person appointed by Council;

(6), (7) two persons elected by the Board of the Faculty of Social Studies.

§ 65. *Reader in Educational Studies*

1. There shall be a Reader in Educational Studies who shall be elected by a board consisting of:

(1) the Vice-Chancellor, or, if the head of the college specified in (2) of this clause is Vice-Chancellor, a person appointed by Council;

(2) the head of the college with which the readership shall be for the time being associated by Council under any decree in that behalf, or, if the head is unable or unwilling to act, a person appointed by the governing body of the college;

(3) a person appointed by the governing body of the college specified in (2) of this clause;

(4) a person appointed by Council;

(5)–(6) two persons appointed by the General Board;

(7)–(9) three persons appointed by the Committee for Educational Studies.

2. The Reader shall engage in advanced study or research and shall, under the general direction of the Committee for Educational Studies,

(*a*) give instruction in every term in Educational Studies; and (*b*) take part in the supervision of research in the Department of Educational Studies.

§ **66.** *Professor of Egyptology*

1. The Professor of Egyptology shall lecture and give instruction on the History, Antiquities, and Language of Ancient Egypt.

2. The professor shall be elected by an electoral board consisting of:

(1) the Vice-Chancellor, or, if the Provost of Queen's College is Vice-Chancellor, a person appointed by Council on the occurrence of a vacancy to act as an elector on that occasion;

(2) the Provost of Queen's College, or, if the Provost is unable or unwilling to act, a person appointed by the Governing Body of Queen's College on the occurrence of a vacancy to act as an elector on that occasion;

(3) a person appointed by the Governing Body of Queen's College;

(4) a person appointed by Council;

(5)–(7) three persons appointed by the Board of the Faculty of Oriental Studies.

3. The professor shall be subject to the General Provisions of the decree concerning the duties of professors and to those Particular Provisions of the same decree which are applicable to this chair.

§ **67.** *Pollock Professor of Chemical Engineering*

1. The Donald Pollock Professor of Chemical Engineering shall lecture and give instruction in Chemical Engineering.

2. The professor shall be elected by an electoral board consisting of:

(1) the Vice-Chancellor, or, if the head of the college specified in (2) of this clause is Vice-Chancellor, a person appointed by Council;

(2) the head of the college to which the professorship shall be for the time being allocated by Council under any decree in that behalf, or, if the head is unable or unwilling to act, a person appointed by the governing body of the college;

(3) a person appointed by the governing body of the college specified in (2) of this clause;

(4) a person appointed by Council;

(5), (6) two persons appointed by the General Board;

(7)–(9) three persons appointed by the Board of the Faculty of Physical Sciences.

3. The professor shall be subject to the General Provisions of the decree concerning the duties of professors and to those Particular Provisions of the same decree which are applicable to this chair.

4. The annual sum received from the endowment provided by Dr. Donald Pollock shall be used towards defraying the professor's stipend.

§ **68.** *Professor of Civil Engineering*

1. The Professor of Civil Engineering shall lecture and give instruction in Civil Engineering.

2. The professor shall be elected by an electoral board consisting of:

(1) the Vice-Chancellor, or, if the head of the college specified in (2) of this clause is Vice-Chancellor, a person appointed by Council on the occurrence of a vacancy to act as an elector on that occasion;

(2) the head of the college to which the professorship shall be for the time being allocated by the Council under any decree in that behalf, or, if the head is unable or unwilling to act, a person appointed by the governing body of the college on the occurrence of a vacancy to act as an elector on that occasion;

(3) a person appointed by the governing body of the college specified in (2) of this clause;

(4) a person appointed by Council;

(5) a person appointed by the General Board;

(6)–(9) four persons elected by the Board of the Faculty of Physical Sciences.

3. The professor shall be subject to the General Provisions of the decree concerning the duties of professors and to those Particular Provisions of the same decree which are applicable to this chair.

§ **69.** *Professor of Electrical and Electronic Engineering*

1. The Professor of Electrical and Electronic Engineering shall lecture and give instruction in Electrical and Electronic Engineering.

2. The professor shall be elected by an electoral board consisting of:

(1) the Vice-Chancellor, or, if the President of St. John's College is Vice-Chancellor, a person appointed by Council on the occurrence of a vacancy to act as an elector on that occasion;

(2) the President of St. John's College, or, if the President is unable or unwilling to act, a person appointed by the Governing Body of St. John's College on the occurrence of a vacancy to act as an elector on that occasion;

(3) a person appointed by the Governing Body of St John's College;

(4) a person appointed by Council;

(5), (6) two persons appointed by the General Board;

(7)–(9) three persons appointed by the Board of the Faculty of Physical Sciences.

3. The professor shall be subject to the General Provisions of the decree concerning the duties of professors and to the Particular Provisions of the same decree applicable to the professors enumerated in Schedule A annexed thereto.

§ **70.** *Professor of Optoelectronic Engineering*

1. The Professor of Optoelectronic Engineering shall lecture and give instruction in Optoelectronic Engineering.

2. The professor shall be elected by an electoral board consisting of:

(1) the Vice-Chancellor, or, if the head of the college specified in (2) of this clause is Vice-Chancellor, a person appointed by Council;

(2) the head of the college to which the professorship shall be for the time being allocated by Council under any decree in that behalf, or, if the head is unable or unwilling to act, a person appointed by the governing body of the college;

(3) a person appointed by the governing body of the college specified in (2) of this clause;

(4) a person appointed by Council;

(5), (6) two persons appointed by the General Board;

(7)-(9) three persons appointed by the Board of the Faculty of Physical Sciences.

3. The professor shall be subject to the General Provisions of the decree concerning the duties of professors and to those Particular Provisions of the same decree which are applicable to this chair.

§ 71. *BP Professor of Information Engineering*

1. The University accepts with deep gratitude funding from British Petroleum Company PLC to endow a BP Professorship of Information Engineering and for the provision of research support costs for the professor.

2. The BP Professor of Information Engineering shall lecture and give instruction in information engineering.

3. The professor shall be elected by an electoral board consisting of:

(1) the Vice-Chancellor, or, if the Warden of Keble College is Vice-Chancellor, a person appointed by Council on the occurrence of a vacancy to act as an elector on that occasion;

(2) the Warden of Keble College, or, if the Warden is unable or unwilling to act, a person appointed by the Governing Body of Keble College on the occurrence of a vacancy to act as an elector on that occasion;

(3) a person appointed by the Governing Body of Keble College;

(4), (5) two persons appointed by Council, one of whom shall be appointed after consultation with BP;

(6) a person appointed by the General Board;

(7)–(10) four persons appointed by the Board of the Faculty of Physical Sciences.

4. The professor shall be subject to the General Provisions of the decree concerning the duties of professors and to the Particular Provisions of the same decree applicable to the professors enumerated in Schedule A annexed thereto.

5. Any part of the income of the endowment which is not required to meet the cost of the professorship may be expended, under conditions to be determined by the General Board, to support the research of the professor.

§ 72. *Professor of Mechanical Engineering*

1. The Professor of Mechanical Engineering shall lecture and give instruction in Mechanical Engineering.

2. The professor shall be elected by an electoral board consisting of:

(1) the Vice-Chancellor, or, if the head of the college specified in (2) of this clause is Vice-Chancellor, a person appointed by Council on the occurrence of a vacancy to act as an elector on that occasion;

(2) the head of the college to which the professorship shall be for the time being allocated by Council under any decree in that behalf, or if the head is unable or unwilling to act, a person appointed by the governing body of that college on the occurrence of a vacancy to act as an elector on that occasion;

(3) a person appointed by the governing body of the college specified in (2) of this clause;

(4) a person appointed by Council;

(5) a person appointed by the General Board;

(6)–(9) four persons appointed by the Board of the Faculty of Physical Sciences.

3. The professor shall be subject to the General Provisions of the decree concerning the duties of professors and to the Particular Provisions of the same decree which are applicable to this chair.

§ 73. *Merton Professor of English Language*

1. The Merton Professor of English Language shall lecture and give instruction in the history and structure of the English Language with special reference to the language of literature.

2. The professor shall be elected by an electoral board consisting of:

(1) the Vice-Chancellor, or, if the Warden of Merton College is Vice-Chancellor, a person appointed by Council on the occurrence of a vacancy to act as an elector on that occasion;

(2) the Warden of Merton College, or, if the Warden is unable or unwilling to act, a person appointed by the Governing Body of Merton College on the occurrence of a vacancy to act as an elector on that occasion;

(3) a person appointed by the Governing Body of Merton College;

(4) a person appointed by Council;

(5) a person appointed by the General Board;

(6), (7) two persons elected by the Board of the Faculty of English Language and Literature;

(8) a person elected by the Board of the Faculty of Medieval and Modern Languages.

3. The professor shall be subject to the General Provisions of the decree concerning the duties of professors and to those Particular Provisions of the same decree which are applicable to this chair.

§ **74.** *Goldsmiths' Professor of English Literature*

1. The Goldsmiths' Professor of English Literature shall lecture and give instruction in the history of English Literature during and since the period of Chaucer, on the works of English authors, and on the principles of literary criticism.

2. The professor shall be elected by an electoral board consisting of:

(1) the Vice-Chancellor, or, if the Warden of New College is Vice-Chancellor, a person appointed by Council on the occurrence of a vacancy to act as an elector on that occasion;

(2) the Warden of New College, or, if the Warden of New College is unable or unwilling to act, a person appointed by the Governing Body of New College on the occurrence of a vacancy to act as an elector on that occasion;

(3) a person appointed by the Governing Body of New College;

(4) a person appointed by Council;

(5), (6) two persons appointed by the General Board;

(7)–(9) three persons appointed by the Board of the Faculty of English Language and Literature.

3. The professor shall be subject to the General Provisions of the decree concerning the duties of professors and to those Particular Provisions of the same decree which are applicable to this chair.

4. The income derived from the capital sum provided for the establishment of a Goldsmiths' Readership in English shall be applied towards the maintenance of the Goldsmiths' Professorship of English Literature.

§ **75.** *Merton Professor of English Literature*

1. The Merton Professor of English Literature shall lecture and give instruction in the history of English Literature during and since the period of Chaucer, on the works of English authors, and on the principles of literary criticism.

2. The professor shall be elected by an electoral board consisting of:

(1) the Vice-Chancellor, or, if the Warden of Merton College is Vice-Chancellor, a person appointed by Council on the occurrence of a vacancy to act as an elector on that occasion;

(2) the Warden of Merton College, or, if the Warden is unable or unwilling to act, a person appointed by the Governing Body of Merton College on the occurrence of a vacancy to act as an elector on that occasion;

(3) a person appointed by the Governing Body of Merton College;

(4) a person appointed by Council;

(5), (6) two persons appointed by the Board of the Faculty of English Language and Literature;

(7) a person elected by the Board of the Faculty of Literae Humaniores.

3. The professor shall be subject to the General Provisions of the decree concerning the duties of professors and to those Particular Provisions of the same decree which are applicable to this chair.

§ 76. *Tolkien Professor of English Literature and Language*

1. The J. R. R. Tolkien Professor of English Literature and Language shall lecture and give instruction in Middle English Literature and Language.

2. The professor shall be elected by an electoral board consisting of:

(1) the Vice-Chancellor, or, if the head of the college specified in (2) of this clause is Vice-Chancellor, a person appointed by Council on the occurrence of a vacancy to act as an elector on that occasion;

(2) the head of the college to which the professorship shall be for the time being allocated by Council, or, if the head is unable or unwilling to act, a person appointed by the governing body of the college on the occurrence of a vacancy to act as an elector on that occasion;

(3) a person appointed by the governing body of the college specified in (2) of this clause;

(4) a person appointed by Council;

(5), (6) two persons appointed by the General Board;

(7)–(9) three persons appointed by the Board of the Faculty of English Language and Literature.

3. The professor shall be subject to the General Provisions of the decree concerning the duties of professors and to those Particular Provisions of the same decree which are applicable to the professors enumerated in Schedule A annexed thereto.

§ 77. *Warton Professor of English Literature*

1. The Thomas Warton Professor of English Literature shall lecture and give instruction on the works of authors who have written in the English Language since the age of Chaucer, on the history of literature in English since that period, and on the principles of literary criticism.

2. The professor shall be elected by an electoral board consisting of:

(1) the Vice-Chancellor, or, if the Master of St. Catherine's College is Vice-Chancellor, a person appointed by Council on the occurrence of a vacancy to act as an elector on that occasion;

(2) the Master of St. Catherine's College, or, if the Master is unable or unwilling to act, a person appointed by the Governing Body of St. Catherine's College on the occurrence of a vacancy to act as an elector on that occasion;

(3) a person appointed by the Governing Body of St. Catherine's College;

(4) a person appointed by Council;

(5) a person appointed by the General Board;

(6), (7) two persons appointed by the Board of the Faculty of English Language and Literature.

3. The professor shall be subject to the General Provisions of the decree concerning the duties of professors and to those Particular Provisions of the same decree which are applicable to this chair.

§ 78. *All Souls (G. M. Young) Lecturer in Nineteenth- and Twentieth-century English Literature*

1. There shall be an All Souls (G. M. Young) Lecturer in Nineteenth- and Twentieth-century English Literature.

2. The lecturer shall be appointed by an electoral board consisting of:

(1) the Vice-Chancellor, or, if the Warden of All Souls College is Vice-Chancellor, a person appointed by Council on the occurrence of a vacancy to act for the Warden on that occasion;

(2) the Warden of All Souls College, or, if the Warden is unable or unwilling to act, a person appointed by the Governing Body of All Souls College on the occurrence of a vacancy to act for him or her on that occasion;

(3)–(5) three persons appointed by the Board of the Faculty of English Language and Literature;

(6) a person appointed by the governing body of the college with which the General Board has agreed that the lecturership shall on that occasion be associated.

3. The lecturer shall lecture and give instruction in Nineteenth- and Twentieth-century English Literature on such conditions and with such duties as the General Board shall from time to time determine.

§ 81. *Curator of the Fielding Herbarium*

There shall be a Curator of the Fielding Herbarium who shall be appointed by the Fielding Curators, who shall also have power to dismiss the curator.

The curator shall be under the direct control of the Sherardian Professor of Botany. He or she shall take charge of the Fielding Herbarium and of other similar collections belonging to the University, and shall supervise the Botanical Library.

The curator shall receive by way of stipend the income derived from the sum of £900 bequeathed to the University by Mrs. Fielding. The Fielding Curators shall have power to increase the stipend of the Curator of the Fielding Herbarium, on the recommendation of the Sherardian Professor of Botany out of the funds at their disposal.

APPENDIX TO § 81

FIELDING HERBARIUM

See *Statuta*, 1914, p. 517.

§ **82.** *Professor of French Literature*

1. The Professor of French Literature shall lecture and give instruction in French Literature and shall promote generally the study of that subject in the University.

2. The professor shall be elected by an electoral board consisting of:

(1) the Vice-Chancellor, or, if the head of the college specified in (2) of this clause is Vice-Chancellor, a person appointed by Council on the occurrence of a vacancy to act as an elector on that occasion;

(2) the head of the college to which the professorship shall be for the time being allocated by Council under any decree in that behalf, or, if the head is unable or unwilling to act, a person appointed by the governing body of the college on the occurrence of a vacancy to act as an elector on that occasion;

(3) a person appointed by the governing body of the college specified in (2) of this clause;

(4) a person appointed by Council;

(5), (6) two persons appointed by the General Board;

(7)–(9) three persons elected by the Board of the Faculty of Medieval and Modern Languages.

3. The professor shall be subject to the General Provisions of the decree concerning the duties of professors and to those Particular Provisions of the same decree which are applicable to this chair.

§ **83.** *Marshal Foch Professor of French Literature*

1. The Marshal Foch Professor of French Literature shall lecture and give instruction in French Literature and shall promote generally the study of that subject in the University.

2. The professor shall be elected by an electoral board consisting of:

(1) the Vice-Chancellor, or, if the head of the college specified in (4) of this clause is Vice-Chancellor, a person appointed by Council on the occurrence of a vacancy to act as an elector on that occasion;

(2), (3) two persons appointed by the Council of the University of Paris;

(4) the head of the college to which the professorship shall be for the time being allocated by Council under any decree in that behalf, or, if the head is unable or unwilling to act, a person appointed by the governing body of the college on the occurrence of a vacancy to act as an elector on that occasion;

(5) a person appointed by the governing body of the college specified in (4) of this clause;

(6) a person appointed by Council;

(7) a person appointed by the General Board;

(8), (9) two persons elected by the Board of the Faculty of Medieval and Modern Languages.

3. The professor shall be subject to the General Provisions of the decree concerning the duties of professors and to those Particular Provisions of the same decree which are applicable to this chair.

§ 84. *University Lecturer in French Philology and Old French Literature*

1. The University Lecturer in French Philology and Old French Literature shall lecture and give instruction in French Philology and Old French Literature under the direction of the Board of the Faculty of Medieval and Modern Languages.

2. The lecturer shall be appointed by the Board of the Faculty of Medieval and Modern Languages in accordance with the provisions of Ch. VII, Sect. IV, § 3.

§ 90. *Professor of General Practice*

1. The Professor of General Practice shall engage in advanced study and research and shall lecture and give instruction in Primary Health Care.

2. The professor shall be elected by an electoral board consisting of:

(1) the Vice-Chancellor, or, if the head of the college specified in (2) of this clause is Vice-Chancellor, a person appointed by Council;

(2) the head of the college to which the professorship shall be for the time being allocated by Council under any decree in that behalf, or, if the head is unable or unwilling to act, a person appointed by the governing body of the college;

(3) a person appointed by the governing body of the college specified in (2) of this clause;

(4) a person appointed by Council;

(5)–(7) three persons appointed by the General Board;

(8), (9) two persons appointed by the Board of the Faculty of Clinical Medicine;

(10) a person holding a clinical appointment appointed by the Oxfordshire Health Authority.

At least three members of the board, of whom one shall be a professor, shall hold clinical appointments.

3. The professor shall hold qualifications entitling him or her to be registered with the General Medical Council as a medical practitioner.

4. The professor shall be subject to the General Provisions of the decree concerning the duties of professors and to those Particular Provisions of the same decree which are applicable to this chair.

§ 91. *Professor of Genetics*

1. The Professor of Genetics shall lecture and give instruction in Genetics.

2. The professor shall be elected by an electoral board consisting of:

(1) the Vice-Chancellor, or, if the head of the college specified in (2) of this clause is Vice-Chancellor, a person appointed by Council on the occurrence of a vacancy to act as an elector on that occasion;

(2) the head of the college to which the professorship shall be for the time being allocated by Council under any decree in that behalf, or, if the head is unable or unwilling to act, a person appointed by the governing body of the college on the occurrence of a vacancy to act as an elector on that occasion;

(3) a person appointed by the governing body of the college specified in (2) of this clause;

(4), (5) two persons appointed by Council;

(6) a person appointed by the General Board;

(7)–(9) three persons appointed by the Board of the Faculty of Biological Sciences.

3. The professor shall be subject to the General Provisions of the decree concerning the duties of professors, and to those Particular Provisions of the same decree which are applicable to this chair.

§ 92. *Reader in Geodesy*

1. There shall be a Reader in Geodesy.

2. The reader shall be elected by a board consisting of:

(1) the Vice-Chancellor;

(2) a person appointed by Council;

(3) a person appointed by the General Board;

(4)–(7) four persons elected by the Board of the Faculty of Physical Sciences;

(8) a person elected by the Board of the Faculty of Anthropology and Geography.

3. The reader shall engage in advanced study or research and shall lecture or hold classes in Michaelmas, Hilary, and Trinity Terms as required by the Departments of Engineering Science, Geography, and Earth Sciences.

§ 93. *Professor of Geography*

1. The Professor of Geography shall lecture and give instruction in Geography.

2. The professor shall be elected by an electoral board consisting of:

(1) the Vice-Chancellor, or, if the Principal of Hertford College is Vice-Chancellor, a person appointed by Council on the occurrence of a vacancy to act as an elector on that occasion;

(2) the Principal of Hertford College, or, if the Principal is unable or unwilling to act, a person appointed by the Governing Body of Hertford College on the occurrence of a vacancy to act as an elector on that occasion;

(3) a person appointed by the Governing Body of Hertford College;

(4) a person appointed by Council;

(5) a person appointed by the General Board;

(6), (7) two persons appointed by the Board of the Faculty of Anthropology and Geography.

3. The professor shall be subject to the General Provisions of the decree concerning the duties of professors and to those Particular Provisions of the same decree which are applicable to this chair.

§ 94. *Halford Mackinder Professor of Geography*

1. The Halford Mackinder Professor of Geography shall lecture and give instruction in Geography.

2. The professor shall be elected by an electoral board consisting of:

(1) the Vice-Chancellor, or, if the Master of St. Peter's College is Vice-Chancellor, a person appointed by Council on the occurrence of a vacancy to act as an elector on that occasion;

(2) the Master of St. Peter's College, or, if the Master is unable or unwilling to act, a person appointed by the Governing Body of St. Peter's College on the occurrence of a vacancy to act as an elector on that occasion;

(3) a person appointed by the Governing Body of St. Peter's College;

(4) a person appointed by Council;

(5) a person appointed by the General Board;

(6), (7) two persons appointed by the Board of the Faculty of Anthropology and Geography.

3. The professor shall be subject to the General Provisions of the decree concerning the duties of professors and to those Particular Provisions of the same decree which are applicable to this chair.

§ 95. *Professor of Geology*

1. The Professor of Geology shall lecture and give instruction in Geology.

2. The professor shall be elected by an electoral board consisting of:

(1) the Vice-Chancellor, or, if the Master of University College is Vice-Chancellor, a person appointed by Council on the occurrence of a vacancy to act as an elector on that occasion;

(2) the Master of University College, or, if the Master is unable or unwilling to act, a person appointed by the Governing Body of University College on the occurrence of a vacancy to act as an elector on that occasion;

(3) a person appointed by the Governing Body of University College;

(4) a person appointed by Council;

(5) a person appointed by the General Board;

(6)–(8) three persons elected by the Board of the Faculty of Physical Sciences;

(9) a person elected by the Board of the Faculty of Biological Sciences.

3. The professor shall be subject to the General Provisions of the decree concerning the duties of professors and to those Particular Provisions of the same decree which are applicable to this chair.

§ 96. *Savilian Professor of Geometry*

1. The Savilian Professor of Geometry shall lecture and give instruction in Geometry or some other branch of Pure Mathematics.

2. The professor shall be elected by an electoral board consisting of:

(1) the Vice-Chancellor, or, if the Warden of New College is Vice-Chancellor, a person appointed by Council on the occurrence of a vacancy to act as an elector on that occasion;

(2) the Warden of New College, or, if the Warden is unable or unwilling to act, a person appointed by the Governing Body of New College on the occurrence of a vacancy to act as an elector on that occasion;

(3) a person appointed by the Governing Body of New College;

(4) a person appointed by Council;

(5), (6) two persons appointed by the General Board;

(7)–(9) three persons elected by the Board of the Faculty of Mathematical Sciences.

3. The professor shall be subject to the General Provisions of the decree concerning the duties of professors and to those Particular Provisions of the same decree which are applicable to this chair.

§ 97. *Taylor Professor of the German Language and Literature*

1. The Taylor Professor of the German Language and Literature shall lecture and give instruction in the history and literature of the German language.

2. The professor shall be elected by an electoral board consisting of:

(1) the Vice-Chancellor, or, if the head of the college specified in (2) of this clause is Vice-Chancellor, a person appointed by Council on the occurrence of a vacancy to act as an elector on that occasion;

(2) the head of the college to which the professorship shall be for the time being allocated by Council under any decree in that behalf, or, if the head is unable or unwilling to act, a person appointed by the governing body of the college on the occurrence of a vacancy to act as an elector on that occasion;

(3) a person appointed by the governing body of the college specified in (2) of this clause;

(4) a person appointed by Council;

(5) a person appointed by the General Board;

(6), (7) two persons elected by the Board of the Faculty of Medieval and Modern Languages.

3. The professor shall be subject to the General Provisions of the decree concerning the duties of professors and to those Particular Provisions of the same decree which are applicable to this chair.

§ **98.** *Professor of German Medieval and Linguistic Studies*

1. The Professor of German Medieval and Linguistic Studies shall lecture and give instruction in German Medieval and Linguistic Studies or in some branch of these studies, and shall promote generally the study of the subject in the University.

2. The professor shall be elected by an electoral board consisting of:

(1) the Vice-Chancellor, or, if the Principal of St. Edmund Hall is Vice-Chancellor, a person appointed by Council on the occurrence of a vacancy to act as an elector on that occasion;

(2) the Principal of St. Edmund Hall, or, if the Principal is unable or unwilling to act, a person appointed by the Governing Body of St. Edmund Hall on the occurrence of a vacancy to act as an elector on that occasion;

(3) a person appointed by the Governing Body of St. Edmund Hall;

(4) a person appointed by Council;

(5) a person appointed by the General Board;

(6)-(8) three persons elected by the Board of the Faculty of Medieval and Modern Languages.

3. The professor shall be subject to the General Provisions of the decree concerning the duties of professors and to those Particular Provisions of the same decree which are applicable to this chair.

§ **99.** *Gladstone Professor of Government*

1. The Gladstone Professor of Government shall lecture and give instruction in empirical politics, and shall promote generally the study of that subject in the University.

2. The professor shall be elected by an electoral board consisting of:

(1) the Vice-Chancellor, or, if the Warden of All Souls College is Vice-Chancellor, a person appointed by Council on the occurrence of a vacancy to act as an elector on that occasion;

(2) the Warden of All Souls College, or, if the Warden is unable or unwilling to act, a person appointed by the Governing Body of All Souls College on the occurrence of a vacancy to act as an elector on that occasion;

(3) a person appointed by the Governing Body of All Souls College;

(4) a person appointed by Council;

(5), (6) two persons appointed by the General Board;

(7), (8) two persons elected by the Board of the Faculty of Social Studies;

(9) a person elected by the Sub-faculty of Politics.

3. The professor shall be subject to the General Provisions of the decree concerning the duties of professors and to those Particular Provisions of the same decree which are applicable to this chair.

§ 100. *Mellon Professor of American Government*

1. The Andrew W. Mellon Professor of American Government shall lecture and give instruction in American Government.

2. The professor shall be elected by an electoral board consisting of:

(1) the Vice-Chancellor, or, if the Warden of Nuffield College is Vice-Chancellor, a person appointed by Council on the occurrence of a vacancy to act as an elector on that occasion;

(2) the Warden of Nuffield College, or, if the Warden is unable or unwilling to act, a person appointed by the Government Body of Nuffield College on the occurrence of a vacancy to act as an elector on that occasion;

(3) a person appointed by the Governing Body of Nuffield College;

(4) a person appointed by Council;

(5) a person appointed by the General Board;

(6)–(7) two persons appointed by the Board of the Faculty of Social Studies.

3. The professor shall be subject to the General Provisions of the decree concerning the duties of professors and to those Particular Provisions of the same decree which are applicable to this chair.

4. Any part of the income of the endowment of the professorship which is not required to meet the costs (including support costs) thereof may be expended, under conditions to be determined from time to time by the Board of the Faculty of Social Studies, on the promotion of research in American Government through such means as fellowship, travel grants, and other appropriate research support.

§ 101. *Lecturer in the Government of New States*

1. There shall be a Lecturer in the Government of New States who shall be elected by a board consisting of:

(1) the Vice-Chancellor;

(2) the Beit Professor of the History of the British Commonwealth;

(3) the Director of Queen Elizabeth House;

(4) a person appointed by Council;

(5) a person appointed by the Board of the Faculty of Social Studies;

(6), (7) two persons appointed by the Inter-faculty Committee for Queen Elizabeth House.

2. The lecturer shall under the direction of the Inter-faculty Committee for Queen Elizabeth House lecture and give instruction on the Government of New States.

§ 102. *Regius Professor of Greek*

1. The Regius Professor of Greek shall lecture and give instruction in the history and criticism of the Greek Language and Literature and on the works of classical Greek authors.

2. The professor shall be subject to the General Provisions of the decree concerning the duties of professors and to those Particular Provisions of the same decree which are applicable to this chair.

§ 103. *Bywater and Sotheby Professor of Byzantine and Modern Greek Language and Literature*

1. The Bywater and Sotheby Professor of Byzantine and Modern Greek Language and Literature shall lecture and give instruction in Byzantine and Modern Greek Language and Literature.

2. The professor shall be elected by an electoral board consisting of:

(1) the Vice-Chancellor, or, if the head of the college specified in (2) of this clause is Vice-Chancellor, a person appointed by Council on the occurrence of a vacancy to act as an elector on that occasion;

(2) the head of the college to which the professorship shall be for the time being allocated by Council under any decree in that behalf, or, if the head is unable or unwilling to act, a person appointed by the governing body of the college on the occurrence of a vacancy to act as an elector on that occasion;

(3) a person appointed by the governing body of the college specified in (2) of this clause;

(4) a person appointed by Council;

(5) a person elected by the Board of the Faculty of Theology;

(6) a person elected by the Board of the Faculty of Literae Humaniores;

(7) a person elected by the Board of the Faculty of Modern History;

(8), (9) two persons elected by the Board of the Faculty of Medieval and Modern Languages.

3. The professor shall be subject to the General Provisions of the decree concerning the duties of professors and to those Particular Provisions of the same decree which are applicable to this chair.

§ 104. *Grinfield Lecturer*

1. The lecture shall be on the LXX version of the Hebrew Scriptures, its history, its philological character, its bearing on the criticisms of the New Testament, and its value as an evidence of the authenticity of the Old and New Testaments.

2. The lecture shall be given three times in each academic year, after due notice, in such place as the Vice-Chancellor shall appoint, and shall be open, without fee, to all members of the University.

3. The lecture shall be delivered by a person to be elected for two years who may be re-elected for further periods of two years. The lecturer shall always enter upon this office at the beginning of Michaelmas Term and shall receive from the trust fund such annual stipend (payable on completion of the lectures for the year in question) and such expenses as the board of electors shall

determine. The person elected shall not be considered as a public university professor or reader.

4. The person who shall deliver this lecture shall be elected by a board of electors consisting of:

(1) the Vice-Chancellor;

(2), (3) two persons appointed by Council;

(4), (5) two persons appointed by the Board of the Faculty of Theology;

(6), (7) two persons appointed by the Board of the Faculty of Oriental Studies.

5. The board of electors may apply any surplus income and balance on the fund to the furtherance of Septuagint Studies within the University, subject to the provisions of clause 6 below.

6. This decree may, but with the consent of the founder during his life, be amended from time to time; so nevertheless, that the main object of the founder, namely the promotion of the study of the LXX version, and, through this, the just interpretation of the New Testament, shall be in no wise set aside.

§ 111. *Regius Professor of Hebrew*

1. The Regius Professor of Hebrew shall lecture and give instruction in Hebrew language and literature.

2. The professor shall be subject to the General Provisions of the decree concerning the duties of professors and to those Particular Provisions of the same decree which are applicable to this chair.

3. The professorship shall not be annexed to a canonry at Christ Church but shall be allocated by Council, to such college as it shall, subject to the provisions of Sect. II, above, from time to time determine.

§ 112. *Cowley Lecturer in Post-Biblical Hebrew*

[1]

1. The Cowley Lecturer shall lecture and give instruction, under the direction of the Board of the Faculty of Oriental Studies, in Post-Biblical and Modern Hebrew.

2. The lecturer shall be appointed by the Board of the Faculty of Oriental Studies in accordance with arrangements approved by the General Board from time to time.

3. The income of the Cowley Memorial Fund shall be used towards defraying the stipend of the lecturer.

[2]

Cowley Memorial Fund

1. The fund shall be called the Cowley Memorial Fund, and the Curators of the University Chest shall be empowered to accept further donations in augmentation of the capital.

2. The lecturership supported by the fund shall be called the Cowley Lecturership in Post-Biblical Hebrew.

3. The annual income of the fund, after payment of any expenses incurred in administration, shall be applied in providing a stipend for the Cowley Lecturer in Post-Biblical Hebrew.

4. During any vacancy in the lecturership, the net income accruing during the vacancy shall be applied in augmentation of the capital of the fund.

§ 113. *Harmsworth Professor of American History*

1. The Harold Vyvyan Harmsworth Professor of American History shall lecture and give instruction in the History of the United States of America.

2. The professor shall be at the time of election a citizen of the United States of America.

3. The professor shall hold office for not less than one nor more than five years, as the electors may determine, but shall be re-eligible.

4. The professor shall be elected by an electoral board consisting of:

(1) the Chancellor of the University of Oxford (provided always that the Chancellor may appoint the Vice-Chancellor to act for him or her);

(2) the Ambassador from the United States of America to the Court of St. James at the time of election, or a deputy appointed by the Ambassador to act from time to time;

(3) a person appointed by Council;

(4) Viscount Rothermere for his life, and thereafter each successive holder of the Viscountcy or an elector appointed by him as his representative at the election; but if the Viscountcy should have become extinct or the holder thereof be a minor or otherwise disqualified from acting as an elector or appointing a representative, then the Lord Chief Justice of England shall be the fourth elector;

(5), (6) two persons appointed by the governing body of the college to which the professorship shall be for the time being allocated by Council under any decree in that behalf;

(7) a person appointed by the Board of the Faculty of Modern History.

5. The professor shall be subject to the General Provisions of the decree concerning the duties of professors and to those Particular Provisions of the same decree as to residence which are applicable to this chair. He or she shall give not less than thirty-six lectures or classes in the year, provided that this obligation may be reduced in exceptional circumstances with the approval of the faculty board concerned and of the General Board.

§ 114. *Rhodes Professor of American History*

1. The Rhodes Professor of American History shall lecture and give instruction in the History of the United States of America.

2. The professor shall be elected by a board of electors consisting of:

(1) the Vice-Chancellor, or, if the head of the college specified in (2) of this clause is Vice-Chancellor, a person appointed by Council on the occurrence of a vacancy to act as an elector on that occasion;

(2) the head of the college to which the professorship shall be for the time being allocated by Council under any decree in that behalf or, if the head is unable or unwilling to act, a person appointed by the governing body of the college on the occurrence of a vacancy to act as an elector on that occasion;

(3) a person appointed by the governing body of the college specified in (2) of this clause;

(4) a person appointed by Council;

(5) a person appointed by the General Board;

(6) a person appointed by the Board of the Faculty of Modern History;

(7) a person appointed by the Board of the Faculty of Social Studies.

3. The professor shall be subject to the General Provisions of the decree concerning the duties of professors and to those Particular Provisions of the same decree which are applicable to this chair.

§ 115. *Camden Professor of Ancient History*

1. The Camden Professor of Ancient History shall lecture and give instruction in some part or parts of Ancient History, but especially in Roman History.

2. The professor shall be elected by a board of electors consisting of:

(1) the Vice-Chancellor, or, if the Principal of Brasenose College is Vice-Chancellor, a person appointed by Council on the occurrence of a vacancy to act as an elector on that occasion;

(2) the Principal of Brasenose College, or, if the Principal is unable or unwilling to act, a person appointed by the Governing Body of Brasenose College on the occurrence of a vacancy to act as an elector on that occasion;

(3) a person appointed by the Governing Body of Brasenose College;

(4) a person appointed by Council;

(5) a person elected by the Board of the Faculty of Literae Humaniores;

(6) a person elected by the Sub-faculty of Ancient History, or, if there be no such sub-faculty, then by the Faculty of Literae Humaniores;

(7) a person elected by the Board of the Faculty of Modern History.

3. The professor shall be subject to the General Provisions of the decree concerning the duties of professors and to those Particular Provisions of the same decree which are applicable to this chair.

§ 116. *Wykeham Professor of Ancient History*

1. The Wykeham Professor of Ancient History shall lecture and give instruction in some part or parts of Ancient History, but especially in the Ancient History of Greece and the Greek lands.

2. The professor shall be elected by an electoral board consisting of:

(1) the Vice-Chancellor, or, if the Warden of New College is Vice-Chancellor, a person appointed by Council on the occurrence of a vacancy to act as an elector on that occasion;

(2) the Warden of New College, or, if the Warden is unable or unwilling to act, a person appointed by the Governing Body of New College on the occurrence of a vacancy to act as an elector on that occasion;

(3) a person appointed by the Governing Body of New College;

(4) a person appointed by Council;

(5), (6) two persons appointed by the General Board;

(7) a person elected by the Board of the Faculty of Literae Humaniores;

(8) a person elected by the Sub-faculty of Ancient History, or, if there be no such sub-faculty, then by the Faculty of Literae Humaniores;

(9) a person elected by the Board of the Faculty of Modern History.

3. The professor shall be subject to the General Provisions of the decree concerning the duties of professors and to those Particular Provisions of the same decree which are applicable to this chair.

§ 117. *Professor of the History of Art*

1. The Professor of the History of Art shall lecture and give instruction in the History of Art.

2. The professor shall be elected by an electoral board consisting of:

(1) the Vice-Chancellor, or, if the head of the college specified in (2) of this clause is Vice-Chancellor, a person appointed by Council on the occurrence of a vacancy to act as an elector on that occasion;

(2) the head of the college to which the professorship shall be for the time being allocated by Council under any decree in that behalf, or, if the head is unable or unwilling to act, a person appointed by the governing body of the college on the occurrence of a vacancy to act as an elector on that occasion;

(3) a person appointed by the governing body of the college specified in (2) of this clause;

(4) a person appointed by Council;

(5) a person appointed by the General Board;

(6) a person elected by the Board of the Faculty of Modern History;

(7) a person elected by the Board of the Faculty of Medieval and Modern Languages

(8) a person elected by the Committee for the History of Art;

(9) a person elected by the Committee for the Ruskin School of Drawing and Fine Art.

3. The professor shall be subject to the General Provisions of the decree concerning the duties of professors and to those Particular Provisions of the same decree which are applicable to this chair.

§ 118. *Beit Lecturer in the History of the British Commonwealth*

1. The Beit Lecturer shall lecture and give instruction in the history of the Commonwealth countries over the seas.

2. The lecturer shall be appointed by the Board of the Faculty of Modern History in accordance with the provisions of Ch. VII, Sect. IV, § 3.

§ 119. *Regius Professor of Ecclesiastical History*

1. The Regius Professor of Ecclesiastical History shall lecture and give instruction in Ecclesiastical History and in the Writings of the Fathers or of later theologians in the Christian Church.

2. The professor shall be subject to the General Provisions of the decree concerning the duties of professors and to those Particular Provisions of the same decree which are applicable to this chair.

§ 120. *Chichele Professor of Economic History*

1. The Chichele Professor of Economic History shall lecture and give instruction in Economic History.

2. The professor shall be elected by an electoral board consisting of:

(1) the Vice-Chancellor, or, if the Warden of All Souls College is Vice-Chancellor, a person appointed by Council on the occurrence of a vacancy to act as an elector on that occasion;

(2) the Warden of All Souls College, or, if the Warden is unable or unwilling to act, a person appointed by the Governing Body of All Souls College on the occurrence of a vacancy to act as an elector on that occasion;

(3) a person appointed by the Governing Body of All Souls College;

(4) a person appointed by Council;

(5), (6) two persons appointed by the General Board;

(7) a person elected by the Board of the Faculty of Modern History;

(8) a person elected by the Board of the Faculty of Social Studies;

(9) a person elected by the Board of the Faculty of Modern History after consultation with the Board of the Faculty of Social Studies.

3. The professor shall be subject to the General Provisions of the decree concerning the duties of professors and to those Particular Provisions of the same decree which are applicable to this chair.

§ 121. *Reader in Economic History*

1. There shall be a Reader in Economic History who shall be elected by a board consisting of:

(1) the Vice-Chancellor, or, if the head of the college specified in (2) of this clause is Vice-Chancellor, a person appointed by Council;

(2) the head of the college with which the readership shall be for the time being associated, or, if the head is unable or unwilling to act, a person appointed by the governing body of the college;

(3) a person appointed by the governing body of the college specified in (2) of this clause;

(4) a person appointed by Council;

(5), (6) two persons appointed by the General Board;

(7) the Chichele Professor of Economic History;

(8) a person appointed by the Board of the Faculty of Modern History;

(9) a person appointed by the Board of the Faculty of Social Studies.

2. The reader shall lecture and give instruction in Economic History on such conditions and with such duties as the General Board shall from time to time determine.

§ 122. *Reader in Recent Social and Economic History*

1. The Reader in Recent Social and Economic History shall lecture and give instruction in Recent Social and Economic History on such conditions and with such duties as the General Board shall from time to time determine.

2. The reader shall be elected by a board consisting of:

(1) the Vice-Chancellor;

(2) the head of the college with which the readership shall be for the time being associated, or, if the head is unable or unwilling to act, a person appointed by the governing body of the college;

(3) a person appointed by the governing body of the college specified in (2) of this clause;

(4) the Chichele Professor of Economic History;

(5) a person appointed by Council;

(6) a person appointed by the General Board;

(7) a person appointed by the Board of the Faculty of Modern History;

(8), (9) two persons appointed by the Board of the Faculty of Social Studies.

§ 123. *Carroll Professor of Irish History*

1. The University accepts with gratitude the moneys offered by the Carroll Foundation to endow a Carroll Professorship of Irish History.

2. The Carroll Professor of Irish History shall lecture and give instruction in the History and Culture of Ireland within the general period covered by the School of Modern History.

3. The professor shall be elected by an electoral board consisting of:

(1) the Vice-Chancellor, or, if the head of the college specified in (2) of this clause is Vice-Chancellor, a person appointed by Council on the occurrence of a vacancy to act as an elector on that occasion;

(2) the head of the college to which the professorship shall be allocated by Council under any decree in that behalf, or, if the head is unable or unwilling to act, a person appointed by the governing body of the college on the occurrence of a vacancy to act as an elector on that occasion;

(3) a person appointed by the governing body of the college specified in (2) of this clause;

(4), (5) two persons appointed by Council, one of whom shall be appointed after consultation with the Carroll Foundation;

(6) a person appointed by the General Board;

(7), (8) two persons appointed by the Board of the Faculty of Modern History.

4. The professor shall be subject to the General Provisions of the decree concerning the duties of professors and to those Particular Provisions of the same decree which are applicable to this chair.

§ 124. *Professor of the History of Latin America*

1. The Professor of the History of Latin America shall lecture and give instruction in the History of Latin America.

2. The professor shall be elected by a board of electors consisting of:

(1) the Vice-Chancellor, or, if the head of the college specified in (2) of this clause is Vice-Chancellor, a person appointed by Council on the occurrence of a vacancy to act as an elector on that occasion;

(2) the head of the college to which the professorship shall be for the time being allocated by Council under any decree in that behalf or, if the head is unable or unwilling to act, a person appointed by the governing body of the college on the occurrence of a vacancy to act as an elector on that occasion;

(3) a person appointed by the governing body of the college specified in (2) of this clause;

(4) a person appointed by Council;

(5), (6) two persons appointed by the Board of the Faculty of Modern History;

(7) a person appointed by the General Board.

3. The professor shall be subject to the General Provisions of the decree concerning the duties of professors and to those Particular Provisions of the same decree which are applicable to this chair.

§ 125. *Chichele Professor of Medieval History*

1. The Chichele Professor of Medieval History shall lecture and give instruction in some part or parts of Medieval History.

2. The professor shall be elected by an electoral board consisting of:

(1) the Vice-Chancellor, or, if the Warden of All Souls College is Vice-Chancellor, a person appointed by Council on the occurrence of a vacancy to act as an elector on that occasion;

(2) the Warden of All Souls College, or, if the Warden is unable or unwilling to act, a person appointed by the Governing Body of All Souls College on the occurrence of a vacancy to act as an elector on that occasion;

(3) a person appointed by the Governing Body of All Souls College;

(4) a person appointed by Council;

(5), (6) two persons elected by the Board of the Faculty of Modern History;

(7) a person elected by the Board of the Faculty of Literae Humaniores.

3. The professor shall be subject to the General Provisions of the decree concerning the duties of professors and to those Particular Provisions of the same decree which are applicable to this chair.

§ 126. *Regius Professor of Modern History*

1. The Regius Professor of Modern History shall lecture and give instruction in some part or parts of Modern History.

2. The professor shall be subject to the General Provisions of the decree concerning the duties of professors and to those Particular Provisions of the same decree which are applicable to this chair.

§ 127. *Professor of Modern History*

1. The Professor of Modern History shall lecture and give instruction in Modern History from 1500 onwards.

2. The professor shall be elected by an electoral board consisting of:

(1) the Vice-Chancellor, or, if the head of the college specified in (2) of this clause is Vice-Chancellor, a person appointed by Council on the occurrence of a vacancy to act as an elector on that occasion;

(2) the head of the college to which the professorship shall be for the time being allocated by Council under any decree in that behalf, or, if the head is unable or unwilling to act, a person appointed by the governing body of the college on the occurrence of a vacancy to act as an elector on that occasion;

(3) a person appointed by the governing body of the college specified in (2) of this clause;

(4) a person appointed by Council;

(5) a person appointed by the General Board;

(6), (7) two persons elected by the Board of the Faculty of Modern History.

3. The professor shall be subject to the General Provisions of the decree concerning the duties of professors and to those Particular Provisions of the same decree which are applicable to this chair.

§ 128. *Reader in Modern South Asian History*

1. There shall be a Reader in Modern South Asian History who shall be elected from time to time by a board consisting of:

(1) the Vice-Chancellor;

(2) a person appointed by Council;

(3) a person elected by the General Board;

(4) a person elected by the Board of the Faculty of Oriental Studies;

(5)–(7) three persons elected by the Board of the Faculty of Modern History.

2. The reader shall lecture and give instruction on the history of South Asia from 1700 onwards.

§ **129.** *Professor of the History of Philosophy*

1. The Professor of the History of Philosophy shall lecture and give instruction in the History of Philosophy including Ancient Philosophy.

2. The professor shall be elected by a board of electors consisting of:

(1) the Vice-Chancellor, or, if the head of the college specified in (2) of this clause is Vice-Chancellor, a person appointed by Council on the occurrence of a vacancy to act as an elector on that occasion;

(2) the head of the college to which the professorship shall be for the time being allocated by Council under any decree in that behalf, or, if the head is unable or unwilling to act, a person appointed by the governing body of the college on the occurrence of a vacancy to act as an elector on that occasion;

(3) a person appointed by the governing body of the college specified in (2) of this clause;

(4) a person appointed by Council;

(5), (6) two persons appointed by the Board of the Faculty of Literae Humaniores;

(7) a person appointed by the Sub-faculty of Philosophy.

3. The professor shall be subject to the General Provisions of the decree concerning the duties of professors and to those Particular Provisions of the same decree which are applicable to this chair.

§ **130.** *Professor of the History of Science*

1. The Professor of the History of Science shall lecture and give instruction in the History of Science.

2. The professor shall be elected by an electoral board consisting of:

(1) the Vice-Chancellor, or, if the Principal of Linacre College is Vice-Chancellor, a person appointed by Council on the occurrence of a vacancy to act as an elector on that occasion;

(2) the Principal of Linacre College, or, if the Principal is unable or unwilling to act, a person appointed by the Governing Body of Linacre College on the occurrence of a vacancy to act as an elector on that occasion;

(3) a person appointed by the Governing Body of Linacre College;

(4) a person appointed by Council;

(5) a person appointed by the General Board;

(6), (7) two persons appointed by the Board of the Faculty of Modern History;

(8) a person appointed by the Board of the Faculty of Physical Sciences;

(9) a person appointed by the Board of the Faculty of Biological Sciences.

3. The professor shall be subject to the General Provisions of the decree concerning the duties of professors and to the Particular Provisions of the same decree applicable to the professors enumerated in Schedule A annexed thereto.

§ 131. *Chichele Professor of the History of War*

1. The Chichele Professor of the History of War shall lecture and give instruction in the History of War.

2. The professor shall be elected by an electoral board consisting of:

(1) the Vice-Chancellor, or, if the Warden of All Souls College is Vice-Chancellor, a person appointed by Council on the occurrence of a vacancy to act as an elector on that occasion;

(2) the Commandant for the time being of the Royal College of Defence Studies;

(3) the Warden of All Souls College, or, if the Warden is unable or unwilling to act, a person appointed by the Governing Body of All Souls College on the occurrence of a vacancy to act as an elector on that occasion;

(4) a person appointed by the Governing Body of All Souls College;

(5) a person appointed by Council;

(6), (7) two persons elected by the Board of the Faculty of Modern History;

(8) one person elected by the Board of the Faculty of Social Studies.

3. Notwithstanding the provisions of Sect. I, § 2, cl. 3:

(i) Council may from time to time, if in the opinion of the electors no suitably qualified person is available, suspend the filling of a vacancy in the professorship for such period not exceeding five years, as it may think fit;

(ii) if any such suspension is approved, the electors may appoint a Reader or Lecturer in the History of War on such conditions in regard to stipend and tenure as Council may determine after consultation with the General Board: provided always that the period of office for which such reader or lecturer is appointed shall not exceed the approved period of suspension of the professorship.

4. The professor shall be subject to the General Provisions of the decree concerning the duties of professors and to those Particular Provisions of the same decree which are applicable to this chair.

§ 132. *Dean Ireland's Professor of the Exegesis of Holy Scripture*

1. The Dean Ireland's Professor of the Exegesis of Holy Scripture shall lecture and give instruction in the Exegesis of the New Testament Scriptures.

2. The professor shall be elected by an electoral board consisting of:

(1) the Vice-Chancellor, or, if the Provost of Queen's College is Vice-Chancellor, a person appointed by Council on the occurrence of a vacancy to act as an elector on that occasion;

(2) the Provost of Queen's College, or, if the Provost should be unable or unwilling to act, a person appointed by the Governing Body of Queen's College on the occurrence of a vacancy to act as an elector on that occasion;

(3) a person appointed by the Governing Body of Queen's College;

(4) a person appointed by Council;

(5) a person appointed by the General Board;

(6), (7) two persons appointed by the Board of the Faculty of Theology.

3. The professor shall be subject to the General Provisions of the decree concerning the duties of professors and to those Particular Provisions of the same decree which are applicable to this chair.

§ 133. *Oriel and Laing Professor of the Interpretation of Holy Scripture*

1. The Oriel and Laing Professor of the Interpretation of Holy Scripture shall lecture and give instruction in the Interpretation of the Old Testament Scriptures.

2. The professor shall be elected by an electoral board consisting of:

(1) the Vice-Chancellor, or, if the Provost of Oriel is Vice-Chancellor, a person appointed by Council on the occurrence of a vacancy to act as an elector on that occasion;

(2) the Provost of Oriel College, or, if the Provost is unable or unwilling to act, a person appointed by the Governing Body of Oriel College on the occurrence of a vacancy to act as an elector on that occasion;

(3) a person appointed by the Governing Body of Oriel College;

(4) a person appointed by Council;

(5) a person appointed by the General Board;

(6), (7) two persons elected by the Board of the Faculty of Theology.

3. The professor shall be subject to the General Provisions of the decree concerning the duties of professors and to those Particular Provisions of the same decree which are applicable to this chair.

§ 141. *Vigfusson Rausing Reader in Ancient Icelandic Literature and Antiquities*

1. The University accepts with deep gratitude the benefaction from Dr. Gad Rausing towards the further endowment of the Readership in Ancient Icelandic Literature and Antiquities, which is partly supported from the income of the fund bequeathed by Dr. G. H. Fowler, and which shall henceforth be known as the Vigfusson Rausing Readership in Ancient Icelandic Literature and Antiquities.

2. The reader shall engage in advanced study or research and shall lecture and give instruction in Ancient Icelandic Literature and Antiquities on such

conditions and with such duties as the General Board shall from time to time determine.

3. The reader shall be elected by an electoral board consisting of:

(1) the Vice-Chancellor;

(2) a person appointed by Council;

(3) a person appointed by the General Board;

(4)–(7) four persons appointed by the Board of the Faculty of English Language and Literature.

4. Council shall have power to alter this decree from time to time, provided always that the object of the two donors, namely to support and endow a readership in Ancient Icelandic Literature and Antiquities bearing the names of Vigfusson and Rausing, shall be kept in view.

§ 142. *Pearson Professor of International Relations*

1. The Lester B. Pearson Professor of International Relations shall engage in advanced study and research and shall lecture and give instruction in International Relations on such conditions and with such duties as the General Board shall from time to time determine.

2. The professor shall be elected by an electoral board consisting of:

(1) the Vice-Chancellor;

(2) the head of the college to which the professorship shall be for the time being allocated by Council under any decree in that behalf, or, if the head is unable or unwilling to act, a person appointed by the governing body of the college;

(3) the Montague Burton Professor of International Relations;

(4) a person appointed by the governing body of the college specified in (2) of this clause;

(5), (6) two persons appointed by Council, one of whom shall be appointed after consultation with the University of Dalhousie;

(7) a person appointed by the General Board;

(8), (9) two persons appointed by the Board of the Faculty of Social Studies.

3. The professor shall be subject to the General Provisions of the decree concerning the duties of professors and to those Particular Provisions of the same decree which are applicable to this chair.

§ 143. *Buchan Reader in International Relations*

1. The University accepts with deep gratitude the covenanted and other moneys known as the Alastair Buchan Appeal Fund and held on behalf of the Oxford Committee for the appeal, together with any moneys subscribed to the fund in future, to be applied to the support of study, teaching, and research in International Relations in the University in memory of the Hon. Alastair Francis Buchan, C.B.E., M.A., sometime Montague Burton Professor of International Relations.

2. To this end the fund shall be employed to establish an Alastair Buchan Readership in International Relations: provided that the income derived from £5,000 of the fund shall be placed at the discretion of the Board of the Faculty of Social Studies for expenditure on the subsidiary purposes of the appeal, as defined in cl. 5 below.

3. The reader shall engage in advanced study or research and shall lecture and give instruction in International Relations on such conditions and with such duties as the General Board shall from time to time determine.

4. The reader shall be elected by an electoral board consisting of:

(1) the Vice-Chancellor;

(2) a person appointed by Council;

(3) a person appointed by the General Board;

(4)–(6) three persons appointed by the Board of the Faculty of Social Studies;

(7) a person appointed by the Board of the Faculty of Modern History.

5. The subsidiary purposes of the fund are: to finance short term visits by outstanding exponents and practitioners in the field of International Relations and to facilitate longer visits; to provide facilities for research in the subject (including travel) and to attract research projects; to provide graduate scholarships in the subject; to advance the study of International Relations generally.

6. This decree may at any time be altered by Council provided always that the main purpose of the appeal, the support of study, teaching, and research in International Relations in the University in memory of Professor Buchan shall be observed.

§ 144. *University Lecturer in Islamic Art and Architecture*

1. This University accepts with deep gratitude from anonymous benefactors an endowment fund of £310,000 and any further sums which may be provided for the establishment of a University Lecturership in Islamic Art and Architecture and the promotion of the study of that subject in the University.

2. The University Lecturer in Islamic Art and Architecture shall lecture and give instruction in Islamic Art and Architecture under the direction of the Board of the Faculty of Oriental Studies.

3. The lecturer shall be appointed by the Board of the Faculty of Oriental Studies in accordance with the provisions of Ch. VII, Sect. IV, § 3.

4. Such part of the endowment as the General Board shall determine is not required to meet the costs of the lecturership shall be applied to the promotion of the study of Islamic Art and Architecture in such manner as the Board of the Faculty of Oriental Studies, with the approval of the General Board, shall from time to time determine.

5. Council shall have power to amend this decree, provided that the main object of the endowment, as set out in cl. 1 hereof, shall always be observed.

§ **145.** *Shamma Lecturer and Assistant Keeper in Islamic Numismatics*

1. The University accepts with deep gratitude from Mr. Samir Shamma a sum for the endowment of a University Lecturership in Islamic Numismatics, to be named the Samir Shamma Lecturership in Islamic Numismatics.

2. The University Lecturer in Islamic Numismatics shall lecture and give instruction in Islamic Numismatics under the direction of the Board of the Faculty of Oriental Studies. He or she shall also hold a post of Assistant Keeper in the Heberden Coin Room of the Ashmolean Museum.

3. The lecturer shall be appointed jointly by the Board of the Faculty of Oriental Studies and the Visitors of the Ashmolean Museum, in accordance with the provisions of Sect. IV, § 3 of this chapter. The provisions of Ch. III, Sect. XI, § 4, cl. 1 concerning Assistant Keepers in the Ashmolean Museum shall also apply to this appointment.

4. The first charge on the net income of the endowment shall be the salary and associated costs of the lecturer. The second charge shall be the provision, under such arrangements as the Board of the Faculty of Oriental Studies may from time to time determine, of support, including teaching materials and research expenses, for the lecturer.

5. Any income unspent in any year on the first and second charges as defined in clause 4 above, whether in consequence of a vacancy in the lecturership or for any other reason, shall, at the discretion of the Board of the Faculty of Oriental Studies, either be carried forward for expenditure in a subsequent year or be spent in any way or ways conducive to the advancement within the University of teaching, scholarship, and research in Islamic Numismatics.

6. Council shall have the power to amend this decree from time to time, provided always that the maintenance of the Samir Shamma University Lecturership in Islamic Numismatics shall remain the first charge on the income of the endowment.

§ **146.** *Fiat-Serena Professor of Italian Studies*

1. The Fiat-Serena Professor of Italian Studies shall lecture and give instruction in the subjects of this chair and shall promote generally the study of Italian in the University.

2. The professor shall be elected by an electoral board consisting of:

(1) the Vice-Chancellor, or, if the head of the college specified in (2) of this clause is Vice-Chancellor, a person appointed by Council on the occurrence of a vacancy to act as an elector on that occasion;

(2) the head of the college to which the professorship shall be for the time being allocated by Council under any decree in that behalf, or, if the head is unable or unwilling to act, a person appointed by the governing body of the college on the occurrence of a vacancy to act as an elector on that occasion;

(3) a person appointed by the governing body of the college specified in (2) of this clause;

(4) a person appointed by Council;

(5) a person appointed by the General Board;

(6) a person elected by the Board of the Faculty of Literae Humaniores;

(7) a person elected by the Board of the Faculty of Modern History;

(8), (9) two persons elected by the Board of the Faculty of Medieval and Modern Languages.

3. The professor shall be subject to the General Provisions of the decree concerning the duties of professors and to those Particular Provisions of the same decree which are applicable to this chair.

§ 151. *Nissan Professor of Modern Japanese Studies*

1. The Nissan Professor of Modern Japanese Studies shall lecture and give instruction in the history and the social and economic development of Japan since the middle of the nineteenth century.

2. The professor shall be elected by an electoral board consisting of:

(1) the Vice-Chancellor, or, if the Warden of St. Antony's College is Vice-Chancellor, a person appointed by Council on the occurrence of a vacancy to act as an elector on that occasion;

(2) the Warden of St. Antony's College, or, if the Warden is unable or unwilling to act, a person appointed by the Governing Body of St. Antony's College on the occurrence of a vacancy to act as an elector on that occasion;

(3) a person appointed by the Governing Body of St. Antony's College;

(4) a person appointed by Council;

(5) a person appointed by the General Board;

(6), (7) two persons appointed by the Board of the Faculty of Modern History;

(8) a person appointed by the Board of the Faculty of Oriental Studies;

(9) a person appointed by the Board of the Faculty of Social Studies.

3. The professors shall be subject to the General Provisions of the decree concerning the duties of professors and to those Particular Provisions of the same decree which are applicable to this chair.

§ 152. *Lector in Japanese Studies*

The balance of the sums generously contributed between 1964 and 1979 by Shell International Petroleum Company Limited, Mitsubishi Bank, Mitsubishi Trading Company, Mitsubishi Petrochemical Company, Mitsui Bank, and other companies for the establishment of a Lectorship in Japanese Studies and the development and furtherance of the aims of the lectorship, and any further sums which may be contributed for these purposes, shall be applied under the direction of the Board of the Faculty of Oriental Studies for lectorial purposes in Japanese Studies.

§ 153. *Reader in Jewish Studies*

1. The Reader in Jewish Studies shall engage in advanced study or research and shall lecture and give instruction in the literature, history, social life, and religion of the Jews from 200 B.C. to A.D. 1500.

2. The reader shall be appointed by an electoral board consisting of:

(1) the Vice-Chancellor;

(2) a person elected by Council;

(3) a person elected by the General Board;

(4) a person elected by the Board of the Faculty of Theology;

(5) a person elected by the Board of the Faculty of Literae Humaniores;

(6) a person elected by the Board of the Faculty of Modern History;

(7), (8) two persons elected by the Board of the Faculty of Oriental Studies.

§ 154. *Professor of Jurisprudence*

1. The Professor of Jurisprudence shall lecture and give instruction in Jurisprudence.

2. The professor shall be elected by an electoral board consisting of:

(1) the Vice-Chancellor, or, if the head of the college specified in (2) of this clause is Vice-Chancellor, a person appointed by Council on the occurrence of a vacancy to act as an elector on that occasion;

(2) the head of the college to which the professorship shall be for the time being allocated by Council under any decree in that behalf, or, if the head is unable or unwilling to act, a person appointed by the governing body of the college on the occurrence of a vacancy to act as an elector on that occasion;

(3) a person appointed by the governing body of the college specified in (2) of this clause;

(4) a person appointed by Council;

(5), (6) two persons appointed by the General Board;

(7)–(9) three persons appointed by the Board of the Faculty of Law.

3. The professor shall be subject to the General Provisions of the decree concerning the duties of professors and to those Particular Provisions of the same decree which are applicable to this chair.

§ 161. *Katrak Lecturer*

1. A lecturership shall be established and maintained in the University of Oxford to be called the 'Ratanbai Katrak Lecturership' and a lecturer shall be appointed and called the 'Ratanbai Katrak Lecturer'.

2. The sum of £1,000 Consolidated 2½% Stock and the stocks, funds, and securities for the time being representing the same and any addition made thereto by accumulation or otherwise shall form a fund to be called the 'Ratanbai Katrak Fund'. The capital thereof shall be invested in the corporate name of the University in trustee securities.

3. The purpose of the fund shall be to promote the study of the religion of Zoroaster and of its later developments from a theological, philological, and historical point of view. The lectures given should as far as possible throw new light on the subject treated.

4. A board of management shall be constituted consisting of:

(1) the Vice-Chancellor;

(2) Dr. Nanabhai Navrosji Katrak, the founder of the fund, during his lifetime;[1]

(3) the Regius Professor of Divinity;

(4) the Boden Professor of Sanskrit;

(5)–(8) four persons appointed for each election, two by the Board of the Faculty of Oriental Studies, and one each by the Board of the Faculty of Literae Humaniores and the Board of the Faculty of Theology. Three shall constitute a quorum.

5. Dr. N. N. Katrak and each of his successors during his tenure of office as a member of the board of management shall have power to nominate a representative to succeed him as a member of the board after his death or resignation. He shall have the name of such nominee registered with the University before his death or resignation. If a member fail so to nominate a successor and have his name registered, or if the nominee refuse to become a member of the board of management, this privilege shall cease and thenceforward no further representative of the donor shall be on the board of management.

6. At intervals of not more than ten years the board shall appoint a lecturer, who may be of any nationality, who shall give a course of not less than six lectures in the English language on some subject connected with the study of the religion of Zoroaster as defined in clause 3 above. They shall fix his or her stipend, which shall be not less than £125, and shall have power in addition to pay his or her travelling expenses, and any other incidental expenses if they think it desirable. In exceptional circumstances the board shall have power to appoint a lecturer after an interval of five years to give three or four lectures at a stipend of not less than £60.

7. Each lecturer shall deliver to the Vice-Chancellor his or her lectures or a verified copy thereof, which shall be retained in the Bodleian Library.

8. The copyright of the lectures shall be transferred to and vested in the University.

9. The board of management shall seek to secure the publication of the lectures, and shall be empowered to make contributions from the fund for this purpose.

10. A copy of the lectures, if printed and published, shall be presented by the University to such institutions as the board of management considers desirable.

[1] Dr. Katrak died on 9 October 1945.

11. If the travelling and other expenses of the lecturer should in any case prove to be greater than the fund can afford, the lecturer may, with the consent of the board, send the written lectures to the Registrar to be read before the University by someone appointed for the purpose by the Vice-Chancellor.

12. In any circumstances which they may consider exceptional the board of management shall have the power to offer a prize for an essay in lieu of the lecturership, such prize to be called the 'Ratanbai Katrak Prize' and the conditions to be such as to carry out the intention of the founder as expressed in clause 3 above; the essay shall become the property of the University and may be printed and published in the manner described in clauses 8 and 9 above.

13. Council shall have full power to alter this decree from time to time, provided that the foundation shall always bear the title of the 'Ratanbai Katrak Foundation' and that its main object be kept in view, namely the perpetuation of the memory of the founder's wife to be associated with the promotion of the study of the religion of Zoroaster, in the manner defined in clause 3 above, in the University of Oxford.

§ 171. *Rupert Murdoch Professor of Language and Communication*

1. The University accepts with deep gratitude the moneys offered by News International plc for the provision of a Rupert Murdoch Professorship of Language and Communication.

2. The Rupert Murdoch Professor of Language and Communication shall lecture and give instruction in Language and Communication.

3. The professor shall be elected by an electoral board consisting of:

(1) the Vice-Chancellor, or, if the Provost of Worcester College is Vice-Chancellor, a person appointed by Council on the occurrence of a vacancy to act as an elector on that occasion;

(2) the Provost of Worcester College, or, if the Provost is unable or unwilling to act, a person appointed by the Governing Body of Worcester College on the occurrence of a vacancy to act as an elector on that occasion;

(3) a person appointed by the Governing Body of Worcester College;

(4), (5) two persons appointed by Council, one of whom shall be appointed after consultation with News International plc;

(6) a person appointed by the General Board;

(7), (8) two persons appointed by the Board of the Faculty of English Language and Literature.

4. The professor shall be subject to the General Provisions of the decree concerning the duties of professors and to those Particular Provisions of the same decree which are applicable to this chair.

§ 172. *Corpus Christi Professor of the Latin Language and Literature*

1. The Corpus Christi Professor of the Latin Language and Literature shall lecture and give instruction on the history and criticism of classical Latin authors.

2. The professor shall be elected by an electoral board consisting of:

(1) the Vice-Chancellor, or, if the President of Corpus Christi College is Vice-Chancellor, a person appointed by Council on the occurrence of a vacancy to act as an elector on that occasion;

(2) the President of Corpus Christi College, or, if the President is unable or unwilling to act, a person appointed by the Governing Body of Corpus Christi College on the occurrence of a vacancy to act as an elector on that occasion;

(3) a person appointed by the Governing Body of Corpus Christi College;

(4) a person appointed by Council;

(5), (6) two persons elected by the Board of the Faculty of Literae Humaniores;

(7) a person elected by the Sub-faculty of Languages and Literature, or, if there be no such Sub-faculty, then by the Faculty of Literae Humaniores.

3. The professor shall be subject to the General Provisions of the decree concerning the duties of professors and to those Particular Provisions of the same decree which are applicable to this chair.

§ 173. *Regius Professor of Civil Law*

1. The Regius Professor of Civil Law shall lecture and give instruction in Roman Law, its principles and history, and in some branch or branches of Common Law.

2. The professor shall be subject to the General Provisions of the decree concerning the duties of professors and to those Particular Provisions of the same decree which are applicable to this chair.

§ 174. *Norton Rose Professor of Commercial and Financial Law*

1. The Norton Rose Professor of Commercial and Financial Law shall lecture and give instruction in Commercial and Financial Law.

2. The professor shall be elected by an electoral board consisting of:

(1) the Vice-Chancellor, or, if the head of the college specified in (2) of this clause is Vice-Chancellor, a person appointed by Council;

(2) the head of the college to which the Professorship shall be for the time being allocated by Council under any decree in that behalf, or, if the head is unable or unwilling to act, a person appointed by the governing body of the college;

(3) a person appointed by the governing body of the college specified in (2) of this clause;

(4) a person appointed by Council;

(5), (6) two persons appointed by the General Board;

(7)–(9) three persons appointed by the Board of the Faculty of Law.

3. The professor shall be subject to the General Provisions of the decree concerning the duties of professors and to those Particular Provisions of the same decree which are applicable to this chair.

§ 175. *Clifford Chance Professor of Comparative Law*

1. The Clifford Chance Professor of Comparative Law shall lecture and give instruction in the comparative study of different legal systems national or transnational.

2. The professor shall be elected by an electoral board consisting of:

(1) the Vice-Chancellor, or, if the head of the college specified in (2) of this clause is Vice-Chancellor, a person appointed by Council on the occurrence of a vacancy to act as an elector on that occasion;

(2) the Principal of Brasenose College, or, if the Principal of Brasenose College is unable or unwilling to act, a person appointed by the Governing Body of Brasenose College on the occurrence of a vacancy to act as an elector on that occasion;

(3) a person appointed by the Governing Body of Brasenose College;

(4) a person appointed by Council;

(5), (6) two persons appointed by the General Board;

(7)–(9) three persons appointed by the Board of the Faculty of Law.

3. The professor shall be subject to the General Provisions of the decree concerning the duties of professors and to those Particular Provisions of the same decree which are applicable to this chair.

§ 176. *Allen & Overy Professor of Corporate Law*

1. The University accepts with gratitude the moneys offered by the Allen & Overy Foundation for the provision of an Allen & Overy Professorship of Corporate Law.

2. The Allen & Overy Professor of Corporate Law shall lecture and give instruction in Corporate Law.

3. The professor shall be elected by an electoral board consisting of:

(1) the Vice-Chancellor, or, if the head of the college specified in (2) of this clause is Vice-Chancellor, a person appointed by Council on the occurrence of a vacancy to act as an elector on that occasion;

(2) the head of the college to which the professorship shall be allocated by Council under any decree in that behalf, or, if the head is unable or unwilling to act, a person appointed by the governing body of the college on the occurrence of a vacancy to act as an elector on that occasion;

(3) a person appointed by the governing body of the college specified in (2) of this clause;

(4), (5) two persons appointed by Council, one of whom shall be appointed after consultation with the Allen & Overy Foundation;

(6) a person appointed by the General Board;

(7), (8) two persons appointed by the Board of the Faculty of Law.

4. The professor shall be subject to the General Provisions of the decree concerning the duties of professors and to those Particular Provisions of the same decree which are applicable to this chair.

§ 177. *Professor of English Law*

1. The Professor of English Law shall deliver lectures and give instruction in English Law.

2. The professor shall be elected by an electoral board consisting of:

(1) the Vice-Chancellor, or, if the head of the college specified in (2) of this clause is Vice-Chancellor, a person appointed by Council on the occurrence of a vacancy to act as an elector on that occasion;

(2) the head of the college to which the professorship shall be for the time being allocated by Council under any decree in that behalf, or, if the head is unable or unwilling to act, a person appointed by the governing body of the college on the occurrence of a vacancy to act as an elector on that occasion;

(3) a person appointed by the governing body of the college specified in (2) of this clause;

(4) a person appointed by Council;

(5), (6) two persons appointed by the General Board;

(7)–(9) three persons appointed by the Board of the Faculty of Law.

3. The professor shall be subject to the General Provisions of the decree concerning the duties of professors and to those Particular Provisions of the same decree which are applicable to this chair.

§ 178. *Vinerian Professor of English Law*

1. The Vinerian Professor of English Law shall deliver lectures and give instruction in English Law.

2. The professor shall be elected by an electoral board consisting of:

(1) the Chancellor of the University (provided always that the Chancellor may appoint the Vice-Chancellor to act for him or her);

(2) the Warden of All Souls College, or, if the Warden is unable or unwilling to act, a person appointed by the Governing Body of All Souls College on the occurrence of a vacancy to act as an elector on that occasion;

(3) a person appointed by the Governing Body of All Souls College;

(4) a person appointed by Council;

(5), (6) two persons appointed by the General Board of the Faculties;

(7)–(9) three persons appointed by the Board of the Faculty of Law.

3. The professor shall be subject to the General Provisions of the decree concerning the duties of professors and to those Particular Provisions of the same decree which are applicable to this chair.

§ 179. *Professor of Law*

1. The Professor of Law shall lecture and give instruction in Law.

2. The professor shall be elected by an electoral board consisting of:

(1) the Vice-Chancellor, or, if the head of the college specified in (2) of this clause is Vice-Chancellor, a person appointed by Council;

(2) the head of the college to which the professorship shall be for the time being allocated by Council under any decree in that behalf, or, if the head is unable or unwilling to act, a person appointed by the governing body of the college;

(3) a person appointed by the governing body of the college specified in (2) of this clause;

(4) a person appointed by Council;

(5), (6) two persons appointed by the General Board;

(7)–(9) three persons appointed by the Board of the Faculty of Law.

3. The professor shall be subject to the General Provisions of the decree concerning the duties of professors and to those Particular Provisions of the same decree which are applicable to this chair.

§ 180. *Jacques Delors Professor of European Community Law*

1. The University accepts with gratitude from the European Commission funds towards the costs of the Jacques Delors Professorship of European Community Law.

2. The net income of the fund shall be applied to the cost of the professorship (including salary, National Insurance, and superannuation), and may also be applied to other costs associated with the professorship (including support costs).

3. The Board of the Faculty of Law shall be the board of management of the fund.

4. The Jacques Delors Professor of European Community Law shall deliver lectures and give instruction in European Community Law.

5. The professor shall be elected by an electoral board consisting of:

(1) the Vice-Chancellor, or, if the head of the college specified in (2) of this clause is Vice-Chancellor, a person appointed by Council;

(2) the head of the college to which the professorship shall be for the time being allocated by Council under any decree in that behalf, or, if the head is unable or unwilling to act, a person appointed by the governing body of the college;

(3) a person appointed by the governing body of the college specified in (2) of this clause;

(4) a person appointed by Council;

(5), (6) two persons appointed by the General Board;

(7)-(9) three persons appointed by the Board of the Faculty of Law.

6. The Professor shall be a member of the Centre for the Advanced Study of European and Comparative Law, and shall have the obligation to accept the directorship of the centre if requested to do so under the provisions of Ch. VII, Sect. I, § 5. B, cl. 5. The centre shall be a constituent centre of the Institute for European Studies, and the director of the centre shall be eligible for appointment as director of the institute under the provisions of Ch. III, Sect. XXXVI, cl. 4.

7. The Professor shall be subject to the General Provisions of the decree concerning the duties of professors and to those particular provisions of the same decree which are applicable to this chair.

8. This decree shall be subject to alteration from time to time by Council, provided that the object of the fund as defined in clause 1 above is always kept in view.

§ 181. *Reuters Professor of Intellectual Property and Information Technology Law*

1. The Reuters Professor of Intellectual Property and Information Technology Law shall deliver lectures and give instruction in Intellectual Property Law and related aspects of Information Technology Law.

2. The professor shall be elected by an electoral board consisting of:

(1) the Vice-Chancellor, or, if the head of the college specified in (2) of this clause is Vice-Chancellor, a person appointed by Council;

(2) the head of the college to which the professorship shall be for the time being allocated by Council under any decree in that behalf, or, if the head is unable or unwilling to act, a person appointed by the governing body of that college;

(3) a person appointed by the governing body of the college specified in (2) of this clause;

(4), (5) two persons appointed by Council, one of whom shall be appointed after consultation with the Reuter Foundation;

(6) a person appointed by the General Board;

(7)–(9) three persons appointed by the Board of the Faculty of Law.

3. The professor shall be a member of the Oxford Intellectual Property Research Centre and shall have the obligation to accept the directorship of the centre for the first five years of the appointment and thereafter for five-year periods (or such other periods as may be decided upon), if requested to do so by Council after consultation with the General Board, the Board of the Faculty of Law, and St Peter's College.

4. The professor shall be subject to the General Provisions of the decree concerning the duties of professors and to those particular provisions of the same decree which are applicable to this chair.

§ **182.** *Chichele Professor of Public International Law*

1. The Chichele Professor of Public International Law shall lecture and give instruction in Public International Law.

2. The professor shall be elected by an electoral board consisting of:

(1) the Vice-Chancellor, or, if the Warden of All Souls College is Vice-Chancellor, a person appointed by Council on the occurrence of a vacancy to act as an elector on that occasion;

(2) the Warden of All Souls College, or, if the Warden is unable or unwilling to act, a person appointed by the Governing Body of All Souls College on the occurrence of a vacancy to act as an elector on that occasion;

(3) a person appointed by the Governing Body of All Souls College;

(4) a person appointed by Council;

(5), (6) two persons appointed by the General Board;

(7)–(9) three persons appointed by the Board of the Faculty of Law.

3. The professor shall be subject to the General Provisions of the decree concerning the duties of professors and to those Particular Provisions of the same decree which are applicable to this chair.

§ **183.** *KPMG Professor of Taxation Law*

1. The University accepts with gratitude a benefaction from KPMG to establish the KPMG Professorship of Taxation Law.

2. The KPMG Professor of Taxation Law shall lecture and give instruction in Taxation Law.

3. The professor shall be elected by an electoral board consisting of:

(1) the Vice-Chancellor, or, of the head of the college specified in (2) of this clause is Vice-Chancellor, a person appointed by Council;

(2) the head of the college to which the professorship shall be for the time being allocated by Council under any decree in that behalf, or, if the head is unable or unwilling to act, a person appointed by the governing body of the college;

(3) a person appointed by the governing body of the college specified in (2) of this clause;

(4) a person appointed by Council;

(5), (6) two persons appointed by the General Board;

(7)–(9) three persons appointed by the Board of the Faculty of Law.

3. The professor shall be subject to the General Provisions of the decree concerning the duties of professors and to those Particular Provisions of the same decree which are applicable to this chair.

§ **184.** *Director of the Centre for Socio-Legal Studies and Professor of Socio-Legal Studies*

1. There shall be a Director of the Centre for Socio-Legal Studies who shall also be Professor of Socio-Legal Studies. Subject to the general supervision of the Board of the Faculty of Law acting through the Committee of Management for the Socio-Legal Studies Centre, he or she shall be responsible for the direction and the efficient working of the centre. The director shall lecture and give instruction in Socio-Legal Studies.

2. The director shall be elected by an electoral board consisting of:

(1) the Vice-Chancellor, or, if the head of the college specified in (2) of this clause is Vice-Chancellor, a person appointed by Council;

(2) the head of the college to which the directorship shall be for the time being allocated by Council under any decree in that behalf, or, if the head is unable or unwilling to act, a person appointed by the governing body of the college; (3) a person appointed by the governing body of the college specified in (2) of this clause;

(4) a person appointed by Council;

(5) a person appointed by the General Board of the Faculties;

(6), (7) two persons appointed by the Board of the Faculty of Law, one of whom shall be appointed after consultation with the Committee of Management for the Socio-Legal Studies Centre.

3. The director shall be subject to the General Provisions of the decree concerning the duties of professors and to those Particular Provisions of the same decree which are applicable to the Professorship of Socio-Legal Studies.

§ **185.** *Reader in Law*

1. The Reader in Law shall lecture and give instruction in Law.

2. The Reader shall be elected by an electoral board consisting of:

(1) the Vice-Chancellor;

(2) a person appointed by Council;

(3) a person appointed by the General Board,

(4)–(7) four persons appointed by the Board of the Faculty of Law.

§ **186.** *All Souls Reader in Law*

1. The All Souls Reader in Law shall lecture and give instruction in Law on such conditions and with such duties as the General Board shall from time to time determine.

2. The reader shall be elected by a board consisting of:

(1) the Vice-Chancellor;

(2) a person appointed by Council;

(3) a person appointed by the General Board;

(4)–(7) four persons appointed by the Board of the Faculty of Law.

§ 187. *Brost Lecturer in German and European Community Law*

1. The University accepts with gratitude the gift of D.M.1,500,000 from Mrs Anneliese Brost and Mr Erich Schumann, through the Stiftverband für die Deutsche Wissenschaft, to establish a fund to be known as the Erich Brost Fund, the net income of which shall be used to maintain the Erich Brost Lecturership in German and European Community Law.

2. The Board of the Faculty of Law shall be the board of management for the fund.

3. The board of management shall before 31 October each year transmit to the Stiftverband accounts of the fund for the period of twelve calendar months which has ended on the preceding 31 July. These accounts shall contain details of the investment of the fund, the income from this investment, and the expenditure incurred from the fund. The board shall, if so requested at any time by the Stiftverband, send to the Stiftverband all documents relating to the fund in respect of any or all of the ten years preceding any such request.

4. Before 31 December each year, beginning in December 1996, the University shall pay from the income of the fund such sum, being initially D.M.4,000, as the Stiftverband may reasonably require to cover the Stiftverband's administrative costs in connection with the lecturership.

5. Council shall have power to amend this decree from time to time, provided always that it may do so only with the Stiftverband's prior written agreement. In the event that the University no longer complies with the provisions of clauses 1–4 above, or with any new provisions which may be effective from time to time as a result of amendments made in accordance with such agreement, the University shall return to the Stiftverband both the capital of the fund and any income to the fund which has not already been expended or committed by the University.

§ 188. *Travers Smith Braithwaite Lecturer in the Law of Corporate Finance*

1. The University accepts with gratitude the moneys offered by the solicitors Travers Smith Braithwaite to fund a lecturership which shall be known as the Travers Smith Braithwaite Lecturership in the Law of Corporate Finance.

2. The lecturer shall be appointed by the Board of the Faculty of Law in accordance with the provisions of Sect. IV, § 3, of this chapter and shall lecture and give instruction in the Law of Corporate Finance.

3. Council shall have power to alter this decree from time to time, subject always to the concurrence of Travers Smith Braithwaite or any successor (whether direct or indirect) to that firm.

§ 189. *Professor of General Linguistics*

1. The Professor of General Linguistics shall lecture and give instruction in the field of General Linguistics and shall promote the study of that subject in the University.

2. The professor shall be elected by an electoral board consisting of:

(1) the Vice-Chancellor, or, if the head of the college specified in (2) of this clause is Vice-Chancellor, a person appointed by Council on the occurrence of a vacancy to act as an elector on that occasion;

(2) the head of the college to which the professorship shall be for the time being allocated by Council under any decree in that behalf, or, if the head is unable or unwilling to act, a person appointed by the governing body of the college on the occurrence of a vacancy to act as an elector on that occasion;

(3) a person appointed by the governing body of the college specified in (2) of this clause;

(4) a person appointed by Council;

(5) a person appointed by the General Board;

(6) a person appointed by the Board of the Faculty of Medieval and Modern Languages;

(7) a person appointed by the Board of the Faculty of Literae Humaniores;

(8) a person appointed by the Sub-faculty of Philosophy;

(9) a person appointed by the Board of the Faculty of English Language and Literature.

3. The professor shall be subject to the General Provisions of the decree concerning the duties of professors and to those Particular Provisions of the same decree which are applicable to this chair.

§ 190. *Wykeham Professor of Logic*

1. The Wykeham Professor of Logic shall lecture and give instruction in Philosophy with special regard to the Problems, Theories, and History of Logic.

2. The professor shall be elected by a board of electors consisting of:

(1) the Vice-Chancellor, or, if the Warden of New College is Vice-Chancellor, a person appointed by Council on the occurrence of a vacancy to act as an elector on that occasion;

(2) the Warden of New College, or, if the Warden is unable or unwilling to act, a person appointed by the Governing Body of New College on the occurrence of a vacancy to act as an elector on that occasion;

(3) a person appointed by the Governing Body of New College;

(4) a person appointed by Council;

(5), (6) two persons appointed by the General Board;

(7), (8) two persons elected by the Board of the Faculty of Literae Humaniores;

(9) a person elected by the Sub-faculty of Philosophy, or, if there be no such sub-faculty, then by the Faculty of Literae Humaniores.

3. The professor shall be subject to the General Provisions of the decree concerning the duties of professors and to those Particular Provisions of the same decree which are applicable to this chair.

§ **191.** *Professor of Mathematical Logic*

1. The Professor of Mathematical Logic shall lecture and give instruction in Mathematical Logic.

2. The professor shall be elected by an electoral board consisting of:

(1) the Vice-Chancellor, or, if the Warden of Merton College is Vice-Chancellor, a person appointed by Council on the occurrence of a vacancy to act as an elector on that occasion;

(2) the Warden of Merton College, or, if the Warden is unable or unwilling to act, a person appointed by the Governing Body of Merton College on the occurrence of a vacancy to act as an elector on that occasion;

(3) a person appointed by the Governing Body of Merton College;

(4), (5) two persons appointed by Council;

(6), (7) two persons appointed by the General Board;

(8) a person elected by the Board of the Faculty of Literae Humaniores;

(9) a person elected by the Board of the Faculty of Mathematical Sciences.

3. The professor shall be subject to the General Provisions of the decree concerning the duties of professors and to the Particular Provisions of the same decree applicable to the professors enumerated in Schedule A annexed thereto.

§ **192.** *Professors of Management Studies*

1. There shall be two Professors of Management Studies, each of whom shall lecture and give instruction in Management Studies.

2. The first professor shall be elected by an electoral board consisting of:

(1) the Vice-Chancellor, or, if the head of the college specified in (2) of this clause is Vice-Chancellor, a person appointed by Council;

(2) the head of the college to which the professorship shall be for the time being allocated by Council under any decree in that behalf, or, if the head is unable or unwilling to act, a person appointed by the governing body of the college;

(3) the Peter Moores Director of the Saïd Business School;

(4) a person appointed by the governing body of the college specified in (2) of this clause;

(5) a person appointed by Council;

(6) a person appointed by the General Board;

(7) a person appointed by the Board of the Faculty of Social Studies;

(8), (9) two persons appointed by the Board of the Faculty of Management.

3. The second professor shall be elected by an electoral board consisting of:

(1) the Vice-Chancellor, or, if the head of the college specified in (2) of this clause is Vice-Chancellor, a person appointed by Council;

(2) the head of the college to which the professorship shall be for the time being allocated by Council under any decree in that behalf, or, if the head is

unable or unwilling to act, a person appointed by the governing body of the college;

(3) a person appointed by the governing body of the college specified in (2) of this clause;

(4) a person appointed by Council;

(5), (6) two persons appointed by the General Board;

(7) a person appointed by the Board of the Faculty of Social Studies;

(8), (9) two persons appointed by the Board of the Faculty of Management.

4. Each professor shall be subject to the General Provisions of the decree concerning the duties of professors and to those Particular Provisions of the same decree which are applicable to these chairs.

§ 193. *Butten Professor of Management Studies*

1. The University accepts with gratitude the moneys offered by Balliol College to support the establishment of a Professorship of Management Studies, to be known as the Ernest Butten Professorship of Management Studies.

2. The Ernest Butten Professor of Management Studies shall lecture and give instruction in Management Studies.

3. The professor shall be elected by an electoral board consisting of:

(1) the Vice-Chancellor, or, if the Master of Balliol College is Vice-Chancellor, a person appointed by Council;

(2) the Master of Balliol College, or, if the Master is unable or unwilling to act, a person appointed by the governing body of the college;

(3) a person appointed by the Governing Body of Balliol College;

(4) a person appointed by Council;

(5), (6) two persons appointed by the General Board;

(7)–(9) three persons appointed by the Board of the Faculty of Management.

4. The professor shall be subject to General Provisions of the decree concerning the duties of professors and to those Particular Provisions of the same decree which are applicable to this chair.

5. The professor shall be expected to act as Director of Studies for Management students within Balliol College for such time as the college wishes. The other duties of the professor shall, if necessary, be adjusted by the University accordingly.

6. Council shall have power to amend this decree from time to time, subject to the concurrence of Balliol College.

§ 194. *Moores Professor of Management Studies*

1. The Peter Moores Professor of Management Studies shall lecture and give instruction in Management Studies.

2. The professor shall be elected by an electoral board consisting of:

(1) the Vice-Chancellor, or, if the Warden of Wadham College is Vice-Chancellor, a person appointed by Council;

(2) the Warden of Wadham College, or, if the Warden is unable or unwilling to act, a person appointed by the governing body of the college;

(3) the Peter Moores Director of the Saïd Business School;

(4) a person appointed by the Governing Body of Wadham College;

(5), (6) two persons appointed by Council, one of whom shall be appointed after consultation with the Peter Moores Foundation or its nominated representative;

(7) a person appointed by the General Board;

(8) a person appointed by the Board of the Faculty of Management;

(9), (10) two persons appointed by the Board of the Faculty of Social Studies.

The above provision regarding consultation with the Peter Moores Foundation shall not be amended or repealed without the prior agreement of the foundation.

3. The professor shall be subject to the General Provisions of the decree concerning the duties of professors and to those Particular Provisions of the same decree which are applicable to this chair.

§ 195. *The Peninsular and Oriental Steam Navigation Company Professor of Management Studies*

1. The University accepts with deep gratitude the munificent benefaction provided by The Peninsular and Oriental Steam Navigation Company to establish a Professorship of Management Studies which shall, unless the company at any time shall request otherwise (in which case any new title attached to the chair shall be subject to the approval of the company), be known as The Peninsular and Oriental Steam Navigation Company Professorship of Management Studies.

2. The Peninsular and Oriental Steam Navigation Company Professor of Management Studies shall lecture and give instruction in Management Studies in the area of International Business.

3. The professor shall be elected by an electoral board consisting of:

(1) the Vice-Chancellor, or, if the President of Templeton College is Vice-Chancellor, a person appointed by Council;

(2) the President of Templeton College, or if the President is unable or unwilling to act, a person appointed by the Governing Body of Templeton College;

(3) a person appointed by the Governing Body of Templeton College;

(4) a person appointed by Council after consultation with The Peninsular and Oriental Steam Navigation Company;

(5), (6) two persons appointed by the General Board;

(7) a person appointed by the Board of the Faculty of Social Studies;

(8), (9) two persons appointed by the Board of the Faculty of Management.

4. The professor shall be subject to General Provisions of the decree concerning the duties of professors and to those Particular Provisions of the same decree which are applicable to this chair.

§ **196.** *American Standard Companies Professor of Operations Management*

1. The University accepts with deep gratitude the munificent benefaction provided by the American Standard Companies Inc. to establish a Professorship of Operations Management which shall be known as the American Standard Companies Professorship of Operations Management.

2. The American Standard Companies Professor of Operations Management shall lecture and give instruction in Operations Management.

3. The professor shall be elected by an electoral board consisting of:

(1) the Vice-Chancellor, or, if the head of the college specified in (2) of this clause is Vice-Chancellor, a person appointed by Council;

(2) the head of the college to which the professorship shall be for the time being allocated by Council under any decree in that behalf, or, if the head is unable or unwilling to act, a person appointed by the governing body of the college;

(3) a person appointed by the governing body of the college specified in (2) of this clause;

(4) a person appointed by Council;

(5), (6) two persons appointed by the General Board;

(7) a person appointed by the Board of the Faculty of Social Studies;

(8), (9) two persons appointed by the Board of the Faculty of Management.

4. The professor shall be subject to General Provisions of the decree concerning the duties of professors and to those Particular Provisions of the same decree which are applicable to this chair.

§ **197.** *Rhodes Lecturers in Management Studies*

1. The University accepts with deep gratitude the munificent benefaction provided by the Rhodes Trust which shall be used for the advancement of Management Studies within the University through the endowment of two Rhodes Lecturerships in Management Studies and through expenditure on their support costs and on related purposes.

2. The Rhodes Lecturers in Management Studies shall lecture and give instruction in Management Studies under the direction of the Board of the Faculty of Management.

3. The lecturers shall be appointed by the Board of the Faculty of Management in accordance with the provisions of Ch. VII, Sect. IV, § 3.

4. The first charge on the net income of the endowment shall be the salary and associated costs of the lecturers. The second charge shall be the provision, under such arrangements as the faculty board may from time to time determine, of support, including teaching materials and research expenses, for the lecturers.

5. Any income unspent in any year on the first and second charges as defined in clause 4 above, whether in consequence of a vacancy in a lecturership or for any other reason, shall, at the discretion of the Board of the Faculty of Management either be carried forward for expenditure in subsequent years or be spent in any other way or ways conducive to the advancement within the University of teaching, scholarship, and research in Management Studies.

6. Council shall have power to amend this decree from time to time, provided always that the main objects of the benefaction, as defined in clause 1 above, shall be kept in view, and that the maintenance of the Rhodes Lecturerships in Management Studies shall remain the first charge on the income of the endowment.

§ 198. *Professor of Marketing*

1. The University accepts with deep gratitude the munificent benefaction provided anonymously to establish a Professorship of Management Studies which shall be known as the Professorship of Marketing.

2. The Professor of Marketing shall lecture and give instruction in Management Studies in the area of Marketing.

3. The professor shall be elected by an electoral board consisting of:

(1) the Vice-Chancellor, or, if the Warden of Green College is Vice-Chancellor, a person appointed by Council;

(2) the Warden of Green College, or, if the Warden is unable or unwilling to act, a person appointed by the Governing Body of Green College;

(3) a person appointed by the Governing Body of Green College;

(4) a person appointed by Council;

(5), (6) two persons appointed by the General Board;

(7), (8) two persons appointed by the Board of the Faculty of Management;

(9) a person appointed by the Board of the Faculty of Social Studies.

4. The professor shall be subject to the General Provisions of the decree concerning the duties of professors and to those Particular Provisions of the same decree which are applicable to this chair.

5. Council shall have power to amend this decree from time to time, provided that the main objects of the benefaction, as defined in clause 1 above, shall always be kept in view.

§ 199. *Cookson Professor of Materials*

1. The University accepts with gratitude funding from the Cookson Group plc for the establishment of a Cookson Professorship of Materials.

2. The Cookson Professor of Materials shall lecture and give instruction in Materials Science.

3. The professor shall be elected by an electoral board consisting of:

(1) the Vice-Chancellor, or, if the head of the college specified in (2) of this clause is Vice-Chancellor, a person appointed by Council;

(2) the head of the college to which the professorship shall be for the time being allocated by Council under any decree in that behalf, or, if the head is unable or unwilling to act, a person appointed by the governing body of the college;

(3) a person appointed by the governing body of the college specified in (2) of this clause;

(4), (5) two persons appointed by Council, one of whom shall be appointed after consultation with the Cookson Group;

(6) a person appointed by the General Board;

(7)–(9) three persons appointed by the Board of the Faculty of Physical Sciences.

4. The professor shall be subject to the General Provisions of the decree concerning the duties of professors and to those Particular Provisions of the same decree which are applicable to this chair.

§ 200. *Reader in Physical Examination of Materials*

1. There shall be a Reader in the Physical Examination of Materials who shall be elected by a board consisting of:

(1) the Vice-Chancellor;

(2) the Head of the Department of Materials;

(3) a person appointed by Council;

(4) a person appointed by the General Board;

(5)–(7) three persons appointed by the Board of the Faculty of Physical Sciences.

2. The reader shall engage in advanced study or research and shall, under the direction of the Head of the Department of Materials, in every term lecture and give instruction in Metallurgy with special reference to the physical examination of materials.

§ 201. *Rouse Ball Professor of Mathematics*

1. The Rouse Ball Professor of Mathematics shall lecture and give instruction in the applications of Mathematics to the Physical Sciences. The professor may also, in accordance with the wishes of the founder, treat from time to time of the historical and philosophical aspects of Mathematics.

2. The professor shall be elected by an electoral board consisting of:

(1) the Vice-Chancellor, or, if the Warden of Wadham College is Vice-Chancellor, a person appointed by Council on the occurrence of a vacancy to act as an elector on that occasion;

(2) the Warden of Wadham College, or, if the Warden is unable or unwilling to act, a person appointed by the Governing Body of Wadham College on the occurrence of a vacancy to act as an elector on that occasion;

(3) a person appointed by the Governing Body of Wadham College;

(4) a person appointed by Council;

(5) a person appointed by the General Board;

(6)–(8) three persons elected by the Board of the Faculty of Mathematical Sciences;

(9) one person elected by the Board of the Faculty of Physical Sciences.

3. The professor shall be subject to the General Provisions of the decree concerning the duties of professors and to those Particular Provisions of the same decree which are applicable to this chair.

§ 202. *Wallis Professor of Mathematics*

1. The Wallis Professor of Mathematics shall lecture and give instruction in Mathematics with special reference to analysis or mathematical probability.

2. The professor shall be elected by an electoral board consisting of:

(1) the Vice-Chancellor, or, if the head of the college specified in (2) of this clause is Vice-Chancellor, a person appointed by Council on the occurrence of a vacancy to act as an elector on that occasion;

(2) the head of the college to which the professorship shall be for the time being allocated by Council under any decree in that behalf, or, if the head is unable or unwilling to act, a person appointed by the governing body of the college on the occurrence of a vacancy to act as an elector on that occasion;

(3) a person appointed by the governing body of the college specified in (2) of this clause;

(4) a person appointed by Council;

(5), (6) two persons appointed by the General Board;

(7)–(9) three persons elected by the Board of the Faculty of Mathematical Sciences.

3. The professor shall be subject to the General Provisions of the decree concerning the duties of professors and to those Particular Provisions of the same decree which are applicable to this chair.

§ 203. *Professor of Mathematics and its Applications*

1. The Professor of Mathematics and its Applications shall lecture and give instruction in some branch of Mathematics and its Applications.

2. The professor shall be elected by an electoral board consisting of:

(1) the Vice-Chancellor, or, if the head of the college specified in (2) of this clause is Vice-Chancellor, a person appointed by Council;

(2) the head of the college to which the professorship shall be for the time being allocated by Council under any decree in that behalf, or, if the head is

unable or unwilling to act, a person appointed by the governing body of the college;

(3) a person appointed by the governing body of the college specified in (2) of this clause;

(4) a person appointed by Council;

(5), (6) two persons appointed by the General Board;

(7)–(9) three persons appointed by the Board of the Faculty of Mathematical Sciences.

3. The professor shall be subject to the General Provisions of the decree concerning the duties of professors and to those Particular Provisions of the same decree which are applicable to this chair.

§ 204. *Professor of Pure Mathematics*

1. The Professor of Pure Mathematics shall lecture and give instruction in some branch of Pure Mathematics.

2. The professor shall be elected by an electoral board consisting of:

(1) the Vice-Chancellor, or, if the head of the college specified in (2) of this clause is Vice-Chancellor, a person appointed by Council;

(2) the head of the college to which the professorship shall be for the time being allocated by Council under any decree in that behalf, or, if the head is unable or unwilling to act, a person appointed by the governing body of the college;

(3) a person appointed by the governing body of the college specified in (2) of this clause;

(4) a person appointed by Council;

(5), (6) two persons appointed by the General Board;

(7)–(9) three persons appointed by the Board of the Faculty of Mathematical Sciences.

3. The professor shall be subject to the General Provisions of the decree concerning the duties of professors and to those Particular Provisions of the same decree which are applicable to this chair.

§ 205. *Waynflete Professor of Pure Mathematics*

1. The Waynflete Professor of Pure Mathematics shall lecture and give instruction in some branch of Pure Mathematics.

2. The professor shall be elected by an electoral board consisting of:

(1) the Vice-Chancellor, or, if the President of Magdalen College is Vice-Chancellor, a person appointed by Council on the occurrence of a vacancy to act as an elector on that occasion;

(2) the President of Magdalen College, or, if the President is unable or unwilling to act, a person appointed by the Governing Body of Magdalen College on the occurrence of a vacancy to act as an elector on that occasion;

(3) a person appointed by the Governing Body of Magdalen College;

(4) a person appointed by Council;

(5)–(7) three persons elected by the Board of the Faculty of Mathematical Sciences.

3. The professor shall be subject to the General Provisions of the decree concerning the duties of professors and to those Particular Provisions of the same decree which are applicable to this chair.

§ **206.** *Aldrichian Professor of Medicine*

The Regius Professor of Medicine shall be *ex officio* Aldrichian Professor of Medicine.

§ **207.** *Regius Professor of Medicine*

1. The Regius Professor of Medicine shall lecture and give instruction in subjects connected with the study of Medicine.

2. The professor shall perform such duties in relation to the teaching and study of Medicine in the University as Council may from time to time by decree determine.

3. The professor shall be subject to the General Provisions of the decree concerning the duties of professors and to those Particular Provisions of the same decree which are applicable to this chair.

§ **208.** *May Professor of Medicine*

1. The May Professor of Medicine shall engage in advanced study and research and shall, under the direction of the Nuffield Professor of Clinical Medicine, assist in the preparation of candidates for the Degree of Bachelor of Medicine.

2. The professor shall be elected by an electoral board consisting of:

(1) the Vice-Chancellor, or, if the head of the college specified in (2) of this clause is Vice-Chancellor, a person appointed by Council;

(2) the head of the college to which the professorship shall be for the time being allocated by Council under any decree in that behalf, or, if the head is unable or unwilling to act, a person appointed by the governing body of the college;

(3) a person appointed by the governing body of the college specified in (2) of this clause;

(4) a person appointed by Council;

(5), (6) two persons appointed by the General Board;

(7) the Nuffield Professor of Clinical Medicine;

(8), (9) two persons appointed by the Board of the Faculty of Clinical Medicine;

(10) a person holding a clinical appointment appointed by the Oxfordshire Health Authority.

At least three members of the board, of whom one shall be a professor, shall hold clinical appointments.

3. The professor shall hold qualifications entitling him or her to be registered with the General Medical Council as a medical practitioner.

4. The income of the endowment fund shall be applied towards the stipend and superannuation of the professor.

5. The professor shall be subject to the General Provisions of the decree concerning the duties of professors and to those Particular Provisions of the same decree which are applicable to this chair.

§ 209. *Field Marshal Alexander Professor of Cardiovascular Medicine*

1. The University hereby accepts with deep gratitude the endowment provided by the British Heart Foundation for the establishment of a Professorship of Cardiovascular Medicine as a memorial to Field Marshal Earl Alexander of Tunis, to be known as the Field Marshal Alexander Professorship of Cardiovascular Medicine, and towards the costs of supporting expenditure in Cardiovascular Medicine.

2. The professor shall lecture and give instruction in cardiovascular medicine.

3. The professor shall be elected by a board of electors consisting of:

(1) the Vice-Chancellor, or, if the Rector of Exeter College is Vice-Chancellor, a person appointed by Council on the occurrence of a vacancy to act as an elector on that occasion;

(2) the Rector of Exeter College, or, if the Rector is unable or unwilling to act, a person appointed by the Governing Body of Exeter College on the occurrence of a vacancy to act as an elector on that occasion;

(3) a person appointed by the Governing Body of Exeter College;

(4), (5) two persons appointed by Council;

(6) a person appointed by the General Board;

(7), (8) two persons appointed by the Board of the Faculty of Clinical Medicine;

(9) a person holding a clinical appointment appointed by the Oxfordshire Health Authority after consultation with the Oxford Regional Health Authority.

At least three members of the board, of whom one shall be a professor, shall hold clinical appointments.

4. The professor shall be subject to the General Provisions of the decree concerning the duties of professors and to those Particular Provisions of the same decree which are applicable to this chair.

5. Such part of the income of the endowment as the General Board shall determine is not required to meet the costs of the professorship shall be expended on supporting expenditure in Cardiovascular Medicine in such manner as the General Board shall direct.

6. Council shall have power, subject to the consent of the donors, to amend this decree, provided always that the maintenance of the Field Marshal Alexander Professorship of Cardiovascular Medicine remains the first charge on the income of the endowment.

§ 210. *Nuffield Professor of Clinical Medicine*

1. The Nuffield Professor of Clinical Medicine shall lecture and give instruction in Clinical Medicine.

2. The professor shall be elected by an electoral board consisting of:

(1) the Vice-Chancellor, or, if the President of Magdalen College is Vice-Chancellor, a person appointed by Council on the occurrence of a vacancy to act as an elector on that occasion;

(2) the President of Magdalen College, or, if the President is unable or unwilling to act, a person appointed by the governing body of the college on the occurrence of a vacancy to act as an elector on that occasion;

(3) a person appointed by the Governing Body of Magdalen College;

(4), (5) two persons appointed by Council;

(6) a person appointed by the General Board;

(7), (8) two persons appointed by the Board of the Faculty of Clinical Medicine;

(9) a person holding a clinical appointment appointed by the Oxfordshire Health Authority after consultation with the Oxford Regional Health Authority.

At least three members of the board, of whom one shall be a professor, shall hold clinical appointments.

3. The professor shall be subject to the General Provisions of the decree concerning the duties of professors and to those Particular Provisions of the same decree which are applicable to this chair.

§ 211. *Professor of Molecular Medicine*

1. The Professor of Molecular Medicine shall lecture and give instruction in Molecular Medicine.

2. The professor shall be elected by an electoral board consisting of:

(1) the Vice-Chancellor, or, if the head of the college specified in (2) of this clause is Vice-Chancellor, a person appointed by Council;

(2) the head of the college to which the professorship shall be for the time being allocated by Council under any decree in that behalf, or, if the head is unable or unwilling to act, a person appointed by the governing body of the college;

(3) a person appointed by the governing body of the college specified in (2) of this clause;

(4), (5) two persons appointed by Council, of whom one shall be appointed in agreement with the Medical Research Council;

(6), (7) two persons appointed by the General Board, of whom one shall be appointed in agreement with the Imperial Cancer Research Fund;

(8)–(10) three persons appointed by the Board of the Faculty of Clinical Medicine;

(11) a person holding a clinical appointment appointed by the Oxfordshire Health Authority.

At least three members of the board, of whom one shall be a professor, shall hold clinical appointments.

3. The professor shall be subject to the General Provisions of the decree concerning the duties of professors and to those Particular Provisions of the same decree which are applicable to this chair.

§ 212. *Wolfson Professor of Metallurgy*

1. The Isaac Wolfson Professor of Metallurgy shall lecture and give instruction in Metallurgy.

2. The professor shall be elected by a board consisting of:

(1) the Vice-Chancellor, or, if the head of the college specified in (2) of this clause is Vice-Chancellor, a person appointed by Council on the occurrence of a vacancy to act as an elector on that occasion;

(2) the head of the college to which the professorship shall be for the time being allocated by Council under any decree in that behalf, or, if the head is unable or unwilling to act, a person appointed by the governing body of the college on the occurrence of a vacancy to act as an elector on that occasion;

(3) a person appointed by the governing body of the college specified in (2) of this clause;

(4) a person appointed by Council;

(5) a person appointed by the General Board;

(6)–(9) four persons appointed by the Board of the Faculty of Physical Sciences.

3. The professor shall be subject to the General Provisions of the decree concerning the duties of professors and to those Particular Provisions of the same decree which are applicable to this chair.

4. If at any time there is a vacancy in the professorship the emoluments shall be added to the capital endowment for the professorship.

§ 213. *Kelley Reader in Metallurgy*

1. There shall be a George Kelley Reader in Metallurgy who shall be elected by a board consisting of:

(1) the Vice-Chancellor;

(2) the Head of the Department of Materials;

(3) a person appointed by Council;

(4) a person appointed by the General Board;

(5)–(7) three persons appointed by the Board of the Faculty of Physical Sciences.

2. The reader shall engage in advanced study or research and shall, under the direction of the Head of the Department of Materials, lecture and give instruction in Metallurgy in every term.

3. If at any time there is a vacancy in the readership, the emoluments shall be added to the capital endowment for the readership.

§ 214. *Professor of Microbiology*

1. The Professor of Microbiology shall lecture and give instruction in Microbiology.

2. The professor shall be elected by an electoral board consisting of:

(1) the Vice-Chancellor, or, if the head of the college specified in (2) of this clause is Vice-Chancellor, a person appointed by Council;

(2) the head of the college to which the professorship shall be for the time being allocated by Council under any decree in that behalf, or, if the head is unable or unwilling to act, a person appointed by the governing body of the college;

(3) a person appointed by the governing body of the college specified in (2) of this clause;

(4) a person appointed by Council;

(5), (6) two persons appointed by the General Board;

(7) the Professor of Pathology;

(8)–(10) three persons appointed by the Medical Sciences Board.

3. The professor shall be subject to the General Provisions of the decree concerning the duties of professors and to those Particular Provisions of the same decree which are applicable to this chair.

§ 215. *Iveagh Professor of Microbiology*

1. There shall be established in the Department of Biochemistry a Professorship of Microbiology to be known as the Iveagh Professorship of Microbiology. The professor shall lecture and give instruction in Microbiology.

2. The professor shall be elected by an electoral board consisting of:

(1) the Vice-Chancellor, or, if the Principal of Linacre is Vice-Chancellor, a person appointed by Council on the occurrence of a vacancy to act as an elector on that occasion;

(2) the Principal of Linacre College, or, if the Principal is unable or unwilling to act, a person appointed by the Governing Body of Linacre College on the occurrence of a vacancy to act as an elector on that occasion;

(3) a person appointed by the Governing Body of Linacre College;

(4) a person appointed by Council;

(5) a person appointed by the General Board;

(6), (7) two persons appointed by the Board of the Faculty of Biological Sciences.

3. The professor shall be subject to the General Provisions of the decree concerning the duties of professors and to those Particular Provisions of the same decree which are applicable to this chair.

§ 216. *Professor of the Physics and Chemistry of Minerals*

1. The Professor of the Physics and Chemistry of Minerals shall lecture and give instruction in the Physics and Chemistry of Minerals.

2. The professor shall be elected by a board of electors consisting of:

(1) the Vice-Chancellor, or if the Principal of St. Hugh's College is Vice-Chancellor, a person appointed by Council on the occurrence of a vacancy to act as an elector on that occasion;

(2) the Principal of St. Hugh's College, or if the Principal is unable or unwilling to act, a person appointed by the Governing Body of St. Hugh's College on the occurrence of a vacancy to act as an elector on that occasion;

(3) a person appointed by the Governing Body of St. Hugh's College;

(4) a person appointed by Council;

(5) a person appointed by the General Board;

(6)–(9) four persons appointed by the Board of the Faculty of Physical Sciences.

3. The professor shall be subject to the General Provisions of the decree concerning the duties of professors and to those Particular Provisions of the same decree which are applicable to this chair.

§ 217. *Collisson Professor of Musculo-skeletal Science*

1. The Norman Collisson Professor of Musculo-skeletal Science shall lecture and give instruction in Musculo-skeletal Science.

2. The professor shall be elected by an electoral board consisting of:

(1) the Vice-Chancellor, or, if the head of the college specified in (2) of this clause is Vice-Chancellor, a person appointed by Council;

(2) the head of the college to which the professorship shall be for the time being allocated by Council under any decree in that behalf, or, if the head is unable or unwilling to act, a person appointed by the governing body of the college;

(3) a person appointed by the governing body of the college specified in (2) of this clause;

(4) a person appointed by Council;

(5), (6) two persons appointed by the General Board;

(7) the Nuffield Professor of Orthopaedic Surgery;

(8)–(10) three persons appointed by the Board of the Faculty of Clinical Medicine;

(11) a person holding a clinical appointment appointed by the Oxfordshire Health Authority.

At least three members of the board, of whom one shall be a professor, shall hold clinical appointments.

3. The professor shall be subject to the General Provisions of the decree concerning the duties of professors and to those Particular Provisions of the same decree which are applicable to this chair.

4. Such part of the income of the endowment as the Medical Sciences Board shall determine not to be required to meet the costs of the professorship shall be expended on support for the professor in such manner as the board shall direct.

§ 218. *Professor of Music and Choragus on the foundation of William Heather, Doctor of Music*

1. The Heather Professor of Music shall lecture and give instruction in the theory and history of Music and the lectures shall be illustrated as need requires by vocal or instrumental performances.

2. The professor shall be elected by an electoral board consisting of:

(1) the Vice-Chancellor, or, if the head of the college specified in (2) of this clause is Vice-Chancellor, a person appointed by Council on the occurrence of a vacancy to act as an elector on that occasion;

(2) the head of the college to which the professorship shall be for the time being allocated by Council under any decree in that behalf, or, if the head is unable or unwilling to act, a person appointed by the governing body of the college on the occurrence of a vacancy to act as an elector on that occasion;

(3) a person appointed by the governing body of the college specified in (2) of this clause;

(4) a person appointed by Council;

(5), (6) two persons appointed by the General Board;

(7)–(9) three persons appointed by the Board of the Faculty of Music.

3. The professor shall be subject to the General Provisions of the decree concerning the duties of professors and to those Particular Provisions of the same decree which are applicable to this chair.

4. The Choragus, who shall be a member of the Faculty of Music, shall be nominated by the professor and appointed by the Board of the Faculty of Music. The Choragus shall be appointed for a period of five years and shall be re-eligible.

5. The Choragus shall perform such duties as are prescribed for him or her by the Board of the Faculty of Music.

§ **219.** *Myres Memorial Lecturer*

1. A biennial lecture shall be maintained in the University of Oxford to be called the Myres Memorial Lecture, and the lecturer to be appointed shall be called the Myres Memorial Lecturer.

2. The lecture shall be delivered on a subject within the field of ancient history, European and Near Eastern archaeology, historical geography, and ethnology, with special reference to Mediterranean lands, and subjects shall, at the discretion of the board of management, be taken from these fields in rotation.

3. The sum of £961·73 and the stocks, funds, and securities for the time being representing the same, and any addition made thereto by accumulation or otherwise, shall form a fund to be called the Myres Memorial Fund.

4. There shall be a board of management consisting of:

(1) the Vice-Chancellor;

(2) the Warden of New College;

(3) the Wykeham Professor of Ancient History;

(4) one person elected by the Board of the Faculty of Literae Humaniores;

(5) one person elected by the Board of the Faculty of Oriental Studies;

(6), (7) two persons elected by the Board of the Faculty of Anthropology and Geography.

The elected members shall hold office for three years but shall be re-eligible. Four members of the committee shall constitute a quorum.

5. The board of management shall appoint the lecturer in every other year and fix his or her stipend.

6. The stipend of the lecturer shall be the first charge on the income of the fund; the next charge shall be the cost of publication of the lecture, and any profits from the sales of the lecture shall be credited to the fund. Any surplus income arising when these charges have been met shall, at the discretion of the board of management, be applied in one or more of the following ways:

(*a*) applied towards the necessary expenses of the lecturer, including the provision of illustrative material if required (such material to remain the property of the University);

(*b*) carried forward for use in a subsequent year;

(*c*) invested in augmentation of the capital;

(*d*) applied in any other way which the board shall think conducive to the object of the fund.

7. Each lecturer shall deliver to the Vice-Chancellor his or her lecture or a verified copy thereof which shall be retained in the Bodleian Library.

8. This decree shall be subject to alteration by Council provided that the main object, namely the delivery in the University from time to time of a lecture to be called the Myres Memorial Lecture, shall be observed and maintained.

§ **221.** *Action Research Professor of Clinical Neurology*

1. The Action Research Professor of Clinical Neurology shall lecture and give instruction in Clinical Neurology.

2. The professor shall be elected by a board of electors consisting of:

(1) the Vice-Chancellor, or, if the head of the college specified in (2) of this clause is Vice-Chancellor, a person appointed by Council on the occurrence of a vacancy to act as an elector on that occasion;

(2) the head of the college to which the professorship shall be for the time being allocated by Council under any decree in that behalf, or, if the head is unable or unwilling to act, a person appointed by the governing body of the college on the occurrence of a vacancy to act as an elector on that occasion;

(3) a person appointed by the governing body of the college specified in (2) of this clause;

(4), (5) two persons appointed by Council;

(6) a person appointed by the General Board;

(7), (8) two persons elected by the Board of the Faculty of Clinical Medicine;

(9) a person holding a clinical appointment appointed by the Oxfordshire Health Authority after consultation with the Oxford Regional Health Authority.

At least three members of the board, of whom one shall be a professor, shall hold clinical appointments.

3. The professor shall be subject to the General Provisions of the decree concerning the duties of professors and to those Particular Provisions of the same decree which are applicable to this chair.

§ **222.** *Professor of Numerical Analysis*

1. The Professor of Numerical Analysis shall lecture and give instruction in Numerical Analysis.

2. The professor shall be elected by an electoral board consisting of:

(1) the Vice-Chancellor, or, if the head of the college specified in (2) of this clause is Vice-Chancellor, a person appointed by Council on the occurrence of a vacancy to act as an elector on that occasion;

(2) the head of the college to which the professorship shall be for the time being allocated by Council under any decree in that behalf, or, if the head is unable or unwilling to act, a person appointed by the governing body of the college on the occurrence of a vacancy to act as an elector on that occasion;

(3) a person appointed by the governing body of the college specified in (2) of this clause;

(4) a person appointed by Council;

(5), (6) two persons appointed by the General Board;

(7), (8) two persons appointed by the Board of the Faculty of Mathematical Sciences;

(9) one person appointed by the Board of the Faculty of Physical Sciences.

3. The professor shall be subject to the General Provisions of the decree concerning the duties of professors and to those Particular Provisions of the same decree which are applicable to this chair.

§ **231.** *Nuffield Professor of Obstetrics and Gynaecology*

1. The Nuffield Professor of Obstetrics and Gynaecology shall lecture and give instruction in Obstetrics and Gynaecology.

2. The professor shall be elected by an electoral board consisting of:

(1) the Vice-Chancellor, or, if the Provost of Oriel College is Vice-Chancellor, a person appointed by Council on the occurrence of a vacancy to act as an elector on that occasion;

(2) the Provost of Oriel College, or, if the Provost is unable or unwilling to act, a person appointed by the governing body of the college on the occurrence of a vacancy to act as an elector on that occasion;

(3) a person appointed by the Governing Body of Oriel College;

(4), (5) two persons appointed by Council;

(6) a person appointed by the General Board;

(7), (8) two persons appointed by the Board of the Faculty of Clinical Medicine;

(9) a person holding a clinical appointment appointed by the Oxfordshire Health Authority after consultation with the Oxford Regional Health Authority.

At least three members of the board, of whom one shall be a professor, shall hold clinical appointments.

3. The professor shall be subject to the General Provisions of the decree concerning the duties of professors and to those Particular Provisions of the same decree which are applicable to this chair.

§ **232.** *Imperial Cancer Research Fund Professor of Clinical Oncology*

1. The University accepts with deep gratitude the endowment provided by the Imperial Cancer Research Fund for the establishment of an Imperial Cancer Research Fund Professorship of Clinical Oncology and for the provision of supporting expenditure for the professorship.

2. The professor shall be elected by an electoral board consisting of:

(1) the Vice-Chancellor, or, if the head of the college specified in (2) of this clause is Vice-Chancellor, a person appointed by Council on the occurrence of a vacancy to act as an elector on that occasion;

(2) the head of the college to which the professorship shall be for the time being allocated by Council under any decree in that behalf, or, if the head is unable or unwilling to act, a person appointed by the governing body of the college on the occurrence of a vacancy to act as an elector on that occasion;

(3) a person appointed by the governing body of the college specified in (2) of this clause;

(4), (5) two persons appointed by Council, one appointed in agreement with the Imperial Cancer Research Fund;

(6) a person appointed by the General Board;

(7), (8) two persons appointed by the Board of the Faculty of Clinical Medicine;

(9) a person holding a clinical appointment appointed by the Oxfordshire Health Authority after consultation with the Oxford Regional Health Authority.

At least three members of the board, of whom one shall be a professor, shall hold clinical appointments.

3. The professor shall hold his or her appointment in a department to be designated from time to time by the Board of the Faculty of Clinical Medicine in agreement with the Imperial Cancer Research Fund. The professor shall lecture and give instruction in Clinical Oncology.

4. The professor shall be subject to the General Provisions of the decree concerning the duties of professors and those Particular Provisions of the same decree which are applicable to this chair.

5. Such part of the income of the endowment as the General Board shall determine not to be required to meet the cost of the professorship shall be applied to the provision of supporting expenditure for the professor in such manner as the General Board and Council, after consultation with the Board of the Faculty of Clinical Medicine, shall direct.

6. Council shall have power, subject to the consent of the Imperial Cancer Research Fund, to amend this decree, provided that the main object of the endowment, namely the establishment of a Professorship of Clinical Oncology and the provision of supporting expenditure, is always kept in view.

§ 233. *Ogilvie's Reader in Ophthalmology*

[1]

1. The Margaret Ogilvie's Reader shall be elected by an electoral board consisting of:

(1) the Vice-Chancellor;

(2), (3) two persons appointed by Council;

(4) a person appointed by the General Board;

(5), (6) two persons appointed by the Board of the Faculty of Clinical Medicine;

(7) a person appointed by the Board of the Faculty of Physiological Sciences;

(8) a person holding a clinical appointment appointed by the Oxfordshire Health Authority after consultation with the Oxford Regional Health Authority.

At least three members of the board, of whom one shall be a professor, shall hold clinical appointments.

2. The reader shall engage in advanced study or research in Ophthalmology, and shall deliver not less than twelve lectures in each academic year.

3. The reader shall submit annually in Michaelmas Term to the Board of the Faculty of Clinical Medicine a brief report on the original research conducted by him or her during the twelve months immediately preceding.

4. The Margaret Ogilvie's Reader, or, during any vacancy in the readership, the Regius Professor of Medicine, shall have charge of the collection of preparations and drawings illustrating the pathology of the eye, presented by Robert Walter Doyne, M.A., F.R.C.S., the first Margaret Ogilvie's Reader, as a further endowment of the readership, together with any future additions thereto.

5. This decree shall be subject to alteration at any time, provided that the main object of the Foundress as set forth in the Decree of Convocation of 10 December 1912 be always kept in view.

[2]

Ogilvie's Readership in Ophthalmology Fund

1. The annual income of the Margaret Ogilvie's Readership Endowment shall be applied in and for the encouragement of Original Research in Ophthalmology, and also for providing at the Oxford Eye Hospital ordinarily, and elsewhere in Oxford when expedient, instruction in the nature and treatment of Eye Diseases and Defects, for members of the University and for members of the medical profession.

2. Three-fourths of the net annual income from the endowment shall be paid to the reader and subject to clause 5 below one-fourth shall be applied under his or her direction in meeting the expenses of the Nuffield Laboratory of Ophthalmology.

3. During any vacancy of the readership so much of the income arising from the trust fund as the Board of the Faculty of Clinical Medicine shall determine shall, subject to clause 5 below, be applied towards meeting the expenses of the Nuffield Laboratory of Ophthalmology.

4. Subject to clauses 2 and 3 above and to clause 5 below, any surplus income of the trust fund shall be invested in augmentation of the capital of the trust.

5. The expenses connected with the maintenance of the collection of preparations and drawings illustrating the pathology of the eye, presented by Robert Walter Doyne, M.A., F.R.C.S., the first Margaret Ogilvie's Reader, as a further endowment of the readership, and with the maintenance of all collections, preparations, drawings, and apparatus purchased out of the income of the Ogilvie Trust Fund shall be defrayed out of the income of the trust fund.

6. This decree shall be subject to alteration by Council at any time, provided that the main object of the foundress as set forth in the decree of Convocation on 17 June 1902, and in this decree, be always kept in view.

§ 234. *Spalding Lecturer in Eastern Orthodox Studies*

1. There shall be a lecturership which shall be called the Spalding Lecturership in Eastern Orthodox Studies.

2. The lecturer shall be appointed by a Board of Electors consisting of:

(1) the Vice-Chancellor;

(2) one person appointed by Council;

(3) one person appointed by the General Board;

(4) one person appointed by the Board of the Faculty of Theology;

(5) one person appointed by the Board of the Faculty of Modern History;

(6) one person appointed by the Board of the Faculty of Medieval and Modern Languages;

(7) one person appointed by the Board of the Faculty of Oriental Studies.

3. Under the direction of the Board of the Faculty of Theology the lecturer shall lecture and give instruction in Orthodox Christianity as related to the culture and society of the Orthodox peoples.

§ 241. *Action Research Professor of Paediatrics*

1. The Action Research Professor of Paediatrics shall lecture and give instruction in Paediatrics.

2. The professor shall be elected by a board of electors consisting of:

(1) the Vice-Chancellor, or, if the Principal of Jesus College is Vice-Chancellor, a person appointed by Council on the occurrence of a vacancy to act as an elector on that occasion;

(2) the Principal of Jesus College, or, if the Principal is unable or unwilling to act, a person appointed by the Governing Body of Jesus College on the occurrence of a vacancy to act as an elector on that occasion;

(3) a person appointed by the Governing Body of Jesus College;

(4), (5) two persons appointed by Council;

(6) a person appointed by the General Board;

(7), (8) two persons elected by the Board of the Faculty of Clinical Medicine;

(9) a person holding a clinical appointment appointed by the Oxfordshire Health Authority after consultation with the Oxford Regional Health Authority.

At least three members of the board, of whom one shall be a professor, shall hold clinical appointments.

3. The professor shall be subject to the General Provisions of the decree concerning the duties of professors and to those Particular Provisions of the same decree which are applicable to this chair.

4. The University accepts with gratitude from the National Fund for Research into Crippling Diseases the sum of £60,000 to form a fund, the income from which shall be applied to purposes of the Department of Paediatrics under the direction of the Action Research Professor of Paediatrics.

§ 242. *Professor of Pathology*

1. The Professor of Pathology shall lecture and give instruction in Pathology. The professor shall also have charge of the Sir William Dunn School of Pathology and of its pathological collections.

2. The professor shall be elected by an electoral board consisting of:

(1) the Vice-Chancellor, or, if the head of the college specified in (2) of this clause is Vice-Chancellor, a person appointed by Council on the occurrence of a vacancy to act as an elector on that occasion;

(2) the head of the college to which the professorship shall be for the time being allocated by Council under any decree in that behalf, or, if the head is unable or unwilling to act, a person appointed by the governing body of the college on the occurrence of a vacancy to act as an elector on that occasion;

(3) a person appointed by the governing body of the college specified in (2) of this clause;

(4) the Regius Professor of Medicine;

(5) a person appointed by Council;

(6) a person appointed by the General Board;

(7)–(9) three persons elected by the Board of the Faculty of Physiological Sciences.

3. The professor shall not be allowed to engage in private medical or surgical practice. He or she shall be subject to the General Provisions of the decree concerning the duties of professors and to those Particular Provisions of the same decree which are applicable to this chair.

§ 243. *Nuffield Professor of Pathology*

1. The Nuffield Professor of Pathology shall engage in advanced study and research and shall, under the direction of the Professor of Morbid Anatomy, assist in the preparation of candidates for the Degree of Bachelor of Medicine.

2. The professor shall be elected by an electoral board consisting of:

(1) the Vice-Chancellor, or, if the head of the college specified in (2) of this clause is Vice-Chancellor, a person appointed by Council;

(2) the head of the college to which the professorship shall be for the time being allocated by Council under any decree in that behalf, or, if the head is unable or unwilling to act, a person appointed by the governing body of the college;

(3) a person appointed by the governing body of the college specified in (2) of this clause;

(4) a person appointed by Council;

(5), (6) two persons appointed by the General Board;

(7) the Head of the Department of Clinical Laboratory Sciences;

(8)–(10) three persons appointed by the Board of the Faculty of Clinical Medicine;

(11) a person holding a clinical appointment appointed by the Oxfordshire Health Authority.

At least three members of the board, of whom one shall be a professor, shall hold clinical appointments.

3. The professor shall hold qualifications entitling him or her to be registered with the General Medical Council as a medical practitioner.

4. The professor shall be subject to the General Provisions of the decree concerning the duties of professors and to those Particular Provisions of the same decree which are applicable to this chair.

§ **244.** *Abraham Professor of Chemical Pathology*

1. The University has accepted with deep gratitude the sum of £430,000 from the Trustees of the E. P. Abraham Research Fund for the endowment of an E. P. Abraham Professorship of Chemical Pathology in the Sir William Dunn School of Pathology and for the provision of supporting costs for the professorship.

2. The E. P. Abraham Professor of Chemical Pathology shall undertake research in Chemical Pathology and shall lecture and give instruction in this subject.

3. The professor shall be elected by a board of electors consisting of:

(1) the Vice-Chancellor, or, if the Rector of Lincoln College is Vice-Chancellor, a person appointed by Council on the occurrence of a vacancy to act as an elector on that occasion;

(2) the Rector of Lincoln College, or, if the Rector is unable or unwilling to act, a person appointed by the Governing Body of Lincoln College on the occurrence of a vacancy to act as an elector on that occasion;

(3) a person appointed by the Governing Body of Lincoln College;

(4) a person appointed by Council;

(5) a person appointed by the General Board;

(6), (7) two persons appointed by the Board of the Faculty of Physiological Sciences;

(8) a person appointed by the Board of the Faculty of Biological Sciences;

(9) a person appointed by the Board of the Faculty of Physical Sciences.

4. The professor shall not be allowed to engage in private medical or surgical practice. He or she shall be subject to the General Provisions of the decree concerning the duties of professors and to those Particular Provisions of the same decree which are applicable to this chair.

5. Such part of the income of the endowment as the General Board shall determine is not required to meet the cost of the professorship shall be applied to the provision of supporting expenditure for the professor in such manner as the Board of the Faculty of Physiological Sciences shall direct, provided that the professor, subject to the approval of the Head of the Sir William Dunn School of Pathology, may personally authorize expenditure in any single academic year up to a limit to be determined from time to time by the Board of the Faculty of Physiological Sciences with the approval of the General Board.

6. Council shall have power, subject to the concurrence of the Trustees of the E. P. Abraham Research Fund, to amend this decree, provided always that the maintenance of the E. P. Abraham Professorship of Chemical Pathology shall remain the first charge on the income of the endowment.

§ 245. *Reader in Experimental Pathology*

1. The University accepts with gratitude a grant from the E. P. Abraham Research Fund of £20,000 towards the establishment of a Readership in Experimental Pathology in the Sir William Dunn School of Pathology.

2. The Reader in Experimental Pathology shall be elected by a board consisting of:

(1) the Vice-Chancellor, or, if the Rector of Exeter College is Vice-Chancellor, a person appointed by the Council on the occurrence of a vacancy to act as an elector on that occasion;

(2) the Regius Professor of Medicine;

(3) the Professor of Pathology;

(4) the Rector of Exeter College, or, if the Rector is unable or unwilling to act, a person appointed by the Governing Body of Exeter College on the occurrence of a vacancy to act as an elector on that occasion;

(5) a person appointed by the Governing Body of Exeter College;

(6) a person appointed by Council;

(7) a person appointed by the General Board;

(8), (9) two persons appointed by the Board of the Faculty of Physiological Sciences.

3. The reader shall engage in advanced study or research, and shall, under the direction of the Professor of Pathology, lecture and give instruction in Pathology in every term.

4. The reader shall not engage in private medical or surgical practice nor hold any appointment which, in the opinion of the General Board, is inconsistent with the duties of this readership.

5. The readership shall be tenable in association with a fellowship at Exeter College unless the person appointed holds a fellowship at another college and wishes to retain it.

§ 246. *Masoumeh and Fereydoon Soudavar Professor of Persian Studies*

1. The University accepts with deep gratitude the sum of £700,000 from Mr. Fereydoon Soudavar for the endowment of the Masoumeh and Fereydoon Soudavar Professorship of Persian Studies and for the provision of support costs for the professorship.

2. The Masoumeh and Fereydoon Soudavar Professor of Persian Studies shall lecture and give instruction in Persian Studies.

3. The professor shall be elected by an electoral board consisting of:

(1) the Vice-Chancellor, or, if the head of the college specified in (2) of this clause is Vice-Chancellor, a person appointed by Council on the occurrence of a vacancy to act as an elector on that occasion;

(2) the head of the college to which the professorship shall be for the time being allocated by Council under any decree in that behalf, or, if the head is unable or unwilling to act, a person appointed by the governing body of the college on the occurrence of a vacancy to act as an elector on that occasion;

(3) a person appointed by the governing body of the college specified in (2) of this clause;

(4) a person appointed by Council;

(5) a person appointed by the General Board;

(6), (7) two persons appointed by the Board of the Faculty of Oriental Studies;

(8) during the lifetime of Mr. Fereydoon Soudavar or thereafter of his wife if she shall survive him, a person nominated by Mr. Soudavar or Mrs. Soudavar, as the case may be.

4. The professor shall be subject to the General Provisions of the decree concerning the duties of professors and to those Particular Provisions of the same decree which are applicable to this chair.

5. The first charge on the income of the endowment shall be the salary costs of the professor. The second charge shall be the provision, under such arrangements as the Board of the Faculty of Oriental Studies may determine, of support, including secretarial support, travelling expenses, and research expenses, for the professor.

6. Any residue not required to meet the expenditure under clause 5 may be expended at the discretion of the faculty board for the promotion of Persian Studies within the University.

§ 247. *Professor of Pharmacology*

1. The Professor of Pharmacology shall lecture and give instruction in Pharmacology.

2. The professor shall be elected by an electoral board consisting of:

(1) the Vice-Chancellor, or, if the head of the college specified in (2) of this clause is Vice-Chancellor, a person appointed by Council on the occurrence of a vacancy to act as an elector on that occasion;

(2) the head of the college to which the professorship shall be for the time being allocated by Council under any decree in that behalf, or, if the head is unable or unwilling to act, a person appointed by the governing body of the college on the occurrence of a vacancy to act as an elector on that occasion;

(3) a person appointed by the governing body of the college specified in (2) of this clause;

(4) a person appointed by Council;

(5) a person appointed by the General Board;

(6)–(8) three persons elected by the Board of the Faculty of Physiological Sciences.

(9) a person elected by the Board of the Faculty of Physical Sciences.

3. The professor shall not be allowed to engage in private medical or surgical practice. He or she shall be subject to the General Provisions of the decree concerning the duties of professors and to those Particular Provisions of the same decree which are applicable to this chair.

§ 248. *Professor of Comparative Philology*

1. The Professor of Comparative Philology shall lecture and give instruction in the history and comparative philology of different languages.

2. The professor shall be elected by an electoral board consisting of:

(1) the Vice-Chancellor, or, if the head of the college specified in (2) of this clause is Vice-Chancellor, a person appointed by Council on the occurrence of a vacancy to act as an elector on that occasion;

(2) the head of the college to which the professorship shall be for the time being allocated by Council under any decree in that behalf, or, if the head is unable or unwilling to act, a person appointed by the governing body of the college on the occurrence of a vacancy to act as an elector on that occasion;

(3) a person appointed by the governing body of the college specified in (2) of this clause;

(4) a person appointed by Council;

(5) a person elected by the Board of the Faculty of Literae Humaniores;

(6) a person elected by the Board of the Faculty of Medieval and Modern Languages;

(7) a person elected by the Board of the Faculty of Oriental Studies.

3. The professor shall be subject to the General Provisions of the decree concerning the duties of professors and to those Particular Provisions of the same decree which are applicable to this chair.

§ 249. *Locke Lecturer in Philosophy*

1. The John Locke Lecturer in Philosophy shall hold office for one academic year.

2. The lecturer shall deliver not less than six lectures on Philosophy during any one or two of the three terms of the academic year.

3. The lecturer shall be appointed, at least biennially, by the Board of the Faculty of Literae Humaniores.

4. The lecturer shall receive a stipend and travel expenses of such value as the board shall from time to time determine.

§ **250.** *Nolloth Professor of the Philosophy of the Christian Religion*

1. The Nolloth Professor of the Philosophy of the Christian Religion shall lecture and give instruction in the Philosophy of the Christian Religion including Apologetics, that is, the setting forth of the reasonableness as well as the authority of the Christian Religion, and shall generally promote the study of those subjects in the University.

2. The professor shall be elected by an electoral board consisting of:

(1) the Vice-Chancellor, or, if the Provost of Oriel College is Vice-Chancellor, a person appointed by Council on the occurrence of a vacancy to act as an elector on that occasion;

(2) the Provost of Oriel College, or, if the Provost is unable or unwilling to act, a person appointed by the Governing Body of Oriel College on the occurrence of a vacancy to act as an elector on that occasion;

(3) a person appointed by the Governing Body of Oriel College;

(4) a person appointed by Council;

(5), (6) two persons appointed by the Board of the Faculty of Theology;

(7) a person appointed by the Board of the Faculty of Literae Humaniores.

3. The professor shall be subject to the General Provisions of the decree concerning the duties of professors and to those Particular Provisions of the same decree which are applicable to this chair.

4. Council shall have power to alter this decree from time to time, provided that the main objects of the foundation of the professorship, viz. the teaching and study of the Philosophy and Apologetics of the Christian Religion, are kept in view.

§ **251.** *Dr. Lee's Professor of Experimental Philosophy*

1. Dr. Lee's Professor of Experimental Philosophy shall lecture and give instruction in Experimental Philosophy.

2. The professor shall be elected by an electoral board consisting of:

(1) the Vice-Chancellor, or, if the Warden of Wadham College is Vice-Chancellor, a person appointed by Council on the occurrence of a vacancy to act as an elector on that occasion;

(2) the Warden of Wadham College, or, if the Warden is unable or unwilling to act, a person appointed by the Governing Body of Wadham College on the occurrence of a vacancy to act as an elector on that occasion;

(3) a person appointed by the Governing Body of Wadham College;

(4) a person appointed by Council;

(5) a person appointed by the General Board;

(6)–(9) four persons elected by the Board of the Faculty of Physical Sciences.

3. The professor shall be subject to the General Provisions of the decree concerning the duties of professors and to those Particular Provisions of the same decree which are applicable to this chair.

§ **252.** *Wilde Professor of Mental Philosophy*

1. The Wilde Professor shall lecture and give instruction in Mental Philosophy, and shall from time to time lecture on the more theoretical aspects of Psychology.

2. The professor shall be elected by a board of electors consisting of:

(1) the Vice-Chancellor, or, if the President of Corpus Christi College is Vice-Chancellor, a person appointed by Council;

(2) the President of Corpus Christi College, or, if the President is unable or unwilling to act, a person appointed by the Governing Body of Corpus Christi College;

(3) a person appointed by the Governing Body of Corpus Christi College;

(4) a person appointed by Council;

(5), (6) two persons appointed by the General Board;

(7), (8) two persons elected by the Board of the Faculty of Literae Humaniores;

(9) a person elected by the Board of the Faculty of Psychological Studies.

3. For the purposes of this professorship the term 'Mental Philosophy' shall be taken to mean the theoretical and conceptual study of the human mind.

4. The interest on the capital sum provided for the endowment of the post shall be used towards defraying the stipend of the professor.

5. This decree may be altered from time to time; provided always that

(*a*) the title of the professorship shall be retained;

(*b*) the main object of the professorship shall be kept in view, namely, the promotion of the study of Mental Philosophy among the Junior Members of the University of Oxford.

6. The professor shall be subject to the General Provisions of the decree concerning the duties of professors and to those Particular Provisions of the same decree which are applicable to this chair.

§ **253.** *Waynflete Professor of Metaphysical Philosophy*

1. The Waynflete Professor of Metaphysical Philosophy shall lecture and give instruction in Philosophy with special regard to the Problems, Theories, and History of Metaphysics.

2. The professor shall be elected by an electoral board consisting of:

(1) the Vice-Chancellor, or, if the President of Magdalen College is Vice-Chancellor, a person appointed by Council on the occurrence of a vacancy to act as an elector on that occasion;

(2) the President of Magdalen College, or, if the President is unable or unwilling to act, a person appointed by the Governing Body of Magdalen College on the occurrence of a vacancy to act as an elector on that occasion;

(3) a person appointed by the Governing Body of Magdalen College;

(4) a person appointed by Council;

(5), (6) two persons elected by the Board of the Faculty of Literae Humaniores;

(7) a person elected by the Sub-faculty of Philosophy, or, if there be no such sub-faculty, then by the Faculty of Literae Humaniores.

3. The professor shall be subject to the General Provisions of the decree concerning the duties of professors and to those Particular Provisions of the same decree which are applicable to this chair.

§ **254.** *White's Professor of Moral Philosophy*

1. White's Professor of Moral Philosophy shall lecture and give instruction in Philosophy with special regard to the Problems, Theories, and History of Ethics.

2. The professor shall be elected by an electoral board consisting of:

(1) the Vice-Chancellor, or, if the President of Corpus Christi College is Vice-Chancellor, a person appointed by Council on the occurrence of a vacancy to act as an elector on that occasion;

(2) the President of Corpus Christi College, or, if the President is unable or unwilling to act, a person appointed by the Governing Body of Corpus Christi College on the occurrence of a vacancy to act as an elector on that occasion;

(3) a person appointed by the Governing Body of Corpus Christi College;

(4) a person appointed by Council;

(5), (6) two persons appointed by the General Board;

(7), (8) two persons elected by the Board of the Faculty of Literae Humaniores;

(9) a person elected by the Sub-faculty of Philosophy, or, if there be no such sub-faculty, then by the Faculty of Literae Humaniores.

3. The professor shall be subject to the General Provisions of the decree concerning the duties of professors and to those Particular Provisions of the same decree which are applicable to this chair.

§ **255.** *Sedleian Professor of Natural Philosophy*

1. The Sedleian Professor of Natural Philosophy shall lecture and give instruction in Mathematics and its applications.

2. The professor shall be elected by an electoral board consisting of:

(1) the Vice-Chancellor, or, if the head of the college specified in (2) of this clause is Vice-Chancellor, a person appointed by Council on the occurrence of a vacancy to act as an elector on that occasion;

(2) the head of the college to which the professorship shall be for the time being allocated by Council under any decree in that behalf, or, if the head is unable or unwilling to act, a person appointed by the governing body of the college on the occurrence of a vacancy to act as an elector on that occasion;

(3) a person appointed by the governing body of the college specified in (2) of this clause;

(4) a person appointed by Council;

(5), (6) two persons appointed by the General Board;

(7), (8) two persons appointed by the Board of the Faculty of Mathematical Sciences;

(9) a person appointed by the Board of the Faculty of Physical Sciences.

3. The professor shall be subject to the General Provisions of the decree concerning the duties of professors and to those Particular Provisions of the same decree which are applicable to this chair.

§ 256. *Halley Professor of Physics*

1. The Halley Professor of Physics shall lecture and give instruction in Physics.

2. The professor shall be elected by an electoral board consisting of:

(1) the Vice-Chancellor, or, if the head of the college specified in (2) of this clause is Vice-Chancellor, a person appointed by Council on the occurrence of a vacancy to act as an elector on that occasion;

(2) the head of the college to which the professorship shall be for the time being allocated by Council under any decree in that behalf, or, if the head is unable or unwilling to act, a person appointed by the governing body of the college on the occurrence of a vacancy to act as an elector on that occasion;

(3) a person appointed by the governing body of the college specified in (2) of this clause;

(4) a person appointed by Council;

(5) a person appointed by the General Board;

(6)–(9) four persons appointed by the Board of the Faculty of Physical Sciences.

3. The professor shall be subject to the General Provisions of the decree concerning the duties of professors and to those Particular Provisions of the same decree which are applicable to this chair.

§ 257. *Wykeham Professor of Physics*

1. The Wykeham Professor of Physics shall lecture and give instruction in Theoretical Physics.

2. The professor shall be elected by an electoral board consisting of:

(1) the Vice-Chancellor, or, if the Warden of New College is Vice-Chancellor, a person appointed by Council on the occurrence of a vacancy to act as an elector on that occasion;

(2) the Warden of New College, or, if the Warden is unable or unwilling to act, a person appointed by the Governing Body of New College on the occurrence of a vacancy to act as an elector on that occasion;

(3) a person appointed by the Governing Body of New College;

(4) a person appointed by Council;

(5) a person appointed by the General Board;

(6)–(8) three persons elected by the Board of the Faculty of Physical Sciences;

(9) one person elected by the Board of the Faculty of Mathematical Sciences.

3. The professor shall be subject to the General Provisions of the decree governing the duties of professors and to those Particular Provisions of the same decree which are applicable to this chair.

§ **258.** *Professors of Experimental Physics*

1. There shall be three Professors of Experimental Physics each of whom shall lecture and give instruction in Physics.

2. Each professor shall be elected by a board consisting of:

(1) the Vice-Chancellor, or, if the head of the college specified in (2) of this clause is Vice-Chancellor, a person appointed by Council on the occurrence of a vacancy to act as an elector on that occasion;

(2) the head of the college to which the professorship shall be for the time being allocated by Council under any decree in that behalf, or, if the head is unable or unwilling to act, a person appointed by the governing body of the college on the occurrence of a vacancy to act as an elector on that occasion;

(3) a person appointed by the governing body of the college specified in (2) of this clause;

(4) a person appointed by Council;

(5) a person appointed by the General Board;

(6)–(9) four persons appointed by the Board of the Faculty of Physical Sciences.

3. Each professor shall be subject to the General Provisions of the decree concerning the duties of professors and to those Particular Provisions of the same decree which are applicable to these chairs.

§ **259.** *Waynflete Professor of Physiology*

1. The Waynflete Professor of Physiology shall lecture and give instruction in Human and Comparative Physiology.

2. The professor shall be elected by an electoral board consisting of:

(1) the Vice-Chancellor, or, if the President of Magdalen College is Vice-Chancellor, a person appointed by Council on the occurrence of a vacancy to act as an elector on that occasion;

(2) the President of Magdalen College, or, if the President is unable or unwilling to act, a person appointed by the Governing Body of Magdalen College on the occurrence of a vacancy to act as an elector on that occasion;

(3) a person appointed by the Governing Body of Magdalen College;

(4) a person appointed by Council;

(5) a person appointed by the General Board;

(6)–(8) three persons elected by the Board of the Faculty of Physiological Sciences;

(9) a person elected by the Board of the Faculty of Biological Sciences.

3. The professor shall not be allowed to engage in private medical or surgical practice. He or she shall be subject to the General Provisions of the decree concerning the duties of professors and to those Particular Provisions of the same decree which are applicable to this chair.

§ 260. *Reader in Human Physiology*

1. There shall be a Reader in Human Physiology who shall be elected by a board consisting of:

(1) the Vice-Chancellor;

(2) the Waynflete Professor of Physiology;

(3) a person appointed by Council;

(4) a person appointed by the General Board;

(5), (6) two persons appointed by the Board of the Faculty of Physiological Sciences.

(7) a person appointed by the Board of the Faculty of Biological Sciences.

2. The reader shall engage in advanced study and research in some aspect of Physiological Sciences relevant to Man and shall

(*a*) lecture and give instruction in Human Physiology under the direction of the Board of the Faculty of Physiological Sciences;

(*b*) assist in the supervision of research in the Department of Physiology.

3. The reader shall not engage in private medical or surgical practice nor hold any appointment which in the opinion of the General Board is inconsistent with the duties of this readership.

§ 261. *Reader in Plant Science*

1. There shall be a Reader in Plant Science who shall be elected by a board consisting of:

(1) the Vice-Chancellor;

(2) the Sibthorpian Professor of Plant Science;

(3) a person appointed by Council;

(4) a person appointed by the General Board;

(5)–(7) three persons appointed by the Board of the Faculty of Biological Sciences.

2. The reader shall engage in advanced study or research and shall, under the direction of the Head of the Department of Plant Sciences, lecture and give instruction in Plant Science.

§ 262. *Professor of Poetry on the Foundation of Henry Birkhead*

1. The Professor of Poetry shall deliver a Public Lecture in each term.

2. The professor shall be elected by Convocation and shall hold office for five years from the first day of the term following the term in which he or she was elected, and shall not be re-eligible.

3. The provisions of Sect. I, § 4, cl. 3, shall not apply to the Professorship of Poetry.

§ **263.** *Drummond Professor of Political Economy*

1. The Drummond Professor of Political Economy shall lecture and give instruction in the principles and history of Political Economy.

2. The professor shall be elected by an electoral board consisting of:

(1) the Vice-Chancellor, or, if the Warden of All Souls College is Vice-Chancellor, a person appointed by Council on the occurrence of a vacancy to act as an elector on that occasion;

(2) the Warden of All Souls College, or, if the Warden is unable or unwilling to act, a person appointed by the Governing Body of All Souls College on the occurrence of a vacancy to act as an elector on that occasion;

(3) a person appointed by the Governing Body of All Souls College;

(4) a person appointed by Council;

(5) one person elected by the Board of the Faculty of Modern History;

(6), (7) two persons elected by the Board of the Faculty of Social Studies.

3. The professor shall be subject to the General Provisions of the decree concerning the duties of professors and to those Particular Provisions of the same decree which are applicable to this chair.

§ **264.** *Nuffield Professor of Comparative European Politics*

1. There shall be a Nuffield Professor of Comparative European Politics who shall lecture and give instruction in Comparative European Politics.

2. The professor shall be elected by an electoral board consisting of:

(1) the Vice-Chancellor, or, if the Warden of Nuffield College is Vice-Chancellor, a person appointed by Council;

(2) the Warden of Nuffield College, or, if the Warden is unable or unwilling to act, a person appointed by the Governing Body of Nuffield College;

(3) a person appointed by the Governing Body of Nuffield College;

(4) a person appointed by Council;

(5), (6) two persons appointed by the General Board;

(7)–(9) three persons appointed by the Board of the Faculty of Social Studies.

3. The professor shall be subject to the General Provisions of the decree concerning the duties of professors and to those Particular Provisions of the same decree which are applicable to this chair.

§ **265.** *King John II Professor of Portuguese Studies*

1. The King John II Professor of Portuguese Studies shall engage in advanced study and research and shall lecture and give instruction in Portuguese Studies, and shall promote generally the study of Portuguese in the University, on such conditions and with such duties as the General Board shall from time to time determine.

2. The professor shall be elected by an electoral board consisting of:

(1) the Vice-Chancellor, or, if the head of the college specified in (2) of this clause is Vice-Chancellor, a person appointed by Council;

(2) the head of the college to which the professorship shall be for the time being allocated by Council under any decree in that behalf, or, if the head is unable or unwilling to act, a person appointed by the governing body of the college;

(3) a person appointed by the governing body of the college specified in (2) of this clause;

(4) a person appointed by Council after consultation with the Instituto Camões;

(5), (6) two persons appointed by the General Board;

(7)–(9) three persons appointed by the Board of the Faculty of Medieval and Modern Languages.

3. The professor shall be subject to the General Provisions of the decree concerning the duties of professors and to those Particular Provisions of the same decree which are applicable to this chair.

§ 266. *Handley Professor of Psychiatry*

1. The W. A. Handley Professor of Psychiatry shall lecture and give instruction in Psychiatry.

2. The professor shall be elected by an electoral board consisting of:

(1) the Vice-Chancellor, or, if the Warden of Merton College is Vice-Chancellor, a person appointed by Council on the occurrence of a vacancy to act as an elector on that occasion;

(2) the Warden of Merton College, or, if the Warden is unable or unwilling to act, a person appointed by the Governing Body of Merton College on the occurrence of a vacancy to act as an elector on that occasion;

(3) a person appointed by the Governing Body of Merton College;

(4) a person appointed by Council;

(5) a person appointed by the General Board;

(6), (7) two persons elected by the Board of the Faculty of Clinical Medicine;

(8) a person elected by the Board of the Faculty of Psychological Studies;

(9) a person holding a clinical appointment appointed by the Oxfordshire Health Authority after consultation with the Oxford Regional Health Authority.

At least three members of the board, of whom one shall be a professor, shall hold clinical appointments.

3. The professor shall be subject to the General Provisions of the decree concerning the duties of professors and to those Particular Provisions of the same decree which are applicable to this chair.

§ 267. *Professor of Child and Adolescent Psychiatry*

1. The Professor of Child and Adolescent Psychiatry shall lecture and give instruction in Psychiatry.

2. The professor shall be elected by an electoral board consisting of:

(1) the Vice-Chancellor, or, if the head of the college specified in (2) of this clause is Vice-Chancellor, a person appointed by Council;

(2) the head of the college to which the professorship shall be for the time being allocated by Council under any decree in that behalf, or, if the head is unable or unwilling to act, a person appointed by the governing body of the college;

(3) a person appointed by the governing body of the college specified in (2) of this clause;

(4) a person appointed by Council;

(5), (6) two persons appointed by the General Board;

(7) the W. A. Handley Professor of Psychiatry;

(8)–(10) three persons appointed by the Board of the Faculty of Clinical Medicine;

(11) a person holding a clinical appointment appointed by the Oxfordshire Health Authority.

At least three members of the board, of whom one shall be a professor, shall hold clinical appointments.

3. The professor shall be subject to the General Provisions of the decree concerning the duties of professors and to those Particular Provisions of the same decree which are applicable to this chair.

§ 268. *Professor of Psychology*

1. The Professor of Psychology shall lecture and give instruction in Psychology in the widest sense.

2. The professor shall be elected by a board consisting of:

(1) the Vice-Chancellor, or, if the head of the college specified in (2) of this clause is Vice-Chancellor, a person appointed by Council on the occurrence of a vacancy to act as an elector on that occasion;

(2) the head of the college to which the professorship shall be for the time being allocated by Council under any decree in that behalf, or, if the head is unable or unwilling to act, a person appointed by the governing body of the college on the occurrence of a vacancy to act as an elector on that occasion;

(3) a person appointed by the governing body of the college specified in (2) of this clause;

(4) a person elected by Council;

(5) a person elected by the General Board;

(6), (7) two persons elected by the Board of the Faculty of Psychological Studies;

(8) a person elected by the Board of the Faculty of Biological Sciences;

(9) a person elected by the Board of the Faculty of Physiological Sciences.

3. The professor shall be subject to the General Provisions of the decree concerning the duties of professors and to those Particular Provisions of the same decree which are applicable to this chair.

§ 269. *Watts Professor of Psychology*

1. The Watts Professor of Psychology shall lecture and give instruction in Psychology in the widest sense.

2. The professor shall be elected by an electoral board consisting of:

(1) the Vice-Chancellor, or, if the head of the college specified in (2) of this clause is Vice-Chancellor, a person appointed by Council on the occurrence of a vacancy to act as an elector on that occasion;

(2) the head of the college to which the professorship shall be for the time being allocated by Council under any decree in that behalf, or, if the head is unable or unwilling to act, a person appointed by the governing body of the college on the occurrence of a vacancy to act as an elector on that occasion;

(3) a person appointed by the governing body of the college specified in (2) of this clause;

(4) a person appointed by Council;

(5) a person appointed by the General Board;

(6)–(8) three persons appointed by the Board of the Faculty of Psychological Studies.

3. The professor shall be subject to the General Provisions of the decree concerning the duties of professors, and to those Particular Provisions of the same decree which are applicable to this chair.

§ 270. *Professor of Public Health*

1. The Professor of Public Health shall lecture and give instruction in Public Health.

2. The professor shall be elected by a board of electors consisting of:

(1) the Vice-Chancellor, or, if the Master of St. Cross College is Vice-Chancellor, a person appointed by Council on the occurrence of a vacancy to act as an elector on that occasion;

(2) the Master of St. Cross College, or, if the Master is unable or unwilling to act, a person appointed by the Governing Body of St. Cross College on the occurrence of a vacancy to act as an elector on that occasion;

(3) a person appointed by the Governing Body of St. Cross College;

(4), (5) two persons appointed by Council;

(6), (7) two persons appointed by the General Board;

(8), (9) two persons appointed by the Board of the Faculty of Clinical Medicine;

(10) a person holding a clinical appointment appointed by the Oxfordshire Health Authority after consultation with the Oxford Regional Health Authority.

At least three members of the board, of whom one shall be a professor, shall hold clinical appointments.

3. The professor shall be subject to the General Provisions of the decree concerning the duties of professors and to those Particular Provisions of the same decree which are applicable to this chair.

§ 271. *Simonyi Professor of the Public Understanding of Science*

1. The University accepts with deep gratitude the sum of £1.5m from Dr Charles Simonyi for the endowment of the Charles Simonyi Professorship of the Public Understanding of Science.

2. The Charles Simonyi Professor of the Public Understanding of Science shall

(*a*) notwithstanding the provisions of Sect. I, § 5. B, cl. 1 (*b*) of this chapter, engage in teaching related to the Public Understanding of Science and in other appropriate forms of provision as agreed between the professor, the head of the appropriate discipline-based department, and the Director of the Department for Continuing Education, such teaching and other forms of provision to occupy no fewer than twelve hours and no more than fifty hours in Oxford in any academic year;

(*b*) promote the public understanding of science both within and outside Oxford.

3. The professor shall be elected by a board of electors consisting of

(1) the Vice-Chancellor, or, if the head of the college specified in (2) of this clause is Vice-Chancellor a person appointed by Council;

(2) the head of the college to which the professorship shall be for the time being allocated by Council under any decree in that behalf, or, if the head is unable or unwilling to act, a person appointed by the governing body of the college;

(3) a person appointed by the governing body of the college specified in (2) of this clause;

(4), (5) two persons appointed by Council, one of whom shall be appointed after consultation with the benefactor;

(6) a person appointed by the General Board;

(7) a person appointed by the Board of the Faculty of Biological Sciences;

(8) a person appointed by the Board of the Faculty of Physical Sciences;

(9) a person appointed by the Committee on Continuing Education.

4. Subject to the provisions of clause 2 (*a*) above, the professor shall be subject to the General Provisions of the decree concerning the duties of professors and to those Particular Provisions of the same decree which are applicable to this chair.

5. Such part of the income from the endowment as is not required to meet the salary and associated costs of the professorship shall be applied for the provision

of support funds for the professor in such ways as the Committee on Continuing Education may determine. That committee may delegate its powers under this clause to a subcommittee consisting of the Chairman of the Committee on Continuing Education, the Director of the Department for Continuing Education, the professor, and the head of any discipline-based department or departments with which the professor is also associated, or their nominees, subject to annual report to the committee.

§ **281.** *Rhodes Professor of Race Relations*

1. The University hereby accepts with deep gratitude the offer of the Rhodesian Selection Trust Group of Copper Mining Companies to provide for the permanent endowment of a Rhodes Professorship of Race Relations.

2. The Rhodes Professor of Race Relations shall lecture and give instruction in interracial relations.

3. The professor shall be elected by an electoral board consisting of:

(1) the Vice-Chancellor, or, if the head of the college specified in (2) of this clause is Vice-Chancellor, a person appointed by Council on the occurrence of a vacancy to act as an elector on that occasion;

(2) the head of the college to which the professorship shall be for the time being allocated by Council under any decree in that behalf, or, if the head is unable or unwilling to act, a person appointed by the governing body of the college on the occurrence of a vacancy to act as an elector on that occasion;

(3) a person appointed by the governing body of the college specified in (2) of this clause;

(4) a person appointed by Council;

(5), (6) two persons appointed by the General Board;

(7) a person appointed by the Board of the Faculty of Social Studies;

(8) a person appointed by the Board of the Faculty of Modern History;

(9) a person appointed by the Board of the Faculty of Anthropology and Geography.

4. Any part of the income of the endowment of the professorship which is not required to meet the costs (including support costs) thereof and such management fee as shall be determined from year to year by the Curators of the University Chest, may be expended, under conditions to be determined from time to time by the Board of the Faculty of Social Studies, to support teaching and research in interracial relations. The board shall appoint a committee to advise it, and that committee shall include a representative of the Board of the Faculty of Anthropology and Geography.

5. The professor shall be subject to the General Provisions of the decree concerning the duties of professors and to those Particular Provisions of the same decree which are applicable to this chair.

6. This decree may be altered with the consent of the founders provided that the main object of the endowment, namely, the development of the study of interracial relations, is always kept in view.

§ 282. *Wilde Lecturer in Natural and Comparative Religion*

1. The Wilde Lecturer in Natural and Comparative Religion shall be elected by a board of nine electors, consisting of:

(1) the Vice-Chancellor;

(2) the Nolloth Professor of the Philosophy of the Christian Religion;

(3) the Spalding Professor of Eastern Religions and Ethics;

(4) one person appointed by the Board of the Faculty of Theology;

(5), (6) two persons appointed by the Board of the Faculty of Literae Humaniores;

(7) one person appointed by the Board of the Faculty of Physical Sciences;

(8) one person appointed by the Board of the Faculty of Oriental Studies;

(9) one person appointed by the Board of the Faculty of Anthropology and Geography.

2. Each of the appointed electors shall hold office for six years, and shall be re-eligible. When an appointed elector vacates his or her seat otherwise than by lapse of time, the vacancy shall as soon as possible be filled up by the persons or body by whom the elector so vacating his or her seat was appointed. If the vacancy shall be filled up before the expiration of the period for which the elector so vacating his or her seat was appointed, the person appointed to fill the vacancy shall hold office for the unexpired residue only of such period.

3. Appointments of members of the board of electors, except those made to fill casual vacancies, shall be made in Hilary Term, unless Council shall by decree appoint another term in any particular year, and the persons appointed shall enter on office at the end of the same term.

4. No member of the board of electors shall be eligible for the office of lecturer.

5. The lecturer shall hold office for one or two or three years, as the electors shall determine. A person may be appointed lecturer more than once; but the same person shall not be appointed twice in succession.

6. The lecturer shall deliver not less than eight lectures in each academical year in Natural and Comparative Religion; these lectures to be delivered either in the course of one term, or so that not less than four be given in each of two terms. The lecturer shall submit to the board of electors, before the end of the fourth week from the beginning of Trinity Term in each year, a statement of the term or terms in which he or she proposes to lecture, and of the subjects which the lecturer proposes to treat during the ensuing academical year.

7. The lecturer shall enter upon office on the first day of Michaelmas Term, and the electors may make an appointment at any time during the preceding year.

8. For the purposes of this lecturership the term Natural Religion shall be taken to mean man's conscious recognition of purposive intelligence and adaptability in the universe of things on which he is dependent for his continued existence and well-being and with which he endeavours to live in harmonious relations. Comparative Religion shall be taken to mean the modes of causation, rites, observances, and other concepts involved in the major historical religions.

9. In each year there shall be paid out of the income of the trust fund in that year:

(*a*) any expenses incurred by the University in the execution of the trust; and

(*b*) such allowance to the lecturer for his or her travelling and other expenses as the electors shall resolve; and

(*c*) the stipend of the lecturer, which shall be the balance of the income of the fund after the expenses in (*a*) and (*b*) shall have been paid.

10. In case of any accidental vacancy in the lecturership, the net income accruing during the vacancy shall be invested in augmentation of the endowment fund.

11. This decree may be altered during the lifetime of the founder with his consent, and, after the lifetime of the Founder, Council shall have full power to alter it from time to time, provided always that the main object of the foundation is kept in view, namely, the promotion in the University of the study of Natural and Comparative Religion.

§ 283. *Spalding Professor of Eastern Religions and Ethics*

1. The sum of £42,000 offered by Mr. and Mrs. H. N. Spalding for the endowment of a Spalding Professorship of Eastern Religions and Ethics, and for the creation of a travelling fund for the use of the professor, is hereby accepted with deep gratitude.

2. The professor shall lecture and give instruction on the religions and ethical systems of the East under the conditions stated at the time of the establishment of the professorship,[1] preferably though not necessarily with special reference to Hindu and Buddhist thought and their comparison with each other and with other religious systems.

[1] The conditions stated were as follows:

'The purpose of the Professorship shall be to build up in the University of Oxford a permanent interest in the great religions and ethical systems (alike in their individual, social, and political aspects) of the East, whether expressed in philosophic, poetic, devotional, or other literature, in art, in history, and in social life and structure, to set forth their development and spiritual meaning, and to interpret them by comparison and contrast with each other and with the religions and ethics of the West and in any other appropriate way, with the aim of bringing together the world's great religions in closer understanding, harmony, and friendship; as well as to promote co-operation with other Universities, bodies, and persons in East and West which pursue the like ends, which purpose is likely to be furthered by the establishment of a Professorship which would in the natural course normally be held by persons of Asian descent.'

3. The professor shall be elected by an electoral board consisting of:

(1) the Vice-Chancellor, or, if the Warden of All Souls College is Vice-Chancellor, a person appointed by Council on the occurrence of a vacancy to act as an elector on that occasion;

(2) a person appointed by the General Board in consultation with the Spalding Educational Trustees;

(3) the Warden of All Souls College, or, if the Warden is unable or unwilling to act, a person appointed by the Governing Body of All Souls College on the occurrence of a vacancy to act as an elector on that occasion;

(4) a person appointed by the Governing Body of All Souls College;

(5) a person appointed by Council;

(6) a person appointed by the Board of the Faculty of Theology and the Board of the Faculty of Literae Humaniores;

(7), (8) two persons appointed by the Board of the Faculty of Oriental Studies.

4. A sum of £500 shall be set aside as a travelling fund from which as long as it lasts the professor may draw such sums as the board of electors may approve from time to time to enable him or her to travel in the East for purposes of study; and if at any time there is a vacancy in the professorship the emoluments up to a total of £500 shall be set aside to replenish the travelling fund.

5. The professor shall be subject to the General Provisions of the decree concerning the duties of professors and to those Particular Provisions of the same decree which are applicable to this chair.

§ 284. *Professor of the Romance Languages*

1. The Professor of the Romance Languages shall lecture and give instruction in the structure and historical development of the languages which are derived from the Latin.

2. The professor shall be elected by an electoral board consisting of:

(1) the Vice-Chancellor, or, if the head of the college specified in (2) of this clause is Vice-Chancellor, a person appointed by Council on the occurrence of a vacancy to act as an elector on that occasion;

(2) the head of the college to which the professorship shall be for the time being allocated by Council under any decree in that behalf, or, if the head is unable or unwilling to act, a person appointed by the governing body of the college on the occurrence of a vacancy to act as an elector on that occasion;

(3) a person appointed by the governing body of the college specified in (2) of this clause;

(4) a person appointed by Council;

(5), (6) two persons appointed by the General Board;

(7), (8) two persons elected by the Board of the Faculty of Medieval and Modern Languages;

(9) a person elected by the Board of the Faculty of Literae Humaniores.

3. The professor shall be subject to the General Provisions of the decree concerning the duties of professors and to those Particular Provisions of the same decree which are applicable to this chair.

§ 285. *Romanes Lecturer*

1. A lecturership shall henceforth be established and maintained in the University of Oxford called the Romanes Lecturership, and the lecturer, who shall be called the Romanes Lecturer, shall be appointed annually by the Vice-Chancellor. It shall be the duty of the Romanes Lecturer to deliver a public lecture in Oxford, on a day and at a place to be fixed by the Vice-Chancellor, on some subject approved by the Vice-Chancellor relating to Science, Art, or Literature, and public notice thereof shall be given to members of the University in the usual manner.

2. The sum of £1,000 and the stocks, funds, and securities for the time being representing the same, and any additions thereto, shall be called 'the Romanes Lecturership Fund'.

3. The capital of the fund shall be invested in the name of the Chancellor, Masters, and Scholars of the University of Oxford, hereinafter referred to as 'The University', in government securities or in other securities in which trustees are by law allowed to invest trust money, with power for the University from time to time to vary such securities for others of a like nature.

4. The income accruing from the fund shall be applied under the direction of the Vice-Chancellor for the time being in payment to the Romanes Lecturer for the time being of an annual sum to be determined by the Vice-Chancellor.

5. Each lecturer shall deliver to the Vice-Chancellor his or her lecture or a verified copy thereof, which shall be retained in the Bodleian Library.

6. Any surplus income of the fund may be applied at the discretion of the Vice-Chancellor in any of the following ways:

(*a*) to form a reserve fund from which the travelling expenses of such lecturers as shall from time to time come from overseas may be paid;

(*b*) in payment of expenses incidental to the administration and delivery of the lecture.

7. From time to time the rules aforesaid may be altered by decree, and council may make and vary from time to time any rules or by-laws for or incidental to the delivery of the lectures and the management of the trust fund; provided always that the fundamental object of the endowment, viz. the delivery in the University once a year of a lecture to be called the Romanes Lecture on some subject approved by the Vice-Chancellor relating to Science, Art, or Literature, shall be always observed and maintained.

8. A copy of this decree having been delivered to each lecturer at the time of his or her appointment, the lecturer shall be deemed to have accepted the office with notice of, and to have consented to, the same.

§ **286.** *Professor of Russian*

1. The Professor of Russian shall lecture and give instruction in Russian Language and Literature.

2. The professor shall be elected by an electoral board consisting of:

(1) the Vice-Chancellor, or, if the head of the college specified in (2) of this clause is Vice-Chancellor, a person appointed by Council on the occurrence of a vacancy to act as an elector on that occasion;

(2) the head of the college to which the professorship shall be for the time being allocated by Council under any decree in that behalf, or, if the head is unable or unwilling to act, a person appointed by the governing body of the college on the occurrence of a vacancy to act as an elector on that occasion;

(3) a person appointed by the governing body of the college specified in (2) of this clause;

(4) a person appointed by Council;

(5) a person appointed by the General Board;

(6), (7) two persons elected by the Board of the Faculty of Medieval and Modern Languages.

3. The professor shall be subject to the General Provisions of the decree concerning the duties of professors and to those Particular Provisions of the same decree which are applicable to this chair.

§ **291.** *Boden Professor of Sanskrit*

1. The Boden Professor of Sanskrit shall lecture and give instruction in the Sanskrit Language and Literature.

2. The professor shall be elected by an electoral board consisting of:

(1) the Vice-Chancellor, or, if the Master of Balliol College is Vice-Chancellor, a person appointed by Council on the occurrence of a vacancy to act as an elector on that occasion;

(2) the Master of Balliol College, or, if the Master is unable or unwilling to act, a person appointed by the Governing Body of Balliol College on the occurrence of a vacancy to act as an elector on that occasion;

(3) a person appointed by the Governing Body of Balliol College;

(4) a person appointed by Council;

(5), (6) two persons elected by the Board of the Faculty of Oriental Studies;

(7) a person elected by the Board of the Faculty of Literae Humaniores.

3. The professor shall be subject to the General Provisions of the decree concerning the duties of professors and to those Particular Provisions of the same decree which are applicable to this chair.

§ **292.** *Idreos Professor of Science and Religion*

1. The University accepts with deep gratitude the benefaction from the late Dr Andreas Idreos, together with any further sums received for the same

purpose, for the establishment of the Andreas Idreos Professorship of Science and Religion.

2. The Andreas Idreos Professor of Science and Religion shall engage in advanced study and research and shall lecture and give instruction in questions raised for Theology by the Natural and Human and Social Sciences, and the impact of Theology on the Natural and Human and Social Sciences.

3. The professor shall be elected by an electoral board consisting of:

(1) the Vice-Chancellor, or, if the head of the college specified in (2) of this clause is Vice-Chancellor, a person appointed by Council;

(2) the head of the college to which the professorship shall be for the time being allocated by Council under any decree in that behalf, or, if the head is unable or unwilling to act, a person appointed by the governing body of the college;

(3) a person appointed by the governing body of the college specified in (2) of this clause;

(4) a person appointed by Council;

(5), (6) two persons appointed by the General Board;

(7)–(9) three persons appointed by the Board of the Faculty of Theology.

4. The professor shall be subject to the General Provisions of the decree concerning the duties of professors and to those Particular Provisions of the same decree which are applicable to this chair.

§ 293. *Barnett Professor of Social Policy*

1. The Barnett Professor of Social Policy shall lecture and give instruction in Social Policy.

2. The professor shall be elected by an electoral board consisting of:

(1) the Vice-Chancellor, or, if the head of the college specified in (2) of this clause is Vice-Chancellor, a person appointed by Council;

(2) the head of the college to which the professorship shall be for the time being allocated by Council under any decree in that behalf, or, if the head is unable or unwilling to act, a person appointed by the governing body of the college;

(3) a person appointed by the governing body of the college specified in (2) of this clause;

(4) a person appointed by Council;

(5), (6) two persons appointed by the General Board;

(7)-(9) three persons appointed by the Board of the Faculty of Social Studies.

3. The professor shall be subject to the General Provisions of the decree concerning the duties of professors and to those Particular Provisions of the same decree which are applicable to this chair.

§ 294. *Chichele Professor of Social and Political Theory*

1. The Chichele Professor of Social and Political Theory shall lecture and give instruction in Social and Political Theory.

2. The professor shall be elected by an electoral board consisting of:

(1) the Vice-Chancellor, or, if the Warden of All Souls College is Vice-Chancellor, a person appointed by Council on the occurrence of a vacancy to act as an elector on that occasion;

(2) the Warden of All Souls College, or, if the Warden is unable or unwilling to act, a person appointed by the Governing Body of All Souls College on the occurrence of a vacancy to act as an elector on that occasion;

(3) a person appointed by the Governing Body of All Souls College;

(4), (5) two persons elected by the Board of the Faculty of Social Studies;

(6) a person elected by the Board of the Faculty of Literae Humaniores;

(7) a person elected by the Board of the Faculty of Modern History.

3. The professor shall be subject to the General Provisions of the decree concerning the duties of professors and to those Particular Provisions of the same decree which are applicable to this chair.

§ 295. *Professor of Sociology*

1. The Professor of Sociology shall lecture and give instruction in Sociology.

2. The professor shall be elected by an electoral board consisting of:

(1) the Vice-Chancellor, or, if the head of the college specified in (2) of this clause is Vice-Chancellor, a person appointed by Council;

(2) the head of the college to which the professorship shall be for the time being allocated by Council under any decree in that behalf, or, if the head is unable or unwilling to act, a person appointed by the governing body of the college;

(3) a person appointed by the governing body of the college specified in (2) of this clause;

(4) a person appointed by Council;

(5), (6) two persons appointed by the General Board;

(7)–(9) three persons appointed by the Board of the Faculty of Social Studies.

3. The professor shall be subject to the General Provisions of the decree concerning the duties of professors and to those Particular Provisions of the same decree which are applicable to this chair.

§ 296. *Professor of Sociology and Social Policy*

1. The Professor of Sociology and Social Policy shall lecture and give instruction on the sociology and social policy of modern society.

2. The professor shall be elected by an electoral board consisting of:

(1) the Vice-Chancellor, or, if the head of the college specified in (2) of this clause is Vice-Chancellor, a person appointed by Council;

(2) the head of the college to which the professorship shall be for the time being allocated by Council under any decree in that behalf, or, if the head is unable or unwilling to act, a person appointed by the governing body of the college;

(3) a person appointed by the governing body of the college specified in (2) of this clause;

(4) a person appointed by Council;

(5), (6) two persons appointed by the General Board;

(7)–(9) three persons appointed by the Board of the Faculty of Social Studies.

3. The professor shall be subject to the General Provisions of the decree concerning the duties of professors and to those Particular Provisions of the same decree which are applicable to this chair.

§ 297. *Reader in Sociology*

1. The Reader in Sociology shall lecture and give instruction in Sociology, on such conditions and with such duties as the General Board shall from time to time determine.

2. The reader shall be elected by a board consisting of:

(1) the Vice-Chancellor;

(2) the Professor of Sociology and Social Policy;

(3) one person appointed by Council;

(4) one person appointed by the General Board;

(5), (6) two persons appointed by the Board of the Faculty of Social Studies;

(7) one person appointed by the Sub-faculty of Sociology.

§ 298. *University Lecturer in Spanish*

1. The University Lecturer in Spanish shall lecture and give instruction in Spanish studies under the direction of the King Alfonso Professor.

2. The lecturer shall be elected by the Board of the Faculty of Medieval and Modern Languages after consultation with the King Alfonso Professor, and subject to approval by the General Board.

3. The lecturer shall be elected for a period of one year in the first instance, with the possibility of an extension for up to nine months in addition.

4. The total cost to the University of the lecturership shall be charged to the Spanish Fund.

§ 299. *King Alfonso XIII Professor of Spanish Studies*

1. The King Alfonso XIII Professor of Spanish Studies shall lecture and give instruction in the subjects of his or her chair and shall promote generally the study of Spanish in the University.

2. The professor shall be elected by an electoral board consisting of:

(1) the Vice-Chancellor, or, if the head of the college specified in (2) of this clause is Vice-Chancellor, a person appointed by Council on the occurrence of a vacancy to act as an elector on that occasion;

(2) the head of the college to which the professorship shall be for the time being allocated by Council under any decree in that behalf, or, if the head is unable or unwilling to act, a person appointed by the governing body of the college on the occurrence of a vacancy to act as an elector on that occasion;

(3) a person appointed by the governing body of the college specified in (2) of this clause;

(4) a person appointed by Council;

(5) a person elected by the General Board;

(6), (7) two persons elected by the Board of the Faculty of Medieval and Modern Languages;

(8) a person elected by the Board of the Faculty of Modern History.

3. The professor shall have power to arrange for special lectures or courses of lectures on subjects connected with Spanish studies such as the history, laws, art, and social and economic conditions of Spanish-speaking countries generally, provided that all expenses incurred on account of such lectures shall be defrayed out of the Spanish Fund, and shall not be a charge upon any other university fund.

4. The professor shall be subject to the General Provisions of the decree concerning the duties of professors and to those Particular Provisions of the same decree which are applicable to this chair.

§ 300. *Spencer Lecturer*

1. A lecturership shall henceforth be established and maintained in the University of Oxford to be called the Herbert Spencer Lecturership, and the lecturer to be appointed shall be called the Herbert Spencer Lecturer.

2. The sum of £1,000 Victoria Government Stock, and the stocks, funds, and securities for the time representing the same, and any additions made thereto by accumulation or otherwise, shall form a fund, to be called the Herbert Spencer Lecturership Fund.

3. The capital of the fund shall be invested in the name of the Chancellor, Masters, and Scholars of the University of Oxford, hereinafter referred to as 'The University', in government securities or in other securities in which trustees are by law allowed to invest trust money, with power for the University from time to time to vary such securities for others of a like nature.

4. The following board of management shall appoint a lecturer in every year, subject to the provisions of clause 7 hereof, fix his or her stipend, which shall not be less than £20, and make such minor regulations as are not herein otherwise provided for:

(1) the Vice-Chancellor;

(2) a person elected by the Board of the Faculty of Literae Humaniores;

(3) a person elected by the Board of the Faculty of Psychological Studies;

(4) a person elected by the Board of the Faculty of Biological Sciences;

(5) a person elected by the Board of the Faculty of Physiological Sciences;

(6), (7) two persons elected by the Board of the Faculty of Social Studies.

The elected members shall hold office for three years but shall be re-eligible. Four members of the committee shall constitute a quorum. The board of management shall have power to co-opt up to two additional members for periods of five years.

5. Each lecturer shall deliver to the Vice-Chancellor his or her lecture or a verified copy thereof, which shall be retained in the Bodleian Library.

6. The Vice-Chancellor may arrange with individual lecturers for the printing and publication of their lectures in some form within two years of their delivery, and from time to time as part of a collected volume of Herbert Spencer lectures; and shall have power, in consultation with the board of management, to apply, if necessary, surplus income of the fund towards the cost of such separate or collective publication.

7. The board of management shall have power, at its discretion, to suspend the annual delivery of the Herbert Spencer Lecture until sufficient income shall have accumulated for the financing, in its place, of a course of lectures to be delivered by one or more Herbert Spencer Lecturers, or of a conference or colloquium in memory of Herbert Spencer.

8. Any surplus income of the fund shall either be invested or applied from time to time in manner hereinbefore authorized or shall be applied in such other way consistent with the object of the founder, as may be determined by the board of management with the approval of the General Board.

9. If at any future time it shall appear to the board of management that the founder's intention (which is to devote an endowment to the honour of the name of Herbert Spencer) can be better carried out by the establishment of a prize to be called the Herbert Spencer Prize, the board of management shall have power, subject to the founder's consent during his lifetime, to establish a Herbert Spencer Prize in lieu of the lecturership.

10. In the event of this power being exercised, the Herbert Spencer Prize shall be awarded to members of the University under regulations to be made by the board of management, provided that the prize shall be awarded for the encouragement of research in Philosophy or Science, and that the successful competitor shall be required to expend the money value of the prize in the purchase of books or apparatus, or in travel for the purpose of research.

11. It shall be lawful for the board of management, if it thinks fit, to arrange for the printing and publication of any dissertation or report of research for which a Herbert Spencer Prize shall have been awarded, and the rules hereinbefore made respecting the printing and publication of Herbert Spencer

Lectures shall apply so far as may be practicable to any such dissertation or report.

12. This decree shall not be altered during the lifetime of the founder without his consent, but, after the lifetime of the founder, Council shall have full power to alter it from time to time, provided that the Foundation shall always bear the title of the Herbert Spencer Foundation, and that its main object, namely, the perpetuation of the memory of Herbert Spencer, shall be kept in view.

§ 301. *Professor of Statistical Science*

1. The Professor of Statistical Science shall lecture and give instruction in Statistical Science and shall generally promote the study of that subject in the University.

2. The professor shall be elected by an electoral board consisting of:

(1) the Vice-Chancellor, or, if the Principal of St. Anne's College is Vice-Chancellor, a person appointed by Council on the occurrence of a vacancy to act as an elector on that occasion;

(2) the Principal of St. Anne's College, or, if the Principal is unable or unwilling to act, a person appointed by the governing body of the college on the occurrence of a vacancy to act as an elector on that occasion;

(3) a person appointed by the governing body of St. Anne's College;

(4) a person appointed by Council;

(5), (6) two persons appointed by the General Board;

(7)–(9) three persons appointed by the Board of the Faculty of Mathematical Sciences.

3. The professor shall be subject to the General Provisions of the decree concerning the duties of professors and to those Particular Provisions of the same decree which are applicable to this chair.

§ 302. *Professor of Applied Statistics*

1. The Professor of Applied Statistics shall lecture and give both instruction and advice in statistical methods.

2. The professor shall be elected by an electoral board consisting of:

(1) the Vice-Chancellor, or, if the head of the college specified in (2) of this clause is Vice-Chancellor, a person appointed by Council on the occurrence of a vacancy to act as an elector on that occasion;

(2) the head of the college to which the professorship shall be for the time being allocated by Council under any decree in that behalf, or, if the head is unable or unwilling to act, a person appointed by the governing body of the college on the occurrence of a vacancy to act as an elector on that occasion;

(3) a person appointed by the governing body of the college specified in (2) of this clause;

(4) a person appointed by Council;

(5) a person appointed by the General Board;

(6) a person appointed by the Board of the Faculty of Biological Sciences in consultation with the Board of the Faculty of Psychological Studies;

(7) a person appointed by the Board of the Faculty of Clinical Medicine in consultation with the Board of the Faculty of Physiological Sciences;

(8), (9) two persons appointed by the Board of the Faculty of Mathematical Sciences.

3. The professor shall be subject to the General Provisions of the decree concerning the duties of professors and to those Particular Provisions of the same decree which are applicable to this chair.

§ 303. *Nuffield Professor of Surgery*[1]

1. The Nuffield Professor of Surgery shall lecture and give instruction in Surgery.

2. The professor shall be elected by an electoral board consisting of:

(1) the Vice-Chancellor, or, if the Master of Balliol College is Vice-Chancellor, a person appointed by Council on the occurrence of a vacancy to act as an elector on that occasion;

(2) the Master of Balliol College, or, if the Master is unable or unwilling to act, a person appointed by the governing body of the college on the occurrence of a vacancy to act as an elector on that occasion;

(3) a person appointed by the Governing Body of Balliol College;

(4), (5) two persons appointed by Council;

(6) a person appointed by the General Board;

(7), (8) two persons appointed by the Board of the Faculty of Clinical Medicine;

(9) a person holding a clinical appointment appointed by the Oxfordshire Health Authority after consultation with the Oxford Regional Health Authority.

At least three members of the board, of whom one shall be a professor, shall hold clinical appointments.

3. The professor shall act as examiner in Part I of the examination for the Degree of Master of Surgery.

4. The professor shall be subject to the General Provisions of the decree concerning the duties of professors and to those Particular Provisions of the same decree which are applicable to this chair.

§ 304. *Gibson Lecturer in Advanced Surgery: Sir Paul Patrick Benefaction*

1. A gift for the general purposes of the University of £1,000 from Sir Paul Patrick, K.C.I.D., C.S.I., M.A., Corpus Christi College, shall be invested and the interest used, in accordance with the desire of the donor, in the first place to maintain a Lecturership in Advanced Surgery to be awarded triennially and

[1] See also § 42, above.

to be in commemoration of John Monroe Gibson, B.A., University College, F.R.C.S.

2. The lecturer shall be appointed by the Board of the Faculty of Clinical Medicine, on the recommendation of the Nuffield Professor of Surgery, on such terms as it shall think fit.

3. The board shall use any income not required in connection with the triennial lecturership for the provision of occasional lectures on surgical subjects.

§ 305. *Nuffield Professor of Orthopaedic Surgery*

1. The Nuffield Professor of Orthopaedic Surgery shall lecture and give instruction in Orthopaedic Surgery.

2. The professor shall be elected by an electoral board consisting of:

(1) the Vice-Chancellor, or, if the Provost of Worcester College is Vice-Chancellor, a person appointed by Council on the occurrence of a vacancy to act as an elector on that occasion;

(2) the Provost of Worcester College, or, if the Provost is unable or unwilling to act, a person appointed by the Governing Body of Worcester College on the occurrence of a vacancy to act as an elector on that occasion;

(3) a person appointed by the Governing Body of Worcester College;

(4), (5) two persons appointed by Council;

(6) a person appointed by the General Board;

(7), (8) two persons appointed by the Board of the Faculty of Clinical Medicine;

(9) a person holding a clinical appointment appointed by the Oxfordshire Health Authority after consultation with the Oxford Regional Health Authority.

At least three members of the board, of whom one shall be a professor, shall hold clinical appointments.

3. The professor shall be subject to the General Provisions of the decree concerning the duties of professors and to those Particular Provisions of the same decree which are applicable to this chair.

§ 311. *Reader in Bibliography and Textual Criticism*

1. The Reader in Bibliography and Textual Criticism shall lecture and give instruction in Bibliography and Textual Criticism, with special reference to the periods after the introduction of printing, on such conditions and with such duties as the General Board of the Faculties shall from time to time determine.

2. The reader shall be elected by a board consisting of:

(1) the Vice-Chancellor, or, if the head of the college specified in (2) of this clause is Vice-Chancellor, a person appointed by Council;

(2) the head of the college with which the readership is on that occasion associated, or, if the head is unable or unwilling to act, a person appointed by the governing body of the college;

(3) a person appointed by the governing body of the college specified in (2) of this clause;

(4) a person appointed by Council;

(5), (6) two persons appointed by the General Board;

(7)–(9) three persons appointed by the Board of the Faculty of English Language and Literature.

§ **312.** *Mackintosh Visiting Professor of Contemporary Theatre*

1. Whereas

(*a*) the Mackintosh Foundation has provided the initial endowment, with St. Catherine's College as trustee, for a visiting professorship associated with the college, to be known as the Cameron Mackintosh Visiting Professorship of Contemporary Theatre; and

(*b*) under a Deed of Trust dated 26 March 1990 which has been entered into by the University, St. Catherine's College, and the Mackintosh Foundation, elections to the professorship are to be made by an electoral committee comprising the Vice-Chancellor or his or her deputy, the Master of the College, one other elector nominated by Council, and three electors nominated by the Foundation, and are otherwise subject to the Conditions of Endowment embodied in the said Deed of Trust:

any holder of the professorship elected as aforesaid shall while holding it be known as the Cameron Mackintosh Visiting Professor of Contemporary Theatre in the University of Oxford.

2. The professor shall not be subject to the provisions of Sect. I, § 5 of this chapter.

§ **313.** *Regius Professor of Moral and Pastoral Theology*

1. The Regius Professor of Moral and Pastoral Theology shall lecture and give instruction in Moral and Pastoral Theology, in the duties of the Pastoral Office, and in such subjects as Christian Ethics, both Social and Individual, Ascetic and Mystical Theology, and the study of the various types of Christian Experience.

2. The professor shall be subject to the General Provisions of the decree concerning the duties of professors and to those Particular Provisions of the same decree which are applicable to this chair.

§ **314.** *Rhodes Professor of Therapeutic Sciences and Clinical Pharmacology*

1. The Rhodes Professor of Therapeutic Sciences and Clinical Pharmacology shall lecture and give instruction in Therapeutic Sciences and Clinical Pharmacology.

2. The professor shall be elected by a board of electors consisting of:

(1) the Vice-Chancellor, or, if the President of Corpus Christi College is Vice-Chancellor, a person appointed by Council;

(2) the President of Corpus Christi College, or, if the President is unable or unwilling to act, a person appointed by the Governing Body of Corpus Christi College;

(3) a person appointed by the Governing Body of Corpus Christi College;

(4), (5) two persons appointed by Council;

(6) a person appointed by the General Board;

(7), (8) two persons elected by the Board of the Faculty of Clinical Medicine;

(9) a person holding a clinical appointment appointed by the Oxfordshire Health Authority.

At least three members of the board, of whom one shall be a professor, shall hold clinical appointments.

3. The professor shall be subject to the General Provisions of the decree concerning the duties of professors and to those Particular Provisions of the same decree which are applicable to this chair.

§ 315. *Professor of Transplantation*

1. The Professor of Transplantation shall lecture and give instruction in Transplantation and shall engage in advanced study and research.

2. The professor shall be elected by an electoral board consisting of:

(1) the Vice-Chancellor, or, if the head of the college specified in (2) of this clause is Vice-Chancellor, a person appointed by Council;

(2) the head of the college to which the professorship shall be for the time being allocated by Council under any decree in that behalf, or, if the head is unable or unwilling to act, a person appointed by the governing body of the college;

(3) a person appointed by the governing body of the college specified in (2) of this clause;

(4) a person appointed by Council;

(5), (6) two persons appointed by the General Board;

(7) the Nuffield Professor of Surgery;

(8) a person appointed by the Board of the Faculty of Clinical Medicine;

(9) a person holding a clinical appointment appointed by the Oxfordshire Health Authority.

At least three members of the board, of whom one shall be a professor, shall hold clinical appointments.

3. The professor shall be subject to the General Provisions of the decree concerning the duties of professors and to those Particular Provisions of the same decree which are applicable to this chair.

§ 316. *Reader in Transport Studies*

1. The Readership in Transport Studies is established under the provisions of Tit. XVI, Sect. XXIX.

2. The reader shall be elected by an electoral board consisting of:

(1) the Vice-Chancellor, or, if the head of the college specified in (2) of this clause is Vice-Chancellor, a person appointed by Council;

(2) the head of the college with which Council shall for the time being have associated the readership, or, if the head is unable or unwilling to act, a person appointed by the governing body of the college;

(3) a person appointed by the governing body of the college specified in (2) of this clause;

(4) a person appointed by Council;

(5), (6) two persons appointed by the General Board;

(7), (8) two persons appointed by the Board of the Faculty of Anthropology and Geography;

(9) a person appointed by the Board of the Faculty of Social Studies.

3. The reader shall lecture and give instruction in Transport Studies on such conditions and with such duties as the General Board shall from time to time determine. The reader shall be the director (without emoluments) of the Transport Studies Unit set up under the provisions of Ch. IX, Sect. I, § 345.

§ 317. *Schultz Professor of Turbomachinery*

1. The University accepts with deep gratitude funding from Rolls-Royce plc, for the provision for one tenure of a Donald Schultz Professorship of Turbomachinery and for the provision of support costs for the professorship.

2. The Donald Schultz Professor of Turbomachinery shall lecture and give instruction in Mechanical Engineering with special reference to Turbomachinery.

3. The professor shall be elected by an electoral board consisting of:

(1) the Vice-Chancellor, or, if the head of the college specified in (2) of this clause is Vice Chancellor, a person appointed by Council to act as an elector;

(2) the head of the college to which the professorship shall be allocated by Council under any decree in that behalf, or, if the head is unable or unwilling to act, a person appointed by the governing body of the college on the occurrence of a vacancy to act as an elector;

(3) a person appointed by the governing body of the college specified in (2) of this clause;

(4) a person appointed by Council;

(5) a person appointed by the General Board;

(6)–(9) four persons appointed by the Board of the Faculty of Physical Sciences.

4. The professor shall be subject to the General Provisions of the decree concerning the duties of professors and to those Particular Provisions of the same decree which are applicable to this chair.

§ 318. *Eastman Visiting Professor*

1. The George Eastman Visiting Professor shall be at the time of election, a citizen of the United States of America eminent in teaching or research in any branch of university study, and shall lecture and give instruction in the subject of study in respect of which he or she is appointed.

2. The professor shall hold office for a period not less than one year nor more than five years, but shall be re-eligible.

3. The professor shall be elected by an electoral board consisting of:

(1) the Vice-Chancellor;

(2), (3) two persons appointed by the Association of American Rhodes Scholars;

(4), (5) two persons appointed by Council;

(6)–(8) three persons appointed by the General Board;

(9) one person appointed by the Governing Body of Balliol College.

4. In making each election the electors shall bear in mind the desire of the donors that successive appointees shall in so far as possible represent different subjects of study.

5. The professor shall be subject to the General Provisions of the decree concerning the duties of professors and to those Particular Provisions of the same decree as to residence which are applicable to this chair. In exceptional circumstances, the faculty board concerned may reduce the professor's residence requirement and/or the number of required lectures or classes.

6. The provisions of Ch. VII, Sect. II, relating to the allocation of professorships to colleges and societies, shall not apply to the George Eastman Visiting Professorship.

§ 319. *Newton-Abraham Visiting Professor*

1. The University accepts with deep gratitude the sum of £400,000 from the Trustees of the E. P. Abraham Research Fund for the furtherance of research in the medical, biological, and chemical sciences within the University, in particular by the endowment of a visiting professorship in those sciences, to be tenable in association with Lincoln College, the costs of which shall be the first charge on the income of the endowment. The professorship shall be known as the Newton-Abraham Visiting Professorship, and shall be held under the conditions set out below.

2. The professor shall be elected by a board of electors consisting of:

(1) the Vice-Chancellor;

(2) one person appointed by Council not being the resident holder of a teaching, research, or administrative post in the University or in any college or other society;

(3) one person appointed by the General Board;

(4)–(7) one person appointed each by the Boards of the Faculties of Clinical Medicine, Biological Sciences, Physical Sciences, and Physiological Sciences;

(8), (9) two persons appointed by the Governing Body of Lincoln College.

Council shall have power to alter the composition of this electoral board by decree, provided that no alteration in the representation of Lincoln College shall be made without the consent of that college.

3. The electors shall normally elect a person resident overseas, but may exceptionally elect a person resident within the United Kingdom.

4. The professor shall hold office for such period not exceeding one year as the electors may determine. It shall be the professor's duty to stimulate and promote research in a subject within the field of the medical, biological, and chemical sciences, and he or she shall perform such other duties as the electors may assign to him or her.

5. The professor shall receive a stipend at the rate applicable to a professor in Schedule A.

6. The income from the endowment remaining after the stipend of the professor and the costs of administration have been met shall be applied by the electors at their discretion towards:

(i) the research expenses of the professor, including the costs of secretarial and technical assistance, the amount required for these purposes being fixed in consultation with the head of the department in which the professor is to work;

(ii) the travelling, accommodation, and other expenses of the professor.

7. Any income not expended on the above purposes in any year may be carried forward for expenditure in a subsequent year.

8. If at any time the electors consider that the income from the endowment is insufficient to provide adequately for the expenditure specified in cll. 5 and 6 above, they may leave the professorship vacant for not more than a year to allow income to accumulate.

9. If at any time the electors consider that the income from the endowment is more than sufficient to provide for an annual visiting professor and for the expenses specified in cl. 6, they may so report to Council, which shall then have power, subject to the consent of the Trustees for the time being of the E. P. Abraham Research Fund, to amend this decree to provide that surplus income may be used by the electors, on conditions to be specified in the amending decree, for the furtherance of research in the medical, biological, and chemical sciences.

§ 320. *Zaharoff Lecturer and Fund*

1. The first charge on the Zaharoff Fund shall be the maintenance of the Marshal Foch Professorship of French Literature, the contribution to the cost of which chair shall be equal to one-half of the total income of the fund from year to year.

2. There shall be an annual lecture on some subject of French Art, Archaeology, History, Literature, Science, or Sociology, to be called the Sir Basil Zaharoff Lecture. The lecturer shall deliver the lecture on a date to be agreed upon between him or her and the Curators of the Taylor Institution. The lecturer shall be nominated in alternate years by the Vice-Chancellor of the University and the Recteur de l'Académie de Paris; and shall receive a fee to be determined by the curators, together with such sum towards travelling and other incidental expenses as may be assigned by the curators who shall have power to allocate a further sum at their discretion for expenses incurred in connection with the entertainment of the lecturer. This shall be the second charge upon the fund. The copyright of the lecture shall be vested in the University and the lecturer shall be required to deliver to the Curators of the Taylor Institution a typewritten copy of the lecture at least one month before the date fixed for its delivery. The lecture shall be advertised and printed out of the income of the Zaharoff Fund, but not published before it is delivered. Any profits which may arise from such publication shall be treated as income arising from the fund and be dealt with or applied accordingly.

3. The balance of the annual income of the Zaharoff Fund, if any, after providing for the Marshal Foch Professorship and the Sir Basil Zaharoff Lecture as prescribed above, together with any moneys unexpended owing to vacancies in these offices, shall in the first place be applied to the establishment of Zaharoff Travelling Scholarships for members of the University for study in France. The number and value of, method of election to, and supervision of such scholarships, the approval of the subjects and places of study, and generally the conditions of their award and tenure, shall be fixed from time to time by the Curators of the Taylor Institution.

4. Any balance of the annual income not required for use under the provisions of clause 3 above shall, at the discretion of the curators, be

(*a*) transferred to a fund to be used by the curators for the purchase of rare French books, autographs, and manuscripts for the library of the Taylor Institution; or

(*b*) spent on travel grants in connection with French Studies; or

(*c*) used on any object connected with French studies in the University; or

(*d*) carried forward for expenditure in subsequent years.

5. Council shall always have power, but subject to the consent of the donor during his life, to alter this decree, provided that the main objects of the foundation, namely, the establishment of a Professorship of French Literature, an annual lecturership, and Travelling Scholarships for study in France are kept in view, and in particular shall have power, subject to any vested interests, to reduce the amount of the second charge on the fund, if the income of the fund should be permanently reduced to a level inadequate to cover the first and third charges on the fund.

§ 321. *Professor of Zoology*

1. The Professor of Zoology shall lecture and give instruction in Zoology.

2. The professor shall be elected by an electoral board consisting of:

(1) the Vice-Chancellor, or, if the head of the college specified in (2) of this clause is Vice-Chancellor, a person appointed by Council;

(2) the head of the college to which the professorship shall be for the time being allocated by Council under any decree in that behalf, or, if the head is unable or unwilling to act, a person appointed by the governing body of the college;

(3) a person appointed by the governing body of the college specified in (2) of this clause;

(4) a person appointed by Council;

(5), (6) two persons appointed by the General Board;

(7)–(9) three persons appointed by the Board of the Faculty of Biological Sciences, of whom one shall be appointed after consultation with the Curators of the Hope Collections.

3. The professor shall be subject to the General Provisions of the decree concerning the duties of professors and to those Particular Provisions of the same decree which are applicable to this chair.

§ 322. *Linacre Professor of Zoology*

1. The Linacre Professor of Zoology shall lecture and give instruction in Zoology.

2. The professor shall be elected by an electoral board consisting of:

(1) the Vice-Chancellor, or, if the Warden of Merton College is Vice-Chancellor, a person appointed by Council on the occurrence of a vacancy to act as an elector on that occasion;

(2) the Warden of Merton College, or, if the Warden is unable or unwilling to act, a person appointed by the Governing Body of Merton College on the occurrence of a vacancy to act as an elector on that occasion;

(3) a person appointed by the Governing Body of Merton College;

(4) a person appointed by Council;

(5) a person appointed by the General Board;

(6), (7) two persons elected by the Board of the Faculty of Biological Sciences.

3. The professor shall be subject to the General Provisions of the decree concerning the duties of professors and to those Particular Provisions of the same decree which are applicable to this chair.

§ **323.** *Hope Professor of Zoology (Entomology)*

1. The Hope Professor of Zoology (Entomology) shall give public lectures and instruction in Zoology (Entomology) at such times as shall be prescribed or approved by Council.

2. The professor shall be elected by an electoral board consisting of:

(1) the Vice-Chancellor, or, if the Principal of Jesus College is Vice-Chancellor, a person appointed by Council on the occurrence of a vacancy to act as an elector on that occasion;

(2) the Principal of Jesus College, or, if the Principal is unable or unwilling to act, a person appointed by the Governing Body of Jesus College on the occurrence of a vacancy to act as an elector on that occasion;

(3) a person appointed by the Governing Body of Jesus College;

(4) a person appointed by Council;

(5), (6) two persons appointed by the General Board;

(7)–(9) three persons appointed by the Board of the Faculty of Biological Sciences, of whom one shall be appointed after consultation with the Curators of the Hope Collections.

3. The Hope Professor shall not hold any other professorship or readership in the University.

4. The Hope Professor shall be subject to the General Provisions of the decree concerning the duties of professors and to those Particular Provisions of the same decree which are applicable to this chair.

Section IV. Readerships, Lecturerships, etc.—General

§ **1.** *General*

1. Except where it has been provided otherwise by statute, decree, or regulation, the provisions of this sub-section shall apply to every appointment of which the holder is required (unless exempted or excluded under the provisions of Tit. X, Sect. I (*g*) (ii)) to be a member of the Federated Superannuation Scheme for Universities or the Universities Superannuation Scheme, in faculties and in departments, institutions, delegacies, or committees which Council has determined shall receive their grants from the General Board.

2. The appointment shall be on such conditions as to duties and tenure as the appointing body may determine; provided that

(i) the appointment shall be for a term of five years in the first instance, at the end of which the holder of the appointment shall be eligible for reappointment and, if reappointed, shall hold office until he or she reaches the retiring age, subject to the provisions of Tit. VIII, Sect. I,

except that in a special case the General Board shall have power to permit the appointing body (*a*) to make an appointment for a shorter initial term than five years, or (*b*) to reappoint the holder of an appointment who has completed his or her initial term for a further limited period, after which if reappointed he or she shall hold office as aforesaid, or (*c*) to appoint to retiring age without initial term a person who has already served an initial term and been reappointed to retiring age under the provisions of this section in respect of some other appointment;

(ii) the appointment or reappointment and the conditions determined by the appointing body shall be subject to the approval of the General Board except when the appointment carries an annual stipend of not more than an amount as determined by the General Board from time to time.

3. The General Board shall fix the stipends of such appointments having regard to the stipends payable to readers and university lecturers.

4. The General Board may reduce the stipend of any person holding such an appointment having regard to any other office or employment for which he or she receives remuneration.

5. All appointments (whether made under the provisions of this sub-section or not) approved by the General Board which carry a stipend rising above the amount determined by the General Board under cl. 2 (ii) above and appointments of C.U.F. lecturers shall be published in the *University Gazette*.

§ **2.** *Readers*

1. The provisions of this sub-section shall not apply to a reader appointed under the provisions of Sect. V, § 2.

2. Readers may either be appointed by the General Board or elected by an electoral board under the provisions of a statute or decree.

3. A reader in any subject may be appointed by the General Board, on such conditions as to duties and tenure as the board may determine; provided that

(i) such a reader shall hold office until he or she reaches the retiring age subject to the provisions of Tit. VIII, Sect. I;

(ii) before appointing such a reader the Board shall consult any board of faculty that in its opinion may be concerned with the subject in which it is proposed to appoint the reader.

4. A university reader elected by an electoral board shall hold office until he or she reaches the retiring age, subject to the provisions of Tit. VIII, Sect. I. The reader shall be subject to the power of the General Board to determine his or her duties and other conditions of service, provided that no duties or conditions of service shall be imposed upon him or her which are inconsistent with the terms of the particular statute or decree relating to his or her readership.

5. A reader shall receive a stipend on a scale as determined from time to time by Council, except that readers in post before 24 April 1972 shall receive stipends on personal scales as determined from time to time by Council, provided that the General Board may reduce the stipend of a reader having regard to any other office, except the office of Proctor or Assessor, or employment for which he or she receives remuneration.

6. Clauses 4 and 5 shall not apply to the James P. R. Lyell Reader in Bibliography whose stipend, duties, and conditions of tenure shall be as fixed by decree.

7. No fee shall be charged for attendance by members of the University at the lectures of any reader, except as provided in Ch. VIII, Sect. I, § 8.

§ **3.** *University Lecturers*

1. The provisions of this sub-section in relation to a university lecturer or university lecturers shall, unless otherwise stated, apply also to the holders of faculty lecturerships, university lecturerships (C.U.F.), and special (non-C.U.F.) lecturerships, but not to university lecturers appointed under the provisions of Sect. V, § 3.

2. University lecturers may either be appointed by a board of a faculty or elected by an electoral board under the provisions of a statute or decree.

3. Subject to clause 4 below, a board of a faculty may appoint a university lecturer in a subject under the supervision of that board, on such conditions as to duties and tenure as the board may determine; provided that

(i) such a lecturer shall be appointed in the first instance for a term of five years, at the end of which he or she shall be eligible for reappointment and, if reappointed, he or she shall hold office until he or she reaches the retiring age, subject to the provisions of Tit. VIII, Sect. I

except that in a special case the General Board shall have power to permit a faculty board (*a*) to appoint a lecturer for a shorter initial term than five years, or (*b*) to reappoint a lecturer who has completed his or her initial term of appointment for a further limited period, after which if reappointed he or she shall hold office as aforesaid, or (*c*) to appoint to retiring age without initial term a person who has already served an initial term and been reappointed to retiring age under the provisions of this section in respect of some other appointment;

(ii) the General Board may, on the recommendation of a faculty board, approve an appointment as temporary university lecturer for a period not exceeding five years, whether required as a substitute for a member of the established academic staff who has been granted extended leave of absence or dispensation from duties, or in circumstances where in the General Board's view there are emergency teaching needs, and the provisions of this clause concerning tenure shall not apply to any such appointment;

(iii) before making any such appointment the faculty board concerned shall satisfy itself that the person it proposes to appoint will be free from any excessive burden of teaching and will have sufficient time for research;

(iv) the appointment or reappointment of such a lecturer and the conditions determined by the faculty board shall be subject to the approval of the General Board;

(v) the appointment or reappointment of a university lecturer to hold office in one of the university laboratories or departments enumerated either in Ch. II,

Sect. XIII, § 2, cl. 7, or in Ch. VII, Sect. V, § 1, cl. 1, shall be made on the recommendation of a committee appointed by the faculty board, of which the head of the department concerned shall be a member and which may include other persons not being members of the board, subject, in the case of appointments or reappointments to university lecturerships associated with Curatorships of the Scientific Collections in the Oxford University Museum of Natural History, to procedures to be approved from time to time by the General Board after consultation with the Committee for the Scientific Collections and with the faculty boards concerned.

4. No faculty lecturership or university lecturership (C.U.F.) shall be held otherwise than in association with a tutorial post at a college, and no special (non-C.U.F.) lecturership shall be held otherwise than in association with a post at a college or other society the members of which are not eligible for appointment to a C.U.F. lecturership. If at any point the appointment to the post specified in the preceding sentence in association with which the university appointment is held is terminated, for whatever reason, then the university appointment shall automatically end on the same date as the effective date of termination of the college appointment.

5. For the purpose of clause 3 above and clause 8 and the General Board may exercise the powers of a board of faculty if it desires to appoint a university lecturer in a subject which is not under the supervision of any board of a faculty.

6. A university lecturer elected by an electoral board shall be elected in the first instance for a term of five years, at the end of which he or she shall be eligible for re-election, and if re-elected shall hold office until he or she reaches the retiring age, subject to the provisions of Tit. VIII, Sect. I,

> except that in a special case the electors shall have power (*a*) to elect a lecturer for a shorter initial term than five years, or (*b*) to re-elect a lecturer for a further limited period, after which if re-elected he or she shall hold office as aforesaid.

The lecturer shall be subject to the power of the General Board to determine his or her duties and other conditions of service, provided that no duties or conditions of service shall be imposed upon him or her which are inconsistent with the terms of the particular statute or decree relating to his or her lecturership.

7. A university lecturer may either receive no stipend as such or may receive a stipend on one of the scales determined by Council from time to time in accordance with the provisions of Tit. X, Sect. I (*c*); provided that

(i) the General Board shall have power to assign a stipend to a university lecturer without placing him or her on the incremental scale;

(ii) the General Board may reduce the stipend of a university lecturer (or a faculty lecturer, but not that of a C.U.F. lecturer or special (non-C.U.F. lecturer) having regard to any other office, except the office of Proctor or Assessor, or employment for which he or she receives remuneration;

(iii) the General Board may, under such arrangements and conditions as are agreed by it from time to time, confer the title of university lecturer, faculty lecturer, or C.U.F. lecturer, as appropriate, on the holder of a tutorial post at a college (or a post at a college or other society the members of which are not eligible for appointment to a C.U.F. lecturership), provided always that the title shall cease to be held at the same date at which, for whatever reason, the college appointment is terminated.

8. Increments on the scale for university lecturers shall become payable from the beginning of the quarterly period next following that during which the lecturer attains the qualifying age.

9. Clauses 6 and 7 above shall not apply to any of the following university lecturers whose stipends, duties, and conditions of tenure shall be as fixed by their particular statutes or decrees:

Sidney Ball Lecturer
Bampton Lecturer
Cherwell-Simon Memorial Lecturer
Ford's Lecturer in British History
Grinfield Lecturer
Halley Lecturer
John Wilfred Jenkinson Memorial Lecturer
Ratanbai Katrak Lecturer
Lecturer in Spanish
John Locke Lecturer
Myres Memorial Lecturer
O'Donnell Lecturer
Romanes Lecturer
Speaker's Lecturer in Biblical Studies
Herbert Spencer Lecturer
Wilde Lecturer in Natural and Comparative Religion
Sir Basil Zaharoff Lecturer.

10. If the board of any faculty has satisfied itself that any university lecturer appointed by it has by reason of neglect or incompetence failed satisfactorily to perform his or her duties as a university lecturer, it shall report the circumstances to the General Board, which shall report in that sense to the Visitatorial Board.

11. No fee shall be charged for attendance by members of the University at the lectures of any university lecturer, except as provided in Ch. VIII, Sect. I, § 8.

§ 4. *University Research Lecturers*

The General Board may, on the recommendation of a faculty board, confer the title of University Research Lecturer without stipend on a member of the University's research-support staff, or on a research worker employed in Oxford by an outside body, who has demonstrated a sustained and continuing contribution to the general academic work of a department or faculty, who is of academic standing equivalent to that necessary to merit appointment to a University Lecturership, and who meets such other criteria as the General Board may from time to time determine. The title shall be conferred for the period for which the individual holds the relevant university appointment or appointment in Oxford with the outside body.

§ 5. *Visiting Lecturers*

The General Board may, on the recommendation of a faculty board, confer the title of Visiting Lecturer without stipend on a member of the staff of a government research establishment or comparable industrial or other institution outside the University, or on an individual not on the establishment of another academic institution who is deemed suitably qualified, who regularly participates in lecturing or any other form of teaching in the University in some department of study which falls within the province of that board. The title shall be conferred for a period not exceeding three years in the first instance, but may be renewed thereafter on the recommendation of the faculty board for a further period or periods not exceeding three years at a time.

§ 6. *Senior Research Officers*

1. A board of a faculty (on the recommendation of a committee appointed by the faculty board, of which the head of the department concerned shall be a member and which may include other persons not being members of the board) may appoint a senior research officer in a subject under the supervision of that board, to engage in advanced study or research in one of the university laboratories and departments to which reference is made in Ch. VIII, Sect. I, § 7, and on such other conditions as to tenure and duties as the board may determine at the time of his or her appointment; provided that

(i) such a senior research officer shall be appointed in the first instance for a term of five years, at the end of which he or she shall be eligible at the discretion of the faculty board, either for reappointment as a senior research officer or for appointment as a university lecturer; if he or she is reappointed as a senior research officer he or she shall hold office until retiring age, subject to the provisions of Tit. VIII, Sect. I,

> except that in a special case the General Board shall have the power to permit a faculty board (*a*) to appoint a senior research officer for a shorter initial term than five years or (*b*) to reappoint a senior research officer who has completed his or her initial term of appointment for a further limited period, after which if reappointed he or she shall hold office as aforesaid:

if he or she is appointed as a university lecturer the appointment shall be subject to the terms and conditions which would apply if he or she were being reappointed after having served an initial term of appointment as university lecturer under the provisions of Ch. VII, Sect. IV, § 3, cl. 3;

(ii) the appointment or reappointment of such a senior research officer and the conditions determined by the faculty board shall be subject to the approval of the General Board.

2. A senior research officer shall receive a stipend on the scale for university lecturers as laid down in Ch. VII, Sect. IV, § 3, cl. 7.

3. The General Board may permit the board of the faculty, or a delegacy, or a committee receiving its grant from the General Board, to appoint a senior research officer to engage in advanced study or research in a department or institution under the supervision of that board, delegacy, or committee which is not among those referred to in cl. 1 hereof, and all the other provisions of this sub-section shall apply to such an appointment, except that the option of appointing as a university lecturer a senior research officer who has completed his or her initial term of appointment shall be exercisable only by the board of a faculty.

§ 7. *Departmental Lecturers*

1. The head of any academic department with responsibilities for teaching and research shall have power to appoint departmental lecturers for a period, to be determined by him or her, which shall not exceed four years. A departmental lecturer may be reappointed for a further period or periods provided that his or her total period of service as departmental lecturer, whether in one or more than one department, shall not exceed six years.

2. A departmental lecturer shall be required to carry out such teaching duties as shall be assigned to him or her by the head of his or her department and to engage in advanced study or research.

3. Subject to the provisions of clause 5 below, the stipend of a departmental lecturer shall be paid out of departmental funds, and shall not exceed the annual stipend referred to under Ch. VII, Sect. IV, § 1, cl. 2 (ii).

4. The head of the department shall give to a departmental lecturer at the time of his or her appointment a written statement of the duties, emoluments and duration of his or her office.

5. The head of any department shall have power to make to a departmental lecturer additional salary payments out of departmental funds, having regard to such guidelines as are issued from time to time by the General Board.

Section V. Academic Posts in Clinical Departments

§ 1. *General*

1. The provisions of this section shall apply to a person required (unless exempted or excluded under the provisions of Tit. X, Sect. I (*g*) (ii)) to be a member of the Federated Superannuation System for Universities or the Universities Superannuation Scheme, who holds qualifications entitling him or her to be registered with the General Medical Council as a Medical Practitioner,

who holds an honorary appointment in the National Health Service, and whose appointment is held in the

Nuffield Department of Anaesthetics
Department of Cardiovascular Medicine
Nuffield Department of Clinical Laboratory Sciences
Nuffield Department of Clinical Medicine
Department of Clinical Neurology
Department of Clinical Pharmacology
Nuffield Department of Obstetrics and Gynaecology
Nuffield Laboratory of Ophthalmology
Nuffield Department of Orthopaedic Surgery
Department of Paediatrics
Department of Primary Health Care
Department of Psychiatry
Department of Public Health
Department of Radiology
Nuffield Department of Surgery,

or in such other departments or institutions as the General Board may determine.

2. The holder of an appointment made under this section shall, subject to the provisions of Ch. VIII, Sect. IV, be required to enter the Universities Superannuation Scheme, unless exempted or excluded under the provisions of Tit. X, Sect. I (*g*) (ii), provided that the University shall bear the cost of the employer's share of superannuation contributions in the case of a holder, who, in accordance with Ch. VIII, Sect. IV, FIRST SCHEDULE (1) (*h*) (i) is permitted to remain subject to the National Health Service Superannuation Scheme.

3. A person holding a full-time appointment under the provisions of this section, and holding an honorary consultant appointment in the National Health Service in any of the clinical departments listed in cl. 1 above, shall be permitted to engage in private practice in the hospitals in Oxford associated with the University or in other hospitals in Oxfordshire on such terms as the General Board may from time to time determine, provided that

(i) the proportion of gross salary which may be retained shall not exceed the proportion which may be retained by full-time consultants in the National Health Service;

(ii) any private practice fee which is not claimed by the individual concerned or which remains after payments have been made up to the annual limit specified above shall be made payable to the University Chest and shall be divided by the Chest so that three-quarters is allocated to the relevant university departmental fund and one-quarter to the General Clinical Fund in accordance with Sect. I, § 5. B, cl. 3 (*e*);

(iii) all persons engaging in private practice under the provisions of this clause shall belong to a medical defence society. Payment of the subscription for such membership shall be permitted to constitute a first charge on the income earned before any calculation is made to determine whether or not the individual concerned has reached the limit of earnings specified under (i) above.

4. Where, in this section, the term 'appropriate health authority' is used, this shall mean the National Health Service Regional or District Health Authority responsible for granting an honorary contract of employment to the appointee concerned.

§ **2.** *Readers in Clinical Departments*

1. Readers to whom this section applies may either be appointed by the General Board, when (unless appointed *ad hominem*) they shall be entitled 'clinical readers', or be elected by an electoral board under the provisions of a statute or decree.

2. A clinical reader may be appointed by the General Board on such conditions as to duties and tenure as the board may determine; provided that

(i) such a reader shall be appointed in the first instance for a term of five years, at the end of which he or she shall be eligible for reappointment and, if reappointed, shall hold office until he or she reaches the retiring age, subject to the provisions of Tit. VIII, Sect. I,

> except that in a special case the General Board shall have power (*a*) to appoint a reader for a shorter initial term than five years or (*b*) to reappoint a reader who has completed his or her initial term of appointment for a further limited period, after which if reappointed he or she shall hold office as aforesaid;

(ii) before appointing or reappointing such a reader the board shall consult any board of faculty that in its opinion may be concerned with the subject in which it is proposed to appoint the reader;

(iii) the appointment or reappointment of a clinical reader shall be made on the recommendation of a committee, appointed by the Board of the Faculty of Clinical Medicine, consisting of not less than five persons, including the head of the clinical department concerned, a medically qualified representative nominated by the appropriate hospital authority, and where appropriate, a person from one of the pre-clinical departments.

3. A reader in a clinical department appointed *ad hominem* shall hold office until he or she reaches the retiring age, subject to the provisions of Tit. VIII, Sect. I.

4. A reader in a clinical department elected by an electoral board shall hold office until he or she reaches the retiring age, subject to the provisions of Tit. VIII, Sect. I. The reader shall be subject to the power of the General Board to determine his or her duties and other conditions of service, provided that no duties or conditions of service shall be imposed upon him or her which are inconsistent with the terms of the particular statute or decree relating to his or her readership.

5. A reader to whom the provisions of this section apply shall receive a stipend on a scale as determined by Council from time to time, or, if he or she holds an honorary consultant appointment in the National Health Service awarded by the appropriate Health Authority, on the scale currently payable to consultants

in the National Health Service, provided that the General Board may reduce the stipend of a reader having regard to any other office, except the office of Proctor or Assessor, or employment for which he or she receives remuneration.

6. No fee shall be charged for attendance by members of the University at the lectures of any reader appointed under this section, except as provided in Ch. VIII, Sect. I, § 8.

§ 3. *University Lecturers in Clinical Departments*

1. University lecturers to whom the provisions of this section apply shall be appointed by the Board of the Faculty of Clinical Medicine.

2. The faculty board may appoint such a university lecturer in a subject under its supervision on such conditions as to duties and tenure as the board may determine; provided that

(i) he or she shall be appointed in the first instance for a term of five years, at the end of which he or she shall be eligible for reappointment and, if reappointed, shall hold office until he or she reaches the retiring age, subject to the provisions of Tit. VIII, Sect. I,

> except that in a special case the General Board shall have power to permit the faculty board (*a*) to appoint a university lecturer for a shorter initial term than five years, or (*b*) to reappoint a university lecturer who has completed his or her initial term of appointment for a further limited period, after which if reappointed he or she shall hold office as aforesaid;

(ii) he or she shall normally have held the post of clinical tutor or clinical lecturer under the provisions of § 4 of this section for an initial term of service of at least three years;

(iii) the appointment or reappointment shall be made on the recommendation of a committee appointed by the faculty board and consisting of not less than five persons, including the head of the department concerned, a medically qualified representative nominated by the appropriate hospital authority, and, where appropriate, a person from one of the pre-clinical departments;

(iv) before making any such appointment or reappointment the faculty board shall satisfy itself that the person it proposes to appoint will be free from excessive burdens of teaching or of the care of patients within the hospitals associated with the University or such other institutions as the faculty board may approve, and will have sufficient time for research;

(v) the appointment or reappointment of such a lecturer and the conditions determined by the faculty board shall be subject to the approval of the General Board.

3. Subject to the provisos to this clause a university lecturer to whom the provisions of this section apply may either receive no stipend as such, or may receive a stipend on a scale as determined by Council from time to time, or, if he or she holds an honorary consultant appointment in the National Health Service awarded by the appropriate Health Authority, on the scale currently payable to consultants in the National Health Service, provided that

(i) the General Board shall have power to assign a stipend to such a university lecturer without placing him or her on an incremental scale;

(ii) the General Board may reduce the stipend of a university lecturer having regard to any other office, except the office of Proctor or of Assessor, or employment for which he or she receives remuneration.

4. Clause 3 above shall not apply to the Litchfield Lecturers whose stipends, duties, and conditions of tenure shall be as fixed by the decree concerned.

5. If the faculty board has satisfied itself that any university lecturer appointed by it has neglected his or her duties as a university lecturer, it shall report the circumstances to the General Board, which shall report in that sense to the Visitatorial Board.

6. No fee shall be charged for attendance by members of the University at the lectures of any university lecturer, except as provided in Ch. VIII, Sect. I, § 8.

§ 4. *Clinical Tutors and Clinical Lecturers*

1. Clinical tutors and clinical lecturers shall be appointed by the Board of the Faculty of Clinical Medicine.

2. The faculty board may appoint a clinical tutor or a clinical lecturer in a subject under its supervision on such terms as to duties and tenure as the board may determine, provided that

(i) such an appointment shall be made for an initial term not exceeding three years, at the end of which the person concerned shall be eligible for reappointment for a further period or periods not exceeding three years in total; the total period of service as a clinical tutor and the total period of service as a clinical lecturer shall not exceed six years each, except that a clinical lecturer who has held for not more than three years a post which is not recognized for the purposes of higher professional training may be appointed for a period not exceeding six years to a post which is so recognized;

(ii) the appointment or reappointment of a clinical tutor shall be made on the recommendation of a committee appointed by the faculty board and consisting of not less than five persons including the head of the department concerned and a medically qualified representative nominated by the appropriate hospital authority;

(iii) the appointment or reappointment of a clinical lecturer shall be made on the recommendation of a committee appointed by the faculty board, consisting of not less than five persons including the head of the department concerned;

(iv) the appointment of a clinical tutor or a clinical lecturer and the conditions determined by the faculty board shall be subject to the approval of the General Board, provided that the initial appointment of a clinical lecturer for a term not greater than one year, and the reappointment of a clinical tutor or a clinical lecturer for a single period of three years, may be approved by the faculty board without the approval of the General Board.

3. Subject to the provisos to this clause a clinical tutor or a clinical lecturer may either receive no stipend as such, or may receive a stipend on scales as determined by Council from time to time, or, if he or she holds an honorary consultant appointment in the National Health Service awarded by the appropriate Health Authority, on the scale currently payable to consultants in the National Health Service, provided that

(i) the General Board shall have power to assign a stipend to such a person without placing him or her on an incremental scale;

(ii) the General Board may reduce the stipend having regard to any other office, except the office of Proctor or Assessor, or employment for which he or she receives remuneration.

4. Clause 3 above shall not apply to the Litchfield Lecturers whose stipends, duties, and conditions of tenure shall be as fixed by the decree concerned.

5. If the faculty board has satisfied itself that any clinical tutor or clinical lecturer appointed by it has neglected his or her duties as a clinical tutor or clinical lecturer, it shall report the circumstances to the General Board, which shall report in that sense to the Visitatorial Board.

§ 5. *Honorary Consultant Appointments in the National Health Service*

An application for the granting of an honorary consultant appointment in the National Health Service to a person appointed under this section shall be initiated by the head of department concerned and considered by the Board ofthe Faculty of Clinical Medicine. The faculty board shall, unless the application is coincident with the appointment or reappointment of the person concerned as clinical reader, university lecturer, or clinical tutor, set up a review committee, consisting of not less than five persons including the head of department concerned and a medically qualified representative nominated by the appropriate hospital authority, to consider the case for recommending an honorary consultant appointment and the financial implications of such a proposal. The faculty board shall, subject to the approval of the General Board, forward the application to the appropriate hospital authority. This procedure shall also apply to a person appointed under a research grant administered through the University, after consultation with the grant-making body concerned.

§ 6. *Title of Honorary Senior Clinical Lecturer and of Acting Clinical Lecturer*

1. (*a*) The Board of the Faculty of Clinical Medicine may confer the title of 'Honorary Senior Clinical Lecturer in [here state the subject]' upon any appropriately qualified individual who takes part, in the hospitals in Oxford associated with the University, in the instruction in clinical subjects of candidates for the Second Examination for the Degree of Bachelor of Medicine or in postgraduate teaching, provided that

(i) such a person shall be appointed for an initial period of five years, with a review at the end of the fourth year, and may be reappointed (subject to such review) for further periods of five years with review at the end of the fourth year of each five-year period;[1]

(ii) the appointment or reappointment of such a person shall be subject to the approval of the General Board;

(iii) such a person shall be deemed to be a member, or associated member as appropriate, of the corresponding university department.

(*b*) The Board of the Faculty of Clinical Medicine may confer the title of 'Honorary Senior Clinical Lecturer in [here state the subject]' upon any appropriately qualified individual who takes part, in hospitals other than those in Oxford associated with the University, in the instruction in clinical subjects of candidates for the Second Examination for the Degree of Bachelor of Medicine, provided that

(i) such a person shall be appointed for an initial period of three years, with a review at the end of the second year, and may be reappointed (subject to such review) for periods of three years with review at the end of the second year of each three-year period;

(ii) the appointment or reappointment of such a person shall be subject to the approval of the General Board;

(iii) such a person shall be deemed to be a member, or associated member as appropriate, of the corresponding university department.

2. The same faculty board may confer the title of 'Acting Clinical Lecturer in [here state subject]' without stipend upon any person who regularly undertakes teaching in clinical subjects of candidates for the Second Examination for the Degree of Bachelor of Medicine provided that

(*a*) such a person shall be appointed in the first instance for a period of not more than three years to be specified by the faculty board at or before the time of appointment, at the end of which period he or she shall be eligible for reappointment for successive periods not greater than one year at a time;

(*b*) such a person shall be deemed to be a member, or associated member as appropriate, of the corresponding university department.

3. Persons shall cease to hold these titles in the event of their resignation or retirement from their substantive appointments.

§ 7. *Title of District Clinical Tutor*

The Board of the Faculty of Clinical Medicine may confer the title of 'District Clinical Tutor' without stipend upon a District Clinical Tutor appointed under the provisions of Ch. IV, Sect. IX, cl. 2 (vii); provided that

(*a*) such a person shall be appointed or reappointed for a period of not more than five years to be specified by the faculty board at or before the time of appointment or reappointment;

[1] This proviso shall be effective from 1 January 1997, save that the provisions of Ch. VII, Sect. V, § 6, cl. 1 as they stood before that date shall continue to apply to any person holding the title of Honorary Senior Clinical Lecturer on 31 December 1996.

(*b*) the appointment or reappointment of such a person shall be subject to the approval of the General Board.

§ 8. *Tutors in General Practice*

1. Tutors in General Practice shall be appointed by the Board of the Faculty of Clinical Medicine on such terms as to duties and tenure as the board may determine, provided that

(i) they shall be appointed for an initial period of three years, with a review at the end of the second year, and may be reappointed (subject to such review) for periods of five years with review at the end of the fourth year of each five-year period, the appointment being terminable by three months' notice on either side;

(ii) the appointment or reappointment of a Tutor in General Practice shall be made on the recommendation of a committee appointed by the faculty board consisting of not less than five persons including the Professor of General Practice, the Professor of Public Health, the Director of Clinical Studies, a representative of the Clinical Medicine Board, and a representative nominated by the appropriate hospital authority;

(iii) the appointment or reappointment of Tutors in General Practice and the conditions of appointment shall be subject to the approval of the General Board.

2. A Tutor in General Practice may receive no remuneration as such, or may receive an honorarium at a rate to be determined from time to time by the General Board.

§ 9. *Joint appointments between hospitals and the University*

1. A joint appointment between a hospital and the University is one in which the health authority concerned and the University each contribute part of the stipend of a person holding a consultant appointment in the National Health Service on the basis of notional sessions, the appointment on the university side being made by the Board of the Faculty of Clinical Medicine with the approval of the General Board. Holders of such joint appointments shall hold the title of 'Senior Clinical Lecturer'.

2. The holder of a joint appointment shall, on the university side, be appointed for a period of five years. No person shall be reappointed unless this be on reapplication in competition with others following advertisement of the post, and no person shall be appointed for more than two periods in all. Each appointment shall be made on the recommendation of a committee appointed by the faculty board and consisting of not less than five persons, including at least one medically qualified representative of the appropriate NHS authority, and where appropriate a person from one of the pre-clinical departments.

3. The notional sessions of a person holding such a joint appointment shall be paid for by the University at the same rate per session as in the National Health Service appointment.

4. Other conditions of tenure shall be laid down by the faculty board for each appointment and shall be set out in writing to the person appointed when the appointment is offered.

§ **10.** *Other appointments*

1. An appointment to which this section applies which is not covered by the provisions of §§ 2–9 hereof shall be made by the Board of the Faculty of Clinical Medicine on such conditions as to duties and tenure as it may determine, provided that the appointment or reappointment and the conditions determined shall be subject to the approval of the General Board.

2. The General Board shall fix the stipends of such appointments having regard to the stipends payable to readers and university lecturers and to equivalent appointments made in the National Health Service.

3. The General Board may reduce the stipend of any person holding an appointment under this sub-section having regard to any other office or employment for which he or she receives remuneration.

Section VI. Promotion of Equality of Opportunity in Appointing to University Posts

All members and employees of the University whenever they participate in the making of a university appointment, or in the arrangements for the making of such an appointment, shall comply in all relevant respects with the code of practice for the promotion of equality of opportunity which was approved by Congregation on 16 June 1987 in relation to academic and academic-related posts and which is appended at A. III to this chapter.

Section VII. Holding of Fellowships

§ **1.** *Persons whose offices entitle them to hold fellowships*

The persons whose offices entitle them to hold fellowships shall be the persons enumerated in the Schedule annexed to this decree, together with such other persons as may from time to time be added to the Schedule by decree.

SCHEDULE

(*a*) Full-time professors (other than titular professors), readers.

(*b*) University lecturers (including C.U.F. lecturers) appointed by the General Board when their appointments have been confirmed to retiring age.

(*c*) Senior research officers appointed by the General Board when their appointments have been confirmed to retiring age.

(*d*) The following persons:

Director of the Ashmolean Museum
Keepers of departments in the Ashmolean Museum
Director of University Library Services and Bodley's Librarian

Keepers in Bodley's Library
Keeper of the Museum of the History of Science
Director of the Oxford University Museum of Natural History
Director of the Pitt Rivers Museum
Librarian of the Taylor Institution
Director of the Careers Service
Director of the Forestry Institute
Director of Postgraduate Medical Education and Training
Director of Queen Elizabeth House
Peter Moores Director of the Saïd Business School

§ 2. *Persons whose offices qualify them to hold professorial fellowships*

The persons qualified to hold professorial fellowships shall be the persons enumerated in Schedule A annexed to this decree together with any persons holding any of the posts enumerated in Schedule B annexed to this decree, and such other posts as may from time to time be added to them by decree, provided that any such person who has been elected to a fellowship shall no longer be qualified to hold such fellowship if he or she ceases to hold the post in virtue of which he or she was elected.

SCHEDULE A

The Vice-Chancellor
The Registrar
The Director of the Ashmolean Museum
The Keeper of the Department of Antiquities
The Keeper of the Heberden Coin Room
The Keeper of the Department of Eastern Art
The Keeper of the Department of Western Art
The Director of the Careers Service
The Librarian of the Taylor Institution
The Director of the Computing Services
The Peter Moores Director of the Saïd Business School
The Director of Postgraduate Medical Education and Training
The Director of the Oxford University Museum of Natural History
The Secretary to the Delegates of the University Press
The Deputy Secretaries of the University Press
The Warden of Rhodes House
The Director of the Educational Technology Resources Centre

SCHEDULE B

A full-time or titular professorship.
A readership.
The directorship of any institute of which the functions are specially prescribed by statute or decree.

The curatorship of any collection or museum of which the functions are specially prescribed by statute or decree.

Any established post the holder of which is paid on the scale for senior library, administrative, and computer staff at Grade 6, or the scale for research staff at Grade IV, or the scale for departmental keepers and Keeper of the Museum of the History of Science.

Section VIII. Payment of Persons during Sickness

1. The University shall pay Statutory Sick Pay to those employees who are eligible in accordance with the appropriate legislation.

2. If entitlement to Statutory Sick Pay is exhausted, or in the case of employees who are ineligible for Statutory Sick Pay, the University (except in the case of C.U.F. lecturers) shall make deductions from full pay of the maximum amount of sickness or other state benefit that would be available (even if it is not claimed). Married women and widows exercising their right to be exempted from the payment of full national insurance contributions shall be deemed, for these purposes, to be insured in their own right, and in their case deductions shall be made from full pay of an amount equal to the benefit that would have been receivable had full national insurance contributions been paid.

3. No deductions shall be made from payments at half pay under the University's sick pay arrangements, as determined by Council from time to time, except that, where the total amount of half pay plus state benefit or other allowances exceeds full pay, a deduction shall be made of an amount equivalent to the excess.

4. Where appropriate, a period of three 'waiting days' shall be allowed before any deductions are made under the provisions of this decree.

Section IX. Removal Expenses

The Curators of the University Chest shall pay contributions towards removal and travelling expenses incurred by persons taking up approved posts in the University on such conditions as Council may from time to time prescribe.

APPENDIX A TO CHAPTER VII
Equal Opportunity Policy and Code of Practice

I. INTRODUCTION

Statutory obligations

The Sex Discrimination Act 1975 and the Race Relations Act 1976 proscribe discrimination in, among others, the spheres of employment and education, on grounds of sex and marriage (in the case of the former Act) and on racial grounds[1] (in the case of the latter Act). According to the Acts, there is direct discrimination where an individual, on the grounds of his or her sex or racial group, is treated less favourably than a member of the other sex or someone of a different racial group would be treated; there is indirect discrimination where a requirement or condition is applied (i) which is such that a considerably smaller proportion of persons of one sex or of the same racial group can comply with it than the proportion of persons of the other sex or not of that racial group who can comply; and (ii) which cannot be shown to be justifiable irrespective of the sex, colour, race, nationality, or ethnic or national origins of the person to whom it is applied; and (iii) which is to the detriment of the person concerned because he or she cannot comply with it. An example of indirect discrimination on grounds of sex might be a rule that applicants must be under a specified age (see below). An example of such discrimination on racial grounds might be a rule that candidates must have a British or European degree.

It is also unlawful for an individual to be victimised for having brought proceedings under the Acts, or for giving evidence or information relating to such proceedings, or for alleging that discrimination has occurred.

The Equal Opportunities Commission and the Commission for Racial Equality, set up by the Acts to work towards the elimination of discrimination and to promote equality of opportunity, have both produced codes of practice on equal opportunities in employment which have been endorsed by Parliament. The codes do not have the force of law, but they can be brought in evidence in industrial tribunals. The University's code of practice, which is set out at III below, is consistent with these codes.

The Disability Discrimination Act 1995 (D.D.A.) introduced measures to prevent discrimination against disabled people in employment, in the provision of goods and services, and in buying and renting land and property. The D.D.A. also requires higher education institutions regularly to publish information about education provisions for people with disabilities at their institutions. The D.D.A. defines a disabled person as a person with 'a physical or mental impairment which has a substantial and long-term adverse effect on their ability to carry out normal day-to-day activities'. A National Disability Council (N.D.C.) was created under the D.D.A. Unlike the Equal Opportunities Commission and the Commission for Racial Equality, the N.D.C. has an advisory role only and has no powers to enforce the legislation. Guidelines on the implementation of the D.D.A. have been issued by the Government, and the code of practice below is consistent with these guidelines.

In order for the University to comply with the Sex Discrimination (Gender Reassignment) Regulations 1999, which amended the Sex Discrimination Act 1975 with effect from 1 May 1999, Council has decided that from 1 May 1999, where the words 'sex' or 'gender' are used in the University of Oxford Equal Opportunity Policy and Code of Practice, the Code of Practice relating to

[1] Racial grounds are the grounds of colour, race, nationality – including citizenship – or ethnic or national origins, and groups defined by reference to these grounds are referred to as racial groups.

Harassment, or other policy documents relating to equal opportunity in employment, they should be deemed to include gender reassignment.

II. POLICY STATEMENT

The policy and practice of the University of Oxford require that entry into employment with the University and progression within employment will be determined only by personal merit and the application of criteria which are related to the duties of each particular post and the relevant salary structure. Subject to statutory provisions, no applicant or member of staff will be treated less favourably than another because of his or her sex, marital status, racial group, or disability. In all cases, ability to perform the job will be the primary consideration.

III. CODE OF PRACTICE

The University seeks to ensure that all candidates for employment are treated fairly, and that selection is based solely on the individual merits of candidates and on selection criteria relevant to the post. In pursuance of this aim and of its statutory duties, the University of Oxford, as an employer committed to the principle of equality of opportunity, will adhere to the following procedure in the conduct of the recruitment and selection process for all posts.

1. *Selection criteria*

Selection criteria for all posts will be clearly defined and reflected in the further particulars sent to candidates, which will also include details of the University's commitment to equality of opportunity. Job qualifications or requirements which would have the effect of inhibiting applications from members of one sex, from persons of a particular marital status, from persons of a particular racial group, or from those with a disability will not be demanded or imposed except where they are justifiable in terms of the job to be done. (For the purposes of this code, 'racial group' means a group of persons defined by reference to colour, race, nationality, or ethnic or national origins.) An age limit which is convenient as opposed to genuinely necessary could constitute unlawful indirect discrimination against some classes of candidate (such as women who have taken time out of employment for child-rearing). Accordingly age limits will not be imposed unless they can be shown to be necessary for the job to be done.

2. *Advertising*

Job advertisements will state the University's commitment to the principle of equality of opportunity, and will be widely publicised so as to encourage applications from a broad range of suitable candidates from all backgrounds. All job advertisements placed on behalf of the University will include a footnote or final note indicating the University's commitment to equality of opportunity. In addition, where further particulars are prepared they should quote in full the University's Equal Opportunities Policy Statement and make reference to the University's maternity leave provisions and the availability of the university nursery. Further particulars should also be made available in large print, tape, or other formats when they are requested by disabled applicants.

3. *Selection methods*

All those handling applications and conducting interviews must be aware of the principles of the Sex Discrimination Act, the Race Relations Act, the Disability Discrimination Act, and other relevant legislation. The University will ensure that training and advice are available in furtherance of this requirement. All candidates will be compared objectively with the selection criteria, and all applications will be processed in the same way. Information sought from candidates and passed to those responsible for appointments will relate only to the qualifications for or requirements of the job. It is recognised that the University has a statutory obligation to make such adjustments to the workplace and to working arrangements as are reasonable to accommodate suitably qualified disabled applicants.

4. *Interviews*

Wherever suitably qualified persons are available, there will be at least one member of each sex on the bodies responsible for short-listing, interviewing, and making or recommending an appointment. Interview questions will relate to the selection criteria. No questions will be based on assumptions about roles in the home and the family, or the assumed suitability of different ethnic groups for the post in question. In particular, questions about marital status, children, domestic obligations, marriage plans, or family intentions will not be asked at interview. Questions about a candidate's ability to 'fit in' with colleagues may also be construed as unlawful discrimination. Where it is necessary to obtain information on personal circumstances (for example, in relation to a selection criterion such as flexibility to work irregular hours) or on whether a candidate will be able to work well with colleagues, questions about this will be asked equally of all candidates and, like other questions, will relate only to the job requirements. In the case of disabled applicants who identify themselves at the application stage, appropriate interview arrangements (such as accessible interview rooms or the assistance of a sign interpreter) should be offered to enable candidates to compete on an equal basis.

5. *Record-keeping*

Details of candidates and of selection decisions will be kept for at least six months after an appointment has been made, in case they are required as evidence by an industrial tribunal or for other proceedings. The University will keep records of the sex of all candidates and of those short-listed and appointed. The composition of selection panels will also be monitored. In addition, the University will investigate the practicalities of extending its system of monitoring recruitment (for example, covering such categories as marital status, ethnic origin, and any disability). (Records may be used to determine whether members of one sex or persons of a certain racial group or those with a disability do not apply for employment, or apply in smaller numbers than might be expected, or are short-listed or appointed in a lower proportion than their application rate, or are concentrated in certain jobs, faculties, or sub-faculties.)

6. *Review of recruitment practice*

Recruitment procedures and practices will be kept under review so as to ensure that this code is being adhered to. The University's Equal Opportunities Officer has responsibility for advising on the operation of this code and for the distribution to those involved in the recruitment and selection processes of information about the Sex Discrimination Act, the Race Relations Act, the Disability Discrimination Act, and other relevant legislation.

Council shall have power to make changes in this code by decree from time to time, under the provisions of Tit. IV, Sect. I, cl. 2.

APPENDIX B TO CHAPTER VII

Regius Professor of Medicine

13 Norham Gardens to be held in trust as official residence or otherwise applied for endowment of Professorship.

13 Norham Gardens shall be held in trust by the University in accordance with the terms of the will of the late Lady Osler as an official residence for the Regius Professor of Medicine for the time being or to be otherwise applied towards the endowment of the said Regius Professorship in such manner as Council shall determine by decree.

The Curators of the University Chest shall accept any sum which may be given by friends of Sir William Osler and of Professor Pickering in the United States towards the cost of adapting (with special reference to amenities which would not otherwise be provided) 13 Norham Gardens as an official residence for the Regius Professor of Medicine, or of work in the department of the Regius Professor in the Radcliffe Infirmary; the money so received to be spent in such a manner as Council shall determine.

Readership in Chemical Crystallography

Until Council shall otherwise determine by decree, the provisions of Ch. VII, Sect. III, § 46, concerning the Readership in Chemical Crystallography, are suspended.

CHAPTER VIII

FINANCIAL MATTERS

Section I. Fees and Dues payable to the University

For this Section, see *Examination Decrees*.

Section II. Payments by the University

§ 1. *Payment of children's allowances to holders of university posts*

An allowance of £50 per annum for each dependent child who is below the age at which compulsory education ceases, or, being above that age, is receiving full-time education, shall be paid to the holders of university posts who under the regulations of a British university, Research Council, or comparable body were entitled to receive, or were in receipt of, such an allowance on 31 December 1964 and who have remained continuously so entitled thereafter; provided that

(*a*) for holders of college fellowships with emoluments, the allowances shall be reduced to £25, unless Council shall authorize otherwise in the case of fellows who do no teaching or administrative work other than for the University.

(*b*) no allowance under this decree shall be payable to

(i) the Vice-Chancellor;

(ii) the Public Orator;

(iii) the Keeper of the Archives;

(iv) C.U.F. lecturers;

(v) members of the Employees' Pension Scheme, and members of the university clerical staffs;

(vi) persons appointed after 31 December 1964 to professorships, readerships, or analogous posts from a lower grade.

§ 2. *Remuneration of Judges, examiners, and assessors*

Judges, examiners, and assessors shall be paid according to scales drawn up by the General Board from time to time.

§ 3. *Remuneration of supervisors*

Persons appointed to act as supervisors of students for a research degree or other graduate course of study, or as directors of studies of Recognized Students, shall be paid according to scales drawn up by the General Board from time to time.

§ 4. *Payments to be made for presenting to Superior Degrees*

On any occasion on which presentation is made to any one of the under-mentioned degrees, there shall be paid out of the University Chest to the person who makes the presentation for the degree of (*a*) Doctor of Divinity or of Civil Law or of Medicine or of Letters or of Science or of Music, or of Master of Arts, if conferred *honoris causa*, £2·10 for each person presented; provided always that, if the person who would have presented has prepared an oration for the purpose which shall have been submitted to the Vice-Chancellor, he or she shall receive £2·10 even if in the event the honorand is not presented;

(*b*) Doctor of Divinity or of Civil Law or of Medicine or of Letters or of Science or of Music, if not so conferred, and Master of Surgery and Bachelor of Divinity or of Civil Law or of Medicine, £2·10 for one or more persons presented.

§ 5. *Examiners (number of)*

Until Council shall by decree otherwise determine the General Board may increase the number of examiners in any Final Honour School on the recommendation of the chairman of the board of the faculty concerned, notwithstanding the provisions of Ch. VI, Sect. II. A, § 1, cl. 2.

§ 6. *Qualifying examinations for the Degrees of Master of Letters and Bachelor and Master of Philosophy*

Expenses in connection with qualifying examinations for the Degrees of Master of Letters and Bachelor and Master of Philosophy shall be met out of the University General Fund. The rates of remuneration to examiners for those examinations shall be as determined from time to time by the General Board of the Faculties.

Section III. Professorial Pension Fund

1. The Professorial Pension Fund shall consist of the sum of £34,000 transferred from the General Reserve Fund.

2. The Professorial Pension Fund shall be held on trust and shall be used to make payments to retired professors or the dependants of deceased professors.

3. All payments from the fund shall be made on the authority of the Curators of the University Chest.

Section IV. Superannuation

§ 1. *Superannuation Schemes*

1. Subject to the provisions of cl. 4 below, every member of the regular teaching and administrative staffs of the University, as defined in the First Schedule annexed to this decree, appointed as such (including appointment by promotion) before 1 April 1975, and every person so appointed on or after 1 April 1975 who at the date of such appointment is already a member of the Federated Superannuation System for Universities, shall be subject to the provisions of Ch. VIII, Sect. IV, § 1, and to the Federated Superannuation

System for Universities as set out in the First and Third Schedules thereto, as these stood on 30 September 1974.[1]

2. Every member of the regular teaching and administrative staffs, as defined in the First Schedule annexed to this decree, appointed as such (including appointment by promotion) on or after 1 April 1975 and not being a member of the Federated Superannuation System for Universities at the time of such appointment, shall become a member of the Universities Superannuation Scheme, provided he or she is eligible to join that scheme under the Trust Deed and Rules thereof.

3. The Curators of the University Chest shall be charged with the general administration of both schemes, and shall exercise all the powers and perform all the duties of the University thereunder.

4. The foregoing provisions of this sub-section shall not apply to any member of the teaching and administrative staff who has been exempted or excluded from membership of the scheme.

§ **2.** *Scheme for the supplementation of superannuation benefits*

The Curators of the University Chest shall give effect to the provisions of the scheme for the supplementation of superannuation benefits contained in the Second Schedule annexed to this decree. For the purposes of ascertaining the benefits payable by the University under the provisions of paragraph 3, the Curators shall take into account any salary (as defined in paragraph 9 (2)) and any pension (as defined in paragraph 6) received from a college as well as the salary and pension received from the University.

§ **3.** *Pensions to dependants of employees*

The Curators of the University Chest shall pay dependants of employees of the University who die while still in the service of the University such pensions and allowances as Council, with the concurrence of the Curators of the University Chest, may consider appropriate.

§ **4.** *Pensions for retired members of the F.S.S.U. and E.P.S.*

The Curators of the University Chest are authorized to pay, with effect from 1 September 1971, increased pensions to:

(*a*) retired members of the F.S.S.U., in accordance with advice received from the Committee of Vice-Chancellors and Principals of the Universities of the United Kingdom or any successor body to that committee;

(*b*) retired members of the E.P.S., according to the same formulae as are used for the increase of F.S.S.U. pensions.

[1] See *Statutes*, 1974, pp. 463–77.

FIRST SCHEDULE

The term 'regular teaching and administrative staffs of the University' shall include

(1) Every professor, reader, lecturer, or other university teacher, including teachers regularly employed by any department of the University, except the holder of

(*a*) any of the following appointments:

The Grinfield Lecturership on the Septuagint;
The Speaker's Lecturership in Biblical Studies;
The Harold Vyvyan Harmsworth Professorship of American History;
George Eastman Visiting Professorship;
Newton-Abraham Visiting Professorship;
Ford's Lecturership in British History;
The Professorship of Poetry;
The Slade Professorship in Fine Art;
The John Locke Lecturership in Philosophy;
The James P. R. Lyell Readership in Bibliography;
The O'Donnell Lecturership in Celtic Studies;
The Wilde Lecturership in Natural and Comparative Religion;
The University Lecturership in Spanish.

(*b*) a teaching or research appointment the holder of which is in one of the following categories, provided that he or she has agreed to be excluded from the Universities Superannuation Scheme or the Federated Superannuation System for Universities:

(i) a member of the National Health Service scheme;

(ii) a temporary employee appointed for not more than three years who is already a member of a final salary scheme, the administrators of which are prepared to allow him or her to remain in it.

(2) The Vice-Chancellor.
Bodley's Librarian, and the Officers of the Bodleian Library.
The Public Orator.
The Keeper of the Archives.
The Registrar.
The Director of the Ashmolean Museum.
The Keeper of the Department of Western Art.
The Keeper of the Department of Antiquities.
The Keeper of the Department of Eastern Art.
The Keeper of the Heberden Coin Room.
The Director of the Pitt Rivers Museum.
The Master and Officers of St. Cross College.
The Clerk of the Schools.

All Administrative Officers employed by the University or by any Department of the University.

SECOND SCHEDULE

1. This schedule defines the limits within which universities and university colleges in Great Britain may supplement superannuation benefits from general university income.

2. The scheme shall be applied as of right to any person who on or after 1 April 1960 retires at the age of 60 or over from full time service remunerated wholly or partly by a university or university college in Great Britain, who immediately before retirement was subject to the superannuation scheme operated under the Federated Superannuation System for Universities, and whose pension as defined in paragraph 6 is less than his or her appropriate rate as laid down in paragraph 7. However, this is subject to the proviso that if, in the case of any member of staff serving on 1 April 1960, this scheme would result in a lower appropriate rate than that under the Scheme for Alleviation of Superannuation Hardships (as revised in 1957), the member shall have a right to have his or her claim to supplementation considered on the basis of what the appropriate rate would have been under that scheme.

3. Any benefit payable under this scheme to a person to whom it applies will be an annual sum equal to the difference between his or her pension and his or her appropriate rate. Benefits should not be expressed otherwise than as an annual sum and beneficiaries should be informed that an award of benefit under this scheme confers no right which can be commuted by a capital sum or assigned to another person.

4. No benefit may be paid to a person unless five years or more of his or her university service was given in the United Kingdom.

5. In any case in which the period of university service, as defined in paragraph 9 (4), exceeds twenty years and the appropriate rate exceeds £500, the aggregate of pension and of benefit under the scheme shall not exceed two-thirds of the annual rate of salary, as defined in paragraph 9 (2), at which the beneficiary was last employed.

6. In this scheme the expression a retired person's 'pension' means the best single annuity on his or her own life which is obtainable (with the capital sum available on retirement) from the company or companies with which the individual F.S.S.U. policies had been effected on his or her behalf, provided that

(i) there shall be excluded such part of such capital sum as may arise from contributions made in respect of service which is not university service; and

(ii) any benefits received under the F.S.S.U. or any other pension scheme with which he or she was connected during his or her period of university service are brought into account.

Where a person to whom this scheme is applied has received in respect of a period of university service benefit from a superannuation scheme other than the

F.S.S.U., account shall be taken of such benefit in arriving at the amount of his or her pension in the same manner, so far as possible, as that in which account is taken of benefits receivable under the F.S.S.U.

7. The appropriate rate of any person shall be one seventy-fifth of his or her terminal salary, as defined in paragraph 9 (3), for each year (not exceeding forty) of his or her university service, as defined in paragraph 9 (4). Periods of service of six months or more but less than a year should be treated as a year, while periods of less than six months' service should be ignored.

8. Retirement pensions under the National Insurance Acts 1946 to 1959 have been taken into account in determining the appropriate rates laid down in paragraph 7; no further adjustment of the rates is required on account of these pensions.

9. In this scheme the following expressions have the meaning hereby assigned to them, that is to say:

(1) 'University or university college in Great Britain' means an institution which receives recurrent grants paid by the Treasury on the recommendation of the University Grants Committee or any successor to that body whether directly or through the Court or Council of a university or a local authority.

(2) 'Salary' means only remuneration taken into account in calculating the contributions payable under the F.S.S.U. and 'remunerated' relates only to such remuneration.

(3) 'Terminal salary' means the average annual salary as defined above, over the last three years of university service, except that, for persons born on or before 1 April 1915 who retire on or after 1 April 1972, it shall mean the salary for whichever year of the last three years of university service is best for the member.

(4) 'University service' means full time service with

(*a*) a university or university college in Great Britain (except that in the case of service in a College of Advanced Technology or Heriot-Watt College this shall relate only to service after 1 April 1965 under F.S.S.U. or similar policy scheme) or with a college of the University of Oxford or the University of Cambridge; or

(*b*) a university or university college outside Great Britain, provided that

(i) service with a university or university college outside Great Britain, which is not service with a university or university college of the British Commonwealth, shall be taken into account in reckoning the period of university service only in the case of a person none of the last twelve years of whose university service was given with an institution outside the United Kingdom; and

(ii) where account is taken of a period of service which is not service with a university or university college of the British Commonwealth, only one-half of that period shall be reckoned as university service; or with (*c*) the Civil Service of the State whether in Great Britain or Northern Ireland and if subject to F.S.S.U. at the time, or for which a Transfer Value has been paid for the purchase of a single annuity F.S.S.U. policy; or with

(*d*) the Association of Commonwealth Universities and if subject to F.S.S.U. at the time, or for which a Transfer Value has been paid for the purchase of a single annuity F.S.S.U. policy; or with

(*e*) one or more of the grant-aided bodies mentioned below during which service the person concerned was subject to the F.S.S.U. or to any other scheme having an insurance policy basis:

Medical Research Council
Agricultural Research Council
The National Institute of Agricultural Botany
The Marine Biological Association of the United Kingdom
The Freshwater Biological Association
The Scottish Marine Biological Association
The Institute of Seaweed Research
The Institute for Marine Biochemistry
The Institute of Development Studies
The Seale Hayne Agricultural College
The Royal Agricultural College
The Harper Adams Agricultural College
The Cranfield Institute of Technology
The Natural Environment Research Council
The Social Science Research Council
The Science Research Council
The Imperial Cancer Research Fund
The Institute for Marine Environmental Research
Animal Diseases Research Association
The Animal Virus Research Institute
The British Society for the Promotion of Vegetable Research
The British Society for Research in Agricultural Engineering
The East of Scotland College of Agriculture
The Glasshouse Crops Research Institute
The Grassland Research Institute
The Hannah Dairy Research Institute
The Hill Farming Research Organization
The Houghton Poultry Research Station
The John Innes Institute
Kent Incorporated Society for Promoting Experiments in Horticulture
Lawes Agricultural Trust Rothamstead Experimental Station
Long Ashton Research Station
The Macauley Institute for Soil Research
The National Institute for Research in Dairying
The North of Scotland College of Agriculture
Plant Breeding Institute
The Rowett Research Institute
The Scottish Horticultural Research Institute
Scottish Society for Research in Plant Breeding
Welsh Plant Breeding Station
The West of Scotland Agricultural College
The National Institute of Economic and Social Research
The Open University
Ruskin College
Cambridge Institute of Education
Commonwealth Agricultural Bureaux
The National Museum of Wales
The Inter-University Council for Higher Education Overseas
The Cancer Research Campaign
The Scottish Agricultural Development Council
The Marine Invertebrate Biology Unit
University College at Buckingham
Nature Conservancy Council
Royal College of Surgeons of England.

(5) 'Service with a university or university college of the British Commonwealth' means service either with an institution included in the fifth edition of the 'List of University Institutions in the British Commonwealth' (otherwise than in Appendix II thereof) published in February 1959 by the Association of Universities of the British Commonwealth, or with an institution which, although not included in that List, was a member or an associate member of that Association at any time during the period of service concerned.

10. Where service with any of the grant-aided bodies listed in paragraph 9 (4) (*e*) is taken into account the terms to be applied will be those of this scheme.

11. Any benefit payable under this scheme will be paid by the university or university college in Great Britain by which the salary of the beneficiary was wholly or partly paid at the time of his or her retirement.

Section V. Pension Schemes for University Employees

§ 1. *Old Pension Scheme for University Employees*

For this sub-section, see *Statutes*, 1982, pp. 474–81.

§ 2. *New Pension Scheme for University Employees*

For this sub-section, see *Statutes*, 1982, pp. 481–8.

§ 3. *Staff Pension Scheme*

1. A Scheme entitled the University of Oxford Staff Pension Scheme has been established under Deed of Trust for the purpose of providing pensions and other benefits for persons in the employment of the University who are not eligible to become members of the Universities Superannuation Scheme, and every such person appointed on or after 6 April 1978 who is eligible under the conditions of the scheme shall, unless he or she has submitted a written request for exemption, be required to join it; provided that the Scheme shall not apply to persons employed by the University Press nor to those excepted from the Universities Superannuation Scheme under the First Schedule to Ch. VIII, Sect. IV, § 4.

2. The scheme shall be administered in accordance with the terms of the Trust Deed by Managing Trustees appointed as follows:

(1)–(5) five persons appointed by Council;

(6)–(10) five persons who are members of the scheme, comprising:

(i) two persons employed in the University's technicians' scales appointed by the University branch of the Manufacturing, Science, and Finance Union;

(ii) two persons employed in the University's clerical and library scales appointed by the staff side of the Clerical and Library Negotiating Committee;

(iii) one person employed in the University's ancillary scales appointed by the staff side of the Ancillary and Gardens and Parks Employees Joint Committee;

(11) a person appointed by the Vice-Chancellor to be chairman, after consultation with the Managing Trustees appointed under (1)–(10) above:

Provided always that any Managing Trustee appointed under (6)–(10) shall resign if he or she ceases to be eligible for membership of the scheme.

3. Each Managing Trustee shall be appointed for a term not exceeding three years and shall be eligible for reappointment at the end of such term.

4. The conditions of the Scheme, including qualifications for eligibility and rates of contributions and of benefits, are laid down in an attachment to the Deed of Trust and may be amended only with the agreement of a majority of the Managing Trustees and the approval of the Curators of the University Chest and Council.

§ 4. *Pensionable salary and pension of Vice-Chancellor*

1. For the purposes of para. 9 (2) of the scheme set out in the Second Schedule to Ch. VIII, Sect. IV, § 4, the salary of a Vice-Chancellor shall always be deemed to be one and one-fifth times that of a Schedule A professor.

2. When a person who has held office as Vice-Chancellor after October 1969 and who immediately before retirement was subject to the superannuation scheme operated under the Federated Superannuation System for Universities finally retires, being aged 60 or over, from university service as defined in para. 9 (4) of the aforesaid Schedule, the University shall pay him or her such amount by way of additional benefit as will make the benefit paid to him or her up to what it would have been had he or she held the Vice-Chancellorship during the three years immediately preceding retirement; provided that if he or she held the office of Vice-Chancellor for less than four years, the amount of additional benefit shall be abated as Council may think appropriate.

Section VI. Payment of Employees

For this Section, see *Statutes*, 1995, pp. 517–18.

Section VII. Capital Fund

1. The Capital Fund shall be formed by carrying to it the moneys held at 31 July 1982 by the Capital Development Fund and by the Reserve and Loans Permanent Fund together with such proportion of the Reserve and Loans Remainder Fund as the Curators of the University Chest may, with the approval of Council, determine. Council may add to the fund from time to time such other moneys as it shall determine after consultation with the Curators of the University Chest.

2. The fund shall be applied to such expenditure as Council may determine, provided that, if such expenditure is of a capital nature for the extension or development of university institutions or departments, the expenditure may at Council's discretion be treated as a loan on such terms, including the method and period of repayment and the rate of interest, if any, to be charged, as

Council shall determine after consultation with the Curators of the University Chest.

Section VIII. Trusts Pool

Note. This Scheme is made as stated in 1 (i) below; it is not made by decree or regulation.

General

1. (i) This scheme is made under Section (2) of the Universities and Colleges (Trusts) Act, 1943.

(ii) Subject to the exceptions and exclusions specified in Article 2 hereof the property of all trusts to which this scheme applies shall be administered by the University as a single fund hereinafter referred to as the 'pool'.

(iii) In this scheme the word 'pool' shall have the same meaning as the word 'fund' in Section (2) of the Universities and Colleges (Trusts) Act, 1943.

Trusts to which the scheme applies

2. (i) This scheme shall apply to those trusts which at the date on which this scheme comes into operation were included in the scheme sealed by the University on 26 February 1957, approved by The Queen in Council on 24 June 1957, as subsequently amended (hereinafter referred to as the 1957 Scheme).

(ii) This scheme may by decree of Council or by resolution of the Curators of the University Chest be applied, subject to such exceptions as may be specified, to any other trusts administered or to be administered by or for purposes connected with the University, unless the terms of the trust expressly provide to the contrary, and subject in the case of any trust not administered by the University to the consent of the trustees.

(iii) Property belonging to trusts to which the 1957 Scheme applied and which at the date on which this scheme comes into operation was excluded from the 1957 Scheme, and property excluded from this scheme by a decree or resolution under Article 2 (ii) hereof, may be included in this scheme by decree or resolution.

Additions to or withdrawals from the pool

3. Shares in the pool may be acquired or disposed of by constituent trusts on 1 August, 1 November, 1 February, and 1 May on the basis of the valuation made on the previous day under Article 6 hereof, provided:

(i) that in the event of there being included in the pool a trust which has a repairs fund, a fund for eliminating or reducing fluctuations of income, or a sinking fund to provide the capitalized value of increases in rents receivable in respect of leasehold properties, such fund or funds may be amalgamated with the funds provided for by Articles 8, 10, and 11 hereof;

(ii) that the appropriate number of Trusts Pool shares shall be issued in respect of all assets transferred to the pool.

Power to invest

4. The pool may be invested and the investment thereof may be changed by the University in its discretion within the range laid down by the University Statutes, Title XIV, Sect. V, cl. 2.

Power to borrow money

5. The University may borrow money for investment on behalf of the pool upon such terms of interest and repayment as it may decide, and may mortgage land or hypothecate securities held on behalf of the pool as security therefor: provided always that interest payable on such borrowed money, and suitable provision for the repayment of the capital, shall be prior charges on the gross income of the pool.

Valuation

6. The University shall cause the whole of the assets of the pool (including any Works and Repairs Fund, Reserve Fund, or Sinking Fund created under Articles 8, 10, and 11 hereof respectively) to be valued on 31 July, 31 October, 31 January, and 30 April in each year and the total value (less any liability for money borrowed under the provisions of Article 5 hereof) shall be divided by the number of shares in issue at the same date, and the value of each share thus determined shall be recorded. Such revaluation shall be made in the following manner:

(i) as to securities at the mid-market price on that day, or if that day is a holiday on the last previous working day;

(ii) as to mortgages at their face value; and

(iii) as to real property (including rent charges secured on land and interests in land) at the value thereof as at 31 July 1967 and thereafter on 31 July in every subsequent fifth year in accordance with a valuation obtained from a firm or firms of chartered surveyors. The managing agents shall also review the value of each property in the course of each year between the quinquennial valuations and shall report to the Curators of the University Chest any substantial variation, and the said curators shall give effect if they think fit to such variation on the occasion of the next valuation of the pool. On the occasion of each quarterly valuation account shall be taken of additions to and reductions in such property since the last valuation, and in the case of leaseholds or other wasting assets of any provision made for the amortization thereof.

Allocation of the income of the pool

7. The net income of the pool in each year including the income of any Reserve Fund created under Article 10 hereof after deducting any sum reserved under Articles 8, 9, 10, and 11 hereof, shall be allocated and distributed among the trusts concerned in proportion to the shares in the pool for the time being belonging to such trusts respectively.

Works and Repairs Fund

8. The Curators of the University Chest may each year out of the income of the pool carry such sum as may seem to them appropriate to a Works and Repairs Fund for expenditure on repairs and improvements to real property held by the pool.

Expenses of administration

9. The Curators of the University Chest may retain in or towards reimbursement of the expenses incurred by the University in the administration of the pool such yearly sum not exceeding 2 per cent of the gross income for the time being of the pool and of any reserve created under Article 10 hereof.

Reserve

10. The Curators of the University Chest may in each year set aside such portion of the distributable income of the pool as they shall think fit to form a reserve to be used at the discretion of the said curators with the consent of the Hebdomadal Council to supplement the income of the pool in any subsequent year or years for the purpose of eliminating or reducing fluctuations of income.

Sinking Fund

11. The Curators of the University Chest may, if they think fit, set up a sinking fund to provide the whole or a part of the capitalized value of any increases in rents receivable in respect of leasehold properties, such sinking fund to be calculated at such a rate of interest as the said curators may decide and for the same period as the unexpired portion of the head lease.

Operation

12. This scheme came into operation on 25 February 1970, and the 1957 Scheme ceased to have effect from the same date.

Section IX. Form of University Accounts and Audit

1. The Curators of the University Chest and each delegacy, board, and committee, and the head of each institution and department to whom funds are entrusted shall respectively ensure that all moneys under their control are safely kept and are used only for the purposes for which they are allocated and that all transactions are recorded in proper accounting records.

2. (*a*) As soon as practicable after the 31 July in each year the Curators of the University Chest shall cause to be prepared and audited and submitted to the Vice-Chancellor Financial Statements of the University for the year to that date. The Financial Statements shall be drawn up in such a way as to give a true and fair view of the state of the financial affairs of the University and its related bodies and subsidiary companies (other than the University Press) at the balance sheet date and of their income and expenditure for the year then ended.

(*b*) Each delegacy, board, committee, and subsidiary company and the head of each institution and department shall as soon as practicable provide or cause to be provided such information as the Curators of the University Chest may require to enable them to comply with the requirements of sub-clause (*a*) above.

3. Council shall annually, having received the advice of the Audit Committee, appoint as University Auditor a person or persons eligible for appointment as a company auditor with Registered Auditor status.

4. The University Auditor shall audit the Financial Statements of the University in accordance with Auditing Standards and shall report to the Vice-Chancellor in writing whether in his or her opinion the Financial Statements give a true and fair view of the state of the financial affairs of the University and its related bodies and subsidiary companies (other than the University Press) at the balance sheet date and of their income and expenditure for the year then ended.

5. If, as a result of the University Auditor's audit of the Financial Statements, the University Auditor considers that there are defects in the systems of financial control, or in their operation, which should appropriately be drawn to the attention of Council, the University Auditor shall report specially thereon to the Vice-Chancellor.

6. The University Auditor shall report to the Curators of the University Chest as to any receipt or payment which he or she may judge to have been accepted or made without sufficient authority, and the Curators shall report to the Vice-Chancellor all cases which they consider should be drawn to the attention of Council.

7. The cost of the audit (including expenses properly incurred in connection therewith) shall be paid out of the University General Fund.

8. The Accounts of the Delegates of the University Press shall be audited as prescribed by Ch. III, Sect. LXXXIV, cl. 8, and nothing in this decree shall be deemed to refer to the accounts of those delegates. Accordingly, the income and expenditure account, balance sheets, and related notes set out in the Financial Statements of the University shall not include the Accounts of the Delegates of the University Press.

Section X. Effecting Contracts

The Registrar, the University's senior administrative officers appointed under the provisions of Tit. IX, Sect. VII, cl. 11, their respective deputies appointed from time to time, and the Land Agent, are authorized to enter into, vary, and discharge on behalf of the University such contracts and such classes of contracts (whether made in writing or by parol), and to sign such other documents and such classes of documents, as may be specified by Council. In addition, any person who has received consent under the provisions of Tit. X, Sect. III to enter into a contract or contracts on behalf of the University has authority to do so.

Section XI. Procedures for the Administration of the University's Intellectual Property Policy

1. Where any person who is subject to the provisions of Tit. X, Sect. IV or of Tit. XV, Sect. VI (a 'researcher') creates intellectual property[1] which is capable of commercial exploitation, he or she shall report its existence to the Head of Department (or equivalent) and to the Director of the Research Services Office, providing the Director with all necessary information concerning the provenance of the intellectual property and and the circumstances in which it was created. The next step shall depend upon the source of funding:

(*a*) whenever the conditions of research council grants require the assignment of intellectual property to the research council or its nominee, or to industrial collaborators, and whenever there is a similar requirement in an agreement for research sponsored by some other party, the research council, industrial collaborator, or sponsor shall be given the responsibility for exploitation;

(*b*) Isis Innovation Limited ('Isis') shall be responsible for the exploitation of research funded with research council grants the conditions of which do not include such a requirement;

(*c*) in all other cases, the University's preferred route to exploitation is through Isis. A researcher who wishes to exploit the intellectual property by some other means may apply to Council for permission to do so.[2] Council shall consider in particular the question of whether the alternative means of exploitation are likely to result in a reasonable return to the University from royalties or equity or other means of sharing profits which may accrue.

2. In the event of a dispute between the researcher and the University concerning the ownership of the intellectual property, the matter shall be referred to an independent expert to be agreed between the researcher and the University. If agreement on the identity of the expert is not reached within thirty days, the expert shall be a barrister specializing in intellectual property law, who shall be nominated for the purpose by the then Chairman of the General Council of the Bar. The expert's fee shall be paid by the University, but shall constitute a first charge on any profits which may accrue, whether to the researcher or to Isis or the University, whichever party or parties is or are held by the expert to be the owner of the intellectual property.

3. Where the University decides to seek exploitation of intellectual property to which it lays claim, discussions between the interested parties shall be held to determine the appropriate action to be taken. This may include one or more of the following:

(*a*) control over disclosure;

(*b*) the filing of a patent application, with the researcher as named inventor;

[1] In these procedures the term 'intellectual property' refers to the items detailed in Tit. X, Sect. IV, cl. 1 and Tit. XV, Sect. VI, cl. 1.

[2] Members of the University who wish to seek approval from Council are asked to contact the Director of the Research Services Office in the first instance.

(*c*) the identification of potential licensees;

(*d*) the formation of a company to exploit the technology.

4. Notwithstanding paragraph (*a*) of clause 3, Isis and the University may consult appropriate experts in the field of the intellectual property in question, in order (for example) to assist with an assessment of innovation or commercial potential.

5. Where the University decides to seek exploitation, the researcher shall provide reasonable assistance in the exploitation process by (for example) promptly assigning his or her rights to Isis and/or to a third party specified by the University, providing information promptly upon request, attending meetings with potential licensees, and advising on further development. The University shall ensure that researchers do not become personally liable for product liability claims arising from the University's exploitation activities.

6. Where exploitation is through the medium of a company formed for the purpose, royalty or sales fee income received by Isis or the University from the company shall be treated in accordance with clause 7. The respective shareholdings in the company of the researchers and the University (or Isis) shall be negotiated at the time of formation or capitalization; and unless otherwise agreed, revenues generated by the shareholdings (both capital and income receipts) shall be retained by the shareholders, and shall not be subject to distribution under clause 7.

7. In this clause the expression 'net revenue' means gross revenue less professional fees and expenses and other costs incurred in protecting the intellectual property and negotiating the arrangements for exploitation.

(*a*) Where there is a receipt by the University which is in the nature of a university milestone payment, no part of the net revenue shall be distributed to Isis or the researcher: the net revenue shall be distributed as to 40 per cent to the General Revenue Account and as to 60 per cent to the department(s). A university milestone payment shall be taken for this purpose to be a payment which is referable to the progress of research or development by the University, but which is not covering or supporting the cost of such research or development; as against a payment for the right to use intellectual property, or a payment referable to the progress of research or developments by a party other than the University (such as a licensee), where the net revenue shall be distributed in accordance with the following paragraphs of this clause.

(*b*) Where responsibility for the exploitation of intellectual property is given to a research council, industrial collaborator, or sponsor under paragraph (*a*) of clause 1, any net revenue received by the University shall be distributed as follows:[1]

[1] For the explanation of the asterisks see clause 7 (*e*).

Total net revenue	*Researcher(s)*	*General Revenue Account*	*Department(s)*
Up to £50K	90%*	10%*	0%
Band from £50K and up to £500K	45%	30%	25%
Over £500K	22½%	40%	37½%

(*c*) Where responsibility for the exploitation of intellectual property is given to Isis, any net revenue received by Isis shall be distributed as follows:

Total net revenue	*Researcher(s)*	*General Revenue Account*	*Department(s)*	*Isis*
Up to £72K	63%*	7%*	0%	30%
Band from £72K and up to £720K	31½%	21%	17½%	30%
Over £720K	15¾%	28%	26¼%	30%

(*d*) Where responsibility for the exploitation of intellectual property is given to the University, then, unless some other arrangement is approved by Council under clause 1 (*c*), any net revenue received by the University shall be distributed as stated in paragraph (*c*) of this clause, save that the 30 per cent share payable to Isis shall be passed instead to the General Revenue Account.

(*e*) The percentages asterisked above are intended to put the University in funds to pay the employer's National Insurance Contribution(s), but otherwise to leave the General Revenue Account out of the allocation of the bands in question. These percentages shall be adjusted to match this intention, as and when the rates of National Insurance Contribution vary.

8. (*a*) The University shall account to researchers for their entitlements under clause 7 on a monthly basis.

(*b*) A researcher's entitlement under clause 7 shall continue to be paid to him or her should he or she leave the University; and in the event of a researcher's death, the entitlement shall continue for the benefit of his or her estate.

9. Where more than one researcher contributes to the creation of the intellectual property, the distribution of their share of the income between themselves shall be a matter for them to determine (and to notify in writing to the Director of the Research Services Office); save that where there is failure to agree, the distribution of income shall be prescribed by the Vice-Chancellor, taking into account each individual's contribution.

10. If the University decides not to seek to exploit intellectual property to which it lays claim; or if, after the University has initiated or sanctioned exploitation, the University decides (in consultation with Isis) that the process of exploitation be abandoned; the University shall not unreasonably withhold or

delay an assignment of the intellectual property to the researcher (at the researcher's expense).

Section XII. Financial Regulations

I. INTRODUCTION

These Financial Regulations are made by the Council of the University in accordance with its statutory responsibilities for the proper control of the financial business of the University. The regulations apply to the conduct of all financial business of the University of Oxford, irrespective of the source of funding.

The Financial Regulations are included as regulations in the Statutes, Decrees, and Regulations of the University.

The primary objective of these regulations is to ensure the proper use of finances and resources in a manner which satisfies the requirements of accountability and internal control and also fulfils any legal or financial obligations as laid down by the Inland Revenue, the Higher Education Funding Council for England (H.E.F.C.E.), Customs and Excise, and other government authorities. The regulations do not extend to non-financial activities of the University nor are they a definitive statement on the governance of the University.

Copies of the regulations are circulated to the heads of all university divisions, departments, and institutions and to the secretaries of all university committees and boards that receive and hold funds. It is their responsibility to ensure that all those to whom any financial authority is delegated are made aware of the existence and provisions of these regulations, and that an adequate number of copies are made available for reference. Those with financial and accounting responsibilities must have their own copies.

Compliance with the Financial Regulations is a requirement for all employees of the University (irrespective of whether their appointment is financed by general university funds, research grants and contracts, or trust or other funds) and for all those not directly employed by the University who have responsibility for the administration or management of university funds.

Additional copies of these regulations may be obtained from the Director of Finance and Secretary of the Chest, who should also be contacted for advice if there is any uncertainty as to their application.

II. DEFINITIONS AND ABBREVIATIONS

The following definitions and abbreviations have been used in the text in order to shorten and simplify the regulations:

Director of Finance refers to the Director of Finance and Secretary of the Chest.

Budgetary units/units/bodies refers to all divisions, departments, institutions, committees, and boards that receive and administer funds disbursed by the

University or received from external sources, and that are subject to the provisions of these regulations.

Head of unit refers to heads of divisions, departments, and institutions and secretaries of committee and boards as defined above.

Finance Committee refers to the Finance Committee of Council.

P.R.A.C. refers to the Planning and Resource Allocation Committee of Council.

R.S.O. refers to the Research Services Office.

Parent body refers to a budgetary unit that allocates funds to other units under delegated authority.

V.A.T. refers to Value Added Tax.

III. THE FINANCIAL REGULATIONS

§ 1. *General*

1. These regulations apply to the conduct of all financial business of the University, irrespective of the source of funding. They do not extend to the non-financial business of the University and are not a definitive statement on the governance of the University. The University is a civil corporation, and the structure of its governance is laid down in the Statutes and Decrees of the University. The University is an exempt charity by virtue of the Charities Act 1993.

2. Compliance with the regulations is a requirement for all employees of the Chancellor, Masters, and Scholars of the University of Oxford (other than those responsible to the Delegates of the University Press) and for all those not directly employed by the University who have responsibility for the administration or management of university funds.

3. The staff of the Internal Audit Section will point out any non-compliance they encounter during the course of their work.

§ 2. *Application*

1. The regulations apply to all bodies included in the University's annual audited financial statements except subsidiary companies and colleges without independence. Such entities are expected to develop their own regulations based on this document, appropriately amended to take account of their differing governance arrangements. The regulations apply to all funds received and held by university bodies from whatever source.

2. The regulations do not apply to those colleges of the University that are independent.

3. The regulations do not apply to the Delegates of the University Press, who have their own internally established financial policies and procedures.

4. Where the Finance Division or any body within the University provides an accounting or other financial service for organizations that are not part of the University, it is acting as a custodian of the funds it is holding and has a duty

to exercise the same care as with its own funds. The regulations apply to these funds while the University holds them.

§ 3. *Distribution*

1. The Director of Finance is responsible for ensuring that copies of the regulations are distributed to the heads of all budgetary units.

2. The heads of all budgetary units are responsible for ensuring that all members of their unit or all those responsible to their committee or board are aware of the regulations, have a proper understanding of their operation, and have access to them and that those with financial and accounting responsibilities have their own copies.

§ 4. *Updating*

Every five years, or more frequently if appropriate, the Director of Finance shall arrange for the regulations to be reviewed and for any proposed changes to be submitted to Council for its consideration.

§ 5. *Financial Responsibility within the University*

1. *Council* is (subject to the provisions of the statutes) responsible for the administration of the University and for the management of its finances and property and has all the powers necessary for it to discharge these responsibilities. To perform these responsibilities effectively, it delegates detailed management to budgetary units and officers, retaining ultimate responsibility subject to the statutes.

2. *Congregation* is the ultimate legislative body of the University and is composed of virtually all academic staff and certain research support staff, administrators, and librarians. It has to approve changes to the Statutes and Decrees of the University.

3. *The Finance Committee* is responsible under Council for the approval of the University's Annual Financial Statements and for consideration of proposed financial regulations.

4. *The Planning and Resource Allocation Committee* is a committee of Council that keeps under review the financial resources and needs of the University, and makes recommendations to Council, in particular on long-term financial planning, the annual budget, the allocation of resources, and the use of the University's capital funds. The committee is also responsible for ensuring that university bodies to which financial management has been delegated exercise proper management over delegated resources.

5. *The Vice-Chancellor* is the chief officer of the University, who normally presides over Congregation and chairs Council. The Vice-Chancellor also chairs P.R.A.C. He or she is the Designated Officer appointed by Council in accordance with the University's Financial Memorandum with H.E.F.C.E., and

may be required to appear before the Public Accounts Committee on matters relating to Funding Council grants made to the University.

6. *The Registrar*, under the Vice-Chancellor, is the head of the central administrative service of the University and is also secretary of Congregation and of Council.

7. *The Director of Finance* is the Chief Financial Officer of the University with right of direct access to the Vice-Chancellor and Council on financial, technical, and professional matters, and is responsible to the Registrar. The Director of Finance is responsible:

(*a*) to Council for ensuring that adequate controls and procedures are in place to record all transactions of the University in an accurate and timely manner;

(*b*) for the provision of financial information and advice to all budgetary units; and

(*c*) for advising the relevant university bodies and officers on financial policies and planning, and the financial implications of any proposals.

8. *Financial Memorandum with the Higher Education Funding Council for England*. Council is responsible for ensuring that the University complies with the memorandum and related guidance. H.E.F.C.E. is required to be satisfied that Council has appropriate arrangements for financial management and accounting and that the uses to which H.E.F.C.E. funds are put are consistent with the purposes for which they were given. Council is also required to ensure that the University has a sound system of internal financial management and control and that value for money is delivered from public funds. The Financial Memorandum sets out detailed guidelines covering a number of areas referred to in these regulations; in such cases the regulations have been framed to incorporate the requirements of the memorandum.

9. *Heads of Divisions, Departments, and Institutions*. Accountability for financial management is delegated from Council, through P.R.A.C., to Divisional Boards. Within divisions, financial management is further delegated to departments and other budgetary units in accordance with rules laid down by each Divisional Board, but within the overall framework of these Financial Regulations. At each level, the body or individual concerned must ensure that funds received or spent by those bodies or individuals are properly controlled and their use monitored. Responsibility for internal control within a budgetary unit rests with the head of that unit, who should ensure that appropriate and adequate arrangements exist to safeguard all assets, that university policies including these Financial Regulations are complied with, and that records are maintained in as complete and accurate a form as possible. Heads of units must ensure that adequate procedures for regular independent checks of financial transactions are in place.

10. Guidance on recommended internal control procedures may be obtained from the Internal Audit Section.

§ 6. *Ethical Policy*

1. University employees and others with responsibility for the administration or management of university funds should never use their authority or office for personal gain and should always seek to uphold and enhance the standing of the University.

2. The University has published Guidelines on Conflict of Interest which employees and others who have responsibility for the administration or management of university funds are expected to follow in order to avoid such conflicts. A Conflict of Interest Committee has also been set up to give formal and informal advice. Enquiries should be directed in the first instance to the secretary of the Conflict of Interest Committee, from whom details of the guidelines are also available.

3. Members of university bodies should declare any relevant interests (financial or otherwise) in matters under discussion and should, if requested by the chairman, withdraw from such discussion.

§ 7. *Audit*

1. The University's audit arrangements are required to be in accordance with the H.E.F.C.E. Audit Code of Practice.

2. *The Audit Committee* is a committee of Council whose members are appointed by Council but are not officers of the University.

The committee reviews the effectiveness of the financial and other internal control systems of the University including the scope and effectiveness of the work of the Internal Audit Section and the audit of the University Financial Statements. The committee must produce an annual report for Council, which, after consideration by Council, must be sent to the Chief Internal Auditor of H.E.F.C.E.

3. *The Internal Audit Section* is responsible for carrying out an independent appraisal of the internal control systems of the University's activities, financial and otherwise. It provides a service to all levels of management by evaluating and reporting to them the effectiveness of the controls for which they are responsible. The section may provide advice concerning controls and other matters in the development of systems but does not have direct responsibility for the development, implementation, or operation of systems. The section is responsible for giving assurance to the Audit Committee, Council, and the Vice-Chancellor on all financial and other control arrangements.

The Internal Audit Section has unrestricted right of access to all vouchers, documents, books of account, computer data, and any other information which it considers relevant to its inquiries and which is necessary to fulfil its responsibilities. This includes the right to verify assets and to have direct access to any employee or person responsible for the administration or management of university funds with whom it is felt necessary to raise and discuss such matters.

4. *External Auditor*. Council shall annually appoint, on the recommendation of the Audit Committee, the University Auditor.

The University Auditor audits the Financial Statements of the University and reports to the Vice-Chancellor whether in his or her opinion the financial statements give a true and fair view of the state of the financial affairs of the University and its related bodies and subsidiary companies (other than the University Press) at the balance sheet date, and of their income and expenditure for the year then ended.

The University Auditor has unrestricted right of access to all vouchers, documents, books of account, and computer data, and any other information. The University Auditor has the right to verify assets and to have direct access to any employee or person responsible for the administration or management of university funds with whom it is felt necessary to raise and discuss such matters. The University Auditor may visit any budgetary unit.

5. *Other Auditors*. The University may be audited by the H.E.F.C.E. Audit Service and may be visited by the National Audit Office. These auditors have the same rights of access as the Internal and External Auditors.

§ 8. *Fraud and Irregularity*

Any suspicion of financial irregularity should be notified immediately to the Internal Audit Section, who will advise the Director of Finance and others as appropriate. Action must not be taken without the approval of the Director of Finance. The Thames Valley Police should not be contacted directly. In cases that involve or may involve students, the Proctors will also be informed by Internal Audit at an early stage.

Serious weaknesses, significant frauds, or any other major accounting breakdown must be reported by the Director of Finance to the Vice-Chancellor as the University's Designated Officer in accordance with H.E.F.C.E. requirements.

§ 9. *Budgets and Forecasts*

1. *University Budget*. P.R.A.C. is required to report to Council on the budget for the ensuing financial year.

All heads of budgetary units must, by the date stated by the Director of Finance, supply the Finance Division with any information requested for the university budget.

2. *Delegated Budgets*. Each body that receives or spends central university funds is required before the start of each financial year to prepare a budget for that financial year, based on its submission to the University's planning cycle, and before the start of the financial year to which the allocation applies to notify its income and expenditure plans to the body to which it is responsible.

3. *Surpluses and Deficits*. Budgetary units are required to keep their expenditure within the resources available to them. A unit may budget for a surplus or deficit for the year provided that this is consistent with the strategic plan for the division and agreed by P.R.A.C. Accounts for funds that are earmarked by the body from which they are received must not be in deficit.

If a unit finds in the course of a year that it will be unable to achieve its budget and is likely to show a worsened outcome at the end of the year, it must report the situation to its parent body without delay. The parent body may agree to allow the variation to stand only if it is satisfied that the unit has plans in place to recover the position.

§ 10. *Staff Establishment*

1. New academic-related and non-academic posts at the grades of P06, Whitley Council MLS01, MT02, and below, Nurse E and below, Administrative and Clerical 3 and below, and outside-grant-funded academic-related RSIA and RSIB may be set up by budgetary units without the prior approval of the grading by the Personnel Services Section of the Central Administration (acting on behalf of the Personnel Committee), provided that if the post is outside-grant-funded the relevant procedures specified by the R.S.O. for the acceptance of the outside grant have been completed. The grading of all other new academic-related and non-academic posts, or changes to the grade of similar existing posts, must be approved by the Personnel Services Section on behalf of the Personnel Committee unless otherwise specifically covered by Council. Advice can be obtained from the Personnel Services Section.

2. A separate panel of the Personnel Committee considers the proposed grading of new posts (or the regrading of existing posts) in respect of all administrative, library, curatorial, and other staff in receipt of salaries in grades ALC6 or RSIV.

3. The setting up of any new posts and any changes to existing posts should also be approved, in the case of academic units, by the Divisional Board with responsibility for the budget of the unit, subject to appropriate consultation with colleges and written confirmation that the anticipated commitment will be within the budget set for the board by P.R.A.C., such confirmation to be obtained from the Finance Division.

§ 11. *Accounting Records, Annual Accounts, and University Financial Statements*

Advice on accounting matters may be sought from the Head of Financial Accounting in the first instance.

1. *Accounting Records*. The head of each body to whom funds are entrusted shall ensure that all moneys under his or her control are safely kept and are used only for the purposes for which they are allocated and that all transactions are properly recorded in the University's central accounting system.

2. *Retention of Financial Documents*. Prescribed periods and recommended guidelines have been published by the Internal Audit Section, as set out in the schedule below.

3. *University Computerized Accounting System*. All members and staff of the University with access to the University's computerized accounting system must comply with the password and other security controls established within the

Central Administration. Advice can be obtained from the Financial Systems Team.

All members and staff of the University must comply with the University Policy and Rules for Computer Use. Advice can be obtained from the Director of Computing Services.

All members and staff of the University must comply with the University Data Protection Policy. Advice can be obtained from the Director of Management Information Services.

4. *Financially related Software*. Heads of budgetary units are required to inform the Director of Finance of any software packages with financial applications that they may be intending to acquire, in order to ensure that such projects have been properly planned and resourced and that the software will provide the required functionality and be compatible with existing financial systems.

5. *New Budgetary Units*. No new budgetary unit may be established with resources from central university funds otherwise than on the authority of the appropriate parent body. No resources from central or divisional funds may be transferred between bodies without the permission of the appropriate central body or Divisional Board.

6. *Annual Financial Statements*. The Finance Committee shall approve, on behalf of Council, audited Financial Statements of the University for each year to 31 July, and report to Council accordingly by the last meeting of Michaelmas Term.

The head of each budgetary unit shall provide such information as the Finance Committee may require to enable it to prepare the Financial Statements.

The Vice-Chancellor, the Chairman of the Finance Committee, and the Director of Finance shall sign the financial statements.

§ 12. *Banking Arrangements*

1. University income comprises all moneys receivable by the University, and any part thereof. University income includes all moneys made available to individuals on the basis of their association with the University. All university income must be paid into a university bank account and properly accounted for, and all university expenditure must be paid from a university bank account. The opening of private bank accounts that result in the diversion of any moneys receivable by the University is not permitted.

2. The setting up of university bank accounts, other than imprest accounts, including the mandate for those bank accounts and subsequent changes to the mandate, must be approved by the Finance Committee. All bank accounts shall be in the name of the University.

3. The Director of Finance may approve the setting up of an imprest bank account. Such an account may be used only for making payments and not for banking receipts other than for the reimbursement of the account. Imprest bank accounts cannot be used for payments that are in the nature of employment or for the settlement of normal commercial invoices. They can be used to

reimburse travel expenses under £30 provided that a travel claim form is used. They must not be overdrawn. The department holding the account is responsible for ensuring regular reconciliation of the account and for providing information required by the Finance Division at the year end. Advice can be obtained from the Head of Treasury.

4. The approval of the Director of Finance is needed in advance for the setting up of any university charge or credit cards. Advice can be obtained from the Head of Treasury.

5. When a unit becomes aware that it will become subject to foreign exchange risk through the future receipt or payment of foreign exchange, it should notify the Finance Division and arrange to discuss how the risk can be reduced or avoided. Advice can be obtained from the Head of Treasury.

§ 13. *Deposit Pool*

1. The University has a Deposit Pool in which units and trust funds may invest certain cash balances for a minimum period of one month. The pool attracts the same income as the University's short-term cash deposits but does not offer investors any capital growth. Investments are made at the discretion of the Investment Committee, which shall determine from time to time the minimum amount that may be invested by a budgetary unit or trust fund and the minimum withdrawal or additional investment. It will also determine the monthly dates when deposits and withdrawals may be made.

2. Every account that has funds in the Deposit Pool must either have a nil or positive balance of cash with the Finance Division, except for those accounts recording expenditure to be reclaimed from a trust fund at the end of the financial year, in which case the calculation will be made on the anticipated income.

3. The Investment Committee shall approve the type of funds that can be placed on deposit in the Deposit Pool. The Director of Finance will approve each individual application to place funds on deposit. No moneys received from central university funds may be so invested. Advice can be obtained from the Financial Accounting Office.

§ 14. *Petty Cash*

Where a petty cash float is provided to pay minor expenses, it may not be used for payments that are in the nature of employment or to regular suppliers. It may be used to reimburse travel expenses under £30 provided that a travel claim form is used. The unit is responsible for the security of the float. Claims for reimbursement must be made using the standard form provided by the Finance Division and be supported by invoices or other supporting documents. Cash receipts are not to be added to the petty cash float. Petty cash floats must not be used for personal expenditure.

§ 15. *Receipts*

1. Each head of a unit that receives cash or cheques is responsible for establishing procedures to ensure that all receipts to which it is entitled are received, properly accounted for and recorded, and banked intact within a week, or more often if large sums are received. The head is also responsible for the security of cash received until banked.

2. All cheques received by budgetary units shall be made payable to 'Oxford University'.

3. The postal service and University Messenger Service must not be used to send cash.

4. Remittance advices and account code details must accompany all receipts advised to either the Financial Accounting Office in respect of centrally banked items, or the Treasury Section in respect of locally banked or electronic receipts.

§ 16. *Acceptance of Gifts, including Gifts in Kind and Benefactions received under a Will*

1. Council has given delegated authority as follows:

(*a*) to the Director of Finance, authority without limit to accept gifts in respect of allocations from the Trustee of the Campaign for Oxford Trust Fund;

(*b*) to the Registrar, authority to accept gifts worth more than £20,000 and up to £100,000, subject to a termly report to Council of action taken;

(*c*) to the Director of Finance, authority to accept gifts worth more than £2,000 and up to £20,000; and

(*d*) to the head of each unit or, if the head so wishes to its administrator, authority to accept for that unit gifts worth up to £2,000;

except in each case:

(i) research grants and contracts covered by procedures agreed by Council;

(ii) any gifts the acceptance of which involves the establishment of a new trust;

(iii) any gifts that bear any restrictive conditions or entail any potential commitment on university funds;

(iv) any gifts that may be considered sensitive for political or other reasons; or

(v) any other gifts in respect of which those given delegated authority may consider Council's approval necessary.

In appropriate cases those exercising delegated authority are expected to ask Council to vote thanks for a gift.

2. Benefactions and endowments made to the University may be given on trust. In order to ensure that the University complies with any conditions attaching to the benefaction or endowment, a decree must be made. The decree should include the purpose of the fund, its aims and objectives, the use to which the income is to be put (including unspent income carried forward to future financial years), whether the capital may be spent, details of the management committee,

and provision for subsequent amendment subject to continuing observation of the purpose of the fund. Advice may be obtained from the Legal Services Office. The capital is usually invested in the Trusts Pool. Advice may be obtained from the Head of Treasury.

§ 17. *Sales*

1. Each head of a budgetary unit that receives income from the sale of goods or services is responsible for establishing procedures to ensure that all sales are authorized and are made only to acceptable credit risks. Customers must be made aware of the University's standard conditions of sale, which must be incorporated into any contracts. Invoices must be prepared for all goods dispatched or services supplied and be properly recorded and processed. Procedures must also be in place to follow up overdue accounts effectively. In the event of prolonged non-payment or dispute, the Finance Division, and/or Legal Services Office, should be informed as appropriate.

2. The liability to V.A.T. of all goods and services supplied must be established and V.A.T. charged and accounted for as appropriate.

3. When a new income-generating activity is set up, the Director of Finance must be consulted to consider whether the activity constitutes trading which might be subject to Corporation Tax and therefore should be conducted through a university company. Failure to do so may result in the activity being investigated by the Inland Revenue and the consequent payment of tax.

4. The University is required by the Financial Memorandum between the University and H.E.F.C.E. when determining the price to be charged for research contracts, residences, catering, conferences, and services to external customers, including consultancy, to assess the full cost to the University. H.E.F.C.E. expects the full cost to be recovered unless it is appropriate to do otherwise having regard to the particular circumstances. Budgetary units are responsible for ensuring that charges make due allowance for overhead costs and that they are aware of the extent, if any, to which they subsidise the cost from their own resources and can give justification for any subsidy. When research grants and contracts are costed, the University's policy on the charging of overheads between unit and central funds must be followed.

5. The head of a unit must approve sales to employees, members of the University, or other customers made without charge or at a charge below that normally made to external customers.

6. The head of a unit should ensure that appropriate charges are made for the use of university premises and facilities for non-university purposes.

7. *Writing-off Bad Debts*. Heads of budgetary units must ensure that procedures are in place properly to monitor all debts and to follow up overdue accounts. A debt is created whenever a sale is made. The following authorities to write off bad debts after all reasonable steps have been taken to recover them apply to all debts.

(*a*) The head of a budgetary unit may write off a bad debt up to £5,000 against its own budget with the permission of the Director of Finance.

(*b*) The Director of Finance has authority to write off bad debts of up to £100,000 against general revenue and also has authority, where he or she considers that the bad debt resulted from unguarded action taken by a unit, to write off the debt against that body's funds.

The Finance Committee will receive an annual report of the total sum written off each year giving details of individual sums over £5,000.

Any V.A.T. included in bad debts that have been written off may be recovered using the procedures prescribed by Customs and Excise.

Any legal action to recover moneys due has to be approved by the Director of Finance. Any action arising will be taken through the Legal Services Office

§ 18. *Authority for the Effecting of Contracts*

1. The Registrar, the University's senior administrative officers, their respective deputies appointed from time to time, and the Land Agent are authorized to enter into, vary, and discharge on behalf of the University such contracts and such classes of contracts (whether made in writing or by parol), and to sign such other documents and such classes of documents, as may be specified by Council.

2. The Director of the R.S.O. is authorized to effect all contracts relating to research and associated matters.

3. Heads of budgetary units have authority to effect contracts in the course of the ordinary business of their unit involving only the funds over which they have delegated control, subject to the Statutes, Decrees, and Regulations of the University including these Financial Regulations. They do not have any authority to enter into any contract which is illegal or which does not comply with obligations laid down by H.E.F.C.E., the Inland Revenue, Customs and Excise, and other government authorities. What is ordinary business will vary but for academic units can be taken to mean teaching and research and (save as otherwise provided) their support. Specific funds may be used only for the purposes given.

4. Heads of units may delegate in writing their authority to effect contracts.

5. Heads of units should obtain the advice of the Director of Finance in the first instance if they are unsure of their authority to effect a particular contract.

6. The regulations for contracts of employment are stated in § 23 below.

§ 19. *Expenditure*

1. Each head of a budgetary unit is responsible for establishing procedures to ensure that goods and services are ordered only in required quantities of suitable quality at the best terms available, after appropriate requisition and approval. Order forms should refer to the University's standard terms and conditions of business.

Procedures must be in place to ensure that goods and services received are inspected and only properly ordered items are accepted before invoices are authorized. Invoices must be properly recorded. Duties of staff should be segregated wherever possible so that more than one member records and processes each transaction. Where only one member of staff is available, procedures for regular independent checks of transactions should be in place.

2. Orders may be placed only when funds are available to pay for them.

3. Each head of a budgetary unit must supply the Departmental Accounts Section of the Finance Division with a register of authorized signatures for the authorizing of documents for payment. The register may have limits to any individual's authority. Each entry on the register must be signed or initialled by the unit head. Where the proposed authorized signatory is not a university employee, the approval of the Director of Finance is also required. The register must be kept up to date. Advice can be obtained from the Departmental Accounts Office.

4. The Central Purchasing Officer in the Central Administration should be consulted for advice and information on all purchasing matters including centrally negotiated purchasing arrangements, to ensure that value for money is obtained. Further information is available in the Oxford University Purchasing Group Buyers' Guide.

5. Heads of budgetary units are responsible for complying with European Union Procurement Directives. All individual procurements and contract arrangements with a value in excess of £150,000 must by law be advertised in the Official Journal of the European Union. The penalties for non-compliance by the University are severe. Further guidance on the E.U. Procurement Directives is available from the Central Purchasing Officer and is included in the Oxford University Purchasing Group Buyers' Guide.

6. Prompt payment for discount must not be made earlier than the date of supply except in cases where the supplier must itself make cash outlays at an early stage or permission has been obtained from the Finance Division. Advice can be obtained from the Head of Financial Accounting.

7. Payments in the nature of employment must be made through the university payroll and not by other means.

§ 20. *Travel and Subsistence: Claims for Reimbursement*

1. Travel and subsistence reimbursement claims should be made on university claim forms or other forms approved by the Director of Finance.

2. The claims must be for the reimbursement of actual expenditure incurred wholly and necessarily on the business of the University and be in accordance with the rates approved by the Director of Finance. The lower mileage rate should be used unless the head of the unit has authorized the use of the higher rate in advance.

3. Supporting vouchers must be provided for the cost of accommodation, fares, and other major items of expenditure.

4. No round-sum allowances may be paid.

5. An owner whose vehicle is being used for travel on university business must ensure that it is adequately insured for that purpose.

6. Employees cannot be reimbursed for the cost of travel to and from their normal place of work otherwise than in exceptional circumstances, when permission from the Director of Finance must be sought.

7. No one may authorize reimbursement of his or her own expenses. Claims should always be approved by an employee senior to the claimant. Where there is no suitable person within a budgetary unit to authorize an expense claim, the Director of Finance must be asked to make alternative arrangements.

8. Those travelling abroad on university business should take out appropriate insurance cover by registration with the University's block travel policy available through the Insurance Office of the Finance Division. This cover includes medical expenses incurred abroad and those costs arising from cancellation or curtailment of the journey.

9. Advice on claims should be sought from the Head of Financial Accounting.

§ 21. *Travel and Subsistence: Advances*

1. Advances will normally be made only to employees and registered students of the University for up to one month's costs. Trips that exceed one month should be funded on an imprest system of topping up the advance against claim forms. Only in cases where this would be genuinely impossible or impracticable will an exception to the time limit be made and then only on consideration of a written application in advance to the Director of Finance.

2. Advances will be limited to 75 per cent of the estimated cost of up to one month's subsistence according to the daily rates for countries abroad approved by the Director of Finance and to the full cost of fares.

3. Requests for advances should be made on university expense claim forms giving details of dates and countries to be visited, and a breakdown of the advance required.

4. Claimants must submit full documentation within seven days of return, and the process of accounting for the claims against advances must be completed within one month of the return date. Advances should not be outstanding for more than two months.

5. Advice on advances may be obtained from the Head of Financial Accounting.

§ 22. *Payments for Entertaining*

1. Entertaining should wherever possible and appropriate be carried out in the University's own facilities in departments or in the colleges.

2. Entertainment expenditure may be an appropriate use of university moneys and avoid tax liability only if it is incurred wholly, necessarily, and exclusively for university purposes. A schedule must be included with the claim that gives details of those entertained and their institutions and the purpose of the entertainment.

3. All expense claims for entertaining, which must be supported by vouchers, must be authorized by the head of the unit (except where the head is the claimant, when alternative arrangements must be made – see § 20, cl. 7 above). The authorizing and submission of a claim for payment for entertaining is a declaration that the cost was incurred wholly, necessarily, and exclusively for university purposes. Only on this basis can the Finance Division pay the claim in full without deduction of tax.

4. In authorizing entertainment expenditure, heads of units are also undertaking that, if in any case tax is subsequently levied, any cost which is not recoverable from the individual beneficiaries will fall on the budget of the unit.

5. Advice on such payments may be obtained from the Head of Tax and Advisory Services.

§ 23. *Salaries and Staff Appointments*

1. No one shall have authority to offer any person employment as a member of the University's staff, or to sign letters of appointment for staff, or to dismiss staff, except with the express consent of Council, and provided that any offer of employment shall be on the appropriate terms and conditions of employment for the category of staff concerned; and any dismissal shall have complied with the appropriate procedures for the dismissal of the member of staff concerned. Council has delegated its powers to the Personnel Committee and to the chairman and officers of that committee.

2. All university employees shall have a properly authorized letter of appointment whose form has been approved by, or under the authority of, the Personnel Committee.

3. No member of staff may be given a contract of employment for a period exceeding that for which funding is available fully to support the post, or posts, to which he or she is appointed.

4. The only payments which may be made to university employees are those which relate to the operation of approved university salary scales and such other payments as have been specifically approved by the Personnel Committee.

5. All university employees shall be paid through the payroll operated by the Salaries Office.

6. Each head of a budgetary unit that has staff paid through the university payroll must supply the Salaries Office with a Register of Authorized Signatures for the authorizing of salary documents. The register may have limits to any individual's authority. Each entry on the register must be signed or initialled by the head of the unit. The register shall be kept up to date. Where the proposed

authorized signatory is not a university employee the approval of the Director of Finance is also required.

7. All documents sent to the Salaries Office authorizing the payment of new employees or subsequent changes to their salary or other details must be authorized in accordance with the relevant Register of Authorized Signatures.

8. If it is proposed to employ a citizen of a country outside the European Economic Area (E.E.A.), it is the responsibility of the head of the unit, or other authorized signatory:

(*a*) in the case of a person at present in the U.K., to ensure that the landing conditions imposed on that person by the Immigration and Nationality Directorate of the Home Office allow the proposed employment; or

(*b*) if the person is not in the U.K., to obtain through the Central Administration a work permit from the D.f.E.E. for the specific employment proposed.

The Work Permit and Immigration Help Desk within the Central Administration will handle centrally any applications that may be necessary and will advise on the detail and documentation required. (It should be noted that the D.f.E.E. normally requires, to support a successful application, evidence that the vacancy was advertised in an approved publication available in the E.E.A.)

The Salaries Office will not add a non-E.E.A. citizen to the payroll unless it is clear that any necessary work permit has been obtained or that the immigration status of the person concerned does not require the University to seek permission for the specific employment proposed.

9. Any circulars issued by the Director of Finance on taxation or national insurance matters must be complied with to ensure that the requirements of the Inland Revenue and Department of Social Security are met and to protect the University from financial loss.

10. Advice on all staff appointments may be obtained from the Personnel Services Section.

§ 24. *Stocks*

1. Each head of a unit is responsible for establishing procedures to ensure that stocks are adequately protected against loss or misuse. Stocks should be maintained at the minimum level required to support operations.

2. A physical stock count must be conducted at least once a year, preferably at 31 July.

§ 25. *Equipment and Furniture*

1. Each head of a unit is responsible for establishing procedures to ensure that all items of equipment and furniture are adequately protected against loss and misuse and that all purchases and disposals of equipment are properly authorized, accounted for, and recorded.

2. Equipment inventories must be maintained and be able to satisfy the requirements of the Internal Audit Section.

3. Equipment bought from research grants and contracts belongs to the University, unless there is explicit provision to the contrary in the relevant contract, and is available for use in the relevant unit on the expiry of the grant subject to any conditions imposed by the funding body.

4. Any proceeds from the sale of equipment will normally be credited to the account of the unit concerned.

5. Where equipment is loaned, units should have procedures in place to ensure that it is returned in good condition, and should consider the need for the borrower to arrange insurance cover.

6. Items of equipment are covered for all-risks insurance if they are included on the asset register which must be updated regularly and a copy supplied to the Insurance Office of the Finance Division annually. Items purchased between annual submissions are automatically covered.

7. Units must not enter into leasing contracts for equipment without taking the advice of the Central Purchasing Office, which has prepared a standard contract.

§ **26.** *University Vehicles*

1. No university-owned vehicle may be used unless it is insured for the purpose for which it is being used and has a valid D.E.T.R. Certificate where required, and the driver is qualified to drive the vehicle.

2. University-owned vehicles may be used only by persons and for purposes authorized in writing by the head of the unit, and a record of authorized drivers should be maintained. University vehicles should not normally be used for travel to and from work and they should be left on university premises at night. Where the use of university vehicles is authorized for travel to and from work and they are not left on university premises at night, any employee of the University is likely to be taxed on the benefit enjoyed.

3. Where private use is allowed, the terms and conditions of use and reimbursement of costs must be authorized in writing by the head of the unit, and the person granting such authorisation is also responsible for ensuring that there is comprehensive insurance cover.

4. University vehicles must be included in the unit's asset register.

5. Sales of vehicles should be advertised beyond the unit making the sale.

§ **27.** *Buildings*

1. The Buildings and Estates Subcommittee shall be responsible to P.R.A.C. for formulating and reviewing the University's programme for all building works, for the execution of all building projects, for maintaining university buildings in a satisfactory condition, and for allocating space within them.

2. All building works, however funded, in university functional buildings require the prior permission of the Director of Estates and University Surveyor, acting on behalf of the Buildings and Estates Subcommittee.

3. The Current Standing Orders for Building Tenders must be observed.

4. H.E.F.C.E. Instructions for Estates Procedures must be complied with for H.E.F.C.E.-funded projects.

5. European Commission public procurement directives on supplies, services, and works must be followed.

6. Advice on building matters can be obtained from the Director of Estates and University Surveyor.

§ **28.** *Investments*

1. The Investment Committee shall, on behalf of Council, arrange for the investment of funds and endowments of the University in accordance with Tit. XV, Sect. V, cl. 2, or in accordance with the Trusts Pool Scheme.

2. The Investment Committee shall report to Council at least annually on its investment policy and the performance of the University's investments.

3. No budgetary unit or trust of the University may invest in any securities or other investments (including land) without the permission of the Investment Committee.

4. The Investment Committee manages the Trusts Pool Scheme, which is designed for long-term investment, and shall approve all new shareholders and increases in shareholdings. The terms of the pool are included in the University's Decrees (Ch. VIII, Sect. VIII).

5. The Investment Committee shall, on behalf of Council, approve the appointment of managers of investments and the investment powers of officers.

§ **29.** *Property*

1. *Functional Property*. The authority of Council is needed for any purchase of land or property (whether freehold or leasehold) for the functional use of the University.

All contracts for the purchase of land or property for the functional use of the University (whether freehold or leasehold) and all sales of existing functional land and property must be effected by the University centrally on the authority of Council.

2. *Non-functional Property*. The Property Management Subcommittee of P.R.A.C. has charge of all real property that is not in use for the functional purposes of the University, nor for investment purposes, and may authorize the purchase, leasing, and sale of real property for non-functional purposes on behalf of the University.

3. Advice on property matters may be obtained from the Director of Estates and University Surveyor in respect of functional property and the Land Agent in respect of non-functional property.

§ 30. *Borrowing Powers*

No budgetary unit may borrow moneys without the permission of Council.

§ 31. *Research Grants and Contracts and Related Matters*

1. All applications to outside bodies for research funds must be submitted for university approval to the R.S.O. before being despatched to the sponsor. The R.S.O. is also responsible for negotiating, and entering into, research and related contracts on behalf of the University.

2. The University's policy of disclaiming liability under research agreements must be complied with.

3. The University's policy on the charging of indirect costs, and the distribution of indirect cost income between departmental and central funds, must be followed when research grants and contracts are being costed.

4. The University's policies covering all aspects of research funding and related activities must be complied with. Further advice on such policies is available from the R.S.O.

§ 32. *Personal Consultancies*

Clauses 1, 2, and 5 below do not apply to C.U.F. lecturers (Ch. VII, Sect. I, § 5. A, cl. 10).

1. Academic staff (other than C.U.F. lecturers) may without loss of stipend engage in personal consultancy work with the approval of the relevant Divisional Board and head of department in departmentally organized faculties, provided that the amount of time spent on these and other outside appointments does not exceed thirty days per annum. Applications for permission to spend more than thirty days per annum on outside appointments (including consultancies) need the same approvals and may result in loss of stipend. Academic-related staff may also engage in personal consultancy work on similar terms with the approval of their head of department, 'line manager', and sponsoring body (if applicable). Such approval is subject to clause 2 below. Advice may be obtained from the R.S.O.

2. The terms of any personal consultancy agreement must be vetted by the R.S.O. prior to signature. Advice can be obtained from the R.S.O.

3. Employees of the University must not hold themselves out as acting on behalf of the University when undertaking personal consultancy work. The University accepts no responsibility for work done or advice given. Once approval to hold a consultancy is given, appropriate disclaimers of liability will

be issued on behalf of the University by the R.S.O. in respect of academic staff and by departments in respect of other staff.

4. Employees of the University engaged in personal consultancy work are covered by the University's professional indemnity insurance only if the permission of the University has been obtained, through the procedures in clauses 1 and 2 above, and the fees receivable declared to the insurers. Advice should be obtained from the Insurance Section of the Finance Division.

5. The University's policy on the payment to employees for consultancy and services to industry must be complied with. Advice is available from the R.S.O.

§ 33. *Intellectual Property*

1. Except with the express consent of Council, no official of the University or any other person employed by the University or working in or in connection with any department of or under the control of the University shall in connection with any invention, discovery, or patent, or (except under the authority of the Delegates of the University Press, in matters falling within their jurisdiction) process, or manufacture have authority to make any representations on behalf of the University or to enter into any contract on behalf of the University or to be concerned in any transaction whatsoever in connection therewith on behalf of the University.

2. Revenue received by the University as a result of the exploitation of any item of intellectual property shall be distributed in accordance with the University's Intellectual Property Policy.

3. Advice on intellectual property matters should be obtained from the R.S.O.

§ 34. *University Companies*

No university company may be set up to exploit any university activity to which the University has rights, or for any other purpose, unless approved by Council. Advice should be obtained from the Director of Finance.

§ 35. *Commercial Activities*

No non-university commercial activities may be carried out on university premises and no university facilities may be used for such activities unless a definite agreement between the University and the persons concerned has been approved by the Director of Finance. In no circumstances may departmental or institutional addresses be used for non-university commercial activities.

§ 36. *Private Work by Departmental Staff for Other Departments*

1. When a member of staff in his or her spare time undertakes private work for other units involving the use of facilities operated by the unit by which he or she is ordinarily employed, proper invoices in respect of any charges which may be made for such work must be prepared, and submitted to the head of the unit by which the member of staff is ordinarily employed for approval and signature.

Payment will be made through the university payroll unless a Schedule D tax reference for the trade has been obtained in writing from the Inland Revenue. Advice can be obtained from the Head of Financial Accounting.

2. Where the head of the unit allows private work to be carried out for other units, written rules should be drawn up and made readily accessible to all members of staff. The cost of any materials provided should be recovered, and care taken that safety procedures are observed. Advice may be obtained from the Internal Audit Section.

§ 37. *Private Patients' Fees*

Persons holding honorary consultant appointments in the National Health Service in clinical departments are permitted to engage in private practice in accordance with the Decrees of the University, which provide for the treatment of private patients' fees. Advice can be obtained from the secretary of the Medical Sciences Division.

§ 38. *Insurance*

1. The University is required by its Financial Memorandum with H.E.F.C.E. to have adequate insurance cover.

2. Central policies are held for the insurance of buildings and contents (except library holdings and certain museum collections) against all risks, public and employer's liability, professional indemnity, and fidelity; these are paid for centrally by the University.

3. Personal accident cover is in place for certain defined categories of personnel.

4. Insurance matters must only be arranged through the Insurance Section of the Finance Division, which can provide all necessary advice.

§ 39. *V.A.T.*

1. The University is a partially exempt registered taxable body and has a legal obligation to account properly for V.A.T. and to make correct returns to the Customs and Excise. Each unit is responsible for its own V.A.T. affairs including ensuring that it is adequately informed about V.A.T. and related aspects of the matters with which it deals. All heads of units must submit correct and timely returns of V.A.T. and other legally required data to the Finance Division for inclusion in the University's returns to Customs and Excise, as well as providing the information needed on invoices and other documents of costs incurred to allow the University to operate its V.A.T. partial exemption scheme.

2. Information on V.A.T. and related matters is available from the circulars produced by the Finance Division, and advice is available from the V.A.T. Officer in the Finance Division.

§ 40. *Waivers*

Where a person entitled to a fee or other payment due from the University decides to waive it, the fee or other payment must be completely waived without condition as to what happens to the waived fee or other payment. The Statutes, Decrees, and Regulations of the University do not in general allow payment to persons and bodies other than the person to whom it is due. Also, unless the waiver is without condition, the payment will continue to be taxable income of the individual to whom it is due. Advice should be sought from the Head of Tax and Advisory Services.

§ 41. *Relocation Expenses*

1. The University shall pay contributions towards removal and travelling expenses incurred by persons taking up approved posts in the University on such conditions as Council may approve.

2. Application must be made to the Director of Finance before expenditure is incurred or authorized by the new post-holder. Advice should be sought from the officer in charge of removal expenses in the Finance Division.

3. Unit funds may not be used to fund relocation expenses except as allowed for by the approved scheme.

§ 42. *Appeals from Charitable Organizations*

1. Council has empowered P.R.A.C., without reference to Council, to make grants from revenue in response to appeals from educational or charitable organizations of direct concern to the University in Oxford or in places where the University owns land or is patron of a benefice, provided that Council is consulted on any case of doubt or difficulty or involving a grant of more than £10,000.

2. Unit funds may not be used to make charitable donations or grants.

§ 43. *Fees*

No person shall be presented for a degree unless he or she has paid all the sums due from him or her to the University.

§ 44. *Sealing*

The Seals of the University shall be used in accordance with the Statutes, Decrees, and Regulations of the University. Documents for sealing must be sent to the Legal Services Office.

§ 45. *Projects*

All proposals for expenditure from university funds of a capital or 'self-financing' nature must be assessed through the University's approved project evaluation procedures, advice on which may be obtained from the Management Accounting Section of the Finance Division.

SCHEDULE

Time to hold Accounting Documents

The period for retaining documents is a complex issue and it is a decision which must be taken by the management of each organization. The most favourable retention period will allow for records to be kept only as long as they are really needed for legal and commercial purposes.

A programme should be drawn up to select records which are to be retained or destroyed in order to keep the volume of records under control. The retention policy should be just one of the elements comprised in a much broader programme covering records management.

In determining appropriate retention periods the following aspects need to be considered:

(*a*) economy;

(*b*) legal and related requirements;

(*c*) potential demand within the organization;

(*d*) historical value.

There are few firmly established regulations to follow in deciding how long to keep documents. However, this guideline covers recommended minimum retention periods for accounting records to discharge the University's legal and statutory obligations in respect of the various taxing authorities and audit requirements.

1. *Purchase Invoices*

All paid invoices are retained at the Finance Division for at least one year, until after the completion of the external audit. They are microfiched one month after receipt, and the microfiche records are retained for fourteen years. If departments take photocopies of the invoices, these are purely for departmental reference purposes and can be destroyed as judged appropriate.

Supporting requisitions, purchase orders, and goods-received notes should be kept for three years.

2. *Sales*

Copies of all sales V.A.T. documents, which include sales invoices and daily till rolls from shops, must be held for seven years, i.e. six years plus the current year. If a department has particular difficulty in keeping six years' worth of till rolls, it is possible to apply to Customs and Excise to request a shorter period of retention.

3. *V.A.T. Returns*

Copies of all V.A.T. returns including the Instrastat and E.C. returns are kept at the Finance Division and therefore there is no requirement for departments to keep copies. However, as only the actual returns are held at the Finance Division, all supporting documentation used to compile the return should be retained by departments for a period of seven years, i.e. six years plus the current year.

4. *Outside Grants*

The Research Services Office holds the original contracts/agreements, related correspondence, and financial documents for at least six years after expiry of the grant. Should a department hold any further relevant original documentation then this should be held for a similar period. Any detailed records supporting charges against the grant, e.g. time sheets, should be retained for a period of three years after the expiry of the grant. Photocopies of any original documents sent to the R.S.O. can be destroyed at the department's discretion. However, any specific terms within a particular contract relating to the retention of records will take precedence. If in doubt consult the R.S.O.

5. *Banking*

The Finance Division keeps copies of all receipt records and as the daily banking sheets are not prime documents supporting individual sales transactions there is no need to keep these sheets beyond three years. Bank paying-in counterfoils should be kept for six years.

6. *Payments to Personnel*

All documents relating to payments to personnel should be kept for at least seven years, i.e. six years plus the current year. Any supporting documentation held in the departments and not copied to the centre should be retained for a similar period.

7. *Equipment Registers*

Equipment registers (i.e. Fixed Asset Registers) should be kept indefinitely. Copies of asset-disposal notes should be kept for three years.

8. *Accounts Printouts*

Departments should keep monthly account printouts for one year plus the current year; these should be evidenced as having been checked by a senior officer from within the department. The Finance Division keeps microfilmed copies of the Accounts Nominal Ledger from 1976 onwards.

9. *Payroll Printouts*

Departments should keep quarterly and monthly printouts for one year plus the current year; these should be evidenced as having been checked by a senior officer from within the department. The Finance Division retains all the past monthly and quarterly salary printouts.

[*Note*. The above is not meant to be a comprehensive list of all the financial documents held in a department and does not imply that all other documentation can be destroyed. The Internal Audit Section can provide guidance on the legal and related requirements for other accounting documentation if required, as well as further information or assistance in connection with any other aspects of these guidelines.]

APPENDIX TO CHAPTER VIII

Annual subscriptions

The Curators of the University Chest shall pay such annual subscriptions as are authorized by Council to the following bodies:

Area Museums Service for South Eastern England
Association of Commonwealth Universities
Association for the Study of Medical Education
British Universities Sports Federation
International Association of Universities
National Institute of Adult Education
Oxford Preservation Trust
Standing Conference of European Rectors and Vice-Chancellors

Organist at degree days and other university ceremonies

The Curators of the University Chest shall pay annually out of the University General Revenue Account a sum determined by Council from time to time to an organist appointed by the Curators of the Sheldonian Theatre for his or her services at degree days and other university ceremonies in the Sheldonian Theatre.

Rector of Helmdon with Stuchbury

The Curators of the University Chest shall pay the sum of £25 a year to the Rector of the United Benefice of Helmdon with Stuchbury, or, during any voidance of the living, to the Sequestrators, such payment to date from the last voidance of the living.

Vicar of Kirkdale

The Curators of the University Chest shall pay to the Vicar of Kirkdale, or, during any voidance of the living, to the Sequestrators, the sum of £15 a year, from the University General Revenue Account, in addition to the sum of £10 a year at present paid from the Botanic Garden Trust.

Vicars' stipends

	£
Holme Cultram	70
St. Cuthbert's	50
St. Paul's	50
St. John's	50

Estates Register, 1964, p. 70

Monetary penalties under Title XIII
Decree (7) of 13 May 1999

The amount of the maximum financial penalty excluding damages which the Proctors may impose in the case of a 'minor university offence' under Title XIII shall be £65 with immediate effect until 30 September 2001, and the amount of the maximum financial penalty excluding damages which they may impose in any other case shall be £1,090 for the same period.

CHAPTER IX

SCHOLARSHIPS, PRIZES, SPECIAL FUNDS, COLLECTIONS, LIBRARIES, AND GRANTS

Section I. Particular Scholarships, Prizes, Special Funds, Collections, Libraries, and Grants

§ 1. *African Humanities Research Fund*

1. The University accepts with gratitude an anonymous benefaction which shall be used, together with any further donations for this purpose, to form a fund for the support of research within the University in African Studies in the Humanities, with reference to any of the regions or peoples of the African continent and its islands.

2. The Inter-faculty Committee for African Studies shall be the management committee for the fund.

3. The first call on the income of the fund shall be the maintenance of up to three scholarships, to be known as the ORISHA Studentships, tenable for up to four years each, by persons registered as graduate students of the University whose work involves the study of Africa in one or more of such of the following disciplines as the management committee for the fund shall from time to time determine using the criterion set out in clause 4 below:

Social and Cultural Anthropology
Archaeology
Egyptology
History
Human Geography
Politics and International Relations
Religious Studies

4. The management committee may add disciplines to those specified in clause 3 above, provided that the main object of the fund as defined in clause 1 above shall always be observed. In considering the disciplines in which scholarships shall be offered and in adding disciplines, the management committee shall take into account whether adequate supervision is available in the field in question, in the form of the presence of one or more permanent members of the academic staff with major research or teaching interests in African Studies.

5. The management committee shall make all necessary arrangements for each of the scholarships, including the determination of their respective values.

6. Any surplus income in the fund arising because scholarships are not awarded on any occasion or for any other reason shall be expended at the discretion of the management committee on the support of African Studies in the Humanities, including any expenditure necessary in subsequent years to cover the costs of

scholarships already awarded, the provision of additional scholarships, the provision of funds for libraries, and the support of visiting scholars.

7. Council shall have power to amend this decree from time to time provided that the main object of the fund as defined in clause 1 above shall always be kept in view.

§ 2. *Aldrichian and Aldrichian-Tomlinsian Funds*

1. The income arising from the Bequest of George Aldrich, Doctor of Medicine, shall be applied as follows:

(*a*) one-third to be paid to the Regius Professor of Medicine who shall *ex officio* become the Aldrichian Professor of Medicine;

(*b*) one-third to be paid to the Aldrichian Praelector and Reader in Chemistry; and

(*c*) one-third to be paid to the Aldrich Tomlins Fund and applied as directed by cl. 2 below.

2. The emoluments arising from the benefactions of Richard Tomlins, Esquire, and George Aldrich, Doctor of Medicine, shall be applied to the payment of a Departmental Lecturer or Lecturers in Zoology appointed by the Head of the Department of Zoology.

§ 3. *Arboretum, Nuneham Courtenay*

The University accepts with gratitude from an anonymous benefactor the sum of £2,000 to establish a fund the capital and accumulated income of which may be used for the benefit of the Nuneham Courtenay Arboretum at the discretion of Council acting on the recommendation of the Curators of the Botanic Garden.

§ 4. *Aris Fund for Tibetan and Himalayan Studies*

1. The University accepts with deep gratitude from the Michael Aris Trust for Tibetan and Himalayan Studies, through the generosity of Hans and Märit Rausing and Joseph and Lisbet Koerner, a sum which, together with any further sums which may be donated for the same purpose, shall be used to establish a fund, to be known as the Michael Aris Fund for Tibetan and Himalayan Studies, the net income of which shall be used for the advancement of Tibetan and Himalayan Studies within the University.

2. The fund shall be administered by a board of management comprising the Chairman of the Board of the Faculty of Oriental Studies (chairman), a person appointed by the faculty board, the Keeper of the Oriental Collections in the Bodleian Library, the Boden Professor of Sanskrit, a person appointed by Council, and a person appointed by the Curators of the University Libraries.

3. The first charge on the net income of the fund shall be the salary and associated costs of a university lecturership in Tibetan and Himalayan Studies. Other charges on the fund shall be the provision, under such arrangements as the board of management may from time to time determine, of support for

Tibetan language instruction, library provision (both for staff and for materials relating to Tibetan and Himalayan Studies), teaching materials and research expenses for the lecturer, research fellowships, and any other purpose approved by the board of management as contributing to the advancement of Tibetan and Himalayan Studies within the University.

4. The University Lecturer in Tibetan and Himalayan Studies shall lecture and give instruction and carry out advanced study and research in Tibetan and Himalayan Studies under the direction of the Board of the Faculty of Oriental Studies. The lecturer shall be appointed by the Board of the Faculty of Oriental Studies, in accordance with the provisions of Ch. VII, Sect. IV, § 3.

5. Any income unspent in any year on the first and other charges as defined in clause 3 above, whether in consequence of a vacancy in the lecturership or for any other reason, shall, at the discretion of the board of management, either be carried forward for expenditure in subsequent years or be spent in any other way or ways conducive to the advancement within the University of teaching, scholarship, and research in Tibetan and Himalayan Studies.

6. Council shall have power to amend this decree from time to time, provided that the main object of the fund, namely the advancement of Tibetan and Himalayan Studies within the University, shall always be kept in view.

§ **5.** *Arnold Prizes*

1. There shall be two prizes in the University of Oxford to be called 'the Arnold Prizes' for the encouragement of the study of history, one for ancient history and one for modern history.

2. The Ancient History Prize shall be awarded each year in Hilary Term to the writer of the best essay or dissertation on some subject of ancient history between 1500 B.C. and A.D. 500, if such essay shall be deemed worthy of a prize. The offer of the prizes for the next year shall be announced before the close of Hilary Term. The candidates shall be members of the University reading for a final honour school. They may choose their own subjects, subject to the approval of the Board of the Faculty of Literae Humaniores, under such conditions as the board may prescribe. The board shall appoint up to three judges, to serve for such terms as it may prescribe.

3. The Modern History Prize shall be awarded each year to the writer of the best thesis in modern history submitted in the Honour School of Modern History, or any joint school in which Modern History is a component, or in the Honour School of Philosophy, Politics, and Economics, if such thesis be deemed worthy of a prize. Modern History shall be defined for the purpose of this decree as the period between A.D. 285 and the latest terminal date for the time being of the subjects of the Honour School of Modern History. The judges shall be the Public Examiners in the Honour School of Modern History in consultation as they shall think fit with the Public Examiners in the other schools referred to in this clause.

4. Each prize shall be of such equal value as the Boards of the Faculties of Literae Humaniores and of Modern History shall in consultation from time to time determine.

5. Neither prize shall be awarded twice to the same person and only one of the prizes may be awarded in respect of any one essay.

6. The judges shall have power

(*a*) to award the prizes;

(*b*) to divide a prize between two candidates whose essays are of equal merit;

(*c*) to make awards of lesser value than the prizes to unsuccessful candidates whose essays have shown special excellence.

7. The judges shall be allowed, subject to the approval of the Vice-Chancellor and Proctors, to appoint one or more assessors.

8. Any surplus income of the fund shall be divided into two sub-accounts to be designated the ancient history account and the modern history account respectively, as follows:

(*a*) whenever either prize is not awarded, the value, less the value of any lesser award made under cl. 6 (*c*) above, shall be credited in full to the respective sub-account;

(*b*) any other surplus income, including any standing to the credit of the fund on the day from which this decree shall be effective, shall be credited in the proportion one part to the ancient history account and nine parts to the modern history account.

9. Moneys standing in the sub-accounts shall be applied by the respective faculty board, either directly or by delegation at its sole discretion, to the following purposes:

(*a*) for the payment of lesser awards made by the judges under cl. 6 (*c*) above when the prize itself is awarded;

(*b*) to pay such fees to the judges of the Ancient History Prize and to any assessors they may appoint as the Board of the Faculty of Literae Humaniores shall determine;

(*c*) on the recommendation of the judges to contribute to the cost of printing the whole or parts of any prize-winning essay;

(*d*) to encourage in any other way as the respective faculty board may see fit the study of ancient and modern history by members of the University.

10. Council shall have power at any time to alter this decree, but only in such ways as shall appear calculated to promote the object of the institution, namely, the encouragement of the study of history ancient and modern.

§ 6. *Arteaga Prize*

1. The Arteaga Prize shall be awarded for distinguished work in Spanish, and shall be open annually to members of the University offering Spanish as sole language or as one of two languages in the Final Honour School of Modern Languages, or as one of their two subjects in the Final Honour Schools of

Modern History and Modern Languages, or Philosophy and Modern Languages, or Classics and Modern Languages, or English and Modern Languages, or European and Middle Eastern Languages.

2. The trustees of the prize shall be the Curators of the Taylor Institution. It shall be the duty of the trustees to determine and announce the value of the prize on each occasion and also to announce the names of successful candidates; and it shall be the duty of the Secretary to the Curators each year to inform the examiners in the Final Honour School of Modern Languages of the procedure for the award of the prize.

3. The trustees shall in each year award the prize to the candidate recommended by the examiners in Spanish in the Final Honour School of Modern Languages, provided that the examiners shall not recommend the award of the prize to a candidate whose work in the use of the modern language they did not consider to be meritorious.

4. The chairman of the examiners in the Final Honour School of Modern Languages shall transmit the recommendation of the examiners in Spanish to the trustees and shall cause it to be published at the same time as the class list for the examination.

5. The income of the fund so far as it is not required for the payment of the prize may be employed at the discretion of the trustees for the remuneration of the examiners, or for any purpose connected with the promotion of the study of Spanish in the University of Oxford.

6. Council shall have power to alter this decree from time to time, provided that the name of the prize be not changed and that its main object be always kept in view, namely the promotion of the study of Spanish in the University of Oxford.

§ 7. *Ashmolean Museum of Art and Archaeology*

Ashmolean Bomford Bequest Trust

The University expresses its gratitude to Mr. H.J.P. Bomford for his generosity in establishing the Ashmolean Bomford Bequest Trust for the benefit of the Department of Antiquities of the Ashmolean Museum; and the Curators of the University Chest are authorized to accept payments made from time to time by the trustees to be used under the terms of the trust for or towards the purchase of antiquities and other objects of artistic merit for the museum.

Bouch Bequest

The sum of £4,741·46 bequeathed by the late Major Thomas Bouch, Magdalen College, shall be used to provide an income for the purchase of pictures, drawings, and other works of art for the Department of Western Art, Ashmolean Museum.

Dell Cabrejos Drawings Fund

1. The University accepts with gratitude an endowment from Mr. David Dell, and any further sums contributed for the same purpose, to establish a fund, to be known as the Dell Cabrejos Drawings Fund in memory of Eliseo Cabrejos, the net income of which shall be used for the upkeep and augmentation of the collections of drawings, including watercolours, in the Ashmolean Museum.

2. The fund shall be administered by a board of management consisting of

(1) a person, who shall be chairman, appointed by the Vice-Chancellor;

(2) the Director of the Ashmolean Museum;

(3) the Keeper of Western Art of the Ashmolean Museum;

(4), (5) two persons appointed by the Visitors of the Ashmolean Museum.

The board shall have power to delegate expenditure to the Keeper of Western Art, such delegation to be reviewed on an annual basis when the Keeper shall report to the board all exercises of his or her delegated authority.

3. The board shall apply the income of the fund towards the following purposes:

(*a*) the acquisition of drawings suitable for collections in the Department of Western Art;

(*b*) the conservation of drawings in the said collections;

(*c*) such other related purposes as the board shall think fit but excluding the payment of salaries of employees of the University.

Income not expended in any year shall be carried forward for expenditure in subsequent years.

4. Council shall have the power to alter this decree from time to time, provided that the main object of the fund, as stated in clause 1 above, is always kept in view.

Eldon Fund

The residue of the sum of £1,200 given in 1868 by the Right Honourable the Earl of Eldon to the Curators of the University Galleries for the purpose of (*a*) maintaining and illustrating the collection of Michelangelo and Raphael drawings, towards the purchase of which in 1845 his father had contributed £4,000, and (*b*) illustrating Italian Art generally shall be held on trust for the Visitors of the Ashmolean Museum and University Galleries to be appropriated to the purposes above mentioned.

Evans Bequest

The Curators of the University Chest shall expend, on the instructions of the Visitors of the Ashmolean Museum, either income or capital of the bequest, accepted under Decree (2) of 11 November 1941, of three-twentieths of the residuary estate of the late Sir Arthur John Evans, M.A., D.Litt., Hon. Fellow of Brasenose College, Honorary Keeper and Perpetual Visitor of the Ashmolean Museum, for the upkeep and augmentation of the collections in the Minoan Room at the Ashmolean Museum.

Evans-Sutherland Fund

The University accepts with gratitude the bequest of Carol Humphrey Vivian Sutherland, C.B.E., M.A., D.Litt., F.B.A., former Keeper of the Heberden Coin Room and Student of Christ Church, for the benefit of the Heberden Coin Room at the Ashmolean Museum. The bequest and the net income derived therefrom, together with Sir Arthur Evans's bequest for the same purpose and the net income derived therefrom, accepted under Decree (2) of 11 November 1941, shall be applied by the Curators of the University Chest on the instructions of the Visitors of the Ashmolean Museum for the augmentation of the collections in the said Coin Room.

Griffith Institute

[1]

Whereas the University did by Decree (2) of 25 January 1938, accept bequests of the late Professor and Mrs. Griffith for the purpose in the first place of furnishing and endowing a home or Institute for Egyptological Study, and in the second place, after the said purposes have been sufficiently accomplished, for the purpose of the expansion of the said home or Institute to Babylonian or other departments of archaeological research.

1. The aforesaid Institute shall be named the Griffith Institute in memory of the principal benefactors.

2. The Griffith Institute and the income of the Griffith Bequests shall be administered by a committee of management consisting of:

(1)–(3) three persons appointed by the Visitors of the Ashmolean Museum of whom at least one shall be a Visitor;

(4) the Professor of Egyptology;

(5) the University Lecturer in Akkadian;

(6) the Lincoln Professor of Classical Archaeology and Art;

(7) one person appointed by the Board of the Faculty of Theology;

(8) one person appointed by the Board of the Faculty of Literae Humaniores;

(9) one person appointed by the Board of the Faculty of Anthropology and Geography;

(10) the Director of the Ashmolean Museum;

(11) the Keeper of the Department of Antiquities of the Ashmolean Museum;

(12) the Librarian of the Ashmolean Library.

The committee shall have power to co-opt not more than three other persons on the committee, and to appoint any one of its members as chairman. The Secretary shall be the Keeper of the Department of Antiquities or his or her deputy.

3. The Institute shall be incorporated in the Ashmolean Museum as provided by Tit. VIII, Sect. IV, cl. 2 and Ch. III, Sect. XI, § 7, cl. 1.

4. The committee of management of the Griffith Institute shall have power to make rules, subject to the approval of the Visitors, for the use of the Institute and to allocate rooms within it.

5. So much of the annual cost of administration and upkeep of the Institute as shall be determined by the Visitors in consultation with the committee of management shall be defrayed from the income of the Griffith Bequests.

[2]

The University gratefully accepts an anonymous gift of £5,000 to the Griffith Institute for the continuation and completion of the *Topographical Bibliography of Ancient Egyptian Hieroglyphic Texts, Reliefs, and Paintings.*

[3]

The University gratefully accepts funds arising from the A. H. Gardiner Settlement for Egyptological Purposes of 10 March 1939, which shall form a fund, the income of which shall be expended for the general purposes of Egyptology at the discretion of the Management Committee of the Griffith Institute.

Hattatt Bequest

The University accepts with gratitude the bequest of £80,000 of the late Richard Hattatt for the Department of Antiquities of the Ashmolean Museum. The net income of the bequest shall be expended for the general purposes of the department.

Jones Bequest

A bequest of £1,000 under the will of the late John Reginald Jones, B.A., Trinity College, for the Department of Western Art in the Ashmolean Museum, shall be used to establish a fund for the purchase of pictures or other works of art not less than one hundred years old, to be known as 'The Reginald Jones Bequest'.

Kemp Bequest

The following decree has been made by Council under the provisions of Decree (1) of 5 March 1940:

1. The Kemp Collection of painting, scrolls, jades, brasses, books, embroideries, pictures, and other objects illustrating the civilizations of China and neighbouring countries, shall be housed in the Ashmolean Museum in space allotted by the Visitors.

2. The Visitors shall have power to make temporary loans from the collection to other institutions within the University at their discretion.

3. The Visitors shall make a catalogue of the collection which shall contain information of any dispersals by temporary loan.

4. If at any time a building is erected devoted to the study of Eastern civilizations inclusive of the Chinese, the Kemp Collection shall be transferred to it, and the whole of the cash bequest for its housing, exhibition, and maintenance shall be devoted to the purposes of that building.

5. If any of the articles referred to in clause 1 above shall become unsuitable for purposes of study in the University, the Visitors may present them to other universities or schools or, with the consent of Council, deal with them in such other way as may most effectively promote interest in Eastern civilizations.

Leigh Bequest

The bequest of £1,000 from the late Miss Vivien Leigh shall be expended at the discretion of the Keeper of Western Art, Ashmolean Museum, in such manner as he or she thinks will best serve the interests of art, including the education of members of the University in artistic matters and the assistance of young artists of promise.

Madan Bequest

Half of the residue of the estate of the late F.F. Madan, M.A., Corpus Christi College, shall be held upon trust to establish a fund for the purchase, out of current or accumulated income, of objects suitable for the Department of Western Art in the Ashmolean Museum.

Milne Bequest

The bequest by the late J.G. Milne, M.A., D.Litt., Corpus Christi College, of his residuary estate shall be held in trust for the maintenance and benefit of the Collection of Coins in the Ashmolean Museum of Art and Archaeology and the Numismatic Library in connection with the said collection.

North Bequest

The University accepts with gratitude the bequest of the late Eric Harrison North for the Department of Eastern Art of the Ashmolean Museum of a collection of Chinese ceramics, seals, books, pictures, and objects of art together with one-half of his residuary estate. The money shall be expended at the discretion of the Visitors of the Ashmolean Museum for the purposes of the Department of Eastern Art, both capital and income being expendable.

Oriental Art (Lecturers in)

Sums given for the provision of lecturers in Oriental Art shall be administered by the Keeper of the Department of Eastern Art, Ashmolean Museum.

Russell Bequest

The income from the residue of the estate of the late A.G.B. Russell shall be expended at the discretion of the Visitors of the Ashmolean Museum as to half for the purchase of 'Old Master' drawings and as to half for the purchase of works of art of major importance for the Ashmolean Museum.

Story Bequest

The University accepts with gratitude the residuary bequest of the late Jeffery Stokes Story for the Ashmolean Museum. The net income from the bequest shall be expended at the discretion of the Visitors of the Ashmolean Museum to purchase Japanese art objects for the museum and to provide grants to the staff and students of the museum for the study of Japanese art.

§ 8. *Astor Travel Fund*

1. The University accepts with gratitude from the trustees of the William Waldorf Astor Foundation the sum of $200,000 to establish an Astor Travel Fund.

2. The fund shall be administered by a board of management consisting of up to five persons to be appointed by Council for such periods as it shall think fit. The chairman of the board shall be nominated by Council.

3. The board shall apply the fund to continue one of the principal activities of the foundation (1) by providing grants to senior members of the University's academic staff and other scholars and scientists from the British Isles to enable them to visit laboratories, hospitals, libraries, and similar institutions in the United States and thus enhance or facilitate their research and teaching efforts, and (2) by enabling the University to invite distinguished scholars and scientists from the United States to visit the University in order to lecture and to carry out research.

4. Council shall have power to alter this decree from time to time provided that the main objects of the fund, defined in clause 3, shall be kept in view.

§ 10. *Baber Studentship Fund*

1. The University accepts with gratitude a gift of £200,000 from Dr. Flora Baber in memory of her husband, Ernest George Baber, which shall be used, together with any further sums accepted for this purpose, to establish a fund, to be called the Baber Studentship Fund, the net income of which shall be used to provide studentships for the support of mature students who have been accepted by the University to read for the First or Second B.M. Examination.

2. The fund shall be administered by a board of management consisting of:

(*a*) Dr. Flora Baber, or such person as she shall nominate as her successor, that person and each subsequent successor having power in turn to nominate his or her successor;

(*b*) Mr. V.J.H. Rees or, in the event of his unwillingness or inability to act, one of the other partners of Winkworth & Pemberton, 16 Beaumont Street, Oxford as may be nominated by the partners or, failing that, a nominee of Dr. Baber or her current successor;

(*c*) the Pre-clinical Adviser;

(*d*) the Director of Clinical Studies.

3. The board shall elect its own chairman and shall determine its own procedure.

4. The studentships shall be awarded by the board of management, which shall determine the value and other terms and conditions of the studentships.

5. In the award of the studentships, preference shall be given (all other things being equal and at the discretion of the board of management) to students resident in the U.K. or in another state of the Commonwealth.

6. Income not spent in any year shall be carried forward for expenditure in subsequent years.

7. The board of management shall attempt to contact former Baber Students (whose whereabouts are known) five years after they have qualified as medical practitioners to ask them to make a contribution towards the Baber Studentship Fund.

8. For the purposes of clause 1 above, a mature student shall be defined as any person over the age of 21 years, with or without a degree, wishing to read for the First or Second B.M. Examination.

9. Subject to the consent of the person specified in clause 2 (1) above, Council shall have power to amend this decree from time to time, provided that the main object of the fund, as defined in clause 1 above, is always kept in view.

§ 11. *Balfour Fund*

The University accepts with gratitude the bequest of the late Lewis Balfour for the benefit of the Pitt Rivers Museum of *objets d'art* and of half the residue of his estate, which shall be known as the Balfour Fund and shall be used for the benefit of the museum in such ways as Council, after consultation with the General Board, shall determine.

§ 12. *Bannister Award in Organic Chemistry*

1. The University accepts with gratitude a gift of $4,000 from Brian Bannister, B.Sc., M.A., D.Phil., Oriel and New Colleges, to form a fund the income of which shall be applied to the establishment of an award to be known as the Brian Bannister Award in Organic Chemistry.

2. The award shall be open to members of the University who are presenting themselves for examination in Part II of the Subject Chemistry in the Honour School of Natural Science, and one or two awards may be made annually for the most meritorious performance in that examination in Organic Chemistry, judged on the thesis and the viva voce examination.

3. The board of management for the award shall be the Board of the Faculty of Physical Sciences, which shall make rules for the administration of the award.

4. Council shall have power to amend this decree provided that the main object of the donor (namely the maintenance of an award in Organic Chemistry to be associated with the name of Dr. Brian Bannister) shall always be kept in view.

§ 13. *Barnett Fund*

1. The sum of £6,982·42, being the accumulated assets of the Barnett House Council, shall form a fund to be known as the Barnett Fund to be administered by the Board of the Faculty of Social Studies and the Department for Continuing Education jointly.

2. The fund (as to either capital or income) shall be used for any or all of the following purposes:

(*a*) in making grants to persons admitted as students for the Special Diploma in Social Studies or to persons engaged in a course of training in social work as part of the M.Sc. in Applied Social Studies, provided that the recipients of such grants may include, in particular, persons who intend in connection with their studies to spend a period of residence at Toynbee Hall or in another such institution in the United Kingdom, or who, being associated with such an institution, intend to pursue a course of study in Oxford;

(*b*) for the development of adult education and social work in Berkshire, Buckinghamshire, and Oxfordshire.

§ 14. *Beaconsfield Prize in Physiological Sciences*

1. The University accepts with gratitude an anonymous gift of £10,000 in memory of Dr. Peter Beaconsfield to create a fund the income of which shall be applied to the establishment of the Peter Beaconsfield Prize in Physiological Sciences.

2. The prize shall be awarded under rules approved by the Board of the Faculty of Physiological Sciences, which shall be the board of management of the prize.

§ 15. *Beattie Visiting Fellowship Fund*

1. The University accepts with gratitude the bequest from the estate of the late May Hamilton Beattie which shall form a fund to be called the Beattie Visiting Fellowship Fund.

2. There shall be a board of management for the bequest composed of the following persons:

(1) the Director of the Ashmolean Museum;

(2) the Keeper of Eastern Art at the Ashmolean Museum;

(3), (4) two persons appointed by the Visitors of the Ashmolean Museum;

(5) Dr. Anthony Clark for his lifetime.

3. The board of management shall from time to time appoint a Beattie Visiting Fellow in Carpet Studies. The board shall determine the frequency, duration, and salary of such appointments.

4. The board of management shall apply the income of the fund, after payment of all proper expenses, for the following purposes:

(*a*) to provide the salary of the Beattie Visiting Fellow in Carpet Studies;

(*b*) to provide travel grants and other expenses incidental to the holding of the fellowship;

(*c*) to support conferences and seminars in the field of Carpet Studies;

(*d*) to support publications arising out of work undertaken by the visiting fellow during his or her period of office;

(*e*) to support the purchase of additional rugs for the Ashmolean Collection;

(*f*) to support the conservation of the collection of rugs and the costs of exhibiting the same;

(*g*) to support any other activities relating to Carpet Studies.

5. Any income not expended in a given year shall be carried forward for use in subsequent years.

6. Council shall have power to alter this decree from time to time, provided that the main object of the fund, namely the establishment of a Beattie Visiting Fellowship in Carpet Studies in the Department of Eastern Art at the Ashmolean Museum, is always kept in view.

§ 16. *Beckit Memorial Prize*

'The Henry Oliver Beckit Memorial Prize' shall be awarded in accordance with regulations framed by the Board of the Faculty of Anthropology and Geography.

§ 17. *Beddington Prizes*

1. There shall be an annual undergraduate prize in English and an annual undergraduate prize in Modern Languages. They shall be called 'The Mrs. Claude Beddington English Literature Prize' and 'The Mrs. Claude Beddington Modern Languages Prize' respectively.

2. The management of the prize in English Literature shall be entrusted to the Board of the Faculty of English Language and Literature and the management of the prize in Modern Languages to the Board of the Faculty of Medieval and Modern Languages; and the boards shall have power to make regulations, not inconsistent with this decree, for their respective prizes.

3. The prize in English Literature shall be awarded, if there is a candidate of sufficient merit, by the Honour Moderators in English Language and Literature in Trinity Term to the candidate whose performance in that examination, or in part 2 of the Preliminary Examination in English and Modern Languages in the same term, they judge to be the best. The prize in Modern Languages shall be awarded, if there is a candidate of sufficient merit, by the Moderators in the Preliminary Examination for Modern Languages in Hilary Term to the candidate whose performance, in the language specified for that year by the Board of the Faculty of Medieval and Modern Languages, in that examination, or in the Preliminary Examination in Philosophy and Modern Languages in the same

term, or in part 1 of the Preliminary Examination in English and Modern Languages in the same term, or in the Preliminary Examination in European and Middle Eastern Languages in the same term, or in part 1 of the Preliminary Examination in Modern History and Modern Languages in the same term, they judge to be the best.

4. The two prize-winners shall each be entitled on award to half the income produced (after meeting any expenses of administration) by the fund in the previous financial year. Any surplus income arising because either prize is not awarded or from any other cause shall be carried forward for expenditure in subsequent years.

5. Council shall have power to amend this decree provided that the main object of the testator, as set out in clause 1 above, is kept in view.

§ 18. *Beit Fund*

1. The administration of the Beit Fund shall be entrusted to a board of management consisting of five persons, who shall be

(1) the Vice-Chancellor;

(2) the Beit Professor of the History of the British Commonwealth;

(3) one person elected by the Board of the Faculty of Modern History;

(4) one person elected by the Board of the Faculty of Social Studies;

(5) one person appointed by Council.

The elected members of the board of management shall hold office for three years and shall be re-eligible.

2. The first charges upon the Beit Fund shall be

(*a*) an annual contribution equal to two-fifths of the total income of the fund from year to year towards the payment of the full stipend of the Beit Professor of the History of the British Commonwealth;

(*b*) the payment of the Beit Prize and of the Examiners for that prize;

(*c*) the payment of an annual contribution of £50 to the Bodleian Library for the purchase of such books and documents as in the opinion of the Curators of the Library are required in the study of the history of the British Dominions over the Seas, exclusive of India and its Dependencies.

3. Any balance of the income, so far as not required for the purposes aforesaid, may be applied to the following purposes:

(*a*) the establishment of Senior Research Scholarships in the History of the British Commonwealth on such terms as the board shall from time to time decide;

(*b*) the provision of a fund to assist the Beit Professor to travel from time to time within the Commonwealth in order to visit the countries with which his or her work is concerned and to study local records;

(*c*) grants made by the board of management for any purposes which in its opinion will promote the study of the History of the British Commonwealth in the University of Oxford.

Any balance of the income not so applied shall be carried forward for expenditure in subsequent years.

4. This decree shall be subject to alteration from time to time by Council, provided that the main objects of the fund as set forth in the preamble to the decree superseded by this decree[1] are always kept in view.

§ **19.** *Beit Prize*

1. The prize shall be called the Beit Prize, and shall be for an essay on some subject connected with the advantages of 'Imperial Citizenship', or on some subject connected with Colonial History. It shall be open to all members of the University who on the day appointed for sending in the competing essays shall not have exceeded twelve years from their matriculation, and who have not previously been awarded either the Beit Prize or the Robert Herbert Memorial Prize.

2. The trustees of the prize shall be the Board of Management of the Beit Fund. It shall be the duty of the trustees to determine the subject of the essays, to give notice thereof in the usual manner, and to appoint judges.

3. The value of the prize, and the annual sum for the payment of the judges, shall be as determined by the trustees from time to time.

4. If in any year the prize be not awarded, the money thus rendered available shall be returned to the Beit Fund.

5. This decree may be altered from time to time by Council with the consent of the trustees, provided that the main object of the prize shall always be kept

[1] WHEREAS the late Mr. Alfred Beit in 1905 offered to contribute the sum of £1,310 a year for seven years (1) for the maintenance of a resident Professor of Colonial History; (2) for Assistant Lecturers in that subject; (3) for an annual Prize of the value of £50 for an Essay on some subject connected with the advantages of 'Imperial Citizenship', or on some subject connected with Colonial History, and for the payment of Examiners; and (4) for the purchase of books on the subject of the Professorship to the amount of £50 a year:

And WHEREAS Mr. Beit made this offer subject to the following conditions:

(1) That the Professor shall be resident and that accommodation shall be provided by the University for the lectures to be given by him.

(2) That in addition to his ordinary lectures he shall deliver annually at least one public lecture open to all members of the University.

(3) That the general subject of the Professorship shall be the History of British Dominions over the Seas, and that it shall be taken to include

(*a*) The history of Imperial Policy towards British possessions;

(*b*) The detailed history of the separate self-governing Colonies, including the American Colonies, before their separation from the mother country, but exclusive of India and its dependencies;

(*c*) The detailed history of all British possessions, past and present, other than India and its dependencies.

(4) That the list of special historical subjects suggested by the Board of the Faculty of Arts (Modern History) shall always include a portion of the History of the British Dominions over the Seas, or a special subject falling within that history.

in view, namely, the promotion of the study of Colonial History in the University of Oxford.

§ **20.** *Berlin Fund*

1. The University accepts with gratitude from Sir Isaiah Berlin, O.M., the sum of $105,000 to establish a fund to be known as the Isaiah Berlin Fund, which shall be used for the furtherance of academic links with Italy in the fields of literature and history, including the History of Art.

2. The fund shall be administered by a board of management consisting of:

(1) the Vice-Chancellor;

(2) one person appointed by Council;

(3) one person appointed by the Board of the Faculty of Medieval and Modern Languages;

(4) one person appointed by the Board of the Faculty of Modern History;

(5) one person appointed by the Committee for the History of Art.

The appointed members shall serve for such periods as the appointing bodies shall think fit. The board shall have power to co-opt up to two additional members on such terms as it shall determine.

3. The board shall apply the income of the fund towards the provision of grants to members of the University to enable them to visit Italy in order to lecture or to undertake research, and to scholars and students from Italy to enable them to visit the University in order to lecture or to undertake research.

4. Council shall have power to alter this decree from time to time provided always that the main object of the fund, as defined in clause 1 above, shall be kept in view.

§ **21.** *Betts Fund*

1. The University accepts with gratitude the bequest from Mrs. John Betts to establish a fund, to be known as the John Betts Fund, to commemorate the activities of Mr. John Betts as a builder and restorer of organs, which shall be used to establish musical scholarships or fellowships related to the study of the organ.

2. The fund shall be administered by the Board of the Faculty of Music.

3. Council shall have power to amend this decree from time to time, provided that the main object of the fund, as defined in clause 1 above, is always kept in view.

§ **22.** *Binyon Prize*

1. The fund shall be invested by the University and the income arising from it shall be devoted to the maintenance of a prize to be called the 'Laurence Binyon Prize'.

2. The prize shall be open to all members of the University, whether men or women, who shall not have exceeded twenty-one terms from their matriculation, and shall be awarded, after consideration of the qualifications of the candidates and of testimonials submitted by them, to enable the prize-winner to travel abroad to extend his or her knowledge and appreciation of the visual arts. Each candidate shall be required to submit a statement of his or her proposed course of travel.

3. If a candidate of sufficient merit present himself or herself, the prize shall be awarded when the income from the fund is sufficient to permit of the purpose for which the prize is awarded being carried out; and if no candidate present himself or herself on that occasion, the prize shall be offered in the following year.

4. The management of the prize shall be entrusted to the Committee for the History of Art which shall determine on each occasion the amount of the prize to be awarded.

5. Any income not expended when a prize is awarded may, at the discretion of the Committee for the History of Art, be either accumulated to increase the sum available from time to time for prizes, or added to the capital of the fund.

§ 23. *Bird Bequest*

Note. This sub-section is not a decree or regulation but an extract from a Scheme concerning the administration of the Charity called or known as The Bird Bequest founded by Will dated 18 August 1774, approved in the Chancery Division of the High Court of Justice on 23 November 1936

Scheme for the regulation and management of the above-mentioned charity and of the funds and property thereof:

1. The above-mentioned charity shall be administered and managed by the Chancellor Masters and Scholars of the University of Oxford (hereinafter called 'the University') in whose name the funds thereof shall remain vested with power for the University from time to time at discretion to vary or transpose any investments for or into others of a nature authorized by law for the investment of trust funds.

2. All the proper costs charges and expenses of and incidental to the administration and management of the charity shall be first defrayed out of the income of the said funds.

3. Subject to the payments aforesaid the income of the said funds shall be applied in or towards the payment of the stipends or stipend of the assistants or assistant for the time being to the Savilian Professor of Astronomy at the Observatory of the University.

4. Any income of the said funds not required for the purposes aforesaid may be applied by the University in the promotion of the study of astronomy in the University in such manner as the University may think fit and if not so applied

shall be invested in the name of the University and added to the capital of the said funds.

§ **24.** *Blackman Lecturership Fund*

1. The Board of the Faculty of Biological Sciences shall be the Board of Management of the G.E. Blackman Lecturership Fund.

2. The departmental committee of the Department of Plant Sciences, acting on behalf of the faculty board, shall appoint a committee to carry out the provisions of clause 3 below, subject to such conditions as the board may lay down. The committee shall consist of the Sibthorpian Professor of Plant Science *ex officio* and up to six persons representative of agricultural crop, animal, and soil science. The elected members shall hold office for three years and shall be re-eligible.

3. The income from the fund shall be used to provide an annual lecture to be called the G.E. Blackman Lecture, to be given on some aspect of the application of science to Agriculture.

4. Income not expended in any year shall be carried forward for expenditure in subsequent years.

5. Council shall have power to alter this decree from time to time, provided that the main object of the fund (namely, to promote the study of Agricultural Science within the University) is kept in view.

§ **25.** *Blakiston Fund*

The £12,000 bequeathed to the University by the late Dr. H.E. Blakiston shall constitute a fund to be known as the Blakiston Fund for the purchase of works of graphic art, subject to payment of an annuity of £52 per annum.

§ **26.** *Blaschko Visiting Research Scholarship*

[1]

1. The University accepts from the Trustee of the Campaign for Oxford Trust Fund the endowment made possible by an extremely generous benefaction from Mrs. Mary Douglas Blaschko, in recognition of the contribution of her late husband, Dr. Karl Felix Hermann Blaschko, to the advancement of science internationally and to the development of the Department of Pharmacology, to establish a fund the net income of which shall be applied in the furtherance of research in Pharmacology within the University by the support of Blaschko Visiting Research Scholarships tenable in the said department or elsewhere under the direction of the head of department.

2. The fund shall be administered by a board of management comprising:
   (1) the Professor of Pharmacology;
   (2) the Principal of Linacre College, or a deputy appointed by the Principal;

(3) one member of the staff of the Department of Pharmacology, or of the Medical Research Council Anatomical Neuropharmacology Unit, appointed by the Professor of Pharmacology to hold office for up to one year and to be eligible for reappointment;

(4) Mrs. Mary Douglas Blaschko;

(5) Dr. Ruth Baker;

(6) Mrs. Ann Campbell.

3. The board shall from time to time award Blaschko Visiting Research Scholarships to graduate students in Pharmacology (or in a related area of study) from a university outside the United Kingdom. Preference shall be given to students from a European university.

4. The scholarships shall be tenable for up to one year, and in exceptional circumstances may be extended for not more than one further year. Each Visiting Scholar shall be required to be a member of Linacre College on taking up the award and shall receive full-time instruction in pharmacological research under the general direction of the Head of the Department of Pharmacology. In addition to the payment of the scholarship emoluments towards the Visiting Scholar's maintenance costs, the board of management is empowered to contribute towards the Visiting Scholar's travelling and other appropriate expenses.

5. Income not spent in any year shall be carried forward for expenditure in subsequent years.

6. Council shall have power to alter this decree from time to time, provided that the main object of the fund, as defined in clause 1 above, is always kept in view.

[2]

1. The University accepts with gratitude from Mrs. Mary Douglas Blaschko the sum of £50,000 to create a fund to supplement the Blaschko Visiting Research Scholarship ('The Blaschko Supplementary Fund').

2. The supplementary fund shall be administered by the Board of Management for the Blaschko Visiting Research Scholarship.

3. The board shall use the income of the supplementary fund for the following purposes:

(*a*) for the provision of travel grants for the Blaschko Visiting Research Scholar;

(*b*) to support publications by the Blaschko Visiting Research Scholar;

(*c*) for the payment of appropriate supplementary expenses incurred in connection with the Blaschko Visiting Research Scholarship as approved by the board.

4. Income not spent from the supplementary fund in any year shall be carried forward for expenditure in subsequent years.

5. Council shall have power to alter this decree from time to time, provided that the main object of the supplementary fund, as defined in clause 1 above, is always kept in view.

§ **27.** *Bodleian Library*

Bannister Bequest

The income arising from the bequest of the late H. M. Bannister shall be used at the discretion of the Curators of the University Libraries; and the University undertakes neither to diminish its customary grants to the Bodleian Library in the light of this additional income nor to take it into account when determining the amount of future grants.

Brister Fund

The residuary bequest of Mr. James Brister shall form a fund, to be known as the Brister Fund, the income of which shall, subject to the approval of the Curators of the University Libraries, be used by the Department of Printed Books for the purchase of printed material for the Library's collections including prints and ephemera.

Cowley Bequest

The residue and remainder of the estate of Sir Arthur Ernest Cowley, M.A., D.Litt., Fellow of Magdalen College, formerly Bodley's Librarian, shall be held upon trust for the general purposes of the Bodleian Library subject to the payment out of the income therefrom of annuities to certain persons mentioned in the will.

Duff Fund

1. There shall be a fund to be called the Gordon Duff Fund into which shall be paid the income of the Gordon Duff Bequest, which is to be held on trust for (*a*) the purchase for the Bodleian Library of old or rare manuscripts, printed books, and book bindings (preferably of date prior to A.D. 1700) and, (*b*) an essay prize of £50 to be awarded triennially.

2. Save as provided in clause 3 below the fund may be used at the discretion of the Librarian for the purchase of manuscripts, printed books, and book bindings of a date earlier than A.D. 1700.

3. In every third year the Curators of the University Libraries shall provide from the income of the fund a prize of £50 or such higher sum as they may determine to be called the Gordon Duff Prize to be offered for competition in accordance with the following procedure:

(*a*) The prize shall be open to all members of the University without restriction of age or standing but shall not be awarded more than once to any one person.

(*b*) The prize shall be offered for a written essay on any of the following subjects, namely, bibliography, palaeography, typography, book binding, book illustration, the science of books and manuscripts, and the arts relating thereto.

(*c*) The curators shall give notice of their intention to offer the prize by advertisement in the *University Gazette* and shall specify (i) the date by which subjects chosen by candidates must be submitted for approval, (ii) the date by which essays must be submitted. No work may be submitted unless the subject is first approved by the curators or by a committee of them.

(*d*) The curators may make and vary such regulations as they think proper regarding the length or method of presentation of essays.

(*e*) The prize shall be awarded by the curators on the recommendation made by a panel of two judges to be appointed by them on each occasion on which the prize is offered.

(*f*) If no candidate submits an essay or if the judges are unable to recommend the award of the prize to any candidate the prize money shall be retained in the fund and made available *pro hac vice* for the purposes indicated in clause 2 above.

(*g*) The remuneration of the judges shall be a charge on the Gordon Duff Fund and shall be determined by the curators.

Grahame Fund

1. The capital of the Kenneth Grahame Fund shall consist of the assets received under the will of the late Kenneth Grahame and accepted by Decree (3) of 25 April 1933, together with the additions provided for by clause 3 below and any other moneys which the University may add to the capital in accordance with any powers enabling it so to do. The capital shall be invested by the Curators of the University Chest, provided that any assets received under the will may, at the said curators' discretion, be retained in kind or sold.

2. The annual income arising from the said capital shall be placed at the disposal of the Curators of the University Libraries subject to the provisions of clause 3 below.

3. One-half of the net annual income arising from royalties forming part of the said capital shall be invested annually by the Curators of the University Chest and added to the capital of the fund.

4. The Curators of the University Libraries shall, on the recommendation of the Librarian, apply the income thus placed at their disposal to the financing of

(*a*) official Library publications, or

(*b*) the reproduction of printed books, manuscripts, and other material, in or connected with the Bodleian Library, or both.

5. If in the opinion of the curators the income thus placed at their disposal shall be more than sufficient to defray expenditure recommended to them by the Librarian under clause 4 above, they may from time to time either make grants therefrom for the purchase of rare books and manuscripts for the Library or

request the Curators of the University Chest to invest temporarily some part of the said income to defray future expenditure on the said purposes or both.

Hebrew Collections

The University accepts with gratitude an initial grant of £10,000 from a foundation requesting anonymity. This grant, together with such further sums as shall be contributed for the same purpose, shall be used towards the creation of an endowment fund for the establishment and maintenance of one or more posts of librarian with responsibility for the Hebrew Collections of the Bodleian Library. The fund shall be administered by the Curators of the University Libraries.

Jenkins Bequest

The income of the residue of the estate of the late Professor C. Jenkins, D.D., shall be paid (subject to two annuities) to the Curators of the University Libraries for the general purposes of the Library, including any special fund for the purchase of rare books or manuscripts at the discretion of the said curators.

Jones Bequest

A bequest of £1,000 under the will of the late John Reginald Jones, B.A., Trinity College, for the Bodleian Library, shall be used to establish a fund for the purchase of books or manuscripts not less than one hundred years old, to be known as 'The Reginald Jones Bequest'.

Lewis Milne Bequest

The University accepts a bequest by the late Mrs. Mary Lewis Milne, subject to certain life interests, of the residue of her estate, to be used for the purposes of the Bodleian Library and the University records its thanks for the generosity of the testatrix.

Presentation Copies, Clarendon Press Books

[1]

The Delegates of the University Press shall be at liberty to present from time to time to institutions within the University a copy of such Clarendon Press Books as they may deem suitable to the uses of such institutions.

[2]

The Delegates of the University Press shall be at liberty, on the application of the Curators of the University Libraries, to supply them with copies of works published by the Press, to be presented at the discretion of the curators to foreign universities, libraries, and other learned institutions.

Sanderson Bequest

The University accepts with gratitude a bequest from the late Lady (Maude Isolde) Sanderson for one-fourth of the residue of her estate, amounting to approximately £19,000, for the expenditure, at the discretion of the Curators of the University Libraries, on the purposes of the library.

Sayce Fund

The University accepts with gratitude the gift of Mrs. Olive Sayce to the Curators of the University Libraries of the sum of £1,000 to be invested in a fund bearing the name of Richard Sayce, late Fellow and Librarian of Worcester College, the income from which shall be used towards the purchase of books in bibliography, history of printing and book production, and library history, or of French books.

Scicluna Bequest

The income of the bequest of £1,500 of the late Lady (Margaret Helen) Scicluna shall be applied at the discretion of the Curators of the University Libraries to the acquisition of books on Malta and the Order of St. John of Jerusalem to be added to the Scicluna Collection of Melitensia in Rhodes House Library.

Sowers Bequest

The University accepts with gratitude the bequest of $87,600 from the late R.V. Sowers for expenditure, at the discretion of the Curators of the University Libraries, on the purposes of the library.

Vaisey Endowment Fund

1. The University accepts with gratitude the sums contributed in recognition of the period in office of Mr. David Vaisey as Bodley's Librarian, together with any moneys which may be subscribed for this purpose in the future, which shall form a fund to be known as the Vaisey Endowment Fund. The net income of the fund shall be applied for the benefit of the Bodleian Library.

2. The fund shall be administered by the Director of University Library Services and Bodley's Librarian in consultation with the Curators of the University Libraries.

3. Income not spent in any year shall be carried forward for expenditure in subsequent years.

4. This decree may be altered from time to time, provided always that the main object of the fund, as defined in clause 1 above, is adhered to.

Vere Harmsworth Library Acquisitions Endowment Fund

1. The University accepts with gratitude an endowment from Nigel and Helen Lovett, together with any further sums contributed for the same purpose, to establish a fund, to be known as the Vere Harmsworth Library Acquisitions Endowment Fund, the net income of which shall be used for the acquisition of library materials in the Vere Harmsworth Library of the Rothermere American Institute.

2. The fund shall be administered by the Curators of the University Libraries. The curators shall have power to delegate expenditure to the Director of University Library Services and Bodley's Librarian, such delegation to be reviewed on an annual basis when the director shall report to the curators all exercises of his or her delegated authority.

3. Income not spent in any year shall be carried forward for expenditure in subsequent years.

4. This decree may be altered from time to time, provided always that the main object of the fund, as defined in clause 1 above, is adhered to.

Winstedt Bequest

The bequest of the late E.O. Winstedt, which was accepted by Decree (4) of 16 October 1956, shall be used, as to capital and income, at the discretion of the Curators of the University Libraries for the upkeep, improvement, and maintenance of the Bodleian Library.

§ **28.** *Boyd Bequest*

1. The University accepts with gratitude the bequest by the late Mrs. A.M.G.J. Boyd of one-sixteenth of the residue of her estate, together with all royalties to which she was entitled on her late husband's publications, for the Taylor Institution.

2. The bequest shall be used by the Curators of the Taylor Institution for the benefit of the Institution.

§ **29.** *British Telecom Research and Technology Prize for Computing Science*

1. The University accepts with gratitude the sum of £5,000 donated by British Telecom to form a fund, the income from which shall be used to provide an annual prize for Computing Science.

2. The prize shall be awarded for specially meritorious performance in the Honour School of Mathematics and Computation.

3. The prize, of a value to be determined from time to time by the Board of the Faculty of Mathematical Sciences, shall be awarded, if there is a candidate of sufficient merit, by the examiners for the Honour School of Mathematics and Computation to the candidate whose performance in that examination they judge to be the most deserving, paying special regard to performance in computation.

4. The administration of the fund shall be under the direction of the Board of the Faculty of Mathematical Sciences.

5. Income not expended in any one year shall be carried forward for expenditure in subsequent years.

6. Council shall have power from time to time to alter this decree, provided always that the purpose of the fund, as defined in clause 1 above, is kept in view.

§ 30. *Bryce Research Studentship in History*

1. The Bryce Research Studentship in History shall be open to members of the University pursuing research in History for the Degree of Doctor of Philosophy. Candidates must by the date on which they take up the studentship have been admitted to and not have subsequently lost the status of Student for the Degree of Doctor of Philosophy, and not have exceeded the twelfth term since they began their research studies at the University.

2. The studentship shall be administered by a board of management consisting of:

(1) the Vice-Chancellor;

(2) the Camden Professor of Ancient History;

(3) the Wykeham Professor of Ancient History;

(4) the Regius Professor of Modern History;

(5) the Chichele Professor of Medieval History;

(6) the chairman of the committee appointed under the provisions of Tit. XVI, Sect. V, cl. 3;

(7) one person elected by the Board of the Faculty of Literae Humaniores;

(8), (9) two persons elected by the Board of the Faculty of Modern History.

The elected members of the board of management shall be the same persons as those elected by the aforesaid faculty boards to serve on the board of management of the Amy Mary Preston Read Scholarship; they shall hold office for five years and shall be re-eligible.

3. The student shall receive the net income arising from Viscount Bryce's endowment subject to the provisions of clause 6 below.

4. The studentship shall be tenable for one year either at Oxford or, with the consent of the board of management, elsewhere.

5. The studentship shall be awarded without examination. Every candidate, with his or her application, shall submit a programme of work in History, either Ancient or Modern, which he or she proposes, if elected, to undertake. He or she shall also

(*a*) state any other emoluments which he or she may already hold and whether he or she is a candidate or prospective candidate for such other emoluments;

(*b*) undertake, if elected to the studentship, to inform the board if, during its tenure, he or she is awarded any other emoluments.

The election of the student shall be made by the board of management after consideration of the past records of the candidates and of the programmes submitted by them, but without having regard to the candidates' financial needs.

6. Every student shall, while he or she continues to hold the studentship, produce from time to time evidence, satisfactory to the board of management, that he or she is carrying out his or her programme of work. The board shall have power to deprive a student who does not comply with this condition of the whole or any part of the emoluments of his or her studentship. The board shall

also have power to modify, at its discretion, the value of the studentship either at the time of an election or at any time during the period of tenure.

7. Income undisposed of from any cause may at the discretion of the board of management be used in any year for the purpose of awarding an additional studentship, or of continuing an existing studentship, or for the payment of expenses, including those of travel or publication, incidental to the pursuit of a definite piece of historical investigation, or otherwise for the encouragement of approved pieces of historical study and research.

8. The election to the studentship shall take place either in Trinity Term or in Michaelmas Term, as the board of management shall determine. No person shall be awarded the studentship a second time.

9. The board of management shall have power to alter this decree from time to time with the consent of Council, and of Lady Bryce during her lifetime, provided that the main object of Lord Bryce in founding the studentship be always kept in view.

§ 31. *Bull Memorial Fund*

1. The University accepts with gratitude the sums contributed in memory of Hedley Bull, Fellow of Balliol College and Montague Burton Professor of International Relations, which shall form a fund to be known as the Hedley Bull Memorial Fund. The net income of the fund shall be applied to support the study of International Relations within the University.

2. The Board of the Faculty of Social Studies shall be the board of management for the fund.

3. The board of management shall have power to use the income of the fund to establish research fellowships in International Relations, and for any purpose related to the study of International Relations within the University.

4. The research fellowships may be held at any college approved by the board of management. The area of research may be any aspect of International Relations.

5. Council shall have power to alter this decree from time to time, provided that the main object of the fund, the support of the study of International Relations within the University in memory of Professor Bull, shall always be kept in view.

§ 32. *Burdett-Coutts Foundation*

1. The Board of the Faculty of Physical Sciences shall be the board of management of the Burdett-Coutts Foundation.

2. The board shall establish a committee to exercise on its behalf the powers conferred by clauses 3 and 4. The committee shall consist of the Professor of Geology and three other persons, of whom two shall be elected by the Board of the Faculty of Physical Sciences and one by the Board of the Faculty of Biological Sciences. The elected members (who need not necessarily be

members of either faculty board) shall hold office for three years and shall be re-eligible. The committee shall report on its activities to the Board of the Faculty of Physical Sciences at least once in each year.

3. The first charge on the foundation shall be the award in each year of a Burdett-Coutts Prize, the value of which shall be determined by the committee but shall not be less than £50. The prize money shall be spent on travel or some other purpose connected with the study of Geology and approved by the Professor of Geology, and shall be paid in accordance with his or her instructions. The prize shall be open to members of the University who have read Geology in the Honour School of Natural Science, have passed the examinations necessary for the Degree of Bachelor of Arts and are of not more than twelve terms' standing. It shall be awarded to the candidate who, after consideration of the candidates' performance in the Final Honour School and of their proposals for the use of the prize money is, in the opinion of the committee, best fitted to receive it. If in any year the prize is not awarded because no candidate of sufficient merit has presented himself or herself, the committee shall report accordingly to the board.

4. Income not required for the prize may be kept in hand or used by the committee in one or more of the following ways:

(*a*) the award of a second prize—the value and conditions to be decided by the committee in each case;

(*b*) the award of a studentship to a member of the University who has (or will have by the time the studentship is taken up) (i) passed the examinations necessary for the Degree of B.A., (ii) not exceeded twenty-seven terms from his or her matriculation, (iii) satisfied the committee that he or she intends to read for the Degree of M.Sc. or D.Phil. in the Department of Geology—the value and conditions to be decided by the committee in each case;

(*c*) the award of a studentship to a member of another university who has been admitted by the Board of the Faculty of Physical Sciences as a student for the Degree of M.Sc. or D.Phil. in the Department of Geology—the value and conditions to be decided by the committee in each case; provided that an award under this sub-clause shall not be made unless the financial state of the fund is such that it can be made without prejudice to the possibility of an award under subclause (*b*);

(*d*) in any way (whether by the making of grants or otherwise) for the promotion of the study of geology, and of other branches of natural science bearing on geology, among members of the University who have not exceeded twenty-seven terms from their matriculation.

5. The board shall, with the consent of Council, have power to alter this decree from time to time, provided always that the main end of the foundation shall be kept in view, namely, the promotion of the study of Geology, and of other branches of natural science bearing on Geology, among the junior members of the University of Oxford.

§ 33. *Burdette Lectures in Surgical Science*

1. The University accepts with gratitude such further sums as shall be donated by Dr. Walter J. Burdette; these shall be added to the fund created by his original gift of $5,500 in 1983 and subsequently supplemented by further gifts from him totalling $4,500.

2. The whole of the income of the fund shall be used, under the direction of the Nuffield Professor of Surgery or that professor's deputy, to provide for lectures in Surgery to be known as the Burdette Lectures in Surgical Science.

3. Any income not expended in any year shall be carried forward for expenditure on the Burdette Lectures in Surgical Science in subsequent years.

§ 41. *Cairns Memorial Fund*

To commemorate the work of Sir Hugh Cairns, late Nuffield Professor of Surgery in the University, £2,700 annually from the Nuffield Medical Benefaction shall, together with any donations that may be received, be paid into the Sir Hugh Cairns Memorial Fund, which shall be administered by the Board of the Faculty of Clinical Medicine, to assist research in neurology and neurosurgery in the Medical School.

§ 42. *Cancer Research Committee*

The Curators of the University Chest shall accept annual block grants for cancer research from the Cancer Research Campaign, to be paid out on the direction of the Oxford Cancer Research Committee composed of the following:

(1) Regius Professor of Medicine
(2) The Head of the Department of Zoology (or his or her nominee)
(3) Dr. Lee's Professor of Anatomy
(4) Waynflete Professor of Physiology
(5) Waynflete Professor of Chemistry
(6) Professor of Pathology
(7) Whitley Professor of Biochemistry
(8) Nuffield Professor of Surgery
(9) Nuffield Professor of Clinical Medicine
(10) Nuffield Professor of Obstetrics and Gynaecology
(11) Professor of Morbid Anatomy

§ 43. *Celtic Studies: Lectures endowed by C. J. O'Donnell*

1. From and after the decease of the wife of Mr. Charles J. O'Donnell and until the expiry of his lease of No. 37 New Bond Street in the County of London (a period of about fifty years), his trustees shall out of the rental of the said premises pay to each of the following universities in turn, namely, the National University of Ireland, the Universities of Oxford, Wales, and Edinburgh, and Trinity College, Dublin, by annual rotation in the above order

the sum of £500 (so that in every year one university will receive a sum of £500).

2. Only such of the said universities as for the time being maintain a Professor of or Reader or Lecturer in Celtic History and Literature shall be entitled to receive any payment under the will.

3. Each of the said universities shall apply the sum paid to it in establishing annual lectures to be called the O'Donnell Lectures.

4. Each of the said universities shall undertake as a condition of receiving any benefit under the will to procure the delivery during each of the five years immediately succeeding the receipt of such benefit of at least one lecture connected with one or other of the following subjects, namely, in the English and Scottish universities (*a*) the British or Celtic elements in the English language and the dialects of English counties and the special terms and words used in agriculture and handicrafts, (*b*) the British or Celtic elements in the existing population of England; provided that if all of the said universities are not qualified to receive or do not accept the sums payable to them under the terms of the will, then such of the said universities as do receive the said sums shall together undertake to procure the delivery as aforesaid of a total of not less than five lectures per annum on one or other of the subjects aforesaid.

§ 44. *The Chancellor's Prizes*

1. The Chancellor's Prizes shall be three in number, one for Latin Prose, one for Latin Verse, and one for an English Essay.

2. The prizes shall be offered for competition annually in Trinity Term, and shall each be of such value, being not less than £250, as Council shall determine from time to time. They shall be open to all members of the University of either sex who, on the day appointed for sending in compositions, have not exceeded four years from the date of their matriculation.

3. No person who has already obtained one of the prizes shall be eligible for that prize again.

4. The examiners for the Latin Prose and Latin Verse prizes shall be the Public Orator, the Corpus Christi Professor of Latin, and one other member of Convocation appointed annually by the Vice-Chancellor and Proctors; the examiners for the English Essay Prize shall be the Professor of Poetry and two other members of Convocation similarly appointed. If in any year any of the offices of Public Orator, Corpus Christi Professor of Latin, or Professor of Poetry is vacant, or if the holder of any of these offices is unable to act, the Vice-Chancellor and Proctors shall appoint another member of Convocation to act as examiner in his or her place. No examiner shall vote on any candidate's merits except at a meeting of the examiners.

5. The subjects for the prizes in any year shall be determined by the examiners for the preceding year and shall be announced not later than the first day of the Michaelmas Term preceding the term in which the prizes are offered.

§ **45.** *Charterhouse European Bursaries*

1. The University accepts with gratitude from the Charterhouse Charitable Trust the sum of £100,000 to establish a fund to be known as Charterhouse European Bursaries Fund, the net annual income of which shall be used for the award of bursaries to junior members working for degrees of the University who wish to undertake a period of study of up to one year in another European country. Priority in the award of bursaries shall be given for study in the areas of Economics, Management, Applied Mathematics in Industry, Engineering, and Technology.

2. The fund shall be administered by the International Committee.

3. Any income not spent in any year under the provisions of clause 1 above shall be carried forward for expenditure in subsequent years.

4. Council shall have power to amend this decree from time to time, provided that the object of the fund as defined in clause 1 above shall always be kept in view.

§ **46.** *Chester Fund*

1. The University accepts with gratitude the bequest of £30,000 from Sir Norman Chester as an accretion to, and to be held upon the trusts of, the fund established in 1979 to commemorate on his retirement as Warden of Nuffield College Sir Norman's services to the college and the University. The combined fund shall be called the Norman Chester Fund, and the income thereof shall be used for the promotion of the study of government and politics and generally to further a science of politics within the University by giving grants on such terms as the board of management thinks fit, preference being given to those engaged in postgraduate work. Part of the income may be used to establish prizes, on such terms and conditions as the board of management thinks fit.

2. The Board of the Faculty of Social Studies shall be the board of management of the fund and shall have power to appoint a committee to act on its behalf in the determination of applications for grants, consisting of not less than three members, one of whom shall always be a member of Nuffield College.

3. Any income not spent in any year under the provisions of clause 2 above shall be carried forward for expenditure in some future year.

4. Council shall have power to alter this decree from time to time, provided always that the purpose of the fund, as stated in clause 1, shall be kept in view.

§ **47.** *Chiles Award Fund*

1. The University accepts with gratitude from the Executors of the Estate of Mavis Stanley the sum of £5,000 which shall be used, together with any further sums accepted for this purpose, to establish a fund, to be called the Ralph Chiles, C.B.E., Award Fund, for the furtherance of legal studies within the University.

2. The fund shall be administered by the Board of the Faculty of Law which shall apply the income of the fund for the award of scholarships, prizes, or grants under such conditions as the board shall from time to time determine.

3. Income not spent in any year shall be carried forward for expenditure in subsequent years.

4. Council shall have power to alter this decree from time to time, provided that the main object of the fund, as defined in clause 1 above, is always kept in view.

§ **48.** *Clough Travel Fund*

1. The balance of the original benefaction received from Mr. S. D. P. Clough, and such further sums as shall from time to time be accepted for the same purpose, shall constitute the Clough Travel Fund.

2. The fund shall be administered by the Japanese Lectorship Committee under the Board of the Faculty of Oriental Studies, and shall be applied towards the provision of travel grants for undergraduate or graduate students of Japanese in the University to enable them to visit Japan or Japan and Korea for the study of the language or literature.

§ **49.** *Cohn Memorial Fund*

1. The sum of £3,000 accepted from Mrs. Isa Cohn primarily to provide for the delivery from time to time of a lecture in memory of the late William Cohn and in later years, failing a lecture, for such purposes as the Keeper for the time being of the Department of Eastern Art of the Ashmolean Museum shall think fitting to commemorate the late William Cohn and to assist the Department of Eastern Art shall form a fund to be called the William Cohn Memorial Fund.

2. The lecture shall be called the William Cohn Memorial Lecture, and the lecturer shall be called the William Cohn Memorial Lecturer.

3. The lecture shall be delivered on a subject relating to Eastern Art.

4. The Keeper for the time being of the Department of Eastern Art of the Ashmolean Museum shall appoint the lecturer from time to time, and shall determine his or her stipend.

5. The income of the fund shall, at the discretion of the Keeper of the Department of Eastern Art, be applied in one or more of the following ways:

(*a*) to provide the stipend of the lecturer;

(*b*) to meet his or her necessary expenses, including the provision of illustrative material, if required;

(*c*) to meet any expenses consequent upon the delivery of the lecture;

(*d*) to assist in defraying the cost of any other form of commemoration of the late William Cohn which the Keeper shall think fit.

Income not so expended in any year may be either carried forward for expenditure in subsequent years, or invested in augmentation of the capital.

6. This decree shall be subject to alteration by Council provided that the main object of the fund, namely the commemoration of the late William Cohn by the promotion of the study of Eastern Art in the University, shall be observed and maintained.

§ 50. *Colin Prize*

1. There shall be an Andrew Colin Prize, consisting of the income of the fund, which shall be awarded annually by the Moderators in the Preliminary Examination for Modern Languages in Hilary Term to the candidate whose performance in Russian in that examination or in the Preliminary Examination in Philosophy and Modern Languages in the same term, or in part 1 of the Preliminary Examination in English and Modern Languages in the same term, or in the Preliminary Examination in European and Middle Eastern Languages in the same term, or in part 1 of the Preliminary Examination in Modern History and Modern Languages in the same term, they shall judge to be the best.

2. The Board of the Faculty of Medieval and Modern Languages shall be the board of management of the prize, and shall have power to make regulations, not inconsistent with this decree, for the award.

3. Any surplus income arising because the prize is not awarded or from any other cause shall be carried forward for expenditure in subsequent years.

4. Council shall have power to amend this decree provided that the main object of the bequest (which was that the bequest should be 'invested on behalf of the Russian Faculty for the award of such prize or scholarship as the said faculty may desire') is kept in view.

§ 51. *Conington Prize*

1. The money contributed for the Conington Memorial Fund shall be invested in the name of the University for the establishment of a prize, which shall have for its object the encouragement of mature classical learning among graduates of the University, and shall be called 'The Conington Prize'.

2. The prize shall be managed by the Board of the Faculty of Literae Humaniores, and shall be offered annually for a dissertation, to be written either in English or in Latin at the option of the writer, on some subject appertaining to classical learning in the field specified for the year in accordance with the provisions of clause 3 below.

3. At least twelve months before the day appointed for sending in the dissertations, the board shall invite competitors to offer dissertations, whether published or unpublished, on subjects chosen by themselves within the field specified for the year and under such conditions as the board may think it expedient to prescribe. The following fields shall be specified for one year each, in rotation:

(*a*) classical literature, textual criticism, and philology;

(*b*) ancient history, religion, art, and archaeology;

(*c*) ancient philosophy and ideas.

In case of doubt the board shall determine the field, if any, within which the subject of a dissertation falls.

4. Subject to the provisions of clause 7 below, the prize shall be open to all members of the University who, on the day appointed for sending in the dissertations, are qualified by examination for a degree of the University, and shall have completed six years, and not exceeded fifteen years, from their matriculation, except that graduates whose first degrees are from other universities shall have completed two years, and not exceeded eleven years, from their matriculation.

5. The prize shall be so much of the annual income of the fund as shall remain after the appropriation of such sum as the board shall determine as an honorarium to the judges and the payment of all other expenses.

6. The board shall each year appoint three judges, to whom the dissertations shall be submitted, through the Secretary of Faculties, and by whom the prize shall be awarded, provided that the board may at its discretion appoint two judges in a year in which there is only one candidate.

7. The prize shall not be awarded twice to the same person. A previously unsuccessful competitor may resubmit his or her dissertation or an amended version of it, on not more than two occasions, subject to the provisions of clause 4 above and provided always that he or she shall do so only within the same field as that within which it was originally submitted.

8. If no award is made in any year because there has been no candidate of sufficient merit or for any other cause, the sums which accrue to the fund during that year, after the payment of any expenses, shall be used by the board for some other purpose consistent with the object of the prize as stated in clause 1 above.

9. Council, with the approval of the board, shall have the power to amend this decree from time to time, provided always that the object of the prize as stated in clause 1 above is observed.

§ 52. *Continuing Education, Department for*

The Lecturers' and Officials' Benefit Fund

1. The Lecturers' and Officials' Benefit Fund shall be vested in the Chancellor, Masters, and Scholars of the University.

2. The administration of the fund shall be entrusted to the Continuing Education Board.

3. The Continuing Education Board shall have power to spend the income of the fund for the purposes hereinafter described, and may, subject to the approval of the department, in a particular case where it appears to them desirable and equitable spend up to one-fifth of the capital for the time being.

4. Persons entitled to benefit shall be:

(*a*) administrative officers and university lecturers[1] who are, or who have been, in the full-time service of the department;

(*b*) part-time lecturers and tutors who, over a period of several years, have undertaken a substantial volume of work for the department;

(*c*) the dependants of deceased persons falling into categories (*a*) and (*b*).

5. Grants or loans, which may be free of interest, may be made:

(*a*) of an eleemosynary nature in cases of need;

(*b*) towards expenses in connection with study, research, publication, or travel;

(*c*) exceptionally, towards the cost of purchasing a house or other approved purpose.

6. Income not required in any year for expenditure under clause 5 above shall be carried forward for expenditure in subsequent years.

Sanderson Bequest

The income from the residue of the estate of the late Lord Sanderson, M.A., Hertford College, which was bequeathed by him to be held 'upon trust to invest the same and to apply the income derived therefrom for the benefit of the Delegacy for Extra-mural Studies to promote the higher education of adult working men and women and, in the event of the said delegacy ceasing to exist, to apply the said income given hereby for the higher education of working men and women', shall be applied to this purpose by the Department for Continuing Education.

§ **53.** *Conway Fund*

1. The University accepts with gratitude a gift from Mrs. Lucinda Stevens, and such further sums as shall from time to time be contributed for the same purpose, to establish a fund, to be known as the Joan Conway Fund in commemoration of the late Mrs. Joan Conway, which shall be used to advance the study of music within the University by supporting performance-related studies.

2. The fund shall be administered by a board of management consisting of:

(1) the Heather Professor of Music;

(2) Mrs. Lucinda Stevens during her lifetime;

(3), (4) two members of the Board of the Faculty of Music appointed by that board.

3. The board of management shall apply the income of the fund for any or all of the following purposes:

[1] The provisions of this clause as they were before 12 October 1990 shall continue to apply to former staff tutors who have been in the full-time service of the department.

(*a*) the award of one or more grants to undergraduate or postgraduate members of the University to enable them to undertake specialised tuition in performance, which grants may include provision for travel and other incidental costs;

(*b*) the provision of lectures and the support of research in performance-related topics;

(*c*) the provision of master classes;

(*d*) the promotion of instrumental studies in the Faculty of Music.

4. Any income not expended in any year shall be carried forward for expenditure in subsequent years.

5. Council shall have power to amend this decree from time to time, subject to the prior approval of Mrs. Stevens in her lifetime, provided that the main object of the fund, as defined in clause 1 above, is always kept in view.

§ 54. *Cooper Fund*

1. The University accepts with gratitude the residuary estate of the late Reginald Fabian Cooper, to be known as the Cooper Fund, for the furtherance of the study of Philosophy within the University.

2. The fund shall be administered by a board of management consisting of:

(1) the Waynflete Professor of Metaphysical Philosophy, or a deputy appointed by him:

(2) the Wykeham Professor of Logic, or a deputy appointed by him; and

(3) the White's Professor of Moral Philosophy, or a deputy appointed by him.

3. The fund may be used:

(*a*) to assist the University's graduate students of Philosophy to pursue their study or research by the award of grants for purposes connected with such study or research, and

(*b*) in such other way or ways as the board of management may from time to time decide, with the approval of Council, for the furtherance of the study of Philosophy within the University.

§ 55. *Corcoran Memorial Fund*

1. The University accepts from the Trustee of the University of Oxford Development Trust Fund the sum of £15,000, being a benefaction from Mr. J.K. Corcoran, and any further sums which may be donated for the same purpose, to establish a fund in memory of Mr. S. Corcoran, Wadham. The net income from the fund shall be applied to provide a prize or prizes, each to be known as a Corcoran Memorial Prize, for award to graduate students of the University in Statistics, and also the annual Corcoran Memorial Lecture (or Lectures) in Statistics.

2. The fund shall be administered by the Board of the Faculty of Mathematical Sciences, which shall appoint a committee to determine the value of the prize

or prizes, appoint judges, and appoint the lecturer or lecturers (who may be the prizewinner or prizewinners). This committee, which shall meet each Michaelmas Term, shall comprise the Professor of Applied Statistics and the Professor of Statistical Science *ex officio* and two other members elected by the board for periods of five years. The elected members shall be re-eligible.

3. One or more prizes of equal value, consisting of a bronze medal and a sum of money, shall be awarded every two years to members of the University provided that there are candidates of sufficient merit.

4. Each prize shall be awarded for outstanding work, as determined by the committee, in the form of a dissertation or thesis, deposited in the Bodleian Library or another library within the University, or in the form of a publication, provided always that the dissertation, thesis, or publication shall have been deposited or published within the twelve terms preceding the date of the award.

5. A prize shall not be awarded on more than one occasion to the same person.

6. The lecturer or lecturers shall be appointed annually by the committee, which shall determine the fee, if any, to be paid from the fund to each lecturer.

7. If in any year a prize is not awarded or there is unexpended income from the fund for any other reason, the surplus income shall be carried forward for expenditure in subsequent years.

8. Council shall have power to alter this decree from time to time, provided that in any change of decree the object of the fund, as stated in clause 1 above, shall always be kept in view.

§ 56. *Cornish Bequest*

1. The Vaughan Cornish Bequest (accepted in accordance with the terms of the will 'as an endowment to be known as "The Vaughan Cornish Bequest" of which the income shall be devoted to the encouragement and assistance of postgraduate students of the University engaged in the advancement of knowledge relating to the beauty of scenery as determined by nature or the arts in town or country at home or abroad'): shall be under the control of a Board of Management composed as follows:

(1) the Vice-Chancellor;

(2)–(4) three persons appointed by the General Board;

(5) one person appointed by Council.

The board may co-opt additional members in such numbers and for such periods not exceeding three years as it may think fit.

2. The elected members of the board shall hold office for three years and shall be re-eligible. When an elected member vacates his or her place otherwise than by lapse of time, the body which elected him or her shall elect another person for the unexpired residue of his or her period of office.

3. The board shall apply the income of the bequest in such ways as it may think fit for the assistance (whether by the making of grants or in such other ways as seem to the board to suit the circumstances of a particular case) of members of

the University engaged on any field of study covered by the terms of the will who have been admitted as students for the Degree of M.Litt., B.Phil., M.Phil., M.Sc., or D.Phil., or having proceeded to a degree in the University, can satisfy the board that they have an appropriate plan of work.

4. If in any financial year the whole income of the fund is not spent, the surplus shall, at the discretion of the board, be either added to the capital of the endowment fund or else carried forward for expenditure in subsequent years.

5. Council shall have the power to amend this decree from time to time, provided always that the main object of the bequest as set out in the will is observed.

§ **57.** *Coulson Memorial Fund*

1. The sums contributed by friends and colleagues in memory of Charles A. Coulson, F.R.S., Professor of Theoretical Chemistry 1972–4, Rouse Ball Professor of Mathematics 1952–72, and Fellow of Wadham College, shall form a fund to be called the Charles Coulson Memorial Fund.

2. The fund shall be managed by the Board of the Faculty of Physical Sciences, which shall appoint to exercise its functions under this degree, subject to report in cases of difficulty, a committee consisting of:

(1) the Chairman of the Board or a deputy appointed by him;

(2) the Head or Acting Head of the Sub-department of Physical and Theoretical Chemistry;

(3) a member of the Sub-faculty of Chemistry;

(4) a member of the Sub-faculty of Physics.

The members of the Sub-faculties of Chemistry and Physics shall serve for a period to be determined by the board.

3. The income of the fund shall be used to further study and research in theoretical chemistry and related subjects, preference being given to the provision of assistance to scholars from abroad who wish to come to Oxford for short periods in connection with their work. Residual income from the fund may be applied for the purpose of making grants to members of the University seeking funds to attend conferences or visit other universities or for such other purposes consistent with the main object of the fund as the Board of the Faculty of Physical Sciences may consider appropriate.

4. Income not expended in any year shall be carried forward for expenditure in a subsequent year.

5. Council shall have power to alter this decree, provided that in any change of decree the object of the fund shall always be kept in view, namely, the furtherance of study and research in theoretical chemistry and related subjects as a memorial to Charles Coulson.

§ 58. *Creweian Benefactions*

See *Estates Register*, 1972, p. 61.

§ 59. *Crown Benefactions*

See *Estates Register*, 1972, p. 60.

§ 61. *Crowther Memorial Prize*

1. The University accepts with gratitude the sum of £2,000, and any further sums which may be contributed for the purpose, to establish a prize in Human Sciences to commemorate the work of Mrs. Wilma Crowther, Fellow of Lady Margaret Hall and University Lecturer (C.U.F.) in Zoology.

2. The Standing Committee for Human Sciences shall be the board of management for the prize and shall determine the value of the prize from time to time.

3. The prize shall be awarded annually, provided that there is a candidate of sufficient merit, for performance in the Final Honour School of Human Sciences on such terms as the standing committee shall from time to time determine.

4. Any surplus income arising from the non-award of a prize, or from any other cause, shall at the discretion of the standing committee either be carried forward for expenditure in a subsequent year or be applied in awarding one or more further prizes of such value as the standing committee shall determine.

5. Council shall have power to amend this decree from time to time provided that the main object of the benefaction, as set out in clause 1 above, is always kept in view.

§ 62. *Crystallography Fund*

1. The Crystallography Fund has been established to foster the study of crystallography in the University.

2. The board of management of the fund shall be the Board of the Faculty of Physical Sciences, which shall have power to appoint a committee to act on its behalf in the expenditure of the income of the fund, subject to report to the faculty board once a year and in cases of difficulty.

3. The fund shall be used:

(i) to facilitate visits to the University by research workers in the field of crystallography from member countries of the European Crystallographic Committee;

(ii) for other purposes consistent with the promotion of the study of crystallography.

4. Income not expended in any year shall be carried forward for expenditure in a subsequent year.

5. Council shall have power to amend this decree provided that the main object of the fund, as set out in clause 1 above, shall always be kept in view.

§ **63.** *Cunliffe Sculpture Prize*

1. The University accepts with gratitude the bequest of Mr. Joseph Solomon, and any further sums which may be contributed for the same purpose, to establish a fund, to be known as the Mitzi Cunliffe Sculpture Prize Fund, which shall be applied to the provision of travel grants for undergraduates reading Fine Art in the University. The capital as well as income of the fund may be expended.

2. The Committee for the Ruskin School of Drawing and Fine Art shall be the board of management for the fund and shall determine the size of the grants from time to time.

3. The grants shall be awarded annually to one or more persons at the discretion of the board of management. Priority shall be given to second-year Bachelor of Fine Art students specializing in sculpture.

4. Council shall have power to amend this decree from time to time, provided that the main object of the fund, as stated in clause 1 above, is always kept in view.

§ **64.** *Curzon Memorial Prize: Founded to commemorate Lord Curzon's Viceroyalty of India and his Chancellorship of the University*

1. The prize shall be called the 'Curzon Memorial Prize' and shall be offered every third year in Hilary Term for an English Essay on some aspect of Indian life or history.

2. A second prize may be offered from time to time at the discretion of the board of management which shall, when a second prize is offered, determine the relative value of the awards.

3. The value of the prize, or prizes, shall be the income of the fund after the remuneration of judges and other necessary expenses of the trust have been discharged.

4. The prize shall be open to all members of the University, whether men or women, who on the day appointed for sending in the essays shall be of not more than fifteen terms' standing.

5. The prize shall be managed by the Board of Management for the Frere Exhibition in Indian Studies. It shall be the duty of the board to determine the subject of the essays, to give notice thereof in the *University Gazette*, to appoint judges, and to determine their remuneration.

6. The prize shall not be awarded a second time to the same person.

7. In the event of the prize not being awarded in any particular year an award shall be made in the next following year if a candidate of sufficient merit presents himself or herself in that year; but the next regular triennial award shall not be postponed by reason of any such special award.

8. In case no award is made in any year in consequence of there being no candidate of sufficient merit or in case of any vacancy arising from any other

cause, the sums which accrue during the vacancy shall be either added to the capital of the fund or used for some other purpose consistent with the object of the trust, as the board of management shall determine.

9. This decree may be altered from time to time by Council provided that the main object of the prize shall always be kept in view.

§ 71. *Davies Bequest*

The University accepts with gratitude the legacy of £100 bequeathed by the late William Twiston Davies for the general purposes of the University.

§ 72. *Davis Prize*

1. The prize shall be called the 'H.W.C. Davis Prize' and shall be awarded either for the purchase of books or for foreign travel or for both.

2. It shall be awarded annually by the Honour Moderators in Modern History for the best performance in Honour Moderations in that subject.

3. Candidates must not, at the time of the examination, have exceeded three terms from their matriculation and must not be Senior Students.

4. The value of the prize shall be fixed at the discretion of the Board of the Faculty of Modern History after allowing for the expenses of management.

5. The holder of the award shall be required to send to the Board of the Faculty of Modern History through the Secretary of Faculties a list of the books purchased and places visited.

6. The board may dispose of surplus income either by making grants to one or more candidates on the recommendation of the examiners for meritorious work in the examination, or by awarding additional prizes.

7. Council may from time to time by decree amend, suspend, or dispense from this decree, provided that the main object of the founders be kept in view, namely, the encouragement of the study of history among younger members of the University.

§ 73. *Davis Scholarships in Chinese*

1. There shall be scholarships to encourage the study of Chinese language and literature, which shall be called the Davis Scholarships in Chinese in memory of the Founder, Sir John Francis Davis, Baronet, K.C.B., F.R.S., D.C.L. The Board of the Faculty of Oriental Studies shall be the board of management of the scholarships.

2. The annual value of the scholarships shall be determined by the board from time to time.

3. Up to four scholarships shall be awarded each year to candidates offering Chinese in the Honour School of Oriental Studies. The scholarships shall be awarded in the term prior to the candidates' compulsory study abroad. The

criteria by which the scholarships are awarded shall be determined by the board from time to time.

4. Any surplus income arising from the non-award of the scholarships, or form any other cause, shall at the discretion of the board either be carried forward for expenditure in a subsequent year or be applied in making grants for other purposes connected with the advancement of Chinese studies in the University.

§ 74. *Davy Research Scholarship*

1. The annual income of a bequest by the late J. Burtt Davy, M.A., D.Phil., University College (for the foundation of a scholarship, to be called the Burtt Davy Research Scholarship, for research in 'Taxonomic Botany and/or Tropical Plant Ecology preferably in connection with Tropical Forestry at the Herbaria of the Department of Botany and of the Imperial Forestry Institute, University of Oxford') after payment of any necessary expenses shall be devoted to the maintenance of a Burtt Davy Research Scholarship, to be awarded from time to time to graduates of the University of Oxford who undertake to carry out research into Taxonomy and Ecology or into the use of biochemical, microscopical, genetical, or such other methods for the classification of plants as may be approved by the Sherardian Professor of Botany and the Director of the Forestry Institute (hereinafter called 'the awarders'), provided that such part of the value of the scholarship as the awarders shall determine may be paid by way of reimbursement of travel, exploration, and other expenses incidental to the scholar's research.

2. The scholarship shall be placed under the general supervision of the Board of the Faculty of Biological Sciences.

3. Scholars shall be selected jointly by the awarders, who shall determine the value and tenure of the scholarship (provided that the tenure of any one holder shall not in any case exceed three years) and any other conditions of award not inconsistent with this decree.

4. The awarders shall on the occasion of each award report to the said faculty board the name of the scholar, the value and tenure of the scholarship, and the subject of his or her research.

5. Surplus income arising from whatever cause may at the discretion of the faculty board either be carried forward for expenditure in future years, or added to the capital of the fund.

6. Council shall have power to alter this decree provided that the main object of the testator shall always be kept in view.

§ 75. *de Osma Studentship*

1. The annual income of the fund presented to the University by Señor Don Guillermo Joaquin de Osma, after discharging the necessary expenses of administration, shall be paid to a member of the University desirous of studying

in Madrid in connection with the Instituto de Valencia de Don Juan, who shall be called the de Osma Student.

2. The de Osma Student shall be appointed by the Vice-Chancellor in Michaelmas Term, and shall hold the studentship till 31 October in the following year. The same person may be appointed student for a second and third year.

3. The student shall undertake to study in connection with the Instituto de Valencia de Don Juan in any subject for which facilities are provided there, for the space of not less than six weeks. The income of the fund shall be paid to the student at such dates and in such manner as the Vice-Chancellor may from time to time determine.

4. Any surplus income shall either be applied to such extent as the Vice-Chancellor may determine in augmentation of the emoluments of the student or shall be invested by the Curators of the University Chest in augmentation of the capital of the fund.

§ 76. *De Paravicini Prizes*

1. There shall be two De Paravicini Prizes each of which shall consist of one-half of one year's income of the endowment.

2. The prizes shall be awarded, provided that suitable candidates present themselves, by the Moderators for Honour Moderations in Greek and Latin Languages and Literature, and Latin Literature with Greek, for performance in such Latin papers in those examinations as shall be prescribed from time to time by the Board of the Faculty of Literae Humaniores.

3. No person who has been awarded the Hertford Prize shall be awarded a De Paravicini Prize.

4. Any income accruing in years when one or both prizes are not awarded may be applied by the Board of the Faculty of Literae Humaniores in any way that it thinks conducive to the study of the Latin Language and Literature.

5. It shall be lawful for Council from time to time to alter this decree, provided always that the object of the foundation namely to found an award in memory of Baron Francis de Paravicini, formerly Fellow and Tutor of Balliol College, with a view to the encouragement of the study of the Latin Language and Literature be kept in view.

§ 77. *Derome Memorial Fund*

1. The University accepts with gratitude the initial endowment, and such further sums as shall be contributed for the same purpose, to establish a fund, to be known as the Andy Derome Memorial Fund, the net income of which shall be applied to promote wider interest within the University in current scientific research.

2. The first charge on the net income shall be the provision from time to time of series of lectures or seminars, to be called the Andy Derome Memorial Lectures (or Seminars, as the case may be), by members of the international

scientific community actively engaged in research. Each series of lectures or seminars shall be given by a person or persons chosen by the Waynflete Professor of Chemistry under such arrangements as shall be approved from time to time by Council. In the selection of the person or persons who will give each series, preference shall be given to those who have spent in aggregate not more than twenty-four years in full-time teaching or research since passing the examinations required for a first degree or comparable qualification.

3. If in any year the moneys available are inadequate to cover the cost of a series of lectures or seminars in accordance with clause 2 above, the net income of the fund in that year shall be carried forward for expenditure on the next series to be given. Surplus moneys in any year in which a series has been given may be applied, within the limitations prescribed by clause 1 above, for such other purpose or purposes as the Waynflete Professor of Chemistry, in accordance with such arrangements as shall be approved from time to time by Council, shall determine.

4. Council shall have power to alter this decree from time to time, provided that the main object of the fund, as defined in clause 1 above, is always kept in view.

§ 78. *de Sola Wright Memorial Fund*

1. The University accepts with gratitude the sum of £5,000 from Francisco de Sola, and any further donations made by him or others for this purpose, to establish a fund, as a permanent memorial to Carlos de Sola Wright, formerly of St. Antony's College, for the furtherance of study or research within the University considered likely to promote the advancement or welfare of the people of Central America.

2. The fund shall be administered by a board of management, consisting of up to six persons, to be appointed by Council for such periods as it shall think fit.

3. The board of management shall apply the income of the fund, after the payment of all proper expenses, towards the provision of grants to be awarded from time to time to members of the University who are in need of financial assistance for the pursuit of postgraduate study or research for a degree of the University, provided that such study or research shall be considered by the board, in its absolute discretion, to be likely to further the advancement or welfare of the people of Central America, with priority for study or research concerning El Salvador.

4. Council shall have power to alter this decree at any time, provided the main object of the fund (namely, to commemorate the life of Carlos de Sola Wright by the furtherance of study or research within the University considered likely to promote the advancement or welfare of the people of Central America) is always maintained.

§ **79.** *Derby Scholarships*

1. The Derby Scholarships shall be open to all members of the University of Oxford who have not exceeded the twenty-first term from their matriculation. They shall be tenable for two years and shall be of the annual value of £100 (provided that the Craven Committee shall have the power, where it thinks fit, to make a supplementary award to any scholar who fails to obtain, or is ineligible for, a state studentship). In any particular case the trustees of the Derby Scholarship Fund, after consideration of a report from the Craven Committee for the time being, may also agree to refund expenses incurred, in their opinion, in the reasonable discharge of the obligations imposed on him or her by clause 3 below, in so far as such expenses cannot be met from another source.

2. One or more scholars shall be elected annually without examination, provided that candidates of sufficient merit present themselves, by the trustees of the Derby Scholarship Fund after consideration of a report from the Craven Committee for the time being, provided that an interval of not less than two complete terms shall elapse between any such election and the next. The Craven Committee shall issue notices respecting the Derby Scholarships in the same manner as the usual notices respecting the Craven Fellowships, and candidates shall send in their names and testimonials and other papers to the Craven Committee in accordance therewith.

3. A Derby Scholar shall be required to undertake a course of research or higher study in some subject connected with classical antiquity, which he or she must submit to the Craven Committee when offering himself or herself as a candidate, and which must be approved by that committee; he or she shall be required also to spend at least six months out of the twenty-six months immediately following his or her election in residence abroad, for the purpose of such approved course of research or higher study, at a place or places sanctioned by that committee, unless the committee think fit to grant the candidate total or partial dispensation from the requirement of residence abroad. He or she shall further satisfy the committee of diligence in the prosecution of his or her studies, and emoluments shall be paid to him or her at their discretion and in such instalments as they think fit.

4. In the election of Derby Scholars, preference shall be given to a candidate who offers a subject connected with the languages and literatures of ancient Greece and Rome (including palaeography and comparative philology) or with one of these, provided he or she be of sufficient merit.

5. Any surplus of the annual income of the fund which may remain over after the scholars have been paid and the necessary expenses of the trust have been defrayed shall remain at the disposal of the trustees, who may, provided a report of all grants made is published in the *University Gazette*, make grants out of it for any purpose connected with the advancement of classical learning. Without prejudice to the powers conferred upon the trustees by this clause, applications for such grants may be made through the Craven Committee, who shall report the same to the trustees together with their observations thereon.

6. The said trustees shall be
(1) the Lord Lieutenant of Lancashire;
(2) the Earl of Derby;
(3) the Chancellor;
(4) the Vice-Chancellor;
(5) the Dean of Christ Church.

§ 80. *Dolabani Fund for Syriac Studies*

1. The University accepts with gratitude from the Trustee of the Campaign for Oxford Trust Fund the initial endowment, made possible by an anonymous payment to the Trustee, and all further sums contributed for the same purpose, to establish a fund, to be called the Dolabani Fund for Syriac Studies, the income from which shall be used for the furtherance of Syriac Studies within the University, and which endowment will help to support students from the Syriac churches in studying their own tradition in working for a formal qualification of the University.

2. The fund shall be administered by a board of management consisting of two persons appointed by the Board of the Faculty of Oriental Studies and one person appointed by the Board of the Faculty of Theology. The appointing bodies shall determine the periods of office of their respective appointees. The board shall have power to co-opt up to two additional members. Any co-opted member shall serve for two years and may be reappointed. The board shall elect its own chairman.

3. The board of management shall apply the income of the fund:

(*a*) in the provision of financial support to graduate students of the University from or originating from the Middle East or the region of the Indian State of Kerala, to assist them in meeting the cost of engaging in courses involving Syriac Studies in the University;

(*b*) in the provision of grants, in such amounts as the board shall from time to time determine, for the purchase of Syriac manuscripts for the Bodleian Library and for the purchase of books in or concerning Syriac for the Bodleian Library and the Oriental Institute Library

4. Any income not required for expenditure under clause 3 hereof may be applied for the furtherance of Syriac Studies within the University in such other ways as the board shall consider appropriate.

5. Council shall have power to alter this decree from time to time, provided that the main object of the fund, namely the furtherance of Syriac Studies within the University, shall always be kept in view.

§ 81. *Dooley Prize in Anatomy*

1. The University accepts with gratitude the sum of £500 donated by Mr. D. Dooley, F.R.C.S., the income from which shall be used to provide for a prize in Clinical Anatomy.

2. The prize, consisting of medical or surgical books or instruments, shall be offered annually for award to one of the trainee demonstrators in the Department of Human Anatomy and Genetics who has passed the Primary Examination for the Fellowship of the Royal College of Surgeons, and whose prosecutions and general performance are judged to be best by the departmental committee of the Department of Human Anatomy and Genetics.

3. If in any year the prize is not awarded, the income of the fund shall be carried forward for use in whole or in part to augment the value of the prize on subsequent occasions at the discretion of the awarders.

4. The prize shall be placed under the general supervision of the Board of the Faculty of Physiological Sciences.

5. Council shall have power to alter this decree from time to time, provided that the main object of the fund, namely the establishment of a prize in Clinical Anatomy, is kept in view.

§ **82.** *Douglas Memorial Prize*

1. The University accepts with gratitude the sum of £25,000 from Mrs. Sheila Colman, and any further sums contributed for the same purpose, to establish a prize to be known as the Lord Alfred Douglas Memorial Prize.

2. The board of management for the prize shall be the Board of the Faculty of English Language and Literature, which shall determine the value of the prize from time to time and shall make regulations for its award.

3. There shall be three judges for the prize, who shall be members of Congregation and shall be appointed by the Board of the Faculty of English Language and Literature. They shall receive such remuneration as the board shall determine from time to time.

4. The prize shall be open to any member of the University who is registered for a degree of the University (whether being an undergraduate or a graduate student).

5. The prize shall be awarded, provided that there is an entry of sufficient merit, for the best sonnet or other poem written in English and in strict rhyming metre.

6. Income not expended in any year shall be carried forward for expenditure in subsequent years.

7. A copy of the winning entry shall be deposited in the Bodleian Library.

8. The prize shall not be awarded more than once to the same person.

9. Council shall have power to amend this decree from time to time, provided that the purposes of the fund, as defined in cll. 1, 4, and 5 above, shall always be kept in view.

§ 83. *Drake Fund for Italian Studies*

1. The University accepts with gratitude the sum of £1,500 from Christina Roaf (née Drake), M.A., D.Phil., Fellow of Somerville College, to establish a fund, to be known as the 'Christina Drake Fund for Italian Studies', and the further sums which she has agreed to contribute to the fund. The net income of the fund shall be applied to the making of grants to students working for a research degree or diploma of the University of Oxford in the field of Italian Studies (with a preference for students of language and literature) to assist them in connection with visits to Italy for purposes of their study or research, in the hope that the cultural benefits they derive from such a visit may thereby be enhanced.

2. The Board of the Faculty of Medieval and Modern Languages shall be the board of management of the fund and shall appoint a committee of three members to award the grants, one of whom shall be the Fiat-Serena Professor of Italian Studies (or, during a vacancy in the professorship, another person appointed by the board) and the other members, not necessarily members of the Faculty of Medieval and Modern Languages, shall be elected by the board to hold office for three years and shall be re-eligible.

3. Any unexpended income may be

(i) applied towards such other purpose or purposes conducive to the promotion or encouragement of Italian Studies (with a preference for language and literature) within the University as the board shall from time to time determine; or

(ii) carried forward for application in future years either towards the provision of grants under cl. 1 above or for any purpose falling within (i) above.

4. Council shall have power to alter this decree from time to time, provided that the main object of the fund, namely the promotion or encouragement of Italian Studies (with a preference for language and literature) within the University is kept in view.

§ 84. *Druce Bequest*

[1]

Decree (20) of Congregation of 15 June 1937

That the University gratefully accepts the bequest of the late George Claridge Druce, M.A., D.Sc., Magdalen College, of certain property and moneys for the purpose of housing and maintaining the Herbarium and Library, now situate at 9 Crick Road, Oxford, together with a bequest of £1,000 for the benefit of the Bodleian Library, and authorizes application to the Chancery Division of the High Court for a Scheme for the administration of the said bequests.

[2]

The following is an Extract from an Order of the High Court of Justice, Chancery Division, made 11 July 1938, in the matter of the Estate of George Claridge Druce, deceased:

7. The University shall from time to time appoint and may dismiss a curator who shall be known as the Claridge Druce Curator to care for and superintend the said [Druce] Herbaria and Library and such curator shall be appointed for such period and upon such terms and conditions as to stipend and otherwise as the University shall from time to time think fit. The University may also from time to time appoint an assistant curator and such other assistants and attendants as the University may from time to time think requisite for the proper care and maintenance of the said Herbaria and Library upon such terms and conditions as to stipend or wages or otherwise as the University may from time to time think fit and the University may dismiss any such assistant curator or other assistant or attendant.

8. The residue of the trust fund after raising and paying thereout the sums referred to in clause 4 hereof together with any interest or income already accrued thereon up to the date of this Scheme shall be invested in the name of the University as and when the same shall be received by the University in any manner authorized by law for the investment of trust funds with power for the University from time to time to vary or transpose any such investments for or into others of a like nature and the investments for the time being representing the same are hereinafter called 'the Invested Fund'.

9. The University shall apply the annual income of the Invested Fund in or towards making the following payments and in the following order:

(1) in payment of all proper costs charges and expenses of the University of and incidental to the administration and management of the charity (including . . . the stipends or wages of any assistant curator or other assistants or attendants and the University's share of any contributions payable to the superannuation fund of the University on their account respectively);

(2) in payment of the stipend of the Claridge Druce Curator and of the University's share of contributions payable to the superannuation fund of the University on his account;

(3) in payment of the cost of further acquisitions for or the preservation or maintenance of or repairs to any of the contents of the said Herbaria and Library or of the cost of the preservation or maintenance of or repairs to . . . the existing buildings of the Department of Botany aforesaid when so reconstructed and enlarged as aforesaid;

(4) otherwise for the encouragement and promotion of the study of and research in systematic or taxonomic botany in the University as the University may think fit.

10. Any income not so applied shall be invested as aforesaid in the name of the University and added to the capital of the Invested Fund.

11. If at any time or times the capital of the Invested Fund shall be more than sufficient to provide by the income thereof for all the payments to be made thereout and specified in subclauses (1) (2) and (3) of clause 9 hereof then and in such case the University may in its discretion from time to time apply the excess of the capital of the Invested Fund or any part thereof in such manner for the encouragement and promotion of the study of and research in systematic or taxonomic botany in the University as the University may think fit.

[3]

1. The Board of the Faculty of Biological Sciences shall be the board of management of the Druce Bequest.

2. The board shall appoint a committee consisting of:

(1) the Sherardian Professor of Botany;

(2) the Claridge Druce Curator;

(3)–(5) three other members elected by it (who need not necessarily be members of the board); to be responsible, on behalf of the University, for expending the income arising from the Druce Bequest in accordance with clause 9 of the scheme for the administration of the bequest.

3. The elected members shall hold office for three years and shall be re-eligible.

4. The committee shall report on its activities to the board at least once in each year.

§ **85.** *Duff Memorial Fund*

1. The University gratefully accepts the sums contributed in memory of the late Dr. Colin Duff, and any further sums which may be contributed for the same purpose, to establish a fund, which shall be known as the Colin Duff Memorial Fund, and both the income and capital of which may be applied for the furtherance within the University of forestry and environmental studies with particular reference to the African environment.

2. The fund shall be administered by the Board of Management for the Trapnell Fund for Environmental Field Research in Africa.

3. The fund shall be used for book grants to graduates of African universities who are nationals of sub-Saharan Africa, who have been accepted as members of the University of Oxford to engage in advanced study or research for the Degree of Master of Science or Doctor of Philosophy, or for another course of study approved for this purpose by the board of management, and who are engaged in advanced study or research in forestry.

4. The books which are purchased with such grants shall be made available to the student concerned for use on course and in the expectation that they will thereafter be deposited in the library of his or her own university or employing institute.

5. Any income not required for the award of grants in any year shall be either carried forward for expenditure in subsequent years or applied by the board of

management in such other way as shall seem to the board best to conduce to the support of the objects of the fund.

6. Council shall have power to alter this decree from time to time provided that the main object of the fund as expressed in clause 1 above is always kept in view.

§ 86. *Dunston Memorial Fund*

1. The University accepts with gratitude the late Miss E.F.I. Dunston's bequests in memory of her grandfather, her father, and her three brothers, for the furtherance within the University of the study of Mycology.

2. The fund established by the bequests shall be administered by the Board of the Faculty of Biological Sciences.

3. Council shall have power to alter this decree from time to time, provided that the main purpose of the fund as defined in clause 1 above is maintained.

§ 87. *Dyson Perrins Fund*

1. Of the whole sum of £25,000 an amount not exceeding £5,000 shall be held in reserve by the Curators of the University Chest, to be spent under the supervision of the Waynflete Professor of Chemistry upon the equipment of the new laboratory or to be drawn upon by the professor for similar purposes.

2. The remainder of the sum shall be invested in the corporate name of the University as a fund to be called 'The Dyson Perrins Fund', and shall be held in trust in perpetuity by the University as an endowment.

3. The income of the said Dyson Perrins Fund shall be applicable under the supervision of the Waynflete Professor of Chemistry, so long as Organic Chemistry shall form the main subject of his or her chair, or if that shall cease to be the case, then of the professor to whom that subject shall be assigned, for the current expenses of his or her laboratory and for the carrying on therein of research and instruction in Organic Chemistry.

4. Any portion of the income in any one year which shall not have been spent within the year shall be carried to the credit of a Reserve Fund, which shall from time to time be invested, so that either the capital or income of this fund shall be available by decree for expenditure upon the same objects as the income of the original fund.

5. Council shall have full power to alter this decree from time to time, provided always that the Dyson Perrins Fund and its title shall be preserved, and that the main object of the foundation, namely the furtherance of the study of Chemistry and the promotion of Chemical Research in the University, shall be kept in view.

§ 91. *Economics of Developing Countries, Travel Fund for*

The Board of the Faculty of Social Studies may make grants to the holders of any of the established academic posts in the Sub-faculty of Economics, to enable them to travel for purposes of the study of the economics of developing countries (broadly conceived), from the moneys earmarked for such purposes in the Higher Studies Fund.[1]

§ 92. *Elliott Memorial Fund*

1. The University accepts with gratitude the sum of approximately £4,300, and any further sums which may be contributed for this purpose, to establish a fund, to be called the Jimmy Elliott Memorial Fund, to assist students or young research workers within the University of Oxford to attend conferences or broaden their professional experience, with consequent benefit to British agriculture.

2. The fund shall be administered by the committee appointed to administer the Mike Soper Bursary Fund, save that the committee shall have power to co-opt one additional member (who need not be a member of the Faculty of Biological Sciences) for the purpose of assisting in the administration of the fund.

3. Council shall have power to alter this decree at any time, provided that the main object of the fund as defined in cl. 1 above is always maintained.

§ 93. *English Library: Raleigh Memorial Fund*

The sum of £400 accepted by the University from the Committee of the Walter Raleigh Memorial Fund on condition that the interest on this sum be paid annually to the Library of the English School shall be expended by the Board of the Faculty of English Language and Literature upon such books as the board may think suitable.

§ 94. *Entomology (Hope Department of): Longstaff Endowment*
Decree approved by Convocation on 26 October 1909

See *Statuta*, 1914, pp. 516–17.

§ 95. *Esson Bequest*

The bequest of the late William Esson, Savilian Professor of Geometry 1897–1916, of half the income of a trust fund created out of the residue of his estate shall be used for the benefit of the University in such a way as Council shall see fit.

§ 96. *European Studies Fund (the Europaeum)*

1. The University accepts with gratitude the initial donations, and all further contributions received for the same purpose, to establish a fund, to be called the European Studies Fund, for the advancement of education through the encouragement of (i) European Studies in the University and, in connection

[1] Authority for the expenditure of these moneys was granted by the Special Resolution of Congregation of 28 January 1992.

therewith, in other European institutions of higher education having links with the University, and (ii) the movement of academic staff and students between the University and those institutions. In its inter-institutional application, the fund shall be known as the Europaeum. European Studies shall include (but without limitation) the study of national and supranational institutions, policies, and relations both within Europe and between countries in Europe and elsewhere, together with the study of the languages, history, cultures, and professions of the people of Europe.

2. The fund shall be administered by a board of management consisting of:

(1) the Chancellor, or a person appointed by the Chancellor for such period as the Chancellor shall determine;

(2)–(6) five Foundation Members, the initial appointments of whom (from among persons other than resident members of the University) shall be made by the Chancellor on the basis of roles performed in the establishment of the fund;

(7) the Vice-Chancellor, or a person appointed by the Vice-Chancellor for not longer than the duration of the current Vice-Chancellorship;

(8)–(11) four persons appointed by Council for such periods as Council shall determine, of whom not more than two shall hold an academic appointment of the University.

On the retirement, resignation, or death of a Foundation Member, the remaining Foundation Members acting jointly with the Chancellor (or, if the Chancellor is not a member of the board, the Chancellor's appointee under (1) above) shall appoint a successor.

3. Without prejudice to the generality of the purpose of the fund as defined in clause 1 above, the board shall further the purpose by applying the fund, within the limitations prescribed by clause 1, in support of provision in the University of one or more of the following:

(*a*) courses designed to enhance understanding of the European dimension in relevant academic disciplines, including Law, Modern History, Modern Languages, and Social Studies;

(*b*) post-experience courses on European affairs for non-academic professional persons, including senior civil servants, diplomats, businessmen, and journalists;

(*c*) graduate courses of relevance to persons intending to pursue a non-academic career in some part of Europe; and

(*d*) conferences on European affairs to be attended by policy-makers, businessmen, and academic specialists.

4. The board is also empowered, in connection therewith, to support the provision of similar courses and conferences at other European institutions within the limitations prescribed by clause 1.

In the provision of such support, whether in the University or elsewhere, the board may apply the fund:

(*a*) in the endowment of relevant university posts and in the funding of fixed-term university appointments;

(*b*) in the funding of scholarships and bursaries to enable (i) attendance at the graduate or undergraduate courses referred to above, or (ii) study or teaching to be undertaken either in the University by persons from other European institutions of higher education having links with the University, or elsewhere in Europe by members of the University (whether holding academic appointments or being junior members);

(*c*) in the funding of conferences; and

(*d*) in meeting, or contributing to, the cost of the provision of both (i) residential and functional accommodation and (ii) relevant library and other facilities.

5. In reaching decisions on the application of the fund, the board shall take into account:

(*a*) the priorities and requirements of the University, as communicated to them from time to time by Council;

(*b*) any representations received from time to time from other European institutions of higher education having links with the University; and

(*c*) any views expressed by donors at the time of their contributions.

6. The Chancellor shall have power to invite the Foundation Members, and such other persons as Council may from time to time recommend, to serve, for such periods as the Chancellor shall determine, on a Founders' Council for the fund. If such a council is established, its members shall be invited to meet from time to time to receive and consider periodic reports from the board on the application of the fund and on the activities, both at Oxford and elsewhere, that have thereby been sustained. It shall also be empowered to invite the University and the other educational institutions concerned to report to it on their respective developments in the furtherance of European Studies and the movement of staff and students between institutions.

§ 101. *Fiedler Memorial Fund*

1. In honour of the late Hermann George Fiedler, M.V.O., M.A., Hon. D.Litt., Taylor Professor of German and Fellow of Queen's College, and for many years a Curator of the Taylor Institution, the fund shall always be called the 'Fiedler Memorial Fund'.

2. The fund shall be administered by the Curators of the Taylor Institution, and the annual income arising from the fund shall be employed by the curators at their sole discretion towards the promotion of the advanced study of Modern European Languages and Literatures among members of the University of Oxford, and the costs of publication of the results of their researches, special consideration being given to German.

3. Subject to the consent of the Curators of the Taylor Institution, this decree may be altered from time to time by Council, provided that the main object of the foundation, namely, the promotion of the Advanced Study of Modern European Languages amongst members of the University of Oxford be kept in view.

§ **102.** *Field Studies Book Prize*

1. The University accepts with gratitude the sum of £500 donated by Dr. H.N. Southern, former Senior Research Officer in Zoology, the income from which shall be used to provide a book prize for the field study of animals.

2. The prize shall be awarded annually to the candidate who has shown the greatest aptitude for zoological field studies in the Honour School of Natural Science (Biological Sciences) and/or in independent project work, provided that his or her work is deemed to be of sufficient merit.

3. The prize shall be awarded jointly by three persons (hereinafter called 'the awarders') who shall comprise:

(1) the Head of the Department of Zoology or his or her nominee;

(2) the Director of the Edward Grey Institute of Field Ornithology or his or her nominee;

(3) a person appointed by the Board of the Faculty of Biological Sciences.

4. If in any year the prize is not awarded, the income of the fund shall be carried forward for use in whole or in part to augment the value of the prize on subsequent occasions at the discretion of the awarders.

5. The prize shall be placed under the general supervision of the Board of the Faculty of Biological Sciences.

6. Council shall have power to alter this decree from time to time, provided that the main object of the fund, namely, the establishment of a book prize for the field study of animals, is kept in view.

§ **103.** *Finch Collection and Fund*

Note. This sub-section is not a decree or regulation but draws attention to a scheme sanctioned by the Chancery Division of the High Court of Justice, 10 December 1918 (Statuta, 1949, pp. 508–10)

§ **104.** *Forestry*

Brooks Memorial Fund

The interest on the sum of £200 generously offered by Mrs. Clara Brooks in memory of her son, Clement C. Brooks (M.Sc. Manchester), formerly an Assistant Entomologist on the Staff of the Imperial Forestry Institute, shall be spent on the purchase of books on entomology or allied subjects, and of insects and other collections for the benefit of the Forestry Institute.

School of Forestry Jubilee Prize

1. The fund shall be invested by the University, and the income arising from it shall be devoted to the maintenance of a prize to be called the School of Forestry Jubilee Prize.

2. The prize shall be offered each year for award by the Board of the Faculty of Biological Sciences on the results of the examination for the Degree of Master of Science in Forestry and its Relation to Land Management.

3. The management of the prize shall be entrusted to the Board of the Faculty of Biological Sciences which shall determine on each occasion the amount of the prize to be awarded. The board shall also have power to pay expenses of management, if any.

4. Any income not expended on the annual prize may, at the discretion of the Board of the Faculty of Biological Sciences, be either accumulated to increase the sum available from time to time for the annual or additional prizes, or added to the capital of the fund.

5. Council shall have power to alter this decree, provided that the name of the prize shall be retained.

§ 105. *Foster Bequest*

1. The fund established with the bequest of the residue of the estate of the late C.A. Foster shall be known as the Cyril Foster Fund.

2. The purpose of the fund shall be the promotion of international peace and the prevention of future wars, which shall include the maintenance in the University of an annual lecture or lectures dealing with the elimination of war and the better understanding of the nations of the world.

3. The Board of the Faculty of Social Studies shall be the board of management of the fund.

4. An annual lecture or lectures on some subject relating to the elimination of war and the better understanding of the nations of the world shall be established and maintained in the University of Oxford to be called the 'Cyril Foster Lecture' or 'Cyril Foster Lectures' and the lecturer or lecturers appointed shall each be called the 'Cyril Foster Lecturer'. At least one Cyril Foster Lecturer shall be appointed in each year by the board of management and each lecturer shall receive from the income of the fund a fee to be determined by the board of management.

5. The board of management may apply the remainder of the annual income of the bequest in any or all of the following ways:

(*a*) in making grants for the assistance of any members of the University who wish to travel abroad for purposes relating to their work;

(*b*) in making grants on the recommendation of a faculty board for the purpose of enabling foreign scholars to spend a period in Oxford,

provided that in weighing the merits of applications for grants under subclauses (*a*) and (*b*) above the board shall keep in mind the purpose of the fund as stated in clause 2 above;

(*c*) in making such grants as they may deem necessary towards travelling or other incidental expenses incurred by the Cyril Foster Lecturer;

(*d*) in any other way which they shall judge conducive to the purpose of the fund.

6. Surplus income in any year may be reserved for expenditure in any future year on the purposes specified in clause 5 above.

7. Council shall have power from time to time to alter this decree provided always that the purpose of the fund, as stated in clause 2 above, shall be kept in view.

§ 106. *Foster Memorial Fund*

1. Sums contributed by his friends in memory of the late M.B. Foster, M.A., Student of Christ Church, shall form a fund (to be known as the Michael Foster Memorial Fund), the income of which shall be used, together with the annual sum generously provided by the Stifterverband für die Deutsche Wissenschaft, to award scholarships tenable at Oxford in any subject for two years by a student from the Federal Republic of Germany, selected in consultation with the German Academic Exchange Service.

2. The German Academic Exchange Service will award scholarships tenable in any subject for one or more years at any university or other institution of higher learning in the Federal Republic of Germany by a student from Oxford recommended to the German Academic Exchange Service by a selection committee consisting of the members of the Board of Management for the Michael Foster and Michael Wills Scholarships.

3. For as long as students holding scholarships under clause 2 hereof are excused university fees by universities or other institutions of higher learning in the Federal Republic of Germany no university fees shall be required from students from the Federal Republic of Germany holding Michael Foster Memorial Scholarships in Oxford.

4. The scholarships shall be administered by the Board of Management for the Michael Foster and Michael Wills Scholarships, which shall consist of up to six permanent members, and one representative of each of the colleges from time to time wishing to participate in the scheme for the reception of scholars under clause 1 above and under § 375 of this section. Invitations to colleges to participate shall be extended at the discretion of the board. College representatives shall be appointed to the board with effect from the beginning of the academic year preceding the period in which their colleges have scholars in residence, until the end of that period. Permanent members shall be elected for a period of three years and shall be re-eligible, the board appointing the first six permanent members under this decree for periods designed to ensure retirement in rotation. The board shall have the power to co-opt up to three additional members for any periods of time it shall specify, and shall have full power to do all things necessary for the administration of the scholarships and to defray its expenses out of the income of the Michael Foster Memorial Fund.

§ 107. *Foundation Trust Fund*

1. The Foundation Trust Fund shall comprise such sums of money as shall be allocated to the University by the Trustee of the Campaign for Oxford Trust Fund for expenditure on general university purposes within the charitable trusts declared in clause 3 of the Campaign for Oxford Trust Deed dated 14 April 1989. There shall be added to the fund such other sums of money as may be

allocated to it from time to time on the authority of Council after consultation with the Curators of the University Chest.

2. The Curators of the University Chest shall make arrangements, under Council, for the investment of the assets of the fund and for the submission to Council of annual accounts relating to the income of the fund, expenditure therefrom, and any capital sums held in the fund.

3. The income of the fund shall be transferred to the General Fund in the year in which it is received.

4. The Curators of the University Chest shall, on the advice of the Investment Committee, submit annually to the Resources Committee, to be taken into account in its consideration of the University's budget, estimates of the income of the fund which will be available in the coming year to augment the income of the University General Fund.

5. Up to 10 per cent of the capital of the fund may be expended. In the calculation of the sum which constitutes the capital for this purpose, income earned on sums received by the Campaign for Oxford Trust Fund prior to transfer to the Foundation Trust Fund shall be disregarded. The calculation of the amount available for expenditure shall take account of any change in the capital value of the assets in which the fund is invested.

6. Expenditure of any part of the capital, within the limit of 10 per cent set out in clause 5, shall require the authority of Council after it has considered the recommendations thereon of the Resources Committee.

§ 108. *French Memorial Fund*

1. The University accepts with gratitude from the Atherosclerosis Discussion Group the sum of approximately £1,000, to establish a fund as a memorial to the late Dr. John French, formerly Reader in Experimental Pathology, the income from which shall be used to provide a lecture to be called the John French Memorial Lecture in the field of atherosclerosis or thrombosis or related problems.

2. The fund shall be administered by a board of trustees consisting of:

(1) the Chairman of the Board of the Faculty of Physiological Sciences;

(2) the Professor of Pathology;

(3) the Chairman of the Atherosclerosis Discussion Group;

(4) a person appointed by the Board of the Faculty of Physiological Sciences;

(5) a person appointed by the Atherosclerosis Discussion Group.

The trustees shall have power at their discretion to co-opt an additional trustee.

3. The lecture shall be given at such intervals as the trustees shall determine and the lecturer, who shall be elected by the trustees, shall normally be chosen from amongst scientists working in Great Britain and under the age of thirty-five who have made a notable contribution to knowledge in the field of atherosclerosis or thrombosis. The lecture shall normally be delivered in Oxford,

though it may on occasion be delivered in some other academic centre in Great Britain. The lecturer shall receive an honorarium to be determined by the trustees on appointment, together with such expenses as the trustees shall determine.

4. Income not expended in any year shall be carried forward for expenditure in subsequent years.

5. Council shall have power to alter this decree from time to time, with the consent of the trustees, provided that the main object of the trust as defined in cl. 1 above is kept in view.

§ 109. *Frere Exhibition for Indian Studies*

1. There shall be an exhibition for the encouragement of the study of matters relating to India, which shall be called the Frere Exhibition for Indian Studies, in memory of Sir Henry Bartle Edward Frere, Bt.

2. The emoluments of the exhibition shall be the net annual income of the endowment fund after deduction of any expenses connected with the exhibition, subject to the provisions of clause 7 of this decree.

3. The exhibition shall be open to all members of the University, whether men or women, who, on the day of election, shall not have exceeded the twenty-first term from their matriculation.

4. The exhibitioner shall be elected by a board consisting of:

(1) the Boden Professor of Sanskrit,

(2) the Reader in Modern South Asian History,

(3) a person appointed by the Board of the Faculty of Modern History,

(4) a person appointed by the Board of the Faculty of Social Studies.

The elected members of the board shall hold office for five years and shall be re-eligible. The board may elect the exhibitioner, either after an examination or otherwise, as it may from time to time think fit.

5. The board shall give at least three months' notice of the time and place at which the names of candidates will be received.

6. The exhibition shall be offered once in each academic year and shall be tenable for one year. Every candidate must undertake to carry out a specified piece of work, to be approved by the board, in the field of Indian studies. The work shall be carried out at Oxford for three terms unless the board shall, in the interests of the work, give leave to the exhibitioner to carry it out elsewhere for one or more terms. The board shall authorize one of its members to report from time to time to the Secretary of Faculties whether the exhibitioner is worthy to receive his or her stipend. If the report is unfavourable, the Secretary of Faculties shall immediately inform the board of electors, which shall have power to withhold further emoluments.

7. The board shall have discretion to diminish or to augment from income previously unspent the emoluments of the exhibition, either at the time of

election or at any time during the period of tenure; to elect an additional exhibitioner in any year; and to make grants for the purpose for which the exhibition was founded, as defined in clause 1 of this decree.

8. Any income not disposed of from any cause shall be carried forward for expenditure at any future time under the board's powers as defined in clause 7 of this decree.

9. The exhibition may be awarded a second but not a third time to the same person.

10. The board shall have power to defray out of the income of the fund any expenses connected with the exhibition, including the remuneration of examiners if appointed.

11. This decree may be altered from time to time by Council, provided that the sole object of the benefaction shall always be kept in view, namely the foundation of exhibitions at the University for encouraging the study of matters relating to India.

§ 110. *Friedman Fund*

1. The University accepts with gratitude a benefaction, together with any further sums which may be contributed for this purpose, to establish a fund, to be known as the Mendel Friedman Yiddish Conference Fund, for the furtherance of Yiddish Studies.

2. The Board of the Faculty of Medieval and Modern Languages shall be the board of management of the fund.

3. The income of the fund shall be applied:

(*a*) to the organizing of conferences in Oxford on Yiddish Studies and the publication of the proceedings thereof;

(*b*) in such other manner as the board shall determine for the promotion of Yiddish Studies within the University.

4. Council shall have power to alter this decree from time to time, provided that the main object of the fund, as defined in clause 1 above, shall always be kept in view.

§ 111. *Fry Memorial Fund*

1. The University accepts with gratitude from the Trustees of the Daphne Somerset Fry Memorial Trust all moneys paid, or which hereafter may be paid, to the trust.

2. All moneys received from the trustees shall be invested and used to form a fund to be known as the Daphne Somerset Fry Memorial Fund.

3. The Regius Professor of Medicine shall make use of the income of the fund, at his or her discretion, to advance knowledge in the field of Bright's disease and cognate problems, such use to take the form, when considered desirable by the Regius Professor of Medicine, of the award of a research fellowship or

scholarship, any such awards being entitled Daphne Somerset Fry Fellowships or Scholarships, as the case may be, and being administered under regulations to be made by the Board of the Faculty of Clinical Medicine.

§ **121.** *School of Geography*

Geographical Endowment Fund

The administration of the Geographical Endowment Fund, which was established by a donation from the Clothworkers' Company accepted by Decree (1) of Convocation of 11 July 1914 and increased by subsequent donations, shall be entrusted to the Board of the Faculty of Anthropology and Geography; and the income of the fund shall be expended for the benefit of the School of Geography in such ways as the board shall from time to time determine.

Tue Bequest

The bequest of the late George Albert Tue of one-third of the residue of his estate to be used by the School of Geography for the purchase of books for its library, such books to be suitably inscribed with his name and to be used in the School of Geography, shall be administered by the Board of the Faculty of Anthropology and Geography on the recommendation of the Professor of Geography.

§ **122.** *Geology and Mineralogy*

The University accepts with gratitude an anonymous benefaction of 404,073 Swiss francs for the benefit of Geology and Mineralogy within the Department of Earth Sciences, which shall be expended in such ways as Council, after consultation with the General Board, shall determine.

§ **123.** *Gerrans Memorial Fund*

1. In honour of the late Henry Tresawna Gerrans, M.A., formerly Fellow and Vice-Provost of Worcester College, Secretary to the Delegates of Local Examinations and for many years a Curator of the Taylor Institution, the fund established with a view to perpetuate his memory and to promote the advanced study of Modern Languages amongst members of the University of Oxford shall always be called the 'Gerrans Memorial Fund'.

2. The annual income arising from the fund, and from any additions which may hereafter be made thereto, shall be paid to and administered by the Curators of the Taylor Institution for the promotion of the advanced study of Modern Languages amongst members of the University of Oxford.

3. The curators shall apply the said annual income to promote the production of research work in any subject connected with Modern Foreign Languages or Literatures which they may deem worthy of receiving financial assistance

(*a*) by contributions towards the cost of publishing such work when it is not likely to be remunerative;

(*b*) by grants of money to enable scholars to visit foreign libraries for the collection of materials which cannot be obtained in this country;

(*c*) by awards for work of value which has been already published.

4. Before making any contribution or award the curators shall have power to obtain the opinion of an expert or experts on any piece of original work submitted to them, and to pay for it out of the income of the fund.

5. At the end of every year the curators shall have power either to authorize the Curators of the University Chest to invest any surplus income in augmentation of the fund or to reserve it to be expended in a subsequent year.

§ 124. *Gilbert-Houston Publications Fund*

1. The sum of £136·28, being authors' royalties on *Urbanization and its Problems*, edited by Dr. R.P. Beckinsale and Dr. J.M. Houston and published in honour of Professor E.W. Gilbert, shall form a fund to be known as the Gilbert–Houston Publications Fund.

2. The fund shall be administered by a committee appointed by the Departmental Committee of the School of Geography, under the chairmanship of the Professor of Geography.

3. The committee of management shall apply the income and, if it thinks fit, the capital of the fund towards the maintenance and improvement of the publication of research papers in the School of Geography.

4. The Curators of the University Chest are authorized to receive additional contributions to the fund.

5. Council shall have power to alter this decree on the recommendation of the committee of management, provided that the object of the fund, namely, the promotion of the study of Geography in the University, is kept in view.

§ 125. *Gildesgame Trust*

1. The University accepts with gratitude from the Pierre and Moniusia Gildesgame Charitable Trust the sum of £45,000 to establish a fund, to be known as the Pierre and Moniusia Gildesgame Trust, for the furtherance of the study of European and Comparative Law within the University.

2. The fund shall be administered by the Board of the Faculty of Law.

3. Income from the fund may be applied for any of the following purposes:

(*a*) to finance visits to Oxford by European Scholars, such scholars to be known as Gildesgame Scholars;

(*b*) to finance visits by members of the Law Faculty to European institutions, such awards to be known as Gildesgame Travel Bursaries;

(*c*) any other purpose consistent with the main object of the fund as defined in clause 1 above.

4. Income not expended in any year shall be carried forward for expenditure in subsequent years.

5. Council shall have power to amend this decree from time to time, provided that the main object of the fund, as defined in clause 1 above, is always kept in view.

§ **126.** *Ginwala Scholarships*

1. The University accepts with gratitude from the Trustees of the Sven Leopold Bengtson Settlement the sum of approximately £90,000 to establish a fund for the maintenance of scholarships, to be known as the Hilla Ginwala Scholarships, and to be awarded from time to time to persons of Indian nationality normally resident in the Republic of India who are or who have been accepted for admission as members of the University, in order to enable them to undertake study or research at or in connection with the University, provided however that no such scholarship may be awarded to persons who were actually resident outside the Republic of India on 7 February 1992.

2. The scholarships shall support either (*a*) the study of, or research into some aspect of, one or more modern European languages and the literatures associated therewith (with a preference for French and Italian, or French, or Italian), or (*b*) attendance on a course of the University in which facility in a modern European language (other than English) is a requirement. The holders of the scholarships may either read for an honour school or work for a graduate qualification of the University.

3. The fund shall be administered by a board of management, the membership of which, and the respective periods of office of the members, shall be determined by Council.

4. The board shall apply the fund and the net income thereof in the maintenance of the scholarships, and the board shall determine the conditions of their award, and their several value and tenure. The board is empowered to provide financial support for up to one year to enable any scholarship-holder to live on the continent of Europe for the purpose of acquiring fluency in speaking one or more of the languages concerned, where this is judged by the board likely to further the purpose of the course of study or research undertaken in accordance with the provisions of clause 2 above.

5. Income not expended in any year shall be carried forward for expenditure in subsequent years.

6. Council shall have power to alter this decree from time to time, provided always that the main object of the fund as defined in clause 1 above is kept in view.

§ **127.** *Gladstone Memorial Prize*

1. The annual gift received from the Gladstone Memorial Trust shall be used for the maintenance of the Gladstone Memorial Prize. The prize shall be awarded for a thesis on some subject connected either with recent British History, Political Science, or Economics or with some problem of British policy—domestic, imperial, or foreign—in relation to finance or other matters,

submitted for examination in the Honour Schools of Modern History, Modern History and Economics, and Philosophy, Politics, and Economics.

2. The prize shall consist of cash or books of such value as the trustees shall determine.

3. There shall be three judges, of whom one shall be the chairman for the time being of the examiners in the Honour School of Modern History and Economics, one shall be appointed by the board of examiners for the time being in the Honour School of Modern History, and one shall be appointed by the board of examiners for the time being in the Honour School of Philosophy, Politics, and Economics.

4. An honorarium, the value of which shall be determined from time to time by the Board of the Faculty of Modern History with the consent of the donors, shall be paid to each of the judges out of moneys provided by the donors.

5. The prize shall not be awarded to the same person a second time.

6. This decree shall be subject to alteration from time to time, but not without the sanction of the Trustees of the Gladstone Memorial Trust for the time being.

§ 128. *Goodger Scholarships*

1. There shall be two Mary Goodger Scholarships and one Henry Goodger Scholarship to assist research into the causes and prevention of disease, with special reference to the study of disease in its early stages.

2. The scholarships shall be administered by a board of management consisting of the following:

(1) the Regius Professor of Medicine or a substitute appointed by the professor;

(2) the Nuffield Professor of Clinical Medicine;

(3) a person appointed by the Board of the Faculty of Clinical Medicine who shall hold office for three years and be re-eligible.

3. The board shall have power to make regulations for the scholarships, not inconsistent with this decree.[1]

4. One scholarship shall be awarded annually, and one scholarship awarded in one year out of three shall be a Henry Goodger Scholarship.

5. The scholarships shall be open to all members of the University; provided that in the award of the Mary Goodger Scholarships preference shall be given to women.

6. The scholarships shall each be tenable for two years, but may be extended for a further year by the board.

[1] The board has made a regulation that holders of the scholarships shall be required to work primarily in Oxford.

7. Each scholar shall be required to engage in research in accordance with the provisions of clause 1 above.

8. Each scholar shall receive his or her emoluments terminally, subject to satisfying the board, at the end of the first year of a two-year tenure and at the end of the first and second years of a three-year tenure, that he or she is satisfactorily pursuing his or her research.

9. The annual emoluments of each scholar shall be fixed by the board and shall not be less than the maximum fixed for a Research Council Studentship nor more than the bottom point of the university lecturer scale as laid down in Ch. VII, Sect. IV, § 3, cl. 7. The board may, at its discretion, contribute towards any expenses incurred by a scholar in connection with his or her research, including university and college fees and dues incurred by a scholar reading for a research degree.

10. A scholarship shall be tenable with another post subject to the approval of the board.

11. Any income from the benefaction in excess of the sum required each year for paying the emoluments of the scholars may be applied by the board in one or more of the following ways:

(*a*) for the award of further scholarships;

(*b*) for some purpose consistent with the object of the fund as set out in clause 1 above;

(*c*) in augmentation of the capital of the fund.

12. The board shall make an annual report to the Board of the Faculty of Clinical Medicine.

13. Council shall have power to alter this decree from time to time, provided that:

(*a*) the object of the bequest as stated in clause 1 above shall always be observed;

(*b*) the title of the scholarship shall be retained;

(*c*) not less than two of the scholarships shall be Mary Goodger Scholarships awarded by preference to women.

§ 129. *Gordon Bequest*

[1]

The bequest of Walter Gordon, M.A., Non-Collegiate Student, who bequeathed to the University the residue of his property subject to the payment of certain annuities upon trust that the income thereof be applied for the benefit of needy members of the University as well junior as senior, and especially to help in providing nursing medical attendance or other aid for senior members of the University who are in need, shall be administered by the Curators of the University Chest in accordance with the intentions of the Testator. By his Will dated 7 March 1928, Walter Gordon bequeathed the residue of his property to the University 'that the income thereof may be applied for the benefit relief and assistance of needy Members of the said University as well junior as senior without distinction of Sex Race Nation Creed or Degree NOT by way of remunerative Scholarships or Exhibitions to reward and promote proficiency in learning BUT by generous and judicious relief of distress due to poverty ill-health or other trouble or misfortune not occasioned by repeated misdemeanour or persistent folly affording no reasonable hope of amendment and in particular when debt has been incurred no aid is to be given from this source in cases where advantage has been or is to be taken of the pleas of minority or lapse of time I desire to assist only such needy students as are in the main honest and honourable MOREOVER it is above all my wish to help to provide nursing medical attendance or other aid for senior Members of the University of Oxford who are in need out of health disabled or otherwise have genuine claims on compassion'.

[2]

Undergraduates Fund

1. The gift of surplus assets, amounting to about £9,000, of the Oxford University Provident Association shall be carried to a separate account called the Walter Gordon (Undergraduates) Fund.

2. Both capital and income shall be available for expenditure.

3. The fund shall be used to further the improvement or maintenance of the health of undergraduate members of the University, and, in particular (but without prejudice to the generality of the foregoing) to help in providing them with nursing, medical attendance, or other aid.

4. The fund shall be administered by the Curators of the University Chest.

5. Any income remaining unspent at the end of any year may be added to the capital of the fund and invested.

§ 130. *Gotch Memorial Prize: Founded by friends of the late Francis Gotch, M.A., D.Sc., F.R.S., Waynflete Professor of Physiology and Fellow of Magdalen College*

1. The fund shall be called the Gotch Memorial Fund and shall be managed by a board consisting of the Waynflete Professor of Physiology, the Whitley Professor of Biochemistry, and a third member appointed by the first two to hold office for such period or periods as they shall determine.

2. The income of the fund shall be applied to the establishment of a prize to be called the Gotch Memorial Prize and to the payment of all expenses concerned in the award thereof. The prize shall consist of one year's income of the fund after the deduction of any expenses of administration. It shall be awarded annually by the board of management to such person, being a member of the University, whose name had previously been placed in the Class List in the Honour School of Natural Science (Physiological Sciences), or in the Honour School of Psychology, Philosophy, and Physiology (provided that he or she had offered Physiology in that examination), and who has produced written evidence of having subsequently conducted meritorious research in a laboratory of the

University during not less than three terms, provided always that no person shall be eligible for the prize who, on 31 December of the academic year in which it is awarded, shall have exceeded twenty-five years of age.

3. The board of management may in any year withhold the prize if there is no candidate of sufficient merit.

4. If, owing to any circumstance, the whole of the income of the fund in any year be not applied as directed in clause 2 above, the board of management shall determine whether the residue shall be carried forward for expenditure in subsequent years, or shall be expended in some other way consistent with the object of the fund.

5. In any change of decree the main objects of the fund, namely, the perpetuation of the memory of Professor Gotch and the encouragement of physiological studies within the University, shall be always kept in view.

§ 131. *Green Moral Philosophy Prize: Founded by Thomas Hill Green, sometime Fellow of Balliol College and White's Professor of Moral Philosophy*

1. The income from the trust shall in every third year be applied, together with the income of the two preceding years and the accumulation thereof (after deducting the expenses incident to the trust including the payment to the examiners of such remuneration as the board shall determine), as a prize for a dissertation on some subject relating to Moral Philosophy.

2. The prize shall be known as the Green Moral Philosophy Prize.

3. The prize shall be open to all members of the University, whether men or women, who have previously been admitted to, or are qualified for, the Degree of Master of Arts.

4. The Board of the Faculty of Literae Humaniores shall be the board of management of the prize.

5. The prize shall be awarded by the following judges:

(1) White's Professor of Moral Philosophy, if he or she consents to act, or, failing the professor, a person appointed by the board;

(2) the Waynflete Professor of Metaphysical Philosophy, if he or she consents to act, or, failing the professor, a person appointed by the board;

(3) a person appointed by the board.

6. In Hilary Term in the second year before a prize is to be awarded, the board shall invite competitors to submit dissertations on subjects chosen by themselves under such conditions as the board may think it expedient to prescribe.

7. If on any occasion no election is made in consequence of there being no candidate of sufficient merit, the sum so accruing shall, at the discretion of the board, either be invested in augmentation of the capital of the fund or used for some other purpose relevant to the study of Moral Philosophy.

§ 132. *Griffith Egyptological Fund*

1. The fund shall be called the 'Griffith Egyptological Fund'.

2. The Board of the Faculty of Oriental Studies shall be the board of management of the fund.

3. The net income of the fund shall be devoted to the promotion of research into the history and antiquities of Egypt and the Nile Valley and the anthropology of north-east Africa so far as it concerns the study of Ancient, Hellenistic, and Christian Egypt and the early pagan and Christian kingdoms of the Nilotic Sudan, including such linguistic, religious, and cultural survivals as may throw light upon these matters, but excluding special studies of Muhammadanism and Islamic art. It may also be employed for the publication of the results of such researches. It may also be employed to enable any person appointed by the board of management, whether the Professor or Reader of Egyptology, or any other person, to travel or conduct exploration with a view to the promotion of Egyptological study, but it may not be employed for the stipend of the professor or reader or for the payment of any lecturer or for providing lectures in the subject.

4. The income not expended in any year shall be carried forward for expenditure in subsequent years.

5. Council shall have full power to alter this decree from time to time, provided always that the title of the fund be preserved, and that the main object of the foundation, as expressed in clause 3 above, be kept in view.

§ 133. *Griffiths Memorial Studentship*

1. The University accepts with gratitude from Mr. and Mrs. John Griffiths a gift of assets to establish a fund in memory of their son, to be known as the Jeremy Griffiths Memorial Studentship Fund.

2. The board of management for the fund shall be the Board of the Faculty of English Language and Literature, which shall make regulations concerning the award of the studentship.

3. The net income of the fund shall be used, if there is a suitable candidate, to provide a studentship to a citizen of the United Kingdom to study for a graduate degree in a field relating to the history of the book in the British Isles before 1625.

4. The selection committee for the studentship shall consist of

(1) the Director of Graduate Studies of the Board of the Faculty of English Language and Literature;

(2) the Reader in Bibliography and Textual Criticism;

(3) the University Lecturer in Palaeography;

(4) the J.R.R. Tolkien Professor of English Literature and Language or his or her nominee;

(5), (6) two persons appointed by the Governing Body of St John's College.

5. The studentship shall be tenable at St John's College.

6. The studentship shall normally be awarded for a period of two years but may be renewed for not more than one further year.

7. Holders of the studentship shall be required to submit an annual report to the board of management, and continued tenure of the award shall depend upon satisfactory progress towards completion of the graduate degree concerned.

8. Income not expended in any year shall be carried forward for expenditure in subsequent years.

9. Council shall have power to amend this decree from time to time, provided that the purposes of the fund, as defined in cll. 1, 3, and 5 above, shall always be kept in view.

§ 134. *Grocyn Fund*

1. The University accepts with gratitude from the Trustee of the Campaign for Oxford Trust Fund donations received, and such further sums as shall be contributed for the same purpose, to establish a fund to be known as the Grocyn Fund, the net income of which shall be applied to promote the teaching and study of Ancient Greek and Latin Languages and Literature.

2. The Board of the Faculty of Literae Humaniores shall be the board of management for the fund.

3. Council shall have power to amend this decree from time to time, provided that the main object of the fund, as defined in clause 1 above, is always kept in view.

§ 135. *Gurden Memorial Fund*

1. The University accepts with gratitude the bequest of the late T.K. Penniman, formerly Curator of the Pitt Rivers Museum, of the sum of £2,000 together with such copyrights, and the royalties therefrom, as belonged to him on the books and writings of which he was the author. The said sum together with the royalties and the net proceeds of the sale of any such copyrights shall form a fund to be known as the Ronald Cyril Gurden Memorial Fund.

2. The first charge on the net income from the fund shall be expenditure at the discretion of the Curator of the Pitt Rivers Museum on the garden of the Pitt Rivers Museum and on plants for the museum. Any surplus income may, at the discretion of the Curator, be either carried forward for expenditure in subsequent years or expended on other purposes for the benefit of the Pitt Rivers Museum.

3. If the University should be precluded from expending the said income as provided in cl. 2 above, Council shall have power to amend this decree, provided that the object of the testator, that the said fund shall be applied as a memorial to Ronald Cyril Gurden, formerly Administrator and Librarian of the Pitt Rivers Museum, is kept in view.

§ 136. *Gutiérrez Toscano Prize*

1. The University accepts with gratitude donations totalling £3,600, and any further sums which may be contributed for the same purpose, to establish a fund, to be known as the Gutiérrez Toscano Prize Fund, for the encouragement of the study of Applied Statistics at postgraduate level within the University.

2. The net income of the fund shall be used for the award of a prize for performance in the examination for the M.Sc. in Applied Statistics.

3. The prize, of a value to be determined from time to time by the Board of the Faculty of Mathematical Sciences, shall be awarded, if there is a candidate of sufficient merit, by the examiners for the M.Sc. in Applied Statistics to the candidate whose performance in that examination they judge to be the best.

4. The administration of the fund shall be under the direction of the faculty board, which may delegate this responsibility to the Standing Committee for the M.Sc. in Applied Statistics.

5. Income not expended in any year shall be carried forward for expenditure in subsequent years.

6. Council shall have full power to alter this decree from time to time, provided that the purpose of the fund, as defined in clause 1 above, shall always be kept in view.

§ 141. *Hall, Hall–Houghton, and Houghton Prizes: Founded by the Revd. John Hall, B.D., of St. Edmund Hall, Honorary Canon of Bristol, and the Revd. Henry Houghton, M.A., of Pembroke College*

1. The purposes for which the trust fund and the income thereof are to be held are the establishment and maintenance of two prizes, to be called the 'Canon Hall Junior and Senior Greek Testament Prizes' respectively; two prizes, to be called the 'Hall–Houghton Junior and Senior Septuagint Prizes' respectively; and one prize, to be called the 'Houghton Syriac Version Prize'; which prizes shall be offered annually to candidates for examination in the Greek Testament, the Septuagint, and the Syriac versions of the Holy Scriptures respectively. The value of each of these prizes shall be as determined from time to time by the trustees.

2. Candidates for the Canon Hall Junior Prize, and for the Hall–Houghton Junior Prize, shall be members of the University who are reading for a final honour school, or are at the time of the examination for the prizes within one term of having sat a final honour school.

3. Candidates for the Canon Hall Senior Prize, and for the Hall–Houghton Senior Prize, shall be members of the University of not more than twenty-four terms' standing.

4. Candidates for the Houghton Syriac Version Prize shall be members of the University of not more than twenty-one terms' standing.

5. Three examiners, who must be Masters of Arts or graduates in Divinity of the University, shall be appointed annually by the trustees. The examiners shall receive payment from the fund for their services at such a rate and under such conditions as the University shall from time to time determine for examiners ordinarily resident in Oxford in the Final Honour Schools.

6. The trustees shall be

(1) the Regius Professor of Divinity

(2) the Lady Margaret Professor of Divinity

(3) the Regius Professor of Hebrew

(4) the Regius Professor of Moral and Pastoral Theology

(5) the Regius Professor of Ecclesiastical History

(6) Dean Ireland's Professor of the Exegesis of Holy Scripture

(7) the Oriel and Laing Professor of the Interpretation of Holy Scripture

together with such other persons, not exceeding two in number, as the trustees may co-opt subject to the approval of the Board of the Faculty of Theology.

7. One examination for each of the four prizes shall be held in Michaelmas Term of each year, or in such other term as the trustees may from time to time appoint.

8. The subject for examination for the Canon Hall Junior Prize shall be the Gospels and the Acts of the Apostles in the original Greek in respect of translation, criticism, and interpretation.

9. The subject for examination for the Canon Hall Senior Prize shall be the New Testament in the original Greek in respect of translation, criticism, interpretation, inspiration, and authority.

10. The subject for examination for the Hall–Houghton Senior Prize shall be the Septuagint version of the Old Testament in its twofold aspect, retrospectively as regards the Hebrew Bible, and prospectively as regards the Greek Testament; and for the Junior Prize such book or books of the Septuagint version of the Old Testament as shall have been previously named by the trustees.

11. The subject for examination for the Houghton Syriac Version Prize shall be the ancient versions of the Holy Scriptures in Syriac in respect of translation, criticism, and interpretation, with special reference to such books as shall have been previously named by the trustees.

12. Each prize shall be awarded by the examiners to the candidate who in their judgement or in the judgement of a majority of them shall have acquitted himself or herself best in the examination for the prize and shall be deserving of it; but if two candidates for any prizes are deemed by the examiners to be of equal merit, they may divide the prize between them.

13. It shall not be lawful for any prize-winner to compete again for a prize of the same kind as that already gained by him or her: but one who has gained the Junior Prize or Prizes shall be entitled to compete for either or both of the Senior Prizes, when duly qualified in respect of standing; and the gaining of one

of the Junior or Senior Prizes shall not disqualify the successful candidate from competing for the other of such prizes, whether in the same or in a future term.

14. The trustees shall have power to use any surplus income to make grants of books or of money to meritorious candidates, or to use it in such way or ways as shall seem most likely to promote the general object of the trust; which general object is the encouragement of the study of the Greek Testament, of the Septuagint version of the Hebrew Scriptures in its relation to the Hebrew Bible and the Greek Testament, and of the Syriac versions of the Holy Scriptures. Any surplus income not so used in any year shall be carried forward for expenditure in subsequent years.

15. If at any time surplus funds permit, the trustees may offer a studentship, tenable by a graduate of such standing and on such conditions as they may from time to time determine, who shall undertake a course of Biblical study or research to be approved by them and consistent with the general object of the trust as defined in clause 14 above.

16. Not less than half the number of the trustees at any given time shall be a quorum for meetings of the trustees, and the decision of a majority of those present and voting shall be valid, except as provided in clause 18 below.

17. The trustees shall have power to make such regulations (if any) as may be necessary for carrying out the provisions of this decree.

18. It shall be lawful for Council from time to time or at any time to alter any of the above provisions with the consent of a majority of the whole body of trustees, provided always that the funds of the trust shall be applied only to promote the general object of the trust as defined in clause 14 above.

§ 142. *Halstead Scholarships in Music*

1. The bequest of the residue of the estate of the late J.I. Halstead shall be invested and the income used for the maintenance of scholarships, to be known as 'The James Ingham Halstead Scholarships in Music', for graduates of any university who intend to proceed to an advanced degree in music of the University of Oxford, such as a B.Mus., M.Litt., or D.Phil., or, if they already hold a sufficient qualification, a D.Mus.

2. The bequest shall be administered by the Board of the Faculty of Music which shall have power to make regulations, not inconsistent with this decree, for the award of the scholarships.

§ 143. *Hanson Research Fellowship in Surgery*

1. The University accepts with gratitude from the Hanson Trust Ltd. an annual sum sufficient to cover the full costs (including National Insurance, superannuation, and a contribution to laboratory expenses) of a research fellowship in the Nuffield Department of Surgery paid on the scale for clinical lecturers.

2. The fellowship shall be tenable for up to three years and shall be awarded by a committee of appointment established by the Board of the Faculty of Clinical Medicine.

§ 144. *Harley Prize of the New Phytologist Trust*

1. The University accepts with gratitude from the Trustees of the New Phytologist Trust the sum of £1,500 which, together with any further donations received for the same purpose, shall establish a fund the income from which shall be applied in the award of a prize each year (provided that a candidate of sufficient merit is forthcoming) for the best all-round academic performance in the field of Plant Sciences in the final year of the Honour School of Natural Science (Biological Sciences). The prize shall be awarded on the nomination of the examiners for that school. The prize, which has been established in memory of Professor J.L. Harley, shall be known as the Harley Prize of the New Phytologist Trust.

2. The fund shall be administered jointly by the Sibthorpian Professor of Plant Science and the Sherardian Professor of Botany, and they shall determine from time to time the basis on which the prize shall be awarded.

3. Income not expended on the prize in any year shall be carried forward for expenditure in subsequent years.

4. Council shall have power to alter this decree from time to time, provided that the main object of the donors, namely the establishment of a prize to be awarded to final-year honour-school candidates for excellence in Plant Sciences, is always kept in view.

§ 145. *Harrison Memorial Fellowship Fund*

1. The University accepts with gratitude the gift of £20,000 from Mrs. E. Harrison in memory of Professor Martin Harrison, and any further sums which may be contributed for the same purpose, to establish a fund, to be known as the Martin Harrison Memorial Fellowship Fund. The fund shall be used to provide fellowships to assist Turkish archaeologists working in any area of the archaeology of Anatolia, from Prehistory to the Ottoman Period, to visit the United Kingdom and Oxford in connection with their research work. Beneficiaries of the fund shall be known as Martin Harrison Memorial Fellows.

2. A committee of five members representative of a broad range of Anatolian archaeology shall be appointed jointly by the Board of the Faculty of Literae Humaniores and the Committee for Archaeology to oversee the administration of the fellowships.

3. The fellows shall be chosen annually by the committee with the assistance of the British Institute of Archaeology at Ankara or other appropriate bodies.

4. The fellowships shall be open to junior archaeologists from Turkey who are unable to take advantage of opportunities for travel that are available to senior scholars, and shall normally be awarded for visits lasting between four and

thirteen weeks. Preference may be given to Turkish archaeologists working on British-funded projects in Turkey.

5. The fellowships shall be tenable at St Hugh's College, which shall provide accommodation for the fellows, and of the Middle Common Room of which the fellows shall be members.

6. The committee shall appoint an appropriate academic host in Oxford for each fellow, and the fellows shall be attached to the university body most appropriate to their field of research, normally the Faculty of Literae Humaniores, the Committee for Archaeology, the Committee for Byzantine Studies, or the Faculty of Oriental Studies, as shall be determined by the committee in each case.

7. Each fellow shall receive a grant of up to £1,500 per annum at December 1999 prices, index-linked, as shall be determined by the committee in each case. For this purpose the income of the fund shall be supplemented from capital if necessary. The grants shall normally be used for living expenses and other associated costs of the visit.

8. Council shall have power to alter this decree from time to time, provided that the main object of the fund, as defined in clause 1 above, is always kept in view.

§ 146. *Havas Memorial Prize Fund*

1. The University accepts with gratitude the sum of U.S. $2,000 to establish a fund, to be called the Eugene Havas Memorial Prize Fund, to be applied to the award from time to time of a prize or prizes for distinguished performance in an examination or examinations for a diploma of the University.

2. The prizes shall be awarded, on the recommendation of the diploma examiners concerned, under arrangements to be determined by Council from time to time.

§ 147. *Haverfield Bequest*

1. The income of the Haverfield bequest shall be applied to the promotion of the study of Roman Britain either

(*a*) by defraying the expenses of excavations, including the adequate remuneration of competent directors; or

(*b*) by contributing towards the expense of collecting and preparing for publication materials for the history of Roman Britain, including inscriptions, works of art or manufacture, maps, plans, etc.; or

(*c*) by contribution towards the expense of printing and publishing works incorporating such materials; or

(*d*) by providing for the delivery, at adequate remuneration, of lectures or courses of lectures in Oxford or elsewhere, with special reference to the work carried on by means of the bequest; or (*e*) in any other manner which the standing committee constituted under clause 2 below may from time to time judge likely to promote the objects of the bequest.

2. The administration of the income of the bequest shall be entrusted to a standing committee of seven persons, who shall be

(1) the Professor of the Archaeology of the Roman Empire;

(2), (3) two persons to be nominated by the Sub-faculty of Ancient History of the Faculty of Literae Humaniores;

(4), (5) two persons to be nominated by the Council of the Society of Antiquaries of London;

(6), (7) two persons to be chosen by co-optation.

3. All the members of the committee shall hold office for five years, and shall be re-eligible.

4. All the powers of the administrators of the bequest may be exercised by a majority of those present and voting at a meeting duly summoned, provided that three of the administrators at least be present.

5. Graduate members of the University of Oxford and past and present members of the women's societies in Oxford shall be equally eligible (but not necessarily to the exclusion of others) for any lecturership or other post, emolument, or remuneration provided from the income of the bequest.

6. This decree shall be subject to alteration from time to time by Council, provided that the object of the bequest as defined in clause 1 above is adhered to.

§ 148. *Head Prize for Ancient Numismatics*

1. The fund created by friends of Barclay Vincent Head, Hon. D.Litt., late Keeper of Coins and Medals in the British Museum, offered to the University, with a view to perpetuate his memory by the foundation of a prize for the encouragement of the study of Ancient Numismatics, shall be invested by the University, and the income arising from it shall be devoted to the maintenance of a prize to be called the Barclay Head Prize for Ancient Numismatics.

2. The prize shall be of the value of £100, and shall be awarded for a dissertation or essay, whether published or otherwise, on a subject connected with Ancient Numismatics, not later than the beginning of the fifth century A.D.

3. The prize shall be open to all members of the University who, on the day appointed for sending in the essays, shall not have exceeded twenty-one terms' standing from matriculation.

4. The prize shall be awarded annually provided that a candidate of sufficient merit presents himself or herself.

5. The prize shall under no circumstances be awarded more than once to the same person, or more than once in any year. If the judge or judges so recommend, the prize may be divided between two candidates.

6. The management of the prize shall be entrusted to the Committee for Archaeology. The committee shall fix days on which the essays are to be sent in, shall appoint a judge or judges who shall award the prize, shall determine the remuneration, if any, of such judge or judges, and shall make such other arrangements as may be necessary for carrying out this decree.

7. If in any year a surplus is available either because the prize has not been awarded or for any other reason, the Committee for Archaeology may either direct that the surplus be carried forward for expenditure in subsequent years, or employ the surplus, in any manner that it may think desirable, in furthering the object for which the fund has been established, namely the encouragement of the study of Ancient Numismatics by members of the University.

§ 149. *Heather Benefaction*

Note. This subsection is not a decree or regulation, but summarizes a deed dated 20 February 1627

William Heather, Mus. Doc., by deed dated 20 February 1627 gave to the University an annuity of £18, issuing out of certain lands at Chislehurst, Kent, of which £15 is paid to the Choragus, £2 to the free school of Stanwell, Middlesex, and the balance to the General Fund of the University.

In November 1964 by the payment of £298 (now in the Trusts Pool) the rent charge of £18 was redeemed.

§ 150. *Heatley Fund*

1. The University accepts with gratitude the sum of $10,500, and any further sums which may be contributed for this purpose, to establish a fund to commemorate the contribution of Dr. Norman Heatley to the development of penicillin. The fund shall be called the Norman Heatley Fund and shall be applied, under the direction of the Head of the Sir William Dunn School of Pathology, to the furtherance of the study of Pathology within that department. The primary use of the fund shall be the establishment of the Norman Heatley Lecture, to be given from time to time. Any surplus in the fund may be applied in any way that the Head of the Sir William Dunn School thinks conducive to the study of Pathology within that department.

2. Council shall have power to alter this decree from time to time, provided that the purpose of the fund, namely the furtherance of the study of Pathology within the Sir William Dunn School of Pathology, shall always be kept in view.

§ 151. *Herbert Memorial Prize*

1. The prize, to be called the 'Robert Herbert Memorial Prize', was founded with a view to encouraging interest in those problems of Imperial Administration to which Sir Robert Herbert devoted his life. Its value shall be determined by the administrators of the Beit Fund.

2. The prize shall be awarded by the examiners for the Beit Prize in Colonial History on the results of the examination for that prize, and shall be open to

such persons only as shall be eligible for the Beit Prize, and upon the same conditions as shall be prescribed for that prize.

3. The above-named examiners may in their discretion award the prize to the candidate to whom they award the Beit Prize, or to any other candidate in the same examination whose work may appear to them deserving of special recognition.

4. The prize shall in no case be awarded to the same person a second time, or to any person who has previously won the Beit Prize.

5. Any income not required for the prize in any year shall at the discretion of the administrators of the Beit Fund either be carried forward for expenditure in subsequent years or be applied by the administrators to the making of grants which in their opinion will promote the study in Oxford of imperial administration.

6. Provided the main objects of the foundation as expressed in clause 1 above are always kept in view, Council may from time to time alter this decree in such manner as it shall deem expedient.

§ 152. *Herbertson Memorial Prize*

1. The Curators of the University Chest shall be authorized to accept a sum of money of about £100 subscribed by past and present members of the School of Geography for the purpose of establishing an annual prize in memory of the late Professor Andrew John Herbertson, and any further sums which may hereafter be subscribed towards the same purpose, and to invest the whole as a separate fund to be called the 'Herbertson Memorial Fund'.

2. The interest thereon shall be used for the maintenance of a prize as aforesaid, to be awarded in such manner as the Board of the Faculty of Anthropology and Geography shall from time to time determine.

§ 153. *Hertford Prize*

1. The Hertford Prize to encourage the study of Latin Literature shall be awarded, provided that a suitable candidate presents himself or herself, by the Moderators for Honour Moderations in Greek and Latin Languages and Literature, and Latin Literature with Greek, for performance in such Latin papers in those examinations as shall be prescribed from time to time by the Board of the Faculty of Literae Humaniores, provided that these shall include papers both in Latin composition and in the interpretation of Latin authors.

2. Any income accruing in years when the prize is not awarded may be applied by the Board of the Faculty of Literae Humaniores in any way that it thinks conducive to the study of Latin Literature in the University of Oxford.

§ 154. *Heuss Research Fellowship*

1. The Theodor Heuss Research Fellowship (subsequently called 'the fellowship') shall be open to young British graduates of the University of Oxford as defined in clause 3 below.

2. The holder of the fellowship shall be required to undertake research in a subject of his or her own choice at a university or other institution of higher learning of his or her own choice in the Federal Republic of Germany.

3. The fellowship may be conferred only on a British subject who is a member of the University of Oxford, and who by the date on which he or she takes up the fellowship has not attained the age of thirty-two years and has either embarked on a course of postgraduate study at the University or has already obtained a postgraduate qualification of the University. The holder of the fellowship must be qualified to carry out research at a German university or other institution of higher learning. The fellowship may be conferred only once on the same candidate.

4. The fellowship shall be tenable for one year, which shall normally run from 1 October of one year to 30 September of the year following.

5. The holder of the fellowship shall be appointed by the selection committee for the Michael Foster Memorial Scholarship under the provisions of § 106, cll. 2 and 4 of this section or by such other committee as the University may determine. The fellowship will be administered by the Alexander von Humboldt Stiftung.

§ 155. *Hicks Fund*

1. The University accepts with gratitude the bequests by Sir John Hicks, sometime Drummond Professor of Political Economy, for the promotion of the study of Economics and Economic History at the University.

2. All sums received in respect of the bequests shall constitute the Sir John Hicks Fund, which shall be administered by a joint committee of the Boards of the Faculties of Social Studies and of Modern History.

3. Council shall have power to alter this decree from time to time, provided that the purpose of the fund as set out in clause 1 above shall always be kept in view.

§ 156. *Higher Studies Fund*

The Curators of the University Chest shall accept donations for the purpose of establishing a fund for the promotion of higher studies, including the purposes mentioned in the draft Declaration of Trust sent to Convocation for sealing on 16 February 1937.

§ **157.** *Museum of the History of Science*

Special Purposes Fund

1. The University accepts with deep gratitude a further benefaction of £100,000 to be added to that of approximately the same value gratefully accepted in 1988, for the support of the Museum of the History of Science by funding research, publications, documentation, and acquisitions to the collections and to the museum's library, and in such other ways as the Committee for the History of Science, Medicine, and Technology shall from time to time determine.

2. Expenditure from the benefaction shall be made on the authorization of the Keeper of the museum in accordance with any general principles agreed from time to time by the Committee for the History of Science, Medicine, and Technology, subject to the prior approval of the General Board in the case of expenditure for any single item or two or more related items in excess of such level, not being less than £5,000, as the board shall from time to time determine.

Stapleton Collection

The collection of books and manuscripts relating to Arabic science given by H.E. Stapleton, B.Sc., M.A., D.Litt., St. John's College, shall be kept in the Museum of the History of Science, or, if Council after the lapse of twenty-five years from 9 December 1947 shall by decree determine, in the Bodleian Library, provided always that the collection is not dispersed.

§ **158.** *Hoare Prize in Computation*

1. The University accepts from the Trustee of the Campaign for Oxford Trust Fund the endowment of £2,500 and such further sums as shall be made available for the same purpose, made possible by a generous donation occasioned by the publication of a *festschrift* for Professor C.A.R. Hoare, James Martin Professor of Computing, to establish a fund, to be known as the Hoare Prize Fund, for the encouragement of the study of Computation within the University by the award of Hoare Prizes in Computation for performance in that subject in an Honour School of the University.

2. The prize, of a value to be determined from time to time by the Board of the Faculty of Mathematical Sciences, shall be awarded, if there is a candidate of sufficient merit, by the examiners for the Honour School of Computation to the candidate whose performance in that examination they judge to be the best.

3. The administration of the fund shall be under the direction of the Board of the Faculty of Mathematical Sciences, which may delegate this responsibility to the Standing Committee for Computation and Mathematics.

4. Income not expended in any year shall be carried forward for expenditure in subsequent years.

5. Council shall have full power to alter this decree from time to time, provided always that the purpose of the fund, as defined in clause 1 above, shall be kept in view.

§ 159. *Hodgson Memorial Fund*

1. The University accepts with gratitude donations totalling £8,000, and any further sums which may be contributed for this purpose, to establish a fund, to be known as the Eoin Hodgson Memorial Fund, as a memorial to the late Dr. Eoin Hodgson, formerly University Lecturer in Occupational Health Medicine, Occupational Health Physician, and Fellow of St. Cross College. The fund shall be used for the encouragement of the study of Occupational Medicine within the University.

2. The net income of the fund shall be used for the provision of an Eoin Hodgson Memorial Bursary for Occupational Medicine.

3. The fund shall be administered by a board of management consisting of

(1) the Head of the Department of Public Health;

(2) the Director of Clinical Studies (or his or her nominee);

(3) a person appointed by the Board of the Faculty of Clinical Medicine in consultation with the Head of the Department of Public Health for such period or periods as it shall determine.

4. The bursary, of a value to be determined from time to time by the board of management, shall be awarded annually to the medical student who, in the opinion of the board of management, submits the most meritorious proposal for an elective project within the field of Occupational Medicine. Alternatively, the bursary may be divided, if the board of management determines that there are candidates of sufficient merit, between two or more students.

5. The board of management may in any year withhold the bursary if there is no candidate of sufficient merit. Income not expended in any year shall be carried forward for expenditure in subsequent years.

6. Council shall have power to alter this decree from time to time, provided always that the purpose of the fund, as defined in clause 1 above, shall be kept in view.

§ 160. *Hosier Fund*

1. The University accepts with gratitude from Mrs. Doreen Ethel King, O.B.E., as Trustee of the A.J. Hosier Educational Trust, the sum of £30,000 which shall form a fund for the promotion within the University of agricultural education in the United Kingdom.

2. The first charge on the income from the fund shall be the provision of postgraduate studentships, to be known as the A. J. Hosier Studentships, which shall be tenable at Linacre College.

3. The fund shall be administered by a board of management consisting of:

(1) the Sibthorpian Professor of Plant Science;

(2) the Head of the Agricultural Economics Unit;

(3) the Chairman of the Board of the Faculty of Biological Sciences, or a deputy appointed by the Chairman;

(4) the Principal of Linacre College, or a deputy appointed by the Principal.

4. The studentship shall be open to all persons who have graduated with Honours in a relevant Final School of any university within the United Kingdom, and who are citizens of the United Kingdom, and the board of management shall determine from time to time whether a particular Final School is relevant for this purpose.

5. Holders of the studentships shall be required to pursue a course of advanced study and research at Oxford in any of the following aspects of British Agriculture:

(i) husbandry, whether animal, dairy, poultry, grassland, or crop;

(ii) agricultural economics, agricultural statistics (either experimental or economic), or agricultural marketing;

(iii) agricultural science (in its more applied aspects).

6. The studentships shall be tenable for one year in the first instance, and may be held for up to a further two years at the discretion of the board of management.

7. Any income not required in any year for the studentships shall either be applied at the discretion of the board of management in some other way consistent with the object of the fund or carried forward for expenditure in subsequent years.

8. Council shall have power to alter this decree at any time, provided that no alteration shall be made to clause 2 hereof without the prior consent of the said Doreen Ethel King, her personal representatives and assigns, and provided further that any amended provisions shall be of an exclusively educational charitable nature and provide for the promotion within the University of agricultural education in the United Kingdom.

§ 161. *Hudson Memorial Fund*

1. The University accepts with gratitude the bequest by the late Mr. Richard Guy Ormonde Hudson, D.S.C., of one-third of the residue of his estate to establish a fund to be known as the Guy Hudson Memorial Fund, the net income from which shall be used for the education of officers of the Royal Navy or Royal Marines at the University.

2. The fund shall be administered by a board of management consisting of:

(1) the Chichele Professor of the History of War;

(2) the Officer Commanding the University Royal Navy Unit (or his or her representative);

(3) the representative of the Admiralty Board of the Defence Council on the Delegacy for Military Instruction;

(4), (5) two persons appointed by the Delegacy for Military Instruction.

3. The board shall apply the annual income of the bequest in such ways as it may think fit for the assistance (whether by the making of grants or such other

ways) of the further education of officers of the Royal Navy or Royal Marines at the University.

4. Any income not spent in any year shall be carried forward for expenditure in subsequent years in accordance with the provisions of clause 1 above.

5. Council shall have power to alter this decree from time to time, provided that the main object of the bequest, as defined in clause 1 above, is always adhered to.

§ 162. *Hunt Travelling Scholarship*

1. The scholarship shall be called the 'George Herbert Hunt Travelling Scholarship', and shall be offered every second year for award without examination to a person who either has been admitted to the Degree of Bachelor of Medicine of the University or has passed the First Examination for the Degree of Bachelor of Medicine of the University and holds a medical degree of another British university qualifying him or her to practise Medicine.

2. The value of the scholarship shall be two years' income of the fund.

3. Candidates shall submit with their applications a statement of their academic record together with testimonials, and an undertaking that if elected they will travel abroad for a period of at least one month for the purpose of Clinical Study or Research in Medicine.

4. The award shall be made by a board of electors consisting of:

(1) the Regius Professor of Medicine (chairman);

(2) the Director of Postgraduate Medical Education and Training;

(3) the Director of Clinical Studies;

(4) the Pre-clinical Adviser;

(5), (6) two persons appointed by the Board of the Faculty of Clinical Medicine, of whom at least one shall be a graduate in Medicine of the University.

The Secretary of the Board of the Faculty of Clinical Medicine shall act as Secretary and Convener of the board.

5. The award shall, so far as possible on each occasion, be published on 9 April, being the birthday of the late Dr. Hunt; and in making the award the electors shall give a preference to such candidates as express the intention of engaging in the practice of their profession either as Surgeons, or as General Practitioners.

6. The scholar shall complete his or her period of travel within twelve months from his or her election, and shall within a reasonable period thereafter submit to the Secretary of the Board of the Faculty of Clinical Medicine for the approval of the electors a detailed report on his or her tenure of the scholarship.

7. Payment of nine-tenths of the scholarship shall be made to the scholar on his or her signifying readiness to proceed abroad, and the remaining one-tenth on the approval of his or her report by the electors.

8. Income accruing from the absence of a suitable candidate for election at any biennial period or from other cause shall be applied, subject to the approval of the Board of the Faculty of Clinical Medicine, to increasing the value of the scholarship, or to the establishment of a second Travelling Scholarship, or to such other purposes in the School of Medicine as the faculty board may determine, provided that such purposes shall always be associated with the name of George Herbert Hunt.

9. It shall be lawful for Council from time to time to alter this decree, but only with the approval and consent during her lifetime of Mrs. Hunt.

§ 163. *Department of Human Anatomy and Genetics*

Craniological Collections from Department of Human Anatomy and Genetics: loan to British Museum

The Craniological Collections forming part of the anatomical and anthropological collection deposited in the Department of Human Anatomy and Genetics under the charge of Dr. Lee's Professor of Anatomy shall be transferred on permanent loan to the British Museum.

Boise Gift

The gift of £25,000 from Mr. Charles Watson Boise (the interest on this sum to be used for research on the antiquity and origin of man and his precursors (with particular emphasis on the continued exploration of appropriate sites in Africa) and on the early migration of palaeolithic communities) shall be administered, until Council by decree shall otherwise determine, by a committee consisting of:

(1) the Professor of Biological Anthropology;

(2) the Professor of Geology;

(3) the Director of the Pitt Rivers Museum

(provided that, if any of these persons is unwilling or unable to act, he or she may appoint a deputy to act for him or her), with power to co-opt up to two additional members for such period or periods as the committee may determine.

§ 164. *The Hussey Lectures*

1. The University accepts with gratitude from the late Very Revd. Dr. J.W.A. Hussey, former Dean of Chichester, the sum of £15,000, the net income from which shall be used in providing annually or biennially a lecture or series of lectures on the Church and the Arts to be known as The Hussey Lectures. In the appointment of lecturers the University shall take note of Dr. Hussey's hope that the lectures may especially strengthen the link between the Church and the Arts.

2. The fund shall be administered by a committee consisting of:

(1) a person appointed by the Vice-Chancellor, who shall be the chairman;

(2), (3) two persons elected by the Board of the Faculty of Theology;

(4) one person elected by the Board of the Faculty of Music;

(5) one person elected by the Committee for the Ruskin School of Drawing and Fine Art.

The member appointed under (1) shall hold office for such period as the Vice-Chancellor shall determine. The members elected under (2)–(5) shall hold office for three years. All members shall be re-eligible. Casual vacancies shall be filled for the remainder of the period of the person demitting office.

3. Council shall have power to alter this decree from time to time, provided that at all times the main object of the founder be kept in view, namely the provision of lectures on the Church and the Arts to be known as The Hussey Lectures.

§ 171. *Irish Government Senior Scholarship Fund*

1. The University accepts from the Trustee of the Campaign for Oxford Trust Fund the initial endowment, made possible by a generous benefaction from the Irish Sailors and Soldiers Land Trust of the Irish Government, and such further sums as may be contributed for the same purpose, to establish a fund, to be known as the Irish Government Senior Scholarship Fund, the income of which shall be used to support the award from time to time of Senior Scholarships in the History and Culture of Ireland.

2. The scholarships shall be open to candidates who have recently obtained a postgraduate degree in an appropriate subject and also those who are in the final stages of work for such a degree (preference shall be given to candidates in the former category).

3. The Board of the Faculty of Modern History shall be the board of management for the scholarships and shall appoint a committee for the exercise of its functions under these regulations, comprising:

(1) the Carroll Professor of Irish History;

(2) one person elected by Hertford College;

(3) one person elected by the Board of the Faculty of Modern History.

The elected members of the committee shall hold office for five years and shall be re-eligible. Casual vacancies shall be filled for the remainder of the period of the person demitting office. The committee shall have the power to co-opt up to two other persons. The committee shall appoint one of its members from time to time to be its chairman.

4. The scholarship, which shall be held at Hertford College under the aegis of the Carroll Professor of Irish History, shall be tenable for one year.

5. Every candidate, with his or her application, shall submit a programme of the work in Irish History or Culture which he or she proposes, if elected, to undertake.

6. Every scholar shall, while he or she continues to hold the scholarship, produce from time to time evidence, satisfactory to the committee, that he or she is carrying out his or her programme of work. The committee shall have power

to deprive a student who does not comply with this condition of the whole or any part of the emoluments of the scholarship.

7. Surplus income arising in any year shall, at the discretion of the committee, either be carried forward for expenditure in subsequent years or be used for one or more of the following purposes:

(*a*) the award of an additional scholarship;

(*b*) the continuation of a scholarship previously awarded;

(*c*) the payment of a scholar's expenses, including those of travel or publication, incidental to the pursuit of a piece of research into Irish History or Culture on a subject approved by the committee;

(*d*) the encouragement in any other way of such research within the University, for submission for a degree of the University or for subsequent publication, on a subject approved by the committee.

8. No person shall be awarded the scholarship a second time.

9. Council shall have power to alter this decree from time to time subject to the consent of the Irish Government, and provided that the main object of the Irish Government in founding the scholarship, namely the encouragement within the University of advanced study of the History and Culture of Ireland, shall always be kept in view.

§ 180. *Janson Prize in Electronic Communications*

1. The University accepts with gratitude a gift of £2,500 from Dr. David Edwards and Mrs. Georgina Edwards in memory of Mrs. Edwards's father, Mr. Ronald Victor Janson.

2. The gift shall be invested to form a fund, the net income of which shall be used for the maintenance of a prize to be called the Ronald Victor Janson Prize in Electronic Communications. The Board of the Faculty of Physical Sciences shall be the board of management for the fund.

3. Provided that suitable candidates present themselves, the prize shall be awarded, on the nomination of the examiners, for the best third- or fourth-year project in Electronic Communications in the Final Honour School of Engineering Science and the associated joint schools. The value of the prize shall be as determined from time to time by the board of management.

4. Income not expended on the prize in any year shall, at the discretion of the board of management, either be used to award an additional prize or prizes subject to the provisions of clause 3 above, or be carried forward for expenditure in subsequent years.

5. Council shall have power to amend this decree from time to time, provided that the main object of the fund, as stated in clause 2 above, is always kept in view.

§ 181. *Jaspars Memorial Fund*

1. The University accepts with gratitude the sums contributed in memory of Dr. Joseph Maria Franciscus Jaspars, which shall form a fund to be known as the Jaspars Memorial Fund. The net income of the fund shall be applied towards the provision of lectures in Psychology to be delivered from time to time within the University.

2. The Medical Sciences Board shall be the board of management for the fund and shall appoint a committee to administer the fund subject to such conditions as the board may lay down. The committee shall consist of up to five members of the Sub-faculty of Psychology and shall have power to co-opt any other person.

3. Council shall have power to alter this decree from time to time, provided that the main object of the fund, the provision of lectures in Psychology to be delivered from time to time within the University, shall always be kept in view.

§ 182. *Jenkinson Fund*

1. The fund for the further encouragement of research work in Embryology shall be called the Elizabeth Hannah Jenkinson Fund.

2. The annual income derived from the fund shall be available for grants, to be made on the recommendation of the Linacre Professor of Zoology, towards the expenses of researches on normal and experimental Embryology of Animals undertaken by graduates of the University who have obtained Honours in Zoology in the Final Honour School of Natural Science.

3. Any balance of income which is not required for the aforesaid purpose shall be invested in augmentation of the capital of the fund.

§ 183. *Johnson Loan Fund*

The assets of the Bertha Johnson Loan Fund shall be administered by the Curators of the University Chest, and shall be applied, both as to income and capital, at their discretion for making loans upon such terms as they shall think fit to women members of the University *in statu pupillari*; each applicant for a loan shall produce a statement from the Principal of her college certifying that she is in need of such assistance.

§ 184. *Johnson Memorial Prizes*

1. The moneys establishing the Johnson Memorial Prizes shall be invested in the name of the Chancellor, Masters, and Scholars of the University of Oxford.

2. Prizes, called the Johnson Memorial Prizes, shall be offered for essays in astronomy and geophysics (including meteorology), the subjects of which have been approved by any one of the trustees. The prizes shall be awarded (if suitable candidates present themselves) annually in Michaelmas Term. One prize shall be open to undergraduate members of the University who are reading for the Degree of Bachelor of Arts or Master of Physics and who, in the term in

which the prize is awarded, have not exceeded the seventh term from their matriculation; and one prize shall be open to graduates of this or another university who are registered for a research or other graduate degree at Oxford and who, in the term in which it is awarded, have not completed four terms of such work. In the event of two or more candidates for either prize being judged to be of equal merit, additional prizes may be awarded. The number and value of the prizes shall be determined by the trustees.

3. The trustees of the prizes shall be:

(1) the Vice-Chancellor;

(2)–(5) four persons elected by the Board of the Faculty of Physical Sciences;

(6), (7) two persons elected by the Board of the Faculty of Mathematical Sciences.

The elected members of the board shall be the same persons as those elected by the aforesaid faculty boards to serve as members of the board of electors to the Halley Lecturership; they shall hold office for five years and be re-eligible.

4. The essays shall be sent to the Registrar marked 'Johnson Memorial Prize' on or before the date fixed for the receipt of entries. The prizes shall be adjudged as soon as the judges find convenient.

5. Neither an undergraduate nor a graduate prize shall be awarded more than once to the same person.

6. Surplus income, however arising, may at the discretion of the trustees be applied in any way consistent with the object of the trust, namely the advancement of astronomical and meteorological science.

7. The trustees shall have power to make regulations or by-laws for the purpose of carrying this decree into effect; and Council shall always be at liberty to alter the decree, provided that the main end of the prizes be kept in view, namely, the advancement of astronomical and meteorological science.

§ **185.** *Jones Memorial Prize*

1. The University accepts with gratitude the sum of approximately £700, and any further sums which may be contributed for this purpose, to establish a fund as a memorial to the late Dr. Cyril Jones, formerly University Lecturer in Spanish, the income from which shall be applied towards the promotion or encouragement of Spanish Studies within the University, and in particular by the provisions of a Cyril Jones Memorial Prize.

2. The Board of the Faculty of Medieval and Modern Languages shall be the board of management of the prize and shall have power to make regulations, not inconsistent with this decree, for the administration of the prize.

3. The board of management shall apply the income, after the payment of all proper expenses, and may in any one year apply up to £70 of the capital towards the provisions of a Cyril Jones Memorial Prize which shall be awarded, if a candidate of sufficient merit is forthcoming, by the Moderators in Hilary Term for the Preliminary Examination for Modern Languages, to the candidate in

Spanish in that examination, or in the Preliminary Examination in Philosophy and Modern Languages in the same term, or in part 1 of the Preliminary Examination in English and Modern Languages in the same term, or in part 1 of the Preliminary Examination in Modern History and Modern Languages in the same term, whose performance they judge to be the best.

4. Any surplus income available, either because the prize has not been awarded or for any other reason, may be

(i) applied in making such travel or research grants to members of the University *in statu pupillari* as shall be conducive to the promotion or encouragement of Spanish Studies within the University, such grants to be known as Cyril Jones grants;

(ii) applied towards such other purpose or purposes conducive to the promotion or encouragement of Spanish Studies within the University as the board shall from time to time determine;

or

(iii) carried forward for application in future years either towards the provision of the prize or for any of the purposes referred to in (i) and (ii) above.

5. Council shall have power to alter this decree from time to time, provided that the main object of the fund, namely the promotion or encouragement of Spanish Studies within the University is kept in view.

§ 191. *King Fund*

The bequest made to the University by the late Mr. Joseph King shall be used for the benefit of the University in such way as Council shall determine.

§ 192. *Kirby Memorial Fund*

1. The fund (founded by friends of the late David R.S. Kirby, University Lecturer in Zoology and Fellow of St. Catherine's College) shall be called the David Kirby Memorial Fund, and shall be managed by a board of management consisting of

(1) the Head of the Department of Zoology (or his or her nominee);

(2) the Master of St. Catherine's College (or his or her nominee),

(3) a person appointed by the Sub-faculty of Zoology for such period or periods as it shall determine.

2. The income of the fund shall be applied to the establishment of a David Kirby Memorial Bursary and to the payment of expenses in connection with the award thereof.

3. The bursary shall be awarded annually in Trinity Term to the person who, in the opinion of the board of management, submits the most meritorious proposal for research to be carried out during the vacation in collaboration with a member of the staff of a university department, research unit, or research group. Preference will be given to projects in the field of reproduction. The bursary shall be open to undergraduate members of the University studying for

the Preliminary Examination in Biology, the Honour School of Natural Science (Zoology), the Preliminary Examination in Human Sciences, or the Honour School of Human Sciences.

4. The board of management shall determine the value of the bursary and the form in which applications for the bursary shall be made and shall arrange for an announcement to be made in the *University Gazette*, in colleges, and in the Department of Zoology, not later than the sixth week of Hilary Term.

5. The board of management may in any year withhold the bursary if there is no candidate of sufficient merit. Income not expended in any year shall be carried forward for expenditure in subsequent years and may be used by the board either to award a second bursary or to make grants to unsuccessful candidates of merit.

6. Council shall have power to alter this decree from time to time, provided that no change shall be made without the approval of the Sub-faculty of Zoology and the Master of St. Catherine's College.

§ 193. *Kirkaldy Prizes: Founded by friends of the late Jane Willis Kirkaldy*

1. The Committee for the History of Science, Medicine, and Technology shall be charged with the duty of awarding the prizes.

2. Save as is provided in clause 6 below the whole of the income of the endowment, after the payment of such expenses incurred in examination as the Committee for the History of Science, Medicine, and Technology shall approve, shall be applied to the Junior Prize.

3. The prize money shall be spent on books unless the express consent of the Committee for the History of Science, Medicine, and Technology be given to the contrary.

4. The Junior Prize shall be called the 'Jane Willis Kirkaldy Junior Prize' and shall be offered for competition annually, on an essay written upon a topic concerning the History of Science or Technology proposed by the candidate and approved by the committee. The committee may also award a *proxime accessit* prize.

5. The Junior Prize shall be open to all undergraduate members of the University and to those who, at the deadline for entries, are within one term of having completed the examination for an undergraduate degree of the University, provided that the Junior Prize shall not be awarded a second time to the same person, nor shall a person who has been awarded the Junior Prize receive on any subsequent occasion a *proxime accessit* award to the Junior Prize. A person who has received a *proxime accessit* award to the Junior Prize may, however, be awarded the Junior Prize for a different piece of work on a subsequent occasion.

6. In the event of there being surplus income, it shall be applied in the first instance to the award of a second prize, to be known as the Jane Willis Kirkaldy Senior Prize. If funds permit, the Senior Prize shall be offered for competition

annually on an essay written upon a topic concerning the History of Science and Technology proposed by the candidate and approved by the committee. The committee may also award a *proxime accessit* prize. The Senior Prize shall be open to all members of the University who are registered as students for the degree of M.Sc., M.Litt., M.St., M.Phil., or D.Phil. in the University and who are not eligible to enter for the Junior Prize. The Senior Prize shall not be awarded a second time to the same person, nor shall a piece of work submitted at any time for the Junior Prize be submitted at the same time or subsequently for the Senior Prize, nor shall a person who has been awarded the Senior Prize receive on any subsequent occasion a *proxime accessit* award to the Senior Prize. A person who has received a *proxime accessit* award to the Senior Prize may, however, be awarded the Senior Prize for a different piece of work on a subsequent occasion. In the event that there is any further surplus income, it shall be applied, at the discretion of the General Board, to any purpose connected with the History of Science which the General Board may approve.

7. In any change of decree regard shall always be had to the intention of the donors of the prize, viz. that the prize should be competed for by a satisfactory proportion of the best students reading Natural Science, it being understood that opportunity to compete be given from time to time to students in all the Schools of Natural Science in the University.

§ 194. *Kirk-Greene Prize*

1. The University accepts with gratitude a gift of £1,250 from Mr. A.H.M. Kirk-Greene, sometime Lecturer in the Modern History of Africa.

2. The gift shall be invested to form a fund, the net income of which shall be used for the maintenance of a prize to be called the Kirk-Greene Prize in Modern African History. The fund shall be administered by the Board of the Faculty of Modern History.

3. The prize shall be awarded on the basis of the best performance in the area of Modern African History in the Final Honour School of Modern History and the associated joint schools, provided that suitable candidates present themselves.

4. Council shall have power to amend this decree from time to time, provided that the main object of the fund, as stated in clause 2 above, is always kept in view.

§ 195. *Knapp Fund*

1. The University accepts with gratitude one moiety, amounting to approximately £25,000, of the residue of the estate of the late Lt.-Col. H.H.G. Knapp, to establish a fund which shall be called the Herbert Knapp Fund.

2. The fund shall be used to promote the efficiency of the Medical School, under the direction of the Boards of the Faculties of Clinical Medicine and Physiological Sciences.

§ **196.** *Kolkhorst Bequest*

The bequest of the late G.A. Kolkhorst, M.A., Exeter College, for the founding of an exhibition in Spanish to be called the 'G.A. Kolkhorst Exhibition', shall be administered by the Curators of the Taylor Institution, and they shall award the exhibition in such manner as, subject to the terms of the bequest, they shall think fit.

§ **201.** *Labouchere Fund*

1. The University accepts from the Trustee of the Campaign for Oxford Trust Fund the initial endowment and such further sums as shall be made available for the same purpose, made possible by a generous benefaction from Lady Labouchere, to establish a fund, to be known as the Sir George Labouchere Fund, for the advancement within the University of learning, scholarship, and research in the field of Spanish Studies, which expression shall include the history of Anglo-Spanish relations, Spanish history, and the literature, language, and other cultural aspects of Spain. While priority shall, where possible, be given to these aspects, similar aspects relating to Hispanic America shall not be excluded.

2. There shall be a committee to administer the income of the fund consisting of:

(1), (2) two persons appointed by the Board of the Faculty of Modern History;

(3), (4) two persons appointed by the Board of the Faculty of Medieval and Modern Languages.

Members of the committee shall serve for such periods as shall be determined by the appointing board at the time of their appointment. They shall elect the chairman of the committee from amongst their own number.

3. The first charge on the income of the fund shall be the maintenance of graduate studentships or travel grants to be awarded from time to time to members of the University to enable them to undertake research in Spanish archives and libraries in the above-mentioned fields for the award of a degree of the University.

4. Income not required for the maintenance of scholarships or grants as aforesaid may be applied towards the purchase of library material relevant to Spanish Studies, including antiquarian books, for the Taylor Institution Library or other appropriate library or libraries of the University.

5. Income not expended in any year shall be carried forward for expenditure in subsequent years.

6. Council shall have power to alter this decree from time to time, provided that the main object of the fund as defined in clause 1 above is always kept in view.

§ 202. *Lee Fund*

The annual royalties and all pecuniary proceeds arising from the Sir Sidney Lee Bequest shall be used in the furtherance of Shakespearian Studies at the discretion of the Board of the Faculty of English Language and Literature.

§ 203. *Lee-Placito Medical Fund*

1. The University accepts with gratitude from Peter John Placito, Anthony Rudolph Placito, and Mrs. Dorothy Grace Placito the sum of £17,500, and any further benefactions contributed for this purpose, to establish a fund in memory of the late Anthony Placito and the late Emanoel Lee to be called the Lee–Placito Medical Fund. The fund shall be used for the general advancement of the science and practice of medicine and surgery by research within the University and the dissemination of the results thereof for the public benefit.

2. The medical research supported by the fund shall have special reference to the field of gastroenterology (which shall be regarded as including the physiology, histopathology, biochemistry, endoscopy, radiology, and cancers and other diseases of the digestive system).

3. The fund shall be administered by a board of management consisting of:

(1) the said Peter John Placito during his lifetime, or a deputy appointed by him from time to time;

(2) the said Anthony Rudolph Placito during his lifetime;

(3), (4) two persons appointed by the Board of the Faculty of Clinical Medicine to serve for such period in each case as shall be determined from time to time by that board;

(5)–(8) four persons to be appointed by Council, of whom one shall be Mr. M.G.W. Kettlewell for so long as he shall be willing and able to act (but not beyond seventy-five years of age), one shall be Dr. D.P. Jewell for so long as he shall be willing and able to act (but not beyond seventy-five years of age), and at least two shall not be members of the Faculty of Clinical Medicine.

The board of management shall have power to co-opt not more than two persons, who shall serve for five years and be re-eligible.

4. Council shall have power to alter this decree from time to time, provided that no alteration shall be made to clauses 2 and 3 during the lifetime of the said Peter John Placito and Anthony Rudolph Placito without their prior consent, and provided also that at all times the main object of the founders be kept in view, namely the general advancement of the science and practice of medicine and surgery by research within the University and the dissemination of the results thereof for the public benefit.

§ 204. *Lef Nosi of Elbasan, Albania, Memorial Fund*

1. The bequest of the late Mrs. M.M. Hasluck shall be used to establish a fund known as the 'Lef Nosi of Elbasan, Albania, Memorial Fund'.

2. The income of the fund shall be administered by the Curators of the Taylor Institution who shall apply it in the first instance to the purchase of books on Albania in accordance with the frontiers in 1939, and shall insert in each book so bought a book-plate with the inscription 'Bequest by Margaret Hasluck in grateful memory of Lef Nosi of Elbasan, Albania'.

3. The Curators of the Taylor Institution may allow surplus income to accumulate and may direct the Curators of the University Chest to apply it:

(*a*) to increase the capital of the fund;

(*b*) to improve the investments held by the fund;

(*c*) to provide a prize or prizes to be administered by the Curators of the Taylor Institution under regulations made by them and to be open to students of either sex attending any university of the United Kingdom who are either

(i) natives of Albania in accordance with its frontiers in 1939 who are proposing to pursue some branch of studies connected with Britain of preferably a linguistic, folklore, historical, sociological, or agricultural nature; or

(ii) subjects of the British Empire and Commonwealth of Nations who are proposing to pursue some branch of studies connected with Albania in accordance with its frontiers in 1939 of preferably a linguistic, folklore, historical, sociological, or agricultural nature.

§ 205. *Lenman Memorial Prize Fund*

1. The University gratefully accepts a gift of £100 from Mrs. E. Lenman in memory of her son Arthur Hamish Lenman.

2. The money shall be invested to form a fund, the income of which shall be applied to the provision of prizes, to be known as Lenman Memorial Prizes, to be awarded by the Committee of Management of the Griffith Institute to members of the University studying Egyptology, under regulations to be made by the committee.

§ 206. *Lewis Fund*

1. The University accepts with gratitude the gift from the Philip Lewis Trust of £10,000, and any further benefactions contributed for this purpose, to establish a fund to be known as the David Lewis Fund, the net income of which shall be applied for the promotion of the study of ancient history, particularly through the use of inscriptional and other documentary sources.

2. The Board of the Faculty of Literae Humaniores, acting on the advice and recommendation of the Director and the Management Committee of the Centre for the Study of Ancient Documents for as long as that centre shall exist, shall be the board of management for the fund.

3. Income from the fund shall be used to pay the emoluments of a scholar invited each year, if funds permit, to give a lecture relevant to the study of ancient history through inscriptional or other documentary sources. The lecturer shall be called, in honour and memory of David Lewis, the David Lewis

Lecturer in Ancient History. The board shall determine the lecturer's duties and fix the amount of his or her emoluments and expenses to be paid from the income of the David Lewis Fund.

4. Any surplus income arising in any year may at the discretion of the board be:

(*a*) carried forward for expenditure in subsequent years;

(*b*) invested in augmentation of the capital, for as long as this shall be permissible in Law;

(*c*) applied to seminars or other activities in the Centre for the Study of Ancient Documents;

(*d*) applied in any other way which the board shall think conducive to the promotion of the study of ancient history through the use of inscriptional and other documentary sources.

5. Council shall have power to amend this decree from time to time, provided that the main object of the fund, as defined in clause 1 above, is always kept in view.

§ 207. *Lienhardt Memorial Fund*

1. The University accepts with gratitude the sums contributed in memory of Peter Arnold Lienhardt to establish a fund, to be known as the Peter Lienhardt Memorial Fund, which shall be applied, together with any further sums accepted for this purpose, to the furtherance of research within the University in Social Anthropology.

2. The fund shall be managed by the Board of the Faculty of Anthropology and Geography.

3. Council shall have power to amend this decree from time to time, provided always that the main object of the fund as defined in clause 1 above is kept in view.

§ 208. *Lindsay Memorial Fund*

1. The University accepts with gratitude the sum of approximately £650, and any further sums which may be contributed for this purpose, to establish a fund, which shall be called the 'Nancy Lindsay Memorial Fund', whereof the income shall be applied to assist women in the study of botany and, in particular, in the collection of plants of possible horticultural value.

2. The fund shall be administered by a board of management consisting of

(1) the Sibthorpian Professor of Plant Science, or a deputy appointed by the professor;

(2) the Sherardian Professor of Botany, or a deputy appointed by the professor;

(3) the Chairman of the Board of the Faculty of Biological Sciences, or a deputy appointed by the chairman, provided always that in neither case shall the

person serving on the board of management be a member of the Department of Plant Sciences.

3. The board of management shall apply the income in making grants to women to enable them to collect botanical specimens and, in particular, plants of horticultural importance provided that the recipients of such grants shall be either

(i) resident members of the University *in statu pupillari*, or

(ii) employed in the Botanic Garden, or

(iii) employed as technicians in the Department of Plant Sciences.

4. Any surplus income arising from whatever cause may be carried forward and made available in future years for grants either

(i) to women qualified as aforesaid, or

(ii) at the discretion of the board of management, towards the general expenses of expeditions organized by the Oxford University Exploration Club in which any women qualified as aforesaid take part for the purpose of collecting plants of possible horticultural value, or otherwise in support of women qualified as aforesaid.

5. Council shall have power to alter this decree from time to time, provided that the main object of the fund as defined in clause 1 above is kept in view.

§ 209. *Littlemore Trust: Advisory Board to administer Funds*

1. The Curators of the University Chest shall maintain a separate account of the assets transferred to the University on the determination of the Littlemore Trust and apply the interest thereof with accumulations for the purpose of aiding by money grants or pensions, any member, or retired former member, of the staff of the University who may be found in straitened circumstances and deserving of pecuniary assistance or the dependants of any such member after his or her decease who may be found in similar circumstances.

2. All such grants shall be made upon the recommendation of an Advisory Board consisting of the Vice-Chancellor and Proctors together with the ex-Vice-Chancellor who for the time being has most recently retired from office.

§ 210. *Lockey Bequest*

1. The Lockey Bequest, which was accepted by the University under Decree (2) of 21 October 1941 shall be invested by the Curators of the University Chest, and shall be known as the Lockey Fund.

2. There shall be a committee to administer the income of the fund consisting of:

(1) a person appointed by the General Board;

(2), (3) two persons appointed by the Board of the Faculty of Physical Sciences;

(4) a person appointed by the Board of the Faculty of Biological Sciences;

(5) a person appointed by the Board of the Faculty of Physiological Sciences;

(6) a person appointed by the Board of the Faculty of Psychological Studies.

Each member of the committee shall hold office for three years and be re-eligible. The committee shall have power to co-opt not more than five persons for periods of two years at a time.

3. The committee appointed under the preceding clause may make grants from the income of the fund for travelling expenses of senior members of the University and of visiting lecturers or for other purposes on the recommendation of the Board of the Faculty of Physical Sciences or the Board of the Faculty of Biological Sciences or the Board of the Faculty of Physiological Sciences or the Board of the Faculty of Psychological Sciences.

4. If in any financial year the income of the fund is not spent, the residue shall be carried forward for expenditure on grants in subsequent years as the committee may determine.

§ 211. *Lubbock Memorial Fund*

1. The two annual gifts of the Maurice Lubbock Memorial Fund shall be offered as prizes to be awarded, one each on the recommendation of the examiners for performance in the Honour School of Engineering Science, and for performance in the engineering and management papers in the Honour School of Engineering, Economics, and Management respectively.

2. The amount made available annually by the Trustees of the Maurice Lubbock Memorial Fund for the purposes of the Maurice Lubbock Memorial Lecture and the Lubbock Lecture on Management shall be awarded to lecturers invited to speak in alternate years on topics related to the industrial applications of Engineering Science and on Management respectively.

§ 212. *Lucas Fund*

1. The University accepts with gratitude the bequests of Hedley Lucas, poet, and Mrs. Gertrude Elaine Lucas, his widow, the net income from which shall be used to provide from time to time one or more scholarships, to be known as Hedley Lucas, Poet, Scholarships, for the benefit of undergraduates of either sex who are reading or proposing to read Theology, preference being given to candidates proposing to enter the Christian Ministry.

2. The fund shall be administered by the Board of the Faculty of Theology, which shall have power, subject to the provisions of this decree, to determine the value and conditions of the awards.

3. Income not expended in any year shall be carried forward for expenditure in subsequent years.

4. Council shall have power to alter this decree from time to time, provided always that the main object of the fund as defined in clause 1 above is kept in view.

§ **221.** *McGinnes British Airways Transplant Fund*

1. The University accepts with gratitude the sum of £30,000 from the staff of British Airways, and such further sums as may be contributed for this purpose, to establish a fund to be called the Ian McGinnes British Airways Transplant Fund, to be applied towards the support of research on transplantation in the Nuffield Department of Surgery.

2. Either the income or the capital of the fund may be spent, at the discretion of the Nuffield Professor of Surgery, on the object of the fund as defined in clause 1 above.

3. Any surplus income arising in any year shall be carried forward for expenditure in a subsequent year.

4. Council shall have power to amend this decree from time to time, provided that the object of the fund as defined in clause 1 above is always kept in view.

§ **222.** *Mackintosh Drama Fund*

1. The University accepts with gratitude a benefaction from the Mackintosh Foundation, and any further benefactions contributed for the same purpose, to establish a fund which shall be called the Cameron Mackintosh Drama Fund and which shall be used for the promotion of interest in, and the study and practice of, contemporary theatre within the University.

2. The fund shall be administered by a board of management consisting of:

(1) the Vice-Chancellor or his or her deputy;

(2)–(4) three persons appointed by Council;

(5) one person appointed by the Mackintosh Foundation.

Any of the members specified in (2)–(5) above may be appointed, and at any time thereafter removed, by the appointing body giving not less than seven days' prior written notice to the Registrar, who shall be responsible for the maintenance of a register of all current appointments.

3. The net income of the fund shall be applied by the board towards fostering, in such manner as it may think fit, interest in, and the general study and practice of, contemporary theatre within the University, and otherwise as stated in the Conditions of Endowment embodied in a Deed of Trust dated 26 March 1990 which has been entered into by the University, St. Catherine's College, and the Mackintosh Foundation; and in particular (but without limitation) towards any appropriate remuneration of persons engaged in running any activities sponsored by the fund, the provision and maintenance of theatrical equipment, stage scenery and properties, and costumes and premises for theatrical productions by resident members of the University, whether or not such productions take place in Oxford, and also in paying any direct costs of the administration of the fund.

4. The board shall from time to time establish arrangements for receiving competitive applications for financial support from the fund, and shall give such arrangements full publicity within the University. In determining how financial support shall be distributed, the board shall bear in mind the desire of the

Foundation in establishing the initial endowment that musical theatre should play a material part in the expenditure programme. Applications may be invited from within the University from student drama and musical societies and other groups (whether university- or college-based), and from individuals.

5. Any surplus income shall be carried forward for expenditure in a subsequent year, provided that the board may at its discretion apply all or any part of the accumulated surplus at any time either towards the maintenance of the Cameron Mackintosh Visiting Professorship of Contemporary Theatre, or in augmentation of the capital of the fund over such period or periods as the board shall determine but not exceeding eighty years from 1 October 1989 or such shorter period as may be prescribed by law.

6. Council shall have power to alter this decree from time to time, provided

(*a*) that the purpose of the fund as defined in clause 1 above, and as otherwise stated in the said Conditions of Endowment, shall not thereby be changed; and

(*b*) that during the continuing existence of the Mackintosh Foundation no alteration shall be effected without the prior consent of the Foundation under seal.

§ 223. *Maritime Archaeology Fund*

1. The University accepts with gratitude the sum of £250, and such further sums as shall from time to time be contributed for this purpose, to establish a fund to be called the Maritime Archaeology Fund to be applied towards the furtherance of study and research in maritime archaeology under the auspices of the University and towards the publication of the results of such study and research.

2. The fund shall be administered by a board of management, to be known as the University's 'Committee for Maritime Archaeological Research', to be appointed by Council for such periods as it shall think fit, which shall have responsibility for:

(*a*) the raising of further contributions to the fund, in accordance with such guidelines as Council may from time to time determine;

(*b*) the provision of financial and other support (including financing the employment of personnel), subject to such conditions as the board shall from time to time determine, for

(i) research projects in maritime archaeology undertaken under the University's auspices.

(ii) the furtherance of approved academic study and research in connection therewith, and

(iii) the publication, where deemed appropriate by the board, of the results of such research projects and any study and research connected therewith.

3. The board shall report from time to time to Council or the General Board, when so requested, on how the fund has been applied.

4. Council shall have power to alter this decree from time to time, provided that the main object of the fund as defined in clause 1 above is kept in view.

§ 224. *Massart Prize in French Literature*

1. The University accepts from the Trustee of the Campaign for Oxford Trust Fund the endowment made possible by a generous benefaction from Lady Blomefield in memory of her sister, Mme. Claude Massart, to form a fund the net income of which shall be applied in the encouragement of the study of French Literature by undergraduate members of the University, through the award from time to time of prizes for specially meritorious performance in French Literature in a university examination.

2. The examiners in the French Literature papers in an appropriate First Public Examination shall be empowered to determine at their discretion which eligible candidates may be recommended to the board of management for the award of Claude Massart Prizes.

3. The Board of the Faculty of Medieval and Modern Languages shall act as the board of management of the fund. It shall determine the recipients and value of the Claude Massart Prizes, and may award prizes of equal value to two or more candidates where the quality of their meritorious performance is not readily distinguishable. Whenever practicable, the board shall arrange for the donor to receive details of the awards.

4. Council shall have power to alter this decree from time to time, provided that the main object of the fund, namely the encouragement of the study of French Literature by undergraduate members of the University, is always kept in view.

§ 225. *Mathematical Prizes*

1. There shall be a Senior Mathematical Prize offered each year in accordance with the following rules:

(*a*) The prize shall be open to any member of the University who on the first day of the Trinity Full Term in which the dissertations are to be submitted has not attained the age of 25 years, and who

(i) has satisfied the examiners in a Final Honour School, or

(ii) is a Probationer Research Student or a Student for the Degree of Master of Letters or Master of Philosophy or Master of Science or Doctor of Philosophy admitted not later than the preceding Michaelmas Term.

(*b*) The prize shall be awarded to the candidate who shall present the dissertation of greatest merit on any subject of Pure or Applied Mathematics, to be selected by the candidate himself or herself.

(*c*) Candidates shall send in their dissertations under their own names to the Registrar not later than the second Friday of Trinity Full Term, and shall state in writing what portions of their dissertations, if any, they claim as original, and shall give references to writings which they have studied in connection with the subjects of their dissertations. They shall at the same time furnish to the Registrar evidence of their eligibility for the prize.

(*d*) The judges shall be the Savilian Professor of Geometry, the Sedleian Professor of Natural Philosophy, the Waynflete Professor of Pure Mathematics, the Rouse Ball Professor of Mathematics, and the Wallis Professor of Mathematics, and each judge shall receive such fee (not being less than £20) as Council shall from time to time determine, to be paid out of the income of the trust fund, on each occasion on which he or she acts.

(*e*) The judges may obtain reports on the dissertations from suitable persons, whose names shall have been approved by the Vice-Chancellor or his or her deputy if he or she shall have appointed one under the provisions of clause 4 below. A person so reporting, not being a trustee, shall receive a fee to be fixed at the discretion of the trustees, to be paid out of the income of the trust fund, for each dissertation on which he or she reports.

(*f*) The judges shall award the prize. In case no dissertations of sufficient merit are sent in, they may withhold the award.

(*g*) In elections to the prize, no regard shall be had to the place of birth, school, parentage, or pecuniary circumstances of the candidate.

(*h*) When the judges have awarded the prize, they shall certify such award to the Vice-Chancellor and shall cause it to be published in the *University Gazette*.

(*i*) The judges may recommend meritorious though unsuccessful candidates for the consideration of the trustees in accordance with the provisions of clause 5 below.

(*j*) The prize shall not be awarded twice to the same person.

(*k*) The award shall be announced before the end of Trinity Term.

2. The prize shall be of the value of £75 or such larger sum as the trustees may determine, exclusive of the emoluments received by the prizewinner from Dr. Johnson's bequest under Tit. XVI, Sect. XXX.

3. Junior Mathematical Prizes shall be offered each year to candidates qualified to obtain honours in the honour schools referred to below, in accordance with the following rules:

(*a*) Not more than four prizes may be awarded in any one year.

(*b*) The maximum value of the prizes shall be as determined by the trustees.

(*c*) One prize shall be awarded (and its amount fixed) by the examiners in the Honour School of Mathematics, if, in their opinion, a candidate submits work of sufficient merit in that examination.

(*d*) Two prizes shall be awarded (and the amounts of each fixed) by the examiners in the Honour School of Mathematical Sciences, if, in their opinion, candidates submit work of sufficient merit in that examination.

(*e*) The fourth prize shall be awarded (and its amount fixed) by the mathematical examiners in the Honour Schools of Mathematics and Computation and of Mathematics and Philosophy for outstanding performance in the mathematical papers, if, in their opinion, a candidate submits work of sufficient merit in either of those examinations.

4. There shall be seven trustees, viz.

(1) the Vice-Chancellor or a deputy appointed by him or her to serve for one academic year,

(2) the Savilian Professor of Astronomy,

(3) the Savilian Professor of Geometry,

(4) the Sedleian Professor of Natural Philosophy,

(5) Dr. Lee's Professor of Experimental Philosophy,

(6) the Waynflete Professor of Pure Mathematics,

(7) the Rouse Ball Professor of Mathematics.

In case of votes being equally divided, the Vice-Chancellor or his or her deputy shall have the casting vote. The presence of three trustees shall be necessary to constitute a board.

5. The trustees shall have power to make presents of money, instruments, or books to meritorious though unsuccessful candidates for the prize, and to apply any surplus income in such other way or ways as they may think fit for promoting the study of Mathematics in the University. In particular the trustees shall have power to offer additional Senior Mathematical Prizes on the same terms as are set out in clause 1 above and with such emoluments (not exceeding the value from time to time determined by the trustees under clause 2 above) as they shall determine.

6. If after experience of this decree any part of it shall be deemed inexpedient, Council shall be at liberty, with the concurrence of the trustees, to make such alterations as circumstances may require.

§ 226. *Maxwell Memorial Fund*

1. The sums contributed by friends and colleagues in memory of J.C. Maxwell, Reader in English Literature and Fellow of Balliol College 1966–76, and formerly Professor of English at the University of Newcastle upon Tyne, shall form a fund to be called the J. C. Maxwell Memorial Fund for the promotion or encouragement of postgraduate studies in English in the Faculty of English Language and Literature at Oxford University and the School of English Language and Literature at the University of Newcastle upon Tyne.

2. The fund shall be managed by the Board of the Faculty of English Language and Literature at Oxford.

3. The board of management shall apply the income, after the payment of all proper expenses, and may in any one year apply up to £120 of the capital, to further the study or research of either:

(*a*) graduates of the University of Newcastle upon Tyne undertaking postgraduate work in English at Oxford;

(*b*) graduates of Oxford University undertaking postgraduate work in English at the University of Newcastle upon Tyne; or (*c*) other members of Oxford University undertaking postgraduate work in English at Oxford.

Preference shall be given to applicants in categories (*a*) and (*b*) above.

4. Applications for grants shall be made for specific research purposes, such as travel in connection with research, or photographic expenses. They shall be supported by the applicant's supervisor and (in the case of Oxford applicants) college.

5. Income not expended in any year shall be carried forward for expenditure in subsequent years.

6. Council shall have power to alter this decree from time to time, provided that in any change of decree the object of the fund shall always be kept in view.

§ 227. *Medical Prizes for award by the Board of the Faculty of Clinical Medicine*

The following prizes shall be awarded under rules made by the Board of the Faculty of Clinical Medicine, which shall be the board of management for each prize.

Duthie Prize in Orthopaedic Surgery

(*a*) The University accepts with gratitude the donations amounting to £5,000 contributed to mark the retirement of Professor R. B. Duthie as Nuffield Professor of Orthopaedic Surgery, to form a fund the net income from which shall be applied in the award of the R. B. Duthie Prize in Orthopaedic Surgery.

(*b*) The prize shall be open to clinical students working in Oxford for the Second Examination for the Degree of Bachelor of Medicine, and shall be awarded annually to the clinical student whose performance during the Orthopaedic Surgery attachment during Year 2 of the clinical course is judged to be the best, provided that candidates of sufficient merit present themselves.

(*c*) Income which is not expended in any year shall be carried forward for expenditure in subsequent years.

(*d*) Council shall have power to modify the provisions of this decree, provided that in any change of decree the object of the fund, as set out in sub-clause (*a*) above, shall always be kept in view.

Freind Prize in Medical History

(*a*) The University has accepted with gratitude donations amounting to £250 contributed to mark the retirement of Dr. A.H.T. Robb-Smith as Nuffield Reader in Pathology, to form a fund the income from which shall be applied to the establishment of a John Freind Prize in Medical History.

(*b*) The prize shall be awarded every second year for an essay on medical history, submitted by a registered medical student of the University on a subject of his or her own choice.

(*c*) Council shall be empowered to modify the provisions of this decree in consultation with the faculty board, and if necessary to transfer the capital of the fund to some other prize of comparable objective.

Johnson Prize in Pathology

(*a*) The object of the Brian Johnson Fund is the establishment of an annual prize for an essay on some pathological subject in memory of Brian Ingram Johnson.

(*b*) The prize shall consist of the annual income of the fund and shall be awarded annually (provided that a candidate of sufficient merit presents himself or herself) for an essay on some pathological subject. The prize shall be open to students on the Register of Clinical Students under regular instruction in Oxford.

(*c*) If in any year the prize is not awarded, the surplus funds shall be reserved for offering a second prize in any future year.

(*d*) Council shall have power to modify the provisions of this decree, provided that in any change of decree the object of the fund shall always be kept in view.

Mallam Memorial Prize in Clinical Medicine

(*a*) The University has accepted with gratitude a gift of £1,000 from Mrs. P. Mallam, to form a fund the income from which shall be applied to the establishment of a prize to be known as the Patrick Mallam Memorial Prize in Clinical Medicine.

(*b*) The prize shall be open to clinical students working in Oxford for the Second Examination for the Degree of Bachelor of Medicine, and shall be awarded annually (provided that candidates of sufficient merit present themselves) to the clinical student who is considered to have cared for his or her patients in the most exemplary fashion.

Pearce Memorial Prizes in Surgery

(*a*) The University has accepted with gratitude a gift of £3,157 from Mrs. J.K. Pearce, to form a fund the income from which shall be applied to the establishment of a prize or prizes to be known as the John Pearce Prizes in Surgery.

(*b*) The prizes shall be open to clinical students working in Oxford for the Second Examination for the Degree of Bachelor of Medicine, and shall be awarded annually (provided that candidates of sufficient merit present themselves) to the clinical students who are considered to have demonstrated care and concern for their patients in the most exemplary fashion.

Potter Essay Prize

(*a*) The University has accepted with gratitude donations amounting to £3,500 to mark the retirement of Dr. J.M. Potter from the Directorship of Postgraduate Medical Education and Training, to form a fund the income from which shall be applied to the establishment of the John Potter Essay Prize.

(*b*) The primary purpose of the prize, which shall be open to clinical students working in Oxford for the Second Examination for the Degree of Bachelor of Medicine and shall be awarded for an essay on a clinical neurosurgical, neurological, or neuropathological topic, shall be the promotion of the sound use of English and clarity of expression in medical writing.

Spray Prize in Clinical Biochemistry

(*a*) The University accepts with gratitude a gift of £1,500 from Mrs. W.A. Spray, to form a fund the income from which shall be applied to the establishment of a prize to be known as the Geoffrey Hill Spray Prize in Clinical Biochemistry.

(*b*) The prize shall be open to clinical students working in Oxford in their second or third year for the Second Examination for the Degree of Bachelor of Medicine, and shall be awarded annually (provided that candidates of sufficient merit present themselves) for an essay on biochemistry as related to the pathogenesis, prevention, diagnosis, or treatment of disease in man.

Stallworthy Prizes in Obstetrics

(*a*) The University has accepted with gratitude donations amounting to £800 contributed to mark the retirement of Sir John Stallworthy from the Nuffield Professorship of Obstetrics and Gynaecology, to form a fund the income from which shall be applied to the establishment of John Stallworthy Prizes in Obstetrics.

(*b*) The prizes shall be open to clinical students working in Oxford for the Second Examination for the Degree of Bachelor of Medicine.

Tizard Prize in Paediatrics

(*a*) The University accepts with gratitude gifts from Mrs. Imogen Smallwood to form a fund, the income of which shall be applied to the establishment of a Peter Tizard Prize in Paediatrics.

(*b*) The prize shall be open to clinical students working in Oxford for the Second Examination for the Degree of Bachelor of Medicine, and shall be awarded annually provided that candidates of sufficient merit present themselves.

Truelove Prize in Gastroenterology

(*a*) The University accepts with gratitude the sum of £8,000 from Dr. S.C. Truelove, to form a fund, the net income from which shall be applied to the establishment of the Sidney Truelove Prize in Gastroenterology.

(*b*) The prize shall be open to clinical students working in Oxford for the Second Examination for the Degree of Bachelor of Medicine, and shall be awarded annually (provided that candidates of sufficient merit present themselves) for an essay on a topic related to diseases of the gastrointestinal tract.

(*c*) Income which is not expended in any year shall be carried forward for use in subsequent years.

(*d*) Council shall be empowered from time to time to modify the provisions of this decree, provided that in any change of decree the object of the fund, as set out in sub-clause (*a*) above, shall always be kept in view.

Vickers Dermatology Prize

(*a*) The University has accepted with gratitude a gift of £1,000 from Dr. H.R. Vickers, to form a fund, the income from which shall be applied to the establishment of a Renwick Vickers Dermatology Fund.

(*b*) The prize shall be open to clinical students working in Oxford for the Second Examination for the Degree of Bachelor of Medicine and shall be awarded annually (provided that a candidate of sufficient merit presents himself or herself) for an essay on a topic relating to Dermatology.

(*c*) If in any year the prize is not awarded, the surplus funds shall be reserved for making one or more additional awards in any subsequent year.

(*d*) Council shall have power to modify the provisions of this decree, provided that in any change of decree the object of the fund shall always be kept in view.

Witts Prize in Haematology or Gastroenterology

(*a*) The University accepts with gratitude donations amounting to £2,020 in memory of Professor L.J. Witts and any additional donations in his memory to form a fund, the income from which shall be applied to the establishment of a prize to be known as the Witts Prize in Haematology or Gastroenterology.

(*b*) The prize shall be open to clinical students working in Oxford for the Second Examination for the Degree of Bachelor of Medicine and shall be awarded annually (provided that candidates of sufficient merit present themselves) for an essay on a topic relating to diseases either of the blood or of the gastro-intestinal tract.

§ 228. *Medical Scholarships for award by the Board of the Faculty of Clinical Medicine*

1. The Curators of the University Chest are authorized to accept contributions for the endowment of medical scholarships and for this purpose shall institute a fund to be called The Medical Scholarships Fund.

2. The scholarships fund shall be administered by the Board of the Faculty of Clinical Medicine.

3. The funds given by, or in commemoration of, the persons named in the schedule to this clause and any other persons whose name may be added by decree to the schedule, shall form part of the Medical Scholarships Fund and the faculty board shall as far as possible ensure that the names in the schedule continue to be commemorated in the scholarships awarded.

SCHEDULE

Frederick G. Hobson

Gustav F.S. Mann

4. The scholarships shall be awarded by the faculty board and shall be open to members of the University, and of other universities in the United Kingdom, who attend the clinical course of the University Medical School, provided that

(i) subject to the approval of the faculty board, a scholar may defer taking up his or her scholarship in order to engage in research;

(ii) a scholar shall not receive emoluments until he or she has started his or her clinical studies;

(iii) a scholar who ceases to pursue his or her clinical studies shall vacate his or her scholarship.

5. The faculty board shall review annually the progress of scholars and may deprive a scholar of his or her award if it is dissatisfied with his or her progress.

6. The faculty board shall inspect the accounts of the fund annually.

7. The faculty board shall have power to make regulations, not inconsistent with this decree, concerning the award of the scholarships, and may delegate any or all of the functions entrusted to it under this decree, except that specified in clause 6 above, to a committee appointed by the board.

§ 229. *Meyerstein Bequest*

1. The bequest of the residuary estate of the late Edward Harry William Meyerstein shall be held upon trust for the University of Oxford absolutely for the purposes of literary or archaeological research.

2. The first charge on the annual income of the bequest shall be the cost of the upkeep of the Meyerstein tomb in the churchyard of the parish church of St. John, Hampstead.

3. The available income from the bequest shall be divided equally between the Board of the Faculty of English Language and Literature and the Committee for Archaeology.

§ 230. *Milburn Memorial Fund*

1. The University accepts with gratitude the bequest of the Revd. R. Gordon Milburn to establish a fund to promote the theological or the philosophical study within the University of mysticism and religious experience.

2. The Board of the Faculty of Theology shall be the board of management of the fund.

3. The board of management shall apply the income, after the payment of all proper expenses, towards the provision of a Gordon Milburn Junior Research Fellowship tenable at Oxford and awarded from time to time under such conditions, conducive to the purposes of the bequest stated in clause 1 above, as the board shall determine.

4. Any surplus income available, either because of a vacancy in the fellowship or for any other reason, may be applied toward such other purpose or purposes conducive to the promotion of the theological or the philosophical study within the University of mysticism and religious experience as the board shall determine, or may be carried forward for expenditure in subsequent years.

5. Council shall have power to alter this decree from time to time, provided that the main object of the fund, as stated in clause 1 above, is kept in view.

§ 231. *Mineralogy: Bowman Library*

1. The scientific library of the late Herbert Lister Bowman, M.A., D.Sc., Fellow of Magdalen College, Waynflete Professor of Mineralogy and Crystallography, which shall be available for the use of students and research workers in Mineralogy, shall be named the Herbert Lister Bowman Library.

2. It shall be housed in the rooms in the Department of Geology occupied by the University Reader in Mineralogy and shall be under his or her control.

3. The Curators of the University Chest may receive any fund which shall be established for the purchase of additions to the library and contributions in augmentation of the fund and the interest of such fund shall be expended by the University Reader in Mineralogy for that purpose.

§ 232. *Molecular Biophysics Fund*

1. The University accepts with gratitude an anonymous benefaction of £20,000, together with such other sums as may be made available for the purpose, to establish a Molecular Biophysics Fund to promote research and teaching in Molecular Biophysics in the University's Molecular Biophysics Laboratory.

2. The board of management of the fund shall be
   (1) the David Phillips Professor of Molecular Biophysics;
   (2) the Iveagh Professor of Microbiology;
   (3) the Whitley Professor of Biochemistry.

3. The fund shall be used to help research students and other members of the Laboratory of Molecular Biophysics through the provision of grants for travel, for financial support, and for promotion of research and teaching in Molecular Biophysics, in circumstances in which other sources of funds are not readily available.

4. Awards shall normally be made from the income of the fund but in exceptional circumstances the board of management shall have power to make individual awards up to a total of £4,000 per annum or a sum equal to 20 per cent of the fund, whichever shall be the greater.

5. Income not expended in any one year shall be carried forward for expenditure in subsequent years.

6. Council shall have power to amend this decree from time to time, provided that the main object of the fund, as stated in clause 1 above, is always kept in view.

§ 233. *Moores Fund*

1. The University accepts with deep gratitude the benefaction of £1,990,000 received from the Trustees of the Peter Moores Foundation to establish a fund for the advancement within the University of education, learning, teaching,

scholarship, and research in the field of Management Studies. In the event of Management Studies ceasing to be either a field of study or one in which it is practicable to maintain both the Directorship of the University's Saïd Business School and a Professorship of Management Studies, the fund shall be applied for further charitable purposes in accordance with a formulation agreed with the said trustees as a condition of the benefaction.

2. The fund shall be managed by the Board of the Faculty of Management.

3. The University shall apply the net income of the fund partly towards the maintenance of the Directorship of the University's Saïd Business School, each successive holder of which is to be known as the Peter Moores Director, and partly towards the maintenance of a Professorship of Management Studies, to be known as the Peter Moores Professorship of Management Studies. Any income not required in any financial year for the maintenance of the directorship and of the professorship may, at the discretion of the Board of the Faculty of Management, either be carried forward for expenditure in a subsequent year or applied in some other way or ways in furtherance of the purposes of the fund, as defined in clause 1 above.

4. Council shall appoint one elector to the professorship and one to the directorship after consultation with the said trustees or their nominated representative.

5. Council shall have power to alter this decree from time to time provided that the main object of the fund, as defined in clause 1 above, is always kept in view and provided that any changes may be made only with the concurrence of the Trustees of the Peter Moores Foundation or their nominated representative.

§ **234.** *Morgan Prize in Finance*

1. The University accepts with gratitude the gift of £30,000 from J.P. Morgan, and any further sums which may be donated for the same purpose, to establish a fund the net income from which shall be applied to provide a prize, to be known as the J.P. Morgan Prize in Finance, for award to graduate students of the University in Management Studies.

2. The fund shall be administered by the Board of the Faculty of Management, which shall make the detailed arrangements for the award of the prize (including the value of the prize and the appointment of the judges).

3. The prize shall be offered annually to members of the University who are at the time of entry for the prize registered as students for the Degree of Master of Business Administration and who will have been so registered for a period of less than twelve months at the date by which essays for the prize are required to be submitted.

4. Provided that there is a candidate of sufficient merit, the prize shall be awarded annually for the best essay submitted on such subject within the general area of Finance as shall be announced in advance each year by the judges.

5. If in any year the prize is not awarded, or there is unexpended income from the fund for any other reason, the surplus income shall be carried forward for expenditure in subsequent years.

6. Council shall have power to alter this decree from time to time, provided that the main object of the fund, as defined in clause 1 above, is always kept in view.

§ **235.** *Morris Prize Fund*

1. The University gratefully accepts the sums contributed in memory of the late J.H.C. Morris, M.A., D.C.L., Reader in the Conflict of Laws, for the furtherance of the study of the Conflict of Laws within the University.

2. The primary use of the fund shall be the maintenance of a prize, to be known as the John Morris Prize, to be awarded annually to the candidate who, in the opinion of the examiners, writes the best paper on the Conflict of Laws in the examination for the degree of Bachelor of Civil Law or for the degree of Magister Juris in European and Comparative Law. The prize shall be of such value as may be determined from time to time by the Board of the Faculty of Law.

3. Surplus income may be applied in any way that the Board of the Faculty of Law thinks conducive to the study of the Conflict of Laws within the University.

4. Council shall have power to alter this decree from time to time, provided that in any change in decree, the primary object of the fund shall always be kept in view.

§ **236.** *Motz Prize in Electrical Engineering*

1. The University accepts with gratitude the bequest of Professor Hans Motz, sometime Professor of Electrical Engineering, of the sum of £3,000.

2. The bequest shall be invested to form a fund, the net income of which shall be used for the maintenance of a prize to be called the Motz Prize in Electrical Engineering. The Board of the Faculty of Physical Sciences shall be the board of management for the fund.

3. Provided that suitable candidates present themselves, the prize shall be awarded, on the nomination of the examiners, for the best fourth-year project in Electrical Engineering in the Final Honour School of Engineering Science and the associated joint schools. The value of the prize shall be as determined from time to time by the board of management, and the prize shall preferably be spent on works of reference in the fields of Classical Electromagnetism, Classical Mechanics, or Plasma Physics.

4. Income not expended on the prize in any year shall, at the discretion of the board of management, either be used to award an additional prize or prizes subject to the provisions of clause 3 above, or be carried forward for expenditure in subsequent years.

5. Council shall have power to amend this decree from time to time, provided that the main object of the fund, as stated in clause 2 above, is always kept in view.

§ 237. *Müller Memorial Fund*

1. The fund shall be called the Max Müller Memorial Fund.

2. The income of the fund shall be applied to the promotion of learning and research in all matters relating to the history and archaeology, the languages, literatures, and religions of ancient India.

3. The administration of the income of the fund shall be entrusted to seven persons, who shall be

(1) the Vice-Chancellor;

(2) the Boden Professor of Sanskrit;

(3) the Laudian Professor of Arabic;

(4) the Warden of All Souls College;

(5) one person to be nominated by the Board of the Faculty of Oriental Studies;

(6), (7) two persons to be chosen by co-optation to serve for five years.

4. All the powers of the administrators of the fund may be exercised by a majority of those present and voting at a meeting duly summoned, provided that four of the administrators at least be present.

5. If in any year the income from the fund be not wholly expended, the administrators may order that the balance so remaining shall be invested temporarily.

6. The accounts of the fund shall be audited and published in each year with the other University Accounts.

7. This decree shall be subject to alteration from time to time by Council provided that the object of the fund as defined in clause 2 above is adhered to.

§ 238. *Murray Fellowship in History*

The bequest of the late Robert Henry Murray, M.A., Litt.D., T.C.D., shall be applied to the endowment of two Fellowships in History at Oxford, for grants to graduates of the Queen's University, Belfast, who are of exceptional promise in historical studies, and for assisting publications.

§ 239. *Music Libraries and Collections*

Bate Collection

1. The University has accepted with deep gratitude the gift of Mr. Philip Bate of his collection of musical wind instruments.

2. Subject to the consent of the Board of the Faculty of Music and of the General Board, there may be added to the collection such other musical

instruments as have been accepted by the University otherwise than on the basis of their retention as a separate collection.

3. A post of lecturer/curator shall be maintained (under the arrangements applicable to university lecturers), the holder of which shall, under the direction of the Board of the Faculty of Music, have charge of the collection and demonstrate it.

4. The Curators of the University Chest are authorised to accept sums contributed towards the cost of maintaining the said post of lecturer/curator, or of maintaining or adding to the collection.

Ellis Memorial Library

The contributions by friends of the late Francis Bevis Ellis, of Christ Church, and any further sums which may be so contributed, shall be applied, both as to capital and income, under the direction of the Heather Professor of Music, in providing accommodation for and maintaining a Library of Music bequeathed by the said Francis Bevis Ellis to the Heather Professor of Music and to be known as the Ellis Memorial Library.

Howes Bequest

The University accepts with gratitude the bequest of the late Frank Stewart Howes of his library of books, music pamphlets, and gramophone records relating to folk music, for the use of the Faculty of Music in encouraging the study of folk music and ethnomusicology.

Morley-Pegge Collection

The University accepts with gratitude from Mr. William Morley-Pegge, in memory of his father, the late Reginald Morley-Pegge, the collection of wind instruments, books, and volumes of music from the estate of his father, the collection to be accommodated with the Bate Collection of Musical Instruments under the charge of its Curator in the premises allocated to the Faculty of Music.

Music Library

1. The books and music given to the University by Sir Hugh Percy Allen, M.A., D.Mus., Fellow of New College, Heather Professor of Music, shall be kept together as a single working library for students of music within the University, and the present custom of borrowing shall be fully maintained.

2. The library shall be under the management of the Board of the Faculty of Music in consultation with the Heather Professor.

3. The University shall provide and maintain free of charge suitable accommodation for the library either in its present quarters or elsewhere.

4. An annual grant shall be made to the library for the provision for payment of a Librarian, for the purchase of music and books on music, and for the purpose of binding, the amount of such grant to be determined from time to time by the General Board.

Retford Collection

The University accepts with gratitude the collection of violin bows and bowmakers' tools from the estate of the late William Charles Retford, Esquire (donated by his legatees), the collection to be accommodated in the premises allocated to the Faculty of Music, and to be in the charge of the Curator of the Bate Collection of Musical Instruments under the supervision of the Heather Professor of Music, who shall carry out the wish of the said William Charles Retford that the bows shall remain intact and on view for serious students of the craft as much and as regularly as practicable, to preserve and illustrate a basic knowledge of the bowmaker's craft.

§ 241. *Napier Memorial Library*

The sum of £112·50, contributed to the Napier Memorial Fund by the Executors and Relatives of the late Arthur Sampson Napier, M.A., D.Litt., Fellow of Merton College, Merton Professor of English Language and Literature, shall be applied through the Board of the Faculty of English Language and Literature towards the upkeep of the Napier Memorial Library, whether by purchase of books or periodicals or in any other way at the discretion of the board.

§ 242. *Naples Biological Scholarship*

For this subsection, which has been suspended since 1974, see *Statutes*, 1982, pp. 577–8.

§ 243. *News International Fund*

1. The University accepts with deep gratitude a benefaction from News International plc to form a fund the income from which shall be used for the support of academic work (including the provision of library resources) by members of the Faculty of English Language and Literature, and in particular for the support of work in the area covered by the Rupert Murdoch Professorship of Language and Communication.

2. The Board of the Faculty of English Language and Literature shall be the board of management of the fund and shall make such arrangements for its administration as may seem to the board to be appropriate from time to time.

3. Council shall have power to alter this decree from time to time, provided that the main object of the fund, namely the support of academic work by members of the Faculty of English Language and Literature, shall always be kept in view.

§ 244. *Nissan Fund for Japanese Studies*

1. The University has accepted with deep gratitude a benefaction of £1,500,000 from the Nissan Motor Company of Japan as an endowment for the furtherance of Japanese studies in the University, principally by the establishment of posts in the subject and the foundation of an Institute of Japanese Studies to be located at St. Antony's College.

2. The benefaction shall be applied to these objects in such ways as Council in consultation with the General Board shall determine.

§ 245. *Norton Bequest*

1. The Board of the Faculty of Social Studies shall be the board of management of the bequest of the late Sara Norton, the income of which is to be used to provide an annual prize 'to any undergraduate or student of the University for the best essay or study in the field of the political history of the United States of America', and shall have power to appoint judges, and to fix their remuneration.

2. The prize shall be offered in Trinity Term each year for an essay upon some subject proposed by the candidate and approved by the board—the subject to fall within the field of the political history and institutions of the United States of America. Candidates shall not be precluded from submitting work which has been or will be submitted for a thesis in an Honour School or for the examination for the degree of M.Phil.

3. Candidates must be members of the University who will not have exceeded eighteen terms from matriculation by the end of the term in which the prize is awarded.

4. In any year in which the best essay submitted is considered by the judges to be not worthy of the award of the prize but nevertheless of merit, a grant may be made from the income of the bequest to the candidate in question.

5. In any year in which the prize is not awarded, the surplus income arising, after the award of any grant as provided for in clause 4 above and the remuneration of the judges, shall be made over in equal parts to the Social Studies Library and the History Faculty Library for the purchase of books in the field defined in clause 2 above, to be placed, appropriately inscribed, in the lending collections of those libraries.

§ 246. *Nubar Pasha Armenian Scholarship*

1. The sum received by the University from his Excellency Boghos Nubar Pasha shall be invested in the name of the Chancellor, Masters, and Scholars of the University of Oxford.

2. The income derived from such trust fund shall be applied to the establishment and maintenance of a scholarship for the encouragement of the study of Armenian History and Literature.

3. The scholarship shall be administered by a board of management consisting of:

(1) the Vice-Chancellor;

(2) the Master of Balliol College, or, if the Master is Vice-Chancellor then a person appointed by the Master and Fellows of Balliol College to act during his or her Vice-Chancellorship;

(3) the Calouste Gulbenkian Professor of Armenian Studies;

(4) a person elected by the Board of the Faculty of Literae Humaniores;

(5), (6) two persons elected by the Board of the Faculty of Oriental Studies.

The elected members of the board of management shall hold office for three years and shall be re-eligible.

4. The scholarship shall be of the annual value of £250 or such larger sum, not exceeding the value of one year's income of the fund after the expenses of management and any examiner's fees have been deducted, as the board of management may, having regard to any other emoluments accruing to the scholar and to the state of the fund, determine. The scholarship shall be tenable for one year in the first instance, but may be renewed at the discretion of the board for not more than two further years.

5. The scholarship shall be open to any member of the University, provided always that no person shall be eligible for election to the scholarship whose vernacular language is Armenian.

6. The board of management shall have power to make such arrangements as they may deem expedient for the election of a scholar either with or without examination, provided that they shall give not less than two months' notice of the time and place at which the names of the candidates will be received.

7. If no election is made in any year in which the scholarship is offered in consequence of there being no candidate of sufficient merit, or if any vacancy occurs from any other cause, the sums which accrue owing to the vacancy shall, at the discretion of the board of management, be applied for any other purpose designed to encourage the study of Armenian History and Literature.

8. The scholarship shall not be awarded twice to the same person.

9. The board of management shall have power to defray out of the income of the trust fund any expenses incurred in connection with the award of the scholarship, and any surplus income remaining after such expenses have been met and the stipend of the scholar has been paid shall be dealt with in the manner prescribed in clause 7 above.

10. The board of management shall have power to alter this decree from time to time with the consent of Council, provided always that the main object of the founder be kept in view, namely the encouragement of the study of Armenian History and Literature.

§ 247. *Nuclear Electric Prize in Mathematical Modelling and Numerical Analysis*

1. The income from the fund established with the gift of £2,000 to the University from the Central Electricity Generating Board shall be used to provide an annual prize which shall be known as the Nuclear Electric Prize in Mathematical Modelling and Numerical Analysis.

2. The prize, of a value to be determined from time to time by the Board of the Faculty of Mathematical Sciences, shall be awarded, if there is a candidate of sufficient merit, by the examiners for the Degree of Master of Science in

Mathematical Modelling and Numerical Analysis to the candidate whose performance in that examination they judge to be the best.

3. The administration of the fund shall be under the direction of the Board of the Faculty of Mathematical Sciences which may delegate the responsibility to the Supervisory Committee for the Degree of Master of Science in Mathematical Modelling and Numerical Analysis.

4. Income not expended in any year shall be carried forward for expenditure in subsequent years.

5. Council shall have full power to alter this decree from time to time, provided always that the purpose of the fund, as defined in cl. 1 above, shall be kept in view.

§ 248. *Nuffield Benefactions*

[1]

Nuffield Benefaction for the Advancement of Medicine

1. (*a*) For the purposes of the trust created by the Deed of Covenant and Trust executed by Lord Nuffield on 24 November 1936 there shall be a body of trustees, and such body shall be composed as follows:

(1) as chairman, a person appointed on the occurrence of each vacancy by the Chancellor of the University, provided that the Chancellor shall have the right from time to time to revoke any such appointment;

(2) the Vice-Chancellor;

(3)–(5) three persons appointed by the Chancellor of the University;

(6) the Regius Professor of Medicine or, whenever he or she is a trustee in another capacity, a person appointed by the Board of the Faculty of Clinical Medicine;

(7) a person appointed by Council after consultation with the Board of the Faculty of Clinical Medicine;

(8) a person appointed by Council after consultation with the Board of the Faculty of Physiological Sciences;

(9)–(10) two persons appointed by Council after consultation with the chairmen of the N.H.S. Trusts in the City of Oxford which are concerned with teaching and research and which include a university-nominated non-executive director on their trust boards.

Provided that (i) no person appointed or being a trustee (except under (1)–(5) or the Regius Professor of Medicine) shall be capable of being also a member of the committee hereinafter referred to, and in the event of any such member being appointed or becoming a trustee (except as aforesaid) his or her appointment as trustee shall be inoperative, and if any trustee (except as aforesaid) becomes a member of the committee he or she shall *ipso facto* cease to be a trustee; (ii) no person shall become or remain a trustee after reaching the age of seventy years; (iii) the person or body appointing any trustee other than the chairman shall have the power from time to time to revoke the appointment in case such trustee becomes of unsound mind or goes to reside abroad or otherwise becomes incapable of satisfactorily carrying out his duties as trustee; (iv) any trustee who desires to retire from his or her trusteeship may do so on giving to the University and to the person appointing him or her two months' notice in writing of such desire.

(*b*) The trustees shall have full power

(i) to determine in their sole discretion from time to time whether any object proposed to be financed out of the income or capital of the trust fund is inconsistent with the terms of the said deed;

(ii) to appoint their own Secretary;

(iii) to make rules or by-laws as to their meetings (including what is to be the quorum for meetings) and from time to time to alter such rules or by-laws;

(iv) to make such arrangements for meeting the necessary remuneration of their Secretary and expenses of his or her office and the expenses of the trustees as they think fit, and the said remuneration and expenses shall be a first charge on the income of the trust.

(*c*) The duties of the trustees shall be

(i) to receive and consider an annual statement of the objects proposed to be financed out of the trust fund in which shall be included an annual estimate of the income and expenditure thereof; to determine whether any of the objects proposed to be financed out of the trust fund are inconsistent with the terms of the trust, and if so to notify in writing the body submitting the statement of such inconsistency and if not to pass such annual statement and estimate;

(ii) to receive annual accounts of the income of the Trust and the expenditure defrayed therefrom and of any capital subject to the Trust and to report to the University on the accounts;

(iii) to approve, in the light of advice to be received under clause 2 (*b*) (i) below and in the light of any representations made by the General Board on the level of contribution, the amount of the annual income of the Trust to be allocated through the General Fund to the General Board as a continuing contribution to the running of the Clinical Medical School and the amount of the annual income to be allocated to the Board of the Faculty of Clinical Medicine for distribution by its Medical Research Fund Committee to promote work in the field of medical research;

(iv) to receive an annual report on the work of the Board of the Faculty of Clinical Medicine and the Clinical School carried out under, or within the purposes of, the Trust and to report to the University on the annual report.

2. (*a*) There shall be a Nuffield Benefaction Committee composed as follows:

(1) the Vice-Chancellor;

(2) the Regius Professor of Medicine;

(3)–(7) the Nuffield Professors of Clinical Medicine, Surgery, Obstetrics and Gynaecology, Anaesthetics, Orthopaedic Surgery;

(8), (9) two persons, not being Nuffield Professors but qualified under Ch. II, Sect. VI to be official members of the Board of the Faculty of Clinical Medicine, appointed by the faculty board;

(10) the Director of Clinical Studies;

(11) the Director of Postgraduate Medical Education and Training.

The committee shall have power to co-opt not more than two persons, for periods of two years at a time.

(*b*) The duties of the committee shall be:

(i) to advise the Trustees how much of the annual income of the Trust should be allocated each year through the General Fund to the General Board as a continuing contribution to the running of the Clinical Medical School and how much of the annual income should be allocated to the Board of the Faculty of Clinical Medicine for distribution by its Medical Research Fund Committee to promote work in the field of medical research; to advise the Trustees on any proposals for capital expenditure out of income or accumulated income of the Trust; to advise the Trustees of any capital expenditure proposed to be met out of the capital of the Trust and the conditions for its repayment; and to prepare annual accounts and submit them to the Trustees under clause 1 (*c*) (ii).

(ii) to consider an annual report on the work of the Board of the Faculty of Clinical Medicine and the Clinical School carried out under, or within the purposes of, the Trust and submit it to the Trustees under clause 1 (*c*) (iv).

(*c*) The committee may act notwithstanding any vacancy or vacancies in its membership.

3. The Secretary of the Board of the Faculty of Clinical Medicine shall act as secretary of the committee.

4. The Curators of the University Chest shall, on the requisition of the committee or in accordance with the provisions of this decree, as the case may be, make payments out of the income of the trust fund in accordance with the estimates prepared by the committee and passed by the trustees, provided always that capital expenditure may be met out of the capital of the trust fund on condition that provisions for its repayment out of the income of the trust fund is made to the satisfaction of the curators.

5. Any of the clauses of this decree may be modified by a further decree, and this decree or any further decree may be modified and/or replaced in whole or in part by a statute, provided that in the case of a modification the trustees shall first have certified in writing to the Vice-Chancellor that the proposed modification is not inconsistent with the terms of the said deed.

[2]

Gifts towards costs of Buildings

The University accepts with profound and renewed gratitude a gift of £200,000 offered to it in trust by Lord Nuffield, subject to the following conditions to which the University agrees, that is to say:

1. The said sum of £200,000 shall be applied to the following purposes, viz.:

(*a*) meeting the costs already incurred or to be incurred by the University in the erection of the following buildings:

(i) two new wards over Cronshaw Ward at the Radcliffe Infirmary for the use in the first instance of the Nuffield Professors of Surgery and Obstetrics and Gynaecology respectively, together with operating and X-ray theatres and office accommodation;

(ii) a new wing of the Maternity Home at the Radcliffe Infirmary;

(*b*) meeting the cost of erection of any further buildings required at or in connection with any of the hospitals associated with the scheme for the development of the School of Medicine which is referred to in Decree (7) of 1 December 1936, solely by reason of the association of such hospital with the scheme;

(*c*) contributing to the cost of erection of any building required at or in connection with any of the said hospitals partly by reason of the said association and partly otherwise.

Provided always that any dispute which may arise between the University and the governing body of any such hospital as to

(1) whether a building which it is proposed to erect is required solely by reason of the association of the hospital with the scheme; or

(2) what proportion of the cost of any building required partly by reason of the said association is properly payable out of the said sum

shall be referred to the trustees appointed in accordance with clause 1 of the said decree, whose decision shall be final.

2. Any part of the sum of £200,000 remaining in the hands of the University from time to time which is not required immediately for any of the aforesaid purposes shall be invested until it is required and the income thereof shall be applied to the aforesaid purposes.

3. Save as is herein otherwise provided the said sum of £200,000, together with any income arising from the investment of any part of it in accordance with clause 2 above, shall be subject to the same conditions as if it had formed part of the annuity referred to in the Deed of Covenant and Trust made between Lord Nuffield and the University on the twenty-fourth day of November 1936.

[3]

Superannuation Contributions chargeable on Funds of Nuffield Benefaction for the Advancement of Medicine

That part of the Superannuation or Pension contribution of the recipient of a salary from Lord Nuffield's Benefaction for the Advancement of Medicine which is not payable by the recipient of the salary shall be a charge upon the funds of the Benefaction.

[4]

Scheme for Oxford Nuffield Medical Fellowships

1. The authority and duties of the University as set out in the Scheme contained in the Deed of Trust, executed by Viscount Nuffield on 20 May 1938,[1] to promote the progress of medical knowledge by co-operation between the Medical School of the University, and such of the Universities of the Dominions of Australia, New Zealand, and South Africa as provide facilities for medical research, shall, unless provided otherwise, be exercised by Council.

2. The Demonstratorships and Assistantships referred to in the Scheme shall be known as Oxford Nuffield Medical Fellowships, but the provisions of the Scheme relating to Demonstratorships and Assistantships respectively shall otherwise remain unchanged and each appointment made under the provisions of clause 3 thereof shall be reported to the General Board and the appropriate board of faculty.

THE FIRST SCHEDULE

(The Scheme)

1. (1) The University of Oxford (hereinafter referred to as 'the University'), subject to the necessary funding being provided by the Trustees, shall establish:

(i) Three Demonstratorships tenable respectively in the Departments of Anatomy, Biochemistry, Pathology, Pharmacology, or Physiology, or with the consent of the Managing Trustees in such other departments participating in the study of medical and allied problems as the University may from time to time determine; and

(ii) Three Clinical Assistantships tenable in such departments as the University, with the consent of the Managing Trustees, may determine; and

(iii) Up to twelve additional posts, or such higher number as the Managing Trustees shall, with the prior agreement of the University, from time to time determine, each being either a Demonstratorship or a Clinical Assistantship tenable on the same terms as the Demonstratorships and Clinical Assistantships referred to above.

(2) The Managing Trustees shall direct payment of such sums as they may from time to time determine to the Curators of the University Chest for each Demonstrator and Assistant for the time being holding an appointment under the provisions of this Scheme, such sums to be applied to the purposes of the department of the University in which such Demonstrator or Assistant is for the time being employed.

2. (1) The qualifications for appointment to a Demonstratorship shall be graduation at one of the Qualifying Universities and relevant experience in research. The Qualifying Universities shall be such educational establishments in Australia, New Zealand, and South Africa (hereinafter referred to as 'the

[1] For the Deed of Trust, as varied by the Charity Commissioners for England and Wales by a Scheme dated 14 July 1980, see *Statutes*, 1989, p. 585.

Qualifying Countries') as the Managing Trustees shall from time to time determine.

(2) The qualifications for appointment to an Assistantship shall be graduation at one of the Qualifying Universities and a medical qualification obtained in one of the said Qualifying Countries or in the United Kingdom.

(3) No person shall be appointed either to a Demonstratorship or to an Assistantship who does not intend to return, immediately after such appointment shall terminate, to the country from which he or she was appointed, to undertake at least three years' work similar in nature to that carried out under the appointment.

3. (1) Appointments to Demonstratorships and Assistantships shall be made by the University on the nomination of the Qualifying Universities as hereinafter provided.

(2) The University shall from time to time determine, with the consent of the Managing Trustees, the order of priority to be accorded to the respective Qualifying Universities in the nomination of eligible candidates for appointment.

(3) At least one Demonstrator and at least one Assistant shall be appointed each year to commence duties during the ensuing academic year, provided that adequately qualified candidates have been nominated for this purpose.

4. (1) Each appointment of a Demonstrator or Assistant shall be for such period, not exceeding three years, as the University shall determine, provided that the University, in exceptional circumstances, is empowered, subject to the prior consent of the Managing Trustees and of the nominating Qualifying University, to extend the appointment for one or more further periods, but only in so far as tenure overall shall not exceed six years.

(2) Each Demonstrator and Assistant shall receive by way of emolument during his or her appointment such sums as shall be provided at the discretion of the Managing Trustees, which emolument shall be paid monthly in arrears. An allowance, to be fixed at the discretion of the Managing Trustees, for each dependent child who is below the age at which compulsory education ceases or, being above that age, is receiving full-time education, shall also be provided.

(3) The Managing Trustees may defray the cost of college and university fees and dues incurred by Demonstrators and Assistants in working for research degrees of the University, and may make payments towards expenses incurred in respect of the association with a college of an appointee who is not working for a research degree of the University. The Managing Trustees may also at their discretion make grants towards expenses incurred by Demonstrators and Assistants in the course of travel in connection with their work.

(4) Each Demonstrator and Assistant shall also be entitled to the full cost of approved travel for the appointee, any spouse, and any children under the age of 18, to enable the appointee to travel to Oxford for the appointment and to return to the country of his or her nominating university thereafter. Payment for travel to Oxford shall at the request of the Demonstrator or Assistant be paid prior to the commencement of such travel, and the second part shall be paid in England on the completion of the appointment.

Provided that in all cases the Managing Trustees if they think fit may direct the payment of the second part of such travelling expenses to a Demonstrator or Assistant who has not completed his or her appointment.

Provided also that the Managing Trustees shall not be required to make payment of the second part if three or more years shall have elapsed between the completion of the appointment and the appointee's return to the country from which he or she was appointed.

(5) The duties of Demonstrators and Assistants shall be determined by the head of the department concerned and no Demonstrator or Assistant shall without the consent of the head of department enter for any professional examination.

(6) Demonstrators and Assistants, during tenure of their appointments, shall be subject to the jurisdiction of the University's Visitatorial Board as prescribed by Tit. VIII, Sect. I of the University's Statutes, and shall be subject to the provisions of Title XVI thereof; provided that no travelling allowance payable under the provisions of sub-clause (4) of this clause shall be forfeited by reason of deprivation of office.

(7) The Managing Trustees may, if they think fit, authorise payment to a Fellow after return to the country of origin of the same emoluments as those payable in Oxford (but excluding any allowances payable under sub-clause (2) of this clause). Any such arrangement shall not exceed one year and shall normally only be granted to Fellows who have spent not more than three years in Oxford. Any such arrangement shall be conditional upon arrangements being made, to the satisfaction of the Trustees, for the Fellow to undertake research or other appropriate employment in an institution approved by the Trustees and the nominating Qualifying University for the period during which the emoluments are to be paid.

5. The Managing Trustees may in any year, in addition to the appointments made under clauses 1–4 above, appoint up to three graduates of the University of Oxford to hold office for not less than one year in any of the Qualifying Universities in this Scheme upon the same terms and conditions as, *mutatis mutandis*, are prescribed for Demonstrators and Assistants except that the maximum period of appointment shall not exceed three years, such appointments to be subject to the concurrence of the Qualifying University or Universities concerned. The persons to fill any such appointment shall be selected by the Managing Trustees in such manner as they think fit.

6. (1) The University, subject as hereinafter provided, may from time to time appoint any person eminent in the study or practice of Medicine or of some allied subject, and whether or not a member of the University, to visit one or more of the said Qualifying Countries and, by delivery of lectures in any of the Qualifying Universities, by informal conferences, and by such other means as may seem expedient, to give information in regard to research in medical and allied subjects in the United Kingdom and to gain information which will assist the University in carrying out the Donor's charitable intention in accordance with the provisions of this Scheme.

(2) The Managing Trustees may provide a grant to any person appointed under sub-clause (1) of this clause to assist the appointee in undertaking the visit (or visits) therein prescribed. Before making any such appointment the University shall consult the Managing Trustees, and the amount of grant to be offered to any appointee, whether by way of stipend or in respect of expenses, or both, and the duration of the appointment, shall be agreed between the University and the Managing Trustees, provided that the Managing Trustees are satisfied that the income of the Trust Fund is sufficient to meet the amount of the grant agreed in addition to all other payments to be made thereout.

(3) Any such appointee shall be appointed for such period and subject to such conditions as the University, after consultation and agreement with the Managing Trustees as aforesaid, shall determine at the time of the appointment.

7. (1) The University, subject as hereinafter provided, may from time to time appoint any person eminent in the study or practice of Medicine or of some allied subject who is a member of any of the Qualifying Universities in the Scheme to visit the University and, by delivery of lectures in the University, by informal conferences, and by such other means as may seem expedient, to give information in regard to research in medical and allied subjects in the country in which the visitor's university is located and to gain information in regard to research in such subjects in the United Kingdom, with a view to promoting the progress of medical knowledge thereby.

(2) The Managing Trustees may provide a grant to any person appointed under sub-clause (1) of this clause to assist the appointee in undertaking the visit (or visits) therein prescribed. Before making any such appointment the University shall consult the Managing Trustees, and the amount of grant to be offered to any appointee, whether by way of stipend or in respect of expenses, or both, and the duration of the appointment, shall be agreed between the University and the Managing Trustees, provided that the Managing Trustees are satisfied that the income of the Trust Fund is sufficient to meet the amount of the grant agreed in addition to all other payments to be made thereout.

(3) Any such appointee shall be appointed for such period and subject to such conditions as the University, after consultation and agreement with the Managing Trustees as aforesaid, shall determine at the time of the appointment.

8. The Managing Trustees may make such payments to the University, towards the cost of maintaining and improving its equipment and other facilities for medical teaching and research, as they consider necessary to sustain and advance effective co-operation between the Medical School and one or more of the Qualifying Universities in the furtherance of medical knowledge.

THE SECOND SCHEDULE

(This schedule contained Decree (4) of 8 March 1938, the enacting part of which, as subsequently amended, is set out in clauses 1 and 2 of § 248 [4] above. For text of the original decree and preamble, see *Statuta*, 1948, p. 720.)

THE THIRD SCHEDULE
(Qualifying Universities)

UNIVERSITY OF ADELAIDE, AUSTRALIA
FLINDERS UNIVERSITY, AUSTRALIA [Added 23 July 1982]
UNIVERSITY OF MELBOURNE, AUSTRALIA
MONASH UNIVERSITY, AUSTRALIA [Added 17 June 1968]
AUSTRALIAN NATIONAL UNIVERSITY [Added 15 June 1956]
UNIVERSITY OF NEW SOUTH WALES, AUSTRALIA [Added 17 June 1968]
UNIVERSITY OF NEWCASTLE, AUSTRALIA [Added 8 June 1994]
UNIVERSITY OF QUEENSLAND, BRISBANE, AUSTRALIA
UNIVERSITY OF SYDNEY, AUSTRALIA
UNIVERSITY OF TASMANIA, AUSTRALIA [Added 1 December 1969]
UNIVERSITY OF WESTERN AUSTRALIA [Added 15 June 1956]
UNIVERSITY OF AUCKLAND, NEW ZEALAND [Added 1 December 1969]
UNIVERSITY OF OTAGO, NEW ZEALAND
UNIVERSITY OF CAPE TOWN, SOUTH AFRICA
UNIVERSITY OF MEDUNSA, SOUTH AFRICA [Added 8 June 1994]
UNIVERSITY OF NATAL, SOUTH AFRICA [Added 14 February 1957]
UNIVERSITY OF THE ORANGE FREE STATE, SOUTH AFRICA [Added 23 July 1982]
UNIVERSITY OF PRETORIA, SOUTH AFRICA [Added 26 January 1951]
UNIVERSITY OF STELLENBOSCH, SOUTH AFRICA [Added 14 February 1957]
UNIVERSITY OF WITWATERSRAND, JOHANNESBURG, SOUTH AFRICA

§ 249. *Nuffield Department of Clinical Medicine: Ulcerative Colitis Research Fund*

Contributions for the support of research on ulcerative colitis shall be spent under the direction of the Board of the Faculty of Clinical Medicine.

§ 251. *Nuffield Fund for Research in Ophthalmology*

The income from the investment of the remaining balance of the sum of £25,000 given to the University by the Viscount Nuffield, O.B.E., F.R.S., M.A., Hon. D.C.L., LL.D., Honorary Fellow of Pembroke and Worcester Colleges, and accepted under Decree (1) of 4 February 1941, shall be expended as follows:

1. There shall be appointed, under the provisions of either Ch. VII, Sect. IV, § 3 or ibid., Sect. V, § 3, a university lecturer whose duties shall be, under the direction of the Margaret Ogilvie's Reader in Ophthalmology, to engage in teaching and research, whether of a clinical nature or otherwise, into the causes and cure of diseases affecting vision and who, if a medical practitioner, shall not engage in private practice otherwise than as permitted under the provisions of Ch. VII, Sect. V, § 1. The research shall be carried out

(*a*) in Oxford in such place or places (which may include the Oxford Eye Hospital) as the reader shall arrange, or

(*b*) elsewhere if approved by the Board of the Faculty of Clinical Medicine.

2. The annual income of the fund shall be applied, so far as is required, towards meeting, to such extent as may be agreed from time to time between the General Board, the Clinical Medicine Board, and the Margaret Ogilvie's Reader in Ophthalmology, the cost of the post referred to in cl. 1 hereof and (subject to similar agreement) of any other research posts in the Nuffield Laboratory of Ophthalmology.

3. Any balance of annual income not required for the purposes of cl. 2 hereof shall be applied to research purposes in the Nuffield Laboratory of Ophthalmology other than the staff costs referred to in cl. 2.

4. Any residual income in the Nuffield Fund at 1 February 1978 which is not required for the purposes specified in cll. 1–2 above, shall be expended by or under the direction of Margaret Ogilvie's Reader in providing accommodation, apparatus, equipment, or other facilities for research in Ophthalmology, subject to the approval of the Board of the Faculty of Clinical Medicine and of the General Board.

5. If it shall at any time appear to the University that Lord Nuffield's intentions would be better carried out by the establishment of a Professorship of Ophthalmology than by the continuance of the arrangements hereinbefore set out, the fund may be devoted to that purpose by decree.

§ 252. *Ophthalmological Research Endowment Fund*

The Curators of the University Chest shall be authorized to expend the income of the Fund for the Endowment of Ophthalmological Research on purposes connected with Ophthalmological Research under the direction of the General Board, provided that the first charge on the income shall be the excess (if any) of the agreed contribution to the costs of posts in the Nuffield Laboratory of Ophthalmology over that available from the Nuffield Fund for Research in Ophthalmology under the provisions of Ch. IX, Sect. I, § 251, cl. 2.

§ 253. *Oppenheimer Fund*

1. The University accepts with deep gratitude the sum of £400,000 from Mr. H.F. Oppenheimer which shall be used, together with any further donations for this purpose, to form a fund, to be known as the Oppenheimer Fund. The net income from the fund shall be applied from time to time to either or both of the following purposes:

(*a*) the assistance of the academic exchange of senior and junior members between the University of Oxford on the one hand and universities and similar institutions of higher education in the Republic of South Africa on the other;

(*b*) the support of studies within the University of Oxford related to sub-Saharan Africa including, but not limited to, (i) work on environmental or development problems and (ii) research, with particular emphasis on research relevant to mining, in the Earth Sciences or in Engineering Science.

2. The fund shall be administered by the International Committee, which shall have power to delegate responsibility for the administration of the fund to a

subcommittee (not all the members of which need be members of the International Committee).

3. Surplus income arising in any year shall be carried forward for expenditure in subsequent years in accordance with the provisions of clause 1 above.

4. Council shall have power to amend this decree from time to time, provided that the purposes of the fund as defined in clause 1 above shall always be kept in view.

§ 254. *Grey Institute of Field Ornithology*

The University accepts with gratitude the bequest of £500 from the late John Strangman Barrington, in memory of his father, the late Richard Manliffe Barrington, M.A., LL.B., F.L.S., M.R.I.A., M.B.O.U., to be used by members of the staff of the Edward Grey Institute of Field Ornithology on such ornithological research project directly related to Ireland as the Director for the time being of the Institute shall determine. In any published report of the results of such research work, it shall be made known that the expense of the project was defrayed from a fund donated in memory of the said Richard Manliffe Barrington.

§ 255. *Osler Memorial Fund*

1. The fund (formed to enable grants to be made from time to time to teachers in the Oxford Medical School to help them to pursue some special study connected with Medicine outside Oxford, and out of which the expenses of the award of a Bronze Medal every five years to the Oxford medical graduate who shall, in the opinion of the board of awarders, have made the most valuable contribution to the science, art, or literature of Medicine may be defrayed), shall be called the Osler Memorial Fund.

2. A Bronze Medal shall be awarded once in every five years to the Oxford medical graduate who shall, in the opinion of the board of awarders hereinafter constituted, have made the most valuable contribution to the science, art, or literature of Medicine, and who has not previously received the medal. The medal shall, unless the Vice-Chancellor direct otherwise, be formally presented at a meeting of Congregation held for the purpose of the conferment of degrees.

3. For the purposes of the preceding clause the term 'Oxford medical graduate' shall mean a person, whether man or woman, who has taken the Degrees of Bachelor of Arts and Bachelor of Medicine at the University of Oxford.

4. The board of awarders shall be constituted as follows:

(1) the Vice-Chancellor;

(2) a Professor of the Faculty of Clinical Medicine elected by the Board of the Faculty of Clinical Medicine;

(3) a professor of the Faculty of Physiological Sciences elected by the Board of the Faculty of Physiological Sciences;

(4), (5) two persons not being members of the University elected by Council on the recommendation of the Board of the Faculty of Clinical Medicine.

The elected members of the board of awarders shall hold office for five years and be re-eligible.

5. All expenses in connection with the award of the Bronze Medal shall be paid out of the income of the fund.

6. The residue of the income of the fund may be used at the discretion of the members of the board of awarders resident in Oxford, other than the Vice-Chancellor, in making grants from time to time to teachers in the Oxford Medical School, recognized as such by the Board of the Faculty of Clinical Medicine, to enable them to pursue some special study connected with Medicine outside the University.

7. Applications for such grants shall be made to the Secretary of Faculties, who shall act as Secretary to the board of awarders.

§ 256. *Oxford Kobe Scholarships*

1. The University accepts with gratitude the sum of £2,000,000 as a munificent benefaction from St. Catherine's College, offered with the approval of the Board of Directors of the Kobe Institute and the Japan Foundation, to be held on trust as a fund the net income of which shall be applied in the funding of scholarships, to be known as the Oxford Kobe Scholarships, for the support of nationals of Japan studying for graduate degrees of the University.

2. The scholarships shall be administered by a board of management consisting of:

(1) the Vice-Chancellor;

(2), (3) two persons appointed by Council;

(4), (5) two persons appointed by the General Board;

(6), (7) two persons appointed by of the Board of Directors of the Kobe Institute;

(8), (9) two persons appointed by the Governing Body of St. Catherine's College.

The members appointed under (2)–(9) shall serve for three years and shall be re-eligible, provided that if a person appointed by the Board of Directors of the Kobe Institute is unable to attend any meeting of the board of management, an alternate may be nominated by the directors to attend in his or her place.

3. At least one scholarship at any time shall be tenable at St. Catherine's College.

4. Any income not spent in any year shall be carried forward for expenditure in subsequent years.

5. Council shall have power to alter this decree from time to time, provided that the main object of the fund, as defined in clause 1 above, is always kept in view.

§ **257.** *Oxford Project for Peace Studies*

1. Upon the kind invitation of the retiring trustees, the University consents to be and act as sole trustee of the charitable trust deed of 21 December 1982 of the Oxford Project for Peace Studies in place of the retiring trustees, who upon their retirement are discharged from the trusts of the charitable trust deed.

2. The Committee for the Cyril Foster and Related Funds shall be the board of management of the trust funds associated with the Oxford Project for Peace Studies and shall apply the trust funds in accordance with the charitable trust deed.

3. Council shall have power from time to time to alter this decree provided that the purposes of the trust funds, as stated in the charitable trust deed, shall always be kept in view.

§ **261.** *Passmore Edwards Prize: Founded by Mr. John Passmore Edwards*

1. This prize shall always be called, in honour and memory of Mr. John Passmore Edwards, 'The Passmore Edwards Prize'.

2. The prize shall be awarded annually, if there is a candidate of sufficient merit, by the Examiners in the Final Honour School of Classics and English to the candidate whose performance in that examination they judge to be the best. A further prize shall be awarded annually, if there is a candidate of sufficient merit, by the Moderators in Honour Moderations in Classics and English to the candidate whose performance in that examination they judge to be the best.

3. The prize shall be managed by the Board of the Faculty of English Language and Literature, which shall appoint to advise it a committee of which one member shall be appointed by the Board of the Faculty of Literae Humaniores.

4. The value of the prize shall be determined by the board on the recommendation of the committee.

5. Any income of the endowment not required for the prize or for meeting the expenses of the examination shall be applied by the board for any purpose consistent with the main object of the foundation as defined in clause 6 below.

6. In any change of decree the main object of the foundation shall be kept in view, namely, the encouragement and promotion of the study of English Literature in its connection with the Classical Literature of Greece and Rome.

§ **262.** *Pathology (Sir William Dunn School)*

1. The gift of Sir William Dunn's Trustees of £2,000 shall be held in trust for the endowment of a Departmental Library at the Sir William Dunn School of Pathology.

2. The Curators of the University Chest shall apply the income arising from the trust fund to the maintenance of, and the purchase of additions to, the Departmental Library of the Sir William Dunn School of Pathology in accordance with such directions as shall from time to time be given in writing

at his or her absolute discretion by the Professor of Pathology for the time being, and in default of such direction at the absolute discretion of the University.

§ 263. *Paton Memorial Fund*

1. The fund shall be called the 'Alexander Allan Paton Memorial Fund'.

2. The capital sum of the benefaction shall be held by Barclays Bank Trust Co. Ltd., which having deducted from the annual income a sum not exceeding one and one-half per cent of the gross income for administrative charges shall pay the balance annually to the University.

3. The sums received by the University shall be applied in making grants to members of the University *in statu pupillari* as specified in clause 4 below to enable them to take part in expeditions organized by the Oxford University Exploration Club and recognized by Council if the committee referred to in clause 5 below is satisfied that they are in need of assistance for that purpose; provided that if the whole sum received in any year is not used for the aforementioned purposes the balance shall, at the discretion of the committee established under clause 5 hereof, be either

(*a*) used for making grants towards the general expenses of any such expedition taking place in that year; or

(*b*) carried forward and made available to the committee in future years for grants to individual members of the University qualified as aforesaid, or for grants towards the general expenses of expeditions organized and recognized as aforesaid; provided that any income made available to the committee under this sub-clause shall be expended within five years of its accrual.

4. Only those members of the University shall be eligible to receive grants who, being *in statu pupillari*, are studying for or have been classed in one of the Final Honour Schools within the Faculty of Biological Sciences or in Geology or in Geography or under the Committee for Human Sciences.

5. A committee composed of

(1) the Head of the Department of Zoology or a deputy appointed by the head;

(2) the Sherardian Professor of Botany or a deputy appointed by the professor;

(3), (4) two other persons nominated by the Board of the Faculty of Biological Sciences

shall meet when required and shall determine what grants shall be made under the provisions of clause 3 above.

6. This decree may be amended by Council subject to the written consent of the aforesaid Barclays Bank Trust Co. Ltd., the trustee of the fund: provided always and it is hereby accepted by the University that it is the donor's express wish that the main object of the benefaction shall be connected with the Faculty of Biological Sciences.

§ **264.** *Pavry Memorial Fund*

1. The University accepts with gratitude from the Most Hon. Bapsybanoo Marchioness of Winchester the sum of £10,000 to establish a fund, to be known as the Dasturzada Dr. Jal Pavry Memorial Fund, to commemorate her brother, Dasturzada Dr. Jal Pavry. The capital sum of £10,000 shall remain intact in perpetuity, and the net income from it shall be used to make an award to a student of the University who in research or study while pursuing graduate studies at the University has achieved distinction in the area of international peace and understanding.

2. The Board of the Faculty of Social Studies shall be the board of management of the fund.

3. The award shall be suitably advertised within the University and shall normally be given annually, provided that candidates of sufficient merit present themselves, under such arrangements as may be approved from time to time by Council.

4. Any net income not expended in any year shall be used to establish an Accumulated Income Fund, and the total net income that has accrued to that fund since the time at which the last award has been made shall be applied in supplementation of the value of the next award that is made.

5. Council shall have power to alter this decree from time to time, provided always that the purpose of the fund, as stated in clause 1 above, shall be kept in view.

§ **265.** *Pelham Studentship*

1. The Pelham Fund shall be invested by the University and the income devoted to the maintenance of a studentship to be called the Henry Francis Pelham Studentship, and to other purposes for the encouragement of the original study of Roman History and Archaeology as hereinafter mentioned.

2. The student shall be a member of the University of Oxford, and shall hold his or her studentship for one year.

3. The studentship shall not be awarded twice to the same person.

4. The student shall be elected by the committee established by Tit. XV, Sect. V, cl. 3 (hereinafter called the Craven Committee), subject to the conditions herein specified, and to any further conditions which that committee may think fit to prescribe.

5. One student shall be elected annually in Trinity Term, provided that a suitable candidate presents himself or herself (or, at the discretion of the committee, when the state of the fund permits, two students).

6. The value of the studentship shall be £75 but the Craven Committee shall have power, if it can arrange for money to be made available from the other funds with which it is concerned, at its discretion to make a supplementary award to any student who fails to obtain or is ineligible for a state studentship.

The emoluments shall be paid in such instalments and on such conditions as the Craven Committee shall prescribe.

7. The student shall be required, for three months during the tenure of his or her studentship, to reside in Rome and to study under the direction of the British School at Rome, unless he or she receive permission from the Craven Committee to reside elsewhere during the whole or any part of such period for the study of Roman History and Archaeology.

8. Any surplus income arising from whatever cause may under the direction of the Craven Committee be devoted to any of the following purposes:

(*a*) augmentation of the emoluments of the student;

(*b*) some purpose connected with the British School at Rome;

(*c*) the establishment of an additional studentship or exhibition; provided that if any additional studentship or exhibition shall at any time be established it shall be tenable by persons whether members of the University or not, either men or women, under such conditions and restrictions as may from time to time be approved by the Craven Committee.

9. It shall be lawful for Council from time to time to alter this decree, provided always

(*a*) that the income shall always be applied to the encouragement of the original study of Roman History and Archaeology;

(*b*) that the name of Henry Francis Pelham shall always be mentioned in the designation of any purpose to which the income shall be devoted.

§ 266. *Philosophy: Waismann Bequest*

[1]

The gift of the literary executors of the late F. Waismann, New College, of royalties payable on papers published since his death, shall be held for use by the Sub-faculty of Philosophy in aid of the study of Philosophy.

[2]

The gift of the literary executors of the late F. Waismann, M.A., New College, and H.R. Harré, B.Phil., M.A., Fellow of Linacre College, Editor of F. Waismann, *The Principles of Linguistic Philosophy*, of the foreign royalties payable on that book, shall be held for use by the Sub-faculty of Philosophy in aid of the study of Philosophy.

§ 267. *Pirie-Reid Fund*

1. The University accepts with gratitude the net income from a trust established by the late Constance Pirie-Reid in memory of her husband, which shall form a fund to be called the Pirie-Reid Fund.

2. The fund shall be used to provide scholarships, to be known as Pirie-Reid Scholarships, for the benefit of students in need of university education which would otherwise be denied them for lack of funds.

3. The fund shall be administered by a board of management consisting of up to six persons, to be appointed by Council for such periods as it shall think fit, which shall determine the conditions of award of such scholarships, their several value and tenure, and the eligibility of candidates.

4. The scholarships may be tenable by any eligible member of the University *in statu pupillari*, but preference shall, so far as possible, be given to candidates domiciled or educated in Scotland.

5. The board shall submit a report to Council each year on the scholarships which have been awarded, for submission to the trustee of the trust referred to in clause 1 above.

6. This decree may be amended from time to time by Council subject to the prior consent of the said trustee.

§ 268. *Plachte Memorial Fund*

1. The University accepts with gratitude the bequest of Miss Erna Plachte to be used for purposes connected with the teaching of art in the University. The capital as well as the income of the fund may be expended.

2. Expenditure from the fund shall be on such purposes as may be approved from time to time by the General Board of the Faculties.

3. Council shall have power to amend this decree from time to time, provided always that the object of the fund as stated in clause 1 above is observed.

§ 269. *Placito Medical Fund*

1. The University accepts with gratitude from Peter John Placito, Anthony Rudolph Placito, and Mrs. Dorothy Grace Placito the sum of £17,500, and any further benefactions contributed for this purpose, to establish a fund in memory of the late Anthony Placito to be called the Anthony Placito Medical Fund. The fund shall be used for the general advancement of the science and practice of medicine and surgery by research within the University and the dissemination of the results thereof for the public benefit.

2. The medical research supported by the fund shall be concerned with oncology, with special reference to the spread of cancer in the human body (which shall be regarded as including the molecular biology of metastasis and the cell genetics of metastasis).

3. The fund shall be administered by the Board of Management of the Lee–Placito Medical Fund as from time to time constituted under the provisions of § 203 of this section.

4. Council shall have power to alter this decree from time to time, provided that no alteration shall be made to clauses 2 and 3 during the lifetime of the said Peter John Placito and Anthony Rudolph Placito without their prior consent, and provided also that at all times the main object of the founders be kept in view, namely the general advancement of the science and practice of medicine and

surgery by research within the University and the dissemination of the results thereof for the public benefit.

§ **270.** *Portuguese Studies*

1. There shall be a Leitor in Portuguese, whose stipend shall be paid by the Instituto de Cultura e Língua Portuguesa, Lisbon, and who shall be appointed by the Board of the Faculty of Medieval and Modern Languages in consultation with the Instituto de Cultura e Língua Portuguesa, upon such conditions as to duties and tenure as the board shall approve.

2. A Director of Portuguese Studies shall be appointed by the Board of the Faculty of Medieval and Modern Languages under such conditions as shall be determined by that board.

§ **271.** *Poulton Fund*

The Edward Bagnall Poulton Fund shall be applied at the discretion of the Curator of the Entomological Collections for the time being in the promotion of the study of Evolution, organic and social.

§ **272.** *Pre-clinical Adviser's Medical Scholarships Fund*

1. The Curators of the University Chest are authorized to accept donations to a fund to be used to provide scholarships for mature students reading, or to enable mature students to read, for the degree of Bachelor of Medicine of the University.

2. The fund shall be administered and the scholarships shall be awarded by a board of management consisting of the Pre-clinical Adviser and the Director of Clinical Studies *ex officio*, and one person appointed by the Board of the Faculty of Physiological Sciences. The appointed member shall serve for three years and shall be re-eligible. The board of management shall have power to co-opt up to two additional members.

3. The board of management shall have power to determine the eligibility of candidates under the terms of clause 1 above, and the value of the studentships, which shall be awarded on such terms as it shall think fit. Both capital and income may be expended for this purpose.

4. Council shall have power to modify the provisions of this decree, in consultation with the board of management, provided that in any change of decree the object of the fund as stated in clause 1 above shall always be kept in view.

§ **273.** *Psychiatric Research Fund*

The Curators of the Chest are authorized to accept donations towards the Psychiatric Research Fund; the income of the fund may be spent at the discretion of the W.A. Handley Professor of Psychiatry on psychiatric research;

and the professor may in any financial year spend on psychiatric research up to half the capital of the fund in hand at the beginning of that financial year.

§ 274. *Experimental Psychology Fund*

1. The gift of £10,000 from Mrs. Hugh Watts accepted by the University under Decree (1) of 5 May 1936 as a contribution towards the founding of an Institute of Experimental Psychology (renamed Department of Experimental Psychology under Decree (6) of 22 January 1970) shall be known as 'The Experimental Psychology Fund'.

2. The fund shall be administered by the Medical Sciences Board, which shall be empowered, on the application of the Head of the Department of Experimental Psychology, to apply the income for any of the purposes of the Department.

3. If in any financial year the whole income of the fund is not spent, the surplus shall be carried forward for expenditure in subsequent years.

§ 281. *Queen Elizabeth House: Gift from Sir Ernest Oppenheimer*

1. The Inter-faculty Committee for Queen Elizabeth House shall administer the balance of the gift of £100,000 accepted by Decree (1) of 29 June 1954 for the development of colonial and allied studies.

2. The committee shall receive applications for grants and shall authorize the payment of grants from the balance of the fund.

§ 282. *Queen Elizabeth House Fund*

1. The University accepts with gratitude a benefaction from the erstwhile Governors of Queen Elizabeth House, to form a fund for the purpose of furthering such of the purposes of the department of the University called Queen Elizabeth House, as specified from time to time by the Statutes of the University, as are charitable.

2. The Inter-faculty Committee for Queen Elizabeth House shall be the management committee for the fund.

3. The management committee shall determine the use to which any net income of the fund is to be put, within the declared purposes of the fund.

4. The capital of the fund shall be available for expenditure, but any proposals by the management committee to spend some or all of the capital shall require the approval of Council.

5. Council shall have power to amend this decree from time to time provided that the main object of the fund, as defined in clause 1 above, shall always be kept in view.

§ 283. *Queen Elizabeth Scholarship*

1. The University accepts with gratitude from the former U.S. Ambassador to the Court of St James's, Mr. W.H. Annenberg, the sum of $250,000 to establish a fund, to be named for Her Majesty Queen Elizabeth The Queen Mother, the net income of which shall be used for the award of Queen Elizabeth Scholarships to support alternate visits of up to one year between the Universities of Pennsylvania and Oxford by junior or senior members of each institution.

2. The fund shall be administered by the International Committee.

3. Provided that candidates of sufficient merit offer themselves, a Queen Elizabeth Scholarship shall be awarded annually, to a member of the University of Oxford and of the University of Pennsylvania in alternate years. It may be held by either a senior or junior member of the relevant university, and shall be used by the holder for the purpose of study at the other university. No person shall hold the scholarship for more than one academic year.

4. Any income not spent in any year under the provisions of clause 3 above shall be carried forward for expenditure in subsequent years.

5. Council shall have power to amend this decree from time to time, provided that the object of the fund as defined in clause 1 above shall always be kept in view.

§ 291. *Radcliffe Meteorological Collection*

The offer to the University by the Radcliffe Trustees of the meteorological instruments and books in the Radcliffe Observatory are assigned to the Department of Geography under the control of the Professor of Geography, save for such books and papers as the University may from time to time think it desirable to present to other libraries.

§ 292. *Radhakrishnan Memorial Bequest*

1. The University accepts with gratitude the sum of £50,000 from the estate of the late Professor Sir Sarvepalli Radhakrishnan which shall form a fund to be called the Radhakrishnan Memorial Bequest.

2. There shall be a board of management of the bequest composed of the following persons:

(1) the Vice-Chancellor;

(2) Dr. S. Gopal during his life-time;

(3) the Spalding Professor of Eastern Religions and Ethics;

(4) the Warden of All Souls;

(5) the Chairman of the Inter-faculty Committee for South Asian Studies.

The board of management shall have power to co-opt up to two additional members for periods of five years.

3. There shall be an electoral board, comprising:

(1) the Vice-Chancellor;

(2), (3) two members of the board of management appointed by the board;

(4) Dr. S. Gopal during his life-time, and thereafter a third member of the board of management appointed by the board.

4. The electoral board shall at least in every other year elect a scholar, with a preference for scholars from outside Oxford, to visit the University either in Michaelmas or Hilary or Trinity Term (but not in more than one) to give a series of lectures in some field of Indian Studies.

5. The lecturer shall be known as the Radhakrishnan Memorial Lecturer.

6. The board of management shall fix the amounts of the lecturer's emoluments and expenses, which shall be paid from the income of the Radhakrishnan Memorial Bequest.

7. Any income not used to pay the emoluments and expenses of the Radhakrishnan Memorial Lecturer may at the discretion of the board of management be

(*a*) carried forward for use in a subsequent year;

(*b*) applied to assist students who are citizens of the Republic of India and who are studying, or wish to study, in Oxford;

(*c*) applied in any other way which the board shall think conducive to the promotion of Indian Studies in the University of Oxford.

§ 293. *Radiological Research Fund*

Donations towards a Radiological Research Fund shall be expended, at the discretion of the Head of the Department of Radiology, on radiological research in the Radiodiagnostic Department of the hospitals in Oxford under the jurisdiction of the Oxfordshire Health Authority.

§ 294. *Sheikh Rashid Diabetes Fund*

1. The University accepts with gratitude from the Oxford Diabetes Trust the sum of £1,017,620, and any further sums which may be contributed for the same purpose, to establish a fund, to be called the Sheikh Rashid Diabetes Fund, which shall be used for the furtherance of research into diabetes and allied metabolic diseases.

2. The fund shall be administered by a board of management consisting of:

(1) the Regius Professor of Medicine;

(2) the Nuffield Professor of Clinical Medicine;

(3) a person appointed by the Medical Sciences Board;

(4) the Secretary of the Medical School.

3. The fund shall be used:

(*a*) for the support of a senior investigator in the field of diabetes and allied metabolic diseases, and appropriate assistance;

(*b*) for other purposes consistent with the furtherance of the study of this field.

4. The board of management shall have discretion to expend the capital as well as the income of the fund.

5. Council shall have power to amend this decree from time to time, provided that the main object of the fund, as defined in clause 1 above, is always kept in view.

§ **295.** *Read Scholarship*

1. In accordance with the will of the foundress, the scholarship shall be entitled 'The Amy Mary Preston Read Scholarship'.

2. The scholarship shall be open to members of the University pursuing research in History for the Degree of Doctor of Philosophy. Candidates must by the date on which they take up the scholarship have been admitted to and not have subsequently lost the status of Student for the Degree of Doctor of Philosophy, and not have exceeded the twelfth term since they began their research studies at the University.

3. The Board of Management of the Bryce Research Studentship in History shall be the board of management of the scholarship.

4. The scholar shall, subject to the provisions of cl. 5, receive such emoluments from the accumulated income of the endowment fund as the board of management shall see fit.

5. The scholarship shall be tenable for one year, either at Oxford or, with the consent of the board of management, elsewhere, and shall be awarded for proficiency in History, Ancient or Modern. Every candidate, with his or her application, shall submit a programme of work in History, either Ancient or Modern which he or she proposes, if elected, to undertake. He or she shall also

(*a*) state any other emoluments which he or she may already hold and whether he or she is a candidate or prospective candidate for such other emoluments;

(*b*) undertake, if elected to the scholarship, to inform the board if, during its tenure, he or she is awarded any other emoluments.

The election of the scholar shall be made by the board of management after consideration of the past records of the candidates and of the programmes submitted by them, but without having regard to the candidates' financial needs.

6. The board shall have power to deprive a scholar of his or her scholarship, or of any part of the emoluments thereof, on account of idleness or misconduct, or failure to comply with any direction of the board.

7. Income undisposed of from any cause may be used in any year, at the discretion of the board of management, for the purpose of awarding an additional scholarship or of continuing an existing scholarship for longer than a year, or for the payment of expenses, including those of travel or publication, incidental to the pursuit of a definite piece of historical investigation, or

otherwise for the encouragement of approved pieces of historical study and research.

8. Council shall have power to alter this decree, from time to time, provided that the object of the foundation, as expressed in the will of the foundress, is always kept in view.

§ 296. *Rhoades Commemorative Fund*

1. The University accepts with gratitude the sum of £1,260, and any further sums which may be contributed for this purpose, to establish a Geoffrey Rhoades Commemorative Fund.

2. The income of the fund, after the payment of all proper expenses, shall be applied to the provision of bursaries, to be known as Geoffrey Rhoades Commemorative Bursaries, to be awarded from time to time to artists of promise studying for the degree of Bachelor of Fine Art.

3. The Committee for the Ruskin School of Drawing and Fine Art shall be the board of management of the fund, and shall determine the conditions under which the bursaries shall be awarded.

4. Council shall have power to alter this decree from time to time, provided that the main object of the fund, namely the provision of bursaries for artists of promise studying for the degree of Bachelor of Fine Art, for the furtherance of their studies, is always kept in view.

§ 297. *Rhŷs Fund for Promotion of Celtic Study and Research*

The fund bequeathed by the late Sir John Rhŷs, sometime Principal of Jesus College, shall be used for the promotion of Celtic study and research in such manner as the Principal of Jesus College, the Jesus Professor of Celtic, and the Vice-Chancellor shall determine.

§ 298. *Rhŷs Prize*

1. The prize shall be administered by the Trustees of the Rhŷs Fund. It shall be awarded by the judges every year to the writer of the best essay or dissertation on some subject relating to Celtic Languages, Literature, History, and Antiquities, if such essay shall be deemed worthy of the prize.

2. The value of the prize shall be determined by the trustees.

3. The prize shall not be awarded twice to the same person.

4. The candidates must be members of the University of Oxford who shall not on the day appointed for sending in the compositions to the Registrar of the University have exceeded eight years from the time of their matriculation.

5. The judges shall be the Regius Professor of Modern History and the Jesus Professor of Celtic; or substitutes appointed by the trustees for either of these professors who may decline to act or during a vacancy in either of the

professorships. The trustees shall determine the remuneration to be paid out of the income of the trust fund to the judges on each occasion when they act.

6. Candidates shall, not later than Friday of the fourth week in Michaelmas Full Term, submit the title of their proposed essay, together with a brief statement of how they envisage treating the subject, to the judges for approval. Essays shall be submitted to the Registrar not later than Friday of the eighth week in the following Hilary Full Term.

7. The judges shall have power to recommend to the trustees that presents of books be made to unsuccessful candidates whose essays have shown special excellence.

8. The judges shall be allowed, subject to the approval of the Vice-Chancellor, to appoint one or more assessors. The amount of remuneration to be paid to an assessor shall in each case be determined by the Vice-Chancellor after consultation with the trustees.

9. The judges shall have power to recommend to the trustees that a contribution be made out of the Rhŷs Fund towards the expenses of printing the whole or parts of an essay.

10. The judges shall have power to recommend to the trustees that a grant be made from the Rhŷs Fund to enable the successful candidate or candidates to carry on the work which has been the subject of the essay.

11. Council shall have the power to alter this decree at any time on the recommendation of the trustees.

§ 299. *Robinson Memorial Fund*

1. The University accepts with gratitude the moneys known as the Robert Robinson Memorial Fund, together with any moneys which may be subscribed to the fund in future, to be applied to foster research in organic chemistry (and related studies) in the Dyson Perrins Laboratory, in memory of Sir Robert Robinson, O.M., M.A., Hon. D.Sc., sometime Waynflete Professor of Chemistry.

2. The purposes for which the fund shall be used shall be *inter alia*:

(*a*) to facilitate the sojourns in the Dyson Perrins Laboratory of visiting research workers from other parts of Great Britain and overseas;

(*b*) to enable members of the staff of the laboratory to make visits elsewhere in support of their researches;

(*c*) to provide short-term assistance for research.

The fund shall be expendable, both as to capital and income, under arrangements to be approved from time to time by Council.

3. Income not expended in any year shall be carried forward for expenditure in a subsequent year.

4. Council shall have power to amend this decree, provided that the main object of the fund, as set out in clause 1 above, shall always be kept in view.

§ 300. *Rolleston Memorial Prize*

1. The Rolleston Memorial Fund shall be expended in the institution of a prize to be awarded every year.

2. The prize shall be given for original research in any subject comprised under the following heads, Animal and Vegetable Morphology, Physiology and Pathology, and Anthropology, to be selected by the candidates themselves.

3. The period during which this prize may be obtained by a candidate shall be limited to ten years after the date of matriculation; and with a view to rendering the prize as widely associated with Professor Rolleston's name as possible, it shall be open to the members of the Universities of Oxford and Cambridge.

4. If no memoir be considered of sufficient merit, the value of the prize for that year shall be carried forward for expenditure in subsequent years.

5. The prize shall be called 'The Rolleston Memorial Prize', and shall consist of so much of the annual income of the fund as shall remain after payment of all expenses incidental to the trust.

6. The trustees of the prize shall be:

(1) the Vice-Chancellor;
(2) the Regius Professor of Medicine;
(3) the Linacre Professor of Zoology;
(4) the Waynflete Professor of Physiology;
(5) the Sherardian Professor of Botany.

They shall fix and give due notice of the time for sending in the competing memoirs to the Registrar and shall appoint judges, who may be either trustees or members of one of the two Universities of Oxford and Cambridge not below the Degree of M.A. or B.M.

7. The trustees shall have power to make regulations or by-laws for the purpose of carrying this decree into effect; and Council shall always be at liberty to alter the decree, provided that the main object of the prize, namely, the encouragement of original research in the above-mentioned subjects, be kept in view.

8. No one shall be eligible who has not either passed the examinations for the B.A. Degree or the B.M. Degree at Oxford, or for the B.A. Degree or the M.B. Degree at Cambridge, or been admitted as a Student for the Degree of Doctor of Philosophy, or as a Student for the Degree of M.Litt. or M.Sc. at Oxford, or as Graduate Student for the degree of M.Litt. or M.Sc. or M.Phil. or Ph.D. at Cambridge.

9. No candidate shall be eligible who has exceeded a period of six years from attaining one or other of these qualifications, or from his or her attaining the first of such qualifications, if he or she has attained more than one, provided also that no candidate shall be eligible who has exceeded ten years from his or her matriculation.

10. No account shall be taken of any research which has not been prosecuted by the candidate subsequently to his or her matriculation.

11. The prize shall not be awarded twice to the same person.

§ 301. *Roth Memorial Prize for Italian Studies*

1. The University accepts with gratitude the sum of £750, to establish a fund as a memorial to the late Dr. Cecil Roth, formerly Reader in Jewish Studies, the income from which shall be applied towards the promotion or encouragement of Italian Studies within the University, and, in particular, by the provision of a prize to be called the Cecil Roth Memorial Prize for Italian Studies.

2. The fund shall be administered by a board of management consisting of:

(1) the Warden of Merton College, or a deputy appointed by the Warden;

(2) the Fiat–Serena Professor of Italian Studies, or a deputy appointed by the professor;

(3) a Fellow of Merton College to be appointed by the Warden of Merton College;

(4) a person appointed by the Board of the Faculty of Medieval and Modern Languages;

(5) a person appointed by the Board of the Faculty of Modern History.

3. The board of management shall apply the income, after the payment of all proper expenses, and may, in any one year, apply up to £75 of the capital towards the provision of the Cecil Roth Memorial Prize for Italian Studies which shall be offered once in every three years for an essay on such subject or subjects, approved by or on behalf of the board, as shall fall within the field of Italian art, history, and literature of the period from the end of the Roman Empire in the west until the end of the eighteenth century.

4. The prize shall be of the value of £50 (or such greater or lesser amount as the board may from time to time determine) and be open to all members of the University reading for a Final Honour School who, on the day appointed for sending in the essay, have not exceeded four years from the date of their matriculation.

5. The board shall appoint two judges, to whom the essays shall be submitted and by whom the prize shall be awarded, upon such terms (as to remuneration, tenure, and otherwise) as the board shall from time to time determine.

6. Any surplus income available, either because the prize has not been awarded or for any other reason, may be:

(i) applied in making such travel or research grants to members of the University *in statu pupillari* as shall be conducive to the promotion or encouragement of Italian Studies within the University, such grants to be known as Cecil Roth Grants for Italian Studies;

(ii) applied towards such other purpose or purposes conducive to the promotion or encouragement of Italian Studies within the University as the board shall from time to time determine; or

(iii) carried forward for application in future years either towards the provision of the prize or for any of the purposes referred to in (i) and (ii) above.

7. Council shall have power to alter this decree from time to time, provided that the main object of the fund, namely the promotion or encouragement of Italian Studies within the University, is kept in view.

§ 302. *Rothermere Scholarships*

1. The University accepts with gratitude from the Trustees of the Rothermere Foundation the sum of £47,000, and such further sums as shall from time to time be received for the same purpose, to be applied (together with any net interest thereon received by the University) in the award of scholarships, to be known as Rothermere Scholarships, for the support of students from Duke University, North Carolina, attending courses provided by the University.

2. The scholarships fund shall be administered by a board of management the membership of which, and the respective periods of office of the members, shall be determined by Council.

3. The Rothermere Scholarships shall be awarded by the board of management on the nomination of the said Duke University to students attending such courses of the University as Council shall from time to time approve, in such amounts and subject to such conditions as the board shall from time to time agree with the said Duke University.

4. Funds not expended in any year shall be carried forward for expenditure in subsequent years.

5. Council shall have power to alter this decree from time to time, provided always that the main object of the fund, namely the support of students from the said Duke University attending courses provided by the University, shall be maintained.

§ 303. *Rouse Memorial Prize*

1. The University accepts with gratitude from Randolph G. Rouse the sum of £200 to endow a Susan Mary Rouse Memorial Prize in memory of his mother.

2. The income from the endowment shall be applied to the award of an annual book prize to the undergraduate whose performance in a university examination, to be determined from time to time by Council, the examiners judge to be the best, provided that a candidate of sufficient merit presents himself or herself.

3. Income not so expended in any year shall be carried forward for expenditure in subsequent years.

§ 304. *Ruskin Trustees*

Extract from regulations of the Declaration of Trust sealed by the University on 3 June 1875 (University Gazette, *vol. v, p. 633*) *as amended by the Ruskin Trustees with the approval of Convocation in 1977* (*ibid., vol. cvii, p. 906*).

1. There shall always be a Master of Drawing, who shall teach in the Ruskin Drawing School, or in a place assigned for that purpose with the consent of the Ruskin Trustees by or by the direction of the Chancellor, Masters and Scholars of the University of Oxford, in the University Galleries, or in some other building within and belonging to the University.

5. For the purposes of this deed there shall be certain trustees, who shall be called the Ruskin Trustees. The trustees shall for the future be the Vice-Chancellor of the University, the Keeper of the Department of Western Art in the Ashmolean Museum, the Ruskin Master of Drawing, and the Chairman of the Committee for the Ruskin School of Drawing and Fine Art.

§ 311. *St. Catherine of Alexandria Prize Fund*

The income of the St. Catherine of Alexandria Prize Fund shall be used for the annual award of a prize by the examiners to the member of one of the Anglican theological colleges (who intends to be ordained in the Church of England and who is not also a member of one of the societies recognized in Title VII) with the best performance in the Honour School of Theology, provided that his or her work is deemed to be of sufficient merit. If in any year the prize is not awarded, the income from the fund shall be carried forward for use in whole or in part to augment the value of the prize on subsequent occasions at the discretion of the examiners for each occasion.

§ 312. *Sasakawa Fund*

1. The University accepts with deep gratitude a benefaction of 200,000,000 Yen from the Japan Shipbuilding Industry Foundation to establish a fund, to be known as the Sasakawa Fund, to be applied to the advancement within the University of knowledge and understanding of Japan by way of academic contact and exchange between members of the University and citizens of Japan.

2. The fund shall be administered by a board of management to be appointed by Council for such periods as it thinks fit.

3. The income of the fund shall be applied to the funding of travel and research in Japan by senior or junior members of the University of Oxford; of study in Oxford by Japanese scholars or students; of the appointment of junior research fellows or research assistants in Oxford; of conferences in Oxford connected with Japan; of publications and of library and other related purposes; or in any other manner which the board of management shall consider will promote the purposes of the fund as expressed in clause 1 above.

4. Council shall have power to amend this decree from time to time, provided always that the main purpose of the fund as defined in clause 1 above is maintained.

§ 313. *Scatcherd Scholarships*

1. The University accepts from the Trustee of the Campaign for Oxford Trust Fund the sum of £621,000, made possible by an extremely generous benefaction from Mrs. Jane Ledig-Rowohlt, to establish a fund, the net income of which shall be applied in the funding of Scatcherd Scholarships for the support of graduate study in science.

2. The fund shall be administered by the International Committee.

3. The scholarships shall be awarded to persons from any European country (other than the U.K. or Turkey but including Russia and all other countries to the west of the Urals) to enable them to study for a graduate degree of the University in a science subject (including mathematics and medicine). The committee shall endeavour to ensure that at any one time one of the scholarships shall be held by a person from a country outside the European Union.

4. Any income not spent in any year shall be carried forward for expenditure in subsequent years.

5. Council shall have power to alter this decree from time to time, provided that the main object of the fund, as defined in clause 1 above, is always kept in view.

§ 314. *Schacht Memorial Prize*

1. The University accepts with gratitude a bequest of £1,000 from the late Mrs. L.D. Schacht to form a fund, the income from which shall be used for the provision of a Joseph Schacht Memorial Prize in Arabic and Islamic Studies.

2. The prize shall be open to candidates offering Arabic in the Preliminary Examination in, or Arabic or Islamic History in the Honour School of, Oriental Studies. It shall be awarded annually on the recommendation of the moderators and examiners provided that there is a candidate of sufficient merit.

3. The Board of the Faculty of Oriental Studies shall be the board of management for the prize, and shall have power to determine the value of the prize and the terms and conditions of its award.

4. Income not expended in any year shall be carried forward for expenditure in subsequent years.

5. Council shall have power to amend this decree, provided that the object of the bequest, as set out in cl. 1 above, is always kept in view.

§ 315. *Schorstein Research Fellowship in Medical Science*

1. A Research Fellowship in Medical Science shall be established in memory of Gustave Isidore Schorstein, D.M., F.R.C.P., Christ Church, Assistant Physician to the London Hospital and Physician to the Brompton Hospital for Diseases of the Chest, and shall be entitled 'The Schorstein Research Fellowship in Medical Science'. The value of the fellowship shall be determined by the Board of the Faculty of Clinical Medicine.

2. The fellow shall be elected, without examination, by the Board of the Faculty of Clinical Medicine, provided that a suitable candidate offers himself or herself.

3. The fellowship shall be tenable for two years at Oxford in any medical department or institute. The fellow shall not undertake any other work, except by permission of the Board of the Faculty of Clinical Medicine given on the recommendation of the head of the department or institute in which he or she is working.

4. The fellowship shall be open to all members of the University of Oxford who have qualified by examination for a degree of the University and who are under the age of thirty-five years on the 1 October in the calendar year in which the election is made.

5. A fellow shall not be re-eligible.

6. Elections shall be made, provided that suitable candidates present themselves, in Trinity Term in every third year or at such time as funds shall permit, and the fellow elected shall enjoy the emoluments of his or her fellowship from the first day of the succeeding Michaelmas Term.

7. The fellowship shall be open to women on the same conditions as apply to men.

8. Unexpended income in any year shall be carried forward for use in a subsequent year.

§ 316. *Scott Prize in Physics and Scott Fund*

1. The fund shall be called the Arthur William Scott Fund.

2. The annual income derived from the fund and from any addition which may hereafter be made thereto shall be used for the furtherance of Physical Science (the object for which the bequest was given) as may be determined by the University from time to time on the recommendation of the Board of the Faculty of Physical Sciences.

3. The income of the fund shall be applied for the support of the following prizes:

(*a*) one or more Scott Prizes for performance in physics in the Final Honour School of Natural Science; and

(*b*) one or more prizes for outstanding work in practical physics by candidates for that examination.

There shall be a committee comprising

(1) Dr. Lee's Professor of Experimental Philosophy (who shall be chairman);

(2) the Wykeham Professor of Physics;

(3) the person to whom for the time being the Sub-Department of Particle and Nuclear Physics is assigned under Ch. III, Sect. LXIII, § 4, cl. 2;

which shall determine annually the number and the value (which shall be not less than £25 for each prize) of the prizes to be offered. The prizes shall be awarded by, and at the discretion of, the examiners in Physics in the Final Honour School of Natural Science.

4. The residue of the income of the Scott Fund may be applied on the recommendation of the aforesaid committee for the purpose of making grants to persons admitted as Advanced Students in Physics by the Board of the Faculty of Physical Sciences towards maintenance, travelling, and other personal expenses incurred in connection with their studies.

5. If there should in any year be any unexpended income of the fund, it may, as the committee may direct, either be invested in augmentation of the capital of the fund or reserved for expenditure in any future year on the purposes specified in clause 4 above.

§ 317. *Secretan Bequest*

The University accepts with gratitude a legacy of £1,000 from the late Hubert A. Secretan, M.A., Balliol College, to be used in such manner as Council shall determine.

§ 318. *Segal Fund*

1. The University accepts with gratitude the gift of the executors of the will of Lord Segal of Wytham, the income from which shall be used for an award for a graduate student preparing for submission to the University a doctoral thesis in Hebrew or Jewish Studies.

2. The Board of the Faculty of Oriental Studies shall be the board of management for the award and shall have power to determine the value of the award and the terms and conditions upon which it shall be offered.

3. Income not expended in any year shall be carried forward for expenditure in subsequent years.

4. Council shall have power to alter this decree from time to time, provided that the object of the benefaction as defined in clause 1 above shall always be kept in view.

§ 319. *Segovia Fund*

1. The University accepts with gratitude from Señor Andrés Segovia the sum of £1,640, being the proceeds of a recital given by him on the occasion of his visit to Oxford in October 1972 to receive the Degree of Doctor of Music *honoris causa*. The money shall form a Segovia Fund to be applied at the

discretion of the Board of the Faculty of Music for the promotion of the study and performance of music in the University.

2. The proceeds of a further recital generously given by Dr. Andrés Segovia on 19 October 1974 shall be added to the Segovia Fund.

§ 320. *Shaw Fund for Chinese Studies*

1. The University accepts with deep gratitude a benefaction of £3,000,000 from the Shaw Foundation of Hong Kong as an endowment for the development of Chinese Studies in the University, principally by the establishment of posts in the subject, and by provision for various support costs. The fund shall be entitled the Sir Run Run Shaw Fund for Chinese Studies.

2. The benefaction shall be applied to these objects in such ways as Council in consultation with the General Board shall determine.

3. This decree shall be subject to alteration from time to time by Council, provided that the purpose of the fund, as defined in clause 1 above, is adhered to.

§ 321. *Shaw Memorial Fund*

1. The University accepts with gratitude sums contributed in memory of the late Phyllis M. Shaw, B.M., M.A., Somerville, which shall form a fund, to be known as the Phyllis Shaw Memorial Fund, the income and capital of which shall be used to pay all expenses (including the lecturer's fee, the lecturer's travel and subsistence expenses, and expenses incurred in the entertainment of the lecturer) associated with a memorial lecture which shall be given from time to time on a subject and by a lecturer to be chosen by the committee of management of the fund. When choosing the subject and the lecturer on each occasion the committee shall bear in mind the interests of Dr. Shaw in the field of psychological treatment.

2. The fund shall be administered by a committee of management which shall consist of

(1) the W.A. Handley Professor of Psychiatry;

(2) a clinical reader in the Department of Psychiatry;

(3) a national health service consultant in the Department of Psychiatry.

The members under (2)–(3), as from time to time required, shall be appointed by the Psychiatric Specialty Group.

§ 322. *Shelley-Mills Prize*

1. The University shall either permit the bequest of Consolidated Stock to remain as invested or at its discretion realize the same and reinvest the moneys arising therefrom in any investments authorized by law for the investment of trust funds with power to vary the investments from time to time with the aforesaid limitations.

2. The University shall hold the investments for the time being representing the Shelley-Mills Prize Fund upon trust to apply the income thereof in perpetuity in providing and awarding an annual prize to be called 'The Shelley-Mills Prize' in manner hereinafter mentioned.

3. It shall be the duty of the Board of the Faculty of English Language and Literature for the time being to give the subject of an essay at least nine months before the date on which the essays are to be sent in in every year, and to nominate and appoint an examiner or two examiners to award the prize. Such subject must relate to William Shakespeare or his works or some part of them, and at least twice in every four years the subject selected shall be of philosophical, aesthetic, psychological, or literary (as opposed to purely technical) interest, but once in every four years may be of philological interest.

4. The Shelley-Mills Prize shall be awarded to the candidate who in the opinion of the examiner or examiners shall be the author of the best essay on the subject selected, and the winner shall receive the income of the prize fund for the current year after the deduction of the examiners' fee and any other expenses incurred in the making of the award.

5. All members of the University of Oxford who shall not, on the day on which the subject for competition shall be announced, have exceeded three years from the date of their matriculation (except as hereinafter provided) shall be eligible to compete.

6. Notwithstanding they possess the above-mentioned qualifications, the following persons shall not be eligible to compete, namely, any persons who have been a member of any university, English or otherwise, except the University of Oxford, for a longer period than one university year or three terms.

7. An examiner shall hold office for two years and shall not be eligible for reappointment until the expiration of four years from the date of his or her previous appointment.

8. The examiner shall be paid out of the income of the prize fund the sum of £10·50 for each examination, and if two examiners are appointed the said sum of £10·50 shall be paid to them in equal shares.

9. In case no candidate shall enter for the prize or no essay be sent in of sufficient merit in the judgement of the examiner or examiners to gain the prize, the prize money for the current year shall be handed over to the Board of the Faculty of English Language and Literature to expend in any way which seems to it most fitted to further the interests of the study of English Literature in the University of Oxford either by the purchase and presentation to libraries within the University of books or in such other way as it in its discretion thinks best.

§ 323. *Sheppee Fund*

1. The fund shall be administered by a board of management consisting of:

(1) the Vice-Chancellor, or a member of Convocation appointed by the Vice-Chancellor from year to year;

(2) the head for the time being of the Department of Engineering Science;

(3) the Wykeham Professor of Physics.

2. The income of the fund shall be applied by the board in the following ways:

(*a*) to maintain one or more Edgell Sheppee Prizes, the number and value to be determined by the board, to be awarded

(i) on the recommendation of the examiners in the Honour School of Engineering Science for performance in Engineering Science in that examination; and on the recommendation of the examiners in the Honour School of Engineering, Economics, and Management for performance in Engineering in the Part II project, and

(ii) on the recommendation of the head for the time being of the Department of Engineering Science for laboratory or drawing office work carried out in the Department of Engineering Science by candidates for the Honour Schools of Engineering Science and of Engineering, Economics, and Management;

(*b*) to make grants, on the recommendation of the head for the time being of the Department of Engineering Science, for the assistance of members of the University engaged on research in Engineering Science in Oxford;

(*c*) at the discretion of the board, so far as not required for the foregoing purposes:

(i) to make grants, on the recommendation of the head for the time being of the Department of Engineering Science, for the assistance of other persons engaged on research in Engineering Science in Oxford;

(ii) for any other purposes consistent with the main object of the fund.

3. This decree may be altered from time to time provided always that the main object of the fund is kept in view, namely the encouragement and promotion of the study of Engineering Science in Oxford.

§ 324. *Shillito Fund*

The income of the Shillito Fund shall be used for the encouragement of the study of Assyriology in the University. The fund shall be administered by a committee established by the Board of the Faculty of Oriental Studies.

§ 325. *Shute Fund*

The income of the Shute Fund shall be placed at the disposal of the Committee on Student Hardship, to be applied in accordance with the provisions of Tit. XVI, Sect. XVI.

§ 326. *Sidgwick Chemical Library Fund*

1. The bequest of two-twentieths of the residuary estate of the late Professor N.V. Sidgwick for the libraries of the Physical and Inorganic Chemistry Laboratories which was accepted by Decree (1) of 10 March 1953 shall be called the Sidgwick Chemical Library Fund.

2. The annual income shall be expended under the directions of Dr. Lee's Professor of Chemistry in equal parts on behalf of the libraries of the

(*a*) Physical Chemistry Laboratory;

(*b*) Inorganic Chemistry Laboratory.

3. The income so received shall be applied to the maintenance of the various series of scientific periodicals bequeathed to the University by Professor Sidgwick, and to the general purposes of the two libraries.

4. Council may, from time to time, alter the provisions of this decree, provided that the fund shall always be used equally for the benefit of the libraries of the said laboratories.

§ 327. *Silva Memorial Prize in Spoken Spanish*

1. The University accepts with gratitude the sum of £1,500 to establish a fund as a memorial to Ramón Silva, the income from which shall be applied towards the promotion of spoken Spanish among undergraduate members of the University who are not native or bilingual Spanish speakers, and in particular to the provision of a Ramón Silva Memorial Prize in Spoken Spanish.

2. The Board of the Faculty of Medieval and Modern Languages shall be the board of management of the prize and shall determine the value of the prize and the occasions on which it shall be offered.

3. The prize shall be awarded, if a candidate of sufficient merit is forthcoming, by the examiners for the Honour School of Modern Languages to the candidate who, not being a native or bilingual Spanish speaker, has in their opinion given the best performance in Spanish in the oral examination among those offering Spanish as sole language or as one of two languages in that honour school, or as one of the subjects in any joint honour school which includes Modern Languages, in the year concerned. Before the prize may be awarded on any occasion to a candidate nominated by the examiners, the King Alfonso XIII Professor of Spanish Studies (or, in his or her absence, the Chairman of the Sub-faculty of Spanish and Portuguese) shall certify that in his or her opinion the candidate is not a native or bilingual Spanish speaker.

4. Any surplus income arising because the prize is not awarded on any occasion or from any other cause shall either be expended at the discretion of the board of management for other purposes within the main object of the fund as prescribed in clause 1 above or be carried forward for expenditure in a subsequent year.

5. Council shall have power to amend this decree from time to time, provided that the name of the prize shall not be changed and that the main object of the fund as prescribed in clause 1 above shall always be kept in view.

§ **328.** *Soudavar Memorial Fund*

1. The University accepts with gratitude the sum of £100,000 to establish a fund in memory of Alireza and Mohammed Soudavar to be called the Alireza and Mohammed Soudavar Memorial Fund. The net income of the fund shall be used to provide scholarships for students from Iran, or from any countries which the University may from time to time regard as 'third world' countries, to enable them to undertake a course of study at the University.

2. The fund shall be administered by a board of management to be designated or appointed by Council, and the board shall determine the conditions of award of such scholarships, their several value and tenure, and the eligibility of candidates.

§ **329.** *Southern Trust Fund for Students with Disabilities*

1. The University accepts with gratitude from the Trustees of the Southern Trust the sum of £10,000, which, together with such further sums as may be contributed for the same purpose, shall form a fund, to be known as the Southern Trust Fund for Students with Disabilities, to be applied towards the advancement of the education of persons with disabilities who are *either*

(*a*) matriculated members of the University working for a degree or other qualification of the University, *or*

(*b*) candidates for admission as either undergraduates or graduate students of the University.

2. Financial support shall be granted to eligible members of the University under clause 1 (*a*) above solely for the purpose of facilitating their studies at the University. Financial support shall be granted to eligible candidates for admission under clause 1 (*b*) above solely in order to assist in meeting the special costs of attending for interview arising out of their respective disabilities. Details of payments from the fund shall be supplied annually to the said trustees for so long as the trustees require.

3. The Committee for Disabled People shall act as the board of management of the fund. The committee shall maintain a subcommittee of up to four persons, not all of whom need be members of the committee, to determine, subject to the provisions of clauses 1 and 2 above, how the fund shall be applied, within such guidelines as the committee shall from time to time determine.

4. Council shall have power to alter this decree from time to time, provided that the main object of the fund, as stated in clause 1 above, is always kept in view.

§ 330. *Spanish Fund*

1. The sum of £25,000 received from the Endowment Committee shall be invested in the name of the Chancellor, Masters, and Scholars of the University.

2. The income arising from the above investment and from any additions thereto, shall be employed for the following purposes:

(*a*) to provide as a first charge upon the fund a contribution towards the cost of the King Alfonso XIII Professorship of Spanish Studies equal to two-fifths of the total income of the fund from year to year;

(*b*) to provide for the total cost to the University of the University Lecturership (established by decree) in Spanish, unless in any one year there is insufficient income after meeting the first charge to provide for the total cost, in which case the whole of such residual income shall be applied as a contribution towards the total cost;

(*c*) to provide for all expenses incurred on account of special lectures or courses of lectures arranged by the King Alfonso Professor;

(*d*) to contribute to the maintenance of the Spanish section of the Modern Languages Faculty Library.

During a vacancy in either of the posts specified in sub-clauses (*a*) and (*b*) above, the contribution from the fund in any one year to the cost of the post concerned shall be reduced *pro rata* to the actual cost of the post to the University in that year, provided that the income of the fund may be used, under the direction of the Board of the Faculty of Medieval and Modern Languages, either (i) to provide in other ways lectures and instruction in Spanish Studies, or (ii) to meet the total cost to the University of the post concerned (inclusive of superannuation, national insurance, and any other similar contributions or taxes payable by the University) during such period as the University would otherwise for financial reasons have had to leave the post vacant.

3. Any balance of the income, so far as not required for the purposes aforesaid, shall be carried forward for expenditure in subsequent years. All other moneys (if any) which may be added to the fund shall be invested in augmentation of the capital.

§ 331. *Stevens Scholarship*

The University accepts with gratitude the gift of Mrs. Olive Stevens of the royalties from the American edition of *Sidonius Apollinaris* by C.E. Stevens to provide a travel scholarship, to be known as the C.E. Stevens Scholarship, open to undergraduate members of the University studying classical languages and literature or ancient history. The Board of the Faculty of Literae Humaniores shall be the board of management for the scholarship.

§ 332. *Stutchbury Scholarship Fund*

1. The University accepts with gratitude the bequest of £3,000 and interest thereon from the late Pearson John Stutchbury to establish a fund, the net income of which is to be applied to a scholarship, to be known as the Stutchbury

Scholarship, for the furtherance of scientific knowledge and investigation in such manner as the University may in its uncontrolled discretion direct.

2. The Board of the Faculty of Physiological Sciences shall be the board of management of the fund and shall determine the conditions of award of the Stutchbury Scholarship, its value and tenure from time to time, and the eligibility of candidates.

3. In any alteration of this decree the main object of the founder, namely the award of Stutchbury Scholarships for the furtherance of scientific knowledge and investigation, shall always be kept in view.

§ 333. *Styles Memorial Prize*

1. The University accepts from the Trustee of the Campaign for Oxford Trust Fund the sum of £6,666, made available by a benefaction from Mrs. Cynthia Styles, which, together with any further donations received for the same purpose, shall establish a fund the income from which shall be applied in the award of a prize from time to time for an outstanding D.Phil. thesis submitted in the subject area of tropical or subtropical plant taxonomy. The prize, which has been established in memory of Dr. B.T. Styles, shall be known as the Brian Thomas Styles Memorial Prize.

2. The Board of the Faculty of Biological Sciences shall be the board of management of the fund and shall determine the value and terms of award of the prize. The prize shall be awarded on the nomination of the Sibthorpian Professor of Plant Sciences, the Sherardian Professor of Botany, and, if he or she is able and willing to act, the Director of the Royal Botanical Gardens, Kew.

3. Income not expended on the prize in any year shall be carried forward for expenditure in subsequent years.

4. Council shall have power to alter this decree from time to time, provided that the main object of the donor, as defined in clause 1 above, is always kept in view.

§ 334. *Sunderland Fund*

1. The University accepts with gratitude the bequest of £10,000 from the late Cristina Sunderland to establish a fund, to be known as the Harold Lister Sunderland Fund, for the furtherance of the study within the University of the Greek language, and of the literature associated therewith.

2. The income of the fund, after the payment of all proper expenses, shall be applied towards the provision of grants to be awarded from time to time to members of the University to assist them in the furtherance of their study of the Greek language, of such period or periods as Council shall from time to time determine, or of the literature associated therewith.

3. The fund shall be administered by the Boards of the Faculties of Literae Humaniores and Medieval and Modern Languages in accordance with arrangements authorized by Council.

4. Council shall have power to alter this decree at any time, provided the main object of the fund (namely, to benefit a student or students of the Greek language, or of the literature associated therewith, in the University of Oxford) is always maintained.

§ 335. *Swan Fund*

1. The fund established out of the bequest from the late J. A. Swan, for research work at the Pitt Rivers Museum in connection with the Batwa and his relatives in Africa and Europe, shall be known as the James A. Swan Fund; and shall be acknowledged in all publications of material and by any person or expedition benefiting from it.

2. The fund shall be used for any work sponsored by the Pitt Rivers Museum on the archaeological, historical, physical, and cultural nature of the Batwa (small peoples of Africa, e.g. Bushmen and Pygmies, and their prehistoric antecedents, wherever they may have been, in Africa, or possibly in the Mediterranean area), and primarily on field-work and publication of such work.

3. The fund shall be administered by the Director of the Pitt Rivers Museum in consultation with the Professor of Social Anthropology and the Professor of Biological Anthropology.

4. Income not spent in any year shall, at the discretion of the curator, be carried forward for use in a subsequent year.

§ 341. *Taylor Institution*

Sayce Fund

1. The University accepts with gratitude a gift of £1,500 from Mrs. R.A. Sayce in memory of her husband, Richard Anthony Sayce, M.A., D.Phil., Reader in French Literature 1966–77, Fellow of Worcester College 1950–77, and Librarian of the college 1958–77.

2. The money shall be invested to form a fund, the income of which shall be paid to the Curators of the Taylor Institution and administered by them at their sole discretion for the purchase for the Library of the Taylor Institution of books and other works in the fields of French language and literature, bibliography, stylistics, and comparative literature.

3. Surplus income shall be carried forward for expenditure in future years.

Slack Bequest

The bequest of the late Professor Samuel Benjamin Slack shall be used at the discretion of the Curators of the Taylor Institution for the general purposes and benefit of the Taylorian Modern Language Library.

Taylorian Special Lectures Fund

1. The gifts of Sir Charles H. Firth, M.A., Fellow of Oriel College, Regius Professor of Modern History, and of Joseph Wright, M.A., Exeter College, Corpus Christi Professor of Comparative Philology, shall be applied to the formation of a permanent fund to be called the 'Taylorian Special Lectures Fund'.

2. The income of the fund shall be administered by the Curators of the Taylor Institution in providing Special Lectures on subjects connected with Modern European Literature.

3. The copyright of the lectures delivered shall be vested in the University and any profits which may arise from the publication of such Taylorian Special Lectures shall be treated as income arising from the fund and be applied by the Curators of the Taylor Institution accordingly.

Taylorian Special Reserve Fund

Whereas the Delegates of Local Examinations desire to place at the disposal of the University the sum of £10,000, being a portion of the Reserve Fund held by the University on behalf of the Delegates, and to express a wish that the sum may be used in the interests of the Taylor Institution, either in relation to the acquisition of a site or as a contribution to the cost of new buildings, or, if these objects are otherwise provided for, in the general interest of the studies associated with the Taylor Institution, the University hereby expresses its gratitude to the delegates for their generous offer and authorizes the Curators of the University Chest to transfer the sum of £10,000, or securities to the value of £10,000, from the Local Examinations Fund I to a Special Fund to be employed by the Curators both as to principal and interest for any of the above-mentioned purposes as directed from time to time by decree.

§ 342. *Thompson Cancer Research Fund*

The University accepts with gratitude a gift of £500 from Mr. Albert Thompson, and any further sums which may be contributed for the same purpose, for the establishment of the Albert Thompson Cancer Research Fund which shall be used, both as to capital and income, at the discretion of the Nuffield Professor of Surgery for the purpose of research into cancer of the colon and rectum.

§ 343. *Thornton Bequest*

The income of the fund bequeathed by the late Mrs. Elfrida Louise Thornton to the University for use by the Nuffield Laboratory of Ophthalmology on the investigation and prevention of blindness shall be applied for these purposes at the discretion of Margaret Ogilvie's Reader in Ophthalmology.

§ 344. *Tovey Memorial Prize*

1. The fund shall be invested by the University and the income arising from it shall be devoted to the maintenance of a prize to be called the 'Donald Tovey Memorial Prize'.

2. The prize shall be open to men or women without regard to nationality, age, or membership of any University.

3. The prize shall be awarded from time to time for original research in music in order to help the holder either to undertake such research or to publish work

already done. The subject of research shall be in the field of the philosophy, history, or understanding of music.

4. The management of the prize shall be entrusted to the Board of the Faculty of Music, which shall determine, on each occasion, the amount of the prize to be awarded.

5. Any income not expended when a prize is awarded may, at the discretion of the Board of the Faculty of Music, be either accumulated to increase the sum available from time to time for prizes, or added to the capital of the fund.

6. Council shall have power to alter this decree from time to time; provided always that

(*a*) the name of the prize shall be retained;

(*b*) the prize shall be open to non-members of the University;

(*c*) the conditions of research as set out in clause 3 above shall not be altered.

§ 345. *Transport Studies Fund*

1. The Transport Studies Fund established by Tit. XVI, Sect. XXIX, cl. 5, shall be administered in accordance with the provisions in this decree.

2. With the exception of such sums as Council may from time to time determine under the provisions of clause 7 below, the entire income of the Transport Studies Fund shall be placed at the disposal of the Board of the Faculty of Anthropology and Geography and shall be applied to the maintenance of the Unit of Transport Studies which shall be under the direction of the Reader in Transport Studies jointly with the Head of the School of Geography.

3. The Board of the Faculty of Anthropology and Geography shall exercise general supervision over the Unit, and the Reader in Transport Studies shall obtain the approval of the board for the research programmes of the Unit.

4. Subject to the provisions of this decree, the Reader in Transport Studies shall have charge of the Unit and shall make provision for the lighting, warming, water-supply, and cleansing of the premises occupied by the Unit out of sums made available to him or her by the Board of the Faculty of Anthropology and Geography.

5. The staff of the Unit shall be appointed, and their duties and conditions of service shall be prescribed, by the Reader in Transport Studies, advised by the Head of the School of Geography, provided that

(*a*) any appointment to a post carrying a stipend of more than the maximum prescribed in Ch. VII, Sect. IV, § 1, cl. 2 (ii) shall be made by the Board of the Faculty of Anthropology and Geography, and the duties and conditions of service shall be prescribed by the board. Such appointments shall also require approval by the General Board;

(*b*) all appointments shall be subject to the provisions of any statute, decree, or regulation of general application.

6. Council may from time to time, after consultation with the Board of the Faculty of Anthropology and Geography, make available such sums from the income of the Transport Studies Fund as it shall think fit to be applied by the board in making grants for the encouragement and advancement of Transport Studies in the University (including the work of the Reader in Transport Studies) provided that:

(*a*) no grants shall be made to those employed in the Unit;

(*b*) no grants exceeding £500 on value shall be made except by decree.

7. There shall be an advisory committee appointed by the Board of the Faculty of Anthropology and Geography, with power to co-opt representatives of transport services or persons knowledgeable about transport problems. This committee shall review and advise on the research programme of the Transport Studies Unit, and shall report to the board as necessary.

§ 346. *Trapnell Fund for Environmental Field Research in Africa*

1. The University accepts with gratitude the initial endowment from Mr. Colin Trapnell, O.B.E., and his wife, and all further sums contributed for the same purpose, to establish a fund, to be called the Trapnell Fund for Environmental Field Research in Africa, for the furtherance within the University of environmental studies. Such furtherance shall be promoted by the support of research concerned with the African environment with reference to all or any of the following:

(*a*) local climatic variation and geomorphology;

(*b*) pedology, soil biology, and soil conservation;

(*c*) the history, composition, and successional phases of the vegetation, and the conservation of indigenous forests; and

(*d*) the carrying capacity of land for human populations.

It shall be a condition of the provision of support for research that the results will be made available for publication.

2. The fund shall be administered by a board of management consisting of:

(1) the Professor of Geography or a deputy nominated by the professor;

(2) either the Sibthorpian Professor of Plant Science or the Sherardian Professor of Botany, as may be agreed between them from time to time, or a deputy with special knowledge of plant ecology, nominated by them jointly;

(3) the IBM Director of the Environmental Change Institute or, if the director is unable or unwilling to serve, a person with special knowledge of geomorphology and climate, nominated by the member at (1) above;

(4)–(6) three persons with special knowledge respectively of pedology and soil biology, plant ecology, and forest botany, jointly nominated by the members at (1)–(3) above;

(7) a senior member of the Oxford University Exploration Club nominated by that club.

The board shall have power to co-opt up to two additional members, at least one of whom may be co-opted for the purpose of facilitating liaison with bodies serving similar purposes outside Oxford. Any co-opted member shall serve for two years and may be reappointed. Nominated and agreed members shall serve for such periods as shall be determined by the person or persons nominating or agreeing them as members of the board. Nominated and co-opted members, other than the member at (7) above, need not be members of Congregation.

3. Within the terms of clause 1 above, the first call on the net income of the fund shall be to support a research post in the subject of African Terrestrial Ecology in the Environmental Change Institute. The fund shall provide the salary costs of the person appointed and a research and travel fund for the holder of the post, and other such support costs on such terms as the board of management shall from time to time determine. The post shall be advertised at such grade and for such periods as the board of management shall determine, taking into account the financial position of the fund. The appointment shall be made by a selection committee appointed by the board of management, which shall normally be chaired by the IBM Director of the Environmental Change Institute. The board of management shall receive an annual report on the research carried out by the holder of this post.

4. The board of management may apply any surplus income remaining, after providing for the post specified in clause 3 above, for purposes within the terms of clause 1 above in the provision of financial support to any of the following:

(*a*) to graduates of British or African universities carrying out, or intending to carry out, either field research in Africa or research in Oxford based upon fieldwork or on previous field-based recording in Africa, and preference under this heading shall be given to applicants working for a research degree of the University, but applicants holding postdoctoral positions at Oxford may also be considered, subject to the availability of funds; and

(*b*) to members of the University intending to undertake an undergraduate expedition approved by the University on the recommendation of the Expedition Council, provided that they pursue a relevant research project.

In considering applications under either (*a*) or (*b*) above, the board shall give priority, other considerations being equal, to research into the ecological aspects either of soils or of indigenous forests and woodlands in the tropical region.

5. Council shall have power to alter this decree from time to time, provided that the main object of the fund, as defined in clause 1 above, is always maintained, and that the majority of members of the board of management shall always comprise persons with special knowledge, and so far as possible field experience, of the topics listed in clause 2 (3) and (4)–(6) above.

§ 347. *Truelove Lecturership Fund*

1. The University accepts with gratitude from Dr. Sidney Truelove the sum of £7,500 to establish a fund to be known as the Dr. Sidney Truelove Lecturership Fund, the income from which shall be used to fund a special lecture in the Oxford Postgraduate Gastroenterology Course. If the course shall cease, the capital sum and any unspent income shall be transferred to the Nuffield

Department of Clinical Medicine Ulcerative Colitis Research Fund under the provisions of § 249 of this section.

2. The Board of the Faculty of Clinical Medicine shall be the Board of Management of the Dr. Sidney Truelove Lecturership Fund.

3. Such proportion of the income as shall be determined from time to time by the Clinical Medicine Board shall be used to fund the Dr. Sidney Truelove Lecture to be given in the Oxford Postgraduate Gastroenterology Course.

4. Income not expended in any year shall, at the discretion of the Clinical Medicine Board, either be accumulated to increase the sum available from time to time for the lecture, or be added to the capital of the fund for so long as that shall be permissible in Law.

5. Council shall have power to alter this decree from time to time, provided that the main object of the benefaction, as stated in clause 1 above, is always kept in view.

§ 348. *Turbutt Prizes*

1. The fund shall be invested by the University, and the income arising therefrom shall be devoted to the maintenance of prizes for excellence in practical organic chemistry, to be called Turbutt Prizes.

2. The Board of the Faculty of Physical Sciences shall be the board of management for the prizes. The board may appoint a committee for the exercise of its functions under these regulations.

3. The value of the prizes shall be determined by the board, which may also make supplementary regulations, not inconsistent with the terms of this decree, for the administration of the prizes.

4. The prizes shall be open to members of the University who are pursuing the course for Part I of the examination in Chemistry in the Honour School of Natural Science. One or more prizes shall be offered in each academic year in respect of each of the first, second, and third years of the course.

5. Recommendations for awards of the prizes shall be made to the board by the Waynflete Professor of Chemistry, after consultation with the readers and lecturers in Organic Chemistry.

6. Surplus income arising from whatever cause may, at the discretion of the board, either be added to the capital of the fund or carried forward for expenditure in future years.

7. Council shall have power to alter this decree provided that the main object of the donors (namely, the establishment of prizes in practical organic chemistry) shall always be kept in view, and that the name of Colonel Turbutt shall always be associated therewith.

§ **349.** *Turnbull Travelling Scholarship*

1. The University accepts with gratitude the sum of £6,100 contributed in recognition of the work of Sir Alec Turnbull, Nuffield Professor of Obstetrics and Gynaecology from 1973 to 1990, together with any further sums which may be contributed for this purpose, to establish a fund for the provision of travelling scholarships, to be known as the Sir Alec Turnbull Travelling Scholarships and to be awarded from time to time to people working in the Nuffield Department of Obstetrics and Gynaecology.

2. The fund shall be managed by the Board of the Faculty of Clinical Medicine, which shall determine from time to time the persons eligible for and the conditions of award of the scholarships, and their several value and tenure.

3. Council shall have power to alter this decree from time to time, provided always that the main object of the fund, as defined in clause 1 above, is kept in view.

§ **350.** *University Challenge Seed Fund*

1. The University accepts with gratitude the sum of £3,000,000 from the Wellcome Trust, the Gatsby Charitable Foundation, and the Secretary of State for Trade and Industry (acting through the Office of Science and Technology). This shall be applied towards the establishment and operation of the University of Oxford University Challenge Seed Fund, in accordance with the University's application to the University Challenge Fund in January 1999, the Guidelines of the University Challenge Competition, and the terms and conditions laid down from time to time by the Wellcome Trust and the Office of Science and Technology.

2. The fund shall be administered by the Curators of the University Chest, acting on the advice of a manager and an advisory board. The role of the manager shall be to advise the curators on the application of the fund. The role of the advisory board shall be to advise the curators on strategic, procedural, investment, and compliance issues; provided always that the board shall not carry on investment business for the purposes of the Financial Services Act 1986.

3. The manager shall be appointed by the Curators of the University Chest, and shall be a member company of the British Venture Capital Association, with authorization under the Financial Services Act.

4. The advisory board shall be appointed by the Curators of the University Chest, after consultation with the Managing Director of Isis Innovation Limited. The board shall comprise two senior persons from industry or commerce, two members of the University's academic staff, a director of a high-technology company which has spun out of the University, and a representative of the manager.

5. The Curators of the University Chest may delegate all or any of the powers conferred on them in this decree to the Secretary of the Chest, and may revoke

any such delegation at any time. For so long as powers are delegated to the Secretary of the Chest he or she shall report to the curators on the exercise of those powers at such intervals as the curators may prescribe, but no less frequently than annually.

6. Council shall have power to alter this decree from time to time, with the consent of the Wellcome Trust and the Office of Science and Technology.

§ 351. *van Houten Bequest*

The bequest of the late Georges van Houten of the remainder of his estate shall be used for the benefit of the University in such way as the Chancellor, the Vice-Chancellor, and Council shall see fit.

§ 352. *Varley-Gradwell Travelling Fellowship in Insect Ecology*

1. The University accepts with gratitude a benefaction from two anonymous donors which shall be used, together with any other donations accepted for this purpose, to form a fund, the net income of which shall be used for the provision of a travelling fellowship for the support of field work, travel, and other activity of direct benefit to the field of insect ecology. The travelling fellowship shall be known as the Varley-Gradwell Travelling Fellowship in Insect Ecology.

2. The fund shall be administered by a board of management consisting of:

(1) the Linacre Professor of Zoology or a person nominated by the professor;

(2) the Professor of Zoology or a person nominated by the professor;

(3) the Curator of the Entomological Collections;

(4), (5) two persons nominated by the Board of the Faculty of Biological Sciences, who need not be members of Congregation.

Nominated members shall serve for such periods as shall be determined by the person or body nominating them as members of the board.

3. The fellowship shall be tenable for the period of one year. It shall not be renewable.

4. Applications shall be made to the board, which shall determine from time to time the persons eligible for award of the travelling fellowship, and its value.

5. Income not expended in any year shall be carried forward for expenditure in subsequent years.

6. Council shall have power to alter this decree from time to time, provided that the main object of the fund, as defined in clause 1 above, is always kept in view.

§ 353. *Vaughan Morgan Prizes*

1. There shall be prizes in English Literature which shall be called 'The Violet Vaughan Morgan Prizes' in memory of Maud Violet Caroline Vaughan Morgan.

2. The Board of the Faculty of English Language and Literature shall be the board of management of the prizes.

3. The prizes shall be open to members of the University, whether men or women, residing within the University on the date fixed for the examination.

4. No person shall be eligible for a prize who, on the date fixed for the written examination, will have exceeded nine terms from matriculation.

5. Each prize-winner shall be presented with a bronze medal having on one side a profile of Maud Violet Caroline Vaughan Morgan and on the other side an engraved statement of the origin of the prizes.

6. All expenses incurred in connection with the award of the prizes, including the bronze medals, examiners' fees, and expenses of administration, shall be met from the income of the fund.

7. In awarding a prize, in addition to scholastic acquirements, the character of the candidates shall be taken into consideration so far as they can be judged from a *viva voce* examination and also from their records at college, and a prize shall not be awarded to anyone who, in the opinion of the examiners, does not show promise of becoming a loyal citizen of the British Commonwealth.

8. The board of management shall, subject to the conditions specified in clauses 3, 4, 5, and 7 above, make such regulations for the award and value of the prizes as it shall deem fit.

9. Surplus income arising from vacancies or from any other cause may at the discretion of the board of management either be invested in augmentation of the capital of the fund or be used for the award of a postgraduate studentship for the study of English Literature.

10. Council shall have power from time to time to alter this decree, provided always that the prizes shall always bear the title of 'The Violet Vaughan Morgan Prizes' and that the conditions specified in clauses 5 and 7 above are adhered to.

§ 354. *Vice-Chancellors' Fund*

1. The University accepts with gratitude from the Trustee of the Campaign for Oxford Trust Fund donations received, and such further sums as may be contributed for the same purpose, to establish a fund to be known as the Vice-Chancellors' Fund, the net income of which shall be applied to the provision of financial aid for those working for a postgraduate research qualification of the University.

2. The fund shall be expendable, as to both capital and income, under arrangements to be approved from time to time by Council.

3. The arrangements for the administration of the fund shall be as determined from time to time by the Educational Policy and Standards Committee.

4. Income not expended in any year shall be carried forward for expenditure in subsequent years.

5. Council shall have power to alter this decree from time to time, provided that the main object of the fund, as defined in clause 1 above, is always kept in view.

§ 355. *Voltaire Foundation Fund*

1. The University accepts with gratitude the bequest of the late T.D.N. Besterman, which shall form a fund to be called the Voltaire Foundation Fund.

2. The said fund shall be applied to the completion or continuation of the publications and research within the field of Enlightenment and eighteenth-century studies begun by the late T.D.N. Besterman, and, as and when progress on these allows, the undertaking of other publications and research projects of a similar nature, the financing of scholarships, lecturerships, and research within the same field and the improvement of research collections and facilities in the Taylor Institution with these aims in view.

3. The fund shall be administered by a committee consisting of the following:

(1)–(2) two persons appointed by Council;

(3)–(8) six persons appointed by the Curators of the Taylor Institution.

The period of office of appointed members shall be four years and they shall be re-eligible. Casual vacancies shall be filled for the unexpired residue of the period. The committee may co-opt not more than three additional members for periods of four years.

4. The committee shall present an annual report and accounts to the Curators of the University Chest and to the Curators of the Taylor Institution.

§ 356. *von Engel and Francis Fund*

1. The University accepts with gratitude the gift of £8,000 donated by Professor R.N. Franklin, C.B.E., Honorary Fellow of Keble College, which together with moneys in the Gordon Francis Fund shall comprise the Hans von Engel and Gordon Francis Fund.

2. The fund shall be used

(*a*) for the award, by such judges as the body responsible for the administration of the fund may from time to time approve, of a prize, to be known as the von Engel Prize, to a person whom they consider to have made an outstanding contribution to the study of phenomena in ionized gases and plasma physics;

(*b*) to foster the study of phenomena in ionized gases and plasma physics in the University by

(i) the award of a prize, to be known as the Gordon Francis Prize, for meritorious performance in the M.Sc. in the Science and Applications of Electric Plasmas;

(ii) encouraging travel in connection with their research by members of the University doing research in the field indicated;

(iii) for other purposes consistent with the promotion of studies in this field.

3. Income not expended in any year shall be carried forward for expenditure in subsequent years.

4. The administration of the fund shall be under the direction of the Board of the Faculty of Physical Sciences, which may delegate the responsibility to an appropriate body.

5. Council shall have full power to alter this decree from time to time, provided always that the purposes of the fund, as stated in clause 2 above, shall be kept in view.

§ 361. *Wainwright Fund*

1. (*a*) The gift (hereinafter called the 'original gift') of £4,000 shall be incorporated in the Trusts Pool and shall be called the Gerald Averay Wainwright Fund;

(*b*) the Curators of the University Chest shall be authorized to accept gifts for the same purposes, and to treat them, subject to any conditions laid down by the donors, as if they were part of the original gift.

2. (*a*) There shall be a board of management (hereinafter called 'the board') composed of the following persons:

(i) *ex officio*:

(1) the Vice-Chancellor;

(2) the Keeper of the Department of Antiquities in the Ashmolean Museum;

(3) the Director of the Pitt Rivers Museum;

(ii) (4)–(6) three mature scholars specializing in the archaeology of the Near East;

(iii) (7)–(8) one or two persons co-opted by the board.

(*b*) When a vacancy occurs on the board (other than among the *ex officio* members) it shall be filled by co-optation by the remaining members of the board, subject to the condition that at least two of the persons described in sub-clause (*a*) (ii) above and at least one of those co-opted under sub-clause (*a*) (iii) above shall not be members of Congregation; provided that any co-opted member who may become a member of Congregation during his or her term of office shall not be required to resign.

(*c*) Co-opted members shall serve for five years and shall be re-eligible.

3. (*a*) There shall be offered for competition annually a prize or prizes, called the Gerald Averay Wainwright Prizes, for the best essay submitted by any boy or girl at any school of which the head is a member of the Headmasters' Conference or of the Secondary Heads' Association.

The board may award prizes, to be apportioned among the candidates according to its discretion, of such value as the board may from time to time determine.

The board may, in addition, make payments for meritorious work to candidates other than the prize winners.

(*b*) The prize shall be spent on some object or objects approved by the board in furtherance of archaeological studies, which objects may include travel, museum study, and the purchase of books.

(*c*) The subjects of the essays which shall be chosen by the candidates themselves shall relate to the non-classical antiquity of the Near East. They shall consist of not less than 5,000 words and shall include maps and illustrations.

(*d*) The board shall appoint examiners to judge the entries. The prize shall be awarded by the board on the recommendation of the examiners.

(*e*) The board may pay such reasonable remuneration to the examiners as the Vice-Chancellor and Proctors may approve, and may also incur expenditure from time to time in giving public notice of the prize.

4. The first charges on the fund shall be

(*a*) the necessary expenses of administration of the fund, which may include the reimbursement of out-of-pocket expenses incurred by members of the board in the discharge of their duties, and

(*b*) the maintenance of the prizes in accordance with the provisions of clause 3 above.

5. Whenever, in the opinion of the board, the annual income of the fund remaining after the award of a prize is sufficient, the board shall offer (in accordance with clauses 6–10 below) one or more research fellowships, to be called the 'Gerald Averay Wainwright Research Fellowships'.

6. Any income remaining after the obligations imposed on the board by clauses 3–5 above have been met shall be available to the board for the making of grants at its absolute discretion for the furtherance of the study of the archaeology of the Near East.

7. The board of management shall have power to award fellowships and prizes on such terms and conditions, not inconsistent with the terms of this decree, as it shall deem fit.

8. Candidates for a fellowship shall normally be resident in the United Kingdom.

9. Council shall have power at any time to alter, at the suggestion of the board, the provisions of this decree provided that the intentions of the donor as expressed in the recitals shall be observed.

§ 362. *Walker Studentship*

1. The fund shall be called the 'Philip Walker Fund', and shall be devoted to the furtherance of original research in Pathology.

2. The fund shall be administered by the Professor of Pathology, in conjunction with a board of managers, consisting of:

(1) the Vice-Chancellor;
(2) the Regius Professor of Medicine;
(3) the Waynflete Professor of Physiology;
(4) the Professor of Pathology.

3. The income of the fund shall be applied, as and when funds permit and the Professor of Pathology considers it appropriate, primarily for the maintenance

of a studentship called the 'Philip Walker Studentship', the holder of which shall devote himself or herself to original research in Pathology. Any surplus income may be used to further original research in Pathology by the award of additional studentships, prizes, or grants.

4. The studentship shall be tenable for such period not exceeding five years, and shall be of such value, as the board of managers shall determine.

5. The studentship shall be awarded by the board of managers either on the recommendation of the Professor of Pathology or, if the board so desires, after the studentship has been advertised.

6. The studentship shall not be awarded by the result of a competitive examination.

7. Subject to the foregoing provision, the Professor of Pathology or the managers may take such steps as they may think fit to ascertain the qualifications of the candidates.

8. The student shall not necessarily be a member of the University of Oxford.

9. Subject to the approval of the board of managers the studentship may be held in conjunction with any other post or source of funds acceptable to the Professor of Pathology, provided that the student during his or her tenure of the studentship shall devote himself or herself to original pathological research. In any books, papers, or publications in which the student may publish the results of the investigations carried on during his or her studentship, the student shall, where practicable, describe himself or herself as the 'Philip Walker Student'.

10. If the Professor of Pathology shall be of opinion that the student is not fulfilling and is not likely to fulfil the objects of the studentship, he or she shall report accordingly to the board of managers, which may, if it sees fit, remove the studentship from the student.

11. The place and nature of the studies of the student shall be subject to the approval of the Professor of Pathology, provided that the student shall be bound to pursue his or her studies within the University during at least three terms of his or her tenure of the studentship, unless the Professor of Pathology shall, with the approval of the board of managers, dispense with this requirement for special reasons. The Professor of Pathology shall take such steps as he or she may think necessary to satisfy himself or herself as to the diligence and progress of the student, and shall require from the student any reports or other information on the subject of his or her studies which the professor may think desirable.

12. Council shall have power at any time to alter this decree on the recommendation of the board of managers, provided always that the main object of the fund, namely the furtherance of original research in Pathology, is kept in view.

§ **363.** *Wallace Bequest*

1. The bequests of the late Mr. P.M. Wallace and Mrs. H.M. Wallace shall form a fund to be called the Nellie Wallace Bequest.

2. The Board of the Faculty of Literae Humaniores shall be the board of management of the bequest.

3. The board of management shall at least in every other year invite a scholar from abroad, with a preference for scholars working in Europe, to visit Oxford for a period of not less than four weeks to lecture and conduct seminars in a subject within the field of Literae Humaniores.

4. Any person visiting Oxford at the board's invitation under clause 3 above shall be known as the Nellie Wallace Lecturer: the board shall determine his or her duties and fix the amount of his or her emoluments and expenses, which shall be paid from the income of the Nellie Wallace Bequest.

5. Any income not used to pay the emoluments and expenses of a Nellie Wallace Lecturer may at the discretion of the board be

(*a*) carried forward for use in a subsequent year;

(*b*) invested in augmentation of the capital;

(*c*) applied in any other way which the board shall think conducive to the promotion of classical learning in the University of Oxford.

§ **364.** *Walling Memorial Fund*

1. The University accepts with gratitude donations to establish a fund to be known as the Roger Walling Memorial Fund, to commemorate Roger Walling, Worcester College, which shall be used to support undergraduate fieldwork in Geology.

2. The Board of the Faculty of Physical Sciences shall be the board of management of the fund, provided that the disbursement of awards from the fund shall be at the discretion of the Professor of Geology.

3. Council shall have the power to alter this decree from time to time, provided always that the object of the fund as defined in clause 1 above shall be kept in view.

§ **365.** *Warwick Travelling Bursary*

1. The award established to enable women students of French to visit France or to attend vacation courses in French shall be called the 'Marjorie Countess of Warwick Travelling Bursary'.

2. It shall be administered by the Board of the Faculty of Medieval and Modern Languages which shall have power, subject to the conditions of the trust,

(*a*) to make regulations as to the award and tenure of the Bursary, and

(*b*) to defray from the income of the trust any expenses incidental to the carrying out of the provisions thereof.

3. Any income not expended under the conditions of the trust in any year may, at the discretion of the board, be either accumulated to increase the sum available from time to time for bursaries or added to the capital of the fund.

4. Council shall have power to alter this decree from time to time provided always that the main intention of the testatrix is kept in view.

§ 366. *Welch Scholarships*

The board of management for the administration of the Welch Scholarships under the provisions of Tit. XVI, Sect. LIX shall consist of:

(1) the Warden of Wadham College or the Warden's representative;

(2), (3) two persons appointed by the Board of the Faculty of Biological Sciences;

(4) one person appointed by the Board of the Faculty of Clinical Medicine;

(5) one person appointed by the Board of the Faculty of Physiological Sciences;

(6) one person appointed by the Board of the Faculty of Psychological Studies.

The members under (2)–(6) above shall hold office for three years and shall be re-eligible.

§ 367. *Weldon Memorial Prize*

1. The prize, founded to perpetuate the name of Walter Frank Raphael Weldon, M.A., D.Sc., formerly Linacre Professor of Comparative Anatomy and Fellow of Merton College, and to encourage Biometric Science, shall be called the 'Weldon Memorial Prize'. The prize shall be awarded every two years, and shall consist of a bronze medal and of a grant of money, being nine-tenths of two years' income of the endowment.

2. The electors to the prize shall be

(1) the Vice-Chancellor;

(2) the Linacre Professor of Zoology;

(3) one person appointed by the Board of the Faculty of Biological Sciences;

(4) one person appointed by the Board of the Faculty of Mathematical Sciences;

(5)–(6) two persons appointed by Council.

Appointees shall hold office for six years and shall be re-eligible.

3. The electors shall have power to appoint, if they think fit, a judge or judges to assist them in awarding the prize.

4. The prize shall in no case be awarded to the same person a second time.

5. The prize shall, subject to the provisions of clause 4 above, be awarded without regard to nationality or membership of any University to the person who, in the judgement of the electors, has, in the ten years next preceding the date of the award, published the most noteworthy contribution to the

development of mathematical or statistical methods applied to problems in Biology. Biology shall, for the purposes of this clause, be interpreted as including Zoology, Botany, Anthropology, Sociology, Psychology, and Medical Science.

6. The electors shall have the power to divide the prize between two individuals who have collaborated in their contribution.

7. If no candidate is considered to be of sufficient merit to receive the award the electors shall at their discretion either direct the investment of the accrued income in augmentation of the next award, or of the fund in cl. 8 below, or assign the grant of money (without the medal) to some person, who shall undertake to carry out some investigation approved by the electors.

8. Ten per cent of the income of the endowment shall be set aside every year to form a fund which shall be employed for

(*a*) paying for the bronze medal, and

(*b*) paying honoraria to judges, or promoting the investigation of mathematical or statistical methods applied to problems in Biology, as the electors may direct.

9. The electors shall have power to make regulations or by-laws for the purpose of carrying this decree into effect; and Council shall have power to alter the decree from time to time in such manner as it shall deem expedient, provided that the main objects of the foundation as expressed in clauses 1 and 5 above are always kept in view.

§ 368. *Welsh Prize*

1. The sum of £103, given as the endowment of a prize for the encouragement of the study of Human Anatomy and, in particular, of the art of drawing, in relation thereto, and the investments for the time being representing the same, shall be held by the University upon an account to be called 'The Welsh Memorial Fund'.

2. The income of the fund shall be used at the discretion of Dr. Lee's Professor of Anatomy, or other principal teacher of Human Anatomy within the University, and shall be offered by him or her once in every year, either in money or books, as a prize for the best set of drawings illustrative of Human Anatomy, the work of a student, being a member of the University, who shall have been bona fide engaged in the study of that subject in the Anatomical Laboratory of the University during not less than one term prior to the term in which the prize is to be awarded, and who on 30 June in the year of award shall not have exceeded 23 years of age; provided always that the Prize shall never be awarded a second time to the same person.

3. In the event of no student submitting a set of drawings as aforesaid, or of no drawings being submitted which shall be in the judgement of the professor of sufficient merit to be deserving of the prize, the professor may at his or her absolute discretion award the sum to any student qualified as aforesaid as a

reward for conspicuous excellence in any other branch of the study or practice of Human Anatomy.

4. If in any year the prize be not awarded, the income of the fund shall be carried forward for use in augmentation of the prize or for the award of additional prizes at the discretion of the professor (or other principal teacher).

5. This decree may at any time be added to, altered, or repealed by Council.

§ 369. *Wetton Fund for Astrophysics*

1. The University accepts with gratitude a benefaction from Mr. Philip Wetton to establish a fund, to be known as the Philip Wetton Fund for Astrophysics, the net income of which shall be used for the establishment in due course of a Philip Wetton Professorship of Astrophysics and otherwise initially for the support of teaching and research in Astrophysics.

2. The fund shall be administered by the Physics Management Committee.

3. Council shall have power to amend this decree from time to time, provided always that the main purpose of the fund, as defined in clause 1 above, shall be kept in view.

§ 370. *White's Estate*

See *Estates Register*, 1972, p. 60.

§ 371. *Whitehead Fund*

1. The University accepts with gratitude the bequest of £10,000 from Sir George Whitehead to establish a fund to be known as the James Hugh Edendale Whitehead and George William Edendale Whitehead Fund, for the promotion of the study of the history and/or literature of England and her colonies.

2. The fund shall be administered by the Boards of the Faculties of English Language and Literature and of Modern History in accordance with arrangements authorized by Council.

3. Council shall have power to alter this decree from time to time, provided that the main purposes of the fund (namely, the promotion of the study of the history and/or literature of England and her colonies, and the association of the names of Sir George Whitehead's sons with the objects at the University of Oxford on which the fund is expended) are always maintained.

§ 372. *Williams University Parks Tree Fund*

1. The moneys raised to mark the notable service of Sir Edgar Williams as Warden of Rhodes House, 1952–80, shall, together with any further sums contributed in future for this purpose, constitute the Sir Edgar Williams University Parks Tree Fund, the net income of which shall be devoted to the planting and cataloguing of trees and shrubs in the University Parks.

2. The fund shall be administered by the Curators of the University Parks.

3. Any income not expended in any year may, at the discretion of the Curators of the University Parks, be either carried forward for expenditure in subsequent years or (until 31 July 2000 only) added to the capital of the fund.

4. Council shall have power to alter this decree from time to time, provided that the main object of the fund as defined in clause 1 above is always kept in view.

§ 373. *Williams and Grant Memorial Fund*

The Nan Williams and Lena Grant Memorial Fund established by the gift of the Revd. Emlyn Williams, R.N., M.A., Jesus College, together with any other gifts made for the same purpose, shall be used to finance research into the prevention and cure of leukaemia and shall be administered by the Board of the Faculty of Clinical Medicine. Eligibility to apply for a grant from this fund shall not, however, be restricted to members of that faculty.

§ 374. *Williams Scholarships in Human Anatomy, Physiology, and Pathology*

[1] *Human Anatomy*

1. The income derived from the trust fund shall be applied to the establishment of three scholarships in Human Anatomy, one to be awarded annually and to be tenable for three years.

2. The scholarships shall be awarded in connection with the study of Human Anatomy in relation to Medicine with a view to the promotion of industry and the recognition of skill and knowledge in the prosecution of that study.

3. The scholarships shall be confined to members of the University who have commenced and continued the study of Human Anatomy within the University.

4. The scholarships shall be called the Theodore Williams Scholarships in Human Anatomy, and shall be awarded annually in Trinity Term.

5. The Board of the Faculty of Physiological Sciences shall be the board of management and shall have power to make regulations, not inconsistent with this decree, concerning the award of the scholarships.

6. The scholarships shall be open to any member of the University, whether man or woman, who on 30 June in the year of award shall not have exceeded 25 years of age and who shall have

(*a*) attended regularly courses of instruction in the Department of Human Anatomy and Genetics for not less than five terms and not more than nine terms;

(*b*) passed the First Examination for the Degree of Bachelor of Medicine and the examination in Physiological Sciences in the Honour School of Natural Science;

(*c*) made to the board a declaration in writing of his or her intention to continue the study of Medicine.

7. Dr. Lee's Professor of Anatomy shall award the scholarships in consultation with the departmental teachers of Human Anatomy and taking into consideration

(*a*) the results of the examination in the aforesaid honour school;

(*b*) the results of the terminal or other usual examinations held in the Department of Human Anatomy and Genetics and the skill displayed by the students in their dissections.

8. The scholar shall employ himself or herself for at least one year in research on a subject approved by the professor, and (unless the board on the recommendation of the professor shall in a particular case allow otherwise) shall begin such research in the term following his or her election.

9. Each scholar shall receive on election one-third of the net income of the fund for the year of award after payment of all expenses incidental to the trust. He or she shall receive a further one-third after the expiration of a period of one year from election and the final one-third after the expiration of a further period of one year.

10. The professor shall notify the board through the Secretary of Faculties of each award and of the research to be carried out by the scholar.

11. If, owing to any circumstance, the whole of the income of the Fund in any year be not applied as directed in clause 9 above, the residue shall be expended in some way consistent with the object of the founder, and may be carried forward for use in subsequent years.

12. In any change of decree the main object of the founder shall always be kept in view, namely, the encouragement and promotion of the study of Human Anatomy in connection with Medicine.

[2] *Physiology*

1. The income derived from the trust fund shall be applied to the establishment of three scholarships in Physiology in relation to Medicine, one to be awarded annually and to be tenable for three years.

2. The scholarships shall be called the Theodore Williams Scholarships in Physiology, and shall be awarded annually in Trinity Term.

3. The Board of the Faculty of Physiological Sciences shall be the board of management and shall have power to make regulations, not inconsistent with this decree, concerning the award of the scholarships.

4. The scholarships shall be open to any member of the University who at the time of award shall not have exceeded fifteen terms from matriculation and whose name has been placed in the class list in the Honour School of Natural Science (Physiological Sciences), or in the Honour School of Psychology, Philosophy, and Physiology, provided he or she has offered Physiology as a subject in that examination.

5. The Waynflete Professor of Physiology shall award the scholarships after consultation with the Whitley Professor of Biochemistry, the Professor of Psychology, the departmental teachers of Physiology and Biochemistry, and the staff of the Department of Experimental Psychology, the examiners in the

Honour School of Natural Science (Physiological Sciences), and the examiners in Physiology in the Honour School of Psychology, Philosophy, and Physiology.

6. The scholar shall employ himself or herself for at least one year in research on a subject approved by the professor, and (unless the board on the recommendation of the professor shall in a particular case allow otherwise) shall begin such research in the term following his or her election.

7. Each scholar shall receive on election one-third of the net income of the fund for the year of award after payment of all expenses incidental to the trust. He or she shall receive a further one-third after the expiration of a period of one year from election and the final one-third after the expiration of a further period of one year.

8. The professor shall notify the board through the Secretary of Faculties of each award and of the research to be carried out by the scholar.

9. If, owing to any circumstance, the whole of the income of the fund in any year be not applied as directed in clause 7 above, the residue shall be expended in some way consistent with the object of the founder, and may be carried forward for use in subsequent years.

10. In any change of decree the main object of the founder shall be always kept in view.

[3] *Pathology*

1. The income derived from the trust fund shall be applied to the establishment of three scholarships in Pathology, one to be awarded annually and to be tenable for three years.

2. The scholarships shall be called the Theodore Williams Scholarships in Pathology, and shall be awarded annually in Michaelmas Term.

3. The Board of the Faculty of Physiological Sciences shall be the board of management, and shall have power to make regulations, not inconsistent with this decree, concerning the award of the scholarship.

4. The scholarships shall be open to any member of the University, whether man or woman, who on 30 June in the year of award has not exceeded twenty-five years of age, who has attended regularly courses of instruction in the Sir William Dunn School of Pathology, and whose name has been placed in the class list in the Honour School of Natural Science (Physiological Sciences).

5. The Professor of Pathology shall award the scholarships in consultation with the departmental teachers of Pathology, taking into consideration the results of the aforesaid honour school.

6. The successful candidate shall make to the board a declaration in writing of his or her intention to continue the study of Medicine.

7. The scholar shall employ himself or herself for at least one year in research on a subject approved by the professor, and (unless the board on the recommendation of the professor shall in a particular case allow otherwise) shall begin such research in the term following his or her election.

8. Each scholar shall receive on election one-third of the net income of the fund for the year of award after payment of all expenses incidental to the trust. He or she shall receive a further one-third after the expiration of a period of one year from election and the final one-third after the expiration of a further period of one year.

9. The professor shall notify the board through the Secretary of Faculties of each award and of any research to be carried out by the scholar.

10. If, owing to any circumstance, the whole of the income of the fund in any year be not applied as directed in clause 8 above, the residue shall be expended in some way consistent with the object of the founder, and may be carried forward for use in subsequent years.

11. In any change of decree the main object of the founder shall be always kept in view.

§ 375. *Wills Scholarships*

1. The Michael Wills Scholarships shall be tenable at Oxford by students from the Federal German Republic who have already pursued a course for at least two years at a university in their own country or at some other approved university.

2. The scholarships shall be of such number and value as shall be agreed by the Dulverton Trustees in consultation with the University, and shall be tenable for two years.

3. For as long as students from Oxford holding scholarships in Germany under the provisions of § 106, cl. 2 and § 154, cll. 1 and 3 of this section are excused university fees by universities or other institutions of higher learning in the Federal Republic of Germany, no university fee shall be required from students from the Federal Republic of Germany holding Michael Wills Scholarships in Oxford.

4. The scholarships shall be administered and the arrangements for the selection of the scholars shall be made by the Board of Management for the Michael Foster and Michael Wills Scholarships under the provisions of § 106, cl. 4 of this section.

§ 376. *Wilson Benefactions*

[1]

Wilson Bequest

1. The University accepts with gratitude the residuary bequest of Dr. S.E. Wilson for the general purposes of the Oxford Forestry Institute (formerly the Department of Forestry).

2. The fund representing the bequest and the net income derived therefrom shall be administered by a board of management consisting of:

(1) the Chairman of the Advisory Committee for Forestry;

(2) the Head of the Department of Plant Sciences or his or her deputy;

(3) the Director of the Forestry Institute.

The board shall also manage any outstanding balance in the fund established by Dr. Wilson in 1983 for scientific research in Forestry.

[2]

Wilson Scholarships in Forestry

1. The Board of Management of the Wilson Bequest shall also act as the board of management of Dr. S.E. Wilson's benefaction, consisting of copies of certain of his books and the copyright therein, for the promotion of the study of Forestry among members of the University reading for a degree.

2. The first charge on the benefaction shall be the funding of a scholarship (to be known as the S.E. Wilson Scholarship in Forestry) which shall be offered each year for award to a person accepted for the course of study leading to the Degree of Master of Science in Forestry and its Relation to Land Use, but who is not in receipt of a full award from a research council or other organization. The scholarship shall be awarded by a committee under the chairmanship of the Director of the Forestry Institute, subject to the approval of the board of management.

3. The value of the scholarships shall be fixed by the board of management in the light of the needs of the scholars and of the funds available after it has met any expenses incurred in making the awards and has made such provision as it shall think fit, in consultation with the publisher if necessary, for the cost of revising and reprinting the books.

4. Income not required for the scholarships may be applied by the board of management to the award, on the recommendation of the Director of the Forestry Institute, of grants to persons (not necessarily being members of the University) who undertake the study of a special branch of forest utilization. The value of each such grant (which may include a contribution towards the travelling and other expenses, to be incurred by the holder), and the conditions of tenure shall be fixed by the board on the recommendation of the professor, provided that no such grant shall exceed £100 in total value.

5. These regulations may be altered from time to time by Council on the recommendation of the Board of Management, provided always that regard is had to the main object of the benefaction, namely, the promotion of the study of Forestry among members of the University reading for a degree.

§ 377. *Winchester Award Fund*

1. The University accepts with gratitude from the Most Hon. Bapsybanoo Marchioness of Winchester the sum of £10,000 to establish a fund, to be known as the Bapsybanoo Marchioness of Winchester Award Fund. The capital sum of £10,000 shall remain intact in perpetuity, and the net income from it shall be used to make an award to a student of the University who in research or study while pursuing graduate studies at the University has achieved distinction in the area of international relations, in particular as concerned with human rights and fundamental freedoms.

2. The Board of the Faculty of Social Studies shall be the board of management of the fund.

3. The award shall be suitably advertised within the University and shall normally be given annually, provided that candidates of sufficient merit present themselves, under such arrangements as may be approved from time to time by Council.

4. Any net income not expended in any year shall be used to establish an Accumulated Income Fund, and the total net income that has accrued to that fund since the time at which the last award has been made shall be applied in supplementation of the value of the next award that is made.

5. Council shall have power to alter this decree from time to time, provided always that the purpose of the fund, as stated in clause 1 above, shall be kept in view.

§ 378. *Winchester Lecturership and Pavry Memorial Lecturership*

1. The University accepts with gratitude from the Most Hon. Bapsybanoo Marchioness of Winchester

(1) the sum of £50,000 to establish a fund the income from which shall be used to defray all costs associated with an annual visiting lecturership to be known as the Dasturzada Dr. Jal Pavry Memorial Lecturership; and

(2) the sum of £50,000 to establish a fund the income from which shall be used to defray all costs associated with an annual visiting lecturership to be known as the Bapsybanoo Marchioness of Winchester Lecturership.

The two capital sums shall remain intact in perpetuity.

2. Each lecturer shall be appointed annually to lecture in International Relations, History, Philosophy, Religions of the World, Theology, Law, or any other academic subject which the Vice-Chancellor, after consultation with the management committee established under clause 3 below, shall consider appropriate.

3. The management of the income of the fund, including all arrangements for the lectures, shall be the responsibility of a committee consisting of eight persons, who shall be

(1) the Vice-Chancellor;

(2) one person appointed by Council;

(3) one person appointed by the General Board;

(4) one person appointed by the Board of the Faculty of Social Studies;

(5) one person appointed by the Board of the Faculty of Modern History;

(6) one person appointed by the Board of the Faculty of Literae Humaniores;

(7) one person appointed by the Board of the Faculty of Law;

(8) one person appointed by the Board of the Faculty of Theology.

The persons appointed by Council and the General Board shall be from subject areas other than those represented under (4)–(8) and shall keep in mind the interests of all subjects not represented by those five members.

The members of the committee of management shall hold office for three years and shall be re-eligible.

4. Any income from each endowment not spent on the appropriate annual lecturership may at the discretion of the committee:

(*a*) be used to meet the cost of a second lecturer in the year in question;

(*b*) be carried forward for expenditure in a subsequent year;

(*c*) be invested in augmentation of the capital, for as long as this shall be permissible in law.

5. Council shall have power to alter this decree, provided that the main object of the two funds, as defined in clause 1 above, is always kept in view.

§ 379. *Witt Fund*

1. The University accepts with gratitude the bequest of £500 from the late Mr. David Otto Witt to establish a fund to be known as the Gertrude Witt Fund, the income from which shall be used for the furtherance of the study of Forestry.

2. The income shall be placed at the disposal of the Professor of Forest Science, or his or her deputy, for the making of grants at his or her discretion to students or student organizations concerned with the study of Forestry.

3. Council shall have power from time to time to alter these directions for the expenditure of the income of the fund, provided always that the main intention of the founder is kept in view.

§ 380. *Women Students Fund*

1. The University accepts from the present trustees thereof the sum of approximately £37,000, which shall form a fund to be known as the Women Students Fund. The said sum shall be held by the University on the trusts of the declaration of trust of 25 March 1933, namely for the benefit of the women students of the University.

2. The Committee for Educational Studies shall be the board of management for the fund.

§ 381. *Woodforde Collection of British Birds: Loan to Bristol City Museum*

The collection of British birds accepted by the University from the late F.C. Woodforde by Decree (5) of 19 March 1921, and exhibited in the University Museum, shall be transferred on permanent loan to the Bristol City Museum, subject to the condition that the collection be kept together and that each specimen be distinctly labelled as having formed part of the collection of the late F.H. Woodforde, M.D.

§ 382. *Wronker Prizes*

1. There shall be an annual prize in Law and an annual prize in Medicine. They shall be called the Martin Wronker Prize in Law and the Martin Wronker Prize in Medicine respectively.

2. The Martin Wronker Prize in Law shall be awarded by the examiners in the Final Honour School of Jurisprudence to the candidate whose work in the examination for that school is of the highest merit, if in the opinion of the examiners his or her work renders him or her worthy of the award, provided that satisfactory evidence shall have been received from his or her college or other society as to his or her character. Grants may be awarded by the examiners to other candidates who distinguish themselves in the examination, under arrangements to be approved from time to time by the Board of the Faculty of Law. Additional prizes may also be awarded by the examiners, for meritorious performance in the honour school in each of the following five subjects: Jurisprudence, Tort, Land Law, Trusts, and Administrative Law.

3. The Martin Wronker Prize in Medicine shall be awarded by the examiners in the Final Honour School of Physiological Sciences in consultation if appropriate with the chairman of examiners for the Honour School of Psychology, Philosophy, and Physiology. The prize shall be awarded to the candidate on the Register of University Medical Students kept by the Board of the Faculty of Physiological Sciences under the provisions of Ch. II, Sect. VIII, § 3, whose performance in either the Final Honour School of Natural Science (Physiological Sciences) or (provided that the subjects offered have included Physiology) the Final Honour School of Psychology, Philosophy, and Physiology is generally most outstanding, provided that satisfactory evidence shall have been received from his or her college or other society as to his or her character. Grants may be awarded by the examiners to other candidates who distinguish themselves in the examinations, under arrangements to be approved from time to time by the faculty board.

4. The endowment shall be divided into two equal parts to be designated the Law Prize Fund and the Medicine Prize Fund respectively.

5. The respective faculty boards shall determine the values of the prizes.

6. The Board of the Faculty of Law may at its discretion award from the Law Prize Fund a Wronker Scholarship to any holder of an Eldon Law Scholarship and shall have power to determine from time to time the value of each Wronker Scholarship.

7. In addition to the annual prize in Medicine and grants to unsuccessful candidates for this prize, the Board of the Faculty of Physiological Sciences may, at its discretion, award annually to members of the University on the Register of University Medical Students the following prizes of a value to be determined by the faculty board from time to time, provided that no person shall be awarded on any single occasion more than one prize or grant from the Medicine Prize Fund:

(*a*) a Wronker Prize in Pharmacology for meritorious performance in Pharmacology in either the Final Honour School of Natural Science (Physiological Sciences), or (provided that the subjects offered have included Pharmacology) the Final Honour School of Psychology, Philosophy, and Physiology;

(*b*) a prize for meritorious performance in the dissertation on either a special topic in the Final Honour School of Natural Science (Physiological Sciences), or a physiological subject in the Final Honour School of Psychology, Philosophy, and Physiology;

(*c*) such other prizes for meritorious performance in examinations under the aegis of the board, or in the Final Honour School of Psychology, Philosophy, and Physiology (provided that the subjects offered have included Physiology), as the board may from time to time determine.

8. In addition to the annual prize in Medicine and other prizes awarded from the fund, the Board of the Faculty of Physiological Sciences may, at its discretion, award from any surplus balance in the fund a Martin Wronker Prize Research Studentship in Medicine as a reward for excellence in the study of Medicine.

9. The Board of the Faculty of Physiological Sciences shall be the board of management for the studentship and shall have the power to make regulations, not inconsistent with this decree, concerning the award of the studentship.

10. The studentship shall be awarded as funds permit, provided that candidates of sufficient merit present themselves, and shall be tenable for one year in the first instance, with the possibility of extension for a second and third year, subject to review by the board. The value of the studentship shall be determined by the board and shall be paid termly.

11. The studentship shall be open to any candidate on the Register of University Medical Students who has passed the First Examination for the Degree of Bachelor of Medicine and has been awarded a first-class honours degree in the Final Honour School of Physiological Sciences.

12. The board shall award the studentship after consultation with the Heads of the Departments of Human Anatomy, Pathology, Pharmacology, and Physiology.

13. Surplus income arising from any cause may at the discretion of the respective faculty boards be reserved for future expenditure by the board concerned under the provisions of cll. 2, 3, 6, and 7.

14. Each board shall make regulations for the award of the prizes consistent with this decree and the decree may at any time be altered by Council, provided always that the main purpose of the testator, that is, the reward of excellence in the study of Medicine or Law, shall be observed and that the name of the prizes shall be retained.

§ 383. *Wylie Prize*

1. The prize established to commemorate the valuable contribution made by Sir Frances and Lady Wylie to the success of the Rhodes Scholarships in Oxford shall be known as the Wylie Prize.

2. The prize shall be offered annually for an essay on a subject (to be chosen by the competitor himself or herself with the approval of the Board of the Faculty of Modern History) connected with some aspect of the history of the United States of America.

3. Any member of the University may compete who has not completed, on the first day of the Trinity Full Term, the twelfth term from his or her matriculation.

4. The prize shall be of such value as may be determined from time to time by the Board of the Faculty of Modern History. The examiners shall be paid such reasonable honoraria as the Board of the Faculty of Modern History shall determine.

5. The income of the fund, in so far as it is not required for the payment of the prize and the payment of honoraria to the examiners, shall be made over to the History Faculty Library for the purchase of books.

6. The Board of the Faculty of Modern History shall make regulations for the award of the Prize consistent with this decree, and the decree may at any time be altered by Council with the consent of the Rhodes Trustees provided always that the main purpose of the trustees as set out in clauses 1 and 2 above is observed.

§ 384. *Yamanouchi Cell Biology Prize*

1. The University accepts with gratitude the sum of £2,500 from the Yamanouchi Research Institute, and any further sums which may contributed for the same purpose, to establish a fund the net income of which shall be used for the award of a prize to be known as Yamanouchi Cell Biology Prize.

2. The fund shall be administered by a board of management consisting of

(1) the Director of Pre-Clinical Studies (or his or her nominee);

(2) a person appointed by the Medical Sciences Board in consultation with the Director of Pre-Clinical Studies for such period or periods as it shall determine.

3. The prize shall be awarded annually, provided that there is a candidate of sufficient merit, for performance in the Honour School of Physiological Sciences on such terms as the board of management shall from time to time determine.

4. The board of management may in any year withhold the prize if in its opinion there is no candidate of sufficient merit. Income not expended in any year shall be carried forward for expenditure in subsequent years.

5. Council shall have power to amend this decree from time to time, provided that the purpose of the fund, as defined in clause 1 above, shall always be kept in view.

Section II. Standing (Adjustment of, for Illness)

Any person who has been allowed by Council to offer himself or herself as a candidate for honours in a Final Honour School under the provisions of Ch. VI, Sect. I. C, § 1, shall, for the purpose of reckoning his or her standing and age in entering his or her name for a university fellowship, studentship, scholarship, exhibition, or prize, be permitted to exclude such additional time as he or she shall have been granted by Council for the purpose of taking the Final Honour School; provided that the provisions of this decree shall not apply to the following university fellowships, scholarships, or prizes (where the University is precluded by the terms of the relevant trust deed from modifying the conditions of age and standing):

Boden Scholarship;
Dean Ireland's Scholarships;
Matthew Arnold Memorial Prize;
Newdigate Prize.

Section III. Division of prizes and scholarships

Notwithstanding the provisions of any statute or decree governing the award of prizes or scholarships, whenever the examiners for any such award are unable to distinguish between the merits of the best candidates, the body responsible for the award may authorize its division, and any consequential adjustment of the emoluments which it thinks fit.

CHAPTER X

EXAMINATION AND INSTRUCTION OF NON-MEMBERS OF THE UNIVERSITY

Section I. Department for Continuing Education

1. The Department for Continuing Education shall promote the provision of opportunities for adult education for non-members of the University and members no longer in residence. It shall be responsible for the provision of lectures, classes, and courses to meet primarily non-vocational cultural needs, hereinafter called Traditional Adult Education; and shall develop or assist in developing, in co-operation with faculty boards, departments, and institutions of the University, opportunities for role education and professional development, including refresher courses.

2. The Director of the Department shall have charge of the Department for Continuing Education including the residential centre, and shall make provision for the lighting, warming, water-supply, and cleansing thereof. The Director's duties shall include original work and teaching in his or her own subject, and the general supervision of teaching and research in the department, and he or she shall be subject to the General Provisions of the decree concerning the duties of professors.

3. The Director shall be elected by an electoral board consisting of:

(1) the Vice-Chancellor;

(2), (3) two persons appointed by Council;

(4), (5) two persons appointed by the Continuing Education Board;

(6), (7) two persons appointed by the Governing Body of Kellogg College.

4. There shall be an Advisory Council on Continuing Education to advise the University and the Director of the Department for Continuing Education on the University's provision of continuing education. Continuing education shall be defined in this context as all education taken up after a substantial break following initial education, except for mature students on courses leading to postgraduate qualifications.

5. The Advisory Council shall meet at least once a year and shall report at least once a year to the Continuing Education Board.

6. The Advisory Council shall have panels on Public Programmes and on Continuing Professional Development, and such other panels or sub-groups as the Advisory Council may establish from time to time at its discretion. The membership of the panels shall be determined by the Chairman of the Continuing Education Board after consultation with the Director of the Department for Continuing Education. Each panel or sub-group shall report to the Advisory Council at least once a year.

7. The membership of the Advisory Council and of its panels shall be determined by the Vice-Chancellor on the recommendation of the Chairman of the Continuing Education Board after consultation with the Director of the Department for Continuing Education, provided that the Advisory Council shall contain at least six persons who are not members of the University, and shall contain two members of each panel (one internal, one external).

8. Members of the Advisory Council and its panels or sub-groups shall serve for periods of up to three years. Retiring members shall be eligible to serve for one or more further periods.

9. The composition and functions of any other committees which may be required for the performance of the duties laid on the department shall be determined by the Continuing Education Board.

Section II. Postgraduate Diploma in Educational Studies and Postgraduate Diploma in Learning and Teaching in Higher Education

For this Section, see *Examination Decrees*.

Section III. Certificate in Management Studies

For this Section, see *Examination Decrees*.

Section IV. Certificate in Theology and Certificate for Theology Graduates

For this Section, see *Examination Decrees*.

Section V. Examinations open to non-members of the University of Students for Diplomas and Certificates

For this Section, see *Examination Decrees*.

[1]**Section VI. Degree of Bachelor of Education and Diploma of Higher Education (Educational Studies)**

For this Section, see *Examination Decrees*.

[1]**Section VII. Courses for the Degree of Bachelor of Theology and Diploma of Higher Education (Theology) at Westminster College**

For this Section, see *Examination Decrees*.

[1] These courses are no longer available except for students admitted prior to 1 April 2000 by the former Westminster College, which has now merged with Oxford Brookes University (see Decree (1) of 20 July 2000).

[1]Section VIII. Degree of Master of Education and Postgraduate Diploma in Education

For this Section, see *Examination Decrees.*

[1]Section IX. Courses for the Degree of Master of Theology and Postgraduate Diploma in Applied Theology at Westminster College

For this Section, see *Examination Decrees.*

[1]Section X. Postgraduate Certificate in Education at Westminster College

For this Section, see *Examination Decrees.*

Section XI. Fees payable by non-members of the University who attend lectures

1. With the exception of those persons specified in clause 2 (*b*)–(*l*) below, a person who is not a member of the University

(*a*) may not attend any lectures given in the University which are described in the lists issued by the boards of faculties or studies as seminars or classes or informal instruction;

(*b*) may attend other lectures given in the University which form a course (or part of a course) of two or more lectures and which are included in the lists issued by the boards of faculties or studies on application to the Registrar and on payment of a fee for attendance to the Curators of the University Chest at the rate of £500 a term; provided that:

(i) Council may refuse the right of attendance to any person or category of persons;

(ii) at any time Council may withdraw the right of attendance, and any lecturer may exclude a person from his or her lectures without reason given; in either case Council shall determine what portion if any of the fee paid shall be refunded;

(iii) he or she shall not attend lectures under the provisions of this clause for more than three successive terms;

(iv) a lecturer may for personal reasons occasionally admit a student to his or her own lectures without fee;

(*c*) may attend without fee any lectures given in the University which are announced as open to the general public or which are given by the following:

O'Donnell Lecturer in Celtic Studies
Romanes Lecturer
Herbert Spencer Lecturer

[1] These courses are no longer available except for students admitted prior to 1 April 2000 by the former Westminster College, which has now merged with Oxford Brookes University (see Decree (1) of 20 July 2000).

Halley Lecturer on Astronomy and Terrestrial Magnetism
Ratanbai Katrak Lecturer
Bampton Lecturer
Sir Basil Zaharoff Lecturer
Sidney Ball Lecturer
Taylorian Lecturer
Cyril Foster Lecturer;

(*d*) may attend without fee any lecture given in the University which does not fall under the terms of (*a*), (*b*), or (*c*), provided that he or she obtains the permission of the lecturer (or, in the case of a lecture sponsored by a professor, reader, lecturer, or other university teacher, of the sponsor).

2. The provisions of clause 1 above shall not apply to

(*a*) students whose names are entered on the Register of Diploma Students;

(*b*) solicitors' articled clerks attending lectures in pursuance of the Solicitors Acts, 1932 and 1935, under arrangements made by the Board of the Faculty of Law;

(*c*) members of societies or institutions in Oxford established for the purpose of higher study and approved by Council;[1]

(*d*) members of the staff of the Atomic Energy Research Establishment at Harwell nominated by the Director of the Establishment; provided that the Director of the Establishment shall pay to the Curators of the University Chest a composition fee for this privilege, fixed in agreement with the said Curators;

(*e*) such other persons or classes of persons as may be from time to time exempted from its provisions by Council, notice of the exemption having been published in the *University Gazette*, provided that Council shall have power to fix a reduced fee to be paid by such persons;[2]

(*f*) such other persons, resident locally, as may from time to time be exempted from its provisions by Council on payment of the reduced fee prescribed by Council under the provisions of sub-clause (*e*) above;

(*g*) persons not being members of the University who are paying a composition fee under the provisions of Ch. VIII, Sect. I, § 7;

(*h*) persons not being members of the University who are paying a composition fee under the provisions of Ch. VIII, Sect. I, § 8;

(*i*) teachers nominated by a Local Education Authority; provided that the Local Education Authority shall pay to the Curators of the University Chest a composition fee for this privilege in agreement with the said Curators;

(*j*) persons whose names are on the Register of Recognized Students;

[1] The following bodies have been approved under this clause: Ruskin College; Plater College; Ripon College, Cuddesdon; and St. Stephen's House.

[2] Classes of persons exempted under this sub-clause are persons currently registered as Students for the Degree of Doctor of Clinical Psychology and as students of Oxford Brookes University, by whom a reduced fee of £15 a term is payable .

(*k*) employees of the University who are not members of the University or otherwise already exempted;

(*l*) schoolmasters and schoolmistresses attached to colleges of the University during periods of study leave from the teaching appointment held by them;

(*m*) any lectures, seminars, or classes not provided by the University.

Section XII. Recognized Students

For this Section, see *Examination Decrees*.

Section XIII. Visiting Students

For this Section, see *Examination Decrees*.

Section XIV. Postgraduate Certificates (Continuing Education)

For this Section, see *Examination Decrees*.

Section XV. Postgraduate Diplomas (Continuing Education)

For this Section, see *Examination Decrees*.

Section XVI. Undergraduate Advanced Diplomas (Continuing Education)

For this Section, see *Examination Decrees*.

Section XVII. Foundation Certificate in English Language and Literature

For this Section, see *Examination Decrees*.

Section XVIII. Foundation Certificate in Social and Political Science

For this Section, see *Examination Decrees*.

Section XIX. Diploma in Jewish Studies

For this Section, see *Examination Decrees*.

Section XX. Postgraduate Diploma in Legal Practice

For this Section, see *Examination Decrees*.

Section XXI. Postgraduate Diploma in Management Studies

For this Section, see *Examination Decrees*.

Section XXII. Foundation Certificate in Modern History

For this Section, see *Examination Decrees*.

Section XXIII. Degree of Doctor of Clinical Psychology

For this Section, see *Examination Decrees*.

CHAPTER XI

OTHER MATTERS WHICH REQUIRE TO BE GOVERNED BY DECREE OR REGULATION

Section I. Religious Services and Sermons

§ 1. *Holy Communion*

In the week preceding each Full Term, the Holy Communion according to the Liturgy of the Church of England shall be celebrated by the Vice-Chancellor or some person appointed by him or her in the Church of St. Mary the Virgin at an hour to be determined by the Vice-Chancellor.

§ 2. *Latin Sermon*

On the first day of Hilary Full Term a Latin Sermon (to be preceded by the Litany read by the Proctors or by two other members of Convocation appointed by them) shall be preached in the Church of St. Mary the Virgin by persons nominated in turn by the heads of colleges, in the customary order of seniority.

Provided always that if the Head of a College to whose turn it falls to nominate the Preacher should fail to do so, or if the Preacher nominated should be prevented by sudden illness or other urgent cause from preaching, the Vice-Chancellor shall appoint some qualified person to supply the place.

It shall be the duty of the person appointed by the Vice-Chancellor under § 7 of this Section, to give notice to the head of the college whose turn it is to nominate the Preacher three months before the date at which the sermon is to be preached, and the name of the Preacher shall be signified to the Vice-Chancellor as soon as may be by the person whose turn it is to nominate.

§ 3. *Sermons to be preached in Full Term in St. Mary's Church*

1. A sermon shall be preached on the morning of every Sunday in Full Term, in the Church of St. Mary the Virgin, except as is hereinafter provided. The preachers shall be members of Congregation resident in Oxford and nominated as hereinafter provided, the Bampton Lecturer (in the event that the Bampton Lectures are delivered on Sunday mornings), persons nominated by the Vice-Chancellor, the preacher nominated, in accordance with the provisions of § 2, to preach the Latin Sermon, and the Select Preachers.

2. At least one sermon in each Full Term, on Sundays to be fixed by the Vice-Chancellor, shall be preached by a member of Congregation resident in Oxford, who shall be nominated by the Committee constituted by § 5 of this section for the nomination of Select Preachers.

3. The eight theological lectures or sermons which by the will of the late John Bampton are to be delivered in St. Mary's Church shall be delivered on such

days in either or both of Full Hilary and Trinity Terms as the Vice-Chancellor may appoint.

4. On Quinquagesima Sunday, on the last Sunday before the Encaenia, on the last Sunday before Advent, and for the sermon on 'Church Extension within the British Commonwealth' the preacher shall be nominated by the Vice-Chancellor.[1]

5. The sermon for which a benefaction (now known as the Ramsden Benefaction) was given to the University by Mr. J.H. Markland in 1847 shall be preached upon 'Church Extension within the British Commonwealth' on a Sunday in Full Term to be determined by the Committee for Select Preachers.

§ 4. *Sermons to be preached elsewhere than in St. Mary's Church*

Sermons shall be preached before the University in certain colleges, on certain days, namely

(1) in the Cathedral Church of Christ on the first Sunday in Advent and on Whitsunday, and, in the years in which the Bampton Lectures are not delivered, on the third Sunday of Hilary Full Term;

(2) in Magdalen College, on the Sunday in Full Term nearest St. Mark's Day, and on the Sunday nearest St. John Baptist's Day, unless that be the Sunday preceding Encaenia, when it shall be the following Sunday;

(3) in Oriel College, on the Sunday after the end of Hilary Full Term;

(4) in Hertford College, the Macbride Sermon on the second Sunday in Hilary Term; on this Sunday, the preacher shall be nominated by the Vice-Chancellor;

(5) in the Cathedral Church of Christ, when a Court Sermon is required. The preacher of this sermon shall be nominated by the Vice-Chancellor;

(6) in rotation, in one of those colleges which have so agreed with the Committee for the Nomination of Select Preachers, on the fourth Sunday of Michaelmas Full Term and on Trinity Sunday.

§ 5. *Select Preachers*

1. Select Preachers shall be nominated by a committee consisting of:

(1) the Vice-Chancellor;

(2), (3) the Proctors;

(4), (5) two professors in the Faculty of Theology elected by the professors in that faculty;

(6), (7) two members of Congregation elected by Congregation.

[1] The Sermons on Quinquagesima Sunday and the last Sunday before Advent are to be preached upon one or other of certain specified texts relative to the grace of humility or the sin of pride, a benefaction for this purpose having been bequeathed in 1684 by the Revd. William Master, Vicar of Preston, near Cirencester.

The elected members of the committee shall hold office for four years and shall be re-eligible.

2. The committee shall nominate Select Preachers in each Michaelmas Term. The consent of four members of the committee, one of whom must be the Vice-Chancellor, shall be necessary to a nomination, and the names of the persons nominated, after their consent has been obtained, shall be published in the *University Gazette*.

3. Select Preachers shall hold office for one academical year. If a Select Preacher should die or resign during his or her term of office his or her place shall be filled by nomination as above prescribed.

§ 6. *The qualifications of Preachers*

The Vice-Chancellor and the committee may use such liberty in nominating preachers as may be exercised by a Diocesan Bishop in accordance with resolutions of the Convocations of the Church of England.

§ 7. *The summons of Preachers*

1. A person shall be appointed by the Vice-Chancellor to summon those who are to preach. Three months' notice where possible shall be given to each person so summoned, and if he or she does not reply within one month after the summons has been dispatched, he or she shall be taken to have declined to preach.

2. If a person who has undertaken to preach is prevented by sudden illness or other urgent cause from so doing, the Vice-Chancellor shall nominate some qualified person to supply his or her place.

§ 8. *Payment of Preachers*

The Curators of the University Chest shall pay to the Preachers of the University Sermons nominated under the provisions of § 2, § 3, and § 4, items (3)–(6) of this section (except the Bampton Lecturer) on each occasion such sum as shall from time to time be determined by the Hebdomadal Council; and if the Preacher is not resident in Oxford he or she shall in addition receive travelling expenses in accordance with scales drawn up by the Hebdomadal Council.

§ 9. *Commemoration of Benefactors*

1. The preacher, in a prayer before the sermon on the first Sunday after the beginning of term and in the sermon on the morning of the Sunday preceding Encaenia, shall make a grateful commemoration of the benefactors of the University, that is to say of Thomas Cobham Bishop of Worcester, Cardinal Henry Beaufort Bishop of Winchester, Prince Humphrey Duke of Gloucester, Cardinal John Kempe Archbishop of Canterbury, Thomas Kempe Bishop of London, Margaret Countess of Richmond, King Henry VII and Elizabeth his Queen, Richard Lichfield, Cardinal Thomas Wolsey Archbishop of York, King Henry VIII, Queen Mary, Queen Elizabeth I, King James I, Sir Thomas Bodley,

Sir Henry Savile, Sir William Sedley, Sir Nicholas Kempe, Thomas White, William Camden, Richard Tomlins, William Heather, William third Earl of Pembroke, John Lord Craven of Ryton, King Charles I, Edward first Earl of Clarendon, William Laud and Gilbert Sheldon Archbishops of Canterbury, Henry Earl of Danby, Elias Ashmole, Henry Birkhead, King George I, John Radcliffe, Nathaniel third Lord Crewe Bishop of Durham, William Sherard, Richard Rawlinson, Charles Viner, George Henry third Earl of Lichfield, Charles Godwyn, John Bampton, Francis second Lord Godolphin, John Sibthorp, George Aldrich, John Wills, Richard Gough, King George III, Joseph Boden, Anne Kennicott, Francis Douce, Sir Robert Taylor, Robert Mason, John Ireland Dean of Westminster, John second Earl of Eldon, Chambers Hall, Frederick William and Ellen Hope, John Hall, Henry Houghton, Felix Slade, John Henry Parker, Martha Combe, Charlotte Sutherland, William fourth Earl of Ilchester, John Ruskin, Joseph Bosworth, Augustus Henry Lane-Fox-Pitt-Rivers, Charles Drury Edward Fortnum, Rebecca Flower Squire, Cecil John Rhodes, Alfred Beit, Charles James Oldham, Charles and Maria Jane Theodore Williams, Christopher Welch, Thomas second Earl Brassey, Walter Morrison, Ingram and Charlotte Bywater, Henry Wilde, Maria Louisa Medley, Charles Day Dowling Gibbs, Arturo Serena, Walter William Rouse Ball, Charles Marten Powell, Walter Gordon, Sir Arthur Ernest Cowley, Thomas Whitcombe Greene, Kenneth Grahame, Charles Frederick Nolloth, George Flood France, Francis Llewellyn and Nora Griffith, Sir Heath Harrison, George Claridge Druce, Alice Mary May, Emily Georgiana Kemp, George Herbert Fowler, John Beeston Lockey, Sir Arthur John Evans, Herbert Edward Douglas Blakiston, Raymond William and Hope ffennell, Amy Georgina Hartland, Antonin Besse, Gaspard Oliver Farrer, John Francis Mallet, Cecil Jackson, Sir John Rhŷs and Olwen his daughter, Edward Harry William Meyerstein, Eric Otto Winstedt, Henry Norman and Nellie Maud Emma Spalding, Florence Weldon, Sir Montague Maurice Burton, Jacob Patrick Ronaldson Lyell, Sir Ernest Oppenheimer, Sir Herbert Ingram, William Richard Morris Viscount Nuffield, Georges van Houten, James Albert Billmeir, Charles Watson Boise, Claude Jenkins, David Randall-MacIver, Henry Lord Sanderson, Francis Falconer Madan, Gerald Averay Wainwright, Rudolph and Ann Light, Wilfred Augustine Handley, Theodore Deodatus Nathaniel Besterman, Emma Frederica Isabella Dunston, Jeffery Stokes Story, Samuel Glasstone, René Hugo Thalmann, John Gilbert Winant II, and Jane Ledig-Rowohlt, together with any further benefactors whose names shall be added from time to time by Council by decree. The list of names shall be divided by the Vice-Chancellor into three sections, one of which shall be read out in turn at each successive commemoration.

2. The names listed in clause 1 above shall also be recorded in the album of benefactors, together with such other names as Council shall determine.

Section II. Procedures of the Visitatorial Board, and other procedures required under Titles VIII and XVI to be determined by decree

§ **1.** *The Visitatorial Board*

1. The Visitatorial Board (hereinafter called the board) shall be constituted in accordance with Tit. VIII, Sect. I, cll. 1 and 2. The members of the panel of twelve persons elected by Congregation shall

(*a*) hold office for four years, except such as shall be elected to fill casual vacancies who shall hold office only for the unexpired portion of the periods for which their predecessors were elected;

(*b*) be capable of re-election;

(*c*) be elected under the provisions of Tit. II, Sect. IX, provided always that, notwithstanding the provisions of clause 4 of that Section, candidates may be nominated by Council as well as by two members of Congregation.

2. The board shall consider any reference made by the Vice-Chancellor under Tit. XVII, cl. 14 (6) (*d*) concerning a person subject to its jurisdiction, namely any person included in the Schedule to Tit. VIII, Sect. I.

3. Whenever a case is referred to the board by the Vice-Chancellor, the Registrar (or a person appointed by the Registrar to act on his or her behalf) shall select by lot four persons from all such members of the panel of twelve persons elected by Congregation as are not ineligible to serve under the provisions of Tit. XVII, cl. 16 (or, in the event that the case is referred to the board under the provisions of Title VIII only, as would have been ineligible if Tit. XVII, cl. 16 had applied), and the four persons so selected shall serve as members of the board for the duration of its consideration of that case; provided always that if the selection by lot of the first three of such members results in all three of those members being persons of the same sex as the Chairman, and if the eligible members of the panel then remaining include a person or persons of the other sex, that person or a person selected by lot from amongst those persons (whichever shall be applicable) shall serve as the fourth member of the board. If any of the four members of the board so selected for the consideration of a case is unable to serve, a further person shall be selected by the same procedure to replace the member who is unable to serve. Once the board has begun to consider a case, the members of the board selected for the consideration of that case shall remain members of the board for the duration of such consideration whether or not their period of office as a member of the panel has expired in the interim.

4. The proceedings of the board in respect of any case referred to it shall be valid only if the Chairman and at least three other members have each attended all of the meetings at which that case was considered, and any member who has been unable to attend any such meeting shall cease to be a member for the further consideration of the same case. If, through the unavailability of the Chairman or other members, the board is unable to comply with the provisions of this clause, the board shall thereupon be dissolved and a new board shall be constituted under the provisions of clause 1 above for the purpose of considering

the case *de novo*; provided that no person, other than the Chairman, who has served on a board previously constituted to consider that case shall be eligible to serve on any further board constituted to consider that case.

5. In the event of equality of voting, the Chairman shall have a second or casting vote.

6. When the Vice-Chancellor under Tit. XVII, cl. 14 (6) (*d*) has directed that a charge or charges be preferred for hearing by the board he or she shall appoint under cl. 15 (2) a suitable person to formulate the charge or charges and to present the said charge or charges before the board (hereinafter called the person presenting the case).

7. The Registrar shall act as secretary of the board or shall appoint a person to act on his or her behalf.

8. The board may direct that charges against more than one person shall be heard together, due regard being given to the principles of justice and fairness.

9. The parties to a hearing by the board shall be

(*a*) the person or persons charged (hereinafter called the person charged);

(*b*) the person presenting the case;

(*c*) such other person, if any, as the board may add, either on application or otherwise. Reference to the person charged shall include, where the context so permits, reference to such other person.

Any person charged shall be entitled to be represented, but at his or her own expense, by another person, who need not be legally qualified. Where a person charged is so represented, references to the person charged shall include, where the context so permits, that person's representative.

PREPARATION

10. The person presenting the case shall notify the person charged in writing that the referral has been made and shall send to him or her a statement of the charge or charges together with any documents therein specified.

11. The Chairman shall appoint a date, time, and place for the hearing, but shall have power, if he or she judges this to be advisable, to cancel a proposed hearing at any time before it has begun and substitute alternative arrangements for the hearing.

12. The secretary of the board shall give to the person charged at least twenty-one days' notice of the date appointed for the hearing by the board. Such notice shall be in writing and shall be accompanied by a copy of Title XVII and of this decree.

13. The person presenting the case shall give to the person charged and to the secretary of the board at least fourteen days before the hearing date a list of the witnesses to be called in support of the charges, statements of the evidence that the witnesses are expected to give, and copies of documents to be submitted in support of the charges.

14. The person charged shall give to the person presenting the case and to the secretary of the board at least seven days before the hearing date a list of the witnesses that he or she intends to call, statements of the evidence that the witnesses are expected to give, and copies of any documents to be submitted at the hearing.

HEARING

15. Subject to the prior consent of the board, either party may introduce witnesses or documents notwithstanding the fact that the appropriate provisions in clauses 13 and 14 above have not been observed, but in that event the hearing may be adjourned to enable the other party to consider the proposed testimony or further evidence and to introduce further evidence in support of its response.

16. No charge shall be determined without an oral hearing at which the person charged is entitled to be present.

17. All hearings of or in connection with proceedings before the board shall take place in camera.

18. The board may proceed with a hearing in the absence of any of the persons entitled to be present, except where, in the case of the person charged, the board is of the opinion that the person's absence was due to circumstances beyond his or her control. The Chairman of the board may exclude any person from a hearing if in the opinion of the Chairman such exclusion is necessary for the maintenance of order.

19. Each of the parties to the proceedings shall be entitled to give evidence at the hearing, to make an opening statement, to call witnesses, and to question any witness concerning any relevant evidence. After all the evidence has been heard, the person presenting the case, and the person charged, in that order, may address the board.

20. The board may dismiss a charge for want of prosecution.

21. The board may remit any charge to the Vice-Chancellor for further consideration.

22. (*a*) The jurisdiction and powers of the board shall not be affected by the fact that the person charged has been, or is liable to be, prosecuted, but has not yet been convicted, in a court of law in respect of any act or conduct which is the subject of proceedings before the board. The board may recommend to the Vice-Chancellor that a matter before it should be referred to the police, if in its judgment the circumstances so require. In the event that the matter has been referred to the police, whether by the Vice-Chancellor or otherwise, the board shall adjourn the proceedings for such periods as the board judges to be reasonable to enable a prosecution to be undertaken.

(*b*) Evidence that a person has been convicted of any offence by or before any court of law, or that any court of law has found proved an offence with which a person was charged, shall, for the purpose of proving that the person committed the offence or was guilty of any act or conduct in respect of which he or she was so convicted or charged, be admissible in any proceedings before the board.

23. Subject to the provisions of Title XVII and of this decree, the board shall determine its own procedure and may make such interlocutory orders for the conduct of the proceedings as it considers appropriate. The Chairman may set time limits for each stage of the proceedings, to the intent that any charge shall be heard and determined by the board as expeditiously as is reasonably practicable consonantly with the principles of justice and fairness. Within the limit of that intent, any meeting of the board may nevertheless be postponed or adjourned at the discretion of the Chairman.

24. The secretary of the board shall be entitled to be present throughout the hearing and at any meeting of the board, and shall keep a sufficient record of the proceedings of the board.

25. No costs shall be awardable by the board to parties to the proceedings.

DETERMINATION

26. In deciding whether a charge has been proved, the board shall apply the civil standard of proof, i.e. the balance of probabilities.

27. If the board decides that a charge has been proved, it shall, after giving the parties to the proceedings or their respective representatives an opportunity to address it concerning the penalty to be imposed, determine its recommendations, if any, as to the appropriate penalty in accordance with the provisions of Tit. XVII, cl. 19.

28. The board's decision shall be recorded in a document signed by the Chairman which shall also contain:

(*a*) the board's findings of fact regarding the charge or charges;

(*b*) the reasons for the board's decision; and

(*c*) the board's recommendations, if any, as to the appropriate penalty or penalties.

The secretary of the board shall ensure that a copy of the document is sent to the Vice-Chancellor, to the person presenting the case, and to the person charged, and also that a copy of Part V of Title XVII and of the associated procedural decree accompanies the document sent to the person charged.

29. The Chairman of the board may, by an appropriate certificate in writing, correct any accidental errors in documents recording the decisions of the board.

§ **2.** *Medical Boards*

1. When a Medical Board is appointed to determine a case referred to it under Tit. XVII, cl. 22 (3), the appropriate officer for the purposes of Part IV of that statute shall appoint a person to present the case to the board.

2. The Registrar shall act as secretary of the board or shall appoint a person to act on his or her behalf.

3. If after the commencement of proceedings a member of a board ceases to be available to serve as a member, the appropriate officer shall discharge the board and a new board shall be appointed in accordance with the provisions of Tit. XVII, cl. 22 (3).

4. The parties to a hearing before a board shall be:

(*a*) the person whose retirement on medical grounds is to be considered by the board, hereinafter referred to as the person concerned, which term shall include any person authorized to act on behalf of the person concerned, in addition to (or instead of) the person concerned, in accordance with Tit. XVII, cl. 21 (4);

(*b*) the person presenting the case.

5. The person concerned shall be entitled, but at his or her own expense, to be represented by another person, who need not be legally qualified, in connection with and at any hearing by the board.

PREPARATION

6. The person presenting the case shall notify the person concerned in writing that a referral has been made.

7. The Chairman of the board shall appoint a date, time, and place for a hearing by the board, but shall have power, if he or she judges this to be advisable, to cancel a proposed hearing at any time before it has begun and substitute alternative arrangements for the hearing.

8. The secretary of the board shall give to the person concerned at least twenty-one days' notice of the date appointed for the hearing by the board. Such notice shall be in writing and shall be accompanied by a copy of Title XVII and of this decree.

9. The person presenting the case shall give to the person concerned and to the secretary of the board at least fourteen days before the hearing date a written statement of the case together with copies of any relevant medical and other evidence, copies of any other documents intended to be produced at the hearing, a list of the witnesses whom it is proposed to call, and statements of the evidence that they are expected to give.

10. The person concerned shall give to the secretary of the board at least seven days before the hearing copies of any medical evidence that he or she intends to produce, a list of the witnesses that he or she intends to call, and statements of the evidence that they are expected to give.

HEARING

11. Subject to the prior consent of the board, either party may introduce witnesses or documents notwithstanding the fact that the appropriate provisions in clauses 9 and 10 above have not been observed, but in that event the hearing may be adjourned at the request of either party to enable the other party to consider the proposed testimony or further evidence in support of its response.

12. A case shall not be determined without an oral hearing at which the person concerned is entitled to be present. Any hearing of or in connection with any case before a Medical Board shall take place in camera.

13. The board may proceed with a hearing in the absence of any of the persons entitled to be present, except where, in the case of the person concerned, the board is of the opinion that his or her absence was due to circumstances beyond his or her control. The Chairman of the board may exclude any person from a hearing if in the opinion of the Chairman such exclusion is necessary for the maintenance of order.

14. Each party to a hearing before a board shall be entitled to give evidence at the hearing and, either personally or through a representative, to make an opening statement, to call witnesses, to question any witness concerning any relevant evidence, and to address the board after the evidence has been heard.

15. Subject to the provisions of Title XVII and of this decree, a Medical Board shall determine its own procedures and may make such interlocutory orders for the conduct of the proceedings as it considers appropriate. The Chairman of the board may set time limits for each stage of the proceedings, to the intent that the case shall be heard and determined by the board as expeditiously as is reasonably practicable consonantly with the principles of justice and fairness. Within the limits of that intent, any meeting of a board may nevertheless be postponed or adjourned at the discretion of the Chairman.

DETERMINATION

16. A Medical Board shall not determine that any person to whom Title XVII applies shall be required to retire on medical grounds unless it is satisfied that the person's physical or mental incapacity has been established, and it shall apply the civil standard of proof, i.e. the balance of probabilities, in so satisfying itself.

17. The secretary of the board shall be entitled to be present throughout the hearing and at any meeting of the board, and shall keep a sufficient record of the proceedings of the board.

18. The board's decision shall be recorded in a document signed by the Chairman which shall also contain:

(*a*) the board's medical findings;

(*b*) the board's other findings of fact; and

(*c*) the reasons for the board's decision.

The secretary of the board shall ensure that a copy of the document is sent to the person concerned, to his or her representative (if any), to the person responsible for presenting the case to the board, and to the Vice-Chancellor, and also that a copy of Part V of Title XVII and of the associated procedural decree accompanies the copy of the document sent to the person concerned.

19. The Chairman of the board may, by an appropriate certificate in writing, correct any accidental errors in documents recording the decisions of the board.

§ 3. *Appeals*

1. The procedure to be followed in respect of the preparation, consolidation, hearing, and determination of appeals under the provisions of Tit. XVII, cll. 24–30 shall be as follows.

2. The person appointed under ibid., cl. 28 (1) to hear and determine this appeal shall be referred to hereinafter as the Chairman. The body constituted under ibid., cl. 28 (iii) shall be referred to hereinafter as the Appeal Body, which term shall also refer to the Chairman in the event that the Chairman sits alone.

3. The Registrar shall act as secretary in the Appeal Body or shall appoint a person to act on his or her behalf.

4. The parties to an appeal shall be

(*a*) the appellant;

(*b*) such person as the Vice-Chancellor has appointed to act as respondent in the proceedings;

(*c*) such other person, if any, as the Chairman may add, either on application or otherwise.

5. Any party to an appeal shall be entitled, but at his or her own expense, to be represented by another person, who need not be legally qualified, in connection with and at the hearing of the appeal.

PREPARATION

6. The Chairman shall appoint a date, time, and place for the hearing of the appeal, but shall have power, if he or she judges this to be advisable, to cancel a proposed hearing at any time before it has begun and substitute alternative arrangements for the hearing.

7. When a hearing has been arranged, the secretary of the Appeal Body shall send to each party, at least fourteen days before the date appointed for the hearing,

(*a*) notice of the hearing, together with information on the right of representation by another person, on attendance, on the right to produce documents, and on the calling of fresh evidence; and

(*b*) a copy of the notice provided by the appellant in accordance with Tit. XVII, cl. 26.

8. The Appeal Body may at any time make such interlocutory orders for the conduct of the proceedings as it considers appropriate, and it shall have power, on application by the appellant, to suspend, in whole or in part, the operation of penalties pending the determination of the appeal.

HEARING

9. An appeal shall not be determined without an oral hearing at which the appellant and his or her representative, if any, are entitled to be present, save

as is provided in clause 11 below. Subject to the provisions of clause 10 below, any hearing of or in connection with an appeal shall take place in camera.

10. If it considers it appropriate to do so, the Appeal Body may hear appeals by two or more appellants at the same hearing.

11. The Appeal Body may proceed with a hearing in the absence of any of the persons entitled to be present, except where, in the case of the appellant, it is of the opinion that that person's absence was due to circumstances beyond his or her control. The Chairman may exclude any person from a hearing if in the opinion of the Chairman such exclusion is necessary for the maintenance of order.

12. Each party to a hearing shall be entitled to make a statement and to address the Appeal Body, but witnesses may not be called without the consent of the Appeal Body. Leave to adduce fresh evidence, or to recall witnesses examined at first instance, shall be given only if the Appeal Body is satisfied that it is necessary or expedient in the interests of justice.

13. Subject to the provisions of Title XVII and of this decree, the Appeal Body shall determine its own procedure. The Chairman may set time limits for each stage of the proceedings, to the intent that any appeal shall be heard and determined as expeditiously as is reasonably practicable consonantly with the principles of justice and fairness. Within the limits of that intent, any meeting of the Appeal Body may nevertheless be postponed or adjourned at the discretion of the Chairman.

DETERMINATION

14. The Appeal Body may allow or dismiss an appeal in whole or in part, may dismiss an appeal for want of prosecution, or may remit an appeal for further consideration in accordance with the provisions of Tit. XVII, cl. 29 (3) and, in the case of an appeal arising under Part III of that Title, may substitute any lesser alternative penalty available under cl. 19 (2) thereof following a finding by the Visitatorial Board on the original charge or charges.

15. The secretary of the Appeal Body shall be entitled to be present throughout the hearing and at any meeting of the Appeal Body, and shall keep a sufficient record of the proceedings.

16. The decision of the Appeal Body shall be recorded in a document, signed by the Chairman, and including:

(*a*) any findings of fact which differ from those reached by any other university authority which has previously considered the case;

(*b*) the reasons for the decision of the Appeal Body; and

(*c*) any penalty determined by the Appeal Body under cl. 29 (3) (*e*).

The secretary of the Appeal Body shall send a copy of the document to the Vice-Chancellor (or to the Chancellor, where the appeal is against a decision reached under Part VII of Title XVII), the appellant, and the other parties to the appeal.

17. The Chairman may, by an appropriate certificate in writing, correct any accidental errors in documents recording the decisions of the Appeal Body.

§ **4.** *Grievance Committee*

1. When reference has been made to the Grievance Committee under Tit. XVII, cl. 34 the chairman of the committee shall invite the aggrieved person, and any person against whom the grievance lies, to submit a written statement to the committee.

2. The grievance shall not be disposed of without an oral hearing at which the aggrieved person, and any person against whom the grievance lies, shall be entitled to be heard and to be accompanied by a friend or representative.

3. After due consideration, the Grievance Committee shall inform Council whether in its opinion the grievance is or is not well founded. If of the opinion that the grievance is justified, the committee shall at the same time make such proposals for the redress of the grievance as it thinks fit.

§ **5.** *Appointment of alternates*

1. Where any person, including the holder of any specified office of the University, is designated to perform any duties or exercise any power under Title XVII, and that person is, for the purposes of clause 7 (3) of that Title, involved in the matter or matters in question, the Vice-Chancellor may, either on application or of his or her own motion, appoint an alternate to act in that person's place.

2. No appointment under clause 1 above shall be effective unless it is made in writing, and a copy is delivered to the Registrar or, if the latter is involved in the matter or matters in question, to a Deputy Registrar. The Registrar or Deputy Registrar (as the case may be) shall ensure that notice of the appointment is given as soon as practicable to any other persons or bodies involved.

3. When the person referred to in clause 1 above is the Vice-Chancellor, the appointment under that clause shall be made by the Chancellor.

§ **6.** *Procedure under Tit. VIII, Sect. I, cll. 8–17*

1. The meetings of the Visitatorial Board for the purpose of an inquiry under Tit. VIII, Sect. I, cl. 8 shall be held at such times and for such periods as may be convenient between the hours of 10 a.m. and 7 p.m.

2. All documents circulated or distributed in connection with any such inquiry shall be marked 'Confidential' and shall be addressed to members of the board, and any other persons concerned, under sealed cover.

3. When notice is given under Tit. VIII, Sect. I, cl. 10 to the person concerned, the latter shall also be informed that under clause 11 of that section he or she has the right (*a*) to appear before the board to make his or her defence and (*b*) to be represented.

4. On the day fixed for the opening of the inquiry, the board may adjourn the inquiry if in its opinion such adjournment is necessary in order to enable the person concerned properly to prepare his or her defence, and for the same purpose the inquiry may be adjourned again for a further period or further periods; provided always that

(*a*) no one period of adjournment shall exceed twenty-one days; and

(*b*) if the person concerned fails to appear before the board on the day fixed for the resumption of the hearing, the board may (unless in its opinion that person's failure to appear was due to circumstances beyond his or her control) proceed with the hearing in that person's absence.

5. The board shall in every case cause statements of the evidence, sufficient to indicate its substance, to be supplied to the person concerned as promptly as may be possible; provided that it shall be at the discretion of the board to determine the form in which the statements, if they are not full transcripts, are presented.

6. The decision of the board shall be communicated in writing to the person concerned.

Section III. Maison Française

1. The Maison Française shall be recognized by the University

(*a*) as a centre for the exchange of information on matters of learning and scholarship;

(*b*) as a centre of social and cultural activities where university societies recognized by the Vice-Chancellor and Proctors can meet;

(*c*) as an academic centre for information required by members of the University who are engaged on French studies, or who desire to visit France in connection with their studies;

(*d*) as a centre to which French academic persons or French students may resort;

(*e*) if practicable, as a place of residence for selected English students engaged on French studies.

2. Council shall appoint

(*a*) a member of Convocation to represent the University on the Comité Directeur, which will be established by the University of Paris to appoint the Director of the Maison, and to control the activities of the Maison;

(*b*) a fellow of a college to assist French graduates in obtaining admission to colleges.

3. There shall be an Oxford Committee

(*a*) to be answerable to the University for the conduct of the Maison;

(*b*) to advise the Director on any problems which may arise from the relationship of the Maison to the University;

(*c*) to consult when necessary with the Comité Directeur in order to ensure that the policy laid down by that Comité shall be in harmony with the policy and regulations of the University.

4. This committee shall be composed as follows:

(1) the Vice-Chancellor;

(2) the Director of the Maison;

(3) the Marshal Foch Professor of French Literature;

(4) the member of Convocation appointed under clause 2 (*a*) above;

(5) the fellow of a college appointed under clause 2 (*b*) above;

(6) one member of Council appointed by Council;

(7)–(9) three members appointed by the Board of the Faculty of Medieval and Modern Languages;

(10) one member appointed by the Board of the Faculty of Modern History.

The appointed members of the committee shall hold office for three years, and shall be re-eligible.

The committee shall have power to co-opt up to two additional members for such periods as it shall think fit.

Section IV. Dress

Graduates of the University shall wear robes, gowns, and hoods of the colours, materials, and shapes as shall be from time to time prescribed in the Register of Colours and Materials of Gowns and Hoods for Degrees of the University of Oxford, prepared by such academic robemakers as Council shall from time to time determine, approved by Council, and deposited in the University Archives; junior members of the University shall wear such gowns and dress as the Vice-Chancellor shall determine, after consultation with the Proctors and, where appropriate, the heads of colleges; and the Vice-Chancellor shall have power to make regulations and give rulings as to the dress of all members of the University on those occasions when, according to the customs and usages of the University, academic dress is worn.

Academic Dress
Rulings by the Vice-Chancellor

1. Persons who are graduates of other universities, and who also *either* hold an Oxford degree[1] (or have M.A. status) *or* are members of this University reading for a degree, diploma, or certificate of this University, may (if they so wish) wear the appropriate academic dress of their other university on any Oxford University occasion on which they would otherwise be required to wear the academic dress of this University, *except* on the following occasions, on which Oxford academic dress shall always be worn by such persons:

(*a*) a Degree Ceremony;

[1] Including the M.A. by Special Resolution.

(*b*) the Encaenia;[1]

provided that, at a Degree Ceremony, candidates supplicating for a higher degree of this University who are graduates of other universities and who do not already hold an Oxford degree may wear the academic dress of their other university before their admission to the Oxford degree (after which they shall immediately put on the full academic dress of their Oxford degree).

2. Any other persons who are graduates of other universities may (if they so wish) wear the appropriate academic dress of their university on any Oxford University occasion on which they would, had they held an Oxford degree or been otherwise entitled to wear the academic dress of this University, have been required to wear the latter.

3. All members of the University are required to wear academic dress with *subfusc* clothing (and candidates who are not members of the University are required to wear *subfusc* clothing) when attending any university examination, except those at Westminster College, i.e.

Men. A dark suit and socks, black shoes, a white bow tie, and plain white shirt and collar.

Women. A dark skirt or trousers, a white blouse, black tie, black stockings and shoes, and, if desired, a dark coat.

Dress for each sex should be such as might be appropriate for formal occasions.

Candidates serving in H.M. Forces are permitted to wear uniform together with a gown. (The uniform cap is worn in the street and carried when indoors.)

Guidance on Academic Dress for Senior Members of the University

Subfusc is defined above.

Bachelors and Masters

Forms:

1. Black gown
2. Black gown and hood
3. Black gown, hood, square (or for women, a soft cap[2] if desired), and *subfusc* (Full Academic Dress)
4. Black gown, hood, square (or for women, a soft cap[2] if desired), *subfusc*, and bands

[1] I.e. the Encaenia itself, and the preceding gathering to partake of Lord Crewe's Benefaction; the academic dress of other universities may however (if desired) be worn at the Encaenia Garden Party in place of the academic dress of this University.

[2] Women members of the University attending university ceremonies shall *either* wear or carry a square, *or* wear a soft cap.

Occasions:

Chancellor's Court of Benefactors	3
Church Services:	
Generally	1
Certain special days specified in the *Gazette*	2
Congregation, Ancient House of: see Degree Ceremonies	
Congregation:	
Debates	1
Orations and Admissions (of Vice-Chancellor and Proctors)	2
Heads of houses presenting (at Admissions)	4
Degree Ceremonies:	
Deans presenting	3
Observers	2
Dinner in colleges (according to status and convention)	1 (generally)
Dinner with Chancellor or Vice-Chancellor present	1 (or as decreed by him or her)
Encaenia:	
Sheldonian Curators and other officers	4
Others	3
Examinations	3
Garden Parties	2
Lectures, major public:	
Lecturer	2
Others	1
Meetings chaired by Vice-Chancellor	1 (otherwise at the discretion of the Chairman)
Proctors, Admission of:	
Proctors, Pro-Proctors, and Assessor	4 (except for Proctors in office)
Others	2
Vice-Chancellor, Pro-Vice-Chancellors, and Clerks of the Market, Admission of:	
Above officers	4
Others	2
'Vice-Chancellor will be present'	1 (unless otherwise stated)

Doctors

Forms:

1. Black gown (laced, except for DD)
2. Black gown and hood
3. Black gown, hood, square (or for women, a soft cap[1] if desired), and *subfusc*
4. Convocation habit (black gown, hood and sleeveless cloak [chemir], square (or for women, a soft cap[1] if desired), *subfusc*, and bands)
5. Scarlet robe and appropriate cap
6. Scarlet robe with *subfusc* and appropriate cap (Full Academic Dress for D.Phil.s)
7. Scarlet robe with *subfusc* and bands and appropriate cap (Full Academic Dress for higher doctorates)

Occasions:

Chancellor's Court of Benefactors:	
D.Phil.s	6
Higher Doctorates	7
Church Services:	
Memorial Services, weekdays, Quinquagesima Sunday, and Lent	1
Others (including the Court Sermon)	2 or 4
Certain special days specified in the *Gazette*	7
Congregation, Ancient House of: see Degree Ceremonies	
Congregation:	
Debates	1
Orations and Admissions (of Vice-Chancellor and Proctors)	2 or 4
Heads of houses presenting (at Admissions)	4
Degree Ceremonies:	
Candidates after admission to higher doctorate	6
" " " " " D.Phil.	6
Deans presenting	4
Observers	2
Dinner in colleges (according to status and convention)	1 (generally)
Dinner with Chancellor or Vice-Chancellor present	1 (or as decreed by him or her)
Encaenia:	
Higher doctorates	7

[1] Women members of the University attending university ceremonies shall *either* wear or carry a square, *or* wear a soft cap.

D.Phil.s	6
Examinations	3 or 4
Garden Parties	2 or 5
Lectures, major public:	
Lecturer	2 or 5
Others	1
Meetings chaired by Vice-Chancellor	1 (otherwise at the discretion of the Chairman)
Proctors, Admission of:	
Proctors and new Proctors (see Masters)	
Assessor	4
Others	2 or 4
Vice-Chancellor, Pro-Vice-Chancellors, and Clerks of the Market, Admission of:	
Above officers	4
Others	2 or 4
'Vice-Chancellor will be present'	1

Section V. Sites, Buildings, and New Developments (see also individual departments)

§ 1. *Arts and Social Studies Faculties*

[For items [1]–[7] of this Sub-section, see *Statutes*, 1995, pp. 703–4.]

[8]

Social Studies, English, and Law Faculties:
Special Resolution (2) of Congregation of 28 May 1996

That the Manor Road site currently leased to the Territorial Army be allocated for a centre for the Faculty of Social Studies and to provide additional space for the Faculties of English and Law.

[9]

Sackler Library (Foundations of the Humanities):
Special Resolution (1) of Congregation of 28 May 1996

That the site between 2–6 St John Street and the west end of the Ashmolean Museum be allocated for the Sackler Library.

[10]

Rothermere American Institute:

Special Resolution (2) of Congregation of 17 June 1997

That a site behind No. 1 South Parks Road be allocated for a building of approximately 2,200 sq.m. to house the Institute for American Studies.[1]

[11]

Saïd Business School:

Special Resolution (3) of Congregation of 17 June 1997

That this House

(*a*) endorse the development of the School of Management Studies, to be renamed the Saïd Business School in the event of a benefaction from Mr Saïd being forthcoming,[2] through the construction of a new building on the Oxford station forecourt site on the broad terms and conditions set out in the explanatory note to this resolution and in the decree published with this resolution;

(*b*) agree, subject to the acquisition by the University of the freehold of the site, to allocate a site of up to 2.4 acres for the construction of a building for the school if planning consent for the building is given; and

(*c*) endorse the terms of the decree set out [in *University Gazette* No. 4441, 12 June 1997, p. 1224].[2]

[§ 2 of this Section has been rescinded by § 16 [19] below. For §§ 3–10 of this Section, see *Statutes*, 1995, pp. 705–7.]

§ 11. *Radcliffe Square*

Decree (4) of Council of 5 February 1970,
as amended by Decree (1) of 31 May 1971

1. Council shall ask the City Council to promote an order under Section 92 of the Town and Country Planning Act, 1968, closing the highway which exists along the south side of Radcliffe Square and up the west side as far as Brasenose Lane to all vehicles except in so far as it may be necessary to make exceptions for vehicles needing access; and Council shall waive any claim the University may have for compensation in respect of such closure. When this order is made, Council shall take such steps as may be necessary to exclude vehicles from Radcliffe Square except in so far as is set out in the annexed rules agreed between Council and Brasenose College and in so far as access is needed for service and emergency vehicles for St. Mary's Church and the Bodleian Library.

2. Council shall not install in Radcliffe Square a mechanical barrier (whether of the 'rising arm' or any other type and whether or not fitted with an 'intercom' device operated by Brasenose) unless and until the exclusion of

[1] Now the Rothermere American Institute.

[2] See now Ch. III, Sect. LIII.

vehicles from the Square by means of a system of bollards unaccompanied by any mechanical device shall have been tried and proved ineffective.

ANNEXE TO DECREE (4)

Rules agreed between the Hebdomadal Council and Brasenose College

(1) Brasenose College accepts the decision of the University that vehicles should be excluded from Radcliffe Square to the greatest practicable extent.

(2) The University accepts that there must be access to Brasenose College for the vehicles of those wishing to deliver goods to, or collect goods from, the college, and access for the vehicles of those wishing to visit the college for other purposes.

(3) Access shall be given at any time to the vehicles of those wishing to deliver goods to, or collect goods from, the college, and such vehicles may be parked outside the college while the unloading or loading takes place.

(4) Access shall be given at any time to the vehicles of those engaged in maintenance or building operations in the college and such vehicles may be parked outside the college either while the operation is in progress in those cases where use must be made of equipment on the vehicles in connection with the operation or for a period of up to one hour. Access shall similarly be given to vehicles of the college doctor and the college nurse, and such vehicles may be parked outside the college while medical attention is being given to persons in the college.

(5) Access shall be given at any time to the vehicles of other persons wishing to visit the college. Such vehicles, and also the cars of the Vice-Chancellor and Proctors, and not more than two cars of the staff of the University Church of St. Mary the Virgin, may be parked outside the college for a period of up to one hour.

(6) All vehicles parked outside the college under (3)–(5) shall be parked on the land (other than the highway) lying between the college and the Radcliffe Camera between Brasenose Lane to the north and the point at which the surround to the Camera begins to curve to the south.

(7) There shall be a Standing Committee consisting of two persons appointed by the Governing Body of Brasenose College and two persons appointed by the Hebdomadal Council. The committee shall supervise the implementation of this agreement (and in particular the observance of the periods laid down in (4) and (5)). If the committee agrees unanimously or by a majority on what the proper action should be, the decision of the committee shall be final (though it shall not be binding should a similar question be brought before the committee on a subsequent occasion). If the committee fails to reach such agreement, the question shall be referred to a person nominated by the Vice-Chancellor and the Principal of Brasenose (or by the Vice-Principal if the Principal is Vice-Chancellor or is otherwise unable to act) and his or her decision shall be final except that, if the question is one which could properly be referred to a Court

of Law, it shall be open to the college or the University so to refer it if it wishes.

(8) The University and Brasenose College accept that either party may wish to vary this agreement temporarily for particular occasions, and each party shall, so far as it reasonably can, meet the wishes of the other in this respect.

(9) This agreement may be varied at any time by the consent of both parties, subject to prior consultation with the City Council.

[For §§ 12–14 of this Section, see *Statutes*, 1995, p. 709.]

§ 15. *St. Mary's Church*

[1]

In consideration of the payment by Oriel College to the University of the sum of £270, the University undertook to put into repair the walls, roof, battlements, and pinnacles of Adam de Brome's Chapel in the Church of St. Mary the Virgin, Oxford, and to maintain the same and the interior of the said Chapel hereafter in proper repair, the college surrendering to the University all its interest in the said Chapel, reserving only right of access to the tomb of Adam de Brome for the purpose of repairing and maintaining the same; and the Curators of the University Chest shall take the necessary steps to carry this undertaking into effect.

[2]

The Curators of the University Chest shall pay to the Churchwardens of the Church of St. Mary the Virgin annually such sum as Council shall determine, provided that the Vicar and Churchwardens make such provision as may be needed for the orderly use of the Church for the customary University purposes.

§ 16. *Science Departments*

[For items [1]–[16] of this Sub-section, see *Statutes*, 1995, pp. 710–12.]

[17]

Oxford University Museum of Natural History:
Decree (2) of Council of 18 February 1993,
as amended by Decree (1) of 5 December 1996

For safety reasons, the playing of games on the grassed area in front of the Oxford University Museum of Natural History is expressly forbidden.

[18]

Genetics and Physiology Institute and University Security Centre:
Special Resolution of Congregation of 1 July 1997

That a site between the Department of Physiology and the Old Observatory be allocated for five years to the Department of Biochemistry for a building of approximately 3,000 sq.m. in floor area to house the first phase of the planned Genetics and Physiology Institute and the University Security Centre; and that this allocation be confirmed on a long-term basis if sufficient funding is raised to cover both the full cost of the construction of the building and its subsequent running costs.

[19]

Chemistry Research Laboratory:
Special Resolution of Congregation of 15 December 1998

That Special Resolution (2) of Congregation of 30 June 1970[1] be rescinded and that the site of the University Car Park at 2–4 South Parks Road, together with that of 12 Mansfield Road, be allocated to the Department of Chemistry for the construction of a research laboratory of about 17,000 sq.m. floor area.

[20]

Department of Materials (Begbroke site):
Special Resolution of Congregation of 15 June 1999

That some 3,268 sq.m. at the Begbroke Science and Business Park comprising buildings numbers 317, 318, 319, and 321 be allocated to the Department of Materials for ten years on payment of an annual charge relating to the cost of capital required to purchase this space, such charge to be set by the Resources Committee or successor body and reviewed every three years or whenever there is a material change in the circumstances.

[For §§ 17–20 of this Section, see *Statutes*, 1995, pp. 713–14.]

§ 21. *Hospital Sites*

[1]

Wellcome Trust Centre for Human Genetics:
Special Resolution of Congregation of 15 October 1996

That an area of the site purchased from the Regional Office of the N.H.S. Executive, comprising approximately 2.5 acres, be allocated to the Wellcome Trust Centre for Human Genetics.

[2]

Trials and Epidemiology Building:
Special Resolution of Congregation of 18 January 2000

That the site on the Old Road Campus, Headington, currently occupied by Building 667, plus sufficient additional space as is necessary to construct a building of up to approximately 6,800 sq.m., be allocated for the Trials and Epidemiology Building.

§ 22. *Ewert House, Summertown*

Special Resolution of Congregation of 4 July 2000

That approximately 1,100 sq.m. net of space within Ewert House be allocated to the Department for Continuing Education provided that 92 Woodstock Road

[1] *Statutes*, 1995, p. 705.

is relinquished, and that approximately 800 sq.m. of space be allocated to the Curators of the Examination Schools for use as an examination hall.

Section VI. Size and Shape of the University

[1]

For General Resolutions on this subject approved in 1969, 1971, and 1974 see *Statutes*, 1982, pp. 679–80.

[2]

General Resolution of Congregation of 1 May 1990

That this House note with approval the broad assumptions adopted by Council and the General Board with regard to the size of the University in the year 2000,[1] and instruct them, in preparing the University's institutional plan, to take account of the responses from faculties, colleges, and other bodies, and of the debate in this House, on the future size and shape of the University.[2]

Section VII. Numbers at Permanent Private Halls

Under the provisions of Tit. VII, Sect. VI, § 3, cl. 2, Council has determined that the total number of home and European Community students studying for the Degree of Bachelor of Arts, Bachelor of Theology, or Bachelor of Fine Art, for a second Honour School, or for the Special Diploma in Social Studies or in Social Administration at each of the following permanent private halls shall not exceed the figure for that hall which is set out below:

Blackfriars	24
Campion Hall	9
Greyfriars	30
Regent's Park	85
(plus 10 full-time-equivalent students for the part-time B.Th. course)	
St. Benet's Hall	37
Wycliffe Hall	55
(plus 6 full-time-equivalent students for the part-time B.Th. course)	

Section VIII. Regulations of the Rules Committee

§ 1. *Clubs, societies, and publications*

1. Junior Members of the University who form a club, society, or an organization for whatsoever purpose (including one for the publication of a journal, newspaper, or magazine), and who wish to use the name of the University in its title (or in the title of a journal, newspaper, or magazine), shall

(*a*) register with the Proctors; and

[1] See *University Gazette*, vol. cxx, pp. 679, 686.

[2] See ibid., pp. 751, 983.

(*b*) obtain the consent of the Vice-Chancellor. The Vice-Chancellor will not consider applications for the use of the name of the University until the club, society, or organization has been registered with the Proctors for two consecutive terms.

2. The consent of the Vice-Chancellor may be withdrawn or withheld if he or she sees fit.

3. A club, society, or organization which does not wish to use the name of the University in its title may also register with the Proctors provided it conforms with the regulations in clauses 6, 7, and 8 below.

4. The Proctors may not unreasonably withhold or withdraw registration.

5. (i) Each club, society, or organization which registers with the Proctors shall be designated, as the Proctors see fit, to be either

(*a*) a non-sports club, society, or organization (hereafter 'non-sports club'); or

(*b*) a club, society, or organization for sport (hereafter 'sports club'); or

(*c*) an organization for the publication of a journal, newspaper, or magazine, whether in hard copy or electronic format (hereafter 'publication').

(ii) Each such non-sports club and publication shall register with the Proctors through the Clerk to the Proctors. Each such sports club shall register with the Proctors through the Head of the Sports Department.

(iii) In this regulation, non-sports club, sports club, or publication mean the members of the club, society, or organization concerned.

6. (i) Each non-sports club which registers with the Proctors shall:

(*a*) establish a constitution and deposit a copy of it with the Proctors;

(*b*) act in accordance with the constitution established under (*a*) above;

(*c*) advise the Proctors promptly of any changes in the constitution established under (*a*) above;

(*d*) notify to the Proctors not later than the end of the second week of every Full Term the programme of meetings and speakers which has been arranged for that term (e.g. by sending them a copy of its term card);

(*e*) appoint a president (or similar principal officer) who shall be a matriculated member of the University in residence for the purpose of fulfilling the requirements of any statute, decree, or regulation of the University, or reading for any degree, diploma, or certificate of the University, or a member of one of the other institutions listed in (*l*) below attending the institution for the purpose of undertaking a course of study (subject in the latter case to the member's signing, on election to office, an undertaking to abide by the provisions of § 1, cl. 6, and to accept the authority of the Proctors on club matters);

(*f*) appoint a secretary who shall be a matriculated member of the University in residence for the purpose of fulfilling the requirements of any statute, decree, or regulation of the University, or reading for any degree, diploma, or certificate of the University, or a member of one of the other institutions listed in (*l*) below attending the institution for the purpose of undertaking a course of study (subject in the latter case to a member's signing, on election to office, an undertaking to abide by the provisions of § 1, cl. 6, and to accept the authority of the Proctors on club matters) and who shall keep a proper record of its activities;

(*g*) appoint a treasurer who shall be a matriculated member of the University in residence for the purpose of fulfilling the requirements of any statute, decree, or regulation of the University, or reading for any degree, diploma, or certificate of the University, or a member of one of the other institutions listed in (*l*) below attending the institution for the purpose of undertaking a course of study (subject in the latter case to the member's signing, on election to office, an undertaking to abide by the provisions of § 1, cl. 6, and to accept the authority of the Proctors on club matters) and who shall keep a proper record of its financial transactions which shall be available for inspection at the request of the Senior Member or the Proctors; and shall forward to the Proctors by the end of the second week of each term a copy of the accounts for the preceding term[1] signed by the Senior Member for retention on the Proctors' files;

(*h*) not appoint several individuals jointly to hold any of the offices specified in (*e*), (*f*), and (*g*) nor allow any individual to hold more than one of these offices at a time;

(*i*) appoint a member of Congregation as Senior Member who shall be an *ex officio* member of its committee;

(*j*) notify to the Proctors by the end of the second week of each term the names of its officers and the names of the members of its committee;

(*k*) notify the Proctors immediately of any changes in holders of the offices specified in (*e*), (*f*), and (*g*);

(*l*) admit to membership only members of the University and, at the discretion of its committee, members of Ruskin College, of Plater College, of Ripon College, Cuddesdon, and of St. Stephen's House;

(*m*) admit to membership, if it so wishes, other persons not being members of the University, or one of the institutions listed in (*l*) above, provided that non-university members shall not constitute more than one-fifth of the total membership;

(*n*) if having a turnover in excess of £15,000 in the preceding year, or if owing to a change in the nature or scale of its activities, confidently expecting to have such a turnover in the current year, submit its accounts for audit by the University's auditors (or other auditors approved in advance by the Proctors). Accounts shall be ready for audit within four months of the end of its financial year and the costs of the audit shall be borne by the non-sports club. If requested by the auditors the non-sports club shall submit accounts and related material as a basis for a review of accounting procedures, the cost likewise to be borne by the non-sports club;

[1] Any transactions in the vacation should be included in the accounts for the following term.

(*o*) maintain a register of current members who shall elect or appoint the officers (including those specified in (*e*), (*f*), and (*g*)) and who shall have ultimate responsibility for the activities of the non-sports club. This register must be made available for inspection by the Proctors on request;

(*p*) notify the Proctors if the non-sports club ceases to operate, and at the same time submit a final statement of accounts.

(ii) Each officer of a non-sports club must, on relinquishing his or her appointment, promptly hand to his or her successor in office (or to another member of the club nominated by its committee) all official documents and records belonging to the club, together with (on request from the club's committee) any other property of the club which may be in his or her possession, and must complete any requirements to transfer authority relating to control of the club's bank account, building society account, or any other financial affairs.

(iii) In exceptional circumstances, at the request of a non-sports club, the Proctors shall have discretion to dispense from requirements of any of the sub-clauses (i) (*e*), (*f*), (*g*), (*h*), (*i*), (*j*), (*l*), (*m*), and (*n*), subject to such terms and conditions as they may from time to time see fit to impose.

7. (i) Each sports club which registers with the Proctors shall:

(*a*) establish a constitution and deposit a copy of it with the Head of the Sports Department. This constitution must provide for the sports club to appoint a president (or similar principal officer), a secretary, and a treasurer as in clause 6 (i) (*e*), (*f*), (*g*), and (*h*) above; must provide for the club to admit members as in clause 6 (*l*) and (*m*) above; and must provide for the club to be run by a committee on which members of the University, both Senior and Junior, are in a majority;

(*b*) act in accordance with the constitution established under (*a*) above;

(*c*) advise the Proctors promptly, through the Head of the Sports Department, of any changes in the constitution established under (*a*) above;

(*d*) be designated or redesignated by the Proctors, as they see fit, to be a 'foundation sport', 'development sport', 'established sport', or 'recognized sport';

(*e*) appoint to its committee a Senior Member (who shall be a person who is a member of Congregation) through whom the club shall be accountable to the Proctors: in the case of a sports club designated by the Proctors to be a 'recognized sport' in accordance with (*d*) above, the Senior Member shall be the Head of the Sports Department *ex officio*, who shall be formally responsible for the affairs of each recognized sports club;

(*f*) unless designated by the Proctors to be a 'recognized sport' in accordance with (*d*) above, present to the Proctors, through the Head of the Sports Department, annual audited accounts together with a copy of the club's current constitution and list of officers (such accounts to be submitted not later than four months after the end of the financial year to which they relate);

(*g*) make all club administrative and coaching appointments through, and with the approval of, the Sports Strategy Committee, appointing only coaches who are accredited by the relevant national governing body.

(ii) Each officer of a sports club must, on relinquishing his or her appointment, promptly hand to his or her successor in office (or to another member of the club nominated by its committee) all official documents and records belonging to the club, together with (on request from the club's committee) any other property of the club which may be in his or her possession, and must complete any requirements to transfer authority relating to control of the club's bank account, building society account, or any other financial affairs.

(iii) Any registered sports club may apply to the Proctors, through the Sports Strategy Committee, for permission to co-operate in the establishment of a federal or representative team.

(iv) There shall be only one registered club for each sport.

(v) In exceptional circumstances, at the request of a sports club submitted through the Head of the Sports Department, the Proctors shall have discretion to dispense from the requirements of any of sub-clauses (i) (*a*)–(*f*) above, subject to such terms and conditions as they may from time to time see fit to impose.

8. (i) A publication which registers with the Proctors shall

(*a*) notify to the Proctors by the end of the second week of each term the names of its editor or editors and the names of any other persons who have agreed to assume financial responsibility and shall promptly notify to the Proctors any changes in its editor or editors;

(*b*) appoint a member of Congregation as its Senior Member who shall be kept informed of the activities of the organization;

(*c*) keep a proper record of its financial transactions which shall be available for inspection at the request of the Senior Member or the Proctors; and forward to the Proctors by the end of the second week of each term a copy of the accounts for the preceding term[1] signed by the Senior Member for retention on the Proctors' files;

(*d*) inform the Proctors when publication ceases and in doing so present a financial statement; and

(*e*) if having a turnover in excess of £15,000 in the preceding year, or if, owing to a change in the nature or scale of its activities, confidently expecting to have such a turnover in the current year, submit its accounts for audit by the University's auditors (or other auditors approved in advance by the Proctors). Accounts shall be ready for audit within four months of the end of the financial year of the publication and the costs of the audit shall be borne by the publication. If requested by the auditors the publication shall submit

[1] Any transactions in the vacation should be included in the accounts for the following term.

accounts and related material as a basis for a review of accounting procedures, the cost likewise to be borne by the publication.

(ii) In exceptional circumstances, at the request of a publication, the Proctors shall have discretion to dispense from the requirements of sub-clauses (i) (*b*) and (*c*) subject to such terms and conditions as they may from time to time see fit to impose.

9. Failure to comply with this regulation may result in the non-sports club, sports club, or publication being deregistered by the Proctors.

§ 2. *Motor vehicles*

No Junior Member of the University shall park a motor vehicle on any land of the University without the express permission of the person or body which has charge of that land.

§ 3. *Defacement of property*

No Junior Member of the University shall intentionally and without lawful authority deface any building, wall, fence, or other structure within six miles of Carfax, by inscribing thereon any writing or posting thereon any bill. Any breach of this regulation will be treated as a university offence. Where the offending matter relates to the activity of a club, society, or publication, the committee of that club, society, or publication will be held collectively responsible.

§ 4. *Behaviour after examinations*

1. No Junior Member of the University, other than a candidate presenting himself or herself for examination, shall, at any time between the hours of 12.15 and 1 p.m. or 5.15 and 6 p.m., or between fifteen minutes before and thirty minutes after the scheduled time for the completion of a Public Examination of the University for ten or more candidates, in the company of one or more other persons either:

(i) gather without the prior permission of the Proctors in a public thoroughfare within 300 metres of any place where such an examination is being, or has just been, held; or

(ii) having gathered in a public thoroughfare within one mile of any such place, fail to disperse after having been requested to do so by one or more of the Proctors, the Marshal, or their constables.

For the purpose of this regulation, persons shall be regarded as having gathered if they assemble, or form part of an assembly, in such a way as to cause, or to be likely to cause, obstruction of a public thoroughfare.

2. (i) No Junior Member of the University shall, in any place or thoroughfare to which members of the general public have access within six miles of Carfax, throw, pour, apply, or use any thing or substance in a way which is intended, or is likely, to cause injury to any person, or damage to, or defacement or destruction of, any property.

(ii) No Junior Member shall be in possession of any thing or substance with intention to commit an offence under § 4, cl. 2 (i) of the Regulations of the Rules Committee.

§ 5. *Overseas sports tours*

No Junior Member of the University shall participate in any sports tours which involve overseas travel during Full Term without the prior permission of (i) the Senior Tutor of that member's college and (ii) the Proctors. The written permission of the Senior Tutor is to accompany any request to the Proctors.

§ 6. *Rowing on the river*

1. No Junior Member of the University (other than a Junior Member currently in residence at All Souls College, Linacre College, Nuffield College, St Antony's College, St Cross College, Templeton College, or Wolfson College) shall participate in rowing on the river between the hours of 8.30 a.m. and 1 p.m. from Monday to Friday inclusive during Full Term without the prior permission of the Proctors.[1]

2. No Junior Member shall knowingly breach any regulation or instruction relating to safety on the river made by or on the authority of the body to which the University has delegated decision-making on sports matters, by Oxford University Rowing Clubs with the consent of the Proctors, or by a responsible external body such as the Environment Agency.

Section IX. Code of Practice on Freedom of Speech

(Issued by Council on 11 June 1987 pursuant to its statutory duty under Section 43 of the Education (No. 2) Act 1986)

I. INTRODUCTION

Statutory obligations

1. The Education (No. 2) Act 1986, Section 43, imposes on the authorities of universities and their constituent colleges obligations to safeguard the lawful exercise of freedom of speech and requires each of them to issue a code of practice to facilitate the discharge of its duties under the Act. The authorities are further required to take such steps as are reasonably practicable (including where appropriate the initiation of disciplinary measures) to ensure compliance with the code of practice. The duties imposed by Parliament, and the interpretation provisions, are as follows:

'43. (1) Every individual and body of persons concerned in the government of any establishment to which this section applies shall take such steps as are reasonably practicable to ensure that freedom of speech within the law is secured

[1] The Proctors are prepared to consider applications for permission in relation to, for example, Christ Church Regatta, Torpids, and Eights Week.

for members, students and employees of the establishment and for visiting speakers.

(2) The duty imposed by subsection (1) above includes (in particular) the duty to ensure, so far as is reasonably practicable, that the use of any premises of the establishment is not denied to any individual or body of persons on any ground connected with

(*a*) the beliefs or views of that individual or of any member of that body; or

(*b*) the policy or objectives of that body.

(3) The governing body of every such establishment shall, with a view to facilitating the discharge of the duty imposed by subsection (1) above in relation to that establishment, issue and keep up to date a code of practice setting out

(*a*) the procedures to be followed by members, students and employees of the establishment in connection with the organization

(i) of meetings which are to be held on premises of the establishment and which fall within any class of meeting specified in the code; and

(ii) of other activities which are to take place on those premises and which fall within any class of activity so specified; and

(*b*) the conduct required of such persons in connection with any such meeting or activity;

and dealing with such other matters as the governing body consider appropriate.

(4) Every individual and body of persons concerned in the government of any such establishment shall take such steps as are reasonably practicable (including where appropriate the initiation of disciplinary measures) to secure that the requirements of the code of practice for that establishment, issued under subsection (3) above, are complied with.

(5) The establishments to which this section applies are

(*a*) any university;

(*b*) any establishment which is maintained by a local education authority and for which section 1 of the 1968 (No. 2) Act (government and conduct of colleges of education and other institutions providing further education) requires there to be an instrument of government; and

(*c*) any establishment of further education designated by or under regulations made under section 27 of the 1980 Act as an establishment substantially dependent for its maintenance on assistance from local education authorities or on grants under section 100 (1) (*b*) of the 1944 Act.

(6) In this section

'governing body', in relation to any university, means the executive governing body which has responsibility for the management and administration of its revenue and property and the conduct of its affairs (that is to say the body commonly called the council of the university);

'university' includes a university college and any college, or institution in the nature of a college, in a university.

(7) Where any establishment

(*a*) falls within subsection (5) (*b*) above; or

(*b*) falls within subsection (5) (*c*) above by virtue of being substantially dependent for its maintenance on assistance from local education authorities;

the local education authority or authorities maintaining or (as the case may be) assisting the establishment shall, for the purposes of this section, be taken to be concerned in its government.

(8) Where a students' union occupies premises which are not premises of the establishment in connection with which the union is constituted, any reference in this section to the premises of the establishment shall be taken to include a reference to the premises occupied by the students' union.'

2. The University's own statutes include under Tit. XIII (Of University Discipline) the following provision:

'2. (*a*) No member of the University shall intentionally

(i) disrupt or attempt to disrupt teaching or study or research or the administration of the University, or disrupt or attempt to disrupt the lawful exercise of freedom of speech by members, students, and employees of the University and by visiting speakers, or obstruct or attempt to obstruct any officer or servant of the University in the performance of his duties;

(ii) damage or deface any property of the University or of any college;

(iii) occupy or use or attempt to occupy or use any property of the University or of any college except as may be expressly or impliedly authorized by the university or college authorities concerned;

(iv) forge or falsify any university certificate or similar document or knowingly make false statements concerning standing or results obtained in examinations.

(*b*) Every member of the University shall, to the extent that such provisions may be applicable to that member, comply with the provisions of the Code of Practice on Freedom of Speech issued from time to time by Council pursuant to the duty imposed by Section 43 of the Education (No. 2) Act 1986 and duly published in the *University Gazette*.'

II. CODE OF PRACTICE

The following provisions constitute the Code of Practice adopted by Council to operate with effect from 1 September 1987 to facilitate the discharge of the duty imposed by Section 43 (1) of the Education (No. 2) Act 1986, in relation to Oxford University.

Part 1—General Duties

General duty to uphold freedom of speech

1. Member[illegible]students, and employees of the University are bound at all times so to c[illegible]emselves as to ensure that freedom of speech within the law is s[illegible]ers, students, and employees of the University and for visiting

2. The freedom protected by para. 1 of this Code of Practice is confined to the exercise of freedom of speech within the law. Examples of statements which involve a breach of the criminal law are incitement to commit a crime, sedition, and stirring up racial hatred in contravention of statute. Statements may also be unlawful if they are defamatory or constitute a contempt of court.

General duty not to impede access to, or egress from, places at which the right of freedom of speech is exercised

3. Subject to such limitations on access as may lawfully be imposed by the competent university or college authorities, it shall be the duty of every member, student, and employee of the University not to impede any person entitled to be present from entering or leaving a place where the right of freedom of speech is being or is to be exercised.

Right of peaceful protest

4. Nothing in this Code of Practice shall be taken to prohibit the legitimate exercise of the right to protest by peaceful means; provided always that nothing is done which contravenes the foregoing general principles, the other requirements of this Code, or the statutes or decrees or regulations of the University.

Part 2—Academic Activities

5. All persons concerned with the organization or conduct of an activity which forms part of the University's teaching, study, or research (such as a lecture, demonstration, seminar, class, conference, research work, or examination) shall immediately give notice to the Proctors of any facts coming to their notice which indicate that such activity is likely to be delayed or disrupted by improper means.

6. The Proctors shall be empowered to give such directions and to adopt such measures as seem appropriate to them to prevent or minimize the delay or disruption of an academic activity, and all persons concerned with the organization or conduct of the academic activity under threat shall co-operate in carrying out the Proctors' directions and in facilitating the measures adopted.

7. In the event that any academic activity is delayed or disrupted by improper means a report shall forthwith be made to the Proctors by the person or persons responsible for the conduct of such activity.

Part 3—Meetings of University Clubs, etc.

8. In this Code the word 'club' means any club, society, or other organization registered with the Proctors, and 'officers' refers to the officers of the club, society, or other organization.

9. The junior members who are the officers of any club shall draw up a programme for the activities of the club in each term, advise the Senior Member of the club of its contents, and deliver a copy of such programme to the Proctors' Office by Friday in First Week in each term (as required by the regulations of the Rules Committee, published in the Proctors' Memorandum).

The programme shall state the intended venue of each meeting of the club, the names of the speakers, and the subject matter for discussion.

10. Any subsequent additions or amendments to the programme (including changes of venue) shall immediately be notified to the Proctors' Office.

11. When any facts come to the notice of any of the officers which indicate that any meeting of the club is likely to be delayed or disrupted by improper means he or she shall immediately report such facts to the Proctors.

12. In relation to any club meeting which they believe to be threatened, the Proctors shall be empowered to give such directions and to require the adoption of such measures as seem appropriate to them to prevent or minimize the improper delay or disruption of the meeting, and all persons concerned shall be bound to co-operate in carrying out the Proctors' directions and in facilitating the measures required to be adopted.

Part 4—Other Meetings and Events

13. Any member, student, or employee of the University who, whether alone or in collaboration with other persons, makes arrangements for the holding of a meeting or the assembly of persons in Oxford to be attended by members, students, or employees of the University, being a meeting or assembly which is not covered by the provisions of Parts 2 and 3 of this Code, and who becomes aware of facts indicating that such meeting or assembly is likely to be delayed or disrupted by improper means, shall immediately report such facts to the Proctors.

14. In relation to any such meeting or assembly which they believe to be threatened, the Proctors may (subject to the provisos to subparas. (1) and (2) of para. 15 below) take such steps as seem to them to be appropriate and practicable in the circumstances to prevent or minimize the improper delay or disruption of the meeting or assembly.

Part 5—Powers of the Proctors in relation to threatened Meetings

15. (1) *Directions and measures to be adopted*

In relation to any academic activity, club meeting, or other meeting which the Proctors believe to be threatened by disruption, the Proctors may give directions and require measures to be adopted pursuant to paras. 6 and 12 of this Code, and may take steps pursuant to para. 14, on the following (amongst other) matters:

(*a*) the number of persons to be admitted to the premises where the meeting is to be held;

(*b*) the issue of tickets of admission;

(*c*) the designation of one or more persons as the official organizers of the meeting with direct responsibility to the Proctors for all the arrangements thereof;

(*d*) the designation of a person as the chairman of the meeting with responsibility for the proper conduct of such meeting;

(*e*) the admission (or non-admission, as the case may be) of members of the public;

(*f*) the appointment of stewards to assist with the control of the meeting;

(*g*) the employment of security staff to ensure the orderly conduct of the meeting and safe access to and egress from the meeting;

(*h*) the carrying of banners, placards, and similar objects into the meeting;

(*i*) the place where the meeting is to be held.

Provided always that where the meeting is to be held on college premises it is expected that the authorities of the college concerned will issue directions and impose requirements as to the arrangements within the college after consulting the Proctors.

(2) *Meetings where serious disruption is anticipated*

The Proctors will as necessary consult with the local police about forthcoming meetings and activities covered by this Code of Practice. In any case where serious disruption may be anticipated the Proctors shall have power, having taken into consideration such advice from the police as may be available, to order or, as may be appropriate, to advise the cancellation, postponement, or relocation of the meeting.

Provided always that this power shall not be available in the case of a meeting which is exclusively a college occasion in the sense that the meeting is held on college premises and no persons other than members of the college are entitled to be admitted.

(3) *Expenses incurred in safeguarding academic activities and other meetings*

Where expenses are incurred (e.g. in the engagement of stewards or the employment of security staff) to safeguard an academic activity under Part 2 of this Code of Practice the cost thereof shall be borne by the University. In all other cases the cost shall be borne by the club or by the person or persons organizing the meeting, save that the Proctors may (if so advised) make representations to Council suggesting that the cost shall be borne in whole or in part by the University and Council may decide the matter.

Part 6—University Premises made available for use by outside Organizations

16. In any case where the University is proposing to grant permission to an outside organization or group to hold meetings on university premises, the attention of such outside organization or group will be drawn to the contents of this Code of Practice and permission to use the premises may be refused unless the outside organization or group both undertakes to secure that the principles embodied in this Code will be upheld and satisfies the university authorities of its ability to discharge its obligations in regard to upholding freedom of speech.

Part 7—Miscellaneous

17. Council is under a duty pursuant to Section 43 (3) of the Education (No. 2) Act 1986 to keep this Code of Practice up to date. No revision of the Code will, however, take effect until after due notice has been given by publication in the *University Gazette*.

18. Failure by members and students of the University to comply with the provisions of this Code of Practice will constitute an offence under Tit. XIII, cl. 2 (*b*) of the University's Statutes. Where the acts of individuals involve breaches of the criminal law the University will be ready to assist the prosecuting authorities in implementing the due process of law, and disciplinary proceedings may be deferred or suspended pending the outcome of criminal proceedings.

Section X. Code of Practice relating to Harassment

(issued by Council on 25 February 1999; amended on 3 February 2000)

PRINCIPLES AND DEFINITION

1. Harassment is an unacceptable form of behaviour. The University is committed to protecting members, staff, and any other person for whom the University has a special responsibility from any form of harassment which might inhibit them from pursuing their work or studies, or from making proper use of university facilities. Complaints of harassment will be taken seriously and may lead to disciplinary proceedings. All members and staff have a personal responsibility to ensure that their behaviour is not contrary to this code and are encouraged to ensure the maintenance of a working environment in the University which is free from harassment.

2. For the purposes of this code, harassment may be broadly understood to consist of unwarranted behaviour towards another person, so as to disrupt the work or reduce the quality of life of that person, by such means as single or successive acts of bullying, verbally or physically abusing, or ill-treating him or her, or otherwise creating or maintaining a hostile or offensive studying, working, or social environment for him or her. Forms of harassment covered by this code include harassment relating to another's sex, sexual orientation, religion, race, or disability.

In order for the University to comply with the Sex Discrimination (Gender Reassignment) Regulations 1999, which amended the Sex Discrimination Act 1975 with effect from 1 May 1999, Council has decided that from 1 May 1999, where the words 'sex' or 'gender' are used in the University of Oxford Equal Opportunity Policy and Code of Practice, the Code of Practice relating to Harassment, or other policy documents relating to equal opportunity in employment, they should be deemed to include gender reassignment.

Unacceptable forms of behaviour may include unwelcome sexual advances, unwelcome requests for sexual favours, offensive physical contact or verbal behaviour, or other hostile or offensive acts or expressions relating to people's sex, sexual orientation, religion, race, or disability. The abuse of a position of authority, as for example that of a tutor or supervisor, is an aggravating feature of harassment.

3. Being under the influence of alcohol or otherwise intoxicated will not be admitted as an excuse for harassment, and may be regarded as an aggravating feature.

Note on confidentiality

It is essential that all those involved in a complaints procedure (including complainants) observe the strictest confidentiality consistent with operating that procedure; an accusation of harassment is potentially defamatory.

ADVICE

4. Advice may be sought or complaints pursued **through any appropriate channel**. In addition to other officers, the following people have been specially appointed to give advice in this connection and to answer questions (whether or not amounting to a complaint):

(*a*) departmental or faculty 'Confidential Advisers', appointed by heads of department or the equivalent. Their names will be publicized within the institution;

(*b*) members of the 'Advisory Panel', serving the whole University. The Advisory Panel is a standing committee of Council consisting of members and employees of the University with special expertise or interest in relevant aspects of staff and student welfare. Members of the panel may be approached on a number specially designated for this purpose (telephone: (2)70760);

(*c*) special college advisers or advisory panels where colleges have established these.

Those protected by this code may appropriately seek advice in relation to harassment even if the conduct in question is not sufficiently serious to warrant the institution of disciplinary proceedings. Any of the advisers listed above may be approached in the first instance; those approached will direct enquirers elsewhere, if that seems most likely to meet the enquirer's needs.

5. Enquiries about harassment will be responded to promptly. University advisers (whether Confidential Advisers or members of the Advisory Panel) will discuss the range of options available to enquirers on an entirely confidential basis and whenever possible assist them in resolving the problem informally in the first instance. College advisers will be guided by college rules.

6. It is emphasized that the role of advisers is advisory and not disciplinary. All disciplinary matters lie in the hands of the relevant disciplinary bodies.

DISCIPLINE

7. If a complaint is not resolved on an informal basis the complainant may refer the matter to the relevant authority, which will determine whether there is a prima facie case under the relevant disciplinary provision and, if appropriate, set in motion disciplinary procedures. In respect of members of the University subject to the jurisdiction of the Visitatorial Board, the relevant procedures are those described under Title XVII of the University's Statutes. The disciplinary procedures which apply to non-academic staff are set out in the *Handbook for Non-Academic Staff*. Complaints against Junior Members shall be dealt with in accordance with the procedures contained in Title XIII of the University's

Statutes (also set out in the *Proctors' and Assessor's Memorandum*). Colleges may have their own forms of disciplinary provision.

8. It may be that a complaint either against a member of staff or against a Junior Member could potentially be heard by more than one disciplinary body. When the person complained against is a Junior Member, the complainant will be expected to choose whether to pursue disciplinary procedures through his or her college or through the Proctors. If a complainant has previously brought or is in the process of bringing a complaint against the same person, founded wholly or in part upon the same matter, before any other disciplinary body, he or she is responsible for revealing that fact when seeking to institute disciplinary proceedings. It is also incumbent upon a disciplinary body to attempt to ascertain, for example by direct enquiry of the complainant, or by consulting other relevant authorities, whether any such other complaint has been instituted; if so, that body must consider whether it is appropriate for the same matter to provide a basis for two separate disciplinary hearings.

INSTITUTIONAL ARRANGEMENTS

9. The appointment of Confidential Advisers within each department or faculty is the responsibility of the head of department, or equivalent, who must designate two such advisers, one of each sex, return the names of those appointed to the Equal Opportunities Officer (or such other officer as may be designated by the Registrar from time to time), and ensure that the Code of Practice and the names of the Confidential Advisers are adequately publicized within the department or faculty. The Advisory Panel on Harassment will provide Confidential Advisers with information, advice, and training opportunities. Confidential Advisers will be expected to make anonymized annual returns to the panel as to the number and general character of complaints they have dealt with. They may refer enquirers to members of the panel, or themselves seek advice either about university provisions on harassment in general or about possible ways of handling individual cases.

10. Members of the Advisory Panel on Harassment will give advice on request to those troubled by harassment and to other advisers. The panel is responsible for supporting, co-ordinating, and monitoring the effectiveness of the University's arrangements for dealing with harassment. Members of the panel may be contacted on a number specially designated for this purpose (telephone: (2)70760).

11. The provisions of this code supplement and do not supersede or override college arrangements.

12. Nothing in this code shall detract from the position and jurisdiction of the Proctors or the right of free access to them by all Junior and Senior Members of the University.

Appendix

List[1] of departments, faculties, and other institutions

Departments and other institutions

School of Anthropology and Museum Ethnography
Institute of Archaeology
Research Laboratory for Archaeology and the History of Art
Ashmolean Museum of Art and Archaeology (to include the Ashmolean Library and the Griffith Institute)
Department of Biochemistry
Bodleian Library (to include the Law Library and the Rhodes House Library)
Botanic Garden
Brazilian Studies Centre
Saïd Business School
Department of Chemistry (laboratories):
 Chemical Crystallography Laboratory
 Dyson Perrins Laboratory
 Inorganic Chemistry Laboratory
 New Chemistry Laboratory
 Physical and Theoretical Chemistry Laboratory
Institute for Chinese Studies
Departments of Clinical Medicine:
 Nuffield Department of Anaesthetics
 Cairns Library
 Department of Cardiovascular Medicine
 Nuffield Department of Clinical Laboratory Sciences
 Nuffield Department of Clinical Medicine
 Department of Clinical Neurology
 Department of Clinical Pharmacology
 Clinical Trial Service Unit
 Department of Medical Illustration
 Department of Medical Oncology
 Nuffield Department of Obstetrics and Gynaecology
 Nuffield Laboratory of Ophthalmology
 Nuffield Department of Orthopaedic Surgery
 Department of Paediatrics
 Department of Primary Health Care
 Department of Psychiatry
 Department of Public Health
 Department of Radiology
 Nuffield Department of Surgery
Computing Laboratory
Computing Services

[1] This list has been drawn up solely in terms of the Code of Practice relating to Harassment, account having been taken of questions such as the size and physical location of various departments and bodies. It does not imply any change in existing organizational arrangements for other purposes.

Department for Continuing Education
Counselling Service
Centre for Criminological Research
Ruskin School of Drawing and Fine Art
Department of Earth Sciences
Department of Economics
Department of Educational Studies
Educational Technology Resources Centre
Department of Engineering Science
School of Geography (to include the Environmental Change Institute and the Transport Studies Unit)
Department of the History of Art
Unit for the History of Medicine
Museum of the History of Science
Department of Human Anatomy and Genetics
Nissan Institute of Japanese Studies
Language Centre
Latin American Centre
Centre for Linguistics and Philology
Department of Materials
Mathematical Institute
Medical School Offices (to include Postgraduate Medical Education and Training)
Laboratory of Molecular Biophysics
Weatherall Institute of Molecular Medicine
Oxford University Museum of Natural History
Sir William Dunn School of Pathology
Department of Pharmacology
Phonetics Laboratory
Department of Physics (sub-departments):
  Sub-Department of Astrophysics
  Sub-Department of Atmospheric, Oceanic, and Planetary Physics
  Sub-Department of Atomic and Laser Physics
  Sub-Department of Condensed Matter Physics
  Sub-Department of Particle and Nuclear Physics
  Sub-Department of Theoretical Physics
Department of Physiology
Department of Plant Sciences
Department of Politics and International Relations
Department of Experimental Psychology
Queen Elizabeth House (International Development Centre)
Radcliffe Science Library
Institute of Russian, Soviet, and East European Studies
Sheldonian Theatre
Department of Social Policy and Social Work
Centre for Socio-Legal Studies

Department of Sociology
Department of Statistics
Taylor Institution (to include the Voltaire Foundation)
Department of Zoology
Careers Service
Examination Schools
St. Cross Building
University Archives
University Club
University Offices (to include the offices of the University Land Agent and of the Surveyor to the University, the Occupational Health Service, the University Safety Office, the Proctors' Office, the Security Services, and the University Police)
University Parks
University Sports Centre
Faculties (to include the relevant faculty centres, offices, and libraries):
- English Language and Literature
- Law
- Literae Humaniores
- Medieval and Modern Languages
- Modern History
- Music
- Oriental Studies
- Theology

Section XI. Public Interest Disclosure: Code of Practice and Procedure

The Public Interest Disclosure Act came into force on 1 January 1999. It provides employees with legal protection against being dismissed or penalized by their employers as a result of disclosing certain serious concerns. It also requires employees who wish to disclose such concerns and who wish to retain the protection offered by the Act to follow the relevant internal procedure provided by their employer, in all but the most exceptional circumstances. The following guidance and procedure have been designed to assist employees who wish to make such disclosures, and to secure their proper investigation. It is also available to members of the University (including students), whether or not employees, although it is appreciated that the specific terms of the Act apply only to employees.

The Proctors perform a historic role as 'ombudsmen' to the University, empowered under the University's Statutes to investigate complaints made to them by members of the University. In addition, members of Congregation have a right under the Statutes to ask a question in Congregation relating to any matter concerning the policy or the administration of the University (Tit. II, Sect. VII, cl. 1). The University also has in place a number of policies and procedures to address problems that may arise for its employees and students, including those relating to grievance, harassment, and discipline.

In many instances where there is a suspicion of improper behaviour, allegations will be such as to be dealt with directly by reference to these procedures. However, there may be occasions when an individual has concerns relating to matters in the public interest which he or she believes to merit particular investigation. The following guidance sets out the way in which the University will address such concerns.

This policy is intended to assist individuals who believe that they have discovered malpractice or impropriety. It is not designed to question financial or business decisions taken by the University; nor may it be used to reconsider any matters which have already been addressed under a harassment complaint or disciplinary procedures. It is reasonable to expect individuals to await the conclusion of any investigation or review instigated under its terms before seeking to air their complaints outside the institution.

The University places the greatest importance on the integrity of its operations. Individuals are encouraged to bring to the attention of the University any matters referred to below about which they are concerned.

Remit

This guidance is directed specifically at the disclosure of information which is in the public interest and which in the reasonable belief of the person making the disclosure tends to show one or more of the following:

(*a*) criminal activity;

(*b*) failure to comply with legal obligations;

(*c*) danger to health and safety;

(*d*) damage to the environment;

(*e*) academic or professional malpractice;

(*f*) failure to comply with the Statutes, Decrees, and Regulations of the University and the codes of practice contained therein;

(*g*) attempts to conceal any of the above.

Protection

An individual making a disclosure relating to such matters to the appropriate person will not be penalized provided the disclosure is made

(1) in good faith; and

(2) in the reasonable belief of the individual making the disclosure that the information disclosed, and any allegation contained in it, are substantially true.

Confidentiality

The University will treat all such disclosures in a confidential manner.

Malicious allegations

In the event of malicious or vexatious allegations, disciplinary action may be taken against the individual concerned.

Procedure

An individual who wishes to make a disclosure should do so in the first instance (1) to the Registrar in the case of a disclosure concerning an employee or employees of the University, or concerning both employees and students of the University, or (2) to the Proctors in the case of complaints concerning a student or students, or concerning a university examination.

The Registrar or Proctors as appropriate shall decide whether the concern is such as may be addressed under existing university procedures, for example in relation to harassment, grievance, or discipline, or whether further investigation is required. Reference to the Registrar shall be taken to mean a Pro-Vice-Chancellor where the disclosure involves the Registrar.

In the event that the Registrar or the Proctors are of the opinion that investigation is necessary, additional steps shall be taken as follows:

(*a*) where the concerns relate to integrity in the conduct of research, investigation shall be carried out under the provisions of the code of practice and procedure relating to academic integrity in research (see Section XII below);

(*b*) in the case of other concerns where the complaint involves Junior Members of the University or the conduct of a university examination, these shall be investigated by the Proctors under their statutory powers;

(*c*) in the case of other concerns, these shall be brought to the attention of the relevant head of department, or faculty board chairman as appropriate, who shall conduct an investigation, or shall establish a small panel to investigate on behalf of himself or herself, drawing on appropriate expertise where necessary (for example in the event of allegations of financial irregularity).

The Registrar or the Proctors, as appropriate, shall inform the person making the disclosure of the nature of the investigation to be undertaken and the likely timescale.

Where the investigation reveals prima facie evidence of misconduct, the matter shall also be referred to the appropriate body for disciplinary action under the terms of the University's Statutes and Decrees.

In all cases, the matter shall be investigated as speedily as is consistent with thoroughness and fairness. The final outcome of the investigation shall be reported to the Personnel Committee, and the committee shall bring issues of general importance to the attention of Council.

Feedback

The action taken, including the outcome of any investigation, shall be reported to the person making the disclosure and in the event that no action is taken that person shall be given an explanation. In the event that no action is taken, the individual shall be allowed the opportunity to remake the disclosure to a Pro-Vice-Chancellor. The Pro-Vice-Chancellor shall consider all the information presented, the procedures that were followed, and the reasons for not taking any further action. The outcome of this will be either to confirm that no further action is required or that further investigation is required, in which case the procedures in (*a*)–(*c*) under 'Procedure' above, as appropriate, shall be followed.

Where a disclosure is made, the person or persons against whom the disclosure is made shall be told of it and the evidence supporting it, and shall be allowed to comment before any investigation, or further action, is concluded.

Section XII. Academic Integrity in Research: Code of Practice and Procedure

Statement of principle

The University expects all members of the University including staff and students, and those who are not members of the University but who are conducting research on university premises or using university facilities, to observe the highest standards in the conduct of their research. In pursuance of such high standards, it is expected that they shall

(*a*) take steps to acquaint themselves with available guidance as to 'best practice' whether in relation to matters of research policy, finance, or safety relevant to their area of research (for example, the statement 'Safeguarding Good Scientific Practice' published by the Director General of the Research Councils and the Chief Executives of U.K. Research Councils in December 1998);

(*b*) observe such legal and ethical requirements as are laid down by the University or such other properly appointed bodies as are involved in their field of research;

(*c*) take steps to secure the safety of those associated with the research;

(*d*) report any conflict of interest, whether actual or prospective, to the appropriate authority;

(*e*) observe fairness and equity in the conduct of their research.

Failure to comply with the code may give rise to an allegation of misconduct. Misconduct in research may be ground for disciplinary action, and if serious, for dismissal or expulsion.

Definition of misconduct

Misconduct for the purpose of this code means fabrication, falsification, plagiarism, or deception in proposing, carrying out, or reporting results of research and deliberate, dangerous, or negligent deviations from accepted practice in carrying out research. It includes failure to follow an agreed protocol if this failure results in unreasonable risk or harm to humans, other vertebrates, or the environment and facilitating misconduct in research by collusion in, or concealment of, such actions by others. It also includes any plan or conspiracy or attempt to do any of these things.

It does not include honest error or honest differences in interpretation or judgement in evaluating research methods or results, or misconduct (including gross misconduct) unrelated to research processes.

Responsibility

All members of the University, and individuals permitted to work in university institutions, have responsibility to report any incident of misconduct, whether this has been witnessed or is suspected. Suspicions reported in confidence and in good faith will not lead to disciplinary proceedings against the person making the complaint. In the event, however, of a malicious allegation, appropriate action will be taken.

Confidentiality

All allegations will be investigated in the strictest confidence. All those who are involved in the procedures for investigating an allegation, including witnesses, representatives, and persons providing information, evidence, and/or advice, have a duty to maintain confidentiality. For an allegation to be investigated fully, and appropriate action taken, it may, however, be necessary to disclose the identity of the person making the complaint to the person who is the subject of the complaint. The person making the complaint will be advised before such disclosure is made.

Advice

(*a*) In the case of concerns regarding a person or persons other than students, information and advice may be obtained from the head of department, or in the case of non-departmentally organized faculties, the chairman of the faculty board, provided that if the concerns relate to the holder of that office, advice should be sought from the Proctors.

(*b*) In the case of concerns regarding a student, information and advice may be obtained from the Clerk to the Proctors.

Procedure in the case of suspected misconduct

These procedures are without prejudice to the normal operation of the relevant disciplinary procedure of the University, and in the event of any conflict between these procedures and the relevant disciplinary procedure of the University, the latter shall prevail. They have been set out by way of guidance only and may be varied to suit the circumstances of a particular case.

1. All members of the University, and individuals permitted to work in the University and institutions, have a responsibility to report to the Registrar or to the Proctors, in the case of complaints relating to staff or students respectively, any incident of misconduct, whether this has been witnessed or is suspected.

2. In the event that further investigation is required, the Registrar or a person duly authorized on his or her behalf, or the Proctors, as the case may be, shall set up a small panel to inquire into the allegations. This shall normally consist of two members, namely a member of the department or faculty with relevant expertise and a member of the University or a college from outside the department or faculty, again, if possible, with relevant expertise. Where it is deemed appropriate by the Registrar, or the Proctors, as the case may be, one

member of the panel may be a person external to the University, but with relevant expertise. Members of the panel must have no conflict of interest in the case and must be unbiased. The purpose of the preliminary investigation is to evaluate the facts of the allegations in order to ascertain whether there is sufficient evidence amounting to a prima facie case of misconduct.

The Registrar or the person duly authorized on his or her behalf, or the Proctors, as appropriate, shall require the production of such records as are necessary to enable the investigation to proceed and shall secure their safe keeping.

3. The respondent shall be informed of the decision to set up the inquiry panel and of the membership of the panel.

4. The panel may interview both the person making the allegation and the respondent, and any other persons who may be regarded as witnesses. Any person attending for interview may be accompanied by another person.

5. The panel shall prepare a report, setting out the evidence which has been evaluated, accounts of interviews, if any, and its conclusions. The respondent shall have an opportunity to comment.

6. In the event that the panel has found no evidence of misconduct, the complaint shall be dismissed. In the event that the panel concludes that prima facie evidence of misconduct exists, the report shall be referred to the appropriate person for action (whether informal or formal) under the University's relevant disciplinary procedure. In the event that the panel takes the view that the allegations, if proved, would constitute good cause for dismissal, and the allegations relate to a person subject to the provisions of Title XVII of the University's Statutes, the panel shall bring the report to the attention of the Registrar under the provisions of Title XVII, clause 14 (1), or if the allegations relate to a person subject to the provisions of the University's disciplinary procedure for non-academic staff, the panel shall bring the report to the attention of the relevant head of department responsible for employing the person. In the event that allegations relate to a Junior Member, the Proctors may take further action under the terms of Title XIII.

7. Subject to availability of personnel and to operational demands, the investigation of the panel should normally be completed within twenty working days of first notification of the allegation to the Registrar or Proctors as appropriate.

8. In cases where the complaint concerns someone who is not subject to the University's disciplinary procedure, the panel shall invite the Registrar to bring the report to the attention of the appropriate disciplinary body.

9. Where the research is funded in whole or part by an outside grant, the University shall have regard to the guidance issued by the relevant funding body and shall ensure that such body is given appropriate and timely information as to the instigation and progress of an investigation.

Section XIII. Conflict of Interest: Statement of Policy and Procedure

Introduction

1. The University, through its research activity, seeks to promote the advancement, preservation, and dissemination of knowledge; the instruction of undergraduate, graduate, and postdoctoral students; and the advancement of the public interest. The University considers that the establishment of links between its employees and outside bodies, whether government departments, commerce, industry, or others, is not only in the public interest but also benefits the University and the individuals concerned. It is however possible that such links may give rise to potential conflict of interest; and the University has therefore prepared the following guidelines and rules to assist individuals in assessing whether or not proposed activities have potential for conflict of interest, and to outline the procedure for disclosure of any perceived or potential conflict which may arise.

Guidelines as to conflict of interest

2. It is not possible to provide a comprehensive definition of circumstances which necessarily give rise to a conflict of interest, but the following are examples of situations giving rise to perceived conflict of interest. The list is not exhaustive, and in any situation where an individual is uncertain as to the propriety of a given arrangement, advice may be sought from the Conflict of Interest Committee, the remit of which is set out in paragraph 4 below.

General examples

(*a*) The use of the University's research or administrative facilities to pursue personal business, commercial, or consulting activities;

(*b*) any attempt to restrict rights governing the timing and content of publications, save in circumstances properly approved by the University to protect privacy, commercially sensitive proprietary information, and patentable inventions;

(*c*) involvement in externally funded activity which might infringe the right of a student engaged in the activity to complete the degree for which he or she is registered and/or to publish freely his or her findings (save in the circumstances referred to in (*b*) above);

(*d*) a financial interest held by an individual, or by his or her immediate relative(s) or household member(s), in an external enterprise engaged in activities closely related to that individual's line of research in the University: examples of such interests are paid consultancies, paid service on a board of directors or advisory board, equity holdings in or royalty income from the enterprise. The existence of such an interest does not necessarily imply conflict, but is likely to give an appearance of conflict, and should be declared (as is set out in more detail in paragraph 5 below);

(*e*) a personal involvement in any company or commercial enterprise which is in a contractual relationship with the University or which is in the process of negotiating the terms and conditions of a contract with the University, where the employee has been concerned or connected with the placing or negotiation of the contract in question or with the research or other activity which the contract might cover.

3. There are in addition certain circumstances which the University feels give rise to such clear conflicts that it has adopted the specific rules which are set out below.

Executive directorships

3.1. It is the policy of the University that no member of staff of the University shall hold any executive directorship without the express approval of both the appointing authority for his or her post and the Committee on Conflict of Interest. Approval of the holding of such directorships may be given in the following circumstances:

(*a*) where a member of staff has satisfied the Committee on Conflict of Interest that the holding of an executive directorship is or will be necessary in order to satisfy the requirements of a recognized stock exchange for the listing of scientific, research-based companies; and/or

(*b*) where the Committee on Conflict of Interest is satisfied that approval will be justified on other grounds, although it should be noted that such approval will only be given in exceptional cases.

In either case consent will be given only if the appointing authority is satisfied that the appointment will comply with the general conditions relating to the holding of other appointments.

For the purpose of this guidance, an executive directorship is one involving an active management role, whether or not including research, in the company concerned.

The holding of directorships and shares by administrative officers of the University

3.2. 'Administrative officers' for the purpose of these rules means members of staff of the University's central administrative service, departmental administrative staff, and others employed by the University in academic-related administrative grades.

(*a*) Unless formally nominated by the University to do so, no administrative officer shall serve in a personal capacity as director or other officer of a company or commercial enterprise, the establishment of which arose out of or was connected with work done in the University, or any company or commercial enterprise in a contractual relationship with the University where the administrative officer was concerned or connected with the placing or negotiation of the contract in question.

(*b*) Any administrative officer nominated by the University to serve as the director of a company shall be deemed to accept the nomination in the discharge of his or her duties as an employee of the University, and shall decline to accept any director's fee.

(*c*) No administrative officer shall hold any shares in a company, the establishment of which arose out of or was connected with work done in the University, or any company in a contractual relationship with the University, where the administrative officer was concerned or connected with the placing or negotiation of the contract in question, unless such shares have been acquired following the listing of the company on a recognized stock exchange.

Conflict of Interest Committee

4. The University has established a Committee on Conflict of Interest to advise university bodies, appointing authorities, and individual staff members (in appropriate circumstances). The remit of the committee is as follows:

(*a*) to monitor the operation of the University's policy on conflict of interest and to make recommendations in the light of experience, and of 'good practice' guidelines published by outside bodies;

(*b*) to review annual declarations of interest and alert the appropriate university body where further clarification or action is required;

(*c*) to determine, for its part, requests for approval for the holding of executive directorships, or other directorships where there is concern as to a possible conflict of interest;

(*d*) to advise Council, or any relevant personnel committees, as appropriate, on cases of difficulty referred to it;

(*e*) to give advice in the case of individual questions referred to it.

Declarations

5. It is the duty of all employees to disclose any actual or potential conflict of interest. The procedures for certain disclosures are laid out below. In any other case, a disclosure should be made in writing and should be directed to the appointing body for the post-holder in question, with a copy to the secretary to the Committee on Conflict of Interest. Failure to disclose an actual conflict of interest may result in disciplinary action.

5.1. A declaration as to any conflict of interest will be sought in the outside grant (O.G.) form in connection with any externally funded research project.

5.2. Application for permission to undertake other activities (under Ch. VII, Sect. I, § 5. A, cll. 10-11) will require a declaration as to any conflict of interest from the individual concerned before a permission will be granted.

5.3. In addition to declaring any conflict or potential conflict in accordance with paragraphs 5.1 and 5.2 above, those persons occupying the following positions shall be required to submit an annual declaration of external interests to the Committee on Conflict of Interest:

(*a*) the Vice-Chancellor;

(*b*) Pro-Vice-Chancellors;

(*c*) the Registrar;

(*d*) members of Council;

(*e*) heads of divisions, departments, or sub-departments;

(*f*) chairmen of faculty boards;

(*g*) heads of division in the University's central administrative service;

(*h*) chairmen of such other bodies which govern the University's affairs as shall be specified by Council in consultation with the Committee on Conflict of Interest from time to time;

(*i*) such other individuals as may be specified by the relevant personnel committees in consultation with the Committee on Conflict of Interest from time to time.

5.4. A confidential record of all declarations made shall be maintained centrally by the secretary to the Committee on Conflict of Interest. In addition to declarations made under the above procedure from time to time, records shall be updated on an annual basis, and members of staff shall be required to provide updated information on request.

6. In the event that a conflict of interest or a potential conflict of interest has been disclosed, the individual concerned shall discuss a possible resolution with his or her line manager or the chairman of the appropriate committee. Any unresolved matter shall be referred to the Committee on Conflict of Interest for advice, and in cases of particular difficulty, the Committee on Conflict of Interest shall refer its recommendations to Council.

Disclosure

7. Persons with bona fide and substantial reasons to inspect declarations shall be allowed access at the discretion of the chairman of the Committee on Conflict of Interest.

INDEX

The figures in bold type indicate the main reference to certain subjects. Professorships and other posts are indexed under the subject. The main reference to trusts and endowments is to the name (normally a surname) of the trust or endowment.

THE QUEENS COLLEGE
LIBRARY
OXFORD